☙ Music of Hi

CHICAGO STUDIES IN ETHNOMUSICOLOGY

A Series Edited by Philip V. Bohlman and Bruno Nettl

Music of Hindu Trinidad

SONGS FROM THE INDIA DIASPORA

Helen Myers

THE UNIVERSITY OF CHICAGO PRESS
Chicago & London

Helen Myers is professor of music at Connecticut State University, New Britain. She is the editor and a coauthor of *Ethnomusicology* (2 vols.) and is Consulting Ethnomusicologist for the *New Grove Dictionaries of Music.*

THE UNIVERSITY OF CHICAGO PRESS, CHICAGO 60637
THE UNIVERSITY OF CHICAGO PRESS, LTD., LONDON

Printed in the United States of America
07 06 05 04 03 02 01 00 99 98 5 4 3 2 1
ISBN (cloth): 0-226-55451-1
ISBN (paper): 0-226-55453-8

Library of Congress Cataloging-in-Publication Data

Myers, Helen, 1946–
Music of Hindu Trinidad : songs from the India diaspora / Helen Myers.
p. cm. — (Chicago studies in ethnomusicology)
Includes bibliographical references (p.), discography, and indexes.
ISBN 0-226-55451-1 — ISBN 0-226-55453-8 (pbk.)
1. East Indians—Trinidad and Tobago—Felicity—Music—History and criticism. 2. Music—Trinidad and Tobago—Felicity—History and criticism. 3. Music—India—History and criticism. 4. Music, Hindustani—Trinidad and Tobago—Felicity—History and criticism. I. Title. II. Series.
ML3565.M94 1998
781.62′914072983—dc21 97-25692
CIP
MN

∞ The paper used in this publication meets the minimum requirements of the American National Standard for Information Sciences—Permanence of Paper for Printed Library Materials, ANSI Z39.48-1992.

To the memory of my father
Henry Alonzo Myers
Professor of English at Cornell University,
Pioneer in American Studies

If thou didst ever hold me in thy heart,
Absent thee from felicity a while,
And in this harsh world draw thy breath in pain,
To tell my story. *A march afar off.*

Hamlet, V, ii

ཱ In India I know I am a stranger; but increasingly I understand that my Indian memories, the memories of that India which lived on into my childhood in Trinidad, are like trapdoors into a bottomless past.

V. S. Naipaul, *India: A Wounded Civilization*

Contents

List of Illustrations xi
List of Musical Examples xv
Preface xvii
Acknowledgments xxiii
A Note on Translations and Transcriptions xxvii
Romanization of Indian Languages xxix
The Narrators xxxi

ONE East Indians of the West Indies 3
TWO Roots 26
THREE Felicity 45
FOUR A Day in the Village 51
FIVE The Seasons 61
SIX Speaking of Music 89
SEVEN Local Musicology 111
EIGHT Wedding Day 151
NINE Wedding Songs 173
TEN A Song for Mr. Biswas 221
ELEVEN Song of Swans and Snakes 242
TWELVE Songs of Love and Longing 263
THIRTEEN The *Rāmāyaṇ* Tradition 274
FOURTEEN Morning at the Temple 294
FIFTEEN Music and Miracles 340
SIXTEEN The Death of Rani 361
SEVENTEEN Chutney 368
EIGHTEEN Sweet Memory 398
NINETEEN Passage to India 404

Glossary, Biographical Dictionary, and Gazetteer 427
Selections on the Compact Disc 433
Bhojpurī Texts in Devanagari Script 441
Notes 459
Bibliography 463
Discography 481
List of Songs by First Line 487
Index 491

Illustrations

Tables

1. Overseas Indian Groups 28
2. Taxonomy of Musical Types in Felicity 92
3. Music for the Wedding, Felicity 156
4. Dube-Naipaul Genealogy 232
5. Form of *Mere Mana Basigayo* 303
6. Form of *Hey Jagata Pitaa Bhagawaana* 306
7. Form of *Shiva Shambhu Deeno Ki Bandhu,* Felicity Version 311
8. Form of *Raama Raama Bhaju Raama* 325
9. Form of *Bhajale Naama Niranjana Kaa* 327

Map

1. Felicity Village 46

Plates

1. Ships on the Hughli, Calcutta, waiting to embark emigrants (Radio Times Hulton Picture Library) 8
2. Coolie children at breakfast. By courtesy of Sea Breezes, the P.S.N. Co. Magazine, Liverpool 10
3. The ships *Elbe* and *Erne* at the Harbor at St. Helena 11
4. Coolie ships in the harbor at Port of Spain (*John Morton of Trinidad*) 13
5. Settlers in Caroni 1872 (Charles Kingsley, *At Last, Christmas in the West Indies*) 15
6. Mangrove Swamp, Caroni 1871 (Charles Kingsley, *At Last, Christmas in the West Indies*) 23
7. Huts of a Coolie village around 1900 (*John Morton of Trinidad*) 25
8. Coolie and Negro (Charles Kingsley, *At Last, Christmas in the West Indies*) 34
9. Outside Mesho's house, the junction of Cacandee Road with Pierre Road 47

10. Board houses in Jangli Tola 47
11. Map of Trinidad, 1900–1911, showing Presbyterian schools in the Caroni Savannah—Felicity is just west of Charlieville (*John Morton of Trinidad*) 49
12. Shrī Shankar Mandir, Cacandee Road 55
13. Shrī Shankar Mandir, Cacandee Road, decorated with *diyā* on Diwālī night 63
14. Lakshmī *pūjā* in the Felicity Hindu School, 1977 64
15. Hindu Sacrificing (Charles Kingsley, *At Last, Christmas in the West Indies*) 73
16. John Morton (*John Morton of Trinidad*) 113
17. Sarah Morton (*John Morton of Trinidad*) 114
18. Coolie instrumentalists around 1900: two *sāraṇgī* players (left and right) and a *tabla* player (center) 121
19. Solo Sangeet Orchestra of San Juan, Trinidad, with Hawaiian guitar, electric guitars, trap set, electric keyboard, bongo drums, and tomba drums, 1974 127
20. Guru Adesh tuning the *jal tarang* to *rāg jaūnpurī,* 15 August 1974 139
21. Amar Rajkumar, student of Guru Adesh, playing the *tabla* drum and singing *bhajan* with his wife, 1990 140
22. Sankey Ramroop offering her son the protection of her *ānchal* on the morning of his wedding, 1977 152
23. Felicity bride 157
24. Dhanlal Samooj playing the *tāssā* drum at a Felicity wedding, 1985 158
25. Felicity drummer plays the heavy bass drum to accompany the wedding *tāssā,* 1985 159
26. Dhanlal Samooj tuning the goatskin head of his earthenware *tāssā* drum at an open fire, Felicity, 1985. The drummer strikes the head with the chupes (thin beaters) until the membrane tightens to the desired pitch 160
27. Village women dancing and singing *lachārī* to the accompaniment of the *ḍholak* during the wedding celebration at Sankey Ramroop's house, 1977 163
28. Channerdaye Ramdhanie's mother playing the *ḍholak* at her grandson's wedding, Felicity, 1985 164
29. Village women singing *byāh ke gīt,* as they watch the wedding ceremony at the home of the bride, 1975 174

30. Coolie Indian women dressed in traditional *lahar pator* outfits with an *oḍhanī* covering the head and tucked in at the waist 179

31. Coolie girls at the turn of the century wearing traditional ornaments 179

32. Channerdaye's son, dressed in the likeness of Rām on the morning of his wedding. The *bahnoī* (sister's husband) is honoring the bridegroom by putting his shoes on for him, in Hindu culture, a gesture of humiliation appropriate to this ritual setting, November, 1985 181

33. Mother of the bride offering a *lotā* of water as a ritual greeting to the groom, while a loudspeaker broadcasts a recorded Indian film song, 1975 184

34. Felicity bridegroom, Channerdaye's son, wearing the *maur* ("crown") of Rām on the morning of his wedding, November 1985 188

35. Kalawatee Permanand, 1985 222

36. In Mahadewā Dube, in 1985, Jagga Nath Dube holds the photo of his grand uncle, Kapil Dev, with his Trinidadian wife, Soogee 224

37. The author in Anandnagar, Gorakhpur District, U.P., en route to Mahadewā Dube village, 1986 229

38. At the market outside Mahadewā Dube, the local bangle seller forces tiny, fragile glass wedding bangles onto the wrist of the author, 1986 230

39. Jagga Nath Dube (left) recites seven generations of the family genealogy for Umesh (seated, right foreground). Mahadewā Dube, 1986 231

40. Moon Ramnarine, 1975 243

41. The earthenware wedding pitcher, *kalasā,* as decorated for a Felicity wedding ceremony, with rows of cow dung embedded with grains of paddy rice; leaves, grain, a ritual cloth, and a *diyā* are placed atop the *kalasā,* 1977 247

42. Trinidad Sevashram Sangha, Nolan Street, Felicity 296

43. *Havan pūjā,* showing the pandit and celebrants offering camphor, water, ghee, and fruits to the ritual fire, as strings of fragrant blossoms dangle over the ritual space. In the foreground, an earthenware *diyā* is mounted on a *kalasā*, 1974 297

44. Divine Life Society, Cacandee Road, Felicity 319

45. Atmaram Maharajh playing the *ḍhantāl* during the recording of *Raama Raama Bhaju Raama,* 1974 320

46. Umesh Pandey and his daughter Alaka, Karimganj, U.P., 1986 406

47. Bhojpurī village women of Banpurwā, U.P., listen to wedding songs from Felicity, 1986 410

48. Rādhā gathering *purain* (lotus) flowers, Rāgamāla miniature, detail (Bundi Rajasthani, 18th century, Prince of Wales Museum, Bombay) 412

49. Pond alongside the road from Mahadewā Dube to Anandnagar, half with flowering *purain,* and half without, 1986 414

50. "White Boy" Ian begins the day in the back row of the fourth form, Felicity Hindu School, 1990 421

Musical Examples

I. Felicity Counting Rhyme 57
II. Boliye Rājā Rāmachandra Kī Jay, verses 4–5 76
III. Saraswatī Vandanā 141
IV. Karnivāl Kā Desh 143
V. *Tāssā* Drumming 161
VI. Āre Nadiyā Kināre 166
VII. Sānkara Koriyā Bahāro 175
VIII. Leu Na Paṇḍiṭa Rāma 182
IX. Dasa Sakhī, verse 1 183
X. Sā̃jhe Chha Sukawā, verses 1–2 190
XI. Hare Hare Bhaiyā, verses 1–2 192
XII. Surāiyā Gaiyā Ke Gobara, verses 1–5 195
XIII. Āī Gailē Ḍala, verses 1–3 199
XIV. Harīhara Bāsawā, verses 1–5 202
XV. Lauwā Na Parichho, verse 1 207
XVI. Bābā Bābā, verses 1–3 209
XVII. Sā̃jhai 211
XVIII. Melodic motifs of *Byāh Ke Gīt* 219
XIX. Ādhe Talaiyā (Number One Song), verses 1–3 245
XX. Āḍheye Ṭalawā (Number One Song), verses 1–2 248
XXI. Āḍheye Ṭalawā (Number One Song), verse variants 250
XXII. *Dīpchandī Tāl* 257
XXIII. Mere Mana Basigayo 304
XXIV. Hey Jagata Pitaa Bhagawaana 308
XXV. Shiva Shambhu Deeno Ki Bandhu, Indian Filmī version 312
XXVI. Shiva Shambhu Deeno Ki Bandhu, Felicity version 316
XXVII. Shiva Shambhu Deeno Ki Bandhu, full-score Felicity version 321
XXVIII. Raama Raama Bhaju Raama 322
XXIX. Bhajale Naama Niranjana Kaa 328
XXX. Heterophony in Bhajala Naama Niranjana Kaa 333
XXXI. Three Versions of Jai Jagadisha Hare 336
XXXII. Ganesha Sharanam, Indian and Felicity versions compared 346
XXXIII. Ganesha Sharanam, Felicity version 348
XXXIV. Aum Bhagawān 350
XXXV. Talawā Bharla Saba Nāga, Mahadewā Dube, U.P. (Number One Song), verse 1 416

Preface

✿ The West Indian Setting

The cultures of the West Indies have been the object of intensive study since World War II by anthropologists, political scientists, and linguists, who have regarded these highly stratified small-scale societies as virtual laboratories for social science research. Ethnomusicologists came later to explore the diverse music of these island cultures, attracted perhaps by the lively carnival arts practiced there, the relatively tame fieldwork conditions, and the proximity to the United States. Although the West Indies lacked the lure of the East Indies, Africa, and the Orient, and presented only the miniature scale of the some fifty societies, with virtual absence of authentic aboriginal traditions, ethnomusicological interest developed in the wake of anthropological studies of the New World Negro, particularly the seminal work of Melville J. Herskovits. His conclusions about cultural change, marginal survival, acculturation, reinterpretation, and syncretism were tested in the world of music by his students, including Richard Waterman (retention of African patterns in Trinidad) and Alan Merriam (Afro-Bahian cult groups).

The West Indies is a crescent-shaped archipelago stretching from near Florida to the Venezuelan coast, separating the Atlantic Ocean on the east from the Gulf of Mexico and the Caribbean Sea on the west. Eleven million people inhabit the more than fifty distinct geographical and political West Indian units, including the independent states of Trinidad and Tobago, Barbados, Dominica, Grenada, Jamaica, and St. Lucia.

Caribbean culture is diverse, reflecting the many racial and linguistic groups that have settled there—African, Asian, and European. Spanish, English, Dutch, and French are spoken in various regions in addition to Creole dialects such as Papiamento (Spanish Creole) in Aruba and Curaçao, Srana (Taki-Taki or English Creole) in Surinam, and Bhojpurī in Trinidad and Guyana. Diverse though the islands are in culture, language, and political organization, they share a common history of monocrop plantation economies governed by European powers but manned by Asian and African laborers.

Musicologists have concentrated their research on the large British islands, Trinidad and Jamaica. Much of the information about the aboriginal population of Trinidad comes from the chronicles of early Spanish settlers, but research on music is rare. Archaeological studies in Trinidad indicate that the first inhabitants were of the Neolithic period, and their culture has been dated back 2,000 years. Arawaks and Caribs apparently engaged in agriculture, ceramics, and weaving, but no musical instruments have been unearthed, possibly indicating that their music was primarily vocal. Nineteenth-century sources from Trinidad mention an Arawak dance, the *arectoe,* performed at sporting events with music by choral groups and accompanied by drums and conch shells. Some authorities have argued, with little evidence to support this view, that calypso has its roots in topical humorous songs *carieto* (or *arieto*) also attributed to the Arawaks. It is unlikely that much music of the rapidly dwindling aboriginal populations survived after the influx of Europeans, Africans, and East Indians throughout the eighteenth and nineteenth centuries.

The most widespread music of the Caribbean islands is of the African-derived black and Creole populations. However, a distinctive musical culture in the Caribbean is preserved by the Hindu populations of Trinidad, Guyana, Jamaica, Grenada, St. Lucia, St. Vincent, St. Kitts, St. Croix, and Martinique.

Since World War II, the music of Caribbean East Indians and West Indians alike has undergone rapid change, following patterns observed in many other societies where the impact of Western culture endangers the survival of indigenous expression. Electronic instruments and urban popular genres are replacing handcrafted instruments and traditional folk song. During the 1980s and 1990s, research on West Indian music documented these substitutions spurred by the quickened pace of urban life, the impact of technology, the introduction of mass media, and the development of global communications. It is not unusual for ethnomusicologists to return to West Indian communities they studied a decade earlier to find the musical scene transformed through modernization and Westernization. Scholars of these upbeat islands, lands of competition and carnival, are able, perhaps, to accept these innovations more gracefully than those working in more rigid societies; students of West Indian music quickly learn to celebrate change and to applaud revitalization as they note the passing of traditional folkways.

A Study of Felicity Village

Felicity village, the setting for this book, is in the heart of the Caroni cane lands of central Trinidad. Even though this community is not marked on any official map of Trinidad, Felicity has been the object of scholarly scrutiny since the 1950s, and belongs to the growing catalog of "much researched communities." This distinguished list also includes the villages of Karimpur in north India, the Mexican village of Tepotzlán, and the Arapesh community of New Guinea. Felicity is populated by fourth- and fifth-generation descendants of indentured laborers who were brought by the British to the island between

1845 and 1917. A veteran of the travails of research in India cannot be criticized for seeking the gentle charm of this village, which promises an opportunity to study a miniature Hindu world nestled in the verdant interior of a tropical tourist resort.

I first visited Felicity village in the summer of 1974, returned in June 1975, November 1977, October 1985, and January 1990, each time for a stay of several months. During these visits I recorded on tape 158 hours of music and 152 hours of interviews (transcribed onto 1,794 typed pages), and compiled 742 pages of fieldnotes. For the picture I present I have also used some 70 local commercial 33⅓ and 45 R.P.M. microgroove discs, tape dubbings of local 78 R.P.M. standard-groove discs dating from the 1940s, and books, pamphlets, music texts, song books, and liturgical writings in Hindi and English, published locally and in India. The villagers permitted me to record everything I requested—religious rituals, music at parties, question-and-answer sessions, conversations. My 300 hours of recording include a number of sessions when the villagers and I listened to earlier recordings together and I recorded their comments.

Between 1986 and 1992 I made eight research trips to northeastern India, visiting the ancestral villages of my Trinidadian friends. During my research in India I played for Indian Bhojpurī villagers the many folk songs from Felicity, and discussed this music with them. The villagers I met in India remembered people having disappeared from their area and being taken by the British to the West Indies. In a tiny village outside the town of Anandnagar ("City of Joy"), I met the relatives of the eminent novelist V. S. Naipaul, and played for them the songs of their Trinidad cousins, Naipaul's aunts of the Dube lineage. I recorded the genealogy of the Dubes, and heard the tale of indentureship from the Dube family both in India and in Trinidad. During the winter of 1990, I returned to the island to renew acquaintance, to gain fresh impressions, and to tell Trinidadian friends of my Indian adventures. For the sake of clear exposition I have combined my original visits to Felicity into one continuous story, making certain to date specific events carefully. In presenting this story I have also drawn from insights and understanding that came only after I had later visited Felicity's ancestral villages in India. My return to Felicity after sojourns in the mother country was doubly poignant and meaningful. This sequence, I trust, is also doubly rewarding on these pages.

Source references for all my texts and recordings in this book can be found in the documentation accompanying the collections of my work deposited in London, New York City, New Delhi, and Port of Spain (see Acknowledgments). These references have been compiled especially to afford scholars easy access to my research material.

The story from Felicity will persuade my reader, I believe, that the study of music cannot be separated from understanding music makers and music lovers and the culture they enjoy. This volume illustrates Alan Merriam's claim that "music *is* culture" and "what musicians do *is* society."[1] Both field and laboratory work have been essential aspects of this study. The design and implementation of the research has been deductive—to posit theories and test them again and again. Through the process of "falsification" I was able to pose ever more interesting questions leading to ever more informative and powerful ideas.[2]

My method incorporates the viewpoints and values of each participant and witness—myself included. Following Merriam's recommendations it takes into account the "multiple facets of music as symbolic, aesthetic, formal, psychological, physical," and "involves study on three analytic levels—conceptualization about music, behavior in relation to music, and music sound." Thus the focus throughout is on "man as music-maker" and not simply on musical sound.[3] Theory and method notwithstanding, the research became very personal as the villagers realized that I understood the meaning of their songs. Thus my family was taken into their lives. This rapport is reflected in my report on these experiences.

Chapter 1, "East Indians of the West Indies," provides a historical introduction to the Hindus of Trinidad, emphasizing those factors that have shaped their musical life. "Roots," Chapter 2, deals with theory and method, and also reviews the writings on the East Indian community with their relevance to the present study. It outlines anthropological models and theories (consensualism, pluralism, acculturation, syncretism, and social constructionism), and discusses their importance in an ethnomusicological study.

"Felicity," Chapter 3, describes the village and its link to the world. "A Day in the Village," Chapter 4, is an exposition of my field techniques, my role as participant-observer, and the informants I worked with. It describes the sounds and music in Felicity during a typical day. Chapter 4 also introduces two issues: aesthetics in Trinidad Indian music and the relationship of Creole music to the music of Felicity.

"The Seasons," Chapter 5, discusses music within the context of the annual cycle, particularly the *chautāl,* sung at the springtime Phāguā festival, and *kajarī,* songs for the Indian monsoon season, Sāwan. "Speaking of Music," Chapter 6, is a folk taxonomy of musical terms, based on a series of interviews.

"Local Musicology," Chapter 7, presents a history of Indian music in Trinidad, drawn from local sources. It describes the impact of films and records from India (imported from the late 1930s onward), and discusses the effects of the Trinidadian music industry on Felicity. Local songs from 78 R.P.M. records dating from the 1940s are presented. It also analyzes the introduction, by Guru H. S. Adesh, of north Indian classical music to the island beginning in 1966 and its ramifications on the local scene.

"Wedding Day," Chapter 8, describes the place of music in the wedding ceremony, and presents *tāssā* drumming and the light-hearted *lachārī* songs. Chapter 9, "Wedding Songs," analyzes the repertory of Bhojpurī *byāh ke gīt,* wedding songs passed down in oral tradition since the earliest years of the indenture. Chapter 10, "A Song for Mr. Biswas," tells how V. S. Naipaul's aunts, Kalawatee and Dhanpatee, learned the wedding songs in Chapter 9, and traces these marginal survivals back to Naipaul's ancestral home in northern India. "Song of Swans and Snakes," Chapter 11, tells of my search for variants of the first folk song sung for me in Felicity, a song of particular meaning and beauty that became my Number One Song. "Songs of Love and Longing," Chapter 12, presents a selection of songs expressing sensual yearning, where similar themes, emotions, and subjects are passed down to us from India and from Trinidad. Chapter 13 outlines the *Rāmāyaṇ* tradition, the philosophical background against which villagers live their lives. "Morning at the Temple," Chapter 14, introduces the repertory of *bhajan* (devotional song) and presents historical data (1910–1996) on the introduction to Trinidad of new Hindu sects together with new musical styles. In "Music and Miracles," Chapter 15, the introduction of a new repertory of Sai Baba songs to the village (1974–75) is discussed. Chapter 16, "The Death of Rani," illustrates the Hindu prohibition against music at the time of cremation. Chapter 17, "Chutney," discusses the history of African-Indian social relations as expressed in song; it illustrates the popular Hindi calypsos of the 1960s and '70s and Indian soca, or *chutney,* of the 1980s and '90s. In Chapter 18, "Sweet Memory," I have offered conclusions. In Chapter 19, "Passage to India," I tell of my return to Felicity after years of research in Indian villages.

And "I beg of you, in courtesy, / Not to condemn me as unmannerly / If I speak plainly and with no concealings / And give account of all their words and dealings, / Using their very phrases as they fell. / For certainly, as you all know so well, / He who repeats a tale after a man / Is bound to say as nearly as he can, / Each single word, if he remembers it" (Chaucer's prologue to *The Canterbury Tales*).

Acknowledgments

My best thanks must go to the villagers—those intelligent, perceptive, warm-hearted, gracious, intuitively kind people who did not refuse me access to any part of their musical life. They provided such a rich store of material that I can hardly do it justice. I shall always be indebted to the people of Felicity for sharing unselfishly their time and their knowledge of music, particularly to Mesho and Matti Rohit, my hosts in the village, who offered me comfort and companionship during my stays and aided in countless ways with my research. My thanks also go to Sulin and Parsuram Ramsundar for their kindness and generosity, to the learned and artistic Guru H. S. Adesh and all his students, particularly tabla specialist Amar Rajkumar and vocalist Tara Usha Bissoondialsingh. I am also grateful to Dhanpatee and Kalawatee Permanand (maternal aunts of V. S. Naipaul), Moon Ramnarine, Siewrajiah Lochan, Rajiah Sooknanan, and the sisters, Sahodare Nanad and Bhagmania George, all of whom sang for me their Bhojpurī wedding song repertories and provided information about the Indian wedding ceremony in Trinidad, past and present. Thanks also are due to members of the Divine Life Society, Unit 1, the Trinidad Sevashram Sangha, and the Shrī Shankar Mandir, for permitting me to record services in their temples, and also for arranging special recording sessions so I might better learn the *havan* and *sanḍhyā* services.

The ideas and observations of many villagers have proven of special value. In this capacity I wish to thank Kamini Ragoo, Channerdaye Ramdhanie, Rookmin Ragbir, Doday Balgobin, Kala Maharajh, Jagdai, Tara, and Rawti Ragoonanan, Popo Chatoor, Mona Deo, Bonnie and Rawti Kassie, Mohani Jagatram, Basraj Bridglal, Rupnarine Jagoonanan, Swami Satchidananda, Suruj and Dolan Maharajh, Kedar Maharajh, Indra, Chandra, and Shama Baldeo, Dotty Bholansingh, Veni Ramroop, Kowsil Jaggesar, Siew Supersad, Ravideen Ramsamooj, Brahmchārī Karmananda, Sharda Ramdhanie, and Shanti Ramnarine. Special thanks also go to Sankalia (Sankey) Ramroop for sharing her knowledge of the Bhojpurī repertory, and to Dhanlal Samooj for his help with the traditions of *ḍholak* and *tāṣṣā* drumming and also to the members of Shrī Samooj's Felicity *Chautāl* Group: Seereeram Balai, Birja Gadju, Motilal Kalpoo, Ramjit Katwaroo, Ramnarine Taman, Heesalal Baldeo, Hasiae Oree, and Ramdass Dowtal. For information on *chatī* and *barahī* childbirth celebrations I am indebted to Sandy Rampersad. I am also grateful to Shrī and Smt. Dhun,

Matti and Mesho Rohit, and Kowsil Jaggesar, who provided background information about the Sai Baba movement in Felicity.

I am particularly indebted to the individuals who aided in the analysis of my field materials. Umesh Chandra Pandey, my Indian research colleague from Karimganj, Mainpuri, Uttar Pradesh, India, read, edited, and translated the Bhojpurī song texts; I am particularly grateful for his explanations of the double entendre of these lovely poems. Without his hours of painstaking work, much of the promise of this unusual, archaic material could not have been fulfilled. His insights into the Indian character of Trinidad traditions are unique treasures, as the following pages reveal. To Dr. and Mrs. Shyam Manohar Pandey of London, formerly of Ballia district, Uttar Pradesh, India, go my thanks for assistance with the texts and translations of the Bhojpurī repertory. Also, I am grateful to Dr. Rupert Snell of the School of Oriental and African Studies, University of London, who helped me with the *bhajan* translations in Chapter 14. To Dr. Peter Cooke, of the University of Edinburgh, I owe thanks for his constant encouragement and for demonstrating how an astute ear applied to transcribing sound can contribute to the understanding of a musical culture. I would like to thank Professor Morton Klass of Barnard College, Columbia University, who introduced me to Felicity village and arranged for me to meet local musical experts and village leaders. Dr. Krister Malm of Musikmuseet, Stockholm, provided advice and guidance for this project and gracious hospitality at the Swedish Festival of India in 1987. Professor Donald Brenneis of The University of California at Santa Cruz read the manuscript and offered rewarding advice on the recent writings of West Indian anthropologists and linguists. And I am especially appreciative of the insightful comments of Professor Bruno Nettl, dean of American musicology, and co-editor of the series of which this book forms a part. Dr. Raymond Monelle, of the University of Edinburgh, has been particularly helpful on matters of musical analysis. The late Professor John Blacking read an earlier draft of the manuscript, contributing his humane and enthusiastic insights into the musical life of displaced populations.

Copies of my original open-reel recordings and supporting documentation are available at the following archives: The National Sound Archive (formerly the British Institute of Recorded Sound), London, England (Myers Trinidad Collections 1975, 1977, 1985; Myers New York City Trinidad East Indian Collection 1975; Myers London Trinidad East Indian Collections 1977, 1979, 1980); the Columbia University, Center for Studies in Ethnomusicology, New York City (Myers Trinidad Collections 1974, 1975; Myers New York City Trinidad East Indian Collection 1975); The University of Edinburgh, School of Scottish Studies, Edinburgh, Scotland (selections from the above-mentioned collections); and the Archives and Research Center for Ethnomusicology, New Delhi, India (all Trinidad collections plus eight Indian Bhojpurī collections).

I wish to express my gratitude to the University of Edinburgh for financial support and for cooperation during all phases of my work; to Mike Steyn, for the loan of his Stellavox SP7 and AKG microphones for the 1977 visit; to the National Sound Archive, London, for blank tapes and working copies of all my material; and to Dr. Stanley Sadie, CBE, and *The New Grove Dictionary of Music* (20 vols.), London, for a sabbatical leave to work in India and to prepare this manuscript. For the India portion of my research I wish to acknowledge grants from the American Philosophical Society, the British Academy, the American Institute of Indian Studies of the Smithsonian Institution, the Wenner-Gren Foundation for Anthropological Research, and the Ford Foundation. I would like to thank the Music Department of the Banaras Hindu University, my academic home in India. Dr. Shubha Chaudhuri and the staff of the Archives and Research Center for Ethnomusicology, Delhi, provided technical, physical, and emotional support before and after my ventures into the interior villages of eastern Uttar Pradesh. Moreover, I applaud their round-the-clock, seven-days-a-week services to copy the recordings of my large Trinidad and India collections for deposit in their institution; for this enormous effort I am particularly grateful, because local Indian scholars may now draw on my research.

I wish to thank Trinity College, Hartford, Connecticut, for a sabbatical leave to complete this book.

Finally, I wish to thank my family: my mother, Dr. Elsie Myers Stainton, retired managing editor of Cornell University Press for introducing me to the Indians of the Caribbean, for nursing me back to health after three particularly debilitating India sojourns, for editing and styling the many drafts of this manuscript, and for joining me on my musical journeys in Trinidad and India. Sound engineer Bob Woolford provided designer equipment for my location recordings, both in Trinidad and India, and gave professional technical assistance with post-production work; he also engineered the recording that accompanies this book, and helped to draft tables 2 and 4 and the Felicity map. Finally I thank my sons, Ian, Adam, and Sean, who have helped me, more than they will ever know, to understand the songs of village mothers.

Helen Myers
Rocky Hill, Connecticut

A Note on Translations and Transcriptions

Standard Western musical notation has been used for the transcriptions in this book, although a number of modifications have been made and special symbols added to accommodate features of the Felicity repertory:

a)
b) 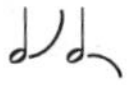
c) 
d) ↓
e) ↑
f)
g) 3+4
h) 7

Attacks incorporating a glide into the target pitch are indicated with a curved line (a). Releases that rise or fall are similarly indicated (b). Pitch glides between notes are shown with a straight line (c). Pitches that are approximately a quarter tone flat or sharp are indicated with arrows: (flat, d) (sharp, e); in a few examples, a half-sharp (f) has been given in the key signature. Sharps and flats that recur throughout a piece are given as "key signatures"; these, however, are not intended to indicate tonality or scale.

It has been possible to notate some of the *bhajan* using conventional European time signatures without distorting the essential character of the piece. For the Bhojpurī repertory, however, time signatures have been avoided, and rhythmic groupings are shown by dotted or half-bar lines with the number of units per division being indicated as in (g, h).

For ease of comparison, all the examples have been transposed so that the *g* above middle *c* serves as the *sa* or tonic. The original pitch is given for each example, as is the tempo and the pitch material of the piece, arranged from low to high (labeled "range" on the transcriptions). This pitch array is not, however, to be interpreted as a scale.

The music (particularly with the Bhojpurī songs) is laid out on the page so as to align vertically similar rhythms and tunes and thus facilitate analysis.

The fundamental problem inherent in all transcriptions of this kind is to decide which pitches should be written out as full-sized melody notes and which as small ornaments. I have aimed to arrive at a reasonable compromise, bearing in mind for each example the purpose of the transcription. Consequently, greater detail is shown in the example of the harmonium accompaniment to a vocal line, intended to illustrate melodic variation, than in, say, some of the *bhajan* scores intended to illustrate form. Those ornaments that can conveniently be described as grace notes, turns, mordents, and inverted mordents have been indicated with conventional symbols. In song texts, syllables that appear in local song books but which are omitted in performance are enclosed in square brackets. Syllables added during performance that do not appear in the Felicity song books are enclosed in parentheses.

For song texts in Indic languages, the *bhajan* in Chapter 14 have been translated according to the longstanding tradition of Hindi and Sanskrit poetry, and use the vocabulary and syntax associated with that tradition. Florid grandiose garlands of words—"diadem'd crown," "bejeweled," "betrothed," "fathomless," "bountiful," "salutations," "obeisance." This style of translation, established with the German Orientalist Max Müller's publication of *The Sacred Books of the East* (51 vols., 1879–1904), invokes the "great" tradition of classic literature of Indian cities and courts through the ages and, analogous to the grand style of the King James Version of the Bible, has literary merit in English.

Translation of the "little" tradition of village poetry is not so simple. I have chosen literal translations to suggest the compact and poignant messages typical of the little tradition as well as the great tradition. I have retained the Bhojpurī postposition (song 22, "Me also world from grant salvation") in many cases rather than converting them to prepositions. Likewise the position of the verb at the end of the phrase or sentences is typical of Hindi dialects (song 6, "This false world is"). For non-Bhojpurī-speaking readers these literal translations offer an opportunity to savor the musical nature of this language.

The transcription and the translation of folk songs recorded in village locations are challenging to the research scholar. Occasionally, where a singer's idiosyncratic pronunciation has rendered a word incomprehensible, I have added the note "obscure" in brackets.

I believe these syllables may denote a passing topical reference that has been lost. One such example shows in Chapter 8 where the syllables "palā̃wā̃ketopi" were puzzling until my Indian associate recalled that decades ago cigarettes were sold in north India in a pack picturing a man in a Panama hat.

Romanization of Indian Languages

Although English is the first language for most Felicity villagers, Bhojpurī, Hindi, and Sanskrit terms are frequently used when discussing music, religion, agriculture, kinship, and for practically all song texts, religious or secular. Most of these Indian terms have been romanized according to the conventional system outlined below (revised from Fairbanks and Misra, *Spoken and Written Hindi,* 1966). I have used local Trinidadian orthography when quoting from island publications, for example, the printed *bhajan* texts in Chapter 14. For ease of comparison of the Trinidad material with that from India, I have favored conventional styles of Indic romanization over local island orthography, for example, the standard Hindi romanization *manjīrā* (finger cymbals) not the various island spellings, including *majeera, manjeera,* and *majira.*

Sung language and spoken language differ, as the reader will note when the singers speak the words of their songs; for example, Rām, the Hindu epic hero, is sung "Rāma̲." Also, in spoken Hindi or Bhojpurī, words of Sanskrit origin ending in *a* are generally pronounced without the terminal letter and are here spelled accordingly, for example *rāg,* the Indian modal system; and *tāl,* the Indian rhythmic system. The words of unpublished Bhojpurī song texts have been transcribed exactly as sung, and the reader may note variant pronunciations of the same word according to dialect or musical setting.

Romanization Table

Vowels	*Consonants*				*Vowel Signs*
अ a	क ka	ट ṭa	प pa	श sha	त ta
आ ā	ख kha	ठ ṭha	फ pha	ष shha	ति ti
इ i	ग ga	ड ḍ	ब ba	स sa	तु tu
ई ī	घ gha	ढ ḍha	भ bha	ह ha	ता tā
उ u	ङ nga	ण ṇa	म ma	त्र tr	ती tī
ऊ ū	च cha	त ta	य ya	ड़ ṛ	तू tū
ए e	छ chha	थ tha	र ra		ते te
ऐ ai	ज ja	द da	ल la		तै tai
ओ o	झ jha	ध dha	व wa		तो to
औ au	ञ na	न na	अं an		तौ tau

The Narrators
(*In Order of Appearance*)

Sean Nine-year-old English boy who emigrated with his family to Rocky Hill, Connecticut, in 1989.

Mummy Sean's American mother.

Adam Twin brother to Sean.

Umesh A wise villager from Uttar Pradesh, India.

Helen A storyteller.

Siewrajiah Felicity grandmother, married age 13, who still remembered the indenture years. Cacandee Road, Felicity.

Jagdai Young wife and mother of Felicity. Born in Claxton Bay. Pierre Road, Felicity.

Veni Unmarried teenage daughter of a Felicity cane worker family. Nolan Street, Felicity.

Doday A Christian Indian housewife and seamstress. Born in south Trinidad. Makan Street, Union Village, Felicity.

Rajiah The wizened grandmother. A Chamār cane worker. Cacandee Road.

Mrs. Maharajh Wife of the village priest Kedar. Born in Couva. Nolan Street.

Guru Adesh The learned and beloved teacher from India. Aranguez, Trinidad.

Kamini Loquacious and smiling nurse trainee. Cacandee.

Shama Shy daughter of an Ahīr family (cattle minder and milk seller). Union Village, Felicity.

Sankey Outspoken grandmother. *Lachārī* singer par excellence. Cacandee.

Channu Kindly village seamstress and singer of devotional songs. Born in Gandhi Village, south Trinidad. Pingle Street, Cacandee.

Tara Music lover in her early twenties. Pierre Road.

Rawti Sister-in-law to Tara.

Moon The sweet singer of wedding songs. Charlieville.

Amar The thoughtful tabla student of Guru Adesh. San Juan.

Suruj Pandit Village priest who has family in London. Cacandee.

Mona Day laborer in vegetable fields. Sole support of her many children. Pierre Road.

Kamini's Mother Soft-spoken, shy, hospitable grandmother to Helen's Felicity family. Cacandee.

Kassie Office Worker. Cacandee.

Rookmin Grandmother. Born in Aranguez. Pierre Road.

Kala Daughter of Kedar Maharajh. Nolan Street.

Indra Sister of Shama. Union Village.

Kalawatee A great singer. Daughter of Kapil Dev. Maternal aunt to V. S. Naipaul, the renowned novelist. St. James, Port of Spain.

Dhanpatee Sister to Kalawatee.

Ramesh Vocal student of Guru Adesh and friend of Amar. San Juan.

Jagga Nath Village elder of Mahadewā Dube, Uttar Pradesh, India. Distant cousin of Kalawatee and Dhanpatee.

Swami Purnananda Hindu Missionary of the London branch of the Bharat Sevashram Sangha, an Indian organization based in Calcutta.

Dhun Businessman and devotee of Sai Baba. Pierre Road.

Chandra Sister of Shama. Union Village.

Kedar Pandit Village priest and prosperous shopkeeper. Nolan Street.

Brahmchari Karma Shy and gentle disciple of Swami Satchidananda of Trinidad. A bachelor. Trained in India. Cacandee, Divine Life Society temple.

Popo Grandmother, cane worker since the age of 10. Born in Felicity. Pierre Road.

Shanti Teenage music lover. Nolan Street.

Mesho School teacher raised by a Swami in the village temple. Host to Helen. Cacandee.

Matti Mesho's wife and mother of four. Helen's friend.

Kowsil Rani's mother. Matti's maternal aunt. Cacandee.

Indra Trinidad distributor at "Jamaican Me Crazy," Queens, New York.

John Storm Roberts Distinguished musicologist. Author of *Black Music of Two Worlds.*

Sundar Popo "Popular Singer of Trinidad and Tobago, West Indies!" Monkey Town, south Trinidad.

Mom Helen's mother.

Veena Gokhale Feature writer for the *Sunday Mid-Day*, Bombay.

Ian "White Boy." Brother to Sean and Adam.

Maa Matti.

Sailor Matti's brother, officeworker in Port of Spain. Cacandee.

ঔ Music of Hindu Trinidad ঔ

☙ Chapter One ❧

East Indians of the West Indies

A man's destination is not his destiny,
Every country is home to one man
And exile to another.

T. S. Eliot, "To the Indians Who Died in Africa"

"Why Felicity?" Sean asked. "Why Felicity, Mummy?"

"You know. That's the village where Ian went. Where they called him white boy. In the Hindu school. In Trinidad," I explained.

"At Mesho's house," Adam said. "Sean, you know Mummy stayed with Mesho and Matti before we were born, us and Ian."

"I *know*," Sean said. "But why Felicity?"

"I love Felicity. I loved it before I arrived there—because of the name. Felicity. Happiness."

"Mummy, you're silly about names," Sean said.

"That may be—but I am happy there."

"What do you do there?"

"Well, I hear Felicity singing."

"What about Number One Song?" Adam asked.

"That's where I learned it. Siewrajiah sang it for me. It came before all the other songs. But it began before that. It began long ago and far away. It began in India."

☙ From India: Islands, Swans, and the Seven Seas

"*Tāpū,*" Umesh explained. "*Tāpū* is island. People in my village might say, 'He left for *tāpū.*' *Tāpū* is the place where there is water around it and people cannot come back from there. Old-time people thought we were going to work at *tāpū* where Marīch was king. Those people who lived on the plains of Uttar Pradesh even could not imagine what would like a *tāpū* be. Our people had information from *Rāmāyaṇ* about Sri Lanka island. God Rām had to build a bridge over the sea to go to there. What simple man could come back from there?"

"Mirīch *tāpū?*" I asked. "Mirich Desh? Morisu? Is 'Marīch' Mauritius?"

"We don't know that. People had fear. People did not come back from *tāpū.* People could not fly. But these kings could fly. They had ships like airships in those days—planes, gliders. Rāwaṇ had one, presented to him by a god, a *dev.* They just like shape of swan. In the middle, where the wings are, they are open at the top and people can sit in it."

"My Number One Song begins with swans," I said. "The male and female swan. What else do swans do?"

"They are never alone. They are always in a pair, husband and wife. They are the symbol of royalty. Swan is the vehicle of Saraswatī, goddess of knowledge. Also, we use them as symbol of justice: *dūdh ka dūdh, pānī ka pānī,* 'milk of milk, water of water.' When you give milk to a swan, he drinks the milk but he leaves that water what is in it away. *Pānī* is a false thing in milk. Lying is water and truth is milk.

"Swans swallow pearls, real pearls," Umesh continued. "They won't eat false pearls, only pure pearls. *Sachchā motī.*"

"What good is the real pearl if the swan swallows it?" I asked.

"That is the identification of the real swan. Another expression is used in the village, *kai hansā motī chune, kai kalank mari jāya.* Either swan picks the pearl or starves. He does not eat anything. In a sense, a good man, either he lives for the truth or he would like to die instead of telling a lie."

"Which is more important, the pearl or the swan?" I asked.

"Both are important. Because swan cannot live without pearl. And without pearl we cannot identify swan."

"Are the swans in Number One Song eating pearls? The song doesn't mention pearls."

"Well the swan doesn't live in the pond, only in the lake. And pearls are not in the pond, they are in the lake."

"How do you explain Number One Song?"

"This is a song, Helen. And song is composed by a village poet based on imagination. Village people won't understand the lake—*jhīl.* They understand pond—*talaiyā.* It contains very little water. For them, *tāl* is a *jhīl. Talaiyā* is a small pond and *tāl* is a big pond and *jhīl* is a great pond. What is the difference between between *jhīl* and *tāl? Jhīl* does not get dried up in summer."

"Do village people have swans?" I asked.

"No, we don't have swans. We have stories about swans. And the spirit is also called swan—*hansā*—very much used in my village. My grandma always said it. 'When *hansā* will fly away, my dead body will be left on this earth.'"

"We think of swans and songs together with death too. We call it 'Swan song.' Shakespeare said 'I will play the swan and die in music.' That is from *Othello.*"

"We have a song in Karimganj, in my village:

ek din ure tāl ke hansā
pheri nahi āvenge
mātī mātī me mili jābe
ūpar harī ghās jami ābe
āi nagar ke pasū bāhi chari jābenge

1 ☙
One day the swan will fly off the pond,
And will not come back again.
The soul will go in the soil,
Green grass will grow on it.
The cattle of the village will come and graze on it.

"It means the person will die. This body is soil. This body of soil will mix in the soil. And on it green grass will grow."

"We say this in America too," I said. "Our poets say that grass is 'the beautiful uncut hair of graves.' And we lie on the grass."

"We don't know what is in there when we lie on the grass," Umesh replied. "Relaxing on the grass. Enjoying on him. And the cattles satisfying their appetite from him. I was four years old when I heard this song. I heard it first in my mother's *naihar,* her mother's village of Nagalā Dhansingh, south of my Karimganj. So Marīch could go anywhere on the swan: he could fly. This is the real beginning of our story, our *Rāmāyaṇ.* Rām had nothing. He had to walk. When Rām won over Rāwaṇ, he took Rāwaṇ's swan-plane and came to Ayodhya, here in U.P., and arrived just in time. We call these planes *pushhpakvimān. Pushhpak* means a ship-like and beautiful flower. *Vimān* is plane. Also, when people die we make bamboo *vimān* to carry them—what goes in air, that is *vimān.*"

"Bamboo is a grass," I said.

"Really? Then a very powerful grass. And *pushhpak* is a flower. Flowers are considered beautiful, light, and pure—the sign of purity, of virgin. I think *Pushhpakvimān* was Indra's plane. He was the most beautiful man. He had hundreds hundreds women in his court. He is *kāmdev,* the god of sex.

"*Rāmāyaṇ* teaches us everything. *Rāmāyaṇ* tells that Marīch was Rāwaṇ's mother's brother. Rāwaṇ, who stole Sītā, Rāwaṇ who was the demon king of Sri Lanka. And Marīch was the king of Marīch. Marīch wanted to be a good person and he had an art to change his body into any kind of animal.

"Marīch was the king who played the role of beautiful golden deer in *Panchwatī,* 'five trees,' the forest where Rām and Sītā lived. Sītā saw this beautiful golden deer, and she asked her husband to bring that deer for her. As Rām left their hut and shot this deer, the deer cried the name of Rām's brother, 'Lakshmaṇ! Lakshmaṇ!' and Sītā thought that Rām was shot with the arrow. As Lakshmaṇ left the hut, Rāwaṇ came and stole Sītā. So this is our story, our *Rāmāyaṇ.*"

"You know, Umesh, in Felicity they still tell these stories. And they perform the Rāmlīlā play each year. And the Bhojpurī songs tell about Rām and Sītā. And the villagers often hold nine-nights *Rāmāyaṇ* readings with singing, chanting, and vegetarian food after the ceremony. Even the modern spicy *chutney* songs tell stories from the *Rāmāyaṇ.* Long ago, for the old Coolies, Trinidad became the most popular *tāpū.* People made the most money there. They called it 'Chīnītāt.'"

"Oh! Chīnītāt!" Umesh laughed. "*Chīnī* is Chinaman. And *Chīn* is China. And *Chīnī* is sugar. And *Chīnīmittī* is china clay. *Tāt* is cloth of jute."

"People in those days believed that Trinidad lay just beyond Fiji," I added.

"They say *sāt samundar pār,* 'across seven seas,'" Umesh continued. "Sea is startling, but Indian people believe that after crossing the seven seas you arrive at a beautiful place, according to your wish, your imagination. And the Coolies were given the same thing, thoughts that they would become rich."

"But what is *kālāpānī* ('black water')?" I asked. "All the books about indentureship mention *kālāpānī.*"

"*Kālāpānī* is sending a person across a sea. It is a lifetime prison," Umesh replied. "At the British period, people were sent to the Andaman and Nicobar *tāpū* for *kālāpānī* prison. After committing a big crime they were not punished to death but sent there to lifetime prison. It is called *kālāpānī.* But when these Coolies learned of *Chīnī,* of gold and sugar, they made castles in the air to come back rich to their villages. When you go *sāt samundar pār,* you are not forced to go. You are not punished to go. But the British gave Coolies a fantasy of *sāt samundar pār.* They were not sent in prison."

"What direction do you go to travel *sāt samundar pār?*"

"Well, Helen, there is only direction for that. The Queen lives in *sāt samundar pār.* You cross one sea, walk on ground or go on horse, cross the second sea and when sun sets, just rest. There is only way to go for *sāt samundar pār.*

"It is not easy to go there. Village people tell how after crossing one sea you find so many hundreds of lions, when you cross another sea the place is full of cobras and scorpion, then third you find some magic witches who makes man like donkey, and one you will find bushes and forest of thorns, and next you will find demons who will eat people up, and in one you find only fire so it is hard to get through, and the last one is the good one where you want to go. A place like heaven. Everything is so nice, beautiful, and Queen lives there."

"What about the king?"

"Never mind king! Queen! And sometimes people get *uṛan khatolā,* a flying cot."

"*Uṛan* what?"

"*Uṛan khatolā.* Don't you know it? All village people know it! A beautiful small rocking *khatolā* is made with edges to hold on. People sit down on it and fly. They get *uṛan khatolā* from beautiful good magic women."

"I thought they were carpets, flying carpets."

"No. Flying cots. Or maybe from some Baba they get *uṛan kharāmūn,* flying wooden sandals. People stand on them and straight! Man flies in the air! You are flying then and you can cross the sea, the forest—only two things to cross, the sea and the forest. There were bad people to hurt and also good people to help."

"Were the British good or bad?" I asked.

"They were never good, were they?"

ఌ

"If you came this way, / Taking any route, starting from anywhere, / At any time or at any season, / It would always be the same: you would have to put off / Sense and notion" (Eliot, *Four Quartets*).

ఌ The Voyage

"Me mother born India, me father born India," Siewrajiah said, "but I born Trinidad." The old women of Felicity remember the particulars of their family and the voyage to Trinidad at the hands of British agents. "Me mother belong to Gorakhpur"—a district of northeastern Uttar Pradesh near the border with Nepal, dotted with hundreds of villages, rich in lore and song, economically impoverished, of cane lands and sugar factories, with streams and rivulets enriching the loam soil while impeding trade, where travel during the monsoon was impossible until the opening of the 78-mile mainline railway from Salempur to Gorakphur city in January 1885. "The English tried to get people from India," Siewrajiah said, "fooling people, telling they sending you somewhere where you *want* to go. And then they take you in the ship and land you in Trinidad. Coolie ain know to read, ain know to write—it is so they fool people. India ain have money. The English say, 'you just have to sift sugar and make plenty money.' They come in big ship. Before they call *jahāj,* a big boat taking three month to reach Trinidad from India. It used to move slow, and everything pack up in that boat, and that boat was never finished when it done land in Trinidad, and that boat still ain finish."

*

Out from Calcutta she sailed—the *Wellesley,* or the *Bucephalus,* the *Sir Robert Seppings,* the *Adelaide,* the *Hereford,* the *Burmah,* the *Scindian,* the *Ganges,* the *Foyle,* the *Fatel Razack,* like graceful swans, these great full-rigged

Plate 1. Ships on the Hughli, Calcutta, waiting to embark emigrants. (Radio Times Hulton Picture Library)

ships—through the unpredictable waters of the first sea, the Bay of Bengal (plate 1). On board, she carried the newly recruited East Indian indentured laborers bound to work the sugar plantations of the New World. And when India and Ceylon and the first sea were left behind, the northeastern monsoon carried her to the storms of the Mozambique Channel. There, with her sorry human cargo unprepared for the icy winds, she turned the Cape of Good Hope to the second sea and headed into the bitter waves of the south Atlantic. She might call at Table Bay, South Africa, to take on fresh water, rations, and laudanum for the sick. Then she rode the southeastern trades past St. Helena (15′58″S, 5′43″W), past Ascension (7′57″S, 14′22″W), and crossed the Equator where, with good luck, she picked up the northeastern trades that would carry her to the final sea, the Caribbean.

With bad luck, she lay becalmed in the doldrums, that equatorial belt of light and baffling winds between the northern and southern trades. Under sail, the voyage could last as many as 188 days or as few as 80 (compare this with the Middle Passage of the African slave trade which took 30 to 40 days). Even when steam came into general use around the 1870s onward, 22 of the 28 immigrant-carrying vessels still were under sail.

Stories of these voyages *sāt samundar pār* are told in Felicity today: "And coming in the ship—there were thousands of people in the ship," my young friend Jagdai told me. "They mess up and they die in the ship together. They throw those who were sick—they throw them away in the sea, just like that."

"They used to pack them like sardines," her sister-in-law Veni explained (plate 2). "In the ships, right? And what lived lived, and what died died."

The infectious tropical diseases (so feared by the British)—typhoid, cholera, dysentery, malaria—swept through the poorly ventilated holds of the great ships. British accounts tell us, for example, that in the year 1851–52, 4.5 percent of the Coolies bound for the West Indies were lost; in 1852–53, 5.6 percent, and in 1855–56, 5.8 percent. In 1856–57, the agents of indentureship were startled by the rising and unconscionable mortality: 17.3 percent died en route; on the *Roman Emperor,* 88 deaths out of a total of 313; on the *Maidstone,* 92 dead of 375; and on the *Merchantman,* 120 dead of 385.

The musicologist cannot escape these tallies of death, these accounts of shipwreck, fire, hurricane, stench and pestilence, epidemic, suicide and despair—history, the stuff of myth. For amid descriptions of these horrors are found the few hints about song.

Dr. De Wolfe of the *Sheila* wrote on the second of March, 1883: "I do not know how the fact became known that cholera was on board. . . . The ship was very quiet, Coolies and crew were very subdued, there was no music and little conversation" (British Consul, Surinam, to Foreign Office).

In the diary of Dr. Wiley, surgeon superintendent of the *Delharree,* 1872, we read:

> *October 25:* Very wet all day, and a heavy storm with lightning; kept the coolies below.
>
> *October 29:* Lovely day, with a little wind; coolies on deck all day, singing and dancing in the evening; invalids improving, with the exception of the children who seem to get worse.
>
> *October 31:* Blowing very hard, with heavy seas all day. Had to keep the coolies down below; unable to give a cooked meal. . . . One of the women killed her child, name Soonmereah—a strong healthy child—and another weak child died, gradually wasted away, although receiving . . . medical comforts. (J. Mackensie, Bengal Government, to Government of India)

F. J. Mouat, Inspector of Jails, Bengal, notes: "The Madrassee is a lively, singing fellow" (*Report on the Mortality of Emigrant Coolies on the Voyages to the West Indies in 1856–57*).

The diary of Captain E. Swinton of the *Salsette* (Calcutta to Port of Spain, 17 March–2 July, 1858), records a description of an epidemic on shipboard together with general comments about music and dance.

PLATE 2. Coolie children at breakfast.

Plate 3. The ships *Elbe* and *Erne* at the Harbor at St. Helena.

May 3: A woman died of dysentery. This makes seventy dead. It is dreadful mortality; still any one who had ever sailed with them would not wonder at it, as they are so badly selected at the depôt, and so many diseased sent on board.

May 20: A little girl died. Jane getting music up to amuse the Coolies.

May 28: The doctor says he wants medicine (chalk-mixture), and two men died of diarrhoea. Coolie blind man dead; a little girl and its mother almost gone also. Doctor asked me if I intended to call at St. Helena, as he was out of chalk-powder and laudanum, both essentially required for the Coolies' complaint. I replied, Not unless he insisted on it, as it would put the ship to considerable expense by doing so.

June 1: One child died of dropsy. The doctor and Jane attending the sick. Doctor wrote me a note, begging me to call at St. Helena for medicine, which I must now do, in compliance with the terms of the charter-party. Woman died.

June 3: Hove to off James Town, St. Helena.

June 8: One man died, age thirty-five. Another man died; this is the last of another family, who said this morning he was much better, and really appeared far from a dying man; but it is most odd, how very suddenly these

> people go off from apparent medium health to general debility, though kept up with port wine and soup; and were it not for the unremitting attention of Jane, many of them would have sunk under the disease. I hope she may not herself fall a prey to her disinterested kindness, but she seems to have no fear.
>
> *June 21:* The Coolies very musical.
>
> *June 22:* Coolies performing.
>
> *June 23:* Coolies having some native games and war-dances.
>
> *June 25:* Little girl, two years old, died of diarrhoea, and neglected by its mother. Coolies performing.
>
> *June 30:* Mustered the Coolies, and find only 108 men, 61 women, and 30 children under ten years of age, 2 infants, and 2 interpreters, left, of the 323 or 324 we sailed from Calcutta with, and 3, I fear, will die before we can get them landed.

Jane Swinton, surely one of the good beautiful magic women foretold in the *Rāmāyaṇ,* offered sympathetic advice in her husband's account. She tells us:

> One day, when ordered by the doctor for all to run round for exercise, one woman *enciente* did not like to go, but was ashamed to tell the doctor why, and came and told me to tell him; by having proper female nurses these difficulties would be obviated. We found exercise, such as their native dances, very useful in keeping up a good state of health—an experiment which we tried. Music is also very desirable, and keeping them employed in any way, to prevent them from thinking and drooping. (*Journal of a Voyage,* 8–11, 14)

ര

"'O voyagers, O seamen, / You who came to port, and you whose bodies / Will suffer the trial and judgement of the sea, / Or whatever event, this is your real destination.' / So Krishna, as when he admonished Arjuna / On the field of battle.

Not fare well, / But fare forward, voyagers" (Eliot).

ര ARRIVAL

From the sailing ship, Trinidad's northern range, some 900 meters high, was the landfall. Passing through the Bocas del Dragón, the "Dragon's Mouths," and into the warmer gentler waters of the Gulf of Paria, the Atlantic behind them, the rounding of the Cape behind them, the disorientation of the voyage, seven lands and seven seas behind them, the humiliation of recruitment, the filth of the depot, the trickery, the loss of family, India behind them, all behind them, they—the East Indian indentured laborers, the new "slaves"—sighted the New World.

For any sailor it is a memorable event, the blue waters of the sixth sea of the Windward Islands mixing with the green of the seventh, awash with silt spillage from the great Orinoco Delta, and the long-awaited sights and sounds of a promised land:

> We became aware of the blue mountains of North Trinidad ahead of us; to the west of them the island of the Dragon's Mouth; and westward again, a cloud among the clouds, the last spur of the Cordilleras of the Spanish Main. . . . To the eastward the northern hills of Trinidad, forest clad, sank to the water; to the south lay a long line of coast, generally level with the water's edge, and green with mangroves, or dotted with coco-palms. That was the Gulf of Paria, and Trinidad beyond. . . . In half an hour more we were on shore, amid Negroes, Coolies, Chinese, French, Spaniards, short-legged Guaraon dogs, and black vultures. (Kingsley, *At Last, Christmas,* 54; plate 4)

Plate 4. Coolie ships in the harbor at Port of Spain. (Reprinted from *John Morton of Trinidad*)

And how does a woman or man feel at this first glimpse of the unknown? The Coolies (perhaps from the Chinese *k'u,* "bitter," and *li,* "strength")[4] never realized that this island, this *tāpū,* would become their home. Their original plan had been to go back, but had they misplaced their trust?—placed their fate mistakenly in the hands of Indian and British strangers, been forced to break the rules of their caste and unwittingly abandoned their villages forever? Had they in fact crossed *kālāpānī* to banishment? How could they know, as the ship, the *jahāj,* came to dock in the harbor of Port of Spain, as they first set foot on Trinidadian soil, that the promised life of ease, "sifting sugar," was never to be? They did not anticipate the back-breaking toil of the cane fields and the relentless passing of the eighteen-month sugar-cane cycle: plant, burn, cut, harvest, grind, plant, burn, cut, and so on and so on and so on.

The Coolies did not know they probably would not see India again. "The journey had been final," Trinidad novelist V. S. Naipaul writes. "How complete a transference had been made from eastern Uttar Pradesh to Trinidad, and that in days when the village was some hours' walk from the nearest branch-line railway station, the station more than a day's journey from the port, and that anything up to three months' sailing from Trinidad. . . . My grandfather had made a difficult and courageous journey. It must have brought him into collision with startling sights, even like the sea, several hundred miles from his village" (*Darkness,* 29–30). Naipaul's grandfather returned to his tiny brahman village, Mahadewā Dube, in northeastern Gorakhpur district, and spun his now legendary tales of Chīnītāt. Then, restless, ambitious, he set out again for the West Indies. The villagers of Mahadewā Dube brought out photos of Kapil Dev and told what an unusual, brave man he was, how such a *tāpū* voyager became prosperous, whereas they who had shrunk behind had sunk deeper into poverty and destitution.

"Grandson Naipaul came to see us," they told me.

Within twenty years of the Trinidad indentureship, Indians began to settle the island. The yearning to go home eased as the new East Indian community grew and, in a restrained sense, flourished. In 1854, only 180 Coolies returned to India; in 1865, 302. In 1865, 25 Coolies who had completed their indenture agreed to commute the value of their return passage, which they had earned, into land grants, setting the precedent for a new policy whereby the Trinidad Colonial Government offered ten acres of land in exchange for the return voyage. In 1872, the option was changed to ten acres of land, or five acres with £5 cash, then in 1881, reduced to £5 and no land. In 1890, the option of either cash or land for the return voyage was withdrawn. Six years after the land-grant policy was instituted, Charles Kingsley saw settlements going up in the plains of central Caroni (plate 5):

Plate 5. Settlers in Caroni 1872. (Reprinted from Kingsley, *At Last, Christmas in the West Indies*)

> We passed another pleasant sight: more Coolie settlers, who had had lands granted them in lieu of the return passage to which they were entitled, were all busily felling wood, putting up bamboo and palm-leaf cabins, and settling themselves down, each one his own master, yet near enough to the sugar-estates below to get remunerative work whenever needful. (Kingsley, 211)

As the years passed most Coolies stayed in Trinidad, joining the established East Indian community and perhaps remembering the troubles in India which they had left behind. British government accounts show the pattern whereby émigrées had evacuated districts in northeastern India where the rains had failed and the annual crop perished. In 1860–61, Coolies had been drawn in great number from the North-Western Provinces (later the United Provinces, today Uttar Pradesh). In 1865–66, they came primarily from Orissa and Bihar, in 1873–75, from Bihar, Oudh (also in modern Uttar Pradesh), and the North-Western Provinces. In 1904 the agents suffered a slack season and reported: "The recent harvest in India has been exceptionally good, and the result is that emigrants are at present almost unobtainable" (*Annual Report* 1904).

❦ TRICKERY AND FILTHY LUCRE

Coolie recruits were vulnerable, unemployed, ailing, hungry, some enticed away during the inevitable family quarrels that force unwieldy four-generation village households to break into smaller groups, some electing indentureship after losing reputation in the village, some escaping condemnation by village elders, some Hindu pilgrims, fasting, often ecstatic, enticed and snatched by agents—all individuals with social and financial problems who had been intercepted by the the *arkatiā* (*arkati, arkattie, arkat;* "recruiter," also "clever, dexterous, ingenious"), the Indian middleman, the trickster who lurked outside the village, who lured the unsuspecting to the *nākā,* the magnet town ("outpost, border"; also cattle exchange)—Allahabad, Faizabad, Agra, Banaras. No one in Felicity today has forgotten the trickery.

"They tell them that they going to Trinidad to sift sugar," Doday explained to me. "They wasn't knowing they was coming to be slave here. My grandfather often said they thief some of them and bring them come. Unknowing to their parents, they catch them by the wayside and they bring them."

"Who ain like you in the village, and they want you to go away from here again," old Rajiah the Chamār cane worker told me. "They fool you on and they bring you come. And they done put you in the ship. And they done take money. And they can't go back. They have to come to Trinidad. So, well, when the old India people come, well, we Trinidadian then."

"They fool them, they fool them," Mrs. Maharajh the brahman housewife said. "Come down in Trinidad and they will work for plenty money. They don't have money to go back. When they see it don't have money down here, those people didn't have, so they had to stay here and stick out with everything."

And in the villages of Uttar Pradesh families still remark on the sudden disappearance of a relative or neighbor. "I heard this word," Umesh said, "and I remembered that my grandfather told me *arkatiā* came and took people away.

"'Hook,' *katiyā*," he explained. "To catch the fish, metal thing to capture, to drag things. We have a lot of stories about it. The Baba came and showed a mirror to young men and boys. Or Baba made the man small and put him in a bag and carried him away. When we young we were told not to go with any Baba, to any jungle, especially at noon when no one is outside watching. When Baba capture someone they don't come back. They vanish. And nobody know where they gone."

The nineteenth-century descriptions of the East Indian indenture only give more details than the stories that Trinidadian people tell today. As I discovered these descriptions, I came to share with my Felicity friends—the grandchildren and the great-grandchildren of those original "Coolies"—their sense of outrage against this inhuman system.

I read the 1871 account of indentureship by the District Magistrate of Ghazipur to Umesh:

> The licenced recruiter has in his employ a number of unlicenced men called arkatias and while the licenced recruiter sits leisurely in some district these creatures of his go out into all the neighbouring districts and collect emigrants. The arkatias entice the villagers with a wonderful account of the place for which the emigrants are wanted and bring in their victims from long distances to the neighbourhood of the headquarters of the licenced recruiter. The licenced recruiter hearing of the arrival of a party goes out a short distance to meet them when the arkatia disappears. On arrival at the sub-depot, the intending emigrants are told the exact facts of their prospects, and on hearing them, decline to proceed. Very well, says the licenced recruiter, you are all at perfect liberty to return, but I have here a little bill against you for road expenses, and as you have no money I must have your lotah [bowl] and dopattah [shawl] and anything else that will procure me a refund of the amount I have expended. The wretched coolie may be a hundred miles from his home, and finding that he has the option of returning penniless . . . and of emigrating, chooses the latter alternative; but this is not voluntary emigration. (District Magistrate of Ghazipur, 1871)

"Whatever you own," Umesh explained. "This man asked for whatever the Coolie owned. 'Give me your *lotā* and your dhoti.' *Dhotī-lotā* comes in rhyme. We say in the village, 'even his *dhotī-lotā* was also gone.' These are the least thing person must have for living."

"Which is the most important?"

"Both," Umesh explained. "Dhoti is the most important thing what people put on under their waist. They didn't have underwear on, only dhoti—one-piece cloth. Without his dhoti he is flat naked. So he couldn't leave dhoti. And if he leaves his *lotā,* then he couldn't drink water and also he couldn't clean himself."

"There was only way to have drinking water out of the well," he continued. "They use *lotā* for this."

"And for the cleaning?" I asked.

"When they sit down mostly they face to the wind. When they wash, they hold the *lotā* with the right hand and pour water on the left hand to wash. They find a clean soil and begin to rub over and under the inside of the *lotā* and also hands until he begin to feel the *lotā* is absolutely shiny. Again do the same procedure because second time when they do it hand is wet and *lotā* is wet and when soil is wet it helps most to clean to *lotā*. This goes three times altogether. And fourth time wash both hands up to the elbow and fifth time feet up to the knee. And sixth time again take the soil to clean hands and *lotā* because hands had touched the feet. This scientific concept is called 'germs.' Seventh time they fill the new fresh water again to clean their face and mouth. It is custom then and now."

"This explanation of yours on Hindu sanitation is longer than the District Magistrate of Ghazipur's discussion of indentureship."

"Indentureshit!"

"Now listen to the report by Nagendranath Gangulee written in 1947:"

> Emigration agents of the British Colonies appointed professional recruiters, who were generally very unprincipled men. They frequented the Indian villages where the crops had failed and also the pilgrim centers where thousands of illiterate and extremely poor people congregated. Here the wily and most unscrupulous recruiters cast their net and entrapped their victims, who were then brought to the recruiting depots for the so-called legal procedures. The recruiter received a gratuity of Rs. 45 (£3) per head for every male and Rs. 55 (£3.13.6) per head for every female whom he successfully enrolled as an emigrant. For the class of people to which the recruiter belonged, the temptation thus given was strong enough to inspire him to use means that were horribly cruel and utterly dishonest. (*Indians*, 43)

"Forty-five, fifty-five silver rupees!" said Umesh. "Niney-two percent silver British Indian coins. For this much money recruiter could do very illegal work against of humanity.

"Village people try to collect these old coins. Mostly they find in the rain when mud house falls down. People hid them inside the mud wall inside old clay pitcher to keep safe from the thief. And they died. Old people always kept secrecy up to the end. If they died by accident or if their throat were caught and couldn't speak family people never knew where the money was, they never even knew they had money. It is always great to buy an old rich man's house! In the rainy weather if the old house falls, you may find silver coins buried in the mud."

"It says here that during 1845, the first year of emigration to Trinidad, Thomas Caird of Calcutta and 300 *arkatiā* searched an area of 5,000 square miles and got 3,000 Coolies."

"They would have been worth about one *lakh* [100,000] and fifty thousand rupees," Umesh calculated. "Divided by 300, each *arkatiā* might have made 500 silver coins."

"Enough to make a dirty person filthy rich in olden days," I said.

Westminster and the Coolies

The British legislators in Westminster, with their humanitarian as well as self-serving motivations, continually refined the indenture system: to avoid winter in the south Atlantic ships were permitted to embark only from the 1st of October through the 28th of February. The Coolies were issued warm clothing; for women, two flannel jackets, woolen petticoat, worsted stockings, shoes, and sari; for men, woolen trousers, jacket, a red woolen cap, and shoes. To deter interracial marriage in the Colonies, in 1870 the English introduced a statutory quota of forty women for each one hundred men, a system that rarely worked since the tales of harassment frightened Indian women. When the quota was strictly enforced, the recruiters turned away men to achieve the four to ten ratio. Rarely did family groups sign up. Most recruits were single and unrelated, and when they reached the depots of Calcutta or Madras, they found themselves alone, in the rush and confusion of the depots, amid hundreds of strangers.

Record keeping by Calcutta administrators was chaotic, and many Coolies out of shame concealed their true identity. The renowned Irish linguist, Sir George Abraham Grierson (1851–1941), B.C.S., Officiating Magistrate of Patna, later M.R.A.S., Bengal Civil Service, Member of the Royal Asiatic Society of Bengal, claimed registration to be a farce: "a disorganized bundle of papers . . . more or less mutilated or destroyed by mice" (*Report,* 1883). The surviving papers document an unusual mixed group—combining skilled and unskilled laborers, high and low castes, Hindu and Muslim, tribal and village—the total understanding of which would explain exactly and entirely the modern Trinidadian social amalgam. But detailed information about individual recruits is scarce and no one has been able to account with certainty for the unmistakable Bhojpurī cultural and linguistic focus of the Indo-Caribbean culture that formed in this century. Could an investigation of Coolie song reveal more about the process of blending and acculturation than the Annual Reports that follow?

For 1872–73: The Protector of Emigrants lists in his Annual Report the departure from Calcutta of 2,521 Coolies of high caste, 4,974 of agricultural castes, 1,537 of artisan castes, and 5,309 of low castes, together with 2,910 Muslims.

For 1877–78: V. Richards gives details about 18,488 emigrants: brahmans, high caste—2,223; agriculturalists—4,438; artisans—763; low castes—8,807; "Mussulmans"—2,250; Christians—7. Of this total, 2,151 went to Trinidad. Half were from the North-Western Provinces, a quarter from Oudh, and the remainder from Bihar, Bengal, Native States, Punjab and dependencies, Central India, and Orissa. One hundred and thirty-one were from "miscellaneous Madras and Bombay, etc."

For 1883: Sir George Grierson records facts about a group of 1,200 north Indian Coolies: Muslims—264; high caste Hindus ("Brahmans," "Rajput," "Chettri")—231; agricultural castes ("Kahar," "Kurmi," "Gowala")—454; low castes ("Chamar")—277. The Calcutta Protector of Emigrants lists 1,995 "Brahmins," 2,454 agriculturalists, 456 artisans, and 2,790 low castes.

For 1908: 1,248 came from the United Provinces, 983 from Oudh, 120 from Bihar, 53 from the Native States, 25 from Central India, 7 from the Central Provinces, 6 from Punjab, 1 from Bombay and Madras, 1 from Bengal, and 2 from "other" places.[5]

What faces did these statistics represent? Many of them, particularly in the early years of the indenture, were the Dhangars, the "janglies," a dark, semi-aboriginal hill people, short of stature, from Chota Nagpur. These tribal folk, outside the caste system, included the Santals, Mundas, and Oraons. They had a long tradition of hiring themselves out as seasonal laborers in the towns and cities of India, and were natural targets for the recruiting agents. But there is no evidence of northeastern Indian tribal music in modern Trinidad.

Then there was the flotsam of humanity, the unemployed and homeless of India's teeming ports—Calcutta, Bombay, and Madras. They, too, were easy targets for the agents. The musical repertory of these urban poor would have derived from adjacent villages which they or their parents had quit during drought years. In the district capitals of eastern U.P.—Banaras, Gorakhpur, Ghazipur, and so on—village song thrives, particularly at the outer perimeter of these sprawling and, with the exception of Banaras, rather undistinguished administrative centers.

On the 30th May, 1845, the *Fatel Razack,* the first ship bearing indentured East Indian labor to Trinidad, dropped anchor in the Port of Spain harbor with 197 males (including one infant) and 28 females. By March of 1846, all of the sugar estates on Trinidad save one had requested indentured laborers, and 812 Coolies had arrived. By 1848, 5,403 East Indian workers were on the island; by 1870, 29,583; by 1892, 93,569. After 1860, immigration from the south Indian port of Madras was halted, and from that time forth the Indian culture of Trinidad incorporated primarily traditions of the *Rāmāyaṇ* belt of the North, following the great plain of the Jamuna and Ganges rivers from Delhi to Calcutta, and focusing on the Bhojpurī-speaking region surrounding Banaras.

The First Publication on Bhojpurī Folk Songs; Felicity is Founded

Grierson was no ordinary civil servant. His penetrating linguistic survey of north Indian languages and his Bhojpurī grammar remain definitive. And Sir George was mindful of the importance of song in understanding the lives of village peoples. In the *Journal of the Royal Asiatic Society of Great Britain and Ireland* he published "Some Bihārī Folk-Songs" (1884) and "Some Bhoj'pūrī Folk-Songs," written in 1886, the same year the first parcel of land adjacent to Felicité estate, Trinidad, was sold to Kakandi and our village was founded. Sir George had a deep understanding of Indian village customs. Most of his transcriptions are of the men's repertory, especially the long and topical *birahā*, still popular in Banaras and environs.

Even so, the images of the opening part of Number One Song found a place in his work: "The pond is dried up, the lotus is withered, and the swan bewails his separation from his beloved. Sar'wan's mother weeps, saying who will carry my *kāwar* [yoke] now." Sar'wan, he notes, is "the hero of a great many poems, principally in the Magahī and Bhoj'pūrī dialects." And the perplexing situation of the brother who must please sister, mother, and wife, the focus of Number One Song, is set out in some detail in another of Grierson's texts. He comments: "The following song is interesting as showing the occupations of a married woman in her husband's house. It narrates how a brother visits his married sister, and returns with news of her to his mother."

2

Seat yourself, my brother, on a sandal stool, and put your arrows and bow in the house.
Seat yourself, my brother, in the verandah of the garland maker, for she knows my sorrows.
I have to plaster a piece of ground measuring a *big'hā* each (morning), and clean enough plates to fill a potter's kiln.
There is the pounding and grinding of a maund [about 82 lbs.] of grain (for me to do), and a whole maund of grain is cooked (daily by me).
My wretched little meal is the first(-cooked) small pieces of inferior bread, and out of that the dog and the cat (must have their share).
Out of that, also, the maid-servant and slave-girls and my husband's younger sister (must have their shares).
Brother, tell not these sorrows to my mother, or she will seat herself upon her stool and weep.

Tell them not to my father, or, seated in the circle of his friends, will he weep.
Tell them not to your wife, or she will taunt me with it when I visit my home.
Tell them not to my uncle, who got me married.
With the weeping of the sister her bordered veil became wet.
With the weeping of the brother, his sheet was wet.
Seat yourself, O son, on a sandal stool, and tell me news of your sister.
Just as, O mother, the jasmine bloomed, so blooms my sister.
Just as, O mother, the Ganges rose and overflowed (its banks), so weeps my sister.
Thank you, my son, for your hard heart, (you) who could leave your sister
weeping behind you.
("Some Bhoj'pūrī," 1886, 231, 240–42; parens. in original)

"Fare forward, you who think that you are voyaging; / You are not those who saw the harbour / Receding, or those who will disembark. / Here between the hither and the farther shore / While time is withdrawn, consider the future / And the past with an equal mind" (Eliot).

TRINIDAD

And what to the Coolie was this "Chīnītāt," this Trinidad? Most southerly island of the West Indian archipelago, it is just beyond the mouths of the Orinoco River, off the northeastern coast of Venezuela. On a bright day, you can see the South American mainland, only 11 miles distant. The island covers only 1,836 square miles; it is 48 miles wide and 65 miles long.

In addition to the northern range, which runs from east to west, there are the Monserrat Hills in the center of the island, and on the southern coast the Trinity Hills from which the country takes its name. The remaining terrain is fairly level. The Caroni mangrove swamp and the Oropuche lagoon, regions of marshland and nesting grounds for thousands of scarlet ibis (the national bird), are found on the western side. These two swamps are bordered by a belt of low-lying treeless savannah, used since the nineteenth century by the East Indians to grow rice (plate 6).

Sugar cane was introduced around 1650. It was the basis of Trinidad's economy when the Indians arrived and is still important today, together with other exports, especially oil, rum, grapefruits, and Angostura Bitters. In the south of the island, the 212-acre Pitch Lake at La Brea is a sedimentary volcano, a seepage of natural asphalt which is used locally and sold abroad. Trinidad has no sizable deposits of precious metals, and for this reason attracted few Spanish colonists after its discovery by Christopher Columbus in 1498.

For nearly 300 years after Columbus's voyage, Trinidad remained a Spanish possession. With Spain's policy of neglect, little economic development was ventured until the late eighteenth century, and the island remained sparsely

Plate 6. Mangrove Swamp, Caroni 1871. (Reprinted from Kingsley, *At Last, Christmas in the West Indies*)

settled. The indigenous American Indians, the Arawaks and Caribs, soon died out from exposure to European diseases, particularly smallpox, and from exploitation on the tobacco plantations. In 1797, Spain peacefully surrendered Trinidad to the British.

As early as the seventeenth century, African slaves had been brought in to work the plantations and during the eighteenth and nineteenth centuries they became the mainstay of Trinidad's labor force. In 1807, the slave trade was outlawed by the British; in 1833, all slaves under the age of six were freed; and in 1838, the practice of African slavery in any form was terminated throughout the Empire. The emancipated slaves tended to move from the plantations to the towns, a hasty migration unanticipated by absentee landlords and resulting in a labor crisis. A crash seemed imminent when Trinidad's dwindling cane exports were suddenly threatened by the introduction on the world market of Cuban beet sugar. No wonder that the indenture scheme was implemented only seven years after emancipation; English legislators moved expeditiously to substitute one wicked practice for another, and their venture succeeded, for within a few decades the East Indian labor force had saved Trinidad from economic ruin.

"You know, before time, Trinidad wasn't cultivate," Siewrajiah told me.

"And Trinidad was just as high wood. It didn't have people to work in Trinidad. Well, they tried to get people from India. Them Negro people don't want to work. Is India people who cultivate Trinidad. And since Indian people come—this is, I don't know how many years—might be thousand years since Indians come, probably more—and then Trinidad get to cultivate, because Trinidad wasn't have nothing."

The newly arrived Coolies were first divided into groups: the shovel gang or cane-cutting gang who did the digging, clearing, and planting, and the weeding gang—the women and weaker men. Smaller jobs were done by the "light" gang or "invalid" gang. There was also a building gang and workers for the mill. Coolies worked by the task, and those who could not complete an entire task forfeited their whole day's wage. For a member of the shovel gang—these, the strongest men—a day's task would be 80 to 90 cane holes five feet by five feet (in heavy soil), or 150 cane holes (in light soil).

The working day began before daybreak. "Morning the head driver from the estate, the overlooker, walking barrack to barrack," Siewrajiah said, "and calling them to come out to work. They come out and they looking out every house. House ain open, they pushing the door and waking you to get ready to go to work." There was a break for lunch when the Coolies returned to the line; then they worked until sunset—in Trinidad, about 5:30 P.M., year round. In the Victorian sugar mills, hours were longer, especially during the crop time (February through June), when they might be expected to work around the clock. During the "slack" season (December to January), the Indians worked to clear the land for the next planting, and they were used as draft animals for the hauling and plowing. Monday was a day off without pay (plate 7).

During their first year, the mortality rate among the indentured population was often as high as it had been on shipboard. The new workers were worn down by the system:

> It is when the rainy season sets in that his heaviest trials commence, when he makes his first essay in weeding, perhaps in high cane and heavy grass. . . . The work is hard, monotonous, and in high canes may almost be called solitary; he loses heart, makes a task in double the time in which an experienced hand would make a whole one, returns at a late hour, cold, wet and fatigued, to renew the struggle on the morrow with decreased vitality till at the end of his first year it is found that his work has not paid for his rations. . . . An immigrant embarks on the second year of apprenticeship saddled with a considerable debt from his first year's ration. (Immigration Agent-General, *Report 1871*)

It was only after the Coolie marked his thumb print on the contract ratifying this, the "meanest and weakest of bonds" (Kingsley, 97)—after his identification papers had been issued, after he had been shown to his quarters on

Plate 7. Huts of a Coolie village around 1900. (Reprinted from *John Morton of Trinidad*)

the Coolie line, after he had been assigned to a work gang, after he had been defeated by the heat of the mid-day, after his hands had become raw, then hardened from the cane, after he had been beaten, fined, jailed, after his rations had been withheld—that the realization came that he had not crossed the seventh sea to paradise, that the beautiful Queen was not to be found, that indeed he had been forced across the black water, across *kālāpānī,* into exile, that this "Chīnītāt," this Trinidad, was the world of slavery.

❧

"Fare forward, travellers! not escaping from the past / Into different lives, or into any future; / You are not the same people who left that station / Or who will arrive at any terminus, / While the narrowing rails slide together behind you; / And on the deck of the drumming liner / Watching the furrow that widens behind you, / You shall not think 'the past is finished' / Or 'the future is before us'" (Eliot).

Chapter Two

Roots

> Sweet memory hid from the light of truth
> I'll keep thee, for I would not have thy worth
> Questioned in Court of Law nor answer for it on my oath,
>
> But hid in my fond heart I'll carry thee
> And to a fair false thought I'll marry thee
> And when thy time is done I'll bury thee.
>
> Stevie Smith, "Portrait"

This is the story of music in a Trinidad village, a portrait, if you will, of the whole musical life of the villagers, of their old Bhojpurī folkways and folk songs, of *byāh ke gīt* and *tāssā* drumming, of *Rāmāyaṇ* and Rām, of holy men and Presbyterians, Sai Baba, Sundar Popo, and Swami Satchidananda, of the Reverend John Morton, of evenings of singing and drumming, dancing, relaxing in burlap hammocks, talking, laughing, eating enormous spicy meals washed down with neat rum, of hot songs, hot days, and hot tempers, whistling, humming, and drumming, of Indian classical music and Hindi *filmī* music, of processes (acculturation, syncretism, revitalization, revival), composition and improvisation, innovations and fascination, of forgetfulness and grief, afternoon walks by the riverside and cool Caribbean nights, of holy miracles and black magic, Chamārs and brahmans, cane laborers, school teachers, teenagers, housewives, priests, taxi drivers, bankers, dentists, of young, of old, of me, of them, of Mesho and Matti and hospitality, of Moon and Siewrajiah, Dhanpatee, Kalawatee and Channu, of the modern and antique and the wise villager from India who is Umesh, of Monkey Town and Monkey Point, of Cuche, Biche, Thick, Poole, Pluck, and Plum, of Green Hill, Orange Valley and Redhead, Brazil, California, Waterloo, Buenos Ayres, of Hardbargain and Tunapuna, of St. Joseph and St. Andrew, St. Mary, Ste. Madlein, San Francique, Santa Cruz, San Juan, Sans Souci, and Felicity—the village of singers and sages, the village that has engaged the attention of scholar after scholar, and whose villagers have taught us about their lives and music, and with generosity led us to understand that "when we try to grapple with another man's intimate need . . . we perceive how incomprehensible, wavering, and misty are the beings that share with us the sight of the stars and the warmth of the sun" (Conrad, *Lord Jim*). I arrived in Felicity on July 5, 1974, and from that day to the moment of writing, I hear Felicity singing—and remember.

The people of Felicity, nearly all Hindus, refer to themselves as East Indians, to distinguish their group from other West Indians (all peoples of the West Indies) and from the American Indians (the indigenous Arawaks and Caribs). The forebears of the East Indians—143,939 in number—were brought by the British from South Asia to Trinidad beginning in 1845. Known originally as the Gladstone Coolies, these people were among the legions of indentured laborers shipped out from India to work the plantations of the Empire: sugar in Trinidad and other colonies of the Caribbean (Jamaica, Grenada, St. Lucia, St. Vincent, St. Kitts, St. Croix, and British Guiana); coffee, tea, rubber, and sugar in Africa, Asia, and the Pacific (Ceylon, Malaya, Natal, Burma, Mauritius, and Fiji). This export of East Indian labor was suspended during World War I and legally abolished by act of Parliament in 1921. The indentureship system had little to recommend it over the system of African slavery that it replaced. Greed prevailed, but Lord John Russell (Whig Secretary of State for the Colonies), opposing indenture before it began, said, "I should be unwilling to adopt any measure to favour the transfer of labourers from British India to Guiana. . . . I am not prepared to encounter the responsibility of a measure which may lead to a dreadful loss of life on the one hand, or, on the other, to a new system of slavery" (15 February 1840).

From 1845 to 1917, East Indian indentured laborers were brought to work on the sugar-cane plantations of Trinidad, and their descendants now constitute over one-third of the population of the island. The villagers of Felicity, nearly all Hindus, have a musical repertory based almost entirely on north Indian genres. The founders of the village came mainly from eastern Uttar Pradesh, and traditional Bhojpurī folk songs and drumming styles from this region have been passed on in oral tradition and are still performed in the village today. These include *byāh ke gīt* and *lachārī* sung at weddings, *sohar* sung at the birth of a child, lullabies, and songs for the cultivation of rice, as well as repertories and performing practices for the *ḍholak* (double-headed barrel drum) and *tāssā* (clay kettledrum).

❧ The India Diaspora

The 430,000 East Indians of modern Trinidad are a segment of the 8.5 million South Asians living overseas. This population includes, first, descendants of Indians who left under various contract labor schemes in the nineteenth and early twentieth centuries, as was the case for Trinidad; second, workers and professionals who immigrated in the twentieth century; and third, secondary migrants, who moved in recent decades from one overseas setting to another. British contract labor systems of the imperialist period included the

Table 1 *Overseas Indian Groups*

Country	Immigration Dates	Original Immigrants	Indian Population 1990s	Total Population
Migration of Contract Laborers, Nineteenth Century and Early Twentieth Century				
British Colonies				
West Indies				
Trinidad	1845–1917	143,939	430,000	1,300,000
Jamaica	1854–85	36,420	50,300	2,513,000
Grenada	1856–85	3,200	4,000	100,000
St. Lucia	1858–95	4,350	3,840	100,000
St. Vincent	1861–80	2,472	6,000	106,000
Guyana (British Guiana)	1838–1917	238,909	424,400	800,000
Southeast Asia				
Burma	to WWII	1,017,825 (1941)	330,000	45,400,000
Singapore	to WWII	12,700 (1864)	169,100	2,900,000
Malaysia	to WWII		1,171,000	14,200,000
Africa				
Tanzania			40,000	29,800,000
East Africa	1895–1901	39,771		
Uganda	(1970)		76,000	19,800,000
Kenya	(1970)		182,000	27,000,000
South Africa Natal	1860–1911	152,184	750,000	41,200,000
Indian Ocean				
Mauritius	1834–1912	453,063	700,712	1,141,900
Seychelles	1899–1916	6,319	5,200	100,000
Pacific				
Fiji	1879–1916	60,969	300,700	800,000
Selected French Colonies				
French Overseas Departments				
Guadeloupe	1854–85	42,326	23,165 (1967)	400,000
Martinique	1854–89	25,509	16,450	400,000
Reunion	1829–1924	118,000	125,000	600,000
French Guiana	1804–76	19,296	66,400	133,376
Selected Dutch Colonies				
Surinam (Dutch Guiana)	1873–1916	34,000	140,000	408,000

TABLE 1 *(Continued)*

Voluntary Migration Since the Early Twentieth Century and Secondary Migration	
Country	Population in Modern Times
Europe and European Cultures	***Number of Indian Immigrants***
UK	1,260,000
Netherlands	102,800
USA	500,000
Canada	228,500
Australia	99,200
The Middle East	
Bahrein	48,050
Yemen (PDR)	103,230
Kuwait	355,947
Oman	190,000
Iraq	85,000
United Arab Emirates	382,302
Total Indians Living Oveaseas	8,691,490

maistry scheme for plantation workers in Burma, the *kangani* system for rubber plantation labor in Malaysia and tea in Ceylon, and—the most widespread—the indentureship whereby hundreds of thousands of Indians were transported to colonial holdings around the world, an event in the history of Empire expansion whereby European powers shifted entire work forces from one colony to another.

In the early twentieth century, and in impressive numbers after World War II, a sizeable group of businessmen, merchants, professionals, and workers, skilled and unskilled, moved to Western countries and the Middle East, a voluntary migration sparked by an infatuation with Western lifestyles and the lure of better living standards.

Since the late 1960s and 1970s, secondary migration has included, within the British Commonwealth, migration from Trinidad and other West Indian communities to Canada, from Fiji to Canada, and the forced mass migration in 1972, under the totalitarian regime of Idi Amin, of Ugandan Indians to Britain. In the Dutch sphere, there has been a steady movement from Surinam to the Netherlands of East Indian descendants of indentured laborers (table 1).[6]

The motivation for all categories of migration has been primarily economic. The major north Indian famines of 1804, 1837, 1861, and 1908 fed the contract labor force as did the twenty localized famines from 1860 to 1908, which devastated various districts in the catchment area of the *arkatiā* recruiters of indentured labor. Other circumstances favored emigration: the overworked soil throughout agricultural districts of the Gangeatic plain consequent to centuries of crowding; the population explosion in eastern Uttar Pradesh and western Bihar from the mid-nineteenth century onward; the British policy, introduced in the mid-nineteenth century, whereby peasant farmers paid rent, not as a percentage of the annual harvest, but in cash to the landowners (*zamidar* or *tālukdār*) and its sudden and devastating effect on rural economies, frequently resulting in the eviction of peasant families from fields they traditionally had tilled for generations.

The total overseas Indian population, less than 1 percent of the 1,000 million South Asian peoples, is small when compared with other ethnic or national groups: 22 million overseas Chinese as compared with 1,000 million in China, 300 million Africans overseas and 540 million in Africa. Though few in number, South Asians are more widely distributed geographically than other overseas groups. Furthermore, they are ideally suited for comparative study because most migrated to the former British colonies and share the British colonial experience whether in Trinidad, Mauritius, or Fiji.

Most immigrants came from north India and spoke the Indo-Aryan dialects of the Hindi belt. Bhojpurī predominated in Trinidad, Mauritius, and Fiji; throughout the diaspora of the colonial era various forms of "plantation Hindustani" evolved. A minority of indentured laborers, from south India, spoke the Dravidian languages, Tamil and Telugu, which for the most part died out in the diaspora. Most immigrants of east and central Africa spoke Gujarati and Punjabi, and those to the French Caribbean and Indian Ocean islands spoke mainly Tamil, as did the *maistry* and *kangani* laborers of southeast Asia.

Eighty-five percent of the overseas population are Hindus, most are north Indian Vaishnavite (followers of Vishnu), some Bengali Shaktis, and the minority south Indian Shaivites (followers of Shiva). The Punjabi Sikhs built the Uganda-Kenya railway, and many Sikh traders moved to east Africa.

Life in their new setting depended on the proportion of migrants to the host population and also on the administrative practices of the host society, which included discrimination against Indians and even institutionalized racism—apartheid in South Africa, the policy of Africanization in Kenya and Uganda, and *bumiputra* in Malaysia. Bending to the forces of prejudice, dominance, and constraints, some linguistically and religiously diverse overseas populations retreated into cohesive groups. Some Indian enclaves tended toward cultural homogenization, as in Trinidad, although the cultural divide between Indians from the north and south of India persisted in settings such as Fiji, where they were brought in approximately equal numbers.

Indentured laborers in Trinidad and other colonies found themselves at the bottom rung of the social system, whereas Gujarati and Punjabi merchants in east Africa were quickly incorporated into the urban middle class. In Burma, Indians arrived as part of the elite, as have the doctors and lawyers, computer specialists and other white collar workers, and college students who continue to arrive in the United States from India.

The survival of caste values and practices has been assumed to indicate the nature of cultural retention in overseas communities, and discussions among scholars on this point have been heated and aggressive. For Trinidad, Morton Klass states in his Felicity ethnography that important caste structures have been maintained; Joseph Nevadomsky, also based in Felicity, and Barton Schwartz, who studied the southern city of San Fernando, argue that the caste system has been abandoned because little occupational speciality has been required in Trinidad. Likewise ritual function disappeared, because the *jajmani* patronage system broke down, as did the Hindu system of purity and pollution, as a consequence of relocation. Nevertheless, in Trinidad, the importance of brahmans has been maintained to the present day, and the ideals of marriage within the social group but outside the village persist, although honored mainly in the breach.

ꕥ

Former British colonies where Indians constituted a substantial segment of the population include Trinidad, Mauritius, and Fiji. Imagine if you will a family with four daughters, one of whom was transported to Trinidad, one to Mauritius, one to Fiji, with one remaining in India. For the musicologist, many questions come to mind about the culture and music of the descendants of these four sisters. If their great-great-granddaughters could meet, would they find any common ground? Who might remember the old Bhojpurī songs—and why?

Trinidad: The Historical and Anthropological Record

Indian immigrants, cut off by time and distance from their mother culture, living in a New World African culture, exploited and abused by English plantation owners, confronted with different traditions, different values, and a whole new way of life—what songs would these people choose to sing? What music would they play? These simple questions puzzled me as I read the anthropological accounts of life in Felicity, Charlieville, Endeavour, Warrenville, and other East Indian villages of Trinidad.

Morton Klass, the first anthropologist to study life in Felicity, had been particularly interested in the questions of acculturation and cultural persistence. During his first stay in Trinidad (1957–58), he had examined these opposing forces in relation to five areas of Indian culture: caste, extended family, religion, economics, and politics. He concluded that cultural persistence had predominated; the Trinidad Indians had managed to reconstruct a South Asian culture in the Caribbean. Would his conclusions hold good for music some two or three decades later?

Much information was available—accounts of the voyages from India, analyses of the indentureship system, its place in the economic picture and its effects upon the Indian émigrées, the diaries of foreign missionaries, the researches of anthropologists who journeyed to Trinidad, the reflections of teachers, religious leaders, novelists, and poets who were born there—to help the musicologist piece together the clues. First, there were the fragments from the logs and diaries of those tortuous voyages: "Coolies on deck all day, singing and dancing in the evening"; "the Madrassee is a lively, singing fellow"; "coolies and crew were very subdued, there was no music"; "should be permitted to play their drums till 8 bells"; "getting music up to amuse the Coolies"; "Coolies having some native games and war dances"; "the Coolies are very musical"; "Coolies performing." Nothing about the steps of the dances, the verses of the songs, the types of drums, the groups of singers; here only the sparsest evidence of cultural persistence and the wonderful image of songs at the very moment in time when they were transported from one world to another.

These glimpses, so incomplete, so wanting in detail, carry one in imagination across those oceans, in those ships, with those emigrants, suggesting the amazement of white captain and crew, hearing traditional north Indian songs sung on deck. Were the passengers themselves also amazed to hear songs—new to them—from other villages, other districts, in other languages? Overnight, these rural folk, leaving home for the first time, became cosmopolitan in outlook. Overnight, the definitions of "them" and "us" had changed, and "us" now could include someone of a different caste, with different traditions, whose song had different words and a different tune. Did the amalgam that has become the Trinidadian Indian music of today originate on shipboard as new songs were passed from one voyager to the next, and strangers learned to dance hand in hand?

The writings of historians and anthropologists provide clues about acculturation and cultural persistence. Of special value are the comments of anthropologist Melville J. Herskovits, whose observations date from the 1930s. The topic of *Trinidad Village* (Herskovits and Herskovits 1947) is life in Toco, a small, remote fishing community on the island's northeastern coast. During his study, he noted the resistance to acculturation between blacks and East Indians. He observed that the Indians spoke their own language (Bhojpurī), dressed "in the Indian manner," and cultivated "their irrigated rice patches." "The Negroes, from the first, resented the importation of the 'coolies' from India as an economic threat; the Indians looked on the Negroes as 'savages,' according to Charles Kingsley, who was on the scene in 1871" (Herskovits, *Man and His Works,* 538).

> No wonder that the two races do not, and it is to be feared never will, amalgamate; that the Coolie, shocked by the unfortunate awkwardness of gesture and vulgarity of manners of the average Negro, and still more of the Negress, looks on them as savages; while the Negro, in his turn, hates the Coolie as a hard-working interloper, and despises him as a heathen; or that heavy fights between the two races arise now and then, in which the Coolie, in spite of his slender limbs, has generally the advantage over the burly Negro, by dint of his greater courage, and the terrible quickness with which he wields his beloved weapon, the long hardwood quarterstaff. (Kingsley, 101; plate 8)

Shango was Herskovits's great example of New World Negro music, and it illustrated his anthropological theories with eloquence. The songs developed during the nineteenth century, combining Nigerian Yoruba religious practices with Roman Catholic and Baptist belief. Shango ritual and theology are similar to other New World African-Christian cults, for example, Vodun in Haiti, Santería in Cuba, and Shango (Xangô) in Brazil. Spirit possession is common in these cults, as is animal sacrifice, drumming, and dancing, and a blend of African and Christian deities. In Trinidad Shango, the powers include Abatala, Ajaja, Elephon, Emanbjah, Eshu, Mama Latay, Ogun, Osain, Oshun, Oya, and Shango (of African derivation); and Gabriel, Raphael, St. Anthony, St. George, St. Joseph, and St. Peter (of Christian derivation). Each deity has his own personality, as do the gods of Hinduism, and distinctive powers, identified by special songs and drum patterns.

In my early days in Trinidad, before Felicity, I lived at Bagshot House north of Port of Spain, a grandiose nineteenth-century landowner's mansion, now a rest house for tourists. Ferdinand Murphy arrived unexpectedly one afternoon, offering to take me to Toco. He introduced himself as Krister's informant, asked for money, told me where to rent a car, and what kind of living cock to buy for sacrifice at the Shango celebrations in Herskovits's remote

PLATE 8. Coolie and Negro. (Reprinted from Kingsley, *At Last, Christmas in the West Indies*)

coastal village. Again unexpectedly, Murphy vanished, together with my hopes of witnessing a cock sacrifice in Toco. Later I found I could learn nothing about Shango in Felicity.

Shango drumming was thought by Herskovits's students Richard Waterman and Alan Merriam, to derive from west African tradition. Some Shango songs are accompanied by a single box drum, others by three double-headed drums similar to Yoruba *bata* types. The larger pair, the *bemba* and congo, are beaten with one stick, the smaller *oumalay* (or *omele*) with two. Drums are usually accompanied by the shak shak calabash rattles. The faithful believe that the two larger drums speak of the gods, one to St. Michael, the other to St. John the Baptist, which believers relate to the Yoruba deities Ogun and Shango. The use of rattles and also of hand clapping (with cupped, rather than flattened, palms) is common to both Nigerian and Trinidadian Shango. Herskovits stressed African retentions in Shango song style, including body swaying and other movements during singing, antiphony between leader and chorus, and polyrhythm.

Other syncretized forms of Trinidad include the bongo, the *bele*, and the reel, dance-songs in English or French Creole. The bongo is sung and danced at all-night wakes for the dead, and believed to placate the spirit of the deceased. The *bele* and the reel, most common on formal secular holidays, are also performed at wakes. The *bele* singing in west African leader–chorus style is led by a "captain" who makes offerings of rum and rice, and performs the sacrifice of a goat and fowls. Participants in the ceremony, drummers and other singers, partake of the sacrificial blood, and the meat is cooked and eaten by all. No wonder that these *bele* performances, intended to ensure the continued benevolence of the dead toward descendants, were strongly opposed by Anglican and Catholic priests.

Herskovits assumed that such "survivals" dated from the preemancipation period, but later research showed that many Africanisms of modern Trinidad cult music were introduced by free blacks who arrived in the second half of the nineteenth century. Merriam found retention of African musical traits in the music of the Rada cult, a community from Benin founded in Trinidad in 1855 by a free black immigrant who had served in Africa as a *bokono* ("diviner"). Richard Waterman examined African musical survivals in Trinidad, drawing on his teacher's concept of reinterpretation (assigning new values to borrowed cultural forms) and syncretism (similarities between distinct cultural forms providing a basis for their fusion). He pointed out that "since there was little reason, in terms of pressure from the rest of the [New World] culture, to change many diagnostic elements of the West African musical style, it changed only through the incorporation of new musical elements that could be reinterpreted to fit it." The anthropological theory that stemmed from the comparison of the Old-World and New-World African culture fueled ethnomusicological studies well into the 1960s. Meanwhile, the East Indian diaspora had not been examined.

It was only when I attended a Wake of the Cross with Daniel Crowley and visited the Shouter Baptist ceremonies at Success Street in Chaguanas that the significance of the Herskovits's research was before my eyes and ears. Here indeed were African retentions mixed with Christian ritual in a thrilling combination that gave the visitor a rush of bizarre emotion. Matti worried about my stays in Chaguanas and about my visit to the lady doctor on Pierre Road who somehow had mixed the darker side of Hinduism with the obeah "black magic" of the African islanders. Many Indians waited at her simple board house all morning for treatment, but she remained as mysterious a figure in my research as did the Kālī *pūjā* with goat sacrifice, which had been popular up to the 1950s. Only Rajiah the Chamār mentioned these old folkways, and then only in a loud raspy whisper, just as in India, where I saw how the upper caste colonies distanced themselves from these primal rites while sponsoring them, laughing at innocent Americans who jumped with deathly fright on the night that black-faced Chamār demons with gleaming lanterns broke into Brahman homes and sanctified them with their evil taunts. If Herskovits's theory of syncretism did work, then the strange old woman doctor on Pierre Road was this revered scholar's only representative in Felicity.

Of course, the situation has changed since Herskovits's generation. Today in Trinidad, Africans and East Indians alike contribute to the fast-paced, Westernized life of the island. At the McDonalds in Port of Spain, Creoles and Indians mingle. Creoles and Indians speak English and wear bluejeans. The casual visitor, walking down Frederick Street in Port of Spain, assumes that the East Indian has assimilated into the mainstream of Trinidadian life: as the national anthem tells him, "Side by side we stand. . . . Every creed and race finds an equal place." To a great extent, our tourist is correct, for Indians as well as blacks are among the doctors, lawyers, and bankers of the country; both Indians and blacks are businessmen, architects, politicians, and government officials.

But, if our visitor continued down the Princess Margaret Highway, past the miles of cane fields, to Felicity village, then the picture would change. For there, we find that the cane land remains the domain of the Indian; sugar, ever still, his benefactor and his master. "Find cane, and you've found Indians," my black friends told me.

There amid the fields of cane, in the villages of Caroni in central Trinidad, we find the sights and sounds that transport us to an Asian world.

> India lay about us in things: in a string bed or two, grimy, tattered, no longer serving any function, never repaired because there was no one with this caste skill in Trinidad, yet still permitted to take up room; in plaited straw mats; in innumerable brass vessels; in wooden printing blocks, never used because printed cotton was abundant and cheap and because the secret of the dyes had been forgotten, no dyer being at hand; in books, the sheets large, coarse and brittle, the ink thick and oily; in drums and one ruined harmonium; in brightly coloured pictures of deities on pink lotus or radiant against Himalayan snow; and in all the paraphernalia of the prayer-room: the brass bells and gongs and camphor-burners like Roman lamps, the slender-handled spoon for the doling out of the consecrated "nectar" . . . the images, the smooth pebbles, the stick of sandalwood. (Naipaul, *Darkness,* 29)

The brass vessels, the string beds, the printing blocks, these artifacts, "never repaired," "no longer serving any function," were these like the wedding songs of the Felicity women, the *gudanā* (tattoo song) Moon taught me, the *sohar* (childbirth song) Charran sang from his great *Rāmāyaṇ,* "cherished because they came from India . . . continued to be used and no regret attached to their disintegration"? (*Darkness,* 29–30). Were these songs from India's past, here locked in time and slavishly reproduced in their Trinidadian exile? These songs from grandfather's Uttar Pradesh—could they be found in India today?

Or would they long since have been altered beyond recognition or abandoned altogether? Naipaul: "How can I explain my feeling of outrage when I heard that in Bombay they used candles and electric bulbs for the Diwali festival, and not the rustic clay lamps, of immemorial design, which in Trinidad we still used?" (36). Were the songs, like the rustic clay lamps, merely marginal survivals of Indian practices, now obsolete in their original home?

A Plural Society

"What is striking," writes John La Guerre, Professor of Government at the University of the West Indies, is "the virtual demise of some of the more crucial features of East Indian culture—of the *panchāyat* [village council] and of caste—and the retention of those with more symbolic value" (*Calcutta,* xiii). These contradictions are the very heart of Indian life in Trinidad, and it is this cultural and social complexity that has drawn so many scholars to the island.

Since Herskovits's generation, two opposing views of the role of Indian culture in Trinidad have been put forward. Both views, "pluralism" and "consensualism," are useful to the musicologist. It is not so much a question of taking a stand on one side of the debate or on the other, but of appreciating the divisions in Trinidad's multi-ethnic society that have led to this discussion. And these issues help in assessing the nature of musical acculturation in Trinidad, and help explain it.

The anthropologists M. G. Smith and L. Despres describe the island's social organization as "plural" because they feel it is characterized by "formal diversity in the basic system of compulsory institutions . . . kinship, education, religion, property and economy, recreation. . . . It does not normally include government" (*Annals,* 769).

The pluralists maintain that in Trinidad and other similar Caribbean societies, including Guyana and Surinam, the Indians and blacks each have individual systems of agriculture, buying and selling, worship, schools, the arts and music, dance, and so on. These separate institutional structures were unified before independence by the European metropolitan powers, England or Holland or France, and now by the local governments. In the pluralist view, Indians and Creoles are antagonistic forces; Indians have always been excluded by Creoles. They have no assigned place in the color–class hierarchy of Trinidad as it is perceived by Creoles, a hierarchy in which white complexion has high status and black low. The reasons for this are historical. The Indians were brought to the Caribbean specifically to work on the estates, and it was to the estates that they were legally bound. No love was lost between the "Coolieman" and the "Nigger" (or the "Honkie" landowner for that matter). The Creoles sought new employment in Port of Spain and San Fernando, abandoning the rural cane lands where the Indian immigrants were assigned. From 1845 to 1917, isolation on the cane estates remolded that ethnically, culturally, religiously, and linguistically mixed Coolie community: by the 1920s they had more in common with each other than with the Indians of India. Geographer Colin Clarke cites Trinidad between 1960 and 1980 as an example of social pluralism with "increased segregation at the national level" ("Spatial Pattern," 133–34). Naipaul describes the pluralist vantage point as he himself perceived it when a child:

> It was easy to accept that we lived on an island where there were all sorts of people and all sorts of houses. . . . We ate certain food, performed certain ceremonies and had certain taboos; we expected others to have their own. We did not wish to share theirs; we did not expect them to share ours. They were what they were; we were what we were. (*Darkness,* 30–31)

The opponents of the pluralist viewpoint, especially Lloyd Braithwaite and R. T. Smith, think that the functional, consensual model of society, developed by Talcott Parsons, best describes these Caribbean societies. Pointing out that Indians and blacks share many concepts, they claim that the Indian community is not a separate enclave, but rather one class in a highly stratified but unified society. "Values are not co-terminous with norms, nor norms with behaviour," David Lowenthal points out; "West Indian social groups often maintain separate institutions and exhibit divergent behaviour while they share underlying values" (*West Indian Societies,* 90).

A most recent theoretical view called "social constructionist" breaks with much social and historical analysis, questioning "that races have a reality independent of human intervention . . . and take the existence of racial groupings as something to be explained and interrogated" (Segal, 82). These theorists regard the mix of Trinidad as a given laboratory for this study.

But any visitor to one of the temples on Cacandee Road in Felicity will feel immediate sympathy with the consensual model of Parsons. Sunday morning, early. The congregation gathers, the hymns are sung, the prayers said, the sermon delivered, the collection taken, the blessing given. How Western, how Hindu. A Christian modus operandi superimposed over an Eastern faith. The village pandits behave like priests—advising families, visiting the sick in hospitals, ministering to the needs of their parishioners. "Competition is the root cause," Lowenthal points out. "To counter Christian proselytization, Hinduism has achieved a comparable conceptual scope and organizational range.... Competition thus led Hindus to emphasize uniqueness in belief and ritual while emulating Christian structure and function" (152).

"Competition" was one of the first musical terms the villagers defined for me—quite by chance—in Felicity. *Q:* "Is this a composition?" *A:* "No, no. Competition is, you know what? Like you and me singing, and I singing with you, and you singing with me. And you sing better than me. And you win me."

This misunderstanding happened so often that the village teachers finally persuaded me to think beyond the accidents of accent—American and Trinidadian—to the question of meaning. *Q:* "Is this a composition?" *A:* "You know what they call competition song? That now she singing and I singing. Now we two are we jostling to better we self. I singing to better she and she singing to better me. So that mean we two are we jostling to better one another. But if I better she, well I win; and if she better me, she win."

Competition for recognition and fame, for money, and simply for its own sake, is a basic feature of the Trinidadian world view. Indians compete with Creoles, and Indians compete with Indians. All Trinidadians compete with the other little islands and with the rest of the world. In the land of Carnival queens and road-march kings, the victory, the win, is everything: "Ainsley Crawford just win the gold," sings Lord Kitchener, "to put Trinbago on top of the world. . . . Our Crawford done win the race, with the Russian beaten into third place" *(Trinidad Calypso 1977).*

District competes with district in the Prime Minister's Best Village Competition. Singers compete with singers and musicians and dancers on *Mastana Bahaar,* Trinidad and Tobago Television's Indian amateur hour; blacks compete with blacks on *Scouting for Talent.* Indians and blacks compete with each other for financial sponsorship from national corporations, who think of musical organizations as teams, for example, the Solo Soda Pop Company ("the lively drink") sponsors the Solo (Soda Pop) Sangeet Indian Orchestra, the Solo Harmonites Steel Band, the Solo Beavers Basketball Team, the Solo Crown United Soccer Team, the Solo Stars Cycling Team, and the Solo Crusaders Table Tennis Team.

Not all the competition is friendly. "We fear the black man is trying to use us for some sinister purpose," Grace Maharaj said. "Every Indian is united today. . . . We are closer together now than we have been for centuries. . . . Approaching us in *your* tightly knit band, will drive us into *our* tightly knit band. . . . We distrust strangers, especially you, who behave like strangers all these years" ("Black People in T'dad," 9). The East Indians of Trinidad share with immigrant minorities of all lands the problem of identity. Charles Wagley and Marvin Harris reflect that "the minority must adopt certain aspects of the culture of the dominant group and of the society at large. . . . On the other hand, the dominant group must recognize the distinctive cultural traits of the minority as acceptable 'specialties'" (*Minorities*, 287).

Roots

The Creoles in Trinidad appreciate many of the East Indian specialties: the spice of the cuisine, the grace of the sari, the melodrama of the films, the rhythmic complexity of the music, and the elegance of the dance. Other specialties baffle the African: the Indians' frugality, their conservative views about marriage, their attachment to the soil, to the cane and rice, their monkey- and elephant-headed icons, their elaborate Hindu liturgy. It is the Indians' sense of time and of history that is most perplexing to the African. For the blacks are Westerners, and like Europeans and the Americans, they expect that every day in every way things are getting better and better. For the Indians, this modern world, this *kalīyug* (the degenerate fourth age), is only a dim shadow of a glorious Asian past, when all men were brave like Rām and all women were virtuous like Sītā, and goodness prevailed. These mythical recollections are as real to the villagers of Felicity as yesterday's headlines.

"The culture of our fathers," writes Trinidadian K. V. Parmasad, "has outlived the stresses and strains of thousands of years. Whereas other ancient cultures have disappeared under the weight of time (in Egypt only the Pyramids stand), Indian culture lives on and as Gandhi said, 'though ancient it is yet not old.' We in this land are the inheritors of this culture, we are the transporters of this way of life to these parts" ("By the Light of a Deya," 288).

Is our heritage imagined? Indeed we can play with our memories. "It seems, as one becomes older, / That the past has another pattern, and ceases to be a mere sequence . . . But the sudden illumination— / We had the experience but missed the meaning, / And approach to the meaning restores the experience / In a different form, beyond any meaning / . . . The past experience revived in the meaning / Is not the experience of one life only / But of many generations" (Eliot).

For Hindu immigrants severed from their oriental roots, cut off from lost Aryan generations, history and heritage lead to an unknown landscape, where they must speculate, invent, and improvise. In the 1970s, Alex Haley's book and the television series *Roots* dramatized and popularized such a situation. His quest, undertaken on behalf of his family and on behalf of his race "for all of us to know who we are," led to rural Gambia. "Later the men of Juffure took me into their mosque built of bamboo and thatch, and they prayed around me in Arabic. I remember thinking, down on my knees, 'After I've found out where I came from, I can't understand a word they're saying'" (*Roots,* 680). Year after year the East Indians of Trinidad reinvent a new past from the myths of ancient Bhārat as portrayed in the popular comic books on sale in all towns or the Technicolor Indian culture promoted by the Bombay film industry—new images to replace the "little tradition," the old rural ways of their forebears which they can still touch and still remember—the "brass vessels," the "string beds," the "printing blocks." Parmasad writes, "West Indians in the truest sense": "We must dig deep into the farthest recesses of our consciousness as a people and discover our true selves, tapping if necessary the limitless reserve at the source of our culture" (287).

When I inquired how it could be that they, the East Indians, had felt an immediate love for the "great tradition," the urban art music of north India, introduced to the island only in 1966, Guru Adesh, the scholar-musician and poet, a resident teacher from India, explained: "It is their heredity, their parentage. The link was not broken since they came here. If the link had been broken, then this love could not exist."

Anthropologist Daniel J. Crowley claims that competition is the motivation behind the Indian's renewed search for his Asian heritage. Quoting the Punjabi Headmistress of Gandhi Memorial High School in Penal, Trinidad, he says: "'this later-day "revival" of Indian culture is not Indian at all.' In the typical competitive Creole way, East Indians are using Indian culture and often mythical caste for 'making style' and as a club with which to beat contemptuous Creoles" (*Annals,* 853).

Felicity villagers have modified and Indianized their culture with ingenuity to meet the changing demands of a Caribbean milieu. But comparison of a diaspora culture with that of rural India poses problems of method for anthropologists such as Chandra Jaywardena who notes: "Since the period of emigration to various countries ranges from three or four decades to more than a century, and since, presumably, society and culture in India were also changing during that time, a question arises as to which point in this flux should be used as the base time to measure change." What represents persistence or change? he asks ("Migration," 438–39).

Picture a simple chart: On the left-hand side of the page is the past—the arrival of East Indians in Trinidad on those ships so long ago, the items they brought with them, also their talents and their memories of India. On the right is the present, the flourishing East Indian community in Trinidad; the Bhojpurī culture they remember fondly; also renewal and revitalization—

from the 1920s onward, the refreshment of their customs by returning to their roots; and revival—from the 1980s onward, the rediscovery of local Indo-Caribbean customs, inspired in large measure by the jubilee celebrations of indentureship landmarks and Trinidad Independence.

Down the middle of the page are the forces of change in human life: simple phenomena like omission and forgetfulness, complex attitudes like rejection (that song is no longer appropriate for this event), syncretism (what they have is similar to what we have), and all the creative acts of man's mind and imagination—improvisation, delight in adventure, a sense of style, a sense of humor.

Social anthropologist David Lowenthal has observed a pattern of revitalization and reinvention in Indo-Caribbean life: "The elaborate *pagadi* head-dresses, the ubiquitous long skirts and *orhnis, dhotis* and *shalwars,* gave way by the time of the Second World War to dress differentiated from Creole mainly by the vestigial head veils of East Indian women and the ceremonial *dhotis* of some men. But imminent independence in India and rising ethnic tensions in the Caribbean impelled many East Indians to adopt imported saris." For language, the loss and revival of Hindi follow the same pattern. East Indians, within a generation of their Caribbean arrival, spoke English. But Lowenthal notes: "National sentiment reanimated by Indian independence spurred prominent East Indians to advocate Hindi instruction in schools, and Hindi has become an anti-Creole focus for urban Indians, even those whose ancestral tongue it was not" (*West Indian Societies,* 154).

Kamini, a Village Teenager, Tells the Indenture Story

"Sometime afterwards the English settled in Trinidad," Kamini said. "They fight Spain and they got Trinidad and they settle. From India to work in the plantation they had this indentureship system. They fool the Indians with glass and metals and anything that shine, and they tell them it have plenty milk, sugar, spice in the West Indies: come and get plenty and be rich! They didn't know, they came down, and they started working hard in the plantation."

"What was it like living here?" I asked.

"Terrible," she said, "houses is just shacks, without any facilities. They even had to sleep on the floor. Only the estate owners, the plantation owners, had a little piece of bench, and they slept on it. But if you saw those slaves, oh, they had it *really* terrible!"

"So the Indians were never slaves?"

"No. They had to work on the plantations for five years. They had to sign an agreement, a contract. It was known as the indentureship period."

The conversation idled on. I asked why the Indians in Trinidad spoke English but generally sang in Hindi.

"The English used to mix them," she said. "They never put a whole group of Indians together, or a whole group of Africans together, because they afraid they rebel. They mixed them and they couldn't speak their language. First they used to communicate by signs, and then they learn a language—a patois—just a 'local,' a mixture of Indian and African languages, and they started communicating. Gradually they started picking up the English language better than the Indian. The English never really understand Hindi. Gradually the Indian, the Hindi, was left out and just one or two people spoke it. Now English and English and English and English."

I persisted with my original question. "But why do they *sing* in Indian?"

"Our ancestors brought down their culture here, and being as Hindus, we have to maintain it."

Professor Adesh's words came to mind, "the link was not broken."

"Keep up the culture," Kamini went on, "and although we speak English through British ruling, we carry on the culture of our forefathers, our ancestors."

"Why bother?" I asked.

"Because my mother grandparents and my father grandparents came from India and they brought their language, their culture with them. Up till the early twentieth century Indians were coming in from India, they brought their culture. The elder people gradually spoke a mixture of English and Hindi and that just inherited in the other generations."

Here poetry illuminates history: "The past experience revived in the meaning is not the experience of one life only but of many generations."

"But you're the younger generation," I said. "Why don't you just give up the Indian ways."

"You see, that's my culture," she said, "and if I don't preserve it, what will I pass on to my generation? That's my religion. I born in it. I growing in it. And I'll keep it." ["Sweet memory hid from the light of truth / I'll keep thee, for I would not have thy worth / Questioned in Court of Law nor answer for it on my oath."]

Kamini criticized the older generation.

"Well, the Indians, the Hindus, how they does carry on when they go to *bhāgwat* service! Always talking and making all kind of noise. At school we are fighting all these bad behaviors, just talk—talking hard hard hard long while the prayers going on. We try to maintain a standard and keep out this noise so we will remain quiet like the other religions. We are trying to build up this idea so the other religions might recognize us."

Perhaps Lowenthal's analysis is correct. Here was the consensual model: "Competition thus led Hindus to emphasize uniqueness in belief and ritual while emulating Christian structure and function."

"You mightn't really notice how the other people of other faiths just laugh at the Hindus and the way we does carry on. I guess they have a right to laugh at us . . . because the Hindus are really . . . it's really . . ." Kamini paused.

"So you'll stick with your Indian ways?" I said.

"And pass it on, 'cause I born in it, growing up in it. That's why I'm trying to learn Hindi—so I'll be able to understand a little better. Long time people never bothered, but now, going to school and with modern trends, we're realizing what our religion mean, getting to understand it better and appreciate it. ["We had the experience but missed the meaning."] "So when we understand it now, we will appreciate it and keep it up and teach it to others. That is why we learn. Now we going back to learn Hindi. We going back to learn our own culture."

Kamini hadn't answered my question about songs. Her story told of Indian forebears, Hindi lessons, Hindu beliefs, and the transformation from survival to renewal that her people had achieved in less than one hundred years. How this amazing process also transformed the music of Felicity village is my story.

Chapter Three
Felicity

> How small, of all that human hearts endure,
> That part which laws or kings can cause or cure!
> Still to ourselves in every place consigned,
> Our own felicity we make or find.
>
> Samuel Johnson, "Lines Added to Goldsmith's *Traveller*"

The village lies midway along the road leading west from the market town of Chaguanas to the cane fields and the sea. Approaching by car, it is easy to miss the turning on the right, Cacandee Road, and the markerless weedy cemetery on the left, to suddenly find yourself lost on a narrowing lane, all vista save the sky cut off by the green stalks and the spiky white arrows of mature sugar cane. The day is hot, the air dusty and dry, the breeze listless, and you cannot help but wonder why the East Indians chose such a spot to build their homes.

It is a young village by European standards, with a history of less than one hundred years. In the Northern Chaguanas Ward, where Felicity is situated, Crown Land was first made available for settlement in 1885. The government record of deeds tells us that the first settler in the area was Kakandi, who bought a plot on the 30th of November, 1886. A few of the old villagers still tell of him. He had left India around 1875, survived the crossing, and endured the indenture, won back his freedom, and decided to settle in Trinidad. The cluster of *adjoupas* that sprang up around his became known as "Kakandi's Settlement," and the main road through the village still carries the old man's name.

It is a long village, some two miles from the junction, at Peter's Field, with its two shops, up to the Cunupia River on the northern extreme (map 1). The land of the village proper is a treeless and marshy savannah, a region of tall bamboo grass, unsuitable for the cultivation of sugar cane.

The village is large by Trinidad standards, with a population of around 6,500 living in some 953 households. Modern Felicity has resulted from the growth and merger of five small adjoining villages ("districts")—Cacandee Settlement, Casacu, Jangli Tola, Union Village, and Peter's Field. Cacandee Settlement is the most fashionable, with paved roads, street lights, and telephone lines (plate 9). "In the back" of the village, simple board houses line the dirt traces of Jangli Tola (plate 10). Ninety percent of the population is

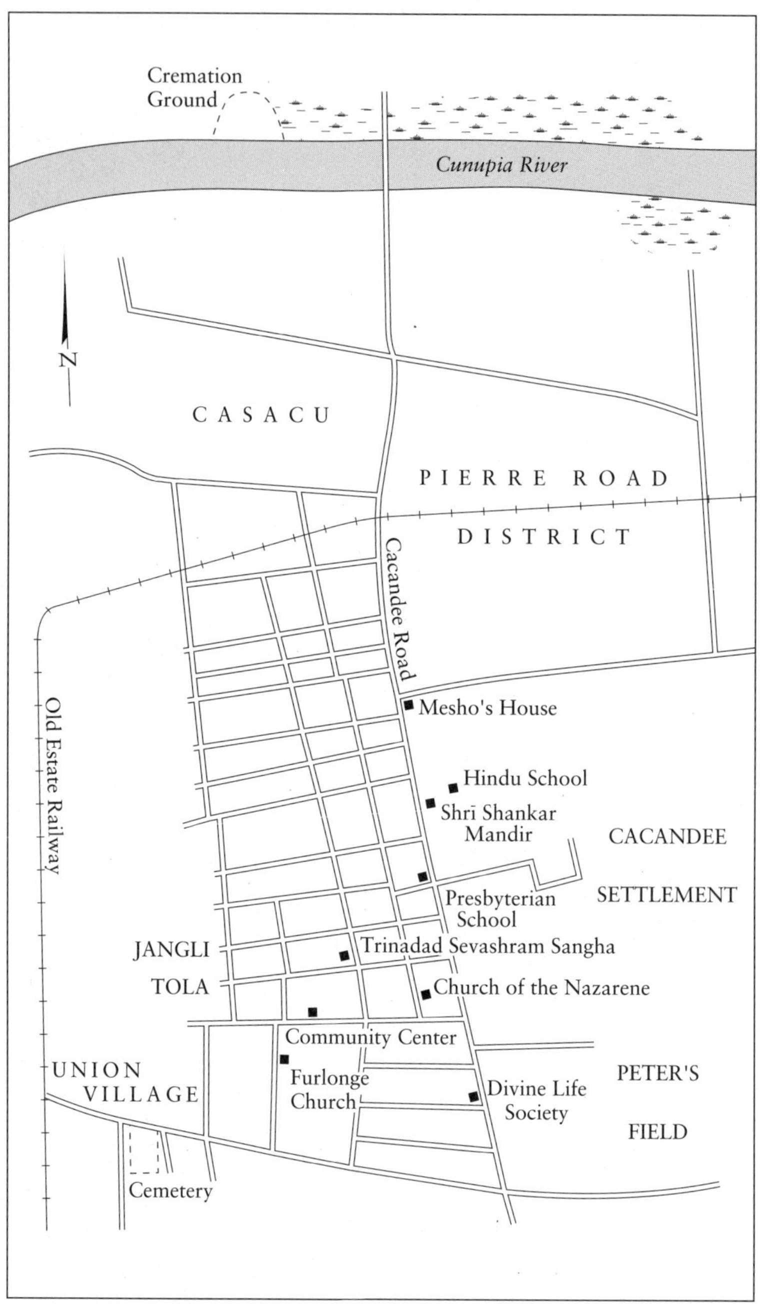

Map 1. Felicity Village

PLATE 9. Outside Mesho's house, the junction of Cacandee Road with Pierre Road.

PLATE 10. Board houses in Jangli Tola.

Hindu, 1 percent Muslim, and 9 percent black. Most of the blacks live in Peter's Field, at the southern end of Felicity.

There are four dry goods shops, eighteen rum shops, two social clubs (with jukeboxes) and many small "parlors" that sell penny sweets and biscuits to the school children. Two primary schools, within sight of each other on Cacandee Road, each accommodate some 1,000 children. There are three temples, two on Cacandee Road, one on Nolan Street, and two small board churches, both on back streets. The three village cricket and football grounds are on land donated by the sugar estate, Caroni, Ltd. The sports ground in Jangli Tola, the westernmost district, also accommodates the village community center. Felicity has no main square or central meeting place; during the early evening hours, villagers congregate at the road junctions, often near a rum shop or club.

Cacandee Road is the heart of the original settlement. Houses, shops, and parlors line it on both sides, thinning out about half a mile before the riverbank. I found the riverside pleasant, cool, quiet, but no one lived there. The girls would walk along in the evening, after the day's cooking, sweeping, and washing were done, but no houses were nearby. The rites of cremation are performed on the farther bank; the little river then carries the ashes of the villagers, the Hindu faithful, away from the village and out to the sea. I never saw anyone wash clothes in the river, or bathe in the river, or swim in the river. Could the Felicity folk understand India's great multipurpose Ganges? Their little waterway knows only one task which it swiftly and silently performs.

Kakandi was happy to buy wetland because he had brought with him the staple crop of his Indian way of life, the seeds of rice that would thrive in marshland. Only four years after the founding of Felicity, the Reverend John Morton, first Christian missionary to the East Indians, saw the rice fields spread across the Caroni savannah (plate 11).

> *April 7, 1890.* Monday. I took early train to Chaguanas. My first duty was to explore a new settlement on the border of an extensive savanna which stretches from the sugar estates of Chaguanas north to the estates on the Caroni, that is, about eight miles. A ride of two miles through cane-fields brought me to a small village on the very edge of this wonderful savanna. The land is low and flat, but capable of being drained. It has never grown trees, but is covered with a crop of tall grass, too dense for man, or horse, to get through it. Nearly all the people are East Indians, and the greater number of them have bought the land upon which they live. . . .
>
> One very interesting feature of the place is the rice-fields. Imagine over one hundred acres of level land divided into fields of several acres each by a low

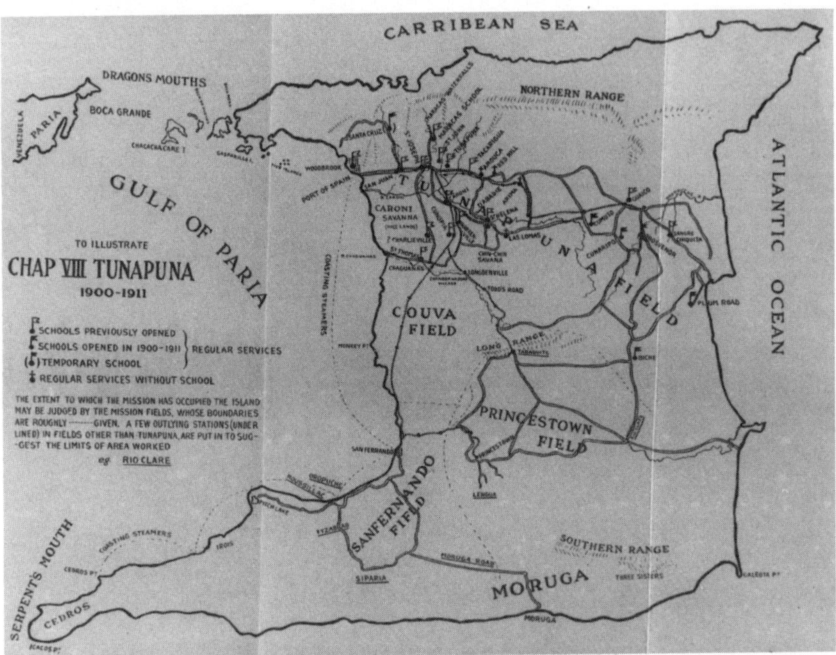

PLATE 11. Map of Trinidad, 1900–1911, showing Presbyterian schools in the Caroni Savannah—Felicity is just west of Charlieville. (Reprinted from *John Morton of Trinidad*)

> bank of earth that can be made to serve as a dam to flood the fields when necessary. Here magnificent crops of rice are grown year after year.[7]

And so on—the savannah, the sugar and the cacao, the rice. How little time has changed the face of the land. Despite the brightly painted houses, the improved roads, the outlook is static, the villagers—great materialists that they are, owners of pressure cookers and color televisions—still stand barefoot in the mud, planting each seedling carefully by hand. There is no other method. The rice dictates a way of life that the Indian understands.

Like all island peoples, the villagers are great travelers. In Felicity, hardly a week passes without an arrival or a departure from foreign parts. All day the BA and the BWIA wide-bodied jets float through the cloudless sky, over the rice and cane, on their final approach to Trinidad's Piarco International Airport, bringing a constant traffic to the island, and taking it away again. Everyone has someone "away"—a sister married and living in Toronto, a daughter in Miami, or a neighbor's son in London. It is not just the traffic in people, but in goods: a Japanese boom box, polyester yard goods, plastic flowers by the bunch, a glass chandelier, blank VHS cartridges, Johnnie Walker Black coming in; home-cooked meals in cool bags, live crabs from the swamp, local East Indian cassettes, fresh mangoes, "Limacol" astringent, Old Oak White rum going out.

The world for Felicity folk looks like those old BOAC route maps: Christchurch and Wellington, Georgetown, Toronto, Cape Town and Durban, Karachi, Lagos, Delhi, Hong Kong—the countries shown in red from the 1950s school atlas mildewed on the shelf. Beyond their many parochial concerns, theirs is the world of the BBC overseas services, and of relaxed afternoons in the shade, listening to the cricket test-match from Islamabad or Melbourne or Lord's. It is the world that hears the Queen's Christmas message and watches the Commonwealth Games, the world of Paddington Bear, Mills and Boon romances, New Zealand cheddar, the eleven-plus, Horlicks for tea, and the ubiquitous orange spines of Penguin paperbacks. It is the old Empire, terra incognita for the American, home ground for the English.

I spent a lot of time discussing with them the writings of V. S. Naipaul, their best-known and most eloquent spokesman in the English-speaking world. Ironically, the villagers look upon him with suspicion, expatriate in London, precisely because they felt he had ignored the Westernized side of their lives, their love of the modern, the fashionable, the up-to-date. They resented being portrayed to the outside as the inheritors of Mr. Biswas, leading the life of the Tulsi family in Hanuman House. Naipaul betrayed them. He defected to the English side and told the world of their hidden treasures, those old Indian ways. He had robbed them of their secret, and they will never forgive him.

Felicity itself is a much-studied village. Almost everyone there remembers the visits of anthropologists Morton Klass in 1957–58, and Joseph Nevadomsky in the early 1970s. They expect scholars to turn up from time to time, and they remain cheerfully optimistic. They welcomed me without hesitation from the very first day, but I could see that they were relieved to learn that this new visitor had come to learn about their music and not about their private lives.

Ironically, when they believed that I had truly come to learn about music, they wanted to tell me about their private lives. But that's another story.

Chapter Four
A Day in the Village

> With the sense of sight, the idea communicates the emotion, whereas, with sound, the emotion communicates the idea, which is more direct and therefore more powerful.
>
> Alfred North Whitehead, *Dialogues*

The village is a noisy place, lacking the pastoral tranquility attributed to agricultural settlements in all lands. The sounds of the night kept me awake during the early weeks of my stay. There were the mongrel dogs—"pot-hounds"—one, sometimes two, per household. Not pets, these: they cowered and scavenged, bickering among themselves, and were constantly prodded and rapped with sticks by the women and children. They barked all day, but as the sounds of the day faded into the darkness, and Matti prepared the children for bed, the village dogs began their noisy vigil in earnest. Like a string of firecrackers, they set each other off. By eight o'clock, the canine alarm passed from one to the next, relaying along the entire length of Cacandee Road and all the way to Nolan Street in the back, as some villager haltingly made his way home from the rum shop.

By ten or eleven o'clock, the "whistle" of the local crapaud frog[8]—"punganak, punganak"—subsided; then the cocks crowed till dawn, shattering the silence at random with their raspy cries.

The sounds of morning were reassuring, repetitive, and rhythmic, the sounds of a household waking to a new day. They began just before the light, around five o'clock, with the "bawling" of the housebird, the bluejean, and the palmist, and, on some mornings, the full-throated ramageing[9] of the picoplat. Next, pots banging in the kitchen, water splashing in the bath-house as one, two, three, four children and one, two adults washed from head to toe, tooth scrubbing and spitting; then, the whispering sounds of sweeping the house with a coconut-rush broom, making the beds, and tying up mosquito nets. The bell sounded from the family altar for the morning prayers, quietly said, the goats were dragged "bawling"[10] to tether, the traffic picked up on the road, the post-boy rang his bicycle bell, and the sound of many little voices passed by under my window. Felicity had awakened to another day, and Felicity's children—more than a thousand of them—were walking down Cacandee Road to school.

For breakfast, there was hot *rotī* (thick bread pancakes) and "tea"—Milo, Horlicks, Ovaltine, or Nescafé. Every morning Matti prepared a different vegetable dish: eggplant or beans or tomatoes or peas, some days pumpkin, some days potatoes, and many others depending on the season. The East Indian diet is extremely varied and healthy, with a lot of garlic, curry, chili pepper, and aromatic spices, especially cumin seeds. It is not unlike the cooking of India, but the differences are telling: little *chāy* (real tea) is drunk in Trinidad, and the small dry whole-wheat *chapātī* of India has mainly been replaced by the larger, thicker and tender *sādā rotī* ("simple bread") made with white flour.

Matti and I would chat about this and that: All the children refused pumpkin this morning. Why? Instead, they were eating bread and cheese or bread and butter. When is she going to get a chance to dry the cashew nuts? Tomorrow Mesho is going to see a film in Chaguanas. We're going to temple tonight. And so on until the business of the morning pressed us both into action. All the weekdays began with this same routine. Then she would get on with washing the "wares" and soaking the clothes, and I would head out of the yard and through the gate, being careful not to let the dogs out.

I turned left down Cacandee Road and walked in the direction of the schools. As I walked, the sounds many, many little voices, singing unaccompanied, grew louder.

DING DING.

The morning prayer ends: "*Aum, shanti, shanti, shanti*" (*Aum,* peace, peace, peace). Teacher hits the desk bell again with the heel of his hand.

DING.

A song, a *bhajan* (Hindu devotional song), begins. "*Seetaa Raama kaho Raadhe Shyaama kaho / Seetaa Raama binaa koi apanaa nahi, / Radhe Shyaama binaa sukha sapana nahi.*" ("Say Seetaa Raama, say Raadhe Shyaama [name for the blue Krishna, lover of Radha] / Without Seetaa Raama nothing is yours, / Without Raadhe Shyaama no happy dreams").

DING, as the last word of that song fades.

DING DING. The next song begins.

DONG DONG. Another desk bell at a different pitch sounds, and another set of voices, these deeper and louder, begin a different *bhajan: "Tumhi ho maataa, pitaa tumhi ho*" ("Oh God, to me you are like my parents"). These must be the voices of the upper form pupils on the second floor.

As I reached the entrance to the Felicity Hindu School yard, the first bell sounded again, then the shuffle of feet, the sound of books taken out onto the desks, whispering voices, and rustling through book bags for pencils. The lower forms had completed their morning prayers and were beginning math. In the distance, I could hear more voices: "Thou preparest a table before me in the presence of mine enemies. . . ."; "all the way my Saviour leads me, for the goodness of his love." This was the Presbyterian School across the street. In the morning, the Hindu children across the street sang hymns, not *bhajan.*

Days earlier I had asked Shama, "Did you go to school here in Felicity?"

"I went to the Hindu School," she said.

"Are all the children in the Presbyterian School Presbyterian?" I asked.

"Majority of them are Hindus," Shama replied.

"Do they convert you when you go?" I asked.

"No, they cannot convert you. But the teachers who are going to work, they have to be converted. I think they supposed to be Christian, Christian names too, before they go to the school." She paused. "But in the Hindu School, I think they only take Hindus too." She laughed at the irony. "Because this Hindu School here, they don't have any Christian teachers. They all are Hindus."

"What is the Presbyterian School like?"

"It's just like the Hindu School, but when the Hindu School have anything, they do Hindu business. They have celebrations for Diwālī, and they teach the children Hindu songs. They teach Hindi. They got a few teachers teaching Hindi, *bhajan,* and closing prayer. But the Presbyterian School have Christian thing."

But oh, what a difference in the music, I thought.

One day I decided to record at the Dorman Nursery School, situated in front of the Hindu School on Cacandee Road. Its big windows were open to the air, and the tiny Indian children, all standing at their desks and in the midst of their singing, had seen me walking toward the school. The three teachers greeted me, but the singing did not stop.

"Good morning to my teacher, good morning to my parents. . . . Are you sleeping . . . Oh my friend . . . morning bells are ringing, ding dong bell . . . pretty little butterfly . . . nothing to do but play . . . Row row row your boat . . . merrily, merrily, merrily, merrily . . . Merrily we roll along, roll along . . . Ring-a-ring . . . the bear went over the mountain, to see what he could see, and all that he could see, was the other side of the mountain, was all that he could see . . . Once I saw a bird going hop, hop, hop . . . Twinkle twinkle little star, how I wonder what you are . . . Mary had a little lamb . . . Jack and Jill went up a hill . . . If I had a donkey . . . The time to be happy is now, the place to be happy is here, and the way to be happy is to make someone happy and you'll have a little heaven right here . . . Three blind mice, see how they run . . . Be careful little eyes what you see, be careful little eyes what you see, there's a father up above and he's looking down at you, oh, be careful little eyes what you see, be careful little ears what you hear . . . little nose what you smell . . . tongue . . . taste . . . brain . . . think . . . hands . . . do" and so on without break, without hesitation, without pause or interruption, those tuneless little voices spun out one song after another.

The order was fixed but without any apparent logic, and it was difficult to tell when one song ended and the next began, for their medley had grown willy-nilly by accretion, a verse a day, a song a week, learned by rote, until the patchwork had expanded to occupy the entire half hour between eight-thirty and nine-o'clock. Each song was rendered complete, with all its verses, complete with its little rhyme or joke, complete with its moral or lesson for the very young. There were hymns and Mother Goose, and what Trinidadians call "folk songs."

Today all the songs were in English—unusual in Felicity; on other days they sang the Hindu *bhajan* as well. They had been learned by rote, by a fixed procedure: performance without regard to the meaning, the same rote learning that was out of fashion when I was a child and still is out of fashion in England and the United States. *Rote.* Was this the key to understanding a musical system in which people sing more songs in Hindi—a language they do not speak, a language they little understand—than in English, their mother tongue? Rote: the foundation, the bedrock of a culture.

"All right, you can sit down now." The little voices had completed their musical pastiche, and it was time for them to turn to other work.

I packed up my tape recorder and said goodbye. The Shrī Shankar Mandir next to the Hindu School stood dark, silent, and empty at this hour of the morning (plate 12). I could make out the black silhouettes of Hindu statuary at the front altar. I passed the cricket ground on the left, with all the goats grazing, the dry-goods shops, the sweets parlors (idle now as school was in progress), and the many "upstairs houses," supported by six or eight sturdy concrete pillars. Hammocks were slung between pillars, and in the shade of the house the dogs loafed, the chickens and ducks scratched around, the toddlers played, and the ladies and the old men "limed" (gossiped). When I reached the Divine Life Society temple, near the junction with Peter's Field Road, I was tired, and I was puzzled by those nursery songs. Everywhere I went in Felicity, I heard only Hindi songs, everywhere except the schools. Why were the children singing in English?

The Divine Life Society temple stood dark and silent. I decided to turn back. My rubber flip-flop thongs slapped along the dusty road. As the heat intensified, the village grew still. The women were preparing lunch—an occasional hiss as a ladle of boiling hot oil and parched garlic was plunged into the cooked *dāl* (lentils). The rice was already boiled and cooling. Lunchtime is early in Felicity. Sulin and her daughter were outside their large house, fanning the unmilled rice. They lifted grain high over their heads in a scoop made

Plate 12. Shrī Shankar Mandir, Cacandee Road.

from an empty cooking-oil tin, and sifted it, allowing the kernels to fall on the sugar sack spread out below, while the breeze carried the chaff away. Across the road, Kowsil was rocking her grandson, Vince, in the hammock.

"Sītā Rām, Miss Helen," I heard from a stray schoolgirl, in uniform, smiling as we passed on the road.

"Sītā Rām," I replied. The village greeting, Sītā and Rām—the eternal godly lovers. Warmer this than the more proper Hindi *namaste* ("I bow to you").

Sankey was stretched out in the hammock by her house, her morning's work done. "Come naa, come naa Helen," she said. Sankey was acknowledged to be the finest woman singer and drummer in the village. "Come lime naa. Come eat crabs naa."

"Sītā Rām," I said. The curried crabs were brought out and I lay back in a second hammock.

"I need a coke bottle to smash these," I said. (The villagers cracked them with their teeth.)

"Mash it, mash the crab for she," Sankey called out, and the crabs were taken away.

WHAM WHAM from the kitchen, and then my lunch was returned. The curry sauce for the crabs was hot, and my eyes watered.

"Sankey," I asked, "how do you make pepper sauce?"

"Well, we make pepper sauce with pepper and acid," she replied, "cooking acid."

"Sankey," I asked, "when they talk about hot songs, when they talk about *chutney* songs . . ."

"*Chutney* sauce?" she asked.

"No, songs."

"Oh, songs, songs! Yes, yes. I know what you mean. A hot song is when you beating the drum hard. And the ladies singing, you know, that they sing on a good voice then, big voice. Well, that is *chutney* song."

"Do they have any cold songs?" I asked.

"It's not sun, it's *song.*"

The accent was always a little problem. And no, there weren't any cold songs.

I shouldered my bag and went home to wash the dust off my feet, and then visit Channu, the seamstress. Channu was making three dresses for me, and she needed my measurements before she could cut the cloth and get on with the sewing. She was a member of the Shrī Shankar Mandir singing group, and liked to discuss music.

The sun was at its full height now, but I felt refreshed from the coke and the crabs and the rest in the shade.

SMASH BANG BANG CRASH, passing the auto mechanics's shop. I hurried along, and the little oil-dipped mechanics grinned.

CRASH CRASH KAWAM, louder this time.

When I reached the Hindu School, a group of children were standing in the playground. They formed a circle around one of their teachers, and they were all chanting a counting rhyme (ex. I).

I found Channu in a chatty mood. She was finishing a piece of work at the sewing machine, and her carpenter husband was home for the afternoon. While I waited, we talked about calypso. "And they have Sparrow," Channu was explaining. "They have Mighty," she paused. "They have certain names, I just can't quite remember." She glanced over at her husband and then turned back to her work.

"The Striker," he said, "Lord Shorty, Almighty Power."

"Do you like calypso?" I asked.

"Yes," she replied, "it's all right, you know, it's . . . for my mind then I always prefer my Indian music."

"Why? Why do you prefer your Indian music?"

"I find it sounds much sweeter," she said. "It gets you. You get a different mood when you sit and you listen. We have some cassettes; my brother has it

Example I: Felicity Counting Rhyme

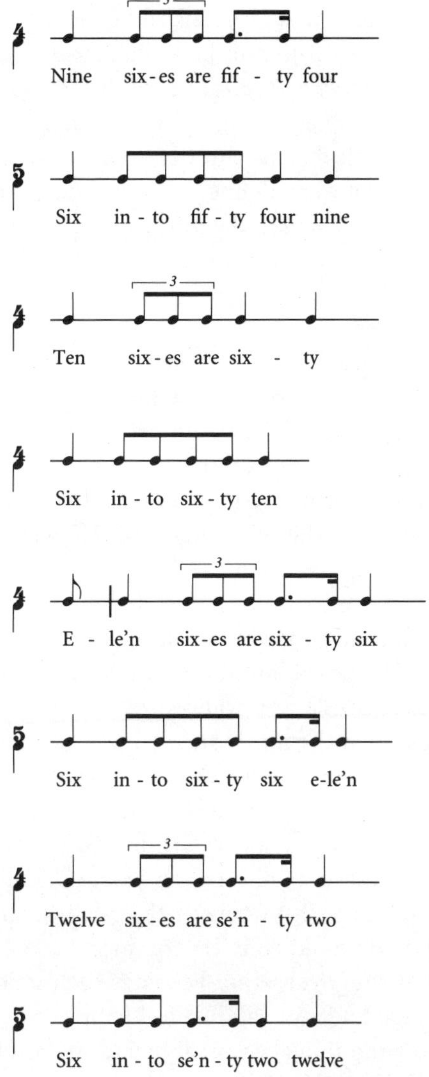

in his car. And they have a cassette based on a *chaupāī* [four-line verse] in the Rāmāyaṇ. When you sit and you listen to that, when he explains it to you. . . ." Channu's hands fell away from the fabric, the machine stopped, and she sank back into her chair as a memory from her childhood began to come alive.

"From the time I was a little girl, I lived together with me parents, always real Indian, you know, Hindu. They do all their prayers and everything in the real Hinduism way. They learn us little little about our religion, so I can understand a little bit of Hindi, and I can talk some too. So when a cassette play, then I can remember when I used to be at Rāmāyaṇ. This *chaupāī*, it starts from where Rām went to *ban* [the forest] with Sītā. This is what Mukesh [popular Indian playback singer] sang. And if you hear the music from that, I sure you will drown with the amount of happiness you will find in you. It must touch your body that you will find, when you hear certain parts, you can see, you can picture, by listening to the music alone, what was taking place in the forest at that time. Your imagination can draw you that amount of attention, you will see true."

"And calypso?" I asked.

"Calypso they only sing," she said. "I just find they have no sense at all of what they sing in calypso because it's just joking to everybody. They will sing something about you, and the calypsonian see me pass and he want to make up a joke about me and he will do it. But these *bhajan* and whatever the Indian sing and whatever music they play, they don't do it of a joke. It's a serious thing for whoever understand it. It's something that will put you to sit down and concentrate, whenever you listen.

"So that is the difference. Probably if I tell somebody that, they might figure because I am an Indian, and I am a more Hindu, I think that way. But a person like you, you have experience about music, and I sure if you sit and you listen to the different types of music, you will realize, and you will see what type of instrument they use to play the music and you will understand for yourself. If a man has not enough experience he would not be able to do that. A person could just take up a pan [steel drum] and knock it as anyhow he want. But a next person could never take up a good drum and beat it as how you want. Whatever music you hear from the Indian side, it's well played. Each and everybody could never do it. But whatever the calypsonian use and the other local people use, anybody could do it. It's common.

"Something that is sung real seriously brings such serious feelings to you. You might hear calypso and you will just feel happy to jump up [traditional Carnival street dance] and thing because it makes you feel like that. But if you hear a real technical piece of Indian music, you might sit down stiff and still and you might be concentrating so much that you mightn't know when it start or when it finish."

After supper that evening, Mesho, Matti, the four children, and I went to their temple, the Divine Life Society, for the weekly Friday service. We got back home just before ten o'clock. Everyone was tired and went straight to bed. I got ready, and tucked the mosquito net under the mattress all around, slipping into bed through the gap I had left in the top corner, taking with me a pencil and my diary. After I had tucked the net in behind me, I settled back and began to write about my day.

Friday Night, 10:30 P.M.

"Busy weeks ahead. Since I go to temple with Mesho and family on Fridays, I can't attend the prayer meetings at the Furlonge Church. The Furlonge group has another service on Sunday morning but this conflicts with the Nazarene Church Sunday School. A typical week in Felicity has many scheduled events:

Friday	7:00 P.M.	Divine Life Society, Unit 1 (Cacandee Road), *sanḍhyā* [Hindu devotional service] (with Matti and Mesho every week)
	8:00 P.M.	Furlonge Church (Makhan Street) Prayer Meeting (these two conflict, but see Wed. P.M. and Sun. A.M.)
Saturday	4:00 P.M.	Trinidad Sevashram Sangha (Nolan Street), Singing Class ("Teacher" leads session till Basraj recovers. Chance to get together with Rawti, Shanti, Baby, and Parvati)
Sunday	6:00 A.M.	Trinidad Sevashram Sangha, *sanḍhyā* (go every week, at least until Swami Purnananda leaves for Guyana)
	7:30 A.M.	Shrī Shankar Mandir (Cacandee Road) *sanḍhyā*
	7:30 A.M.	Divine Life Society, *sanḍhyā* (conflict again, but attend DLS on Fri. P.M.)
	9:00 A.M.	Furlonge Church Sunday School
	10:00 A.M.	Furlonge Church Morning Worship Service
	10:00 A.M.	Church of the Nazarene (Lyle Lane Street), Sunday School
	11:00 A.M.	Church of the Nazarene, Morning Worship (can record one *sanḍhyā* and one church service every Sunday A.M., recharge Stellavox before P.M.)
	7:00 P.M.	Church of the Nazarene—"Evangelistic"
Monday	5:00 P.M.	Guru Adesh's classes (Hindi, Sanskrit, music, dance) (in Montrose Vedic School, Chaguanas—transportation a problem)
Tuesday	Nothing special (to Port of Spain?)	
Wednesday	6:30 P.M.	Shrī Shankar Mandir, *sanḍhyā*
	7:30 P.M.	Furlonge Church Worship Service (alternate weeks?)
Thursday	6:30 P.M.	Trinidad Sevashram Sangha, *sanḍhyā* and *Rāmāyaṇ* (only weekly *Rāmāyaṇ* session in Felicity)
	6:30 P.M.	Sai Baba group (Mr. and Mrs. Dhun) Pierre Road, *sanḍhyā* and chanting)
	6:30 P.M.	Sai Baba group, Montrose, Chaguanas (amplified) (go with Matti or Kowsil—Mesho will drive)

"The *pūjā* at the Divine Life Society tonight combined the performance of Durga *pūjā* [traditional service] with a full moon *kathā*. The entire service lasted about two-and-one-half hours. The most interesting part was the consecration of the *jhaṇḍī*—a long green bamboo pole, about 12 feet long, with a triangular yellow flag tied at the top. Yellow symbolizes the goddess Durga. *Jhaṇḍī* can be seen flying everywhere. They mark all the temples and Hindu homes on the island. Mesho has five or six in the front yard.

"Tonight, the pole was blessed at the altar with oblations of ghee, oil, water. No *bhajan* were sung during the blessing. The pole was then carried out to the temple yard. More offerings were made while the Brahmchārī chanted mantras addressed to various deities. The pole was implanted in a tin and now stands there with other *jhaṇḍī* from other *kathā.* The stalk will dry out and turn yellowish-brown, the leaves will fall off, the flag's color will fade, but the pole will stand.

"There was a surprise tonight. The congregation sang some *bhajan* from the *Divine Life Bhajans,* the book they gave me last year. But for the first hour they sang from a new book, *Bhajans and Chants of Satya Sai Baba.* These songs are all responsorial in form. Mesho explained, 'Each line is sung four times, two times by the leader and two times by the group. The leader gives the group a chance to learn the words and tune.' During the singing, the congregation claps on the beat. As I looked around, everybody was singing, and many were clapping, especially the children. The sound was very loud, louder than last year" . . .

ஐ

I must have fallen asleep there. When I awoke in the morning, the diary and the pencil were beside me on the bed.

ᘓ Chapter Five ᘐ

The Seasons

> Asārh has commenced; the clouds of the sky are thundering, and the lightning flashes therein. I start in fright, look round, and sit and think within my mind.
>
> In Sāwan Shām has deceived me, and made love with Kubjā. The frightened peacock cries in the forest, and the frog makes its sound heard. O Naud Lāl, how can I keep my life? Shame on my life to remain within this body.
>
> Bhādo has come, nor can we see the paths, as the frogs croak in the courtyard. Let me become a cuckoo and roam from forest to forest. The marshes of Brindāban are dried up.
>
> In Kuār I receive no news of Shām, no letter has come from Madhuban. Sāūr (sings) "Let Shām meet me, otherwise let me leave my life in an instant."
>
> (Grierson, "Some Bihārī Folksongs")

This is the calendar that Siewrajiah, Dotty, Tara, Rawti, Rajiah, Savtri, Ramesh, and Amar gave me.

The evenness of the year in Felicity is difficult for people from northern climes even to imagine: the ever-hot days, the constant breeze, the equal division of the day into twelve hours of darkness and twelve hours of light, year round. The seasons in Trinidad are marked by the rain and, in harmony with the rains, the seasons are marked by the crops.

It is the agricultural calendar that the old folks know so well, the relentless timetable dictated by cane and rice. In most years, the dry season begins sometime in January and lasts until mid-June. The older generation calls this "crop time" or "in the crop," the period of intensive labor in the cane fields. In June, the rains begin. The short afternoon cloudbursts usually continue right up until Christmas. During June and July, the rice is planted. Then follows the "post-crop time," from July to September, when the cane laborers weed, plow, plant, and spray the fields for the next crop. In October or November, a short dry season is known as the "petit carime." The rice is harvested, beaten, dried, and fanned at this time. The "slack season" in the cane begins in October and ends in early January.

But for the younger generation, many of whom have escaped the inevitability of the plantation cycle, the seasons are distinguished one from the other by fruits and vegetables, festivals of different religions, and children's games. The dry season is cricket season, and when the rains come, cricket is abandoned for football. The old folk might be shocked to learn, if ever they thought to ask their children and grandchildren, that "in the crop" was known as "pitch" season or mango time, that the sweat and agony of the indenture years, the time of isolation in the high cane, was now associated with the juicy yellow flesh of ripe fruits or a game of marbles. But young and old alike agree that this yearly cycle begins anew on the evening when Lakshmī Mātā, the goddess of prosperity, good fortune, and illumination is believed to enter into every home and bless it. Her coming is called Diwālī, the Hindu festival of lights.

DIWĀLĪ

Diwālī falls on the 13th day of the first half of the month of Kārtik in the Hindu calendar (usually around November).[11] During the week preceding the festival, every house is scrubbed spotless, for it is believed that Lakshmī will not visit a dirty house or a dirty person. At sunset on Diwālī night, the villagers light small clay *diyā,* primitive oil lamps with cotton wicks and coconut oil. Each family displays as many *diyā* as it can afford, sometimes several hundred. They are arranged in rows and in ornate patterns around the house, in the yard, along the windowsills, doorsills, roof, fences, and gate. There is a friendly competition to see which home can produce the most effective display. By nightfall on Diwālī eve, the contours of Felicity village are outlined by thousands of tiny flickering points of light (plate 13). After supper, while the small children and old people stay at home to replenish the lamps, the teenagers and married couples stroll up and down Cacandee Road to admire the magic effect of "lighting up."

Diwālī is an important occasion for village music. The large repertory of *bhajan* devoted to Lakshmī is heard throughout the day on the radio. Indian religious films, with many *bhajan,* may be shown on television and in local theaters. Many families hold a *pūjā* to Lakshmī, consort of Vishnu and goddess of prosperity, or to her more fearsome sister, Durgā, consort of Shiva, to bless and purify their freshly cleaned home and to ensure happiness and prosperity for its occupants. Diwālī is a busy day for the village pandits, each of whom performs more than a dozen hour-long *pūjā,* intoning the ancient Sanskrit mantras in an inflected monotone. This recitation follows the rhythm of the Sanskrit poetry, an uninterrupted oral tradition that dates back some 3,000 years.[12] Hindus believe that mantras must be correctly pronounced and intoned to ensure the successful outcome of the *pūjā.* In India, this belief has encouraged a continuity of tradition over

PLATE 13. Shrī Shankar Mandir, Cacandee Road, decorated with *diyā* on Diwālī night.

the millennia, as has the secrecy surrounding the teaching of vocal techniques for mantra chanting (these performing practices have often been jealously guarded by brahman pandits). Before World War II in Trinidad, the chanting of Sanskrit mantras was the exclusive domain of brahmans; today, with the liberalization of the caste system, lower-caste villagers chant mantras.

On the day before Diwālī, the Felicity Hindu School celebrates a Lakshmī *pūjā* for the students (plate 14). A village pandit chants the prescribed mantras and the children sing *bhajan* to honor Lakshmī. On Diwālī eve, Lakshmī *pūjā* are also held in the village temples, although these are not well attended as most villagers are occupied with the lighting up.

The entire month of Kārtik is a time for ritual bathing, and on Kārtik Nahān, the full-moon day, many Felicity families go swimming at the Maracas Bay, Mayaro, or Manzinilla beaches. A few families go to temple. There is no special music for Kārtik Nahān.

PLATE 14. Lakshmī *pūjā* in the Felicity Hindu School, 1977.

ꕤ HOSAY

Around the time of Diwālī and Kārtik, the Muslim festival of Hosay is celebrated in full splendor in Port of Spain, San Fernando, and smaller Trinidad cities. This spectacular ritual—called Taziya in the Middle East—commemorates the martyrdom in A.D. 684 of Imam Hussein, the grandson of Mohammed. The festival is held on the tenth day of the Islamic lunar month of Muharram, and is in the Islamic world a solemn and mournful ritual incorporating breast-beating, wailing, and self-flagellation with small whips.

In Trinidad, during the 1850s, Hosay became the outlet for East Indian national feeling, Hindu and Muslim, culminating in the San Fernando Hosay Riots of 1884. In modern times, Trinidad Muslims have transformed Hosay into a high-spirited season that vies with Christian Carnival and Hindu Holī for color, drama, and excitement. Families or neighborhoods set up tents in the privacy of which they erect elaborate floats of paper rosettes decorating a bamboo frame 10 to 20 feet high. These complicated *taziya* constructions, replicas of the tomb of Hussein, take some six weeks to construct, are decorated with giant birds, columns, turrets, cornices, and topped off with a large onion dome. The finished *taziya* are brought out for three days to a week, and the fête concludes with a procession to the nearest stream or river where the floats are immersed in the water and pushed out to sea. Gone are the austere nineteenth-century practices and the spectacular fire rod dances with 12-foot poles, flaming rags attached at either end. In today's processions, trained men carry large, shining, half-moon cutouts across their shoulders and bedazzle onlookers with their swirling dances. The march is accompanied by *gatak* stick fighting, jumping-up, rum drinking, all to the rhythm of *tāssā* drummers, the same groups who perform at Hindu weddings. The rhythmic patterns or "hands" for Hosay, however, are unique including *sāda mahatam,* signifying preparation for the battle of Karbela, *tīn chopa,* indicating the beginning of the battle, *chalta mahatam,* suggesting the full rage of the battle of Karbela, and *nabbie sarrwar,* the solemn pattern that marked the burial procession for Imam Hussein.

Hindu and Muslim festivals were incorporated into the Trinidad national calendar in the 1960s. In this fête-infatuated society, the sectarian nature of these street festivities has broken down as people of all religions join in for fun. But Felicity is off the beaten track, and its Hindu villagers don't have much to say about Hosay, and were silent about my visits to the beautiful mosque in St. Joseph, the Silver Jubilee Function at the Nur-e-Islam Mosque in San Juan, and a morning at the Five Rivers Islamia School, where I learned *kaseeda,* Muslim devotional songs. The children sang:

3

Muhammad Mustafa

Be it wealth, or be it power,
Be it strength, or be it youth,
Everything will vanish.
As anything that comes must go.
One day your proud self,
Will also lie in the bowels of the earth.
Therefore, seek and remember Allah,
And you shall surely find him.
The past never returns,
Do not depend on this world,
Whose end is a matter of fact.
Why waste your valuable existence,
By relying on dreams?
So search for Allah,
And you shall find him.
Bear patiently the difficulties,
Since they must have been in your fate.
And with the aid of your faith,
Tread the path of righteousness.
This path when found,
Will lead to all righteous paths.

So fear Allah, who is God.
Remember him. Serve him.
And you shall surely find him.

The children ranged in age from ten to thirteen, boys and girls, Hindus and Muslims alike, as the list of choir members revealed: Rosalind Mohammed and Donna Maharaj, Seema Khan and Ria Ramnarine, Loraida Ali and Patricia Sing; every creed and race, a Creole teacher conducting at the front of the choir and an East Indian Presbyterian-Muslim teacher, curiously, conducting at the back, and all the while Felicity seeming quaintly, provincially Hindu by comparison.

4 ☙
Duniya Say Dil
A full moon has risen over us.
And overshadows the other moons.
We never saw the like of your beauty.
Or the face of gladness.
You are a sun. You are a moon.
You are a greater light than other lights.
You are gold, and high above.
You are a light of hearts.
Oh, beloved, oh, Mohammed.
Oh, groom of East and West.
Oh, supporter, oh, praised one.
Oh, leader of Mecca and Jerusalem.
Whoever sees your face succeeds.
Oh, descendant of noble parents.
Your clear and cool fountain is our goal on the day of reckoning.
We never saw the camel crawl on earth but for you,
And the clouds above shaded you,
And the people prayed for you.

☙ Christmas and New Year's Day

Beginning in December, most of the Felicity cane laborers have a six-week holiday. The rains continue every afternoon, and pigeon peas, a favorite food, come into season. Christmas is celebrated by Hindu, Muslim, and Christian families, and the preparations take up a great deal of time.

"Tell me about Christmas," I asked Tara and Rawti, two young housewives who lived near Mesho.

"The day before Christmas," Tara began, "if people have a goat to kill, they kill it the day before Christmas. Christmas mean happiness for the people. The day before, who eat pork, they kill their pig the day before. Who eat goat, they kill their goat before. Who eat cattle, they . . . they . . ." Tara paused, perhaps not wishing to discuss such a serious transgression against Hinduism. "And the housewife and them," she went on, "they start mixing they cake and baking."

"Is there any singing on Christmas eve?" I asked.

"Yeah," Rawti replied, "people have *parang* [Spanish Christmas songs]."

"Do you know how to sing *parang?*" I asked.

"No," she replied, "I enjoy it. On the radio they have it. People have dance."

Parang evolved during the eighteenth and nineteenth centuries among the African-Spanish cocoa workers of Trinidad. The term derives from the Venezuelan-Spanish *parada,* "to stop" or "to put up," signifying the strolling of from four to six men, serenading from house to house, accompanied by *cuatro,* violin, mandolin, guitar, and shak shak, with ballroom-style dancing, all-night waking, and ginger-beer drinking.

The center of Venezuelan music was Cedros village, at the southwestern tip of the island, in sight of the Venezuelan mainland. Traditional *parang* sessions included Spanish genres, most in leader–chorus style, such as the *aguinaldo pasión (serenaldo, serenal)* about the birth of Christ, *joropo* with dancing, *galerón, estrebio,* and *paseo, manzanare,* and the triple-meter *castillian.* Before Independence, *parang* flourished mainly in the villages of Trinidad. During Advent 1967, the first *parang* competition was held, with five contestant groups; in 1969 the National *Parang* Champions staged a contest in Woodford Square in Port of Spain, drawing big audiences and various groups with commercial sponsorship, including Bermudez Biscuits, Agfa Film, Pepsi Cola, Readymix Cement (Readymix *Parang* Group), and Angostura Rum (Old Oak Serenaders).

In modern Trinidad, *parang* is growing in popularity, thanks to radio, television, the local record industry, and island-wide competitions. With national acclaim from Africans and East Indians alike, *parang* style has become more unified, including less village serenading, more standardized hit tunes, and rehearsed shows on city stages.[13]

"Christmas," Rawti said, "we fête and thing. Some days before Christmas people start drinking and getting drunk. They done have the 'breeze' already. The Christmas breeze. You wake up Christmas morning feeling happy. Cutting up your cake and fixing it nice, buying ice from the truck—big chunk of ice. You have everything. Who killing chicken, you kill the chicken and they feather it and they pluck it. And they cook stewed chicken, curry chicken, fried chicken, baked chicken, curry goat, stewed goat, anything, *dālpūrī* [*rotī* with lentil filling], ice cream, anything. Whole day, people come to your home and you invite people. You go to people home that day. You just keep coming and going by people home. Eating and drinking. Friends, neighbors, relatives, everybody."

"What do they have on the radio?" I asked.

"It is really nice. *Parang* whole day."

"Not Christmas carols?" I asked.

"Christmas carols too, yes."

"Do they have any *bhajan* on the radio?" I asked.

"No, no," Tara replied.

"On the television Christmas day you see people dancing to *parang* and thing," Rawti said.

"And on Christmas day," Tara said, "from England and from Canada, from the universities, they get Trinidad students sending Christmas greetings to their parents."

"Do you go to the temple?" I asked.

"No. The Christians go to church," Tara replied. "We just stay home and cook and eat and spree and fête."

"And Christmas night?" I asked.

"Visiting people," Rawti said. "Who get tired, they go to sleep, and who ain tired, they still go visiting."

"Then the 26th?"

"Boxing Day," Rawti answered. "That day they have horse racing and all this sort of thing going on."

"In Felicity?"

"No," Rawti replied. "Valencia, Arima. And people still keep on coming by your home. Who doesn't come Christmas, they come for Boxing Day. Who doesn't come for Boxing Day, they come the next week. Eating and drinking endlessly. Christmastime is the best time, the most happiest time for people."

"Happier than Diwālī?" I asked.

"Happier than Diwālī. Because they ain have to fast and all of that. Anything they feeling to eat, they eat and they drink; but at some homes people don't cook flesh on Diwālī."

"What happens on New Year's Day?" I asked.

"Well, that is the first day of the year. Everybody happy to be living for the next year."

"There's New Year's Eve," I said.

"That is Old Year's Day they call it."

"Old Year's Day?"

"And they always have Old Year's fête," Tara said. "They have bunches of bamboo. They make something like—it have a noise like a gunshot. People bake and all of that to prepare for the New Year's Day. You wake late and be baking."

"And you buy apples again and balloons," Rawti said. "They blow balloons up and hang in the house. They put decorations in the houses. Christmas and New Year is actually the same kind of happiness, same preparations. Everything new. Endless new sheets, new floors, new vase, tablecloth. And some people paint up the house."

"What if you can't afford all that?" I asked.

"You know," Tara said, "Christmas is a time the poorest person does have things in their house."

"If they don't have food the whole year," Rawti explained, "they have food that day and they have everything nice. It does be really great, you know, in Felicity."

Carnival and Phāguā

January and February are uneventful months with no major national or religious festivals. But with the approach of Lent, Carnival preparations preoccupy the entire Creole population. Indians also participate in Carnival—it is always emphasized that this is a national, not a racial celebration—but their feelings are often ambivalent about this non-Hindu revelry.

"After Christmas," Rawti went on, "if you don't hear Christmas carols, you're hearing this Carnival. Carnival calypso and steel band. Tents and thing all over the place. Calypso tents. That is when the New Year comes and, well, is only Carnival preparation."

"Where is the nearest calypso tent?" I asked.

"I am not too acquainted, you know. I don't like Carnival too much," Rawti said.

"In Enterprise they have a pan," Tara answered.

"What's the name of the group?"

"I don't know."

"And St. Augustine has one," Rawti added. "You know, they say every company have to have steel band group."

"Any big firm," Tara explained, "they just sponsor a side to play music, to play pan."

The invention of the steel band in Trinidad is a Cinderella story in music history, in which poverty and a local ban on drums dating from the nineteenth century inspired lower-class rebellious teens to contrive a unique melodiously percussive combo that took them from the back streets of Port of Spain to London, where they were hailed at the 1951 Festival of Britain as The

Trinidad All Stars Percussion Orchestra. Journalists wrote of their triumphant debut: "It seemed impossible that music could come out of such unlikely instruments."

Legend tells that the steel band evolved from masquerade bands of Carnival processions, particularly the tamboo bamboo bands of "Hell-Yard," Port of Spain, that had enlarged by the 1930s to include such ad hoc instruments as soapboxes, biscuit tins, dustbins, gin bottles, and odd bits of iron. After World War II, bandsmen developed a technique whereby an American 55-gallon oil drum could be fashioned into a tuned idiophone whose tempered steel extended the range and musical versatility of their groups. Bandsmen became local stars in their own right as the "Bar-20" players: "Batman," Anderson, "Scribo" Maloney, "Red Ozzie" Campbell, "Big Dick" Barker, "Red Pops" Smith, "Battersby," "Long Grant," "Big-Head John" Pierre and his brother "Bitter-Man." The "band wars" of 1945 between "Hell-Yard" and "John-John" led to widespread street fights between rival bands—a notorious urban problem, whereby membership in a band was thenceforward interpreted as hooliganism signaling Creole disdain for European norms. A 1963 survey by the Ministry of Community Development reported that steel bands drew their members from the teenage group that tended to mistrust the upper classes and show a high incidence of delinquency and unemployment.

The manufacture of pans is a highly specialized skill. Instruments are not standardized, as fierce competition between rival bands has fostered innovation and experimentation in design and tuning. Drums are made in families: bass pans (formerly called booms), rhythm pans (including double second pans, double guitar pans, treble guitar pans, and cello pans; formerly tune boom or kittle), and tenor pans (formerly ping-pongs) for the melody. Instrument makers begin by "sinking," beating the top of the oil drum into a concave shape, then "burning," tempering the metal, "cutting," to the required length, "seaming" radii from equidistant points around the circumference of the pan, and tuning, hammering each section of the drumhead to the desired pitch. The layout of the notes on the surface of the head is never in scale order (as on keyboard instruments) but varies from maker to maker.

Modern groups have added vibraphones, cowbells, congas, bongos, triangles, and other percussion instruments to the basic pan family. In Carnival processions, the small high drums are slung from the player's neck, and large drums are mounted on enormous movable frames.

By the 1970s, an estimated 200 bands, with some 5,000 players, were established in Trinidad. Steel bands have overcome their antisocial stigma, and island-wide government-sponsored competitions have led to rigorous standards of performance in both village and city groups, and to virtuoso overseas performances at Radio City and Carnegie Hall, with programs including well-known pieces from the Western classical repertory as Strauss's "Voices of Spring," Tchaikovsky's "First Piano Concerto," Chopin's "Minute Waltz" and "Nocturne in E♭," and a Bach concerto performed in the presence of the legendary Spanish cellist Pablo Casals, who is reported to have exclaimed "Bravo! Bravo! It's much better than I thought!" (*Life,* 14 March 1960).

"When Carnival day comes, what happens in Felicity?" I asked.

"Well," Rawti replied, "you see, there are two days, right? People buy clothes and they go up to see Carnival in Chaguanas because Felicity don't have any celebration. That day on Cacandee Road, you could sit down outside you house and see all your friends and relatives passing. They dress up and they going to Chaguanas. The young people like it. Go jump up and dance."

"Did you go last year?" I asked.

"No," Rawti replied, "long time I never go to see Carnival. But in the school, when I used to take part in the bands, once I took part. The name of the band was 'Somewhere in Hawaii.' We dress up the bag—bag they make hammock with. We strip it and make skirts. And we put flower in the hair like Hawaiian people. And plait up our hair, and we put plenty makeup in the face to look red. This blue thing on top of the eyes, and you know, we dress up like real Hawaiians. And we have the hula hoop—put it around the waist and we dancing up with it. When the steel band playing the music, we dancing to that music. I enjoy it, but mostly Creole people take part in it, not Indians."

"Do Indians ever play in steel bands?" I asked.

"Yeah," Rawti replied, "most are Creoles, but they have Indians too."

"And on the radio on Carnival day?" I asked.

"Endless calypso," Rawti answered. "You hearing calypso that happening in the big city like Port of Spain and San Fernando. It comes through the radio what band going now up on stage, and on television from morning till twelve o'clock the night you seeing bands go up. You don't bound to go to Port of Spain to see Carnival. You can see it on television. You see all the people jumping up and drinking up and all that."

"Sometimes it have fight, you know," Tara added. "When it have some bad people drinking, it does be dangerous."

"Do you ever go to temple on Carnival day?" I asked.

"No," Rawti said. "People who are accustomed praying and they go every day, well, they will go. It's not a religious thing. Trinidad is a cosmopolitan society, right? They show that all the different nations [in Felicity usage Hindu castes, also races] could play together. They live in unity. Or like a Carnival theme going through all of that. Carnival is for everybody. That is the time when everybody could participate. It is not for any special race."

Shivrātrī, commemoration of the birth of Shiva, is an important Hindu springtime festival, the most active day of the year at the Felicity temples. Many villagers told me that if they could attend temple only once a year, they would go on Shivrātrī, observed on the 13th day of the first half of the month of Phāgun, around March. The temples are decorated with streamers. Beggars come from outside the village and wait in the temple yards to receive alms (the auspicious benefits of alms donation are described in the wedding song, example XII, song 53). Villagers start going to the temple about midnight and the procession continues until noon of the following day. The Trinidad Sevashram Sangha on Nolan Street has a 24-hour *kīrtan* devotional session on Shivrātrī, with groups of singers performing in relay to complete a whole day and night of continuous singing.

"And what do you do for Shivrātrī?" I asked.

"Well," Tara said, "when you wake up in the morning, you bathe, you throw a *lotā* of water [an act of worship; plate 15], and then you fast for the whole day. You wait until twelve o'clock in the night. They all them singing *bhajan* and *Rāmāyaṇ* till twelve in the temple. Anywhere have temple, all the temples have the same thing that day. From seven they start singing, until twelve, right? All the *bhajan,* but most is Shiva *bhajan.* Steady *bhajan* singing right through. You must wake whole night. You hearing *bhajan* this side; you throwing *jal* [oblation of holy water] that side, and everybody talking."

"And give beggars rice and money," Rawti added.

On the last day of the month of Phāgun (usually March), Hindus celebrate Phāguā (also called Holī). The religious significance of this springtime festivity commemorating the destruction of the demon Holikā is still remembered, but is of little significance in Felicity (or in India). The day is one of music and merriment, often referred to as the "Indian Carnival." The villagers "play" Phāguā by sprinkling *abīr,* a red dye, on their friends and relatives as an expression of affection, even reconciliation. Normal social barriers are transcended and old grudges set aside in the excitement, the mess, and the confusion of the festivities.

"Phāguā morning you wake up as usual and it have a powder called *abīr* powder," Tara explained. "And you mix it in some warm water for that powder to melt. And usually people start playing after lunch.

"With the *abīr,* this red liquid, after lunch they really start it because that is a messy thing. They full up a little bottle and they make some little holes on the cork and they start wetting you with it. You're all red that day. They have a red powder to throw on you too, and they use ordinary white powder. And in the savannah in the back they does have big celebration. Everybody wetting one another and they singing song and they dancing."

PLATE 15. Hindu Sacrificing. (Reprinted from Kingsley, *At Last, Christmas in the West Indies*)

"What kind of songs do they sing?" I asked.

"They call them *chautāl.* Kinda fast fast kind of song for Phāguā."

☙ CHAUTĀL

Chautāl is a seasonal Hindu genre, and the bands rehearse only once a year, beginning several weeks before the Phāguā celebrations. Groups usually consist of eight or more male singers, all of whom play *jhāl* (brass cymbals), and one *ḍholak* player. Until recent decades, the *chautāl* bands used to proceed through the village on Phāguā day, pausing to play at houses along the way. As they performed, the women of the house came out and sprinkled the musicians with *abīr.* Men who had not practiced with the group might join in on the day, either singing or playing the *jhāl.* Morton Klass observed some half-dozen groups during his visit in 1958. Today the number of bands has declined, and street processions have been abandoned in favor of performances in the village savannah and nationwide competitions in the larger towns.

"From morning the band does start," Tara explained. "They does start drinking their liquor, and they start playing, all by the corner. They does go to San Juan in the savannah. And they does have a competition there. More than one band does go."

"Do they walk along Cacandee Road?" I asked.

"No," Tara replied, "they more going in the back, in the savannah, the playground. Just around the time it start getting dark, they stop playing."

"What is the meaning of Phāguā?" I asked.

"They say that there was a bad man," Rawti answered, "and that is the day that they fought and destroy him. That is why the *abīr,* the *abīr* is to signify blood—bloodshed."

The term *chautāl* refers to the entire repertory of Phāguā songs, and also to one of the three main subtypes of this genre, that also includes *jhūmar* and *ulārā.*[14] Most songs in the Phāguā repertory relate episodes from the *Rāmāyaṇ,* the *Māhābhārata,* and the *Purāṇas* (all Hindu epic texts), often describing incidents from the life of Rām or Krishna. In the villages of eastern Uttar Pradesh, men perform many types of Bhojpurī songs for Holī, including *chautāl, cahakā, kabīr, jhūmar,* and *jogīrā.* Usharbudh Arya heard *jhūmar* and *ulārā* at Phāguā in Surinam during the 1960s.

Chautāl singing is responsorial. A song may have as many as 20 verses, each of which is repeated some 10 or more times. The distinguishing feature of this style is accelerando, gradual accelerando during the first four to eight repetitions of the verse; then a sudden burst of speed called *dugun,* "double," is cued by the drummer and characterized by increased density and volume of the drum part. The verse is repeated again six to eight times at this fast tempo (about quarter note = M.M. 120), hence Tara's description, "kinda fast kind of song." Crescendo and accelerando also characterize the *chautāl* singing in eastern Uttar Pradesh, where these musical techniques are cultivated to induce states of religious ecstasy. To heighten the effect of Holī songs, north Indian musicians drink *bhāng,* an intoxicating mixture containing *cannabis.* The association of *chautāl* with heightened states of religious awareness seems to have been lost in Trinidad, as does the custom of taking *bhāng* (but, in Trinidad the villagers drink rum at Phāguā). When I inquired about the striking accelerando effect of the *chautāl* songs, Kamini simply explained: "It is written like that in the *Rāmāyaṇ* and the *Bhāgawad Gītā* [the best-loved portion of the *Māhābhārata*]. When the song starts to speed the drummer takes the lead and the singer just follow on."[15]

A *chautāl* is sung by two groups of men, each playing a pair of *jhāl.* At the beginning of the song, and again with each new verse, the leader starts alone with the first few words of the text; halfway through the verse he is joined by the other members of the leading group, and by the *ḍholak.* Then the chorus group repeats the entire verse. After six or so repetitions, the group stops abruptly, usually for an eighth rest on beat one; immediately afterward, the leader introduces a new verse. Toward the end of the verses the lead singer may call out to end the verse, or to sing louder. Example II, "Boliye Rājā Rāmachandra Kī Jay" (Shout Victory to King Rāmachandra), recorded in Felicity, has 17 verses, each starting slowly and accelerating from quarter note = M.M. 96–116 to quarter note = M.M. 120. In this example, the opening verse has a rhythmic structure of seven beats (3+2+2), followed by two verses in four. The fourth verse is in seven, the first and sixth in four and so on for the 17 verses of this *chautāl:* 7 4 4 7 4 4 7 4 4 7 4 4 and so on (see example II). The text of this example and other items of the Phāguā repertory is in Awadhī (Oudhī), the dialect of north-central and central Uttar Pradesh, some 200 miles west of the Bhojpurī area. Awadhī songs are unusual in Felicity even though this language was spoken by a fair number of the original indentured laborers. That the important men's repertory has survived in this dialect and the important women's repertory has survived in Bhojpurī presents a mystery for the scholar.

These *chautāl* generally begin with the cry *(jaykārā)* "Speak of King Rāmachandra's Victory." Sets of *chautāl* with related texts are often sung in an uninterrupted series, with a change in melody indicating the start of the new song. As with many songs in the archaic Felicity repertory, each line of the song refers to an episode of the *Rāmāyaṇ,* thus in example II, line 4, referring to a story of the crocodile and the elephant (see also chap. 7, songs 22 and 24) or line 5 referring to the story from the *Māhābhārata* when Krishna saved

Example II (song 5, CD track 1): Boliye Rājā Rāmachandra Kī Jay

♩ = M.M. 96–240

4. 7

Leader

ā - he ga - ja ke-(e) ja - ba gā - ha pa - kā - re ka -

Chorus

Leader

ha - ta cha - lo pyār ______

Chorus

ā - he ga - ja ke-(e) ja - ba gā - ha pa -

5. 8

Leader

f

e dru-pa-da su-tā ke chī - ra ba-ḍhā -

Chorus

kā - re ka - ha-ta cha - lo pyār

Leader

ye ga-ṇi-ka su-tā ta-na-hāy[e] _

Chorus

ā - ho dru-pa-da su-tā ke chī - ra ba-ḍhā -

Leader

etc.

Chorus

ye ga-ṇi-ka su-tā ta-na-hāy[e] _

etc.

Dhropatī from the humiliation of nakedness by providing her with a sari *(chīra)* of unending length. These stories are well known to Indian villagers and a single line calls their entire meaning to mind.

EXAMPLE II
Boliye Rājā Rāmachandra Kī Jay

[*jaykārā,* "shout of victory"]
boliye rājā rāmachandra kī jay!
[*Sung verses*]
siyā rāma nāma dina rahana kahata chalo pyāre
e grīdhad ajāmila ganikā tārī sewarī kīnha sukhārī
dekhahu dhrupa prahalāda nayana bhaye
āhe gaja ke jaba gāha pakāre kahata chalo pyār
e drupada sutā ke chīra baḍhāye gaṇika sutā tanahāye
bhārata mẽ baradora māchāo
ahe ganṭā tere se krishana murāre kahata chalo pyāre
o jaba-jaba gāra pare bhaktana para taba-taba harī awatāre
kahan lage karahu bayāna eka mukha
āhe sārada pāwaka nāhī pārye kahata chalo pyāre
e sesha mahesha ganeshha adi saba baranahī bārahi bāre
sundara brajahi amāhi basabahu
aye dasaratha suta rāma udāre kahata chalo pyāre
sumirõ mana rāma sahita sītā
he dashmukha yesā bhūpa mahābala
he indra kubera waruna se kānpẽ
sumirõ mai rāma-sahita sītā
[*jaykārā*]
boliye-boliye ajodhyānāth siyā bar rāmachandra kī jay

5
[*jaykārā*]
Shout victory to King Rāmachandra!
[*sung verses*—literal translation]
Sītā Rāma name day and night speak keep loving.
Those vulture Ajāmil [sinner from *Rāmāyaṇ*] and to Ganikā [temple dancer, *devadāsī*] and to Sevarī [prostitute from *Rāmāyaṇ*] deliver from sin.
Look how Dhrupa [son of king] and Prahalād [son of another king] great became.
Oh, elephant to when crocodile caught saying go dear.
Yes, the sari of King Drupada's daughter increased [in length], Ganikā daughter cured.
In India all this took place.
Oh, bell your, repeat the name of Krishna Murārī saying walk dear friend.
Look, whenever lightning [bad time] falls, devotee only, then God has taken incarnation.
To say begin do explanation with one mouth [together].
Oh, Saraswatī not fire got, saying walk dear.

Oh, Sesha [Vishnu], Mahesha [Shiva], Ganesh, and others all, repeat time and time again.
Keep beautiful Braj [region of Uttar Pradesh where Krishna lived] within your heart.
Oh, King Dasaratha's son, Rāma, is very generous; speak walk, dear friends.
Always remember Rāma and Sītā in your heart.
He ten mouth [Rāwaṇ] like emperor powerful.
Oh, Īndra [Vedic god of rain], Kubera [god of air], Waruna [god of water], like trembling.
Pray I Rāma with Sītā.
[*jaykārā*]
Say, say Ayodhyānāth [Rāma], Siyā bridegroom Rāmachandra of victory!

Other Felicity *chautāl* texts draw on themes from the *Rāmāyaṇ* and the *Māhābhārata:*

6 ☙
[*jaykārā*]
Shout victory to King Rāmachandra!
[*sung verses*]
God of God ours false world is.
Oh, false world is, oh, false world is.
Oh, only his moon light when spreading, Brahmā constructed creation.
Yes, false world is, yes, false world is.
Yes, even then you pray to Shyām Sundar [Krishna].
Waiting with the hope of your *karma* [fate].
This world lust is, unending pain is, false world is.
Look, only God is parents, son, brother, only God is clan, family.
Oh, only He is clan, family Savariya [Krishna], only He is clan, family.
Yes, only He is Lord of various powers.
Look, He is pervading everywhere.
This false world is, oh, false world is.
He is pervading everywhere, false world is.
Oh, if you want well being yours pray Siyāwara [Sītā's bridegroom, i.e., Rāma] dear friend.

"These *chautāl* from Trinidad are very old," Umesh said. "My grandfather loved these religious poems. In modern times our village Holī songs include both religious and some lusty songs.

"At the end of this next song it tells a famous story of the black bee. There was a king. He fell in love with his new beautiful wife and didn't come out of the Queen's palace for a long time. All the work of the court began to shake, and courtiers became concerned. Who would tell the king? But there were poets, and one of them wrote this *dohā* ('couplet'):

nahī parāg nahī madhup madhu hili vikās yahi kāl
alī kalī hī saũ bindhyo āgẽ kaun hawāl

Neither juice nor bee's honey nor progress for this time. / In the tender bud only to be wrapped up. In the future what will be?

"Indeed, you will find several hundred songs about bees in India, because they are a symbol of love—bee and lotus. In my village we know this poem, the *gopīs* [milkmaid lovers] complaint to Krishna with examples:"

prīti kari kāhū sukh na lahyo
prīti patang karī dīpak sõ
āpuhī prān diyo
alisut prīti karī pankaj sõ
sāmput mānjhi gayo
ham jo prīti karī shyām tum sai
madhuwan chhoṛi gayo
madhuwan ri gayo
prīti kari kāhū sukh na lahyo

7 ☙
Fall in love no one happiness gains.
Fell in love moth flame to,
Own life sacrificed.
Bee fell in love lotus with,
Trapped by closing petals in the evening.
We fell in love Shyām [Krishna] to you.
Madhuwan [forest near Brindāban, where Krishna played his *līlā* (love "play")] left.
Fall in love no one happiness gains.

"So to understand a single line of our folk poetry you must know many many stories from the *Rāmāyaṇ*, the *Māhābhārata*, and the *Purāṇas*. We do not take many stories from the *Upanishads* or the ancient *Vedas*, even though these are the old books Western people seem to read the most. In the village we prefer our rich and colorful and sweet stories. See this next song from Felicity."

8 ☙
[*jaykārā*]
Shout victory to King Rāmachandra!
[*sung verses*]
This is an epithet of Prayag [Allahabad, U.P., confluence of the Jamuna and Ganges Rivers], salvation giving happiness.
Pray do many thanks to Queen Ganges.
That at still imperishable banyan tree decorated.

This in every way auspicious bliss mine, salvation giving happiness.
This is salvation giving happiness, oh, salvation giving happiness.
In every way auspicious bliss mine, salvation giving happiness.
Yes, in every way auspicious bliss, salvation giving happiness.
Salvation attain auspicious place say such *Vedas* explained.
Sins, virtues, lies—all can be seen in the water.
Oh, as the sun also rises, darkness fails, salvation giving pleasure.
This salvation giving pleasure, oh, salvation giving pleasure.
As the sun also rises, darkness fails, salvation giving pleasure.
Oh, seeing the lovely wave, happiness cannot be explained.
As the large black bee in a pond easily, out of love, got caught.
Increasing pleasure seeing the water beautiful.
Oh, as talks wave to swell, salvation giving pleasure.
Oh, say begin to praise together qualities several ways.
Uma [Sītā], Rāma, Saint Shesha cannot explain.
Brahma God there thank the goddess of world.
Oh, whatever dwelling place of enchanting kinds, salvation giving pleasure.
Yes, whoever dwelling place of enchanting kinds, salvation giving pleasure.

In Banpurwā village, a Kurmī farmer community south of Banaras, I heard in 1987 many Holī songs. Some, like those of Felicity, draw on themes from the *Rāmāyaṇ*, or combine archaic stories of the epics with a quiet mention of married love:

9 ☙
God already has written it down about Sītā and Rāwaṇ.
God already has written it down about Sītā and Rāwaṇ.
God already has written it down,
God already has written it down,
God already has written it down about Sītā and Rāwaṇ.
And Sītā was put on the chariot.
Saint began to move and the vulture was watching.
Rāwaṇ is carrying away lady Sītā.
Oh, taking away lady,
Oh, taking away lady,
Rāwaṇ is carrying away lady Sītā.
Oh, came [Rāwaṇ] secretly in the costume of a saint.
As the vulture saw, he blocked Rāwaṇ.
Going in the chariot.
Rāwaṇ is taking away Sītā with him.
Rāwaṇ is taking away Sītā with him.
As the vulture saw, he blocked Rāwaṇ.
Going in the chariot.
Sweetheart do not play a trick.
You accepted me by your heart.
Rāwaṇ is taking away Sītā with him.

Burn the body of the vulture.
Set fire [to the vulture] and took Jānakī [Sītā] ahead.
He [vulture] made [Rāwaṇ] to leave a sign [of Sītā's].
Sītā was taken to Lankā with demon.
Tricked by a tricker.
Sītā's [golden] bangle is shown.
Sītā went to Lankā with a demon.
Tricked by a tricker.

Other Holī songs from Banpurwā address the purely sensual:

10 ♪
Phāgun has come and it is Holī.
Phāgun has come and it is Holī.
Sparrow hawk swears everyday.
Having listened, it shoots my heart like a bullet.
How can I live in my tender age?
Phāgun has come and it is Holī.
The fire [Agni; Vedic god of fire] of sex gives me pain every day.
Sleep doesn't come to me in the night.
Oh, can't sleep in the bed.
Oh, can't sleep in the bed.
Phāgun has come and it is Holī.
Phāgun has come and it is Holī.
Oh, can't sleep in the bed.
The bed to me is lonely.
Phāgun has come and it is Holī.
Try hard to come back and quench the fire of my body!
Phāgun has come and it is Holī.
Phāgun has come and it is Holī.

Other Banpurwā Holī songs liken nature to love, in simple and sweet metaphors of flowers and fruits.

11 ♪
The season of blooming of the marigold is come.
Oh, gardener friend, plant the marigolds in the garden.
The season of the marigold flower is come.
The season of blooming of the marigold is come.
Plant *belā* [of the jasmine family], plant *chamelā* [also jasmine family].
Holī is! Is! Is! Is! Is! Look!
Somebody plants bananas and *anār* [pomegranate].
Oh, gardener friend, plant the marigolds in the garden.
The season of blooming of the marigold is come.
Oh, Rām plants *belā-chamelā.*
Oh, *belā-chamelā.*
Holī is! Is! Is! Is! Is! Look!

Somebody plants bananas and *anār.*
Oh, gardener friend, plant the marigolds in the garden.
The season of blooming of the marigold is come.
With what will you irrigate *belā-chamelā?*
Belā-chamelā oh!
Holī is! Is! Is! Is! Is! Look!
With what will you irrigate *anār,* oh, gardener friend?
Oh, gardener friend, plant the marigolds in the garden.
The season of blooming of the marigold is come.
With milk *belā-chamelā* is irrigated.
With milk *belā-chamelā* is irrigated.
Belā-chamelā oh!
Holī is! Is! Is! Is! Is! Look!

"What else is left to irrigate the *anār?*" Umesh joked.

Somebody irrigate [meaning obscure].

"How could the meaning be obscure just there?" I asked.

"Well it is obscure," Umesh replied. "They sang obscure so only they could understand what they sang."

Oh, gardener friend, plant the marigolds in the garden.
Holī is! Is! Is! Is! Is! Look!
The season of blooming of the marigold is come.
The season of blooming of the marigold is come.

"Is that the end?" I asked.

"They repeat that last line eight times. The gardener is three things. Gardener is a caste in northern India called *mālī.* They used to work under the *jajmānī* patronage system; they used to work at wedding time to serve flowers. God is also gardener of this earth. He is also gardener of our heart. We think of flowers as a holy thing. The virgin maid was measured against the flower—she had to weigh only as much as one flower. Then she is holy. We say 'Mother Earth.' And in India we are all gardeners. We plant beautiful things. A song tells, 'God, you are the only gardener of my flower garden.'"

Arya's Bhojpurī collection includes a Phāguā song from Meerzog village, Surinam (Arya 1968):

12 ꕥ
Beloved, do not go abroad; the spring (season) has come close.
The mango (trees) have begun to blossom, the bumblebees are seen in the groves.
The trees have become leafy (and the) *ṭesū* flowers are blooming (in their) minds.
The birds are starting out on (their) journeys on the wing—
(And) these days are getting warmer daily.
Oh Kṛṣṇa, listen to just this request; O thou with (a generous) heart, stay home.

"'Oh, sweetheart Krishna, pay attention to me a little bit; stay inside the palace.' is a better translation," Umesh said.

Without you (my) sixteen adornments (are futile); who (can) know my
  suffering?
With whom shall I play (when) in separation?
(My) beloved knows not at all the pains of (my) body.
(*Ritual Songs*, 101–2)

Wherever Indians live and wherever they have journeyed, these springtime messages of loving Holī, of god and man, of man and nature, have lingered in heart, memory, and song.

☙ The Rainy Season

April is a quiet month in Felicity. Easter is celebrated by the handful of Christian families, but is not important to Hindus.

"We don't do anything special on Easter," Tara told me. "It is Christian people go to church. On Good Friday, we burst a egg and we throw it in a glass of water. The white of the egg. If it form like a coffin, they say somebody will leave soon to go away. Sometime it form like a church. When it form like a church, they say somebody gonna get married in the family."

As in India (and the United States), many weddings are held in June. During the early months of the rainy season in Trinidad—June, July, and August—there are no special celebrations. But Moon, Sankey, and the other Felicity ladies urged me to record their *kajarī*, also sung in India during the monsoon month of Sāwan (July–August). They told me these months are the sweetest of the year.

In July, Moon explained, the monsoon rains begin and many a Bhojpurī song draws the analogy linking the downpour with the consumation of marriage. The month of Sāwan is a romantic time when nature renews itself through the restorative power of the rains. Sāwan is also the music season, especially for girls, who in India hang primitive rope and plank swings from the limbs of village trees. A common sight in Uttar Pradesh is three or four girls, catching the breeze as the songs tell us, swinging together, laughing, some seated, some standing holding the ropes, lazily, their saris floating in the air. The Sāwan songs that Felicity women remember use rich images from nature to tell of love and the irony of the human condition—that humans are not honorable like Rām and Sītā of old, that love brings longing and longing brings pain, that love begets jealousy, that rivalry, deception, separation wound the wife. The "sweet pain" (an Indian term for sexual pleasure, including childbirth) of love is illustrated.

The *kajarī* songs of Felicity describe these Indian scenes, even though the rainy season of Trinidad is minimal compared to the Oriental monsoon, and the Felicity trees not majestic enough for traditional swinging.

Moon sang:

13

Oh, came Sāwan most charming.
Forest in begin speak peacock.
Came Sāwan most charming.
Forest in begin speak peacock.
Mango in branch speak parrot.
Cold breeze shake violent.
Mango in branch speak cuckoo.
Cold breeze shake violent.
Mango in branch speak parrot.
Cold breeze breeze shake violent.
Mango in branch speak parrot.
Cold breeze breeze shake violent.
Oh, as forest in speak cuckoo.
Exactly the same time sang frog, peacock.
As in forest speak cuckoo.
Exactly the same time sang frog, peacock.
Came Sāwan most charming.
Forest in speak peacock.
Oh, joyfully I ask to *sakhiyān* (pl., female friend to female friend).
Listen *sakhiyān* thou talk mine.
Joyfully this ask to *sakhiyān.*
Listen *sakhī* (sing., female friend), thou talk mine.
Oh, swing hand *kadam* [tree] of branch [cf. ex. VII].
Having come play *kajarī.*
Swing hand *kadam* of branch.
Having come play *kajarī.*
Came Sāwan most charming.
Forest in begin speak peacock.
Came Sāwan most charming.
Forest in speak peacock.
Oh, mother-in-law not house in, father-in-law not house in.
How tell story mine?
Mother-in-law not house in, father-in-law not house in.
How to tell story mine?
Oh, how to tell this who me understand.
Rival wife sleeps in bed mine.
Oh, how to tell this who me understand.
Rival wife sleeps in bed mine.
Came Sāwan most charming.

Forest in begin speak peacock.
Came Sāwan most charming.
Forest in begin speak peacock.
Oh, gathering of black clouds roaring cloud.
Lightening look glow powerfully.
Oh, gathering of black clouds roaring cloud.
Lightening look glow powerfully.
Oh, Bandhuk Nath says begin like this.
Nothing is left life in mine.
Oh, Bandhuk Nath says begin like this.
Nothing is left life in mine.
Came Sāwan most charming.
Forest in speak begin peacock.

In Felicity, *kajarī* can be sung at weddings and at the celebrations following the birth of a child—*chatī* (six days after the birth) or *barahī* (twelve days after the birth). In Bhojpurī villages, *chatī* and *barahī* are typically held only after the birth of a son, but in Felicity, these parties are also held to celebrate the birth of daughters. August is a common month for birth in India and Bhojpurī wives will laughingly tell about the long nights of winter (December–January) with their intense cold, and the scarcity of quilts in the household. Men are better rested, don't have to plow their fields. Hence the *byāh ke gīt* verse, "your son walks like a plowman," is at once insult and praise, suggesting that the groom, although clumsy, is also a virile rugged farmer and a powerful partner (see ex. XV, lines 5–6).

A group of Felicity ladies sang several songs for Sāwan, at a *chatī* party. The texts tell of the rain, the breeze, and the ominous black clouds of the monsoon.

This Felicity *kajarī* suggests that the husband has taken a mistress ("wetting the other side") and comments (with sarcasm and inuendo) that if this wife had anticipated her husband's lustings she would have pitched a tent, even thatched the roof of the bungalow to stop the rain.

14 ♫
My husband and king wetting the other side in the drops of the Sāwan rain.
Look, of Sāwan drops, of Sāwan drops.
My husband wetting the other side in the drops of the Sāwan rain.
If I knew my husband will wet,
Look, I would have covered Uṛaniya in the Sāwan drops.
Look, of drops, oh, of drops.
Oh, husband wetting the other side in drops of the Sāwan rain.
Look, if I knew my husband will wet,
Look, I would have pitch the tent in drops of the Sāwan.

Look, of drops, oh, of drops.
My king and husband wetting the other side Sāwan of drops.
Look, if I knew my husband and king will wet,
Look, I would have thatched the bungalow.
Oh, of drops, oh, of drops.
My husband and king wetting the other side the Sāwan drops of rain.
My husband wetting the other side in drops of the Sāwan rain.

The next Felicity *kajarī* invites lovers to the lanes to take the breeze, to play the flute.

15 ♫
Our lanes in come on lovers.
Come on lover, come on lover.
Our lanes in come on lovers.
Our flute of breeze take lovers.
Breeze take lover, breeze take lovers.
Our lanes in come on lovers.

In the next Felicity *kajarī,* the black clouds of the monsoon are likened to the dark complexion of the husband. Even though fair skin is favored in north India, the gods Rām and Krishna were both *shyāmla*—blue, dark blue. In this song, another woman is blinking (flirting) at her husband (possibly this text could be interpreted that the husband is blinking, glancing at another woman [several text lines obscure]).

16 ♫
I am fair beautiful, you black cloud.
I am fair beautiful, you black cloud,
Black cloud, black cloud,
I am fair beautiful, you black cloud.
I am [obscure passage] lover (husband) blink glance.
I fair, look black cloud.
Blink, blink.
I fair beautiful, black cloud.
I fair beautiful.

Sankey sang this *kajarī* during a Felicity wedding:

17 ♫
Blow eastern breeze, pain comes up!
Oh! pain comes up, oh! pain comes up!
Blow eastern breeze, pain comes up, oh!
What city at search my husband?
Now heart feels city go to, oh!
City go to, oh! city go to, oh!
Blow eastern breeze, pain comes up!

What master to stop my husband?
Master should die, oh! master should die!
Blow eastern breeze, pain comes up, oh!

Umesh explained this song. "In India, when the eastern wind blows it is painful for the joints of the body. The eastern wind is always damp; the western wind is dry and good for health, useful for farmers when they are threshing because dry wind dries their stalk of the harvest to make good fodder and take the grain out easily. The deep meaning is that the eastern wind brings to the wife the deep sweet pain of longing for her absent husband."

Independence, Janamāshhtāmī, Rāmlīlā

In August, Trinidadians and Indians (and many other members of the Commonwealth) celebrate their Independence Day.

"Independence. That is the 31st August," Tara explained. "That is the day Trinidad get Independence. I don't know from where."

"From England," I said.

"Oh," she said. "They just give them a public holiday. Schools get eight weeks holiday just for Independence. The people cook a nice lunch like chicken, rice, and they sit down home and they eat. Who have their own car, they just go by the beach and relax."

"Any singing?" I asked.

"No."

"On the streets," Rawti explained, "the government who wear uniform, they have march-past. The policemen, the nurses, and all the firemen. They go on the street and they march, and from morning they have special programs on television for Independence."

Janamāshhtāmī, the birth of Krishna, is celebrated on the 8th day of the first half of the month of Bhādõ, usually in August. Many villagers attend temple, although apparently not as many as in years past. The baby Krishna is represented as a cucumber which is rocked to sleep in a tiny hammock. *Bhajan* dedicated to Krishna are sung.

Rāmlīlā, the commemoration of Rām's victory over the demon Rāwaṇ, is celebrated on the first to tenth days of the second half of the month of Kūār (around September–October). The main activity is a play performed in the evenings during the entire ten days. It is staged in the savannah by the village children (usually only those of upper caste). They are tutored by a pandit in the principal roles—Rām and his three brothers, also Sītā, Rāwaṇ, Hanumān, and the monkey army. Rehearsals are held in one of the village temples. Elaborately decorated costumes are sewn by the village ladies.

"Rāwaṇ side is the bad side," Tara explained. "And Hanamān side does wear red. The black side always bigger than the red side. The black side always want to fight with the red side."

"Does anyone sing songs?"

"The pandit sings *bhajan* at Rāmlīlā."

Around the time of Rāmlīlā, the short dry season, "petit carime," begins. Families throughout Felicity begin the serious task of harvesting their rice. At the same time, they prepare for the renewal of the annual cycle by cleaning their houses in readiness for the visit of the goddess of prosperity, Lakshmī Mātā, on Diwālī night.

ꕥ

This is the annual calendar the villagers outlined for me. The dry season, January through June, is the most important for music. It begins with the music for Carnival: calypso and steel band. Then, in February, the *chautāl* bands start practicing as the East Indian community prepares for its "Indian Carnival," Phāguā. Around March, there is all-night *bhajan* singing for Shivrātrī. The first six months of the year are also the "wedding season," so "mike" trucks with their large speaker horns are often heard playing film songs. Indian orchestras are hired to play in the village, and the traditional wedding songs are performed almost every Saturday night and Sunday afternoon. During the post-crop time, July through September, there are no special musical activities, although the bitter-sweet Bhojpurī monsoon songs are remembered and sung at get-togethers and childbirth celebrations. Then, in the slack season, October to January, the *bhajan* for Lakshmī are sung at Diwālī and the Spanish *parang* at Christmas.

When I asked people about the seasons, I discovered that older people, like Rajiah and Siewrajiah, described the Hindu festivals in enormous detail, especially Rāmlīlā and Shivrātrī. The girls in their twenties thought it was more important to emphasize Christmas and Carnival. No one volunteered long descriptions of music. Is this because the village jukeboxes and radios never stop, because the temple services with their singing and chanting go on regardless of the season, the villagers play records and cassettes at home every day—because the music never stops? Occasionally there are events without music, like Christian weddings, but I never experienced any real silence in Felicity. When you ask anyone in the village about the special days of the year, you are more likely to get detailed descriptions of stewed chicken, curried goat, and *dālpūrī rotī*—the real specialties—than descriptions of music, which, for them, is so much a part of life.

☙ Chapter Six ❧
Speaking of Music

> I wish he would explain his explanation.
>
> Lord Byron, *Don Juan*

Continuing my research, I was soon caught up in the rhythm of village life, and it became harder to set out every morning with my list of prepared questions. Like the rest of the villagers, I too began to complain about the heat of the day. As time slipped by it was more and more difficult to isolate music from the panorama of life around me. Interviews became conversations, and informants became friends. The village became my home, and I began to think of my book not only as their story, but as my story as well.

People grew accustomed to seeing me make my way along Cacandee Road in the afternoon, loaded down with tape recorders and cameras. Each day I ventured a bit farther from Mesho's house, and each day I made new friends. We chatted about songs and singers. They sang songs for me, and I started to sing the wedding songs and *bhajan* I had learned for them.

No one in Felicity likes to walk very far. They find it a hot sticky business, and prefer to be seen driving or riding in a private car, or at least a taxi. I was conspicuous less from the color of my skin, less from the equipment I always carried, than because I walked farther than anyone else. Gradually I began to vary my walks, exploring different districts of the village: one day through "Casacu" and down toward the river, the next day in the opposite direction down Cacandee Road to the "Junction," the next day to "Jangli" in the back.

☙ Music and Singing

On all my walks, I never found anyone in Felicity who said they didn't like music. Some people preferred wedding songs, while others liked English songs, or reggae, or pop music, but everyone agreed that music is a good thing. Suruj Pandit told me, "Whenever music is playing, no matter if you are worried or anything, you just feel a different happiness come into you by listening to music. Music is a charm. If a person don't like music, they're considered to be half alive and half dead."

I tape-recorded a great deal of music; in fact, I kept the recorder turned on nearly the whole day. I wanted to capture all the sounds of the village: the music and the noise, the silences, the people, the animals, the sounds of the day, the sounds of night. I recorded services in the village churches, and Hindu *pūjā* in private homes. I recorded the oldest songs of the East Indians, the Bhojpurī repertory, including *byāh ke gīt* and *lachārī* (sung at weddings), *sohar* (for the birth of a child), *kajarī* (for the rainy season), and *gudanā* (for tattooing), all passed down in oral tradition since the indenture years. I recorded the music of the Hindu temples: *bhajan, dhun,* and *kīrtan* (devotional songs) as well as mantras and prayers and the recitation form known as *jap.* I recorded Indian film songs, which have been popular since the end of World War II. I recorded Sai Baba songs—a new addition to the village devotional repertory. I recorded school activities and playground rumpus, music classes, informal sessions with singers and drummers, as well as discussions about everything from building houses to growing rice and feeding chickens. I recorded mothers talking to their children and children talking to each other. I recorded myself talking to everyone (see table 2 on p. 92).

Some of the best recordings from my Felicity collections are simply of conversations, and much of the talk is about words. I had never realized how interested I was in words—just plain words—until I went to Felicity. Perhaps it was because we shared a common language, at least so we thought at the beginning.

"Will there be music tonight?" I asked.

"No," they might reply, "no music tonight at all. Next week, not tonight." But I soon learned not to leave the tape recorder behind, knowing that an occasion with "no music" might have hours and hours of singing.

As in many cultures, when Felicity villagers specifically mention music, they usually mean instrumental music or instrumental accompaniment to singing. The word "musical" may also mean an instrumental accompaniment or an instrumental piece. For instance, when a villager hears a tabla solo, she might remark, "That is a nice musical." Occasionally, the word music is used to refer to musical notation (either the text or tunes) that is in printed books or handwritten out in their own personal copies.

Villagers do not agree if there is a word that includes instrumental music, song, and dance, that is, a word which corresponds to the Hindi term, *sangīt.* Some people told me that term would be music, but others felt that "Indian culture" or "Hindu culture" would better express the complex of activities that includes singing, playing, and dancing.

Singing is not considered an unusual ability (any more than speaking is), and everyone in Felicity can sing at least a few songs. People enjoy singing. They told me that some people sing better than others, and some people have better voices than others. Solomon, for example, has a superior voice: he sings as if he "had swallowed a microphone." Well-known singers are called "songsters"; people who play instruments are called "musicians" or "drummers."

Children sing and grandmothers sing. People sing while they walk and while they work. They sing in temple, at school, at home, and on the road in their cars. They sing when they are alone. They sing with instrumental accompaniment (with "music") and they sing unaccompanied. Often they hum—usually when alone. Occasionally they whistle tunes, although whistling indoors is thought to be rather rude and particularly unbecoming for women and girls.

Most songs are learned informally, and people don't feel that there is any particular age when a child should begin to sing, any more than there is a specific time when he should begin to play cricket or tell jokes. It is considered good to be able to sing and to sing well, but parents told me that they would never scold a child if, for some reason, he or she didn't learn how. *Bhajan,* film songs, "composed songs," and pop songs are considered easy to "pick up"; wedding songs, *Rāmāyaṇ* (epic song), and Indian classical songs are considered difficult. Any song a child is taught in school is considered a "school song," whether Indian or English. Some school songs, particularly those in English, are called "folk songs," for example, "Oh, Susannah," "Old MacDonald Had a Farm," "Old Black Joe," and "Three Blind Mice." A clever child who hears a new song will "catch it up" or "pick it up" quickly, particularly if he or she can "well carry a tune."

Indian Songs and English Songs

Conversations about words are always a bit clumsy, since we can only describe one word with other words, and explanations can easily be misunderstood. It took me a long time to realize that nearly all the songs from Felicity are "Indian songs." Understandably enough, that usually goes without saying and they are just called "songs." Indian songs have Indian words (Hindi, Sanskrit, Bhojpurī, and occasionally Bengalī) or have Indian "music" (that is, are accompanied by Indian instruments such as the *ḍholak* drum and *manjīrā* (finger cymbals). Indian songs are usually sung by Indians, but not always. If a visitor asks, "Is that song"—say a *bhajan* or a *sohar*—"an Indian song?" anyone would immediately reply, "Yes, of course." But you would never hear a villager saying, "I just heard an Indian song on the radio," or "Let's sing some Indian songs."

"You see," Amar explained, "whatever is understood we don't say. If we were speaking to someone who is non-Indian and referring to a song, we say 'Indian song.'"

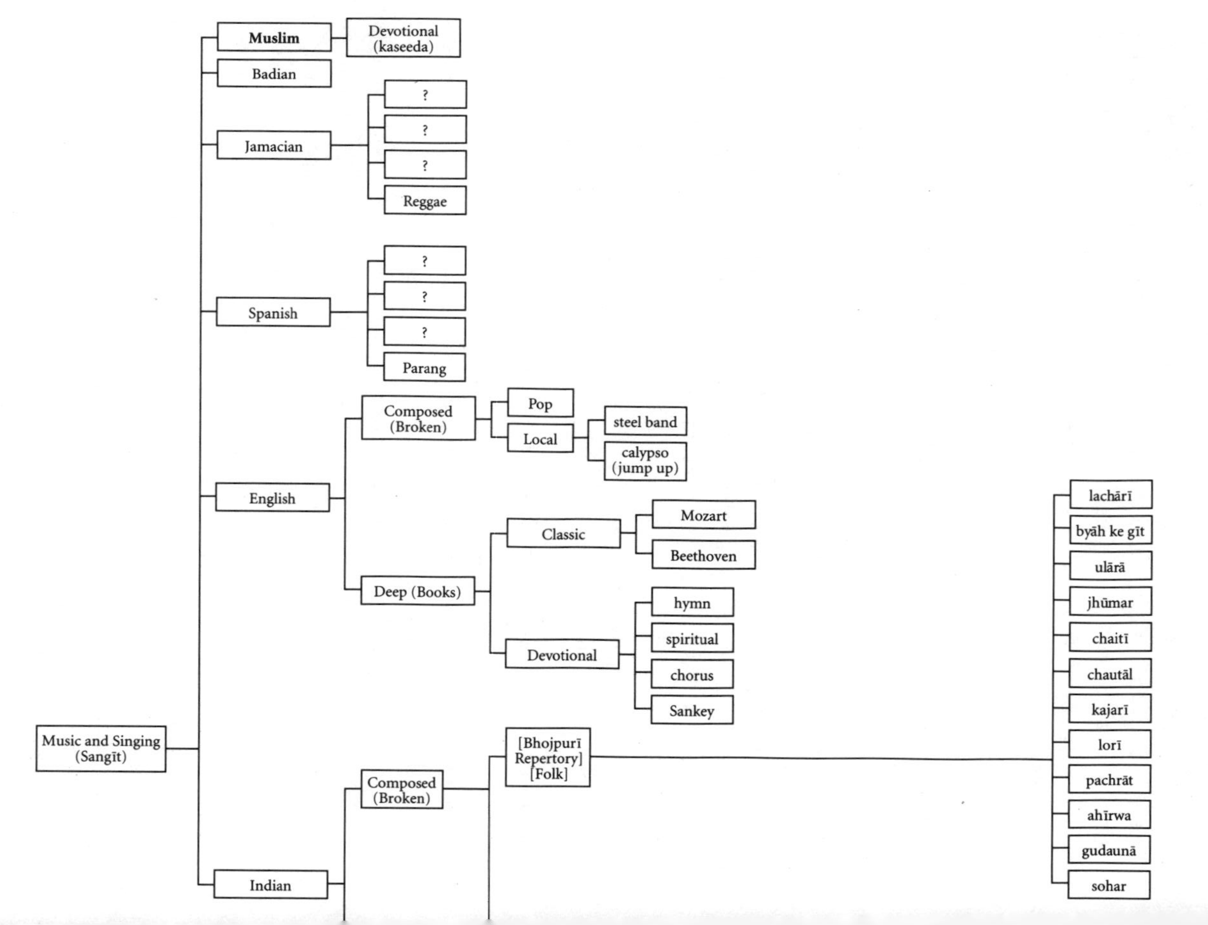
Music and Singing (Sangīt)
Muslim
Devotional (kaseeda)
Badian
Jamacian
?
?
?
Reggae
Spanish
?
?
?
Parang
English
Composed (Broken)
Pop
Local
steel band
calypso (jump up)
Deep (Books)
Classic
Mozart
Beethoven
Devotional
hymn
spiritual
chorus
Sankey
Indian
Composed (Broken)
[Bhojpurī Repertory] [Folk]
lachārī
byāh ke gīt
ulārā
jhūmar
chaitī
chautāl
kajarī
lorī
pachrāt
ahīrwa
gudaunā
sohar

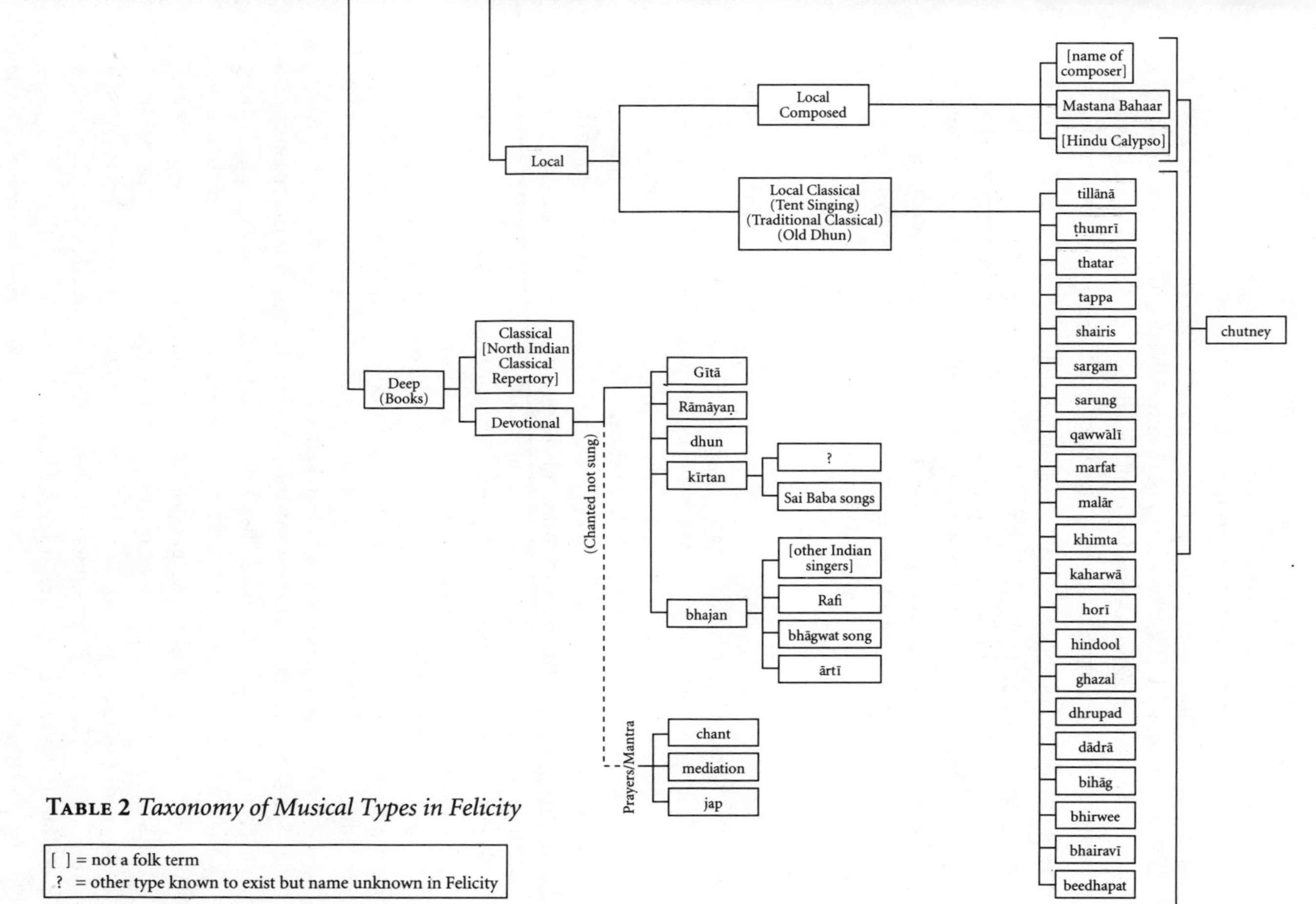

TABLE 2 *Taxonomy of Musical Types in Felicity*

[ ] = not a folk term
? = other type known to exist but name unknown in Felicity

Most songs that are not thought of as Indian songs are "English songs." English songs are in the English language and come "from away"—sometimes from England and sometimes from the United States. But there are some exceptions to these rules. The national anthem, "Forged from the Love of Liberty," is sung in English, but is not an English song (or an Indian song) I was told, since it applies equally to all the people of Trinidad and Tobago. Every one I asked agreed on this important point. Reggae from Jamaica are sung in English Creole but are thought of as Jamaican or Rasta because of the language. Songs from Barbados are "Badian."

"Spanish music" is another category, but it is not as important as Indian and English. Although Venezuela is very near, only one Spanish form, *parang*, is popular in Trinidad. *Parang* is sung at Christmas time throughout the Caribbean. A few people think *parang* is an English form, possibly because it is usually sung by Creoles, and not Indians.

Calypso

Calypso is a special category. Some villagers say calypso is "English"; others say it is "broken English," "Creole," "Negro," "local," "composed," "Trinidadian," or "common." Most people associate calypso with steel band (or "pan") and "jumping up." But everyone I spoke to in Felicity had very definite opinions about it: most were negative. For the outside world, calypso is the famous music of Trinidad. The form developed on the island during the nineteenth and early twentieth centuries, and although it retains African elements, it is an highly eclectic style, uniquely Creole in nature, in which Hispanic, British, French, and African musical and poetic influences have blended. Calypso has spread from Trinidad to the entire circum-Caribbean area and beyond.

Calypso is primarily an urban form and its early development is entwined with the history of Carnival celebrations in Port of Spain. During the eighteenth century, the Trinidad Carnival was a holiday for the European ruling classes. After emancipation, it was taken over by the freed slaves, Creoles, and Spanish peasants, who transformed this sedate religious observance into a lively and disorderly festival. They introduced the *canboulay* (*cannes brûlées*, "cane burning"), a nighttime torchlight procession, with raucous stick-fights between *bationiers* and the singing of kalindas, the antecedent of the calypso. The kalindas in the processions celebrated black liberation; the principal singers, *chantuelles (shantrelle, shantwell),* were accompanied by horns, conch shells, rattles, and African hourglass drums (called *doun doun* in Trinidad; a relative of the Yoruba *dundun* hourglass drum ensemble).

In the 1850s and 1860s, the white ruling classes tried to suppress these masquerades and revelries because they often ended in violence and street riots. Whites protested against the obscenity of the kalindas, with their lewd dancing and noisy instruments. In 1881, conflict between blacks and whites resulted in two days of rioting in Port of Spain (the Cannes Brûlées Riots) and subsequently led to the prohibition of torchlight processions. The Peace Preservation Act of 1884 banned the playing of African drums. But this political opposition did not prevent the growth of Carnival into a national celebration.

From 1890 to 1900, the "band" system developed. Masqueraders from different neighborhoods of Port of Spain, in preparation for Carnival, formed groups wearing costumes based on themes from history and on current events. These included "historical bands," "sailor bands," "military bands," "fancy-dress bands," "Jamét bands" (underworld or prostitute), "Moko Jumby" (stilt dancers), "wild Indians, red, blue, and black Indians" and "fancy Indians" (with elaborate feather headdresses).

To circumvent the ban on African drums, *tamboo bamboo* bands were formed. These musicians played stamping tubes—bamboo of various lengths struck together—which they hit with small pieces of wood or metal, or beat against the ground. Early calypsos and kalindas were sung in French patois; by the time local bands were formed, the common language was a Creole English. Late nineteenth-century songs dealt with topical events from the Port of Spain underworld, the lyrics commenting on current gossip and political events. The social function of calypso is thought to derive from west African tradition in which songs are used for social comment and satire. Other traits that link calypso to west Africa are responsorial patterns, occasional litany forms, and the frequent use of repeated short phrases. Calypso melodies tend to be European-derived (there are some fifty common melodies that are continually being set to new texts). Since 1930 and the rise of the recording industry, calypso has become commercialized, and the great singers—Lord Executor, Lord Beginner, Attila the Hun, Mighty Sparrow, the Lion, Mighty Zebra, Edward the Confessor—have international reputations.

As the days passed I asked villagers to describe their impressions of calypso. Many people in Felicity don't like these Creole songs. Doday, a Christian East Indian, objected on moral grounds: "Calypso have too much robust things in it. Sometimes they have some raw raw rude words in a calypso. But it not proper for a Christian to listen to these things and to concentrate on it—it is evil. The steel band music is nice, but the words they say! Indian people wouldn't put a raw rude word or bad language and a song to sing it, but the Creole put it on the table!"

Mrs. Maharajh, a Hindu, also objected to the texts: "I grow in my Indian culture, so that's why I wouldn't like these. They have a lot of different wordings in it that shouldn't put at all. All different exposed words, you know."

Suruj Pandit agreed that the words were usually indecent: "Sometimes they sing calypso that is very displeasing to the ears. The wording, they use all types of words. I really don't like to listen to it. Some they make all right, they have a lot of meaning in it, but others they make cause a scandal."

"In calypso they give you the facts of life," Kamini said.

I didn't know, and my ignorance surprised Mona: "'Down by the seaside sifting sand,'" she said. "You know what that mean? 'Whole day, whole night, Miss Mary Ann?'"

"No," I replied, "what does that mean?"

"Whole day, whole night, you know, and they're sifting sand. But that mean—you know, they're by the seaside."

"Yeah?"

"And having a good time."

"What kind of a good time?"

"Sex."

"Oh!"

*

"What do you think about calypso?" I asked Kamini's mother.

"All right for who like it, but me ain like calypso," she said. "I don't just hate it. I feel it's nigger song."

"What about the words?"

"Sometime they go good and sometime they say something out of the way. I feel it don't suit me so I don't like to listen."

"What is the difference between Negro music and Indian music?" I asked.

"Sometime something wrong come and they say it in the calypsos—they aren't hiding anything. If a girl or a boy or some kind of thing like that, they sing it out. But the Indian, no. They don't explain it, you know?"

*

"Do you like it?" I asked Kassie.

"No. I don't like that music," he said. "I like Indian music. Is a choice. A lot of them like calypso. You see, Indian music are more sweet, more mild. And the calypso a little rash. You know that the Indian music is clean; a calypso is plenty different."

*

Then I asked Moon.

"What do you think of calypso?"

"Calypso? Calypso is good, too," she said.

"You *like* calypso?" I was surprised.

"Yes," she replied, "I like anything once. Yeah. Pop music and thing. I like calypso. I like everything."

I asked Moon's daughter, "How about you?"

"I don't follow calypso much, you know," she replied. "Some of the calypsos really have good meaning and some again, they call bad words and make up a song so."

"And do you like those?" I asked.

"I don't too much like calypso."

"Moon," I asked, "have you ever heard one with words you don't like?"

Her daughter answered. "She don't follow the words. The words is English. Some of the calypsos have bad wording."

"I like music," Moon said. "Once it's hot music, well it is all right. You know, I make a little song with English."

"Will you sing it?" I asked.

Moon began to sing:

18 ♫
Dr. William[s] well proud and glad,
Trinidad and Tobago independent *ho gayee* [have become].
Dr. William well proud and glad,
Trinidad and Tobago 'dependent *ho gayee.*

Some say yes, and some say no.
Some say Dr. William you'll go.
Some say yes, and some say no.
Some some say Dr. William will go.
Since Dr. William take over Trinidad,
How many fly over, you see in Trinidad.

Dr. William well proud and glad,
Trinidad and Tobago 'dependent *ho gayee.*

Come from the east, you go to the west,
How far you see Dr. William do the best.
Since Dr. William take over Trinidad,
Everybody flying independent flag.

Dr. William well proud and glad,
Trinidad and Tobago 'dependent *ho gayee.*

"That is song when Independence," Moon explained when she had finished. "This is English. Isn't in Hindi."

"This is like a calypso," her daughter explained.

"That come as an Indian," Moon added, "I mean as an Indian thing naa.

If I going anywhere and we singing I sing that with drum and thing too. If you know how them boys and that like when I singing that one, clapping and dancing and thing. They like that, you know."

☙ COMPOSED SONGS

All calypsos are "composed" songs, that is, written by Trinidadians. Some Indian songs, such as Moon's song about Dr. Eric Williams, the late Prime Minister of Trinidad and Tobago, are also classified as "composed songs"; but most Indian songs are identified by the villagers as "coming from books." It is very easy to distinguish one type from the other. There is a general understanding in Felicity that books are written in foreign countries (especially India) by famous people (especially "saints and sages"). Songs whose texts come from books carry the authority of the printed page. They are considered "old" or "from every since" (older still, ancient). Composed songs are "local," they are homemade, "ordinary." Anybody can compose a song. They should not be taken too seriously. Songs from books are almost invariably religious, while composed songs are entertaining. People hear composed songs all the time on radio and television and they can buy them on records. Many local songs, like Moon's, mix Hindi words with English words. They have simple catchy tunes and usually include the accompaniment of the "drum" or "hand-drum" (*ḍholak*, double-headed barrel drum) and "organ" (harmonium, a portable reed organ). Some local songs are accompanied by a whole "orchestra" (combo).

One day I played Moon's song about Dr. Williams for Jagdai and Tara (song 18).

"What kind of song is that?" I asked.

"It's a composed, English and Indian and everything in one," Jagdai said.

"Is a composed song ever in a book?" I asked.

"Naa," Tara exclaimed, "they compose that."

"What's the opposite of a composed song?"

"Well, classic music," Tara answered. "These is not from books. They take their own words and they make that."

"They make that in they own head," Jagdai added, "they own brain they compose that. That is ordinary, they compose that they own self."

"Is it a Negro song?" I asked.

"Negro songs does be different," Tara said. She paused. "Negro don't have a song really. If it was a Negro song, the Negro really wouldn't put the Hindi word in it."

"Is it popular music?" I asked.

"No, popular music is something you hearing every day."

"Is it English music then?"

"No, that is Indian music," Jagdai explained. "The words in English but the music in Indian. The tune is in Indian way."

"Is it an Indian song then?" I asked.

"Well, you have to call it an Indian song," Tara said. "Is a mix-up, they mix it up."

"The words in English, the tune and the music in Indian," Jagdai said.

*

Dolan really didn't like composed songs, but she had heard that the people who wrote them made money: "You know, it have a lot of people who do this thing. Now, they just compose song just for the tune and the music and to keep other people happy. They make a record. Now, they get something out of that, at least when the record sell. They buy the record. So they make their money one side. And they don't care: whatever they put in the record is all well and good. It's just a money-making business, to make a record."

Kamini could tell a local song by the language: "Composed song sort of have a local accent to it. It don't have real Indian words in it."

Mrs. Maharajh suspected that portions of local compositions might actually be taken from books: "Sometimes they compose it down here. They have the book and they compose it. They take a part from this, a part from that page and they make up like a calypso."

But most other people agreed with Tara that "when you say 'composition,' they mean they use they own words."

Amar's analysis was the most thorough, a serious student's reasoning. "Of course all songs are composed," he pointed out, "but if you say 'composed,' we will think automatically 'local composed.' We substitute the word 'composed' for 'local,' right? We will call them 'local' also if it's the traditional local classical, what they call 'tent singing.'"

"Would the traditional classical be a 'local composed' or just a 'local'?" I asked.

"Well, that is debatable. They will think about that. But it is definitely local, because it has been here for so long. They would say, it's 'Trinidad local' or 'classical.' If it's locally composed in recent times, we will use the term 'local,' 'local song,' 'locally composed.' But to differentiate the 'classical' from the classical music from India we will say 'local classical.'"

"So," I asked, "within the larger category 'local,' you would have a smaller group, 'local composed,' which refers to newer things?"

"Yeah, which they know definitely someone has made it up. But if it's something that has been there as far back as you can remember, they will call it 'local classical.' They wouldn't necessarily say 'composed' for that."

ঌ CLASSICAL SINGING

"Local classical" singing in Trinidad dates back to the late years of the indenture period. It is sometimes called "tent" singing after the *marawā* (Bhojpurī: "tent" or "canopy"; Hindi: *maṇḍap*) in which the events, usually a wedding, take place. Tent singing is still heard in Trinidad, and is experiencing a revival in the 1990s. Villagers own records, cassettes, and CDs of this local music, although no one in Felicity sang "classical." Some of these tent songs have taken the names of Indian genres *(ghazal, ṭhumrī, dhrupad),* some of well-known *rāgs (bihāg, bhairavī, hindool),* and some of *tāl* (time cycles) common in north India *(dādrā, kaharwā).* But they are very different from any South Asian counterpart.

Amar had heard a few "classicals."

"There is an old man that we know," he said, "in fact he came from India, but when he was very very small. And he know about 'a *bihāg.*'"

"Does he remember that from India?" I asked.

"I don't know how he knows it because he came very small. But he puts the indefinite article. He will say 'a' *bihāg* or 'a' *bhairavī.* Of course, they must stem from something, but it has changed along the way."

Kamini felt that local classicals couldn't compare with "real" Indian songs. Songs from India are sung in "proper" Hindi or "deep" Hindi and give her a special feeling, a "vibration," that the local songs never inspire.

"Some classical song they compose it down here and some they don't," she explained.

"Is there a difference between the two?" I asked.

"Not really. But in Trinidad it can't really meet the standard of the real Indian classical, because down here people not as conversant in Indian languages. They just can't pronounce the words as how the real Indian would. And then they don't do it like the Indian—real Indian people. It don't have this real Indian beat to it. When they come down from India, you get a sort of vibration. You can go on listening and listening and listening. It sort of make you feel different then, and the music, you just absorb the music on your body and let your body go."

When a "classic" isn't local, it is necessary to be more specific. Symphonies by Beethoven and Mozart are "English classics"; a sitar performance by Ravi Shankar is an "Indian classic" or an "Indian classical."

ঌ MANTRAS AND PRAYERS

Books are considered a rich source of both songs and "prayers" or "mantras." People in Felicity have much more confidence in the reliability of literary transmission than in oral transmission, and they have an immense respect for books and for literacy. Reading opens the door to a world of music, formerly the exclusive domain of pandits and other "big people." "Who learn to read, they gonna read it and sing it."

The most important books known in Felicity—the *Vedas,* the *Rāmāyaṇ,* the *Māhābhārata,* and the *Bhāgawad Gītā,* even the Koran—come from abroad. Rookmin explained, "When them Swamiji and them big people go out, they go anywhere to study, they get the book. They come back here and sell it for the children. The children learn it and they read it and so how they sing it at the temple and all about."

Prayers are always from books, they are never "composed" or "local" or "make-up." "It can't be a make-up prayers," Channu said. "They must learn that from some of our great books. The pandits, they are learned. They have to learn all these prayers, and they have to learn the ways in saying it, the ways in doing it, and then they will go out now so that everybody who would like to follow will follow on."

Prayers and mantras are never sung, they are "said." A devotee will "say" the prayers of the *havan* service or the *sanḍhyā* service; he will "say" the *gāyatrī* mantra, an important Hindu prayer. I found this terminology confusing because the way they "said" their prayers sounded just like singing to me, and I assumed that the prayers were a somber type of religious song. But I soon learned how wrong I was. In no sense would villagers ever consider prayers as songs or praying as singing. There are several "ways" or styles of saying prayers; the most usual is an inflected monotone, but the style a devotee chooses is not thought to alter the essential nature of the prayer. Setting a prayer to a tune, or melody, and singing it would distract the mind of the worshipper from the text: this is considered wrong.

Mantras are special prayers. Usually they are short—a line or two or just a few words such as *Aum Namo Narayana* ("I bow to Thee Narayana"). The villagers know that mantras come from the *Vedas* (most ancient Aryan scriptures) and other great books. The text of the important *pūjā* services, such as the *jhanḍī* or *Durgā pūjā,* are composed of a series of mantras.

All the Felicity pandits have memorized hundreds of mantras to perform the many services of the Hindu liturgy. But each villager also has his own personal mantra, whispered to him by his godfather during the christening ceremony, a personal mantra should be kept secret.

Jap ("repetition") is the performance of a single mantra many times (ideally 108), while the devotee keeps count with his fingers or with a *jap mālā* (string of prayer beads). *Jap* can be whispered quietly alone or recited with others in unison on a monotone. There are also more elaborate performance styles, but conservatively disposed individuals consider these inappropriate to prayer. Since it is a prayer, *jap* is never considered a song, even if it is set to a melody.

Rookmin explained, "They does have the bead, the *mālā.* Now you sit down to do your prayer. You check that *mālā* hundred time. Every time you move a bead, you say '*Aum.*' Well that is what they call *jap.*"

"*Jap* is the repetition of the mantras," Suruj Pandit said. "Speaking it, not singing. And you take a *mālā,* and every time you recite one mantra, you just pull a bead. You can recite it aloud, you can recite it in your mind, in anyhow you want."

"Could you 'sing' a *jap*?" I asked.

"You could say it and you can sing it," he replied. "But when you sing it you don't really call it a song or *bhajan* or *dhun.* You say it in a tune."

This distinction between "saying," "talking," and "singing," particularly when pertaining to prayers, is difficult for the villagers to explain. Sometimes they use the term *chant* to describe this performing style.

One afternoon, I was playing a *havan pūjā* (worship service) for Tara and Jagdai. We came to a passage where the congregation was delivering a spoken English translation of the Sanskrit prayer they had just intoned. The recitation was accompanied with a drone played on the *tambura.*

"Are they singing or are they talking?" I asked.

"They look like they talking," Tara replied.

"Is it a song?" I asked.

"No," she answered, "just praying, just talking."

"Are they chanting?" I asked.

"Not really," Jagdai replied. "They just talking like, you know, when a chorus singing, all singing together."

I played the same recording for Kamini.

"Are they talking or are they singing?" I asked.

"Talking. They're saying it in a rhythm to the music. They're timing the music and they're saying."

"What is the difference between that kind of talking and the way we are talking now?" I asked.

"You see, they timing their words to the music. But we just talking without any music. We don't have to time anything."

"Why isn't it singing?" I asked. "If they are timing and there is music?"

"No, it's not."

We continued listening to the service. After another Sanskrit prayer was "said," I asked:

"Is this a chant?"

"It could be," she replied. "It depends on how you interpret it. It is really a religious chant, a prayer."

"When you do a chant, do you sing or do you talk?"

"You see, different people have different ways of doing it. Some of them just say it out. Some of them sing it. Well, I feel I does sing it."

"Then, chanting can be talking or singing?" I asked.

"Yes."

I asked Jagdai: "What is the difference between a chant and a prayer?"

"Chant is something when you sing fast," she replied, "on a fast kind of way. When you chanting all the way round. Not slow slow slow."

I asked Kala: "Can you talk a chant?"

"Yes," she replied, "you could sing it, you could talk it, anything, but it sounds better when you sing it with the music."

Deep and Broken Hindi

Villagers distinguish between spoken and written Hindi. Great books like the *Vedas,* which contain important prayers and mantras, are written in "deep" Hindi. Hindi devotional songs, such as *bhajan, dhun,* and *kīrtan,* are from books and are thought to be in deep Hindi.

Suruj Pandit explained: "'Deep' is Hindi that is written in the books. Now you observe that the people would speak a different type of Hindi. It is broken Hindi, and a person is speaking broken Hindi."

I asked Kamini, "What is deep Hindi?"

"Deep Hindi come out from the scriptures and the *Bhāgawad Gītā,*" she said. "They use Hindi, the real Indian words, because they were written long ago by the saints and sages. Then they were transcript in Sanskrit, but now they have the English version. But deep Hindi is the Hindi that was written long ago, the first set of Hindi."

"That is deep Hindi," Rookmin said. "That is from the book. They print it, they sell it for the children. They read it. They know it."

"Well," Kala said, "deep Hindi is, I should say, Sanskrit."

*

The opposite, both of written and spoken deep Hindi, is "broken" Hindi, the Bhojpurī dialect still spoken by the older villagers. It is thought that the songs of the Bhojpurī repertory do not come from books. Wedding songs present a perplexing case for the villagers because they are in Bhojpurī ("broken Hindi") but they tell stories from the *Rāmāyaṇ* epic (a book). Nevertheless, villagers classify wedding songs as composed Indian songs in broken Hindi. Jagdai, Tara, and Channu explained that deep Hindi is also the language spoken by all Indians born in India.

"Deep Hindi is what them India people does talk," Jagdai said. "Like them Bombay people and thing does talk deep Hindi—them Bombay in Chaguanas in the store."

"Them Patel, them Patel people," Tara said, "they does talk deep Hindi."

Channu explained: "The real Indians from India, they talk Hindi. They talk it in a proper kind of way. My tongue won't be able to say the words as good as they would be able to say. If they will say the same thing, they will say it in a way that will sound as if it's real good English—it's a bit deeper. Now, you will talk English and your tongue will sound the English much more different than I will say it. I will say it flat, but you will say it in a way that it will sound as if it's something much higher than what I say."

The Muslim and Christian Repertory

"Muslim songs" are in a class by themselves. Because they are sung in Arabic or Urdu, not Hindi, Hindus do not consider them Indian songs. Sometimes the villagers refer to a Muslim song as a "Khan." And although everyone realizes that the Muslims of Trinidad are Indians, this is sometimes difficult to express, probably due to the similarity of the words Hindi, Hindu, and Indian.

"Are Muslims Indians?" I asked Kamini, "or are they Negroes?"

"Well," she replied, "I guess they are Indians. But on the whole, Indian Indians, right? when you say 'Indians' they are referred to as the Hindus."

About a dozen Muslim families live in Felicity, but most Hindu villagers don't like talking about Islam or about Muslim songs: they claim ignorance. When I tried to persuade them to tell me more, they offered a few of the facts.

"Probably we use the *Rāmāyaṇ,* the *Gītā,*" Indra told me, "so they use the Koran. They write in Arabic and I think they know a few words in Arabic."

"It composed in Arabia," Kamini explained. We were listening to a Muslim song sung by school children (song 3). "The Muslim script is written in Arabic, right? I don't know how much B.C. that the Prophet Mohammed was born there, and from there they started believing. And then in India too, it have some Muslims."

Everyone I spoke to advised tolerance: "Because, to my knowing, everybody is sectionalized in this universe," Channu told me. "I am a Hindu. You are a Christian maybe. Then we have Muslims and then we have Arya and then we have Seven Days and Adventists and so. But each one of them pray to God. They pray to God in their own way. So this is the way Muslim is praying to their God."

But these conversations about Islam made people uncomfortable. What a contrast Christianity! Everybody knows something about Jesus Christ, church weddings, lighting candles, the eating of the flesh, the drinking of the blood.

Most of the villagers accept "Lord Christ" as an avatar, a reincarnation of God on earth like Lord Rām, Lord Krishna, or Lord Shiva, and his picture is often amidst theirs on the family altar or in the temple. People in Felicity do not doubt that he walked on water, fed the multitudes with a few loaves and fishes, caused the blind to see, and raised Lazarus from the dead; for, like the other saints, Christ was a "great yogi." This openness of thought is the strength and wonder of Hinduism.

At least half of the village children go to the Presbyterian School, where they say prayers, read from the Bible, and sing hymns. Everyone I spoke with understood that hymns and *bhajan* had a great deal in common. Often they would draw an analogy from one to the other: "Well, *bhajan* is hymn," Suruj explained. "In English, we call them hymns."

"It's somewhat similar to the *bhajan* because it almost have the same meaning," Kamini said. "They sing it in English; we sing it in Indian."

Felicity Christians feel that *bhajan* are "good" songs and Felicity Hindus feel that hymns are "good" songs. "I love *bhajan,* you know," Doday told me. "Never mind I am a Christian. I love them. I love to sing. If I get a *bhajan* book, I could sing *bhajan.*"

It is understood that Hindu songs, Christian songs, and Muslim songs are all "religious songs," "godly songs," and "devotional songs," but Hindu villagers are not familiar with the various types of Muslim songs sung in Trinidad, for example, the *kaseeda,* a devotional form similar to the *bhajan.* Muslim songs are simply called Muslim songs. Another form, the Urdu *ghazal,* which might be classed as Muslim, is usually called "classical" or "local classical" because it is similar to *ṭhumrī.* Villagers assume that most Christian songs are hymns, though some know of "spirituals" or "choruses" and several of the Christians own a "Sankey"—the hymnal, *Sacred Songs and Solos* by Ira D. Sankey (1840–1908)—and can sing a Sankey or two like "Hold the Fort for I Am Coming" or "What a Friend We Have in Jesus." Doday and a few others remembered Christian hymns with Hindi texts they had learned in the Canadian Presbyterian Mission schools. Channu's husband could sing "While the Shepherds Watched Their Flocks by Night" in Hindi. Even though songs are identified by the language of the "wording," even though it is commonplace to describe a *bhajan* as a hymn, Hindi hymns are never called *bhajan.* They are "Hindi hymns," and belong to bygone years.

The Hindu Repertory

Many genres of Hindu devotional songs—*bhajan* and *kīrtan, dhun,* chants, *Rāmāyaṇ,* and *ārtī*—are sung in Felicity. *Bhajan* are the most loved; villagers sing them in temple, listen to them on the radio, buy *bhajan* records imported from India, and watch Hindi religious films to learn new ones. Everyone knows several by heart, but often "copies" or books are needed since *bhajan* have long Hindi texts: a one- or two-line refrain and five or more verses. Villagers like to sing them with instrumental accompaniment, but they can also be performed unaccompanied or with just a *ḍholak.*

No clear distinction is drawn between *bhajan* and *kīrtan.*

"*Kīrtan* is just a religious song, you know, but sing in a different tune," Kamini said. "It just like a *bhajan,* but it in a deeper sound, a deeper note they sing it in."

"All *bhajan* is *kīrtan,* because they all going with drum, organ, and a little put on," Rookmin said.

"*Kīrtan* is something they sing fast and something like a *bhajan,*" Jagdai said.

"Our *bhajan* are *kīrtan* because we use all our *bhajan* as *kīrtan,*" Channu explained. "That is how it's composed on. *Kīrtan* is part of the music together with the *bhajan*—that is what they call *kīrtan.*"

"*Kīrtan* is *bhajan,*" Indra said.

The term *kīrtan* sometimes refers to a session of group singing. Some villagers told me it was unison singing. "*Kīrtan* is when everybody forms themselves in a group and they sing the *bhajan* together," Suruj explained. "Now sometimes you see everybody in a group and one person singing—it is a *bhajan,* but that one person singing and the others following. But when everybody singing together, then is a *kīrtan.*"

Others thought it referred to responsorial singing: "A *kīrtan* is a different sort of song then," Kamini said. "Everybody don't sing it, right? One of them lead and the others follow."

Some people believe that a lengthy session in *kīrtan* style can lead the devotee to ecstasy. A song sheet published by the St. James Mandir, largest Hindu temple in Port of Spain, describes the power of *kīrtan:* "Kīrtan is loud chanting of God's name. The value of this joyful exercise increases in proportion as the voice is raised to a higher and higher pitch. Kīrtan is closely related to musical. In kīrtan harmony of the voices is essential in the beginning. No words can describe the glory of kīrtan. The thrill of joy that it sends into the heart is known only by those blessed souls who practice it."

Amar's explanation drew on his understanding of Indian classical traditions, learned in Guru Adesh's classes: "*Kīrtan* is devotional singing, but the songs are short and repetitive, just repeating the name of the Lord over and over in a fast tempo, usually *kaharwā tāl* [rhythmic cycle of eight beats divided into 4+4] or *dādrā tāl* [six beats divided into 3+3]."

"And *bhajan?*" I asked.

"*Bhajan* is different. *Bhajan* is a song, a devotional song."

"But Indra said '*kīrtan* is *bhajan.*'"

"Well, you see, they are closely related. There is a fine difference between them, a subtle difference. *Kīrtan* is like what they sing at the Sai Baba sessions."

"But some villagers call the Sai Baba songs *dhun,*" I said.

"No, they are not *dhun* really. Perhaps they may say so, but it isn't really. A *dhun* is a little melody, usually in *kaharwā tāl* or *dādrā tāl* whereas a *bhajan* is a complete devotional song, a whole song with *sthāyī* [antecedent phrase or verse], and *antarā* [consequent phrase or chorus]."

The Felicity villagers had many different definitions for the term *dhun.* Some agreed with Amar that the term referred to a short repetitive melody similar to *kīrtan.* Channu thought of it as a mood or state: "When you concentrating, that mean you in a *dhun.* You have to get into a *dhun* to concentrate or to sing something." Channu also used *dhun* to indicate "style" (possibly also "tune"): "The *dhun* in Sai Baba is a little bit different than the *dhun* in ordinary *bhajan* that we sing. They use a lot of clapping and meditating and more tempo like. They put some more action to them; they take on more speed."

Rookmin also used the term *dhun* to refer to tune and singing style: "*Dhun* is only just how you carrying it, I mean what tune you carrying it."

Jagdai said *dhun* refers to old songs: "A classical is when them old man singing—the old *dhun.*"

Some of the *bhajan, dhun,* and *kīrtan* are "from every since"—brought from India with the original indentured laborers—but most are learned from films and records, and new *bhajan* have been composed by Guru Adesh. Most *bhajan* familiar in Felicity are from older films (from the 1940s and 1950s) and are also called "film songs" (by the younger generation) or "theater songs" (by the older). Or they may be identified by the name of the famous playback singer who first sang the song, hence "a Lata," "a Mukesh," "a Rafi" (ex. XXVIII), "a Manna Dey," "a Hemant Kumar," "a Talat," or "a Mohindra Kapoor."

The Bhojpurī Repertory

Many songs of Felicity were passed on in oral tradition and date back to the rural culture of nineteenth-century north India. This Bhojpurī repertory includes wedding songs, *sohar* sung six or twelve days after childbirth, *gudanā* songs for administering the arm tattoo, *ahīrwā* songs of the Ahīr "nation" (caste of cattle minders), *pachrāt* songs for Kālī *pūjā* (goat or pig sacrifice), *lorī* lullabies, *kajarī* songs for rice planting, and *chautāl, ulārā, chaitī,* and *jhūmar* songs for the springtime Phāguā festival. Of these, only wedding songs and the Phāguā repertory are still commonplace in modern Felicity. The villagers do not have a term to distinguish these older traditions from newer songs learned from films, records, and books. Local scholars like Usha and Ramaya classify them as "folk songs," but a foreign scholar might regard this repertory as the "authentic" music of Felicity. The villagers would disagree, since to their ears those old Bhojpurī pieces sound less "Indian," less authentic than a song from a new Indian film or record.

Most of the old songs are sung by women, for in Trinidad, as in so many parts of the world, custom dictates that men don't sing wedding songs or lullabies. There are two important types of songs for the wedding, *byāh ke gīt* and *lachārī.* When a villager refers to "wedding songs," she is probably thinking of the more serious *byāh ke gīt,* unaccompanied responsorial strophic songs with long texts that comment on the various stages in the wedding ceremony.

The *lachārī* are fast lively songs with instrumental accompaniment; the villagers often describe them as "hot" or "*chutney.*" The terms are similar but not synonymous. Both hot songs and *chutney* songs have risqué texts, but the villagers do not think that these "suggestive" poems are as "bad" as the "rude" calypso texts. Amar explained "hot" and "*chutney*" for me. "When we say *chutney,* we mean the rhythm is peppy, fast, and fast tempo. *Chutney,* right? But hot means spicy enough, full and suggestive, for fun, you know? *Chutney* describes more the melody, the rhythm or the melody; hot implies the contents, the text, the meaning." By the 1990s, *chutney* had come to refer to those soca- and disco-influenced spicy dance songs sung in Indian clubs around the island. "Nothing to be proud of," Amar said.

"What is pop?" I asked.

"Pop? Well, songs we hear on the radio or like these pop groups. Songs from England or America."

"Are there any pop songs that are not English songs?" I asked.

"Local? No, no," Amar replied.

"Can pop songs be hot?" I asked.

"No, no. We'll just call them pop songs. We wouldn't describe a pop song as being hot."

Many families in modern Felicity have hi-fi systems and collections of records and cassettes. Most popular are recordings made in Trinidad studios of local East Indian artists, especially productions of Windsor Records, owned by the Mohammed brothers of Port of Spain. Some families have albums of American and European popular music; no one I met owned calypso or steel band albums. In the late 1970s, Kala gave me a list of the records in her diverse collection: Dennis de Souza, *After Hours,* Olivia Newton John, *Have You Never Been Mellow?,* Ace Cannon, saxophone *'Cool 'n Lady,* two albums by Guru H. S. Adesh, *Lata Mangeshkar Recites the Bhagwad Gita,* ABBA, *Greatest Hits, The Beatles/1969–1970, Excerpts from the Holy Ramayan,* spoken and sung by Nirmal Maharajh, *Souvenir of the West Indies, Hari Om Sharan Devotionals,* and *Blast from Your Past,* Ringo Starr.

Theory and Aesthetics

There are three criteria by which villagers evaluate the different ways (styles) of singing: the timing (rhythm and tempo), the scaling or tune (melody), and the wording (text). They can also identify a song by its beat.

"A *kīrtan* is a different sort of song then," Kamini said. "It have a different sort of beat. *Bhāgwat* song is different. They have a faster music beat to it. In Trinidad, when it composed down here, it don't really have a good rhythm or a good beat to it, nothing really lively. It could be lively in how they saying it, but I find when they come out from India they have a more lively beat to it."

"Beat" can also be used as a verb: "For calypso time, they sing and they beat pans, steel pans," Indra said.

"They telling the drummers to beat the drum now at its full pitch," Kalawatee said. "Come on drummers, our brother, beat the drum."

Songs and singers may also be identified by their "pitch": "They sing it at a normal pitch," Channu said.

"They is classical singers does sing these things," Dolan explained. "They is a very high pitch in singing."

Beautiful songs, especially Indian songs, are described as "sweet," "smooth," or "nice": "You can carry something smooth, slowly, and nice," Rookmin said. "Well, the *dhun* is like, I talking hard," she continued. "It mean that I speaking loud. If I speak soft, it mean I speaking soft. That goes smooth and nice. *Rāg* is something slowly and smoothly and very nice."

"It is *sloka* [scriptural passage]," Kala said. "But they recite it as a song so it sound sweet."

"So, the man who is playing the organ, he is just giving a smooth, soothing background with the organ alone," Channu explained. "And then that corresponding together with the pandit's voice."

A beautiful song is "pleasant" and "enchanting." Serious songs can be "dry." Hot songs, *chutney,* and *lachārī* have a "nice taste." A song that is performed badly is "harsh" or "loud": "A harsh and a loud singing voice, you know, a heavy voice," Kamini said. "My sister has a very hoarse voice," Kalawatee said. "Oh, see how the voice chokes," Dhanpatee added.

A "good" song is a meaningful song: "It have meaning in it," Indra explained. "It is just something make up, not hot, but meaningful, right? So I feel it is good."

"'Mother's Love.' That is a good song," Ramesh said. "That is the only song on this record with meaning."

A good song "catches the ear quickly," for example, the Sai Baba tunes that "make you feel joy" because they are "catchy" or "lively" and are sung in a "sing-song way." "Catchy" songs are often "fast," that is they accelerate and are accompanied by loud hand clapping. They "put some more action," Channu explained, "they take on more speed: fast, fast, fast."

Tempo is important to the villagers. Indra said, "Anywhere I hear the Sai Baba songs, I hear them fast." I played a *bhajan* recorded in Felicity and she said, "It's a bit slow, I find." When I played a *sohar* sung by Felicity women for Mrs. Maharajh, she said, "This is slow motion. Some *bhajan* they sing it, you know, in a nice way, not in slow motion."

The opposite of fast is "slowly and soft," Channu said, "more concentrating, in a smoothing kind of way, you know."

A performance might be "a bit too fast": "Well, you see, I would say it's too fast," Indra commented when she heard my recording of a *bhajan* recorded in the Divine Life Society temple. "Probably different groups sing it in a different way. Because in our temple [Trinidad Sevashram Sangha] we didn't learn it so. We learn it as slow and easy way." When we discussed the Sai Baba songs, she explained, "In the temple, if we sing a Sai Baba song we sing it very slow." When I played the recitation of a Hindu prayer, she remarked, "Yes, it could be a chant, if they say it slow. They could be slowing down."

ꙮ

After many days and hundreds of hours of tape recording, we were still speaking of music. My village friends had become accustomed to the many questions and to the intrusion of a live microphone in their homes and temples and schools. I was much more aware than they that a recording was being made, and I soon came to feel as if I were living on two planes: the real-now world of people and places and that little-forever world of recorded sound. Before long, I had collected enough data to construct the taxonomy of folk terminology given in table 2. But in the midst of these many conversations about music, I found myself thinking ahead to the playback and the listening-after-the-event; the hours of analysis, transcription, writing, and teaching to come; the repeated review, as I shared with others fleeting moments I lived in Felicity.

☙ Chapter Seven ❧
Local Musicology

> The body travels more easily than the mind, and until we have limbered up our imagination we continue to think as though we had stayed home. We have not really budged a step until we take up residence in someone else's point of view.
>
> John Erskine, *The Complete Life,* "Foreigners"

After completing my study of the village response to and classification of music in Felicity, I became impatient to discover how local scholars and teachers viewed that music and its link with the music of India. Perhaps this information was to be found in the University Library. In addition, I had begun to long for silence—just an hour or two away from the dogs and goats, the traffic on Cacandee Road, the jukeboxes, and the constant prattle of toddlers, an afternoon of real silence. Perhaps that too was to be found at the library. One day after lunch, I packed up some papers, pen, and sunglasses, and traveled to the University of the West Indies.

In Felicity, "traveling" means taking a taxi. Since the phasing out of the railways in the 1950s and '60s, taxis are the form of public transportation. They are licensed to carry five passengers—two in front, three in back. You learn that the best seat is front-window and the worst middle-back, especially during a long hot afternoon. The taxis have stereo systems with loud, loud mega-bass thumping out island music. There are regular routes and stops, but passengers can ask to be let down anywhere, and drivers will often go off their route if it is a slack period or if you are carrying heavy packages. Fares are low, and anyone can afford to ride to work and home again.

An hour and several taxi changes later, I arrived at the St. Augustine campus, University of the West Indies, eight miles east of Port of Spain. I passed the magnificent modern John F. Kennedy College of Arts and Sciences, completed in 1969 and financed out of compensation payments that the United States made to the Government of Trinidad for use of military bases.

The University of the West Indies is housed on three main campuses: at St. Augustine, in Trinidad, are the faculties of engineering, agriculture, and liberal arts. In the 1970s, information about the music of India was scarce in that library. The card catalog listed nothing under "India—Music" or "Music—India." In the stacks were a few books: *A Historical Study of Indian Music* by Swami Prajanananda, *My Music, My Life* by Ravi Shankar, *Great Musicians of India* by Dolly Rizvi, *Muthuswami Dikshitar* by T. L. Venkatarama Aiyar,

Pandit Vishnu Digambar by V. R. Athavale, *Musical Instruments of India* by S. Krishnaswamy, *Indian National Songs* edited by R. K. Prabhu, *The New Oxford History of Music* edited by Egon Wellesz (volume 1, *Ancient and Oriental Music;* chapter 4, "The Music of India"), *The Pelican History of Music* edited by Alec Robertson and Denis Stevens (volume 1, *Ancient Forms to Polyphony;* chapter 3, "India"), *Grove's Dictionary of Music and Musicians,* 5th ed., edited by Eric Blom ("Indian Music" by A. H. Fox Strangways, revised by Arnold Bake), *Musical Instruments through the Ages* by Anthony Baines (included two Indian instruments), and *Folk Chants and Refrains of Trinidad and Tobago* compiled by M. P. Alladin (contained one or two Indian songs)—in all, seven books on Indian music, three works with chapters or articles on Indian music, and two books with references to Indian music.

In a different section of the library, *John Morton of Trinidad,* the diary of the first Canadian Presbyterian missionary to the East Indians, was on the shelf, a work compiled and edited by his wife, Sarah, and published in 1916 (plates 16, 17). John and Sarah Morton first came to Trinidad in 1868 and remained their entire working lives, converting the East Indians to Christianity and organizing church congregations. Most importantly, they established the first primary schools for East Indian children. From Morton's descriptions of his daily routine, long and full of detail, can be seen how music fitted into life on the sugar estates of nineteenth-century Trinidad. The picture of typical Indian music is sketchy, but Christian hymns in Hindustani are carefully described.

For the Hindu side of the historical picture—the old religious festivals, the family celebrations, and the popular singers of the nineteenth century—there were two Trinidadian manuscripts, one by the violinist, Narsaloo Ramaya, and another by Usha Tara Bissoondialsingh, a vocalist, school teacher, and student of India-born Guru H. S. Adesh. *Saptak* and *Jyoti,* two publications of Guru Adesh's organization (the Bharatiya Vidya Sansthhaan) added to the information available.

From all these works one could recreate the history of Indian music in Trinidad from the early years of the indentureship to modern times. The Morton book was written by a visitor, an outsider looking in. The Adesh publications reflected the viewpoint of another, unique, category of outsider—the musician from India. And the two Trinidadian manuscripts paint a picture drawn from an insider's perspective—a product of local musicology.

The Missionary: Morton

The Morton diary begins with description of the countryside, the sugar mills, and Coolie barracks, setting a picturesque scene that has now vanished.

PLATE 16. John Morton. (Reprinted from *John Morton of Trinidad*)

Plate 17. Sarah Morton. (Reprinted from *John Morton of Trinidad*)

Here we learn how the missionary used music as an enticement to attract potential converts.

> From door to door of the barracks the missionary would pass, speaking with individuals, teaching small groups, and finally, by invitation, or by the singing of a native hymn, drawing as many as he could to a more formal preaching in the gallery (a little open or half open extension) of a barrack, or in the hospital. (68)

From the beginning of their mission, the Mortons saw music as a tool for conversion. Every mission service included the singing of Christian hymns, translated into Hindustani. Mrs. Morton describes the usual order of worship.

> Mr. Morton opened the service in the Hindustani language, with praise, reading of the Scriptures, and prayer. I then followed briefly in an English service and read the Ten Commandments in the Hindustani. Mr. Morton then followed in an address to the Indians and two or three hymns were sung in their language. (104)

As they traveled from village to village in rural Trinidad, the Mortons always found the Indians receptive to music. The missionaries spared no effort to turn this to advantage, but this is not surprising for, in countries all around the world during the last two hundred years, music and proselytization have gone hand in hand. Morton found that the natives remembered the songs long after they had forgotten the preaching.

> I did not intend to sing, as I had so much speaking in the open air, but one man urged me to sing a particular hymn, repeating the chorus of it. When asked how he knew that I could sing it, he replied, "Oh, you sang it in the Castries Hospital about three years ago when I was sick there." . . . Roseau was our next place of meeting. . . . Perspiration streamed from every pore, but the people listened very attentively, urged me to sing two hymns, and joined in the request that a fellow countryman should be sent to Roseau Valley as their teacher. (280–81)

As soon as he came to Trinidad, Morton learned Hindustani. He soon was able to preach in the language and to translate hymns. Yet despite his obvious facility, he made scant use of everyday vocabulary, for example, the English terms "feast" *(pūjā)*, "sacred book" *(Gītā, Rāmāyaṇ)*, "altar" *(bedī)*, and "tom-toms" *(ḍholak, nagārā, tāssā)* appear instead of their Hindusṭani equivalents in his account of a Hindu ceremony.

> April 18, 1868. In the evening went up to Thakurdas' [house]. Found them preparing a feast for their gods. An altar with flowers all round it, a candle in a bottle on each side; a sacred book in the middle; three babujees [or priests], heaps of cocoa-nut cut up, betel, sugar, etc. They said it was their church, same

> as ours; Deenawa's mother came in. The babujee pointed to the book and up toward heaven. She then laid two shillings on the book, bent down and held her hands together near the ground, and looked at the babujee's face. He looked at hers, bowed slowly three times, she doing the same; then the ceremony ended. They kept tom-toms beating till far into the night. At 12 o'clock the god is believed to come and accept the offering; then the feast begins. (53; square brackets in original, indicating Sarah Morton's editorial additions to John Morton's diary)

The Mortons never fully adjusted to local ways, even after living and working with the East Indians for forty years. On page after page, we see the missionary pictured in the heavy black frock-coat of the day and his wife in high button boots and a poke bonnet, so unsuited to the tropical climate. These misunderstandings between members of the two cultures, north and south, had its lighter side.

> We had difficulty both among the children and adults who, with their earliest English vocabulary, contracted the use of improper words. . . . A little boy, hearing me say "If you come to church you will hear sweet Hindi hymns," and wishing to recommend our singing, put in, "Oh yes. They sing like a hell." (5)

The Mortons often mention music when describing local Hindu festivals. Mrs. Morton described weddings, but does not offer details about the drums "beating far into the night." Most likely, they were the *tāssā,* single-headed kettledrums, still used in modern weddings. However sketchy, these observations are the only contemporary record from this period of East Indian musical history.

> May is a favourite month for weddings; the schools are consequently smaller than usual; those children who are not getting married themselves are helping to marry the rest. Drums are beating far into the night; girls who never had any attentions before become centres for smiling groups, to whom the festivities of a marriage are a welcome break in the monotony of their lives. (244)

John Morton's most important contribution to local music history was the compilation of a Hindi hymn book. The project was undertaken early in the mission and took up a great deal of time. Sarah Morton writes:

> In 1872 Mr. Morton began to be much engaged in translating and preparing hymns, with a view to printing a small collection for the use of our worshipping people. This work was not allowed to interfere with his daily duties; he notes:
>
> May 9th. Papering house [No. 62] and hymn work; very weary.
>
> May 16th. Preparing hymns for press and measuring painter's work [in church]—461 yards at 15 cents.
>
> May 17th. Preparing hymns; visiting among San Fernando Indians.
>
> May 25th. Finished and mailed 30 hymns to be printed in Halifax.

> The little book was printed with care and accuracy in the Hindustani language, employing the Roman character. Many of the hymns had been obtained in imperfect form or even in fragments from the mouths of Indians who had learned them in India, and were completed and corrected by Mr. Morton with the help of Thomas Walter Cockey, then teacher at Iere Village. Five hundred copies were printed in Halifax and welcomed joyfully by both adults and children. (110–11; square brackets in original. I never came across a copy of Morton's hymnal in Felicity)

Throughout their ministry, the Mortons stressed education. By 1878, fifteen state-aided Canadian Mission primary schools were operating in Trinidad to serve the children of the East Indian cane laborers. In the early years, the missionaries found it difficult to attract students because child labor was so valuable. By 1891, the number of Canadian Mission schools had grown to 52; by 1974 to 73, officially known as "Presbyterian." Many of the early teachers were Indians who had been tutored by Morton. Like other denominational schools in Trinidad (Hindu, Muslim, Roman Catholic, and Anglican), they receive two-thirds of their operating funds from the state and one-third from the governing religious body, in this case, the Presbyterian Board. In Felicity, the Presbyterian primary school on Cacandee Road has over one thousand pupils.

In Morton's early schools, the curriculum emphasized Christian education, reading, writing, and arithmetic, but singing and Hindi were also included. Sarah Morton explained the rationale for Hindi instruction:

> Mr. Morton always regarded instruction in the vernacular as an important element in any effort for raising the Indian people. The child would in very many cases be obliged to leave school long before he was able to read with intelligence in English. Hindi being phonetic, is easily learned, better understood, would help in the homes and in religious services, which of necessity were all in Hindi. On our frequent visits to the schools Mr. Morton would usually examine in English branches, leaving the Hindi to me. In the assisted schools the teaching of Hindi had to be confined to the first hour, which has always been allowed by the Government for religious instruction. Beautiful hymns composed by native Christians in India were carefully taught and sung on Sabbath by the children, to whom we looked for choir service. A simple catechism used was obtained from India. It was specially adapted to the needs of India's children. (266)

Singing in the schools is mentioned again and again throughout the pages of the diary. Mr. Morton says:

> One day I took some half dozen of the best boys in Tacarigua School and went out in the village to sing and preach the Gospel. We had three meetings. The singing of the boys gathered the people, and then I read and preached to them. (240)

Mrs. Morton writes:

> Before leaving San Fernando Mr. Morton had succeeded in opening a school on Cedar Hill Estate. An interest was thus awakened that was found very helpful at The Mission, especially in establishing our Sabbath services there. Arthur Tejah, the teacher, attended these services, bringing with him a band of his older scholars, who were very proud to be looked upon as our choir; the hymns were Hindi, sung to the native music as taught by ourselves, and they rendered them well and heartily. (165)

And another entry:

> Sep. 5, 1876. There are so many beginners that I have to help the teachers and monitors every day. Sometimes I get tired of hearing "S-o so," "O-x ox," and "go up," "go on," but after all some of the little fellows do "go up" and "go on" very nicely. They learn hymns and catechism and about forty attend Sunday School. (160)

From the diary I could see five conclusions the missionaries might have drawn about the early music of the East Indians.

1. During the second half of the nineteenth century, music was a regular part of everyday East Indian life in Trinidad. It was especially important during religious celebrations.

2. The sung language as well as the spoken language of the period was Hindustani.

3. The East Indians had a tradition of drumming as well as of singing, but we do not know if the drums were brought from India or made locally.

4. The influence of Creole music on Indian music was minimal.

5. The Indians loved music, and were receptive to new musical ideas introduced by the missionaries. Indians preferred songs in their own language; Christian songs in Hindustani were not rejected, even by Hindus who refused to convert.

Local Artist: Ramaya

The Ramaya manuscript, "Indian Music in Trinidad" (1965), gives a different insight, a valuable point of view from the 1960s. Narsaloo Ramaya was a member of the National Cultural Council and a founder of Naya Zamana ("New Era"), a popular Indian orchestra from the 1940s. At the National Cultural Council, he was the chief researcher for East Indian music, and his duties included collecting folk songs from Trinidad villages for the Council archives. Many of Ramaya's articles have appeared in local publications including the leading national newspaper, the *Trinidad Guardian.* He plays the violin, and has made an LP record, "Cherished Melodies" (quotations from "Indian Music in Trinidad," 4–11, 20–21, 26–27, 31, 73–74, 88).

Unlike Morton, Ramaya sees the early indentureship years as a period of great hardship during which music played a relatively minor role. Toiling on the sugar plantations left the indentured immigrant with little time or energy for song. As the conditions of their lives improved, however, laborers found more time for entertainment. Prior to 1900, Indian music in Trinidad was based on regional folk traditions of north India. On the estates, an English planter might hear many local styles of the subcontinent, and see a variety of regional dances.

> The time was now propitious for the development of latent talent and undeveloped skills, and to give expression to their feelings and emotions. They began to indulge in some form of cultural activity which they brought with them from their Motherland. This was done mainly in the form of songs and dances. The songs they sang were chiefly folk songs such as the Rasiya and the Dhola; in addition, there were the Rajasthani songs of the Rajasthan and Pachhanhiyas (people of Western Uttar Pradesh in North India), the Punjabi songs of the Punjabis and the Madrassi songs of the Tamils and Telugus. The dances at this time were also traditional. There were many varieties and they originated from different parts of India. These were the Ahir dance, the Rahasmandal dance, the Rasdhari dance from Uttar Pradesh and Bihar, and the Madrassi dance.

Then as now weddings were the most important occasions for music and dance. Ramaya describes the dances of the Ahīr (caste of cattle tenders), accompanied by *nagārā* kettledrums and *birahā* songs, a folk genre from northeastern India.

> On such a night large crowds of people from the village would gather to witness the entertainment. The Ahir dance seemed to have been the most popular. This style of dance was forceful and virile with well coordinated steps and movements. The participants were only men and the combination of drummers, singers and dancers, presented a fascinating scene in which the dancers with naked backs and willows on their feet made rhythmical movements of the body to the beating of the Nagara drums while the singer, with fingers in his ears sang his Biraha songs with great gusto, the total effect of the performance giving much pleasure to the spectators. The Ahir dance has always been one of the main attractions on wedding nights and its performance survived until quite recently.

For Ramaya, the turn of the century marks the second phase of Indian music in Trinidad. This period, lasting until the outbreak of World War I, saw the rise of local celebrities—itinerant singers and instrumentalists—most of them former indentured immigrants who had acquired their skill in music and singing in India.

> They assumed a new role, that of roaming all over the country entertaining people everywhere with their songs. They found great enjoyment and satisfaction

> in this occupation and they were welcomed to stay at the homes of people who were willing to have them and be entertained by them.

These itinerant songsters performed a variety of genres that Ramaya calls "classical." During the nineteenth century, local Trinidadian classical genres, sung primarily for entertainment, were considered distinct from the folk repertory—the village songs that accompanied the life cycle and annual cycle. Some of these classical forms borrow the names of north Indian classical genres *(dhrupad, ṭhumrī, tillānā),* while others carry the name of popular *rāgs (bhairavī)* or *tāls (dādrā).* Several forms that Ramaya lists are still common, particularly the *ṭhumrī, tillānā,* and *dhrupad.*

> The songs that were sung at this time were those immortal classics as the Sargam, the Tappa, the Sarang, the Dhrupad, the Tilana, the Hori, the Thumri, the Dadra, the Marfat, the Gazal and the Bhairavi. Feelings and moods were expressed in these songs by the singer and many possible variations in style and tempo were executed by him during the course of his rendition. The improvising quality called for in the song gave him ample scope to display his art. Thus he was able to produce an effect both spiritual and esthetic which filled the hearts of his listeners with profound joy and satisfaction.

These singers developed a distinctively Trinidadian style, differing from the classical singing of India in ways that demonstrate for Ramaya that retention and change are two inevitable and complimentary forces in the history of Indian music in Trinidad.

> Perhaps these early songsters could not match the brilliance of their great contemporaries of classical singing in India, but whatever knowledge they possessed in music and singing, and this was impressive enough, they developed and perfected a style and manner of singing which they passed on to another generation and which in time became peculiarly Trinidadian.

Ramaya describes the specialties of early East Indian music in Trinidad. Some indentured laborers established reputations as instrumentalists. He mentions the playing of the *sāraṇgī,* sitar, and tabla, but we do not know if these instruments were made locally or brought from India. (They had largely died out by the 1960s, when Professor Adesh reintroduced them.) The *ḍholak* (double-headed barrel drum), *ḍhantāl* (literally "stick"; iron-rod idiophone struck with a U-shaped beater), and *manjīrā* (finger cymbals) have had a continuous tradition from the indentureship period to modern times (plate 18).

> The musical instruments that were played at this time were the sarangi, the sitar, the tabla and the dholak. In addition to these there were also the Dhantal and the Majeera; these last two were mainly used by the singers to keep time. The harmonium came sometime later.

Plate 18. Coolie instrumentalists around 1900: two *sāraṇgī* players (left and right) and a *tabla* player (center).

One of the best-known early songsters was India-born Phiramat (also called Phiranta, "vagabond"), a professional musician, able to support himself from his performances. He and his troupe established an island-wide reputation. Professional musicians are rare in modern Trinidad, and Felicity has none.

> The skill with which Phiramat rendered his songs was unmatched and he became the acknowledged master of the art of classical singing. Whenever he sang at weddings or at other religious ceremonies large crowds gathered to hear him and even followed him to distant parts of the island where he sang. He wandered from place to place seeking the patronage of prominent people, to entertain them with his songs. . . . His favourite resort was Moklejan (Mount Pleasant, Forres Park), where he and members of his small troupe notably Imami the singer and Sarangi player, and Ramcharan Ostad the drummer, were frequent guests of Babu Ramsingh. . . . This practice of roving from place to place seemed to have become fashionable and was followed by almost all the classical songsters of the period.

During this period, most singing took place at night; public contests between rival artists might last until dawn. Song duels, still popular in Uttar Pradesh villages, were fought out by the early Trinidad songsters. Each hour of the night had a prescribed song form, just as the theory of classical Indian music assigns each *rāg* to a particular time of day.

> The leading protagonists of the time rendered their songs with the most consummate skill, adhering to the pattern laid down in the rules sanctified by custom and tradition, that every hour of the night demanded a special type of song to be sung, and any deviation from this practice was an indication of the singer's inability to cope with the true meaning of classical singing, so that a songster who wished to remain within the scope of that exclusive and classical fraternity must be able, not only to render his songs well to the satisfaction of his hearers, but his repertoire must be such as to enable him to battle his way throughout the night with suitable and appropriate songs. Quite often two or three top songsters would clash on such a night and vie against each other for supremacy and in this battle of the giants the mastery and technique of classical singing were fully demonstrated to the great enjoyment and satisfaction of the audience. So keen was the interest and attention shown by the audience that the faintest whisper or the slightest movement by anyone who interrupted the performance was deemed to be an unpardonable offence and a stern look from one of the elders in the audience was sufficient to put the offender in his place.

The most important song forms performed during these musical evenings were the *sargam, dhrupad, tillānā,* and *ṭhumrī.*

> At the commencement of his performance, the singer on entering the Mahfil takes up his Dhantal or Majeera and opens his singing with an invocation to the goddess of music—Saraswatee, somewhat in a similar manner as the poet who is about to write an epic invokes the Muse of Poetry for his inspiration. The singer makes this invocation by singing a poem or Doha. After this he goes on to sing a Sargam, which is one of the most difficult songs to sing. The Sargam is the purest form of improvisation and calls for the highest skill and technique by the singer and it is in the rendition of the Sargam that the singer's

> ability is proven. The next song in the order is the Dhrupad, then the Tilana, the Thumrie and so on.

This pattern was followed by all contestants, and at each succeeding hour of the night until daybreak they sang the appropriate songs.

After World War I, a new generation of native Trinidadian singers gained popularity. The rising stars were Benny Sewnath, Jhabwah, Yacoob, Poman, Hardeo, Loorkhoor Ramjattan, Jugrue Quaval, Ramdhani Sharma, and Seebalack. The favorite setting for music was still the wedding.

> Hindu weddings at that time took place in the night, the actual wedding ceremony being performed somewhere around midnight. A special tent was provided some yards away from the bride's home and this was known as the Janwasa. Here the bridegroom and the wedding guests remained for a night while entertainment was provided either by a dance troupe or by songsters. The singing here followed a regular pattern of classical songs and as the night progressed a keen contest of classical singing developed among the songsters. The singing continued thus until daybreak. . . . If the parents were well to do and were prominent citizens in the community then it was certain that for three days there would be lavish entertainment of drum beating and the best in singing, and music and dancing.

The musical life of Indians in Trinidad was transformed in the mid-1930s with the importation of full-length feature films from India. The first "talkie" (with Hindi dialogue) was *Bala Joban,* which opened at the Gaiety Theatre, San Fernando, on 7 December 1935. Its immediate success is attested to by the sudden popularity of "Bala Joban" earrings and veils, and "Pandu" haircuts (after the leading actor). During the following year, more Hindi films, each with five or more songs, were imported, including *Bhārat ki Betī* (Daughter of India), *Shadi ki Rāt* (Wedding Night), *Judgement of Allah,* and *Chandidas.* These new songs were quickly taken up by local singers.

Films from India also stimulated interest in learning Hindi; at the same time they reinforced the notion, quite incorrect, that the Bhojpurī dialect which many Trinidadians spoke was a corruption of Hindi. Many local singers studied Hindi and Urdu in order to understand the words of the latest *filmī* songs from India.

The new film songs undermined the popularity of the local classical style.

> Classical singing as it was rendered by the old masters was hopelessly on the decline. . . . The people were now interested in the modern songs of the films which were not without some appeal even to the classical tastes of Jhagroo and Ramdhani. For this reason, and not to appear to be opposed to any change, Jhagroo and Ramdhani met the new challenge with great adroitness. They utilised their talents to conform to the new tastes of the people and in no time they were able to render modern songs with the most consummate ease.

> But a new generation of songsters had entered the stage. They were young people who had become steeped in the film songs and anything classical was distasteful to their modern minds.

Month by month from the 1940s onward, the Hindi films screened in Trinidad were a source for local singers to enrich their repertory with songs directly from India, albeit from the glitzy Bombollywood studios, themselves much influenced by the Latin American and U.S.A. pop scenes. Hitherto, musical influences had been primarily from the West, either Creole (calypso, steel band), or English and American (blues, jazz, big band). Film songs provided Trinidad musicians with the material with which to Indianize their repertory by imitating the popular music of India. Did the upbeat Bombay songs have more appeal than Bhojpurī village music—their genuine Asian heritage?

Ramaya sees the period of local classical singing, before the advent of films from India, as one of musical stagnation, typical of an immigrant people whose music is an unchanging marginal survival of a larger and continuously evolving tradition.

> During the classical period there was virtually no improvement or development in singing. The first set of singers who were pioneers in the field of classical singing came from India. They reigned for about thirty years, singing the same songs throughout their entire singing career. Their repertoire, though consisting of various types of classical songs, was severely limited. They had no means of replenishing their stock for they were virtually cut off from the land of their cultural heritage. The singers that followed them (all Trinidadians) in the later classical period, got their inspiration and guidance from these pioneers and sang the same songs in the same manner. They too had no contact with the source of their culture (this contact only came with the arrival of Indian films) and were unable to make any addition to their repertoire. They were left with what they had and made the best use of it. The whole period was stagnant in that no appreciable development took place in terms of quality and form as the selfsame songs were sung over the years. The people nevertheless loved to hear them and continued to show their warmth and fervour and appreciation for both singer and song.

During the same years, 78 R.P.M. records of Indian film songs were exported to Trinidad. These provided new songs and styles for imitation, particularly *bhajan* and light classical genres such as *ghazal* and *qawwālī*. The first shipment of records in 1936 included songs that were adopted by local artists and became hits in Trinidad (notably two songs, "Allah hoo" and "Betak Ye Dil Mere Kamli Wale" and one piece by Bhai Afzal Hosse).

In 1939, Trinidad Indian singers made their first recordings. Artists Ramdhani Sharma, Jugrue Quaval, Benny Sewnath, and Tarran Persad recorded on the Decca label. Very few copies of these 78 R.P.M. records are extant, but the Mohammed brothers of Port of Spain amassed a collection that has survived (see "A Sample from the 1940s," later in this chapter).

Ramaya kept track of the record industry at the time. Although records from India tended to sell better than those produced in Trinidad, the local music industry flourished during the years of World War II. Singing competitions and live stage shows were held in the new cinema houses. The musical *Gulshan Bahar* (Orchard of Pleasure), one of the first and most popular of these shows, was produced during the war for the India Famine Relief Committee; it included Indian songs, music, and dancing by the local star, Champa Devi. The show was a success in Port of Spain, San Fernando, and on the U.S. Naval Base; it then toured towns and villages throughout Trinidad. In 1945 following on their success with *Gulshan Bahar,* the leading artists organized a second play, *Naya Zamana* (The New Era), and an Indian orchestra of the same name—the first of many such combos in Trinidad. Ramaya participated in the *Gulshan Bahar* and *Naya Zamana* plays and the Naya Zamana Orchestra.

In 1947, Radio Trinidad, the island's first radio station, opened, and on 26 September of that year the first program of local Indian music, *Indian Talent on Parade,* was aired. This Sunday-afternoon spot featured Jugrue Quaval, Tarran Persad, and Jang Bahadoor, Saigal, K. C. Day, Pearu Quaval, and the talented teenager Yankarran, from the isolated Caroni village of Waterloo. Later that year producer Pat Mathura brought out *Songs of India,* also a half-hour program, devoted, however, to imported film songs rather than local talent. These programs provided an opportunity to broadcast and stimulated a revival of the old, local classical style.

> Youngsters who had hitherto been interested in the modern songs of the films now switched over to classical singing. Every week now classical songs were heard on the radio and appreciation developed for them among the people. It now formed a major attraction in singing competitions and other performances. Young people now began to appreciate this new form of the old songs, for undoubtedly . . . the young men who sang the classical songs, almost all of them had no acquaintance with them or even heard them as they were sung by the singers of old. Consequently, they sang not as of old, nor according to the rules laid down for classical singing. They unwittingly disregarded conventional patterns and developed a form and style quite apart from the original and the songs thus lost much of the old form. . . . If perchance visitors from India heard them (as happened on divers occasions) they were very often flabbergasted at the strange mixture that passed for classical singing. . . . In Trinidad, an inordinate love for this so called classical singing grew among the population, a great many of whom vaguely understood its true meaning.

Ramaya sees this cross fertilization of ideas from India as stimulating for local artists, and he envisages as a great source of inspiration and promise for the future the growing fondness for calypso rhythms, Latin American tempos, and "pan."

> Since [1962] the tempo of Indian music rose considerably. . . . Indian music assumed greater dimensions and added meaning was given it in the context of the cosmopolitan nature of our society . . . and an appreciation for it developed among the population as a whole as the latest pop tunes of the Indian films were being sung with the syncopation and swing of the calypso tempo. . . . Even Indian bands mixed their playing and some of their selections often included calypsos, Latin American music and other popular hit tunes of the day. The steel band, too, became the medium through which Indian music was played, and Cyril Raymond and his unique and talented family started to beat out lovely Indian tunes on the "pans" to the great delight of many an audience.
>
> There is vast scope for the improvement of Indian music through the adaptation of western techniques of harmony, especially in orchestration, and one can hopefully contemplate an era of synthesis in eastern and western forms of music.

From the Ramaya manuscript of 1965 I could draw a number of conclusions.

1. The East Indians of Trinidad have had a continuous tradition of vocal and instrumental music based on Indian models. Music has always been important.

2. Professionalism developed, together with a style, known locally as "classical." Both declined after World War II.

3. The relationship between the "classical" music of Trinidad and north Indian classical music is not clear. Trinidad classical forms often carry the names of Indian *rāg*s, *tāl*s, or genres.

4. The wedding has always been the most important occasion for music.

5. Local musicians have preferred to emulate what they understand to be authentic models from India (mainly film music), even rejecting their old Bhojpurī folksongs. Scholars who characterize the "local classical" music of Trinidad as a corrupted or distorted version of the classical music of India have mistakenly assumed that Trinidadian composers had heard Indian classical music before the 1960s.[16]

6. The history of Indian music in Trinidad is a story of continuity and change. The changes are of two types—Indianization and Westernization. The rate of change has accelerated since the introduction of Indian films to Trinidad and the development of a local music industry.

To take the story further, a conspicuous manifestation of Indian film music in modern Trinidad has been the formation during the 1950s, '60s, and '70s of more than a hundred Indian combos, "orchestras," among them Naya Zamana, Solo Sangeet, Satara Hind, Bena Sangeet, Mal Sangeet, Choti Sangeet Saaj, Hum Hindustani, Central Merry Makers, Sisons Naya Sansar, Acme Dill Nadan, and the National Indian BWIA Orchestra. These groups of from ten to fifteen players are found all over the country, in Port of Spain and San Fernando as well as small villages. The Felicity orchestra, Nau Jawan, led by Chanderbally, was one of the nation's leading groups during the 1950s and 1960s, but did not play together thereafter.

Indian orchestras usually include electric guitars, electric keyboards, a drum set, sometimes mandolin, congo drums, bongos, trumpet, violin, and saxophone, as well as the occasional traditional Indian instrument, for example the *bānsurī* (flute), and *ḍholak* and tabla drums (plate 19). The groups play at weddings, parties, and bazaars, and on radio and television, especially the program, *Mastana Bahaar,* an hour-long weekly Indian talent show with contestants from all parts of Trinidad.

At orchestra rehearsals teenage musicians experiment with music—Western and Indian. Most of the instrumentalists are male; young women provide vocals; neighbors hang around and watch the rehearsals, chat, and drink. Throughout Trinidad, evenings are lively with music, in cities and villages, as bands (including calypso groups and steel bands) rehearse. African groups

PLATE 19. Solo Sangeet Orchestra of San Juan, Trinidad, with Hawaiian guitar, electric guitars, trap set, electric keyboard, bongo drums, and tomba drums, 1974.

compete with Indian groups for commercial sponsorship from the business sector. The Indian groups attract less sponsorship than the African groups, a contentious issue since electronic instruments are so expensive.

During the last thirty years, Trinidadians have kept in touch with the musical scene in India, pop and recently classical. A few scholarships have been awarded to study classical music in India. Indian playback superstars tour the island (Hemant Kumar in 1964; Manna Dey in 1965; Mohammed Rafi in 1969; more recently Kanchan and Babla from the 1980s onward). Indianization of pop music in Trinidad has accelerated, as has the process of Westernization, a paradoxical situation, since the film songs from India are themselves Westernized. Western and Indian influences notwithstanding, no one would mistake the Trinidadian sound of local bands.

A SAMPLE FROM THE 1940S: LOCAL 78 R.P.M. RECORDS

A collection of recordings from the 1940s—now very rare—owned by the Mohammed brothers, features selections by local artists, such as Benny Sewnath, Jugrue Quaval, Sayyeed Mohammed, Rambarose Pancham, Pandit Kasi Parsad, and Tarran Persad, the last a gifted singer who had access to the latest and best Indian records and evolved his own unique style. The singers were accompanied by local orchestras including R. S. Narayansingh's Orchestra, Jit Seeshai's Indian Orchestra, Gopi's East Indian Orchestra, Nazir Mohammed's Orchestra—all on the Decca label. The recorded items, *bhajan*, and songs, include explanations of Hindu philosophy, prayers, patriotic expressions, contributions of some poets, as well as stories from the *Rāmāyaṇ*. The languages used are Hindi and Urdu.

I listened to these records later at home in Connecticut, with Umesh, who had journeyed from India to the United States to teach a course entitled "Indian Village Life: Conversations with a Native." I asked Umesh what he thought of these 78 R.P.M. recordings.

"Seems the collection is a mixture. Seems their culture is a mixture. They have Hindu and Muslim mixed in the texts of these songs. For example, I don't think the Trinidad Muslims have the concept of a boat of life stuck crossing the whirlpool of this world. 'Oh Maula help me to cross the river—this world. My heart is trembling, my boat is shaking in the middle of the ocean, and east wind is blowing.' Maybe some Hindu composed it? Maybe it was sung by a Muslim? Did Hindu people link Hindu and Muslim, so when they live on a small island they can live as a community against other people?

"In India, during the Mughal period Muslim composers—Rahim Khan, Raskhan—used Hindu ideas. They composed their poems based on Hinduism. They lived among Hindu people and they were fascinated by Hinduism.

Under Emperor Akbar, people had freedom to learn Hinduism or Islam. At the same time Tulsī Dās, Kabīr, Rahim Khan, Sur Dās—these were the poets of Mughal time.

"These Trinidad people around 1850, 1870, and after that—the concept of joining culture was already among them and most of the Hindus were converted by the Mohammedism so they could not exactly accept pure Islam. When they went to Trinidad this concept could grow a little bit more because they truly were Indian. They had to face other people. This collection is around the '40s when Trinidad was not well developed. It still was under the British Empire. Indian people were living for brotherhood—Hindus and Muslims. Some of the songs in the collection are pure Hindu, some pure Muslim, some mixed. I never saw such kind of songs in India. The Trinidad songs are shorter. Do you think they carried these songs from India?" Umesh asked.

"No," I replied, "as far as we know they were composed in Trinidad. But the records are in bad shape, it is almost impossible to make out the words, and the Bhojpurī usage is unusual, practically unintelligible. What meaning is locked in these old songs?"

"Free me out of prison," Umesh said. "I felt that these people took the songs from their parents. Because of pain when they went to Trinidad they felt they were in prison."

"These musicians of Trinidad were called 'songsters,'" I mentioned.

"In India that would be *gāyak*," Umesh answered. "These people sing in competitions, also without competition. Everywhere in northern India singers always begin to compete, never mind they win any prize or not, but they want to compete. A kind of fight begins among singers—like those people who fight in battle, they want to show their superiority. It is not for money, only to show who is a better singer or composer."

"In Trinidad they have what is called a 'side'—a team," I said.

"We call it *taraf*—'side,' Umesh replied. "Like on a football team: what *taraf* you will play? If anyone goes from my village to sing I will be on the *taraf* of my singers. I do remember my grandfather used to sing. He used to go different places to sing—ten, fifteen, twenty miles from our village on foot and used to come back at night. He used to work in the day and sing competition at night. But it's not very common now."

☙ THE SONGS

Record label: "Quawal Song," *Mora Ji Ghabaraya*, sung by Sayyeed Mohammed; accompanied by Nazir Mohammed's Orchestra; recorded in Trinidad.

"In this song the composer tried to raise love above anything else," Umesh explained. "This is not a *bhajan*, this is a song."

19 ℬ
Let us foreign land go now love.
You without, my heart troubling [*ghabarana*].
Love whirlpool in better found ["I found myself better in the whirlpool of love"].
Love whirlpool in better found.
Let us foreign land go now love.
You without my heart troubling.
Far from here at the river bank.
Sitting in a battlefield.

Umesh commented, "I think it should be 'jungle' or 'forest' but he sang 'battle.'"

Me you are, and nobody is.
Me you are, and nobody is.
Battlefield in is this happiness.

"'*Jangal mai mangal*' is like an idiom," Umesh explained. "In Hindi 'even happiness in bad days,' but he sang *dangal* which means battlefield."

Battlefield in is this happiness.
Let us foreign land go now love.
You without my heart troubling.
Beautiful talk [meaning obscure].
Walking is like [meaning obscure].
Therefore this mine at river bank [i.e., "So therefore at the bank of the river my love is more wonderful than the world."]
Therefore this mine at river bank.
Love worldly than wonderful.
Love worldly than wonderful.
Let us foreign land go now love.
You without my heart troubling.

*

Record label: "Quawali Song," *Sab Nabio Me Vo Allah,* sung by Jugrue Quaval; accompanied by the Jit Seeshai's East Indian Orchestra; recorded in Trinidad, Decca.

This short and unusual fragment combines the story of Mīrābāī, the famous Rajasthani Hindu queen, the *bhaktī* poet of the Mughal period, with praise for the Muslim prophet Mohammed.

20 ℬ
Among all prophets is the the great [Mīrābāī].
Four long hours you made nectar in the bowl of suffering.
That one nectar you made.
Blessed bowl poisoned of made drink.
Oh Mohammed, you are the greatest of God's prophets.
Mohammed is the beloved of everyone.

*

Record label: *Bhajan*, Benny Sewnath; accompanied by the Jit Seeshai's East Indian Orchestra; recorded in Trinidad, Decca.

Of this song, Umesh writes: "The poet is trying to give a lesson to people against their religious dogma that you won't find God worshipping a mountain and in beads of a *mālā*. He also does not live in the temple. You will not find God in your elders or in your friends or in your parents. The poet says that this world is like an ocean but God is in your heart. We have the same kind of thinking and feeling in our village *bhajan*."

21 ☎

Will find Shyām [lit. "blue," name for Krishna] own inside.
Will find Shyām own inside.
Neither grandfather [*dādā;* also wise old man] find in, auspicious friend find in ["We will not find God in our grandfather (wise old man) or in our auspicious friend"].
Neither grandfather find in, nor auspicious friend find in.
Not *parvat* mountain [perhaps stone icons] inside aah aah.
Will find Rām own inside.
Will find Rām.
Tap ["sacrifice," "penance"] of garland [rosary, beads] squeeze [as in pressing of rosary beads] cannot.
Tap of garland squeeze cannot.
Not temple of corner in.
Place in living spirituality lost.
World in living spirituality lost.
Naked middle ocean in.
Will find Rām own of inside.
Will find Shyām own of inside.
In the same trouble Dhrub [son of the king] found.
In the same trouble Dhrub found.
Devotion of pleasure in.
In the same trouble Dhrub found.
In the same trouble Dhrub found.
Devotion of pleasure in.
Kashinnath [composer] chant a hymn Krishna Chandra to.
Kashinnath chant a hymn Krishna Chandra to.
Will find Shyām own inside.
Will find Shyām own inside.
Will find Shyām.

*

Record label: *Apnay Gully Bolewanah* ["Call me in your lane"]; Hindu *bhajan*, Ameer Shah, Tarran Persad; arranged by Amrai Khan, San Fernando.

Of this song, Umesh writes: "This song is about Lord Krishna. In this *bhajan* the poet explains his thoughts and feelings of Krishna by giving examples about those to whom he has given salvation, and the poet is also requesting salvation for himself. You Krishna have give salvation to Bakasur and made succeed Arjun. You saved Dhropatī's dignity by not let her be naked. You saved the elephant from the crocodile and you gave salvation to the crocodile [as in songs 5, 24, and 28]. You help your parents to get out from prison. Please grant salvation to your devoted poet."

22 ☙
Hey Brindāban of living one [i.e., Krishna; he played in the forest *(ban)* of Brindā (according to old Indian villagers of U.P., "*tulsī* plant")].
Brindāban of living one.
Own lane call ["Krishna call me to you"].
[obscure] to killed *giraya* [fall].
Demon Bakasur salvation got [i.e., from Krishna].
Who Arjun made succeed [in the *Bhāgawad Gītā* of the *Māhābhārata*].
Who Arjun made succeed.
Me also give salvation.
Drupad Queen [*sic;* in the *Māhābhārata,* the term "Dhrupad (a king) Sutā" ("daughter") refers to Dropadī, of the Pandava clan] pain increased [*sic; mitaye* ("destroyed") not *baraye* ("increased")].
Dushasan [king from the *Māhābhārata*] of pride destroyed.
Elephant to crocodile from help to escape.
Elephant to crocodile from help to escape.
Me also grant salvation.
Me also world from grant salvation.
[Obscure] killed flat.
King [obscure] of dignity kept.
Parents of prison released [Krishna was born in prison and struggled to free his parents].
Parents of prison released.
My also prison released ["grant me salvation"].
Brindāban of living one.
Brindāban of living one.
Own lane to cause to call.
[*Spoken*]
Merā nām hai Tarran Persad. ["My name is Tarran Persad."]

*

Record label: *Kawalie,* Rambarose Pancham; accompanied by Nazir Mohammed's Orchestra; recorded in Trinidad, Decca.

Umesh writes: "I know how important Haj, when they go to Mecca, is to Muslim. I know they believe they will attain salvation by going to Mecca. 'Navajī Haj' refers to the pilgrim. When he returns from Mecca he becomes Hajī Sahab and is no longer called by his name."

23 ☙
Oh, Prophet, you who sing about *Haj* is.
Oh, Prophet of name at devoted *Haj* is.

Having made drink the liquor of love.
Having made drink the liquor of love.
Made me follower [drunk].
Mohammedan today is that also.
Navajī Haj become is.
Prophet, you who sing about *Haj* become is.
Me world in always.
He only sun showed.
He, oh, sun become is.
He, oh, sun become is.
Prophet. . . .
Me world in always.
He only sun showed.
He, oh, sun showed.
Prophet, you who sing about *Haj* become is.
Prophet of name at devoted who *Haj* become is.

*

Record label: *Hindi Ghazal,* Ramdhani Shyma; accompanied by Gopi's East Indian Orchestra; recorded in Trinidad, Decca.

24 ☙
[*Vocables*] Aah aah aah . . .
Beloved, see my lord.
Came where crazy [for love] being [i.e., How crazy God is that he has come to help].
Beloved, see my lord.
Came where crazy [for love] being.
Pole holding guard in prison.
Lord of concentration made loose.
Powerful love [concentration] then come for you.
Childhood in lad to cause to play.
Lankā King Rāwaṇa to kill.
Mathurā Krishna made leave.
[Meaning obscure but perhaps "Full man saint now Pitam (proper name)"].
Crocodile to across [gave salutation].

"There is a story behind it," Umesh said. "When crocodile hold one leg of an elephant, when he—the elephant—went to drink water in the river, both animals fought hard. The elephant couldn't save himself. A bit of the elephant the size of *jau,* a barley seed—that is an old measurement—so a *jau*-size piece of trunk was above the water. Then the elephant remembered God, and Lord Krishna appeared here and used his *sudarshan chakra,* his weapon like a saw, and he did cut the neck of the crocodile. He saved the elephant. He also saved the crocodile because when God kills someone the person or animal never goes to hell—straight to heaven. In this type of song any single line can have a long meaningful story behind it. In the Indian village everyone knows these stories, but they are puzzling for strangers."

The song continues:

Bharoch Dās [the poet-composer] joining hands as in prayer and says.
[obscure] inside forgotten.
Beloved see my lord,
Came where crazy [of love] being.

Umesh: "These songs are old and these are new. These are never old really. These were before and these are now, and people keep continue composing songs on the base of religious texts."

*

Record label: "Urdu Ghazal," Tulsi Dass; accompanied by Gopi's East Indian Orchestra; recorded in Trinidad, Decca.

Of this song, Umesh writes: "I write according to my understanding because this song is not very clear. In this song the poet is trying to show his feelings by giving facts about English people as well as explaining the condition of people they are ruling over. He says, 'What condition we are living in? You have become ruler of India and rule all over the world. We are poor. Don't wake me up. All the world is under your shadow of ruling. How did you do this wonder?' I think this is a kind of patriotic song."

25 ꩜

[Recording damaged; text obscure]
That life more beloved country to made into graveyard.
See we all of what condition go see,
See we all of what condition go see.
One world of [obscure] own made.
India of country own made,
India of country own made.
Enemy killed [obscure],
Enemy killed [obscure].
[obscure] stolen [obscure] how separate did.
English your light world on showed,
English your light world on showed.
Poor of this way you [obscure] did.
Lived remained in sleep no reason made awake.
All world on shadow on wonder did.

Umesh writes further: "As you can hear, this one seems incomplete and has several obscure passages. It is also a patriotic song of freedom fighters. These are some of the feelings of those people—flow of blood in the nerves of their people so they can wake up and fight. I have heard such songs in India which explain that when somebody die in simple death only a few people go to participate in the funeral. But when you sacrifice for your nation, thousands, millions follow the body, to take *darshan.* It means this slain freedom fighter has become God because we only take *darshan* of God. The song continues:"

Beauty of bargain become is, rest heart wish is.
Beauty of bargain became is, rest heart wish is.
Sacrificed we nation to [obscure] moonlight.
Today is what [obscure] how many *darshan* [vision, sighting] doing.
One dish for *darshan* me sacrifice is.
One dish for *darshan* me sacrifice is.
Is nothing with me only one faith.
Again where are any recollection me not.
Name your wonder is, he empty [obscure] is.
Hand on those wrinkles [of fate] given.
Hand on those wrinkles given were empty is. [Man goes to God empty handed.]
Not any [obscure] Lord on you alone have to go.

*

Record label: *Narw Bhawurr May* ["The Boat in Whirlpool"], Jugrue Quaval; accompanied by the Jit Seeshai's East Indian Orchestra; recorded in Trinidad, Decca.

Of this song, Umesh writes: "This is a song where the poet personifies life. Here the boat is a soul and whirlpool is the world. Poet says that the boat of my life is stuck in worldly whirlpool so, oh, God, help me to get out of it. Grant me salvation. This song is not really a *bhajan* because it does not praise God. It is a kind of prayer."

26
Boat whirlpool in has stuck, Lord [help to] cross.
Boat whirlpool in has stuck, Lord [help to] cross.
Waddle [obscure] heart shaking sun of.
Middle sea in boat waddles wind bowing east.
Step on favor you do my Lord boat make cross.
A great favor you grant my Lord boat make cross.
Mother my broken sin of [boat].
When death of loop get to neck have to come to all sense.
Only request [pray], this is mine.
Only request, this is mine.
Ah, my help, you came.

*

Record label: *Dadra,* Master Rameswak; accompanied by Gopi's East Indian Orchestra; recorded in Trinidad, Decca.

Of this song, Umesh writes: "This songs gives straight information about the social system of the Indian family. Here is a woman asking her husband or her love before dawn that they will separate soon and won't see or talk with each other for all the day or for a long time although living in the same family. So she is asking, 'So embrace me to your neck,' means give me a sweet hug. 'I don't know when we will get together again.'"

27 ♫
[*Vocables*] Aah aah aah . . .
Early in the morning separate will love.
Happily embrace me to the neck.
Early in the morning separate will love.
Happily embrace me to the neck.
House from lost, outer from also lost.
Helpless made, hold me up.
House from lost, outer from lost.
Helpless made, hold me up.
Early in the morning separate will love.
Happily embrace me to the neck.
Happily embrace me to the neck.
Happily embrace me to the neck.
Early in the morning separate will love.
Happily embrace me to the neck.
Do not know when again both will meet.
Making excuse, do not avoid me.
Do not know when both will meet.
Making excuse do not avoid me.
Making excuse do not avoid me.
Out of entire night now little is left.
So you with call me.
So you with call me.
Happily embrace me to the neck.
Happily embrace me to the neck.
Happily neck to embrace me.
Early in the morning separate will love.
Happily neck to embrace me.
Happily neck to embrace me.

*

Record label: *Jazal Ghazal,* Bejulah; accompanied by the Jit Seeshai's East Indian Orchestra; recorded in Trinidad, Decca.

Of this song, Umesh writes: "In this song the poet is giving examples of how many God has given salvation and also saved their life. The poet says, 'This is my turn.' So he is requesting for his number for salvation. This *kathā* ('religious story') of elephant and crocodile is coming again and again. It seems to me it is very important story for these people in Trinidad. In India we also have such kinds of *kathā* in northern India and my village as well. And everybody knows the elephant and crocodile story."

28 ♫
[*Vocables*] Aah aah aah . . .
Lord, how the elephant trouble from got released?
Lord, how the elephant trouble from got released?
The elephant and the crocodile fought in water.
Fighting elephant lost.
The elephant and the crocodile fought in water.
Having fought elephant lost.
A bit trunk left water out.
Then Lord name called.
Lord, how the elephant out trouble from got released?
Lord, how the elephant trouble from got released?
Sibarī's fruits Lord tasted first ate.
Pious Sudāmā praised.
Sibarī's fruits Lord tasted first ate [i.e., from the *Rāmāyaṇ*, Sibarī tasted the fruits first to see if they were sweet enough for Lord Rām].
Pious Sudāmā praised.
Driyodhan home royal food [dry fruit] denied.
Vegetable Bidur [name of Krishna's friend] home ate.
Lord, how the elephant trouble from got released?
Lord, how the elephant trouble from got released [damage on record]?
Rām *charan* ["feet"] of [obscure; record damaged] always [obscure].
Rām *charan* always served [worshipped].
Vedas, Purāṇas chanted.
Tulsī Dās always worshipped Rām.
Lord's feet song sang.
Lord, how the elephant trouble from got released?
Lord, how the elephant trouble from got released?

*

Record label: Hindi Kawali, Master Rameswak; accompanied by Gopi's East Indian Orchestra; recorded in Trinidad, Decca.

Of this song, Umesh writes: "This is a modern song. It explains a person who loves drinking and feels comfortable and loved while he is drunk. But I don't know why he mentions February. Perhaps during February something very important happened to the composer. In India, a song would mention the Hindu month, not the English."

29 ♫
Do not know [obscure] love keep doing.
Your what hand in liquor to cause to drink [before] go.
Now month February sorrow show.
Now month February sorrow show.
We guilty [sinful] for sake [obscure].
Do not know [obscure] love keep doing.
We guilty for sake of sorrow heart [obscure].

[record damaged; obscure]
[record damaged; obscure]
Now keep flowing.
Do not know [obscure] love keep doing.
Your wrist hand in [obscure] make drinking.

ꕥ

So, a true Indian, in a New England college setting far from his homeland, listens to old songs from a place he knew as Chīnītāt and remembers his grandfather in India long ago.

ꕥ Guru from India: Adesh

Guru H. S. Adesh came to Trinidad in 1966 as a representative of the Indian Council for Cultural Relations, New Delhi, India. He held this position for ten years. In 1976, he became the principal of Ashram College, San Fernando. Shortly after Adesh arrived, a group of student-disciples gathered around him. Usha Bissoondialsingh soon became a leader within this group. The focus of their work in the early years was the teaching of Hindi, Urdu, and Sanskrit, these being the subjects which his predecessors from the Indian Council had taught. Then Adesh added Indian classical music including instrumental traditions, vocal forms, music theory, and dance. By 1968, his group had incorporated itself as the Bharatiya Vidya Sansthhaan of Trinidad and Tobago.

Adesh brought a new perspective on the East Indian experience: "India is a grandmother, Trinidad a mother," he said. "The mother must be worshipped, but the grandmother also should be loved. Anyone who is born in Trinidad or who has accepted Trinidad as his land must first be loyal to Trinidad. But everyone has a link with the land of their forefathers, it is natural."

"Here I am seeing a small India of his imagination," said the famous Indian singer Hari Om Sharam on his 1973 visit to the Adesh Ashram.

The Guru is one of those rare personalities encountered from time to time in the world of music. Perhaps the many challenges of a musical life, practical and aesthetic, attract such exceptional individuals who combine extraordinary personal energy with creativity, administrative capabilities, and a way with people. Adesh is single-minded in his wish to educate Trinidad youth, likes to make things happen, and has a broad world view, reflected in his poetry on social and religious harmony on the island.

His students call him "Guru" ("teacher"), the "Revered Gurudev" ("godly" guru), and "Guruji" ("honored" guru). To these he protested, "I haven't reached that stage yet. I don't deserve that much reverence." He be-

PLATE 20. Guru Adesh tuning the *jal tarang* to *rāg jaūnpurī,* 15 August 1974.

longs to the Shankar *gharānā* ("school," "tradition"), which claims its origins in the Gwalior, Agra, and Rampur *gharānā* of the North and, in typically Indian fashion, traces its members and their musical style back to the fifteenth and sixteenth centuries and the great fathers of Indian music, Swami Hari Dās and the famous Mayan Tansen. The vocalist and tabla player, Dr. Tara Shankar Rakesh from Uttar Pradesh, was guru to Adesh.

Adesh calls himself "a musician by chance," and refers to music as his "hobby," but he is a fine vocalist in the north Indian tradition and a gifted performer on the sitar, tabla, *santūr* (box zither of Kashmir), and *jal tarang* (lit., "water wave"; an idiophone, a chime of china bowls tuned with water and beaten with two sticks; plate 20). He has written poems, stories, and tales, as well as impressive theoretical works on music and the dance. But his greatest love is music composition.

Adesh delegated many teaching responsibilities to his senior students, especially Usha, Amar, and Uma. Some 25 centers of the organization around the country, are run by his students. The center nearest Felicity is in Chaguanas, and classes in Hindi and music are held there. Adesh estimated that 1,000 new students joined the institute each year, and that of these, some 200 took the first-year Hindi examinations. In 1974 he reckoned that a total of 5,000 students had registered with the organization. The core of true devotees

PLATE 21. Amar Rajkumar, student of Guru Adesh, playing the *tabla* drum and singing *bhajan* with his wife, 1990.

that met on week nights for the advanced classes and *Swar Sansār* recitals was small—say 20 or 30. But Saturday morning brought hundreds of children to the gathering under the palms outside the Adesh Ashram, to learn language, to practice music, and to dance. During the 1980s, Adesh moved to Canada, but he visits both India and Trinidad on a regular basis. Amar, Usha, Uma and the other advanced students now run Trinidad centers (plate 21).

Adesh is fond of saying that his students range in age from eight to eighty—the younger pupils still in primary school, most of the older ones working. Uma, one of the best vocalists, was a salesgirl in Kirpilani's Department Store in Port of Spain. Usha was a school teacher. Amar worked for British West Indian Airways.

The students helped to prepare the Institute's many publications which include booklets of poems, songs, stories, and epics by the Guru. The most important perhaps is *Saptak* ("octave"), the core of the music curriculum. It consists of a series of eight graded texts written by Adesh; they take the student from the basic beginner's vocal exercises and easy songs through intermediate pieces to advanced compositions in difficult *rāgs* and *tāls.* The early volumes are in Hindi (Devanagari script), with Roman transliterations and English translations given for nearly all the material. For important songs, both a literal word-by-word translation and a free translation are given. The later volumes are exclusively in Hindi.

The eight volumes all follow the same pattern. Each opens with three or four *vandanā* (sung prayers) or *bhajan* composed by the Guru. Pitches are notated with *sargam* (solfeggio) syllables in Hindi following the widely used system introduced by Pandit V. N. Bhatkhande *(sa, re, ga, ma, pa, dha, ni, sa).* The *tāl* is indicated in the usual manner with Hindi numerals under the pitch syllables. The Hindi text in Devanagari script is given separately, and if a Roman transliteration or a literal translation is included, these are laid out below it.

Each session at the Adesh Ashram begins with the singing of the "Saraswatī Vandanā" (Prayer to Mother Saraswatī, goddess of music and learning), from the first volume of *Saptak* (ex. III: *swar lipi* ["notation"], *tāl rupak* [*rupak* rhythmic cycle], 7 *mātrā* [beats]).

Example III (song 30, CD track 2): Saraswatī Vandanā

Sa Sa 3	Dha – *Pa* 0 X	Ma Ma 2	Re – 3	Gare Ga Re 0 X	Sa – 2
Sa – 3	Ma Ma Pa 0 X	Dha – 2	Ni Sa 3	Dha – Pa 0 X	Ma – 2

Dha Ni	Sa – Ni	Sa –	Dha Ni	Sare Ga Re	Ga –
Sare Gama	Re – Ga	Sa Ni	Dha Ni	Sare Ga Re	Sa –
Sa Sa	Dha – Pa	Ma Ma	Re Re	Gare Ga Re	Sa –
Sa –	Ma Ma Pa	Dha –	Ni Sa	Dha – Pa	Ma –
3	0 X	2	3	0	2

SOURCE: *Saptak,* vol. 1, p. 7.

30 ♫
Prayer to Mother Saraswatī
Oh, Mother Saraswatī, grant me a boon of a new awakening.
Oh, Mother Sharada whose vehicle is the swan.
Oh, Goddess of speech, player of the *vīṇā*, Oh, Mother Saraswatī, grant me the boon of limitless knowledge of music.
Oh, Mother Saraswatī, grant me the boon that all ignorance shall be removed, *maya* [illusion] should not overpower me and my mind should not be entangled in delusion.
Oh, Mother Saraswatī, grant me the boon that my desires and thoughts should be free from lust, my *sadhana* should be fruitful, and a new phase, rhythm, and melody.
Oh, Mother Saraswatī, grant me the boon that truth be the charioteer of my life.
I shall do thy *ārtī* every day; and of prosperity, happiness, and honor.
Oh, Mother Saraswatī, grant that my mind and intellect and heart be pure, my character be impeccable, grant to me knowledge, modesty, and strength.
Oh, Mother Saraswatī, grant that we may live a hundred years drinking the nectar of happiness, giving us a secured place at thy feet.
Oh, Mother Saraswatī, grant that this universe be one family, their being equal love for all. Adesh the poet says grant me this high aim.
(*Saptak,* vol. 1, *Sangam,* 18)

Other songs by Adesh emphasize the beauty of Trinidad and its distinctive cultural integrity, as with "Karnivāl Kā Desh" (Country of Carnival). More advanced students use *sargam* musical notation in Devanagari script (ex. IV).

31 ♫
Country of Carnival
May this country of Carnival be always green and prosperous.
May the spring of happiness be in all directions.
May every flower be ever blossoming beautifully.
May the intoxication of love be in every heart.
May the zest for friendship be in every heart.
May not the cruel wheel of time defeat this country.
This land of chirping birds, this the land of flourishing rice.
This the heart's pride in the chain of the Western continent.
Mountains stand on her forehead.
In every direction, in South and North, engulfed in the net of the sea.
Loaded with fruits in every branch.
This the country of the young, old, and babe says the poet, Adesh.
(*Saptak,* vol. 3, *Rishabh,* 7)

Adesh's *bhajan* about Trinidad emphasize equality of races and respect for all religions as in "The Country of Trinidad."

Example IV (song 31, CD track 3): Karnivāl Kā Desh

कार्निवाल का देश

प स -। स रे स। रे ग -।ग ग -।ध प -।म ग -।स रे -।स ग -।
प स -। स स -।प ध -।प म -। म प
म प ।म ग -। स रे -। स ग

अन्तरा

प ग-।म प-।म प-।म प-।प ग-।म ध-।

---।म नि-।नि नि-।नि नि-।स ग-।रे स-।नि स-।

---।ग ग म।ग रे स।स नि स।नि ध म।म ध-।ध स-।

---।स स ग।रे-स।स नि स।नि ध प।म प-।म ग-।

---।स स-।स रे-।रे ग-।ग म म।म प-।म ग-।

---।प स-।स स-।प ध-।प म म।-प-।म ग-।स रे-।स ग-।

32 ☙
The Country of Trinidad

The charming island of Trinidad is beautifully situated in the yard of the ocean. In the chain of the Caribbean Islands, Trinidad has the same place as harmonic notes in a beautiful song.

The church of Mt. St. Benedict which smiles in the arms of the mountain, the Ethel Street of Lord Krishna, the Mosque of Noor-E-Islam and the beautiful beaches of Tobago are the attraction of this country, where there is no sign of conflict among the different races.

The country which is loved by two seasons, wet and dry, and where the clouds shower water abundantly. Its verdure removes the feelings of sadness and weariness from the heart of the spectator.

It seems as though this prosperous country is specially created by the hands of the Goddess of Nature. The poet Adesh says this country of cricket, calypso, soul, and humming bird looks like a living poetry of natural beauty.
(*Saptak*, vol. 4, *Gandhār*, 7)

Following the devotional songs, a large section is given over to the introduction of new *rāgs*. The text explains their *vādī* (principal important note), *saṃvādī* (secondary important note), *vivādī* (forbidden note), *ṭhāt* (family), *jāti* (class or category of the *rāg* according to the number of notes), *āroha* (ascending) and *avāroha* (descending) forms, *pakaḍ* (characteristic phrases), and *gāyan samay* (appropriate time for performance), followed by a number of practice pieces, usually *barā* (big) and *chhotā* (small) *khyāl* (an important classical vocal genre of north India).

The vocal material is followed by a section for string instruments, mainly sitar and mandolin. New *gat* (compositions) in different *rāgs* are introduced in *sargam* notation. A tabla section follows. It introduces new *tāls* and short practice pieces with their *bols* ("words," mnemonic syllables). Each volume closes with a page or two of definitions for important Indian musical terms.

The basic musical course contained in *Saptak* is supplemented by many smaller publications. *Jyoti* ("flame of knowledge"), "The First Hindi, Urdu, and Indian Music Monthly of Trinidad and Tobago," is the magazine of the Institute. Each issue contains the text and musical notation of a *bhajan* composed by the Guru. There are articles on Indian instruments, famous musicians, stories and poems, and news of individual members and forthcoming events. Some space is always devoted to the performances of the Guru or his students on radio and television.

In volume 8, numbers 1–12 (July 1975 to June 1976), for example, *Jyoti* contained twelve *bhajan,* five stories in Hindi, a Vedic (Sanskrit) prayer with English translation, one Urdu lesson, articles on the tabla and *tamburā,* an outline of the Hindi and music examinations of the Institute and (months later) the exam results, a special camp issue, four items concerning the relationship of guru and disciple, and the following feature articles: "Kabir Das" and "Tulsi Das" (saints), "Ameer Khusaro" (musician and composer), "Dusserah in Mysore," "Diwali in Maharashtra," "Kumbh Mela" (religious festivals), "Why Learn Sanskrit," "Children's Corner—The Lazy Man and a Thief," "Life Sketches of Some Great Musicians," "Definitions of Musical Terms," "Temples and Mosques in Trinidad," and "Hindi in Trinidad."

In addition to the publishing program and weekly classes, the Institute sponsors a week-long camp every April at Balendra on the eastern coast of the island. Some two hundred students of all ages attend. The main camp activities are instrumental and vocal music classes, lectures on Indian culture by the Guru, Hindi, Sanskrit, and Urdu poetry recitations, formal debates ("Mothers are the real protectors of moral values," "The study of Indian languages and music is the only means of preserving Indian culture in the Western hemisphere"), dramatic productions by the campers, outdoor games (swimming is prohibited), and films supplied by the India High Commission.

Adesh modeled the curriculum, the examinations, and the degrees of the Institute after the music courses at several Indian schools and universities: four degrees offered in vocal or instrumental music and three in dance, instrumental examinations offered on the sitar, mandolin, violin, *esrāj, sarod, sāraṇgī,* tabla, *pakhāwaj,* and *ḍholak.*

The exams are based on the eight parts of *Saptak* as well as *Hindustānī-Sangīta-Paddhati* and *Kramik-Pustak-Mālikā* of V. N. Bhatkhande. Up to the sixth year, the examinations are in two parts, theoretical and practical (performance). The theory paper always included definitions of important terms in Indian music, the notation of songs in Hindi with English translations, and the writing of *tāl* and their *ṭhekā* (basic pattern) in Hindi notation. Beginning with the second-year "Sangeet Pravesh" exam, short essays are required, for example: second year—"Film Music," "My Favorite Singer," "My Favorite Ragas," and "My Favorite Concert Instrumental Player"; third year—"Importance of Vadi Swar in a Raga," "Indian Classical Music," "Any Music Conferences Which You Have Attended," "Importance of Taal in Music," "Music and Human Life," and "Indian Music in Trinidad"; fourth year—"Folk Music of India," "Music is the Best Source of Devotion," "Nature and Music," "Music and Life," "Taal is the Soul of Music and Sam is the Soul of Taal," and "Kinds of Indian Instruments"; fifth year—"Khyal and Dhrupad," "Classical Music and Folk Music," and "Utilities and Scope of Indian Music"; sixth year—"Harmonium and Tanpura," "Music and Health," "Literature and Music," "Music is a Universal Language," and "Short History of Indian Music up to the Eighteenth Century."

The seven-year degree is considered equivalent to a university bachelor's degree, and the exam is more advanced, with its administration strictly controlled. A thesis of fifty typewritten pages or an exam essay of fifteen handwritten pages (in Hindi or English) is required in addition to the theoretical and practical portions. The theoretical section includes essays on the principles and philosophy of Indian music, the comparative study of north and south Indian music, and also the writing of Indian songs in Western notation and Western songs in Indian notation. Outside examiners from India grade the practical performance section, which the candidate records on a cassette.

When I first met the Guru I had been in Felicity for just six days. On one of my taxi rides I met a driver who volunteered to take me to a "musical function." With no idea of what to expect, I packed up my tape recorder, microphones, some tape, and we set out. Those were to be the first field recordings I ever made. I later learned much about what the tapes contain: the musicians, the songs, *rāg, tāl,* style, the significance of the occasion—Guru

Pūrnimā—the night of the full moon of the Hindu month of Ashhar (July) set aside each year to honor teachers. I made hasty notes during the course of the evening:

> This appears to be a religious function—men and women in traditional Indian dress are seated on the floor. Songs are accompanied by tabla drums and *tamburā.* While the girl sings she holds a sheet of music. Her voice is overpowered by the instruments. The song is a *bhajan.* People keep drifting in, all in formal Indian dress. Applause after each number. A concert, not a religious function? They are following a program. A very "renaissance" affair.

Having anticipated her idea, I was not surprised later to read Usha Bissoondialsingh's article, "A Renaissance of Indian Music in Trinidad" (*Jyoti* 9, no. 1: 10).

> The last decade between the years 1966 and 1976 has seen not only a musical but a whole cultural renaissance in Trinidad. These were the years when Hindi, the religious and cultural language was almost dead, particularly where the younger generations were concerned. There no longer was love for the language nor the desire to learn. Even the Hindi dialects (different provincial languages brought here by our various ancestors) were dying out with the older heads. . . . Since there was a total absence of the true classical forms of Indian music and since there was no basis on which to teach or carry on the tradition except by ear, our musical forms were fast being assimilated in Western music, especially since almost the entire film world of India is moving after Western music.
>
> It is at this crucial point that a son of mother India in the person of Prof. H. S. Adesh, M.A., arrived on this soil to place the Indian culture on the high pedestal on which it now stands. . . . On his arrival here . . . seeing the almost total absence of Hindi as a language and the total absence of the music forms of India, he there and then vowed to introduce Indian music to a people who could not tell anything about raagas or taals or anything what they know about Indian music except what they know from films or records.

Usha's thesis, "Dhrupad Singing in Trinidad," written in 1973, gives some of the background for this "renaissance," including a short history of Indian music in Trinidad (the quotations that follow are from pages 42–49).

ჯ MUSIC STUDENT: USHA

Like Ramaya, Usha begins by describing the hardships of the indenture years and the paucity of music. Both accounts agree that the Indian music of this early period was folk music, but Usha chooses to stress the importance of oral transmission as a criterion of folk culture.

> When our people were brought into their new home, music was brought with them from the paguna (village) the zilla (or districts) or the shahar (town) from which they came, but weighing this against the background of hardships, sup-

> pression, neglection and separation which they had to undergo as a people, what could be expected out of their musical forms but "folk music." . . . Whenever they had the opportunity, they gathered together singing their folk songs. These folk communities did not have the means to record their music or songs, they had no choice but to tell their songs and tales through "word of mouth."

Usha uses evidence from modern folk practices in Trinidad to reconstruct a picture of the musical life of the nineteenth century: songs, including *sohar* and wedding songs, accompanied the events of the life cycle; songs for the annual cycle included *kajarī* for rice planting, *birahā, chautāl, ulārā,* and *jhūmar* for the Holī festival, and many others. Usha concludes that Trinidadian folk songs are a degenerated form of Indian classical music.

> Indian classical music, though to a limited extent, found at the beginning of the 20th century, lived through two generations with constant change, and then degenerated into nothing more than folk music with the passage of time. . . . With the coming of the "Matla Jahaj" . . . to Trinidad about 1910, some Musicians like Imami, Firamat (known in his day as "Firimtad"), Bel Begai ("Gulam Hosein"), Bahadur Syne, Ali Jaan, Kalloo . . . and Fakir Mohammed came. Earlier than their arrival was Ustad Ramcharan and his brother Lakshman etc. These were the men directly responsible for the introduction of some classical forms into this country. To what extent, however, these forms, after a mere generation and a half, could stand the test against the authentic classical forms of India, will be seen by the knowledge of these forms amongst the acclaimed classical musicians and singers here.

As part of her research, Usha did fieldwork among the descendants of these early classical singers. She asked them what *rāg*s their parents and grandparents knew, and about the latest instruments they brought from India or made in Trinidad. Usha discovered that musicians only knew the names of a few well-known north Indian *rāg*s, and that only a few popular instruments had found their way to Trinidad before 1900.

> Through the many interviews with the local "classical singers" . . . it can be clearly seen that these men who came around 1910 brought with them the knowledge of a few popular raagas like bhairav, bhairavi, kaffee, malhar, kalingara (they call it "kalangara"), desh, malkosh, pelu, shyam-kalyan, bihag, saarang, poorvi (called here "poorbi") and assawari. These were the names of the raagas which I came across during my interviews. . . . On the instrumental side, sitar, sarange (mention of one local tanpura, made and used by "Imami"), dholak, mangeera, tabla and mridang found their way here. (A miniature sarangi made by the father of Jhagru Qawal, a traditional classical singer, was shown to me.)

Usha assumes the original function of the *rāg* as a modal form had been forgotten in Trinidad, that the second generation of performers used the name *rāg* simply to identify melodies or well-known local compositions. She outlines the transformation of the repertory from the original versions of the early indentured laborers to distinctively Trinidadian forms.

> Using the tunes of these "compositions" as the main "melody" of the raagas, the new generations of singers put tunes to the poems of Surdas, Tulsī Dās, Mīrābāī, Mahatma Kabir, etc. (whose books of poems with only name of raaga printed next to them which either found their way here or were imported from India), and sang them, calling them by the names of raagas. With the passage of time and the lack of knowledge, all these tunes were mixed up, resulting in the name of a raaga being given to a song or composition which bears no resemblance to the melody of that particular raaga.

In many cases, the names of *rāgs* were forgotten until their re-introduction in recent years through Indian films, books, and records, and by the teachings of Guru Adesh.

> Today, after a mere 50 years or a generation and a half, even the "names" of these raagas were recalled with difficulty; and it must be born in mind that the knowledge of raagas have been introduced authentically since 1966 all over the country to the thousands of students who learn them.
>
> Apart from this, the availability of books, magazines, music albums (of records) and films etc., have all helped in recent times to keep alive the names of these raagas.

During her interviews Usha found little resemblance between local Trinidadian compositions named after traditional *rāgs* and the corresponding classical Indian *rāg.*

> From my interviews with the cream of the remaining "traditional" classical singers here (Ustad Jhagroo Kawal, Mr. Ramcharitar, Mr. Hanniff Mohammed, Mr. Edoo Khan (aged 82), Mr. Abdul "Kush" Rajah, and others like Mr. Asgar Ali (dealer in books), Mr. Ramdeen Chotoo (chowtal expert) etc. and by detailed examination of the specimens of the styles of singing (dhrupad, dhamaar, khyal, thumri, tarana, tappa, chaturang etc.) I have found no authentic piece, except thumris and gazals. There is a slight trace of dhrupad (which is known as "dhurpat") but it does not resemble the authentic dhrupads. Among the remaining classical singers, a little picture of raaga bhairav could be given by Mr. Ramcharitar (being remembered as an "air" or "tune"). When the difference between bhairav and bhairavi was asked, between kaffee and bihag, no answer could be obtained, either by way of explanation or by demonstration.

In conclusion, Usha finds vast differences between the system of local music in Trinidad, past and present, and the classical music of India.

> In the words of Pundit Adhikari (famous pakhawaj and tabla player who visited Trinidad in the 1960s, "Brother, I am unable to accompany you as we don't have these styles of singing in India."

> After the earliest pioneers left their compositions of dhrupads, taranas, thumris, etc., these songs were learnt and the future generations tried to carry on these styles by putting tunes to the poems of the great poets, found in books. Compositions in verse form only were taken from these books and, on the basis of the tunes of the existing dhrupads, gazals etc., tunes were put to these new compositions. With the course of time, one tune was mixed with another, the taals were forgotten because they were never understood beyond imitation, one raag was mistaken for another, and the outcome today is a music which cannot be comprehended by the musicians of India who cling firmly to the authentic classical system handed down to them through the ages. The music which is found in Trinidad, Guyana and Surinam are entirely different, as the language of the compositions have become outdated, the language of Hindi became less known to the singers and musicians, and above all, the little art form which was brought was lost with time.

ဢ

By the time I got back to Felicity after my silent day in the library, it was evening, and the darkness was, as always, filled with the night sounds of the village—the tree toads, the jukeboxes and the dogs. After supper, I escaped to my room to sort out my notes. Ramaya's account had much in common with Usha's—the descriptions of the folk songs of the nineteenth century, the ambiguity over the exact nature of the local classical style (and its relationship with north Indian classical music), and above all, the constant interplay between continuity (even stagnation) and change. Their findings coincided only in part with my own in Felicity. The folk songs which survived in the village seemed surely to date back to the indenture period, and I hoped that my collection of variants would reveal something of the changes over the intervening years. I had not heard the local classical repertory in Felicity, although people remembered it. The interplay between continuity and change was evident in all types of music, the love of the old and the fascination with the new, clinging to tradition and craving the novel.

Both Ramaya and Usha understood the need of local musicians for new material from India. This too, was true of Felicity village: the many Indian records and cassettes, the families gathered around the television on Sunday afternoons to watch the Indian films, the trips to the theater in Chaguanas every Saturday to see Indian films, the journeys to India, the adoption of the Sai Baba faith—the songs, the films, the icons, the tears of honey: all evidence of an inescapable link with their motherland. It was inconceivable to the Felicity villagers, as it was to Ramaya and to Usha, that Trinidad should ever be cut off from South Asia—this, for them, the ultimate source of musical inspiration. For these two local scholars, the landmarks of local music history were the contacts with this source—films and records beginning in the 1930s and Guru Adesh's arrival in the 1960s.

Much as they agreed about the past, the changes for the future they envisaged were quite different. The change Usha sought was a purification of local music, a rejection of local developments, and a return to authentic Indian classical forms. The change that Ramaya sought was in the direction of innovation and acculturation—adding harmonies to Indian melodies, using calypso rhythms in Indian film songs—combining the traditions of the East with the best of the West.

Musical developments since their writings show that it is Ramaya's hopes for change that are being realized at the end of the twentieth century.

ঌ Chapter Eight ঌ
Wedding Day

My father has cut green bamboo;
He has thatched the wedding canopy with betel leaves.

Traditional Bhojpurī Song

One Sunday morning, halfway through my first visit, I awoke alert with anticipation. This day I would not be making my usual dawn visit to one of the Felicity temples. This Sunday was the wedding day of Sankey's son, and it would be my first opportunity to hear many songs of the traditional wedding repertory. I walked down Cacandee Road and could see at a distance the crowd of women already gathered outside Sankey's house. As I arrived, she was seated in the center of the group, amid her many friends and relatives. Her sun-toughened skin, prematurely aged, and her furrowed brow revealed the toil of years in the cane fields. She held her small body rigid and upright. Only her eyes were turned downward. She was wearing a new dress, made especially for the occasion; on her head was the *māur,* the crown of Rām, white and sparkling with bits of mirror and glass.

Her son was dressed entirely in white, in the costume of Rām, the prince. He sat at his mother's feet, facing away from her, looking out toward Cacandee Road. As I drew near and began to photograph the scene, I could see that Sankey was touching her son's head with the end of her *oḍhanī* ("veil"; Indian Bhojpurī *āchalwā,* the end of the sari), held in her left hand (plate 22). His face showed no emotion. The couple remained silent and motionless as the aunts, the sisters, and the sisters-in-law came forward one by one to perform the ritual washing and dressing of the groom—bathing his feet, offering him socks and shoes, placing rings on his fingers and gold *mālā* (chains) around his neck. The singers, a group of older women, stood behind Sankey. (At other village weddings, Sankey herself, one of the finest singers in Felicity, would have been the leader of this group.) When the crown was taken from her head and placed on her son's, the ladies began to sing one of the many traditional wedding songs about the marriage of Sītā and Rām and about events attending that perfect love.

ঌ The Wedding Ritual

Thirty or forty years ago, Hindu weddings in Trinidad always took place at night. The complex process of calculating an "auspicious" date for the marriage was undertaken by the family pandit who, in order to determine the

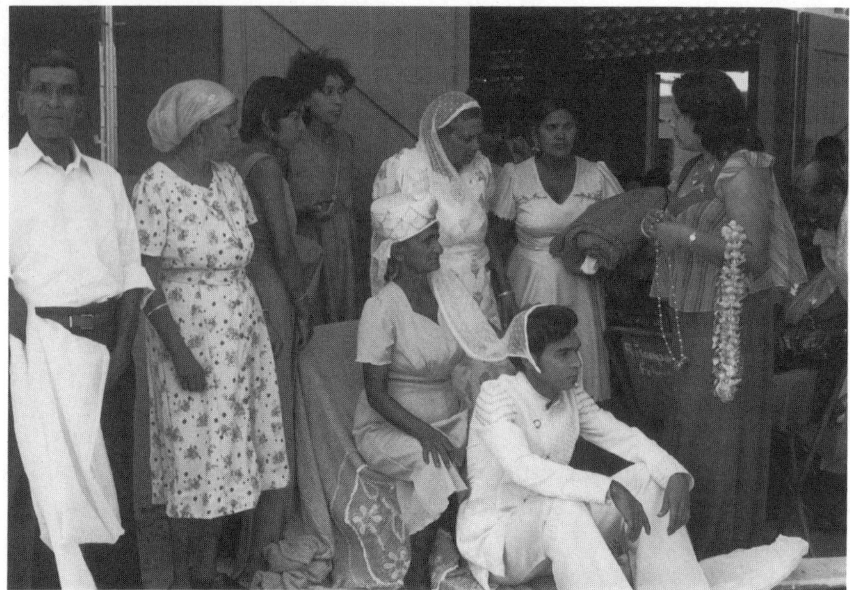

Plate 22. Sankey Ramroop offering her son the protection of her *ānchal* on the morning of his wedding, 1977.

exact time of year and day of week when conditions would be most favorable for the ceremony, studied the horoscopes of the *dulahin* (bride) and the *dulahā* (bridegroom) in his great astrological compendium, the *Patrā*.

In India auspicious dates still are taken very seriously: for certain years, only two or three auspicious dates are available, while for other years many appropriate dates can be determined according to the astrological charts. In modern Trinidad the calculation of wedding dates has become somewhat of a formality. Indeed, most Trinidad weddings conveniently occur on a Sunday. "Every Sunday is a wedding day. Every Sunday is auspicious day now," Suruj Pandit told me.

In India local pandits jealously guard their astrological knowledge and are not willing to announce wedding dates months in advance. To choose a date a pandit analyzes the horoscopes of both bride and groom and collates these findings with the celestial charts. The wedding parties expect this information to be auspicious, and are willing to pay the pandit and wait for the insurance it provides the couple. In Indian cities, the younger generation, who practice "love marriages," dismiss this custom as backward superstition, but in Bhojpurī villages you would be hard put to find a family willing to ignore the time-honored tradition.

On such an auspicious day in a Bhojpurī village, the villager will hear songs for the bride from one family home, songs for the groom from another wedding nearby, brass bands of the *bārāt* (groomsmen) processing into the village, women's singing, all-night drumming from many courtyards, firecrackers from here, gunshots from there, all at once—nothing resembling the systematic analysis of a musicologist. Indian village families have spent years of their lives arranging what might appear to the visitor a cacophony of noise and social disarray.

In Trinidad, following three days of of ritual preparation, the couple are married at the home of the bride's parents. These weddings "under the bamboo" ("My father is cutting green bamboo," ex. XIV; so named for the *marawā,* the wedding canopy or "tent," erected for the celebration) were not recognized by the British colonial government in Trinidad until 1945. In recent years, the traditional weeklong ceremony has been shortened. Whatever day and date the horoscope suggests, for convenience the ritual preparations almost always begin on a Friday night with the *tāssā* procession to a village pond or well for the *mātīkonwā* ceremony. This is followed by application of turmeric to the bride and groom, the *hardī uthāway,* a ritual to lighten and beautify the skin. Saturday night is the "cooking night," *bhatwān ki rāt* (preparation of the special wedding foods), and Sunday is the day of the wedding with ritual, feasting, and celebrations at the homes of the bride and the groom.

Kamini described the *mātīkonwā* and *hardī uthāway* as follows: "Friday of the wedding: Mother prepare a tray with *sindūr* [vermilion], *khurma* [sweets], *dāl* [lentils], *pān* [betel] leaves, oil. Proceed with a procession of ladies accompanied with *tāssā* drumming [ex. V; plates 24 and 25] and singing to a well or a house some distance away from wedding house. The tray is carried on the bride or groom unmarried sister's head. If no unmarried sisters, an unmarried cousin (person must be unmarried). Sister also carry a 'cutlass.' A clean site is chosen, mother dips ring finger in oil and place in five places, then she places five *pān* leaves on top of oil (one leaf for one drop of oil). Mother places *dāl* soaked in sugar *khurma.* Sister dig a hole in the dirt in five places and give some dirt to mother who tie it to her *oḍhanī* and place it on the tray. Sister then share *khurma* with all guests present. Mother places *sindūr* on all married women heads who husband had already put *sindūr* for them on their wedding day [ex. XVI]. Return to wedding house. On arrival, father's sister take dirt and place it on a *kalasā* [see text of exx. XIX, XX]. Mother brings *lotā* of water from well and put the water in a *kalasā* and light a *diyā* and pandit starts the *pūjā.* Five unmarried girls each rub the bride and groom from head to toe with *hardī.*"

Moon sang this song for the ritual of the *hardī:*

33 ꧋

Where of *haldī,*
Our bride goddess such tender is.
Bear not with not know,
Haldī of jealousy.
Bear not with not know,
Haldī of jealousy.
Saṭhī of fresh rice cook.
Kiss she walks whose Rāma daughter are.
Kiss he walking,
Whose Rāma daughter is.
Forehead she kiss-kiss.
Gives blessings.
Live long my bride-bridegroom,
Million years.
Live long my bride-bridegroom,
Million years.

For the Saturday, Kamini explains: "Mother, aunts, neighbors, friends, sisters, relatives help peel mangoes, melongenes [*bigan*], pumpkin, and other things to cook. Night—put *hardī* three times five people. Once before breakfast. Once before lunch. Once before supper." For the *bhatwān ki rāt* she says: "Father sisters parch *lāwā* (puffed rice). Sing and dance [ex. VI]. Mother give aunt gifts and money for parching *lāwā* [text of exx. XIX, XXI]. Indian orchestra if desired. Mike is playing Indian records." For the Sunday morning *lāwā* ceremony she explains: "Mother, sister with tray on head, accompanied by ladies singing to beat of *tāssā* drums return to well or house they went to on Friday night [ex. XV]. The same process is repeated. Return to wedding house. *Hardī* is rubbed on three times. Boy washes and after, *hardī* is rinsed off. Some of the water from final wash is collected in a bottle. Groom dresses and accompanied by his father and sister in the wedding car to proceed to bride's home. The sister takes the ring and gift to bride. They are accompanied by mike, *tāssā,* and guests to bride's home. Groom's mother, friends, and relatives to beat drum, dance, and sing while waiting for groom to bring his bride home. At the bride's home, the groom arrive, bride's father goes out on road to welcome groom and father."

A village song describes this part of the ceremony:

34 ꧋

Father, what bridegroom kept searching.
Father, what bridegroom kept searching.
Father, the same bridegroom stand in wedding tent.

Father, the same bridegroom stand in wedding tent.
Father, bring the sandalwood stool.
Father, bring the sandalwood stool.
Father, arm holding make sit.
Father, arm holding make sit.
Father, his *ārtī* perform.
Father, his *ārtī* perform.

Kamini continues: "*Kanyādān pūjā* [donation of the virgin daughter] with bride wearing yellow sari [ex. XIV], ceremony with bride now wearing red sari and groom in *kurtā* and dhoti. *Pārv pūjā, kicharī* [money given to groom by the bride's family], bride then change into white wedding dress and groom change into a suit, or bride remain in red sari and groom in *kurtā* and dhoti. Bride and groom leave for groom's home. Welcome by groom's mother. Friday night, Saturday night, and Sunday morning is the same procedures for both bride and groom."

Every Hindu wedding in Felicity includes a considerable variety of music—both live and recorded. Music is performed at the home of the bride ("the girl's side") and at the home of the groom ("boy's side"), and also in various processions from one side to the other, as shown in table 3.

❦ TĀSSĀ

Today, as a guest of the groom, I would hear *lachārī,* lively leader–chorus songs, some with slyly bawdy texts, accompanied by north Indian folk instruments such as the *ḍholak, manjīrā, ḍhantāl,* and *kartāl,* blending coherently with the clattering West Indian shak shak rattles. And I wanted to dance with the ladies. On other Sundays, as a guest of the bride, I had photographed the bride, dressed in her red wedding sari and adorned with jewels (plate 23), had witnessed the somber rituals of the marriage ceremony, and had recorded the unaccompanied *byāh ke gīt,* the serious wedding songs, relating events from the great *Rāmāyaṇ* epic (exx. VII–XXI). The distinction between sober *byāh ke gīt* and light-hearted *lachārī* derives from northeastern villages where the unaccompanied ritual songs are called *vivāha* or *vivāh* (cognate with the Trinidad term *byāh*) and the bawdy and abusive type are known variously according to district as *lachārī, lachī, nakaṭā,* and *jhūmar.* In Banaras and its environs, *lachārī* are sung with verve.

After spending an entire day at Sankey's, the groom's house, my bag was bulging with recordings of the laughter and the shouting, the singing and the drumming.

After the ritual of dressing the groom, Sankey performed *ārtī* (the offering of fire) for her son by circing a *diyā* before him. While she did this, the ladies

TABLE 3 *Music for the Wedding, Felicity*

Friday	Saturday	Sunday
Evening (home of bride and groom): *Mātīkonwā Ceremony* (Procession to the well) procession with tāssā lachārī byāh ke gīt dancing *Hardī Uthāway (Chumay Hardī)* (Rubbing of saffron) byāh ke gīt	Evening (bride and groom): *Bhatwān ki Rāt* (Cooking night, rice night) hired Indian orchestra (live Indian film songs) or "Mike" playing recorded Indian film songs lachārī dancing	Morning (bride and groom): *Lāwā Ceremony* (Parching of rice) procession with tāssā lachārī byāh ke gīt dancing *Hardī Uthāway* (Rubbing of saffron) byāh ke gīt Afternoon (bride's house): *Wedding Ceremony Proper* (including kicharī khawaryā, pārv pūjā, and kanyādān) byāh ke gīt hired Indian Orchestra (Indian film songs) Afternoon (groom's house): Ladies' Party lachārī dancing

sang the appropriate *byāh ke gīt* for the offering of *ārtī.* Then he was driven off in a procession *(bārāt)* with the family men to the bride's home, while other cars with wedding guests and an entourage of musicians and guests went on foot. The *bārāt* is led by drummers.

Two villagers play *tāssā* (clay kettledrums about 35 cm in diameter and 20 cm deep) and a third plays the large double-headed cylindrical drum known in Trinidad as the "bass" (plates 24, 25). The *tāssā* are suspended from the drummer's neck by a strap and struck with two sticks ("chupes"). The bass is hollowed out from a solid section of tree trunk, and has heads about 60 centimeters in diameter. The drum is suspended on a strap slung over the shoulder and across the back, and is struck with a short curved stick. Both

PLATE 23. Felicity bride.

Plate 24. Dhanlal Samooj playing the *tāssā* drum at a Felicity wedding, 1985.

tāssā and bass have goatskin heads, firmly laced to the shell. The bass weighs about 50 pounds, and therefore, I was told by village drummers, cannot be played for more than twenty minutes. The *tāssā* must be tuned about every twenty minutes by heating the head over an open fire (plate 26), so the drum ensemble takes a break two or three times an hour. The drums are

Plate 25. Felicity drummer plays the heavy bass drum to accompany the wedding *tāssā,* 1985.

accompanied by two men playing *jhāl,* brass cymbals about 20 centimeters in diameter, adding a shimmering zing to the punctuated, driving drumming.

More than a dozen "hands," rhythmic cycles with variations, are played on the *tāssā* (also on the *nagārā* and *ḍholak*). Many hands are named for the genre they accompany: *tillānā, ṭhumrī, ghazal, chautāl, jhūmar, laig, naichal, kabīr,*

PLATE 26. Dhanlal Samooj tuning the goatskin head of his earthenware *tāssā* drum at an open fire, Felicity, 1985. The drummer strikes the head with the chupes (thin beaters) until the membrane tightens to the desired pitch.

and *ulārā.* Some are named after the religious festival they accompany ("wedding," "Rāmlīlā," "Hosay"). Some hands have old Bhojpurī names (such as *bhāratī,* a popular *ḍholak* hand often used to accompany *bhajan*) and others modern English titles ("one-way drum," also for *ḍholak*). Some have been borrowed from popular Indian films ("Kohinur"); others take their names from Creole culture ("kalinda," "calypso-steel band"). Hands may also be named after the type of drum on which they are most frequently played such as the *nagārā* and *tāssā.* "*Tāssā* hand" has several subcategories including "wedding drum," "olé," *tikura,* and "steel band."

The drumming for Sankey's son typifies *tāssā* style, consisting of a series of hands, each lasting two or three minutes. The leading *tāssā* player introduces every new hand ("to cut"); the bass and *jhāl* join in as soon as the complete pattern has been played once. The second *tāssā* "takes up" the pattern played by the lead player ("to fulay"), another example of the typical leader–chorus form of Felicity music. Both *tāssā* play variations on the basic pattern,

Example V: *Tāssā* Drumming (CD track 4)

a. Hand 1

b. Hand 2

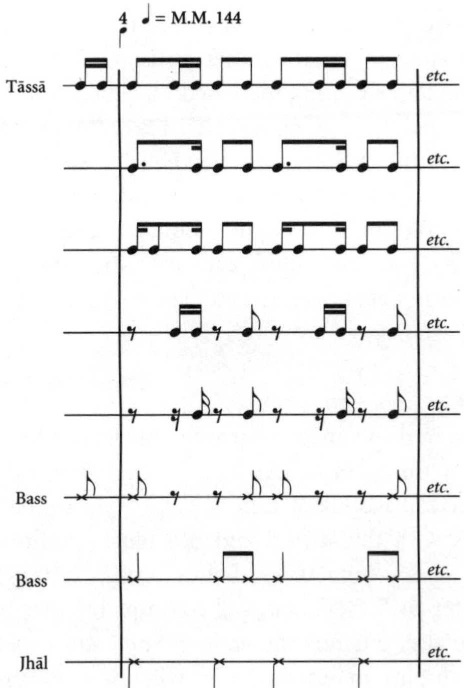

sometimes the two drums play in unison, but interlocking patterns are most common.

Every hand is subdivided into several sections, each 20 to 50 seconds long, and ending in a cadence that village drummers call the *tāl.* After several subsections in a hand have been played, the lead drummer moves on, without break, to the next hand, usually with a tempo change, as in example V, in which hand 1 is around a quarter note = M.M. 176 and hand 2 a quarter note = M.M. 144.

Sunday Afternoon, the Boy's House

The *bārāt* procession had left Sankey's house around one o'clock. Hindu custom dictates that Sankey and her sisters would not witness the actual moment of marriage, when the couple are covered with a large cloth and the groom smears the blood-red *sindūr* in the parting of the bride's hair. Sankey had said farewell to a bachelor son, and there were now three or four hours to occupy before she would greet him for the first time as a married man. And nothing to do but eat and drink, sing and dance.

So engaged, the hours passed rapidly for our group of ladies. Seven or eight of them soon gathered around Sankey with their instruments and began to sing *lachārī* (plates 27, 28), taking turns choosing songs and playing the various instruments. The session grew livelier and louder as the afternoon progressed. As they sang, women in the gathering listened, chatted, ate, and drank, and, as the laughing and shouting increased, they began to dance, sometimes alone, sometimes in pairs, dragging their friends up to join them, two or three dancing at the same time. Never had I seen Felicity women behaving so candidly—for some dances they used crude props! With no men around the women felt free to joke about the male mentality, and the gags and gestures were sexy and funny. I ate and drank rum with the others, and watched the dancing. Then the ladies dragged me up to dance with them. The *lachārī* songs were fast, hot, and exciting.

Lachārī

Most *lachārī* are in duple meter. Each line of the Bhojpurī text is repeated responsorially many times (*saiyā̃ lāge hamār / kaise ke mārõ nazariyā?*; "he is my husband / how can I blink at him?"). The texts are based on jokes and abuse and love, as with the *lachārī* and *gālī* (*gārī*) traditions of Uttar Pradesh. *Āre Nadiyā Kināre* (ex. VI, see below in this section) tells of a wife's jealousy of her sister-in-law *(nanadī).* She complains that her husband is in love with someone else, possibly the *nanadī.* She casts a spell of night blindness (*rataunī:* nyctalopia) on him so that he will not love another woman. The

PLATE 27. Village women dancing and singing *lachārī* to the accompaniment of the *ḍholak* during the wedding celebration at Sankey Ramroop's house, 1977.

PLATE 28. Channerdaye Ramdhanie's mother playing the *ḍholak* at her grandson's wedding, Felicity, 1985.

wife eventually removes the spell and sings, "Oh, I love him, I love him, I love him. . . . He is walking along the road with his balls swinging!" (repeated as a refrain, with hearty laughing). *Lachārī* such as this are sung with a loud robust vocal timbre. The women sang seventeen *lachārī* during the festivities at Sankey's house.

Lachārī are great fun for women in both Trinidad and India, surprising perhaps since their texts often express the poignant loneliness, fear, and disillusionment of the village wife. One evening Matti held a party and the ladies sang laughingly to entertain me and themselves:

35 ☙
Night husband not arrived. Who bewitch?
Night food not ate. Who bewitch?
Night husband not arrived. Mohan bewitch.
Night Gerua not drank. Who bewitch?
Night husband not arrived. Who bewitch?
Night betel not chewed. Who bewitch?
Own husband betel not chewed. Who bewitched?

Who bewitch? Who bewitch?
Night husband not arrived. Who bewitch?
Bed spread, incense lit.
Night bed not slept. Who bewitch?
Night husband not arrive. Who bewitch?

What makes the women laugh? That it should come as no surprise that men are fickle and women fools for their men? That misunderstandings between husband and wife—lover's quarrels—are common enough and indeed funny when compared with the real tragedy of life in village India—poverty, hunger, sudden death from tropical illnesses, infant malnutrition, and the extremely high incidence of infant mortality?

The *sanātan dharma* ("eternal doctrine") to which villagers, Trinidadian and Indian, claim allegiance incorporates in its system of social organization and religious doctrine both good and evil, mixed and conflicting feelings, and the conflict of the unpredictable and predictable forces of nature. Hinduism advises the appeasement of the forces of evil and teaches that no creation can occur without destruction.

Lachārī draw on that style of Hinduism reflected in the *Māhābhārata,* the tales of Krishna, rather than the stories of the *Rāmāyaṇ,* India's other great epic, telling of the exploits of Rām. Most *byāh ke gīt* focus on the honor of Rām and the faithfulness of Sītā. Embedded in *lachārī,* however, are the playful and mischievous exploits of Krishna, who was the archetypical playboy with his entourage of *gopī* (milkmaids) making love under the new moon in the pleasant groves of Brindāban. The many classical dance styles of India depict, with graceful and explicit gesture, the actions and emotions of Rādha the favorite *gopī,* preparing for Krishna's arrival in the night. She bathes, washes and combs her hair, applies *kājal* around her eyes, puts on ornaments, looks in the mirror. Krishna arrives late, perhaps drunk, with the scent of another woman's perfume on his person. Rādha pushes him away, but when he plays his flute (a phallic symbol) Rādha forgives him all and succumbs to his romantic advances. Village women understand the lessons of these ancient tales, and there is every opportunity in the 1990s to review these myths through religious films and via the two extremely popular television series, launched in India in the mid-1980s, first the *Rāmāyaṇ* and then the *Māhābhārata,* running to over 100 episodes.

Perhaps the serious epic *byāh ke gīt* repertory is dying out, but the *lachārī* repertory seems very much alive. The ladies have no difficulty in recalling the words (a common problem with the *byāh ke gīt*), since the *lachārī* texts have shorter lines that the women repeat again and again, probably because they

Example VI (song 36, CD track 5): Āre Nadiyā Kināre

Example VI Concluded

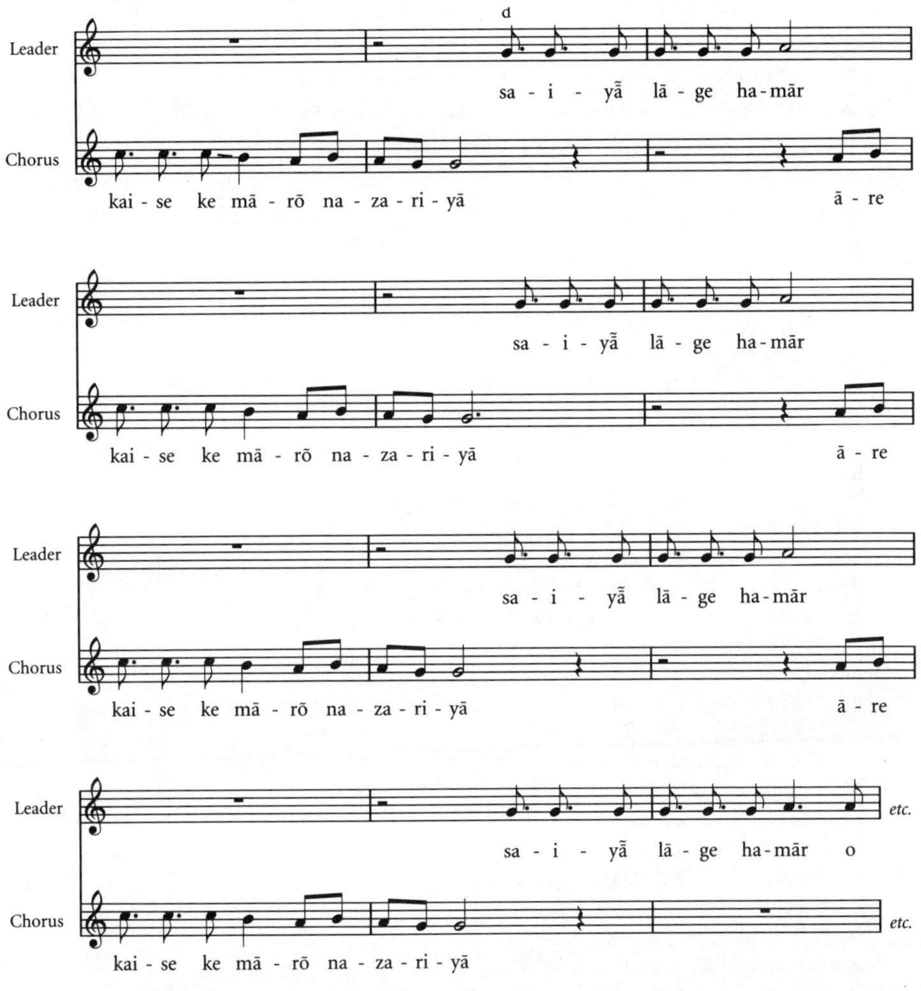

d

Leader
sa - i - yā̃ lā - ge ha - mār

Chorus
kai - se ke mā - rõ na - za - ri - yā ā - re

Leader
sa - i - yā̃ lā - ge ha - mār

Chorus
kai - se ke mā - rõ na - za - ri - yā ā - re

Leader
sa - i - yā̃ lā - ge ha - mār

Chorus
kai - se ke mā - rõ na - za - ri - yā ā - re

Leader
sa - i - yā̃ lā - ge ha - mār o *etc.*

Chorus
kai - se ke mā - rõ na - za - ri - yā *etc.*

are fun to sing. The tunes are well-known, perhaps due to their metrical simplicity. The accompaniment of drum and idiophones together with the frequent repetition of short lines and the overlap of parts (often two beats) lend the performance a vitality and immediacy and zest lacking in the *byāh ke gīt.* As the party progressed some women began singing both parts, starting with the leader's part and then jumping immediately to the chorus. Might the *lachārī* repertory outlast the *byāh ke gīt?* Could any of these arcane Bhojpurī songs endure? Worries of the ethnomusicologist. And of the older women I sang with.

EXAMPLE VI
Āre Nadiyā Kināre

āre nadiyā kināre chhāye bāgalā
opar baiṭhe nabāb, opar baiṭhe nabāb
āre kaise ke mārõ nazariyā, o kaise ke mārõ nazariyā
saiyā̃ lāge hamār
kaise ke mārõ nazariyā
bāke [?mistake, lāge] hamār, jiyā lāge hamār, jiyā lāge hamār
kaise ke mārõ nazariyā, o kaise ke mārõ nazariyā
hāya hamār kaise ke charaiyā
nanadī ke bhatār [?bukhār], nanadī ke bhatār [?bukhār]
āre saiyā̃ ke āwa rataunī, o saiyā̃ ke āwe rataunī
hāy dinā ṭūṭe [?sūjhe] na rār [?rāt]
saiyā̃ ke āwe rataunī
ṭūṭe [?sūjhe] na rār [?rāt], dinā ṭūṭe [?sūjhe] na rār [?rāt], dinā ṭūṭe [?sūjhe] na rār [?rāt]
saiyā̃ ke āwe rataunī, o saiyā̃ ke āwe rataunī
kāhe ka jhārõ jagahiyā
kaise ke bokhār, kaise ke bokhār
āre kaise ke jhārõ rataunī, o kaise ke jhārõ rataunī
hāy dinā ṭūṭe [?sūjhe] na rār [?rāt]
kaise ke jhārõ rataunī
āre bāhõ [?bāro] se jhāre jagahiyā
mantra se bokhār, mantra se bokhār
āre ãcharā se jhārõ rataunī, o ãcharā se jhārõ rataunī
hāy dinā ṭūṭe [?sūjhe] na rār [?rāt]
ãcharā se jhārõ rataunī
dinā sūjhe na rāt
ãcharā se jhārõ rataunī
dinā sūjhe na rāt, dinā sūjhe na rāt, dinā sūjhe na rāt, dinā sūjhe na rāt
ãcharā se jhārõ rataunī, o ãcharā se jhārõ rataunī
dinā sūjhe na rāt, sāsu ke thore jagaiyā, nanadī ke bokhār, nanadī ke bokhār
saiyā̃ ke chhore rataunī, o saiyā̃ ke chhore rataunī
hāy dinā sūjhe na rāt
saiyā̃ ke chhore rataunī
hāy mana lāge hamār

saiyā̃ ke chhore rataunī
āre boke palā̃wā̃ [?panāmā] ke topī
gala bā̃dhe rūmāl, gala bā̃dhe rūmāl
āre laṭakata [lachakata] āwe galine mẽ, o laṭakata [lachakata] āwe galina mẽ
hāy mana lāge hamār
laṭakata āwe galina mẽ
mana lāge hamār
laṭakata āwe galina mẽ
[*laughter*]

36 ꕤ
On the bank of the river there is a bungalow.
On top of that the king is sitting. On top of that the king is sitting.
How can I blink at him? Oh, how can I blink at him?
He is my husband.
How can I blink at him?
He is my beautiful one. I have lost my heart to him.
How can I look at him? Oh, how can I look at him?
How can he come, because he is fickle [meaning unclear]?
The husband of my sister-in-law, the husband of my sister-in-law [line of abuse].
Oh, my husband will suffer from night blindness. Oh, my husband will suffer from night blindness.
Oh, I cannot count days and nights past.
My husband will suffer from night blindness.
All day and night this spell does not break. All day and night this spell does not break. All day and night this spell does not break.
My husband will suffer from night blindness. Oh, my husband will suffer from night blindness.
How can I sweep the place?
How can I cure the fever? How can I cure the fever?
Oh, how can I dispel night blindness? Oh, how can I dispel night blindness?
Oh, all day and night this spell does not break.
How can I dispel night blindness?
Oh, I will sweep the place with my hand.
With mantras, I will remove the fever.
Oh, with my breast I will dispel night blindness! [with a waving motion] Oh, with my breast I will dispel night blindness!
Oh, all day and night this spell does not break.
Oh, with my breast I will dispel night blindness!
He does not see in day or night.
With my breast I will dispel night blindness!
He does not see in day or night. He does not see in day or night. He does not see in day or night. He does not see in day or night.
With my breast I will dispel night blindness! Oh, with my breast I will dispel night blindness!
He does not see in day or night. My mother-in-law has a small place. The sister-in-law will suffer from the fever. The sister-in-law will suffer from the fever.

My husband will be free from night blindness. Oh, my husband will be free from night blindness.
Oh, he does not see in day or night.
My husband will be free from night blindness.
Oh, I love him.
My husband will be free from night blindness.
Oh, I will give him a Panama hat [decades ago Panama cigarettes were sold in north India in a pack picturing a man in a Panama hat].
He puts a beautiful hankie around his neck.
Oh, he is walking along the road with his balls swinging! Oh, he is walking along the road with his balls swinging!
Oh, I love him.
He is walking along the road with his balls swinging!
Oh, I love him.
He is walking along the road with his balls swinging!
[*Laughter*]

Rajiah sang for me this fragment of Sankey's *lachārī.* Alas, only a "piece piece hot *chutney* naa" the ladies told me, not the entire song. How much more could be lost before this king of the bungalow with his Panama hat and his beautiful hankie and his swinging balls would be forgotten forever?

37
On the paved road there is a bungalow.
On it sits the king.
How can I look at him?
Does not see day and night.
How can I look at him?
Mother-in-law is suffering from fever.
Sister-in-law is suffering from fever.
Husband is suffering from night blindness.
Does not see day and night.
Husband is suffering from night blindness.
Does not see day and night.

Another *lachārī* by Rajiah tells of the humiliation men endure in the search for a suitable wife ("come here swimming in the river").

38
Oh, bridegroom, if you wish to have a wife,
Come here swimming in the river.
Oh, father-in-law will wet my pair of garments [shirt and trousers],
Because of your daughter.
Oh, groom I will give a pair of garments,
Own daughter for.
Oh, bridegroom, if you wish to have a wife,
Come here swimming in the river.

Oh, *māmū* [mother's brother] will wet my pair of garments,
Your sister for.
Oh, dear I will give a pair of garments,
And head turban.
Oh, dear I will give a pair of garments,
Our sister for.
Brother-in-law will wet my pair of garments,
My sister for.
Oh, bridegroom, if you wish to have a wife,
Come here swimming in the river.

Toward evening, the ladies began listening for the return of the wedding procession. Around five o'clock, we could hear the "mike," a hired car with an enormous speaker horn mounted on the roof, hailing the return of the *bārāt.* We heard the procession turn onto Cacandee Road and proceed slowly toward the house, blaring out the distorted image of an Indian film song. When the *bārāt* drew nearer, the dancing stopped but the singers went on regardless to finish their song. When the pedestrians arrived, and the line of cars began to pull up in front of the house, Sankey stepped forward to greet her son and his bride. Her friends scattered, pausing only to catch a glimpse of the bride, who had changed from her traditional red sari into a Western-style white wedding dress and veil. This was the end of the public wedding celebration. I packed my recording equipment and walked lazily down Cacandee Road. I had laughed hard and, like all the other ladies, had drunk too much rum. I felt at one with the world and full of insight into the human condition.

Hard to imagine a wedding, any wedding in any land, without music, I thought. All mankind seems agreed that marriage calls for song. To be more specific, calls for two kinds of songs: the fun variety like these fast and lively *lachārī* and more solemn types like the unaccompanied and subdued *byāh ke gīt* they sang during the ritual portions of the ceremony. And marriage calls for great loud outdoor music—the trumpets and oboes and the drums (or a horn loudspeaker).

Matti had supper waiting, and while I ate, she listened to the *lachārī* songs through headphones. Later, Mesho came in and listened too, hearing those bawdy women's songs at a distance, just as he had all his life: from down the road, from the next room and now, from a tape recorder, for they were not intended for a male audience. After he had listened, he smiled and said, "Now you've really got what you came for."

All mankind seems agreed? Should we reject ideas like these, the occasional intuition that tells us we do share feelings with all peoples of all times? New World thinkers as we are, untutored by the integrated world view of the antique Eastern philosophies, we train as specialists and tend to ignore what is common to all. Ours is an age for scientists, not humanists.

All mankind seems agreed? Probably not. Yet I couldn't resist the thought, on that particular Sunday evening, that the laughter and the singing at Sankey's was as ancient as love itself, and that despite the barriers of culture and race, of dialect and habit, I did belong in Felicity.

Chapter Nine
Wedding Songs

In the evening the clouds come in the sky,
  and at midnight it starts to rain.
Mother, open the sandalwood door and let Rāma
  enter the *kohabar.*
Mother, open the sandalwood door and let Sītā
  enter the *kohabar.*

Traditional Bhojpurī Song

On the morning after the wedding, I went to Port of Spain to meet with Dhanpatee and Kalawatee Permanand, the elder sisters of V. S. Naipaul's mother. In 1919, their father, Kapil Dev, had arranged for their double wedding to the Permanand brothers of Claxton Bay, southern Trinidad. Now nearing seventy and both widowed, they were everywhere affectionately called "*Ājī*" (father's mother). The Felicity ladies—Moon, Rajiah, Siewrajiah, Sankey, Channu—had encouraged me to record the exceptional singing of these two women who had been neighbors.

Every important moment in the elaborate Hindu marriage ceremony has a designated *byāh ke gīt.* The songs comment on the ritual, often drawing an analogy between the wedding and that of Rām and Sītā. Decades ago, a wedding guest might have heard thirty or forty *byāh ke gīt* (plate 29), but recently these songs are abbreviated or omitted, the singing group is small and often is drowned out by an orchestra or recorded film music blasted out on the "mike." The orchestra (electric guitar, electric keyboard, drum set, male and female vocalists, sometimes trumpet, flute, violin, accordion, and other Western instruments) plays arrangements of Indian film songs. When this loud ensemble interrupts the *byāh ke gīt* willy-nilly, the ladies cannot complete their singing.

Kalawatee asked, "What would you like us to sing?"

"Just some wedding songs would be fine," I said. I did not know that the *byāh ke gīt* they went on to sing were to become the heart of my musical world when later I heard them sung from village to village in the impoverished countryside of eastern Uttar Pradesh.

"These are all sung at the bride side on Sunday—when the groom and his men arrive," they explained.

PLATE 29. Village women singing *byāh ke gīt,* as they watch the wedding ceremony at the home of the bride, 1975.

ARRIVAL OF THE GROOM

"When the bridegroom is coming in, then they sing this song" (ex. VII), Dhanpatee explained.

"They ask the bride's father to sweep the way," Kalawatee continued. "'Sweep the way as the bridegroom is coming.' Then they ask, 'how is the bridegroom coming?' They say 'he is coming with horses and elephant.' Then they ask 'where he is going to? He is going to the house of the virgin. *Jinhi ghara kanyā kuwā.*'"

EXAMPLE VII
Sānkara Koriyā Bahāro

sānkara koriyā bahāro ho panḍiṭa rāma
bahāro ho panḍiṭa rāma
haṭhiyā̃ līna paiṭhāri ho
haṭhiyā̃ līna paiṭhāra

ki ḍala uṭarele āma amilī ṭare
āma amilī ṭare
kiya re kadama jūrī chhā̃ha
āho kiya re kadama jūrī chhā̃ha

Example VII (song 39, CD track 6): Sānkara Koriyā Bahāro

ohī ḍala uṭare panḍiṭa rāma ḍūarawā
panḍiṭa rāma ḍūarawā ho
jinhi ghara kanyā kuā̃rī ho
jinhi ghara kanyā kuā̃rī ho

39 ☙
Sweep the way, Pandit Rāma.
Sweep the way, Pandit Rāma.
They bring the elephant in.
They bring the elephant in.

The whole wedding party will come near the mango tree,
Or the tamarind tree,
Or under the shadow of the kadam tree,
Or under the shadow of the kadam tree.

Pandit Rāma, the wedding party will come only to the door,
Pandit Rāma, come to the door,
Of the house where there is a maiden to be married.
Of the house where there is a maiden to be married.

William Archer recorded a similar verse in western Bihar in the 1930s: "Sweep clean your lane, O Lāl, / Your bridegroom son-in-law is coming" (*Songs for the Bride,* 37). In 1972, in the Awadhī-speaking district of Kanpur, U.P., Laxmi Tewari recorded "Someone should have the lanes swept with roses / The groom is coming" ("Folk Music," 55).

"Are the elephants and horses important?" I asked the sisters.

"Yes, they are royal animal and kings ride on them," Kalawatee replied.

For the arrival of the *bārāt,* Moon also sang of an entourage riding on elephants:

40 ☙
Oh, elephant invite to sit.
Elephant invite to sit.
If the groomsmen come under the mango or *imiliā.*
Yes, mango, *imiliā.*
Or the groomsmen come to the brother's gate.
Oh, or the *kadam* of shade.
Or the groomsmen come to the brother's gate.
Oh, father's gate.
Oh, whose home daughter virgin is.
Whose home sister virgin is.
Or the groomsmen come to the grandfather's gate.
Oh, grandfather's gate.
Oh, whose home daughter virgin is.
Whose home daughter virgin is.
Put on father, na, oh father dhoti.

In hand betel leaf.
Go meet own gentlemen.
Bow your turban.
Go meet own gentlemen.
Bow your turban.
Bamboo not shake, bunch of bamboo not shake.
Mountain never shakes.
Own loving pet daughter because of,
Bow your turban.
Own loving pet daughter because,
Bow your turban.

In Ghazipur district Henry recorded: "Fuck your sister; you didn't bring elephants!" (*Chant,* 44). But I never found an example or a mention of these abusive *gālī* in Felicity, only the gently teasing *lachārī.* The *gālī* are easy to remember! Are they new to Indian villages, say a twentieth-century development? Did the Trinidad émigrées find them too offensive?

The arrival of a noisy *bārāt* in Ballia district, U.P., is included in Hari S. Upadhyaya's collection:

41 ☙
"A long and noisy wedding party arrives at your gate, O father.
The wedding party looks like an army of ants.
O father, this wedding party comes to your gate."
Mr. So-and-so puts a handkerchief over his face and weeps:
"O, I have been cursed with a daughter."
Mr. So-and-so laughs and strikes his thigh:
"O, I have been blessed with a son."
The wife of Mr. So-and-so weeps, covering her face with the skirt of her sari:
"O, a fire is ablaze in my heart."
Mrs. So-and-so smiles while chewing betel:
"O, here comes a daughter-in-law into my kitchen."
("Joint Family," 302)

Moon's song, like that of the Felicity women (song 34), tells how the bridegroom is received by the bride's father. She extends the song to invoke the uncle's name; in village India these songs are drawn out as various kinfolk are named. "Don't double the line too often," Mesho would sometimes tell the women.

42 ☙
Father, what bridegroom kept searching.
Father, the same bridegroom stand in wedding tent.
Father, the same bridegroom stand in wedding tent.
Father, bring the sandalwood stool [*piḍahiyā*].
Father, bring the sandalwood stool.

Father, arm holding, make to sit.
Father, arm holding, make to sit.
Father, his *ārtī* performed.
Father, his *ārtī* performed.
Uncle of, his *ārtī* perform.
Uncle of, his *ārtī* perform.

"Sweep the way, Pandit Rām," Dhanpatee had repeated. "They bring the elephant in." Later in India I sang this antique Felicity song in every village we visited. And its flowing melody and vivid images did "sweep the way" for me to learn the deeper meaning of Hindu marriage customs. By the time I had sung "*Sānkara koriyā bahāro ho pandiṭa rāma*" I had reached through to a village woman—as much as one song can achieve this, that is.

"Your father Kapil Dev did sweep the way for Indians in Trinidad," I said to the sisters.

"As indentured. He came as indentured," Kalawatee explained. "Gorakhpur, Anandnagar, Gaun Dube Ka. From the countryside."

☙ Dube Daughters

I wanted to believe that Dhanpatee and Kalawatee's song, *sānkara koriyā* came from Dube, from their father's village. That would make my story perfect. But this was romantic wishful thinking, since they normally would have learned wedding songs from their mother, Soogee, and her womenfolk. And she was Trinidad born, and perhaps Bengalī, suggests Fr. Anthony de Vertuil, C.S.Sp. (b. 1932) of the old Trinidad family.

Nevertheless I asked and hoped. "Who did you say taught you these songs?"

"From the estate. There were indentured laborers from India. And they used to sing it all the time home Chaguanas. They used to come from February till May. They had singing every night, the wedding songs. They sang when the *bārāt* come, and they had other wedding songs they used to sing. This was around 1919, the year I was married (plates 30, 31).

"And how old were these ladies?" I asked.

"Well they were grown-ups. They must have been around twenty-five. They sang it and I learned it and I sang it. Whenever they went to weddings I went and sang."

"Do you know what part of India they came from?" I asked.

"No. I never asked them because we were not allowed to get in between with them and ask questions. They were laborers, working on the sugar estate. But they were from India, and they came indentured. I grew up in that kind of atmosphere—so settled and nice."

Plate 30. Coolie Indian women dressed in traditional *lahar pator* outfits with an *oḍhanī* covering the head and tucked in at the waist.

Plate 31. Coolie girls at the turn of the century wearing traditional ornaments.

"Could you sing another song you learned from the cane workers?" I asked.

And they began "Greeting the Bridegroom."

ঃ Greeting the Bridegroom

"They're asking the girl father," Kalawatee explained. "Now he is going to meet the bridegroom and his entourage. The father carries a *lotā* with water. He is saying, 'In all my life, I have never bowed my head. But to marry my daughter now, I have to bow my head to the bride and bridegroom'" (ex. VIII; plate 32).

Example VIII
Leu Na Paṇḍiṭa Rāma

leu na paṇḍiṭa rāma gerūwā
hā̃ṭhe pāna ke bīrā
hā̃ṭhe pāna ke bīrā

karahu na binaṭī samaḍhī rāma se
sīra pāga jhukāye

karahu na binaṭī samaḍhī rāma se
sīra pāga jhukāye

ḍillī na e parabat na e
hamta kabahū̃ na niwalī
hamta kabahū̃ na niwalī

betī kawana ḍeī ke kāranā
aju shīsha niwāyo

betī kawana ḍeī ke kāranā
aju shīsha niwāyo

43 ঃ
Pandit Rāma, take a jug of water in your hand,
Betel leaves in hand.
Betel leaves in hand.

Go and request of Rāma's father.
Bow to him and request of him.

Go and request of Rāma's father.
Bow to him and request of him.

Wherever I went,
I never bowed to anyone.
I never bowed to anyone.

Because of my daughter,
Today I bowed.

Because of my daughter,
Today I bowed.

Plate 32. Channerdaye's son, dressed in the likeness of Rām on the morning of his wedding. The *bahnoī* (sister's husband) is honoring the bridegroom by putting his shoes on for him, in Hindu culture, a gesture of humiliation appropriate to this ritual setting, November, 1985.

Example VIII (song 43, CD track 7): Leu Na Paṇḍiṭa Rāma

Meter of phrase beginnings is indeterminate.

Pitch Range

Example IX (song 44, CD track 8): Dasa Sakhī

"And here is the next song," Dhanpatee went on.

"The women sing the names of Rām and Sītā," Kalawatee explained, "because this is how we look at the bride and groom. It is the *Rāmāyaṇ,* the wedding of Rām and Sītā. When the women came out to greet the groom, the mother-in-law came with the *ārtī* [offering of flame and incense]. And she did that [she demonstrated by waving her hand in a clockwise direction]. She did the *ārtī* to Rām with all her women folk." She turned to her sister.

"She's saying 'I am going to greet my beloved son-in-law to be,'" Dhanpatee added. "'And I am going to do the *ārtī* myself. I don't want nobody to take part in that. I am going to greet him my own self'" (ex. IX; plate 33).

EXAMPLE IX
Dasa Sakhī

dasa sakhī agawā̃ dasahī sakhī pachhawā̃
dasahī sakhī pachhawā̃ ho
dasa sakhī gohanē̃ lagāī
o dasa sakhī gohanē̃ lagāī

kanchana ṭhāra kapūra ke bātī
kapūra ke bātī
ho rāmajī ke āratī utāre
o rāmajī ke āratī utā

Plate 33. Mother of the bride offering a *lotā* of water as a ritual greeting to the groom, while a loudspeaker broadcasts a recorded Indian film song, 1975.

parichhana chalale ho sāsu kawana deī
sāsu kawana deī
parachhata bara ke lilāra
ho parachhata bara ke lilāra

pahile mãī parachhahu mānṭhe ke māura
manṭhe ke māura
pīchhe se bara ke lilāra ho

apana rāma mai apane parichhibõ
mai apane parichhibõ
ho jani koi pariche more rāma ho
jani koi pariche more rāma ho

44 ☙
Ten female friends are in front [of the bride],
Ten female friends are following [her],
Ten female friends are following [her],
Ten female friends are beside [her].

Now you take the golden tray,
The lighted camphor.
Offer *ārtī* to Rāma,
Offer *ārtī* to Rāma.

The girl's mother is now coming to receive the groom.
She comes to perform the *parachhan* [ritual to drive away evil spirits] for the groom,
The girl's mother performs the *parachhan* of the bridegroom's forehead,
The *parachhan* of the bridegroom's forehead.

First I will perform the *parachhan* of the bridegroom's crown,
The *parachhan* of the bridegroom's crown.
After that the *parachhan* of his whole head.

I will do the *parachhan* of the bridegroom myself.
I will do the *parachhan* of the bridegroom myself.
If no one else does this *parachhan* don't do it.
I will do it myself.

"Your songs are like classical music," I said.

"Exactly," Kalawatee replied. With subdued voice, she went on to the important point. "You have to go up and you have to go down. You see the meaning is there, and once you get at the meaning the voice come out to that. If you don't sing with feelings you cannot get that melody that you get. This is my explanation of it. Because I understand and I sing to my feelings as if I was in the person place how I would feel."

Moon's version of this song goes on to describe the grief of the bride's mother as she contemplates a life apart from her daughter.

45 ☙
Ten female friends [*sakhī*] walk ahead, ten female friends behind her.
Oh, ten female friends behind her.
Oh, ten female friends beside her.
I will do the blessing [*parichhagum*] of the bridegroom myself.
Own blessing.
If no one else does this blessing don't do it.
Mother give blessing, sister give blessing,
Father's sister give head bowing.
Come out my mother Kõnsiliyā.
Oh, mother Sumitra, oh, mother Kakahieya,
Offer *ārtī* to Rām.
In this manner my mother offers *ārtī.*
Oh, offer *ārtī.*
Oh, eyes flooded with tears.
Tonight how will I pass?
Oh, how will pass?
Oh, thou going to groom's home.
What we mistook, oh mother.
Oh, mistook, oh mother.
Oh, what drip tears,
Tonight how will I pass?
Oh, how will pass?
Oh, thou going to groom's home.
Tonight gate of Janaka.
Gate of Janaka, mother.
Again will worshipper your.
Again will worshipper your.
Own Gorī married.
Oh, Gorī married.
Oh, milk of [obscure].
Milk of [obscure].
Cow of milk market sold.
Oh, mother of milk priceless is.
Thou, oh my mother not know.
Oh, not know.
Oh, how give milk of price?
How give milk of price?

Sir George Grierson recorded a wedding song in Shahabad in 1883 telling of the five matrons performing the *parichhan,* five matrons who "sang auspicious songs":

46 ☙
Five matrons arranged the lamp with four wicks, and went to perform the *parichhan.*

Five matrons invoked Gauri and Ganes and went to perform the *chumawan.*
Five matrons fed the bridegroom with rice and milk as they sang auspicious songs.
Five matrons seat Rām and Sītā and apply odorous paste to their bodies.
Five matrons are apparelling him with ornaments while they gaze upon Rām's beauty.
Five matrons are jesting with him, saying "Tell us the name of your father."
Siddhī [wife of Sītā's brother] laughs and says to her comrades, "How can he tell the name of his father?
"Saint Sriṇgi came and gave rice and milk (to the wives of Rām's father), and that is how the four brothers came to be born.
"His mother was a great *rang rasiyā* [woman of bad character]: what certainty is there as to his father?"
(*Seven Grammars,* 112–13)

THE EVENING STAR: RĀM HAS COME TO WED

Then Kalawatee and Dhanpatee began another song from the *Rāmāyaṇ,* how at midnight the evening star came out, that Rām had come to wed, come to wed with his friends and brothers (plate 34).

"Rām is here to get married," Kalawatee translated. "He came with himself and his brothers, Lakshmaṇ, Shatrughn, and Bharat. And he come with his friends. *Sājan* mean 'friends' and *bhāī* mean 'brothers.' Then they describe Rām, how he is dressed. He has the crown [*maur, maura, mawara*] on his head. And he has the gold beads [*mālā*] around his neck. And then they saying he has the earring [*kuṇḍala*] in his ears. And the beauty mark of sandalwood paste [*chandana*] on his forehead. And then you saying that they drill the teeth and fill it with gold. That is shining. And the lips are red when they eat the betel leaf [*pān, pānana*]. And then he has the bow [*dhanushha*] and arrow in his hand. And his waist is tied with the yellow sash [*pīṭāmbara*]" (ex. X).

EXAMPLE X
Sā̃jhe Chha Sukawā

sā̃jhe chha sukawā udaye bhaye
sā̃jhe chandra udaye bhaye
sukawā uge ādhī rāṭa

rāma āye biāhan
rāma āye biāhan
sajana sahiṭa chāro bhāi rī

rāma āye biāhan
rāma āye biāhan
sajana sahiṭa chāro bhāi rī

PLATE 34. Felicity bridegroom, Channerdaye's son, wearing the *maur* ("crown") of Rām on the morning of his wedding, November 1985.

mā̃ṭhe maura jo sohai
mā̃ṭhe mawara jo sohai
gala baijantī ke mālā jī

mā̃ṭhe mawara jo sohai
mā̃ṭhe mawara jo sohai
gale baijantī ke mālā jī

kāne kuṇḍala jhalake
kāne kuṇḍala jhalake
chandana khora lalāṭa lasī

rāma āye biāhan
rāma āye biāhan
sajana sahiṭa chāro bhāi rī

dā̃te jhalake batisiyā
dā̃te jhalake batisiyā
pānana oṭha ke lālī jī

rāma āye biāhan
rāma āye biāhan
sajana sahiṭa chāro bhāi rī

hāṭhe dhanushha jo sohai
hāṭhe dhanushha jo sohai
pīṭāmbara se kamara kasī

rāma āye biāhan
rāma āye biāhan
sajana sahiṭa chāro bhāi rī

47 ℬ
In the evening six stars come out,
In the evening the moon comes out,
The evening star comes out in the middle of the night.

Rāma has come to wed,
Rāma has come to wed,
His friends and four brothers.

Rāma has come to wed,
Rāma has come to wed,
His friends and four brothers.

On the bridegroom's forehead there is a beautiful crown,
On the bridegroom's forehead there is a beautiful crown,
Around his neck he has the garland of five colors.

On the bridegroom's forehead there is a beautiful crown,
On the bridegroom's forehead there is a beautiful crown,
Around his neck he has the garland of five colors.

Example X (song 47, CD track 9): Sā̃jhe Chha Sukawā

In his ears earrings are resplendent,
In his ears earrings are resplendent,
The sandalwood paste adorns his forehead.

Rāma has come to wed,
Rāma has come to wed,
His friends and four brothers.

His lips are red with the betel leaves,
His lips are red with the betel leaves,
In this way he has come to wed.

Rāma has come to wed,
Rāma has come to wed,
His friends and four brothers.

In his hand he has the bow,
In his hand he has the bow,
Around his waist he is wearing the yellow sash.

Rāma has come to wed,
Rāma has come to wed,
His friends and four brothers.

Archer's 1930 version from western Bihar also describes the resplendent bridegroom:

48 ☙
Friend, come and see
How grandly he is dressed.
On his head a marriage crown,
Fine his tassels,
In his ear a ring
Fine his pearl,
His garments shining on his person
Grand his sash.
(*Songs,* 75)

❧ BEAT THE DRUMS! BRING THE GOLDEN PITCHER! LIGHT THE RUBY LAMP!

Music is essential for the wedding, and many songs tell of wedding drums, encouraging the drummers to play enthusiastically to announce the arrival of the *bārāt.*

The sisters sang: "Oh, brother, beat the drums! Play the instruments!"

Kalawatee explained: "This is when they telling the drummers to beat the drum now at its full pitch. The bridegroom is coming. And they're telling the bride father, 'put the canopy over him, he is coming in.' And they're telling

Example XI (song 49, CD track 10): Hare Hare Bhaiyā

the girl's mother, 'put your *oḍhanī* [*ãchalwā, ãcharawā*] over his head. He is coming in.'"

"So that he must not get the drizzle of rain," Dhanpatee added. "The ladies are sitting inside on the girl's side, and the *tāssā* drums are coming. '*Hare hare bhaiyā bajaniyān ṭo bajanā bajāwā ho.*' This is 'Come on drummers, our brother, beat the drum!'" (ex. XI).

Example XI
Hare Hare Bhaiyā

hare hare bhaiyā bajaniyā̃
ṭo bajanā bajābahu ho

bhaiyā āi gaile rājā ke kuwa
ṭa bajanā bajābahu ho

hare hare bābā kawana rāma ṭamuā ṭanābahu ho
bābā bhīje na rājā ke kuwar ṭamuā ṭanābahu ho

hare hare mā kawana dei ancharawā ṭū̃ ṭānahu ho
maiyā bhījẽ na rājā ke kũwara ancharawā ṭū̃ ṭāni deu ho

49

Oh, oh, brother who plays the musical instruments,
Play the instruments.

Oh, brother, the son of the king is coming,
Play the instruments.

Oh, oh, Rāma's father, put up the wedding canopy.
Put a canopy so that the king's son will not get wet from the rain.

Oh, oh, mother of the bride, come now and give the protection of your *ãcharwā* [end of the sari].
Give the protection of your *ãcharwā* so that the son of the king will not get wet.

Moon also sang of drums:

50

Whose tent is pitched and whose tent is thatched.
Whose gate drum is being played, sounds beautiful.
Whose gate drum is being played, sounds beautiful.
The carpenter pitched the tent and the leatherworker thatched it.
Oh, grandfather's [*ājā*] gate drum is being played, sounds beautiful.
Oh, uncle's [*kākā*] gate drum is being played, sounds beautiful.
My father's [*bābā*] gate drum is being played, sounds beautiful.

Barua gives a drum song from Tripura, in which the village women address the drummer, "Beat the drum":

51 ♫
Beat the drum, beat the drum,
Beat the drum to such a rhythm,
Beat, it may please the ears,
You will get a good reward.
Beat the drum, beat the drum,
Beat that it might please the ears.
(*Folksongs,* 32)

Rajiah's song about wedding musicians describes the ritual of chewing the sour herb *imili (imili chumawan).*

52 ♫
Brother seated on the cot.
Sister seated at the *chauk* [ritual design].
Brother open the money tied in the cloth knot.
Then perform the ritual of chewing the *imili* herb.
Oh, oh, brother musician,
Then play the instruments.
Look, my people will listen.
Then perform the ritual of chewing the *imili* herb.
Oh, oh, brother musician,
Then play the instruments.
Look, if will listen parent's home people.
Then perform the ritual of chewing the *imili* herb.

"In the next song they are saying 'plaster, smear the wedding place with cow dung and mud to prepare for Rām,'" Kalawatee said. "In my wedding we had to *līpā* the whole yard for the ceremony," she explained. "My father got people for it. The women wasn't like today. They was all helpful. Today the atmosphere is rush, rush, rush, rush, rush. Not everybody can dip their hand there. Today they consider theyself too high faluting because they went to school.

"So Rām and Lakshmaṇ, the bridegroom with his littler brother, are walking to take a seat. They are describing how Rām is looking. They say, 'Rām is shining like the sun. Just as diamonds sparkle in the bazaar, so he is shining.' They ask Sītā, 'what penance, what *ṭapa,* you did to get such a bridegroom?' She says, 'I bathed in the Gangā every Sunday and I gave alms to the brahmans and my father in the cane lands, he gave away a calf. This is the benefit I derive from doing these things. That is why I'm getting married to Rām'" (ex. XII).

Example XII
Surāiyā Gaiyā Ke Gobara

surāiyā gaiyā ke gobara māgāyo
chāro khoṭā beḍēiyā lipāye ho

Example XII (song 53, CD track 11): Surāiyā Gaiyā Ke Gobara

sone ke kalasā ḍharāye more bābā
suruja chhakita hoi jāy
sone ke kalasā ḍharāye more bābā
suruja chhakiṭa hoi jāy
jaise bajāre ke moṭī jo jhalake
awarū dakhinawān ke chīra ho
rāma lachhana ḍauno maraye mẽ jhalake
suruja chhakita hoi jāy
rāma lachhana ḍauno maraye mẽ jhalake
suruja chhakita hoi jāy
dekhana āye re sakhiyā sahelari
nayanana gaile murajhāi ho
kawana-kawana ṭapa kihalo sītala deī
rāma se hobelā biāha
kawana-kawana ṭapa kihalo sītala deī
rāma se hobelā biāha
gangā nahāyo suruja mā̃ṭhā lāgau
bidhi se rahau iṭawāra ho
nibulā sarāphala brāhmana ke dihalaū
ohī se more rāma se biāha
nibulā sarāphala brāhmana ke dihalaū
ohī se more rāma se biāha
nibulā sarāf . . . [*False start*]
bhukhala-ḍukhala hama bipra jībailau
ohī se more rāma se biāha
urakhe ṭe bābā more bachhiyā sākalapai
ohī se more rāma se biāha
urakhe ṭe bābā more bachhiyā sākalapai
ohī se more rāma se biāha

53 ❧
Get the dung of a beautiful cow;
Smear it on the four corners of the square altar.
My father, put the golden pitcher on top [of the altar];
The sun will be surprised [at the beauty].
My father, put the golden pitcher on top;
The sun will be surprised.
As the pearl in the bazaar shines,
The silk cloth from the south.
Both Rāma and Lakshmaṇ shine in the wedding canopy;
The sun will be surprised.
Both Rāma and Lakshmaṇ shine in the wedding canopy;
The sun will be surprised.
The female friends of the bride have come to see;
They are stunned [to behold the beauty].
Sītā Dei, what are the penances you performed
That you might wed Rāma?

Sītā Dei, what are the penances you performed
That you might wed Rāma?
I bathed in the Ganges. I bowed my head to the sun.
I fasted for twenty Sundays.
I fed the brahmans who received a bad spell;
That is why I am going to wed Rāma.
I fed the brahmans who received a bad spell;
That is why I am going to wed Rāma.
I fed the hungry sad brahmans;
That is why I am going to wed Rāma.
On top of this, my father gave a young cow;
That is why I am going to wed Rāma.
On top of this, my father gave a young cow;
That is why I am going to wed Rāma.

As the *bārāt* arrives in splendor and the "sun disappears" in shyness, the bride watches trembling with fear at the procession of the one hundred elephants and the fifty horses. "Roaring comes the drum," Moon sang:

54 ꕤ
Crowd of the groomsmen [*bārīatiā*]
Sun disappears becomes.
Daughter of the father climbed high and looked.
How many in the army of groomsmen?
Daughter of the father climbed high and looked.
How many in the army of groomsmen?
One hundred came on elephant, fifty came on horse.
Roaring comes the drum.
This daughter of father, if this much look,
Closed the stone door.
This daughter of father, if this much look,
Closed the stone door.
If daughter the bride listen this much,
Father, listen to my request.
Brother, sister-in-law together bridegroom adorn.
Uncle, if give donation of the virgin [*kaniyāḍān*].
Brother, sister-in-law together bridegroom adorn.
Uncle, if give donation of the virgin.
Neighbor woman, bridegroom adorn.
My uncle, give donation of the virgin.
If daughter of father listen this much,
Open the stone door.
If daughter of father listen this much,
Open the stone door.

"Auspicious is the lot of the lady Sītā," Grierson recorded in 1883. "By the mercy of the god . . . we adore the brow of Sītā."

55 ☙
Auspicious time, the day, the hour; auspicious is the lot of the lady Sītā.
By the mercy of the gods, the heroes, and the saints, we adore the brow of Sītā.
After adoring Gauri and Ganes we take curds and rice and apply them to Sītā's (forehead).
We also apparel her in ornaments and garments, while all her bridesmaids sing marriage songs.
They are chanting the Beds [Vedas], while bards sing her praises and every one offers her their benediction.
Ambikā Prasād (says) now that Sītā has obtained Rām for a husband, may her happiness increase through endless ages.
(*Seven Grammars*, 114–15)

The new bride is brought out under the wedding canopy and seated on a ritual design of elephant pearls (ivory). Attendants bring the golden pitcher and light the ruby lamp so the ceremony can begin. Moon sang:

56 ☙
Courtyard praises King Janaka of,
He only wedding tent gets thatched.
Sandalwood trunks have pitched.
The wedding tent is thatched with betel leaf.
Sandalwood trunks have pitched.
The wedding tent is thatched with betel leaf.
Sandalwood trunks have pitched.
The wedding tent is thatched with betel leaf.
Bring the golden ritual stool [*pirawā*].
The daughter sits on the ritual design [*chaiuke*].
Bring the golden ritual stool.
The daughter sits on the ritual design.
Bring the golden ritual stool.
The daughter sits on the ritual design.
The ritual design is made of elephant pearls.
Bring the golden pitcher [*kalasā*].
Bring the pitcher of elephant pearls.
Bring the golden pitcher.
Bring the golden pitcher.
Light the ruby lamp.
Bring the golden pitcher.
Light the ruby lamp.
Mother explain who is the queen.
A daughter was born to her.
Bring the golden pitcher.
The daughter sits on the ritual design.
Bring the golden pitcher.
The daughter sits on the ritual design.

To perform, get *mãga* pearls.
The daughter sits on the ritual design.
To perform, get *mãga* pearls.
The daughter sits on the ritual design.

ꕤ THE EXCHANGE OF GIFTS: NOW MY DAUGHTER BELONGS TO SOMEBODY ELSE

The songs also include the topic of gifts, the exchange of ornaments, clothing, and finery between the families of the bride and bridegroom. The barter, the dowry: "They bring gold and silver. Now my daughter belongs to somebody else."

"This is when they bring the gifts for the bride in the *ḍāl*," Kalawatee explained. "They call the *ḍāl*. This basket business. Then they sing, 'now she get her gifts, from now on, she belongs to somebody else. She's not mine anymore'" (ex. XIII).

EXAMPLE XIII
Āī Gailẽẽ Ḍala

āī gailẽ ḍala maunī
āī gailẽ sira maurī

āī gailẽ beṭī ke sĩgāra ṭa
beṭī morī parāī bhailẽ

āī gailẽ beṭī ke sĩgāra ṭa
beṭī morī parāī bhailẽ

sone ḍalawā sona ailẽ
rūpe ḍalawā rūpe ailẽ

Example XIII (song 57, CD track 12): Āī Gailẽ Ḍala

bā̃se ḍalawā ḍhiyā ke sīgāra ṭa
ḍhiyā morī parāī bhailē

bā̃se ḍalawā ḍhiyā ke sīgāra ṭa
ḍhiyā morī parāī bhailē

57 ♪
The wedding party has come;
The crowned head [radiant bridegroom] has come.

The ornaments of the daughter have come;
Now my daughter belongs to somebody else.

The ornaments of the daughter have come;
Now my daughter belongs to somebody else.

They bring gold and silver in the big cane basket.
They bring money in the big cane basket.

They bring ornaments of the daughter in the big cane basket;
Now my daughter belongs to somebody else.

They bring ornaments of the daughter in the big cane basket;
Now my daughter belongs to somebody else.

A song from the Archer collection tells: "The wedding basket and the marriage hat / The joy of the bride / Have come" (*Songs,* 41).

Moon's repertory included several songs about the donation of the *ḍāl.* One describes the gift each of Rām's mother and step-mothers (Kaushalyā; Sumitrā and Kaikeyī) had contributed to the *ḍāl* that is presented to the bride:

58 ♪
Everyone comes.
Someone presents money.
Oh, someone presents precious stones.
Completely fill the winnowing basket.
Kaushalyā presents finger and thumb rings.
Sumitrā presents money.
Oh, Kaikeyī precious stones.
Completely fill the winnowing basket.
Oh, Kaikeyī precious stones.
Completely fill the winnowing basket.

As the bride accepts wedding ornaments from the groom, she no longer belongs to her *gotra* ("tribe," "bloodline"). Moon sang, "Then my daughter is partnered to another."

59 ♪
The basket of ornaments came, oh father, basket came.
Father has come, daughter of ornaments.

Then my daughter is partnered to another.
Then my daughter is partnered to another.
Then my daughter is partnered to another.
The basket of ornaments came, oh father, basket came.
Basket [obscure] came.
Father, the vermilion [*sendurawā*] of Kāshi [ancient Banaras] has come.
Then my daughter is partnered to another.
Father, this came and Kaikeyī came.
Father, all sixteen ornaments have come.
Then my daughter is partnered to another.
Father, all sixteen ornaments have come.
Then my daughter is partnered to another.
Father, all sixteen ornaments have come.
Then my daughter is partnered to another.

Under the Wedding Canopy

As the Permanand sisters sang on and on that morning, the hours passed and the singers lapsed more and more into the old Bhojpurī texts.

"*Basawā kaṭāye more bābā,*" Kalawatee repeated. "My father is cutting green bamboos. And then he is putting up a tent [*marawā*] where he is covering it with the leaves of betel [*pān*]. And under that, *harīhara basawā kaṭāye more bābā pānana marawā chhawāyelā, ṭehī ṭare baiṭhele beṭi ke bābā,* underneath that tent my father is sitting. *Beṭī ke bābā* is sitting. And now the time come for he to give away his daughter. Now he is trembling. How he is going to give away his daughter? Everything is trembling. The *lotā* is trembling. *Kā̃pela ḍhoṭiyā kā̃pela loṭiyā.* The fine *kus* grass is trembling. Everything is trembling."

"How is he going to give away his daughter?" Kalawatee was saying. *Kā̃pela ḍhotiyā kā̃pela loṭiyā kā̃pela kusawā ke ḍābha ho. Maraye mẽ kā̃pela beṭī ke bābā.* He's trembling. 'How I'm going to give away my daughter?' And the daughter is replying, 'Get gold and silver and put it in the flour and give that away. And me now, take me and put me on your leg, your *janghiyā* [*jā̃ghā* in the sung version], and then give me away. *Sonawā̃ au rūpalī ke gupṭa sā̃kalapau ḍeao gaurā deī ke dāna.* Give it to the Gods. And then me, *hamake ṭū more bābā jā̃ghā baiṭhāo.* Put me on your leg and so give me away. *Waise-waise deao kanyādān.*' You are marrying a maiden, a *kanyā.* If you get your period they would not put on father's lap, on his *janghiyā.* Never again" (ex. XIV).

Example XIV
Harīhara Bā̃sawā

harīhara bā̃sawā kaṭā̃ye more bābā
pānana marawā chhawā̃yelā ho
ṭehī ṭare baiṭhele beṭī ke bābā

Example XIV (song 60, CD track 13): Harīhara Bāsawā

āī gaye ḍharamawā̃ ke jūn
ṭehī ṭare baiṭhele beṭī ke bābā
āī gaye ḍharamawā̃ ke jūn
kā̃pelā ḍhotiyā au kā̃pelā loṭiyā
kā̃pelā kusawā ke ḍābha ho
maraye mẽ kā̃pelā beṭī ke bābā
kaise-kaise ḍebo kanyāḍān
maraye mẽ kā̃pela beṭī ke bābā
kaise-kaise ḍebo kanyāḍān
sonawā̃ au rūpalī ke gupṭa sā̃kalapau
ḍeao gaurā deī ke dāna ho
hamake ṭū more bābā jā̃ghā baiṭhāo
waise-waise deao kanyādān
hamake ṭū more bābā jā̃ghā baiṭhāo
waise-waise deao kanyādān

60 ꩜
My father has cut green bamboo;
He has thatched the wedding canopy with betel leaves.
The daughter's father is sitting underneath the wedding canopy;
The time for the religious ritual has arrived.
The daughter's father is sitting underneath the wedding canopy;
The time for the religious ritual has arrived.
His dhoti [loincloth] is trembling, his *lotā* [brass pot] is trembling,
The bunch of *kus* grass is trembling.
In the wedding canopy the daughter's father is trembling.
How will I give away my virgin daughter?
In the wedding canopy the daughter's father is trembling.
How will I give away my virgin daughter?
I will make secret offerings of gold and silver [coins] to Pārvatī [Gaurā Dei];
After that offering you can give me away [Permanand interpretation].
[S. M. Pandey translation: I will offer gold and silver secretly; In that way I will give away my daughter (likened to Gaurā Dei)].
[Umesh translation: Gold and silver rupees donate from your private heart. Donate Gaurā Dei (me, your daughter; as Pārvatī); note that the bride is here speaking to her father).]
My father, you can put me on your lap;
In this way you can give away your virgin daughter.
My father, you can put me on your lap;
In this way you can give away your virgin daughter.

Many Felicity women sing this song for the *kanyādān* ceremony, the centerpiece of the wedding when the father gives his daughter in marriage. Moon's version of the *kanyādān* song continues without interruption to the song for the *ḍharia* ceremony, when the brother must pour a continuous stream of water from a *lotā* into the joined cupped hands of the newlyweds.

61 ☙
Mother kept this daughter as a ghee pitcher [i.e., mother is kind, loving].
Oh, father then to will daughter as a water fly [i.e., father is heartless].
Oh, father then to will daughter as a water fly.
Trembling *lotā,* oh, trembling dhoti.
Trembling ring of grass.
Trembling ring of grass.
In the tent the daughter of father is trembling.
How can give donation of virgin daughter [*kaniyā̃dāna*]?
How can give give donation of virgin daughter?
His trembling *lotā,* his trembling dhoti.
His trembling ring of grass.
His trembling ring of grass.
Not you tremble, oh, daughter of father.
These are religious duties.

Oh, oh, brother, the stream of water [*ḍhariā*] must not break.
Brother, this stream of water will break.
Sister will be stolen.
Brother, this stream of water will break.
Sister will be stolen.
Whole day quarreled brother, quarreled brother.
Oh, evening time when arrived.
Sister had been stolen [i.e., the sister had been married].
Oh, evening time when arrived.
Sister had been stolen.

The Felicity ladies sang the *kanyādān* song in a concise form and after a brief interruption continued with the *ḍharia* song. Their performance illustrates the iterative nature of call-and-response form in village wedding songs, locally called "doubling the line":

62 ☙
LEADER The *lotā* is trembling, the *ḍhotiā* is trembling.
The blade of grass is trembling.
CHORUS Oh, the blade of grass is trembling.
LEADER Oh, the blade of grass is trembling.
CHORUS Oh, the blade of grass is trembling.
LEADER In the wedding tent, the daughter's father is trembling.
How can I give my virgin daughter?
CHORUS Oh, how can I give my virgin daughter?
LEADER Oh, how can I give my virgin daughter?
CHORUS Oh, how can I give my virgin daughter?
LEADER The *ḍhotiā* is trembling, the *lotā* is trembling.
The blade of grass is trembling.
CHORUS Oh, the blade of grass is trembling.
LEADER Oh, in the wedding canopy, the mother's daughter is trembling.
How can I give my virgin daughter?

Chorus Oh, how can I give my virgin daughter?
Leader How can I give my virgin daughter?
Chorus Oh, how can I give my virgin daughter?

63 ꩜

Leader Oh, oh, brother Rām,
Your *ḍhariā* [stream of water] should not break.
Chorus Oh, oh, brother Rām,
Your *ḍhariā* should not break.
Leader Oh, oh, brother Rām,
Your *ḍhariā* should not break.
Oh, oh, brother Rām,
Your *ḍhariā* should not break.
Chorus Oh, oh, brother Rām,
Your *ḍhariā* should not break.
Leader *ḍhariā* break, tear,
Sister will be stolen.
Chorus *ḍhariā* break, tear,
Sister will be stolen.
Leader *ḍhariā* break, tear,
Sister will be stolen.
Chorus This *ḍhariā* break, tear,
Sister will be stolen.
Leader My sister will not be stolen so easily;
The bridegroom will win and bring.
Chorus My sister will not be stolen so easily;
The bridegroom will win.
Leader My sister will not be stolen so easily;
The bridegroom will win and bring.
Chorus My sister will not be stolen so easily;
The bridegroom will win and bring.

Evidence suggests that Felicity villagers have faithfully preserved songs from India, for we find a fragment of the *ḍhariā* song in Archer's 1930 collections from Shahabad:

64 ꩜

O brother, pour the water
In a single jet,
If the jet is broken
You will lose your sister.
(*Songs*, 43)

Villagers believe that the donation of a virgin daughter in marriage is a holy and auspicious act that will benefit her parents. Rajiah's *kanyādān* song describes an eclipse casting its shadow over the wedding. Only the donation in marriage of the virgin can lift this curse:

65 ☙
As the eclipse influenced moon at,
Same way sun at,
Look, same way the eclipse influenced daughter at.
Fell down in wedding tent.
Mother, cure the influence of the eclipse.
This way influence of the eclipse will be over.
Patience keep, oh daughter, patience keep.
Some more patience keep.
Daughter, when father will give donation of the virgin daughter,
Only then the effect of the eclipse will be over.

Henry's Ghazipur collection also includes the metaphor of the eclipse under the wedding canopy: "The eclipse of the daughter occurs under the wedding canopy when half the night is passed" (*Chant,* 48, 254).

I heard the Felicity *kanyādān* song with the same tune and text many times in the Bhojpurī villages of India. Archer's 1930 collection includes:

66 ☙
On the thatching grass the father sits
The girl with loosened hair is in his lap,
O praise the thighs that bore a girl
Who holds her with a pearl in her hair.
(*Songs,* 43)

In Ghazipur, U.P., the brahman women sang for me the *kanyādān* song at such a slow and majestic tempo as if to delay forever the act of separation ("How will I give away my virgin daughter?").

"The Felicity women have a different way of singing," I commented to the sisters. "You sing high and low. They only sing low," I added, having noticed that their songs usually had a range of one octave, and those of the Felicity ladies a fifth.

"They sing it in one, only in one," Dhanpatee explained.

"I couldn't sit down there and hear them not doing it in the right way," Kalawatee added. "They say 'Now we can sing!' 'No!' I say. 'All you go and sit down now. I say I staying in Delhi and all you going to Calcutta so then all you will hear what I sing!' Next is the *lāwā* song, the popped rice."

☙ Ceremony of the Popped Rice

Dhanpatee explained: "This is when they throwing the *lāwā.*"

"When they going around the fire," Kalawatee added, "and they throwing the *lāwā,* the parched rice."

"The paddy rice," Dhanpatee said.

"It burst like the corn," Kalawatee continued. "This song tells, 'Don't parch the *lāwā* because this is your sister. When you do that you're giving away your sister. *Lauwā* [variant pronunciation in the song] *na parichho kawana bhaiyā ho, oṭo bahinī ṭohār.* It's your sister. Why you doing that for? You give away your sister. Don't do it.'"

Lāwā, popped rice, is a popular food in Uttar Pradesh, and this wedding tradition is performed throughout the Bhojpurī-speaking region. Many versions of this song are sung in the villages.

"But what is *amuthā* [sung *ãguṭha*]," I asked.

"*Amutā* means the toe," Kalawatee said. "When they do the *lāwā* they put a grinding stone under the *dulahin* foot. The *dulahā* have to kick out the stone from under her foot. 'But she is your wife now! Don't kick like that!' See where the meaning come. 'You must not kick like that because she is your wife now.' It means never to hit because she is your wife. 'She is dearer to you than your own soul.' See I raise my hair on my own body when I talk that. Who honor their wife like that?" (ex. XV).

EXAMPLE XV
Lauwā Na Parichho

lauwā na parichho kawana bhaiyā ho
oṭo bahinī ṭohārai ho
lauwā na parichho kawana bhaiyā ho
oṭo bahinī ṭohārai ho
hala-bala, hala-bala dulahā chale
harabāhe ke pūtau ho
ṭhumuki-ṭhumuki mori dhiyā chale
rajabāre ke dhīyāu ho

Example XV (song 67, CD track 14): Lauwā Na Parichho

ãguṭha na māro dulahe rāmā ho
uṭo bahinī ṭohārai ho
ãguṭha na māro dulahe rāmā ho
uṭo dhaniyā̃ ṭohārai ho

67 ꕤ
Brother, welcome the popped rice;
That is your sister.
Brother, welcome the popped rice;
That is your sister.
The bridegroom walks clumsily;
He is the son of a plowman.
My daughter is walking slowly and delicately;
She is the daughter of a king.
Hit the bridegroom Rāma on the toe;
That is the sister [the sister still belongs to the bride's family].
Hit the bridegroom Rāma on the toe;
That is the wife [the sister has been given away].

Archer's collection includes a *lāwā* song:

68 ꕤ
Mix the parched paddy [rice], O brother,
For she is your sister.
Touch the girl's toes, you little bastard
For she is your wife.
(*Songs,* 44)

Henry's collection from the 1970s includes a *lāwā gālī,* a sexually abusive song for the popped rice ceremony. When the rice of the bride and groom are mixed together, the ladies sing, "Have our father and your mother sleep together. / Have our father's brother and your father's brother's wife sleep together" (*Chant,* 51).

ꕤ The Vermilion Ceremony

"This is when he is going to put the *sindūr* [vermilion] on her hair," Kalawatee said. "She is calling on the father. He's not answering. She say, 'By the strength of you that he's doing me this now. I will belong to him.' She is calling the mother and repeating the same thing. 'By the strength of the mother the bridegroom is putting the *sindūr.*' And she is calling the brother and repeating the same thing. 'By the strength of the brother he has the authority to put the *sindūr* on her'" (ex. XVI).

"She is all gone," Dhanpatee said.

"Now she is his," Kalawatee concluded.

Example XVI (song 69, CD track 15): Bābā Bābā

Example XVI

Bābā Bābā

bābā bābā pukāre ta bābā nā bolelā ho
āho bābāi ke bariyāī sīdura bara ḍārei ho
māī māī pukāre ta māī nā bolelā ho
āho māīya ke bariyāī sīdura bara ḍārelā ho
bhāī bhāī pukāre ta bhāī nā bolelā ho
āho bhāīya ke bariyāī sīdura bara ḍārelā ho

69 ꟿ

She is calling, "father, father," but the father does not speak.
Oh, by the authority of the father the groom puts the vermilion [in the parting of the bride's hair].
She is calling, "mother, mother," but the mother does not speak.

Oh, by the authority of the mother the groom puts the vermilion.
She is calling, "brother, brother," but the brother does not speak.
Oh, by the authority of the brother the groom puts the vermilion.

Moon's version of the *sindūr* song was virtually identical:

70 ❧
Daughter thy father calling, father does not speak.
Father by what authority the groom puts the vermilion [*sindūra*].
Father by what authority the groom puts the vermilion.

The Ballia version from the collection of Hari S. Upadhyaya comments on the unbreakable bond between bride and groom after the vermilion ritual.

71 ❧
"O father, the month of Chaet ends and Baesakh begins.
"O father, go into a forest and cut fifty bamboos.
"O father, have four pillars posted in the four corners,
"And one in the center of the altar.
"O father, light four lamps in the four corners,
"And one in the center of the altar."
"O girl, you hold the vermilion pot and ripe leaf in your hands."
The girl crawls over and sits on the thigh of her father.
"I belong in part to you, O father."
"You belong, O daughter, fully to me.
But after accepting a pinchful of vermilion, you belong to others."
("Joint Family," 287)

I heard this final cry of the bride for her family's help in every Indian village I visited ("Father! Father! . . . Mother! Mother! . . .").

❧ Entering the Ritual Bedroom

Dhanpatee began: "It say the rain is set up and it will fall just now. So open the big door which is make of sandalwood. And let Rām enter. And let Sītā enter the *kohabar*. This is where they go inside" (ex. XVII).

"That is the end of the wedding," Kalawatee concluded.

Example XVII
Sā̃jhai

sā̃jhai baḍharā umari aile
ādhī rāti barasai ho

maiyā kholi deu chanana kewariyā
ramaiyā jaihāi kohabara ho

maiyā kholi deu chanana kewariyā
sītalā jaihāi kohabara ho

Example XVII (song 72, CD track 16): Sãjhai

72 ꙮ
In the evening the clouds come in the sky.
At midnight it starts to rain.

Mother, open the sandalwood door.
Let Rāma enter the *kohabar* [room in which wedding rituals are performed].

Mother, open the sandalwood door.
Let Sītā enter the *kohabar.*

"You will find this in Tulsī Dās *Rāmcharitmānans,*" Kalawatee said, and she went out to fetch a heavy volume printed in Gorakhpur. "If you check 'Bālakānda' it tells the wedding of Rām and Sītā."

I turned over the pages and began to read the English glosses aloud to the sisters:

"All the fourteen spheres were filled with joy at the news of the forthcoming wedding of Janaka's daughter with the hero of Raghu's race. The king said, 'Go and prepare the horses, elephants, and chariots and start at once in procession for Rāma's marriage.' On magnificent elephants were mounted splendid seats with canopies wrought in a manner beyond all description. Elephants in rut, adorned with clanging bells, headed like beautiful rumbling clouds in the rainy month of Sāwan."

"We sing 'they bring the elephant in,' and we mention that 'at midnight it starts to rain,' and Sītā's mother must 'protect her beloved son-in-law from the drizzle of rain,'" Kalawatee said.

I continued to read. "There were palanquins on which rode companies of noble brahmans, incarnations, as it were, of all the hymns of the *Vedas*. The elephants trumpeted and their bells clanged with a terrific din. The clash of kettledrums would drown the peal of thunder."

"We mention 'come on drummer, our brother, beat the drum.'"

"When it was learnt that the procession of the bridegroom's party was approaching and the tempestuous clash of kettledrums was heard, a deputation went out to receive it with elephants, chariots, footmen, and horses duly equipped. Rāma's swarthy form possessed the glow of a peacock's neck. His bright yellow raiment outshone the lightning."

"That is what we mention the yellow *pitambar,*" Dhanpatee said.

"Wedding ornaments of every kind, all auspicious and graceful, adorned his person."

"We sing 'in his ears, earrings are resplendent,' and we sing his crown, the *maur,*" Kalawatee said.

"His countenance was as delightful as the moon in a cloudless autumnal night; his eyes put to shame a blooming pair of lotuses. Kindling lights of various kinds, a bevy of graceful women proceeded joyfully to perform the ceremony of waving lights round the bridegroom."

"We sing the girl's mother comes to perform the *parachhan* of the bridegroom's forehead," Kalawatee said.

"The elder ladies of the family sang charming festal songs."

"These are the wedding songs, all what we sing today," Kalawatee said.

"The glorious king Janaka gave his daughter to the bridegroom."

"This is the *kanyādān* when the groomsmen are trembling, 'how he will give the maiden daughter.'"

"He then bathed Shrī Rāma's lotus feet, that are enshrined in the lotus-like heart of Shiva."

"This is what we sing, 'because of my daughter today I bowed.'" Kalawatee said.

"Those who lovingly sing or hear the story of Sītā and Rāma's marriage shall ever rejoice; for Shrī Rāma's glory is an abode of felicity."

❧ Kalawatee's Wedding, Chaguanas, 1919

"So these were songs you learned on the estate. And when you sisters were married, people were still working as indentured laborers?" I asked.

"Yes, yes. This was in Chaguanas."

"Were you married from the Lion House?"

"No. The Lion House was not built when we were married," Dhanpatee replied.

"I was married in 1919," Kalawatee went on. "I was ten-and-a-half years. Because Indian people will never marry after you get your period. You are marrying a maiden."

From what house were you married?"

"Well, it was an old house. It was a shop house because they used to run a shop. My father used to go and work in the fields and do his lay *panditāī* [priestly work]. But my mother used to run a shop. With all her children she used to run his shop."

"And you remember your wedding?"

"No. My father took all my vows. I slept. You see it was about midnight and I slept all the while. They bathed me about half-past nine in the night. The *dulahā* [groom] came and he bring the water. They catch the water when he is bathing and they bring it in a bottle. When he come they put him to sit down and they give him food to eat. Then they prepare you, the *dulahin* [bride]. They rubbed me with saffron for five days and all the time you in these saffron clothes. You have to bathe in the night because you have to wait for that water. They bathe you with *dahī,* yogurt, to take out the saffron quickly, and then they soap you down and bathe you clean. Then they throw that water from the *dulahā.* Then you get dressed in a yellow sari and you go to the wedding.

"So my father say I was sleeping and he had to take all the vows. Where I have to say 'yes,' well, he said it. When he was going to India, he said, 'Now I did it for you. You got to maintain those vows.' And sometime when me and husband get angry, I say, 'You damn lucky, you know! If I had given those vows I'd have break it now. But it's my father and he reminded me, "I give your vows, and don't let me down no way." And I promise him now. You know when I promise something I mean it. I could mind myself you know! Don't mind I ain go to high school!'"

"And what was married life like in those days?" I asked.

"I married in Claxton Bay. My father-in-law built a house and he bought some 17 acres of land, part with cocoa and part without cocoa. I used to pick cocoa and cutlass cocoa. I cut virgin land to plant rice. I used to cut a piece of grass measured so and so. And I would cut three time with that cutlass before I get to the ground. The grass was so thick because it was virgin soil. I didn't have to plow because it was virgin soil. I just scraped up the dirt and I sprinkled the rice seed.

"And I used to cut rice, beat it, pound it, and send it to my mother-in-law. I used to cut cane. This is why sometimes I get pain. My husband used to crack one thousand coconuts in his hand like that! I used to sit down and dig out all and dry *kopra* ("head"). When I cut cane I loaded it up using a crowbar. I had that crowbar, that souvenir, until recent days when some workmen stole it."

"I bore two sons and two daughters. And my two sons, they dead."

❧ Bhojpurī Poetry

By World War I, Bhojpurī had been adopted as a lingua franca by the Indians of Trinidad, prevailing over the dozen or so Dravidian and Indo-Aryan languages spoken by the immigrants. As suggested by linguist Mridula Adenwala Durbin, Bhojpurī "shares characteristic features with Bengalī on the one hand, and with Oudhī and Hindi on the other, and hence was capable of being used as a 'common language'" ("Formal Changes," 1301).

Archer describes Bhojpurī as "characterized by long drawled vowels, its fondness for labials, and its musical rhythms. An English which favored words like 'candle,' 'dangle,' 'ladle,' and 'meddle' would be an appropriate analogy" (*Songs*, xxxviii).

The Trinidad linguist Peggy Mohan recounts of her fieldwork in India: "I observed that the Bhojpurī spoken in all but the poorest villages of eastern U.P. differed strikingly from my own West Indian Bhojpurī in that while my Bhojpurī had preserved a pristine purity away from Hindi assault, Indian Bhojpurī was strongly affected by Hindi." What does the Indian villager see when confronted by the Trinidad Indian "searching for her roots?" "Does he see the face of the *angrez* [English]? Does he see the city Indian, come to mock him? No. The very purity of our Bhojpurī, which broke before it bent, marks us as *purabiyas* [eastern peoples]. Our very innocence about India, our curiosity about India, marks us as not what we appear to be, not Indians from the city. Hindi comes to us with difficulty as a genuinely foreign language ("Two Faces," 140–43).

These archaic nineteenth-century Bhojpurī song texts present a challenge for the ethnomusicologist, since usage, pronunciation, and vocabulary have changed in India over the years while the Trinidad language has been maintained as a marginal survival of bygone generations. The Felicity women found it practically impossible to translate song texts into English. Since they all spoke English, it surprised me that they only told the "meaning," the gist of the song. I soon realized this was a practiced skill they had learned from their mothers and grandmothers—the generations of exiled Indian women who had tried to provide simple explanations of this complex Asian heritage to Africans and Englishmen.

The meaning often begins "this is when ..." because singers associate each song with the ceremonial event it accompanies. The ceremony cues the song, and the ladies are commentators, likening the here and now—the imperfect and real—to the ideal, to the splendor of the ancient past, and to the perfect wedding of the perfect individuals, Rām and Sītā.

My native Hindi-speaking colleagues who heard the Trinidad songs invariably remarked on the lack of retroflex plosives (particularly *d* and *t*, made with the tip of the tongue touching the hard palate farther back than for English), and attributed this to the influence of English, which does not have these forms of *d* and *t*. Several talented English- and American-born Hindi scholars found these Felicity songs incomprehensible, because they differ radically from modern Hindi, and also because the words have been molded in the songs to accommodate the undulating melodies, sometimes with extra syllables, such as *lā* and *yā*, interpolated (*rāma* becomes *rāmaiyā*, *sītā* becomes *sītāla* in Example XVII, both to suit the melody and to suggest the sweet nature of these lovers). Bhojpurī is a musical language, and the predominance of speech particles such as *bā*, *wā*, *bū*, and *wū* function in song to float the melody. The most common method of adjusting the text to the melody is to add an *a* or an *i* (ex. XVI) as *bābā* becomes *bā-bā-ī* (three syllables) and *sindūr* becomes *sin-dū-rā* (adding an extra syllable). Sir George Grierson notes distinctions between sung and spoken language, that in Bhojpurī song "there are no silent final consonants, as there are in prose. Thus *subh* is pronounced in poetry *subha*, while in prose it is *subh*. In poetry, also, there is no neutral vowel. Thus, while in prose for 'you saw' we should say *dekh'las*, in poetry we should say *dekhalasa*." For songs he continues: "Each line contains a certain number of instants. . . . A short syllable contains one instant, and a long syllable contains two. . . . Sometimes a long syllable is read as a short one." He also notes that many songs "contain words like ai, nā, o, rām, which are mere expletives, used to fill up the meter," and also that "several old oblique forms will be found noted in these songs" (*Seven Grammars*, 109).

In Indian folk songs, the grammar of the sung language generally is different from that of the spoken, just as poetry is different from prose. The poetry of these songs depends on metaphor; they have a surface meaning and a second intent, often charming, loving, sexual, or allusive, referring to the ancient myths of India. The texts of the songs are dense, layered with meaning, as each item mentioned in the song represents a whole world of values. In example XII—"as the pearl in the bazaar shines, and the silk cloth from the south, so both Rām and Lakshmaṇ shine in the wedding canopy"—all the attributes of Rām (bravery, honor, strength) are understood and, with Lakshmaṇ, the constant devotion of a younger brother.

The deep cultural values preserved in these songs embody core beliefs. They conserve the rituals of a wedding, clarify the role of each participant, and illuminate the relationships. The groom, son of a king, radiant, resplendent on an elephant, superior to the bride, arrives with brothers and male relatives as for battle. The bride's father, supplicant to the groom, trembles in his presence, but defends the daughter's dignity and abuses the groom in a passage signifying loving abuse: "The bridegroom walks clumsily" (ex. XV, verses 3–4). The bride is shy and frightened, supported by virgin girl friends who are stunned by the radiant groom and ask what penance she performed to win him. The groom's mother, awaiting conquest of the bride, greets her son in a new role.

Men in an Indian household typically command the respect of the whole family, but in the wedding ceremony the father of the bride always has to lower his head to the father of the groom as acknowledgment of the superior social status of the groom over the bride. In example VIII, the father of the bride says: "Because of my daughter today I bowed." But in the fourth verse the melody and text take a happier turn, with a new melody phrase that is more animated and ornamented and in the upper tetrachord of the octave, as he remembers, "Wherever I went (even to Delhi) I never bowed to anyone." In other songs, the groom's father defends his son's innocence. The Felicity ladies sang:

73

[*Father of bride*]
"*Samadhī*, my daughter is an innocent,
"She knows nothing.
"Oh, *samadhī*, my daughter is an innocent,
"She knows nothing."

[*Father of groom replies*]
"*Samadhī*, my son is a lotus flower,
"They will sleep together happily.
"Oh, *samadhī*, my son is a lotus flower,
"They will sleep together happily."
[Father of the bride and father of the groom address each other as "*samadhī*."]

Details in the songs—flowers, fruits, trees, village well, places—refer to India, not Trinidad. In example VIII, the text would never be changed to read "Even when I went to Port of Spain."

In example XI, the mother of the bride steps forward and protects the groom using the end of her sari *(ãchalwā)*. The *ãchalwā* is a poignant symbol of womanhood and motherhood. Girls eligible for marriage choose a sari according to the price (expensive being good), the quality of the cloth, the legitimacy of the style (a Banaras sari had better be from Banaras), and especially the beauty of the *ãchalwā*, or *pallū* as the younger girls call it. At her wedding this beautiful *pallū* becomes the *purdah* (Urdu, "curtain") which separates her from her husband and older men, especially his older brothers. As a mother, the end of the sari creates a space for intimacy and privacy of mother and child in the open courtyard. Indians understand the importance of this garment, and in ritual have selected the image of the *ãchalwā* as the ultimate sign of acceptance and protection. In a Hindu wedding, a song is sung when the bridegroom's mother covers his head with her *ãchalwā* to signal the end of a stage in their relationship ("he'll never enjoy mother's milk again").

This idea is particularly meaningful for Felicity women. Rajiah sang:

74 ♫

You go son, *gaurī* marry, *gaurī* marry,
Milk of price make give.
Oh, milk of price make give.
Cow, buffalo of milk.
Elephant sell in bazaar sell.
Oh, mother of milk priceless.
Oh, mother of milk priceless.
You go son, *gaurī* marry, *gaurī* marry.
Milk of price make give.
When I come back mother *gaurī* marry.
Oh, *gaurī* marry.
Oh, then give milk of price.
Oh, then give milk of price.
Heaven stars mother count does not know,
Oh, count does not know.
Oh, how to give milk of price?
How to give milk of price?

Likewise, when the groom arrives at the bride's home, her mother steps forward to cover his head with her *ãchalwā* "so that the son of the king must not catch the drizzle of rain." Another song presents the bride's mother greeting her "beloved son-in-law-to-be" through the ritual of *parachhan* to drive away evil spirits (ex. IX, line 5).

But even these most meaningful of symbols may be invoked in fun, as in the *lachārī* (ex. VI) in which the jealous wife has cast a spell of night blindness over her husband so that her husband will not stray into the sister-in-law's bed. The wife regrets her impulsive mischief (he cannot find her bed either) and lists the possible remedies she can take, all of deep cultural and religious significance: "I will sweep the place with my hand" [as for the groom's procession, ex. VII, "Sweep the way (for) Pandit Rām, sweep the way"], "With mantras I will remove the fever" [as in ex. XII, Sītā's list of penances to win Rām], and most important, "With my *ãcharwā* ["breast;" playful pun on *ãchalwā*, the end of the sari, "veil of breast"] I will dispel the night blindness, oh, with my *ãcharwā* I will dispel the night blindness." This is a funny popular Felicity song.

I don't know what will happen to the wedding songs of Felicity. Many of them have already died out in India, the land of their origin. Laxmi Tewari has commented on the loss of traditional folk songs in central Uttar Pradesh:

> I remember one old widow named Bahureu Amma, who lived in my hometown of Kanpur, just twenty yards away from our family home. My mother always called for her at every ceremony, as did the other neighboring families, for she knew hundreds of songs for each ceremony, as well as all of the rituals. At every religious occasion, my family offered *sīdhā* [gifts of food and money] to her. Unfortunately, she died before my field trip, taking with her all the songs she knew. My vague memories of her singing style and song texts do not correspond with the songs of the present collection. In my opinion, folk songs have undergone revolutionary changes within two generations. The old generation is dying out and young people have not learned the old songs; many young couples have moved away from their family homes and modern trends have caused a lack of interest in the old traditions. ("Folk Music," 63)

"My memory is going now, you know," Kalawatee said.

"I don't think so," I replied.

"I forget a lot. I never wrote it down. I learn it from the people and I sing it like that. I just kept it in my head. And they don't care. Today people don't care."

"I care."

"Your feeling is my feeling," she answered.

Musical Style

I spent a great deal of time recording the *byāh ke gīt*. The style of this repertory conforms with that of central and eastern Uttar Pradesh. Wedding songs in northeastern India, the Trinidadians' ancestral homeland, are also in a leader–chorus form. Like the songs of Felicity, most have a range of less

Example XVIII: Melodic motifs of *Byāh Ke Gīt*

than an octave (none more than a ninth) and the melodic movement is primarily conjunct, yet upward leaps of a third and fourth are fairly common. Although a drone is absent, a strong sense of tonicity is clear. The character of the melodies depends on the tonic; they end on the tonic and generally move above and around the tonic. The melodies are often constructed from short repeated motifs, characterized by upward leaps followed by a slow downward drift, as shown in example XVIII.

Many of the songs have a metrical pattern based on four syllables (often one short and three long); rhythmic groupings of 3+4 and 2+3 are most frequent, and 2+2 occurs in several examples. In some songs the regular pattern of 3+4+3+4 resembles *dīpchandī tāl* (ex. XXII; Professor Adesh pointed this out to me). In other examples the groupings of seven might be heard to resemble *rūpak tāl.* Interruptions in the regularity of these patterns can usually be explained by the taking of breath or the overlap of the leader and chorus part. Most wedding songs in Uttar Pradesh likewise have metric structures of 2+2 and 3+4. Some of the Trinidad wedding songs take the form of *sthāyī* (chorus) and *antarā* (verse), the *sthāyī* lying in the lower half of the octave and the *antarā* in the upper (exx. VIII, X, XI, XIV, XVI, XVII, and XVIII).

Musical Feelings

When I asked the Felicity villagers what they thought of the *byāh ke gīt,* I encountered mixed reactions. Some girls giggled with embarrassment when they heard a wedding song. Others were confused and thought that any song the older ladies sang was for the wedding. Since the girls did not understand the Bhojpurī texts, they sometimes told me that a *sohar* (for childbirth) or a *kajarī* (for the rainy season) was a wedding song. But many people told me that their favorite songs were wedding songs. Some villagers told me they always cried when they heard wedding songs, because they were so beautiful. Many people in Felicity felt it was important for this repertory to be recorded for posterity and they were glad I had undertaken this task. As I worked, my enthusiasm for these songs grew, and before long I found that, like the folksong collectors of the late nineteenth century, I too was caught up by that special fascination with a vanishing tradition.

I say vanishing tradition, but in fact, I have no proof that this is a correct appraisal of the situation regarding Indian wedding songs in Trinidad. Perhaps it only seems that way. The villagers would tell me that the songs were dying out because the young girls were not learning them. And often enough during weddings it did seem as if they were disappearing right then and there as they were drowned out by the *tāssā* drummers or interrupted by a film song played by the hired orchestra on electronically amplified instruments. At a distance, it had been easy enough to dismiss the death of a tradition as a natural feature of culture change, but at close proximity, it became a sad possibility.

The villagers of Felicity also fear that traditional wedding songs will not survive past the next generation, but their view may be overly pessimistic. Whenever did it seem to the elder generation that the younger generation was picking up the right sort of songs?

Chapter Ten
A Song for Mr. Biswas

> Wherever I went, I never bowed to anyone.
> Because of my daughter, today I bowed.
> Because of my daughter, today I bowed.
>
> Traditional Bhojpurī Song

The conversation with the Permanand sisters had lingered on.

"So your father, Kapil Dev, came from India. He made the voyage?"

"Yes," Kalawatee replied with a hushed fascination. "He came as an indentured. And if you know how much trouble he go through in the estate. He went back to India. He died in India. I went to where he was born you know. Gorakhpur, Anandnagar, Gaun Dube Ka. It's a whole *gaun* [village] in the countryside. My father was a brahman, so the whole village. They name it after them, because all of them is related to one another and that spot where they live is twenty-four generation" (plate 35).

Kapil Dev

From Trinidadian sources we learn that Kapil Dev, known in Trinidad as Pandit Capildeo, was born in the village of Mahadewā Dube, Gorakhpur District, in 1873. Family members in Dube and in Trinidad concur that his father was Raghunath of the Dube lineage. Kapil signed up for indentureship and registered with a Bengali clerk in the immigrant ledger on 7 August 1894 at the Banaras sub-depot, falsely identifying himself as Kopil of the Johhattri caste, occupation "laborer." He sailed from Calcutta for Trinidad on the *Hereford* in late September on a three-month voyage during which 40 Coolies died. The *Hereford* put into the harbor of Port of Spain on 27 December 1894. Ten years after Sir George Grierson published his "Bhoj'pūrī Folksongs," ten years after Kakandi bought his plot on the site of Felicity, Kapil Dev was assigned to the Woodford Lodge Estate, west of Chaguanas and neighboring Felicité Estate. Verteuil reports that Capildeo, frail and pious, was assigned to the shovel gang, failed physically, was demoted to the weeding gang, and demoted further to cleaning animal pens.

According to Verteuil, an opportunistic Indian overseer at Woodford, Sirdar Gobinda, spotted the young brahman as a suitable groom for his fifteen-year-old daughter Soogee. Apparently Gobinda bargained with Capildeo: Verteuil reports that Capildeo, clever, shrewd, married Soogee and Gobinda "cut"

PLATE 35. Kalawatee Permanand, 1985.

Capildeo's indentureship, buying back his papers for ten pounds five shillings. The newlywed couple ran Govinda's shop on the main street of Chaguanas (*Eight East Indian Immigrants,* 114ff.).

Soogee bore fourteen children, of whom three died in infancy. Seven daughters, including Dhanpatee and Kalawatee, were born before the first son, Shambhu Nath, arrived. Then followed a second son, Rudra Nath, and two younger daughters including Droapatie, mother of the renowned novelist V. S. Naipaul.

In arranging the marriages of his first seven daughters, Pandit Capildeo was able to solve several problems at once, arranging three times for two of his daughters to marry brothers. For Dhanpatee and Kalawatee he found Ramnarine Permanand and Ramnarace Permanand from Claxton Bay in southern Trinidad. The other son-in-law pairs were Aknath and Dinanath Ramcharan from Fyzabad and Hargovind and Ramjattan Deepan from Carapichaima. The Lion House was replete with inlaws, and the tradition, humiliating to Indians, of their daughters' husbands living in their *sasurāl,* seems to have passed down for three generations in some lines of the family. But with this arrangement, the family prospered, gained wealth, and a degree of political clout on the island over the years. The Pandit visited India once in May 1909 and again in early 1926 (plate 36). Dube villagers built and maintained daily prayers in shrines honoring his name, and tell of his return—they among the few who ever learned of the fate of an *arkatiā* victim. Pandit died in India in '26 en route back to Trinidad.

※ The Mystery of the Lion House

"The Lion House was built in 1922," Kalawatee explained. "It's the Indian people from India who build it. The lion? You see the *devī* Durgā rides a lion. And my father was a devotee of her."

It was Droapatie's son who told fantastic stories of life in a house much like the Lion House, which he describes in *A House for Mr. Biswas* (1964). My village friends told me: "The pond, the pond where Biswas father did drown is in Felicity. Naipaul put us in the story. You can find Felicity named."

Mr. Biswas (said to be patterned after Naipaul's father), an itinerant sign painter, had approached Shama while working at Hanuman House. Biswas was caught by Mrs. Tulsi and forced to marry Shama—a 'love match'—in India and in olden Trinidad a social disgrace beyond remedy, and here a double disgrace since Biswas moved into his *sasurāl,* home of his *sasur,* father-in-law, Pandit Tulsi.

Biswas turned bitter. The rules of Indian culture dictate this as clearly as do many passages in *A House for Mr. Biswas.*

"'How the little gods getting on today, eh?'" he would ask.

"He meant her brothers. The elder attended the Roman Catholic college in Port of Spain and came home every weekend; the younger was being coached to enter the college. At Hanuman House they were kept separate from the turbulence of the old upstairs" (Naipaul, *A House for Mr. Biswas,* 94).

"'And what about the two gods? It ever strike you that they look like two

PLATE 36. In Mahadewā Dube, in 1986, Jagga Nath Dube holds the photo of his grand uncle, Kapil Dev, with his Trinidadian wife, Soogee.

monkeys? So, you have one concrete monkey-god outside the house and two living ones inside. They could just call this place the monkey house and finish. Eh, monkey, bull, cow, hen. The place is like a blasted zoo, man'" (108).

According to custom, Biswas could never have due respect in "Hanuman House" (after Hanumān, the monkey devotee of Lord Rām). The intercepted love note that he sent to Shama, "I love you and I want to talk to you" sealed his fate. Naipaul likely knew that in India "talking" is the euphemism not for the feeling but for the act of love. Like his father-in-law Tulsi, Biswas, through his own action, became a prisoner of Hanuman House.

Was the case for self-deprecation in V. S. Naipaul's writing laid long before his birth? Was the humiliation of family men by family women hurtful, although disguised in public by wealth and success? Only behind the closed doors of that now crumbling edifice, with its balconies and verandas so like the wealthy townhouses of Gorakhpur, the shop façade and its back rooms, the formal downstairs parlors, and the labyrinth of crowded family rooms upstairs for the sons-in-law and their wives and children, with noise and confusion everywhere—only from its ghosts could answers come.

Alas for Naipaul senior, his wife was younger. Living crowded in the Lion House with his wife's sisters and their husbands was for an East Indian a humiliation no Westerner can appreciate. What pent-up rage could ensue, as such a man could not exercise an Indian husband's typical male dominance—shouting, bullying, even beating. His dealings with the sisters' husbands were cynical and cold, as they should be, for this *saṛū-bhāī* interaction is said by Indian men to be the worst and most difficult of the Indian "avoidance" relationships. Inevitably the relationships may worsen, as husbands vie aggressively for superiority.

In *A House for Mr. Biswas,* most humiliating for Biswas was bearing witness to the *jījā-sālī* relationship, the "joking" relationship, flirtatious and dangerous, whereby the husband of a woman's older sister can make outright sexual advances to the younger sister, here Biswas's wife Shama. In this relationship, the woman can retaliate, can pinch him, tease, and assert: "Come on then, I'm your *sālī.*" More commonly she runs in shyness from the room. Occasionally there is more—older sister's husband with younger sister; *Sālī ādhī gharwālī:* "*Sālī* is half wife." Custom suggests the younger husband might well endure the abuse in silence.

Chance and choice together set V. S. Naipaul's fate. Soogee gave birth to nine powerful daughters. The Dube genealogy in India terminates with Kapil Dev's two sons, but the Trinidad genealogy begins with those nine women. According to Indian village custom the heir has to be the oldest son of the oldest son of the oldest son. But the lion author of our time and language happens to be the son of the younger daughter—a position of low respect according to the customs of India. Could such a Naipaul ever love Trinidad where these customs were broken? Could such a Naipaul ever love India where these customs were formed?

Naipaul never turns to romance in his novels. Whence this aversion in one who writes of other passions? The old aunt Dhanpatee told me about wedding nights and the great sandalwood doors, about Rām and Sītā, about the *kohabar* love chamber, the breaking of the virginal *kangan* from the wrists of bride and bridegroom, about the feeding of round brown and sensual sweets, about the shyness, the fear, the lust, the hesitation, the haste. "Well this is the world. This is nature. This is what really is," she explained.

What visions from Lion House have passed down from Naipaul's childhood? What contradictions and confusions of a double inheritance have contaminated the pleasures either homeland could offer? What forces have created for him the trapdoor he named "that India which lived on into my childhood in Trinidad?" "In India I know I am a stranger" (*India,* xi).

Nor was he pleased with Trinidad upon his return after Oxford: "As soon as the *Francisco Bobadilla* had touched the quay, ship's side against rubber bumpers, I began to feel all my old fear of Trinidad. I did not want to stay. . . . I had no assurance that I would ever leave the island again. . . . I had never liked the sugarcane fields. Fat, treeless and hot, they stood for everything I had hated about the tropics and the West Indies" (*Middle Passage,* 40, 62).

It was Kalawatee who cared for the Lion House. She told me of an accident that she had in 1974 while repairing the Lion House. "The taxi knocked me right down there."

"You were repairing the Lion House?"

"Yes, I did. It is my responsibility. I rent below. Upstairs is empty. Well I repairing it, but it still want repairs and I can't make it now; this is my problem. I asking my sister and she was going to help, but since she young Shiva son die, she like she not catching."

∾ MAHADEWĀ DUBE

Kalawatee and Dhanpatee never mentioned Droapatie's older son, V. S., to me, nor I him to them. But in Dube, villagers told of his visit, showed me the family pictures, and asked to be photographed holding them. Yet the genealogy Jagganath recited in December 1989 does not mention his name, only those of his mother's brothers. What abuse!

The Bobina Hotel in Gorakhpur lay outside the town center and backed onto a swamp. The local inhabitants used this wetland as a latrine. And so did I, I realized the first morning when I flushed the toilet and heard water draining out of an open pipe on the outside of the bathroom just behind the wall. The infestation of mosquitoes was not beyond belief, but beyond endurance. Umesh lit green coils in my room at night and had the room swept, aired, and sprayed in the morning. He did not like me taking chloroquine, and believed more in the toxic fumes of the sprays and the coils.

"We get used to these chemicals since the Green Revolution," he said. "They are in our food and they give us gas trouble."

I was reading *An Area of Darkness.*

"Umesh, we must search out every clue if we are going to find this Dube place. There are tens of Dube villages around here. Listen here. Naipaul 'turned off onto an embankment of pure dust. It was lined with tall old trees.' That's in his chapter 'The Village of the Dubes,' here on page 252. On the next page he says, 'The tall, branching mango trees shaded an artificial pond, and the floor of the grove was spotted with blurred sunshine.' What beautiful writing."

"Going good, Helen," Umesh said. "Dust, trees, mangoes, and sunshine. We should be able to find that. Now I'm going out for more coils and then to the Post Office. Read another page in your book."

After two hours Umesh returned with the coils.

"Where were you!" I hollered.

"If you want to see Dube, your rickshaw is waiting downstairs."

"Naipaul went in a jeep with the IAS man—page 254."

"Well, if *you* want to go, you are going on the local train, and you are going with me."

"You're not the IAS!"

"Well, you're not Naipaul."

The train took five hours to reach Anandnagar Junction.

"*Darkness* says that a woman called Jussodra lived in Dube. Naipaul spoke with her. And she had been to Trinidad. She gave most of the information about Kapil Dev. Here on page 255, listen—"

"Yes, yes."

"When he was a young man (Jussodra said) my grandfather left this village to go to Banaras to study, as brahmins had immemorially done. But my grandfather was poor, his family poor, and times were hard; there might even have been a famine. One day my grandfather met a man who told him of a country far away called Trinidad. There were Indians in Trinidad, labourers; they needed pundits and teachers. The wages were good, land was cheap and a free passage could be arranged. The man who spoke to my grandfather knew what he was talking about. He was an *arkatia,* a recruiter; when times were good he might be stoned out of a village, but now people were willing to listen to his stories. So my grandfather indentured himself for five years and went to Trinidad. He was not, of course, made a teacher; he worked in the sugar factory. He was given a room, he was given food; and in addition he received twelve annas, fourteen pence, a day. It was a lot of money, and even today it was a good wage in this part of India, twice as much as the government paid for relief work in distress areas. My grandfather added to this by doing his pundit's work in the evenings. Banaras-trained pundits were rare in Trinidad and my grandfather was in demand. Even the sahib at the factory respected him, and one day the sahib said, 'You are a pundit. Can you help me? I want a son.' 'All right,' my grandfather said. 'I'll see that you get a son.' And when the sahib's wife gave birth to a son, the sahib was so pleased he said to my grandfather, 'You see these thirty *bighas* of land? All these canes there are yours.' My grandfather had the canes cut and sold them for two thousand rupees, and with this he went into business. Success attracted success. A well-to-do man, long settled in Trinidad, came to my grandfather one day and said, 'I've been keeping my eye on you for some time. I can see that you are going to go far. Now I have a daughter and would like her to be married to you. I will give you three acres of land.' My grandfather was not interested. Then the man said, 'I will give you a buggy. You can hire out the buggy and make a little extra money.' So my grandfather married. He prospered. He built two houses."

"Umesh," I said. "This account is different from the more recent accounts in Verteuil, Yelvington, and Mohammed."

A nod. It seemed the local train was moving slower than walking pace, and the romance of Indian steam trains was diminished by the coal dust blowing in through the open windows and the louvers of the shutters. "Umesh, it mentions Kapil Dev's return to India. Listen."

"Soon he was wealthy enough to come back to this village and redeem twenty-five acres of his family's land. Then he went back to Trinidad. But he was a restless man. He decided to make another trip to India. 'Come back quick,' his family said to him. . . . But my grandfather didn't see Trinidad again. On the train from Calcutta he fell ill, and he wrote to his family: 'The sun is setting'" (256).

Umesh was asleep when the train ground to a halt at Anandnagar Junction. I jumped out and photographed all the signs declaring "City of Joy Junction, City of Joy Junction!" I photographed the old *sāraṇgī* player on the platform and gave him too much money. But even the fervor of my song quest could not convert Anandnagar into anything more than a confused and dusty *tashil* town with no hotel, no restaurants, and no bottled drinks.

Umesh led me to the jeep stand (plate 37).

"Now you'll see your pure dusty and your mangoes," he laughed.

A long, straight, tree-lined and well-trafficked road. Tea stalls along the way invited, but there was no possibility of unpacking the human cargo of that jeep. Dube was near the end of the route. The driver dropped us at a junction

Plate 37. The author in Anandnagar, Gorakhpur District, U.P., en route to Mahadewā Dube village, 1986.

where a weekly market was open. Umesh paid our fare while I dashed off to the bangle seller (plate 38).

"Now I will wear glass bangles for you! No more fussing about ugly bare wrists!" I shouted with enthusiasm until the boy started to force the tiny red glass hoops over my hands and drops of blood appeared and broken bangle pieces fell to the ground. "Ouch!! And I will buy you seven cotton undershirts! OUCH!!"

"I only use two," Umesh said. "One to wash, one to wear."

"No, it should be seven, one for every day of the week. Anything, I can do anything today. I will wear *sindūr!* I have seen the whole pond and the half lotus and now I am at the gate of Dube."

A crowd was gathering. One man stepped forward and introduced himself to Umesh.

"Come on Helen. We must sleep here tonight. This man is a village teacher and he has offered his roof."

Plate 38. At the market outside Mahadewā Dube, the local bangle seller forces tiny, fragile glass wedding bangles onto the wrist of the author, 1986.

The Genealogy

"Who can tell of the Dube lineage?" Umesh asked on our second day in Dube. And the younger farmers went to search out Jagga Nath. *Pāgal,* the mentally retarded bachelor, had been following me since I arrived.

Kohī bāt nahī. Woh to pāgal hai: "Never mind. He is just crazy," they reassured me. *Hoshiyār rahanā woh pāgal hai.* "Be careful he is mad," they warned Umesh.

Probably the title of Naipaul's book made us feel darkness in the village. The *pāgal* didn't help. Umesh and I were given coffee. Halfway through Jagga Nath's recitation of the lineage, Umesh decided that his coffee had been laced with opium.

"And Param Din had four sons, Dudha Nath, Mewa Nath, Bhup Narayan, and Shambu Nath." Jagga Nath recited each name in a monotone, shouting each one stacatto as if he was giving the scores of a football game. "And Dudha Nath had three sons, Gopal and Saraju and Jamana." And so on and so on and so on (plate 39; table 4).

Plate 39. Jagga Nath Dube (left) recites seven generations of the family genealogy for Umesh (seated, right foreground). Mahadewā Dube, 1986.

"I'm dizzy in the head," Umesh whispered.

I was perched on the back of the *charpāī,* absolutely still as the received wisdom, the village *sruti* ("what is heard"), was being recorded on tape and, by Umesh, with ink on paper. How hard I had searched to finally learn that Anandnagar (City of Joy) was nowadays Pharenda, that this particular Dube village was *the* Dube village. How I glowed as the jeep had bumped along the dusty road, to see ponds half covered with the lotus flowers, and half empty.

"And Bhup Narayan had four sons, Ganesh, Jagat, Jagdish, and Ganpati, and Ganesh had one son, Rām Subhag." And so on and so on and so on.

"What about the daughters," Umesh asked, having understood something of my interest in women's songs.

"Never mind the daughters," Jagga Nath laughed. "If we do the daughters, we will never finish!"

"And Dhore Dube had two sons, Rām Piyare and Rām Jit. And Rām Piyare had two sons, Janardan and Rajendra. And Janardan had three sons, Sanjay, Vijay Kant, and Anil." And so on and so on and so on.

Table 4 *Dube–Naipaul Genealogy*

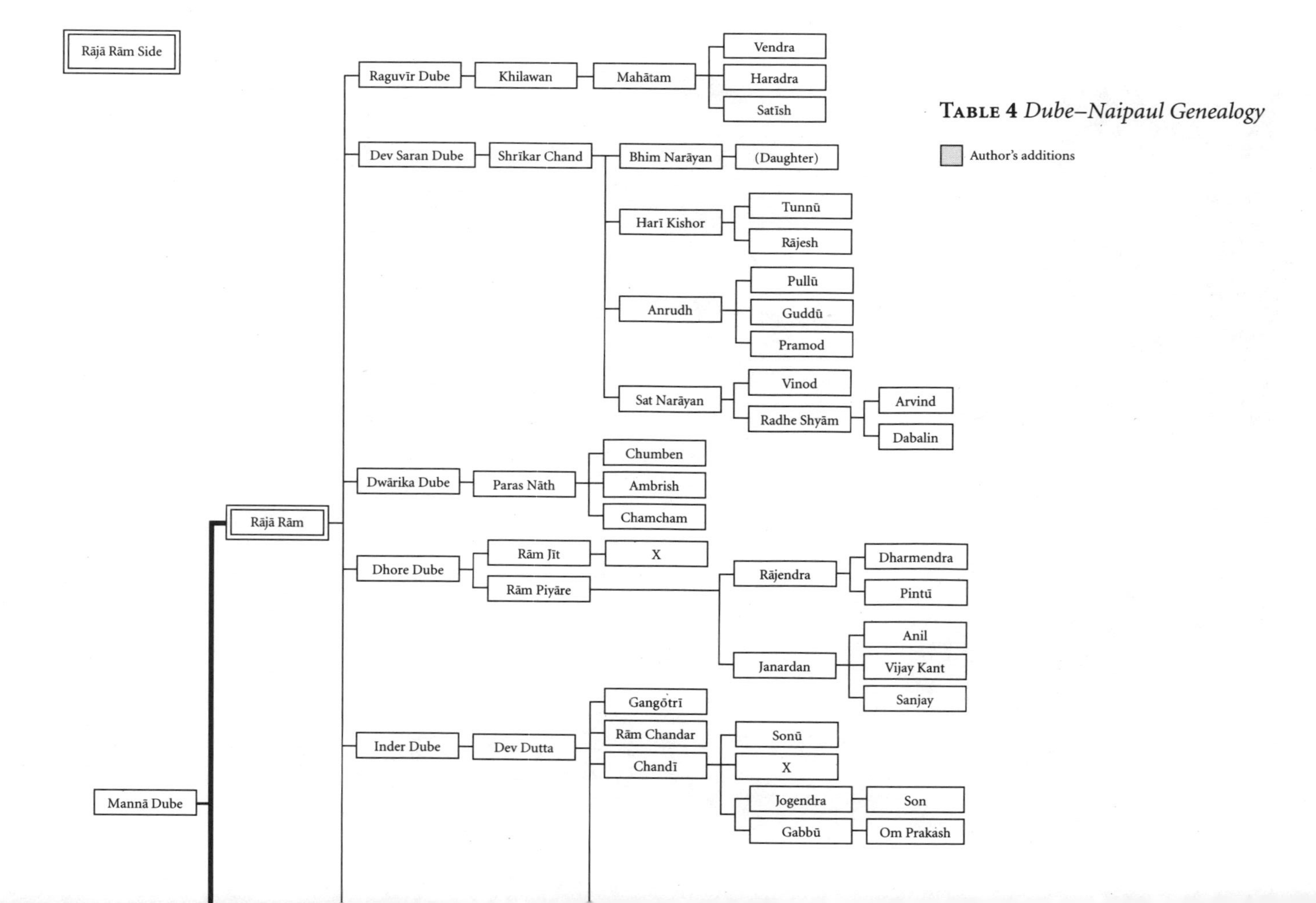

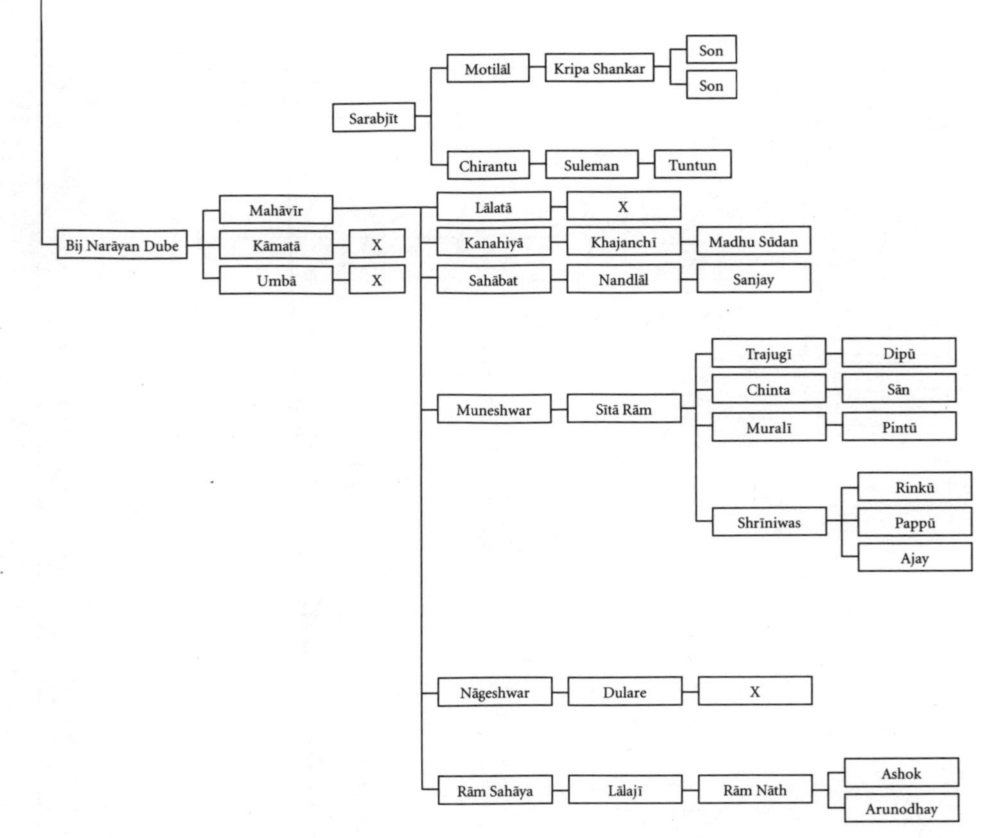

Sarabjīt
Motilāl
Kripa Shankar
Son
Son
Chirantu
Suleman
Tuntun
Bij Narāyan Dube
Mahāvīr
Kāmatā
X
Umbā
X
Lālatā
X
Kanahiyā
Khajanchī
Madhu Sūdan
Sahābat
Nandlāl
Sanjay
Muneshwar
Sītā Rām
Trajugī
Dipū
Chinta
Sān
Muralī
Pintū
Shrīniwas
Rinkū
Pappū
Ajay
Nāgeshwar
Dulare
X
Rām Sahāya
Lālajī
Rām Nāth
Ashok
Arunodhay

(Table 4 continued)

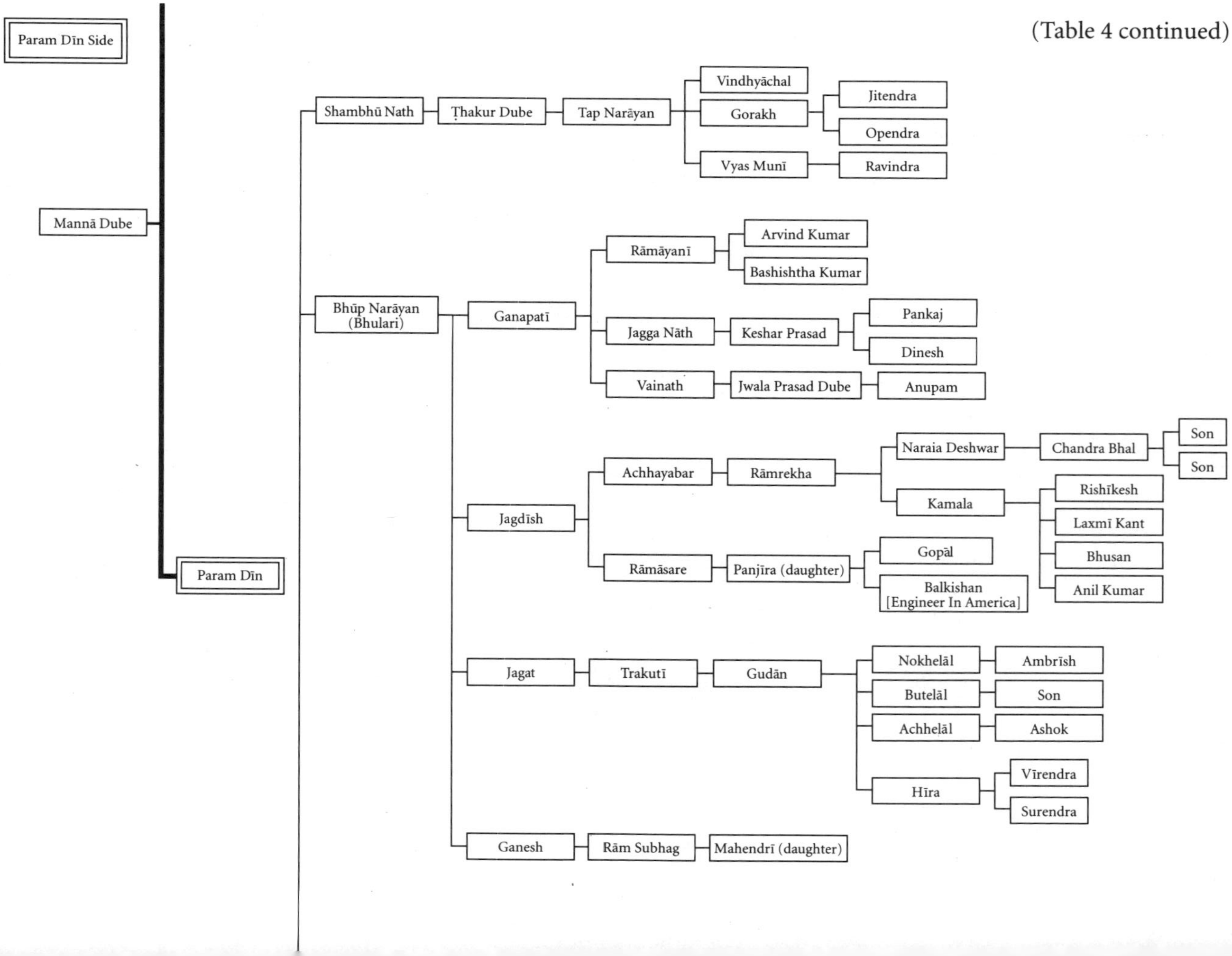

Param Dīn Side

- Mannā Dube
- Param Dīn
  - Shambhū Nath
    - Ṭhakur Dube
      - Tap Narāyan
        - Vindhyāchal
        - Gorakh
          - Jitendra
          - Opendra
        - Vyas Munī
          - Ravindra
  - Bhūp Narāyan (Bhulari)
    - Ganapatī
      - Rāmāyanī
        - Arvind Kumar
        - Bashishtha Kumar
      - Jagga Nāth
        - Keshar Prasad
          - Pankaj
          - Dinesh
      - Vainath
        - Jwala Prasad Dube
          - Anupam
    - Jagdīsh
      - Achhayabar
        - Rāmrekha
          - Naraia Deshwar
            - Chandra Bhal
              - Son
              - Son
          - Kamala
            - Rishīkesh
            - Laxmī Kant
            - Bhusan
            - Anil Kumar
      - Rāmāsare
        - Panjīra (daughter)
          - Gopāl
          - Balkishan [Engineer In America]
    - Jagat
      - Trakutī
        - Gudān
          - Nokhelāl
            - Ambrīsh
          - Butelāl
            - Son
          - Achhelāl
            - Ashok
          - Hīra
            - Vīrendra
            - Surendra
    - Ganesh
      - Rām Subhag
        - Mahendrī (daughter)

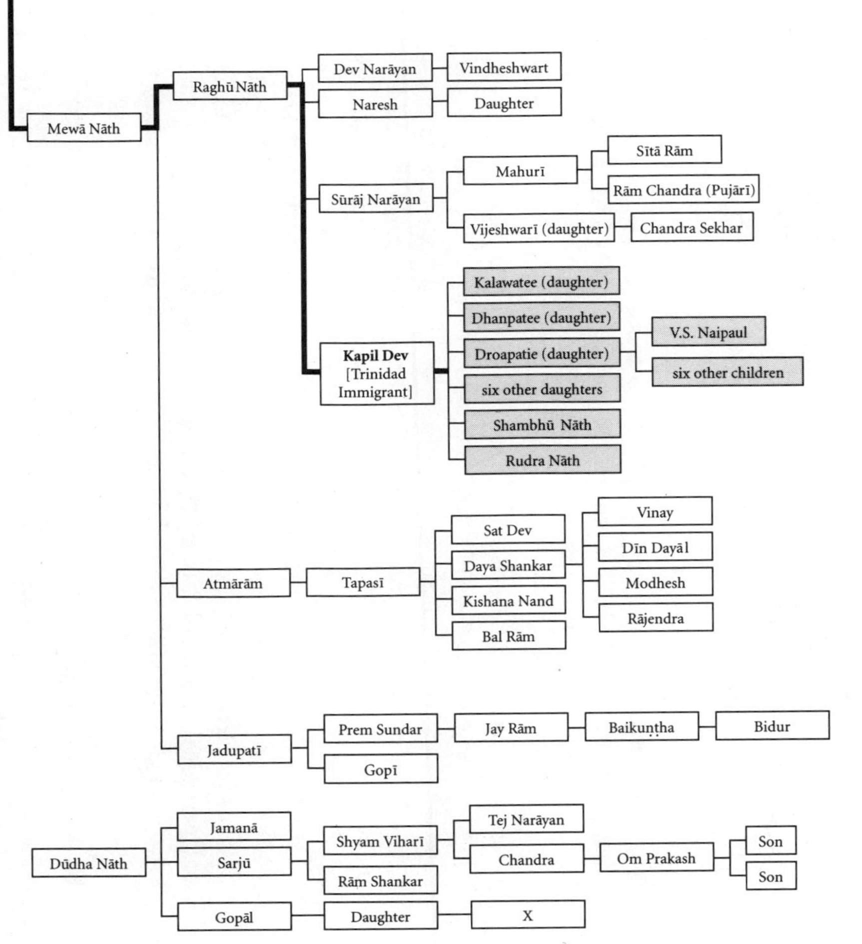

Mewā Nāth
Raghū Nāth
Dev Narāyan
Vindheshwart
Naresh
Daughter
Sūrāj Narāyan
Mahurī
Sītā Rām
Rām Chandra (Pujārī)
Vijeshwarī (daughter)
Chandra Sekhar
Kapil Dev
[Trinidad
Immigrant]
Kalawatee (daughter)
Dhanpatee (daughter)
Droapatie (daughter)
V.S. Naipaul
six other children
six other daughters
Shambhū Nāth
Rudra Nāth
Atmārām
Tapasī
Sat Dev
Daya Shankar
Kishana Nand
Bal Rām
Vinay
Dīn Dayāl
Modhesh
Rājendra
Jadupatī
Prem Sundar
Jay Rām
Baikuṇṭha
Bidur
Gopī
Dūdha Nāth
Jamanā
Sarjū
Shyam Viharī
Tej Narāyan
Chandra
Om Prakash
Son
Son
Rām Shankar
Gopāl
Daughter
X

"I am getting hot," Umesh whispered. "I am fainting."

"Just write the names," I said. Ponds with lotus I was thinking. I could see the *pāgal* staring out from the crowd around us.

"My tongue is coming out. I can't even speak. I am dying here!"

"Then write. You are allergic to coffee," I snapped with impatience. I fumbled in my bag. Take this antihistamine. You are allergic to everything."

"No more medicine, no more medicine," Umesh mumbled.

"And Dev Saran had one son Shrīkar Chand, and Shrīkar Chand had four sons, Sat Narayan, Anrudh, Hari Kishor, and Bhim Narayan. And Anrudh had three sons, Pramod, Guddu, and Pullu." And so on and so on and so on.

Jagga Nath began to ask the younger men, and then the children for the names of teens, boys, then infants, up to the youngest Dube babe. Thus Umesh and the old farmer documented the lineage of older and some younger sons of Dube Village, a patriarchy that is faithfully recorded in table 4.

Umesh collapsed back on the *charpāī* into a drugged sleep. The *pāgal* came up to me again, crawling and grinning. The girls then actually dragged me off to find out if I was a man or a woman (I was wearing a T-shirt and jeans). They pulled me into the back room and took off my clothes. They played with my bra and waved it like a flag. They wrapped me into the best family sari. Like a doll, they played with me, adding ornaments and makeup and then covered my face with the *ăchal* of the sari as is proper for married women. They led me out into the courtyard and took photos of me with my own cameras. They woke Umesh and shouted, "She is dressed in sari! She is dressed in sari! Come see your new Kashmiri bride!" That night they told me the room I had was no longer available. They covered their veranda with straw from the rice harvest and gave us quilts. Everyone in the village could see that he and I had been put to sleep together outside, just a few feet from the lane.

Umesh was angry and worried. "He offered roof, not veranda. We are the only people sleeping out-of-doors in this whole bloody Dube village. This is a red alert area—I learned it today. You might be taken by a bandit. So don't speak a single word and tie those bangles so they wouldn't jingle in the night."

An Area of Darkness

The next morning we headed back for Pharenda, loaded down with records of the Dube generations. I decided to leave *An Area of Darkness* in the village, as a kind of presentation to Naipaul's closest relative. Umesh was unwilling to take me to Ramchandra's house. I insisted. I wanted to make something of a formal speech. "I give you this book . . . a token . . . appreciation . . . hospitality and song . . . your family and the world." Umesh would translate.

"Don't go into that house!" Umesh warned.

When we reached the turn in the lane, I could see through the open door that *pāgal* was shackled, lying on the floor inside the house. As I walked up the path, *pāgal* made a lunge for the door and dragged himself out onto the ground, bound hand and foot. He was was shouting and crying and drooling. Ramchandra was not in sight.

"We'll go now," I said, and I stuffed *Darkness* into my backpack.

At Pharenda I read more long passages to Umesh and he replied yes and yes and yes and yes.

"Listen here on page 257. He is telling about his evening back in Gorakhpur after visiting the village. He wrote a letter—"

"Yes, yes."

"'In the hotel in the town that evening I wrote a letter. The day had provided such unlikely adventure. It distorted time; again and again I came back, with wonder, to my presence in that town, in that hotel, at that hour. There had been those images, those photographs, those scraps of Trinidad English in that Indian village' (257)."

"Yes."

"But Umesh, perhaps this was the Bobina Hotel where we stayed. And perhaps those were the same photos that we saw yesterday."

"Yes, yes. But why is this V. S. so important to you?"

"Oh! I say he is the greatest living writer in the English language. And his aunts sang for me. Listen here, he has a song in it: 'The act of writing released not isolated memories but a whole forgotten mood. The letter finished, I went to sleep. Then there was a song, a duet, at first part of memory, it seemed, part of that recaptured mood. But I was not dreaming; I was lucid. The music was real.

> "'Tumhin ne mujhko prem sikhaya,
> "'Soté hué hirdaya ko jagaya.
> "'Tumhin ho roop singar balam.'" (257)

"I *love* this song," Umesh said. "I want it, I want a copy of it so I can have this song. It is hard to get such kinds of songs you know."

"Naipaul says it was a song from the 1930s. Listen to what he writes: 'I had ceased to hear it years before, and until this moment I had forgotten it. I did not even know the meaning of all the words; but then I never had. It was pure mood, and in that moment between waking and sleeping it had recreated a morning in another world, a recreation of this, which continued' (257).

"Listen Umesh, he walked in the bazaar here in Gorakhpur: 'I saw the harmoniums, one of which had lain broken and unused, part of the irrecoverable past, in my grandmother's house, the drums, the printing blocks, the brass vessels. Again and again I had that sense of dissolving time' (257–58)."

"Yes, yes."

☙ Dube Song

Knowing that Kalawatee and Dhanpatee in fact should not be carriers of the Dube (their father's) musical traditions, the first song I heard in Dube had everything of their style in it, and, most remarkably, the unmistakable melodic strains of the *kanyādān* song (ex. XIV). It was a wedding song, *vivāh,* to be sung any time before marriage, set to a *Rāmāyaṇ* text. The researcher must accept what she finds.

The Dube girls sang these words to the familiar strains of the Trinidad tune. Umesh translated the words:

75 ☙
King Janak a garden plant,
Flowers bloom *kachanār* [type of Indian flower].
King Janaka a garden plant,
Flowers bloom *kachanār.*
Rām, Lakhan, Dasrathjī of son,
Garden to see go.
King Janaka,
Garden to see go.
House in from came out daughter Sītālī Rānī,
Hand a flower basket, mouth betel.
House in from came out daughter Sītāli Rānī,
Hand a flower basket, mouth betel.
Hastily arm hold Shrī Rām Chand,
Come Sītā for tonight.
Hastily arm hold Siya Rām Chand.

"Umesh, what does this mean?" I asked.

"Why for the night? Because this song tells of a love marriage between Rām and Sītā. They met in the garden when Rām went to pluck flowers. Tulsī Dās never said this. He only mentions that they saw each other and they were lost in each other eyes. This Dube song is the imagination of a different poet who felt they fell in love."

"The same Dube poet who put us sleeping on the straw I suppose?"

"This poet was certainly not from Dube. There are no poets in Dube village. But this song goes on":

Leave leave darling, small my arm,
Arm small tender.
Leave leave darling, small my arm,

Arm small tender.
When Janak king question will begin,
That moment what will reply?
When [obscure] ask will begin,
That moment what reply?
Where passed Sītā entire noon?
Where passed entire night?
Where passed Sītā entire noon?
Where passed night?
Flower plucking took entire noon.
Vessel filling night.
Way walking too entire *paharawā* [noon hours],
That is why passed so delay.
Way walking passed entire *paharawā,*
That is why passed so delay.
Oh, take the father bulb turmeric.
Why not take yellow *janeū* [sacred cord]?
Take father bulb of turmeric.
Why no yellow *janeū?*
East search for father, search for west,
Searched out country around.
East searched father, west searched,
Searched out country around.
You suit, oh daughter, bridegroom not found,
Now Sītā stay maiden.
You suit, daughter, bridegroom not found,
Now Sītā stay maiden.
Oh, go na father Ayodhya city,
King Dasarath of gate.
Go na *bābā* Ayodhya city,
King Dasarath of gate.
King Dasarathjī of four sons,
Four all young unmarried.
King Dasarathjī of four sons,
Four all young unmarried.
King Dasarath daughter big is wicked,
Keep will not respect our.
King Dasarath daughter big is wicked,
Keep will not respect our.
Gate at gold of biggest dish.
Gate at gold of biggest dish.
Marawā in come will father Sītā,
Will remain respect your.
Marawā in come will father Sītā,
Remain will respect your.
To whom, oh daughter, so much not I will have,
He how arrange wedding?

To whom, oh daughter, so much not I will have,
He how arrange wedding?
To whom, oh father, so much not will have,
He should father search for a farmer!
To whom, oh daughter, so much not will have,
He should bridegroom search for a farmer!
Moves Shrī Rām Chand own wedding,
Left and right caws crows.
Moves King Rām Chandra own wedding,
Left and right caws crows.
Come on, brother Lakshmaṇ, omen think over,
Come on, brother Lakshmaṇ, omen think over,
What reason caws crows?
Come on, brother Lakshmaṇ, omen think over,
What reason caws crows?
Come on, brother Lakshmaṇ, omen think over,
What reason caws crows?
[Obscure] home would be taken away.
Left and right caws crows.
How would be taken away?
Three from Rām Chand home came back,
Mother open hard door.
Three from Rām Chand home came back,
Mother open hard door.
How to open son hard door?
Till now not sit.
How I open son hard door?
Till now not sit.
Now, oh mother, my with head,
Later will sit to eat.
Heart to a great pain feel,
Heart to a great pain feel.
If you, oh mother, such pain feel,
Not me will go to wed.
If you, oh mother, such pain feel,
I won't get wed.
That you betel sell my father,
Then arrange daughter of wedding.
That you betel sell my father,
Then arrange daughter of wedding.
When *bāriātiyā* [groomsmen],
When *bāriātiyā* [obscure],
Slept Janak, oh awake, sit down,
Gaurā flew in the sky.
Slept Janak, oh awake, sit down,
Gaurā flew in the sky.
When *bāriātiyā* [at] gate,

When *bāriātiyā* [at] gate,
Slept mother, oh got up looked.
Gate at arrived *bārāt,*
Slept mother, oh got up looked.
Gate at settled *bazār.*

ஐ

"Then what kind of village is this Dube?" I asked Umesh.

"I found this village usual. They have enmity with each other. They have cooperations with each other. They have social problems and political."

"They have my *pāgal!*"

"Never mind your *pāgal.* They all look the same—cast in the same pot."

"Maybe they all go to the same barber."

"I haven't seen any real healthy person in the village. Just like sticks, whether is old or young. Do they carry some kind of illness all together? All were yellowish. And I haven't seen any smiling faces in this village? Have you? Laughing smiling people? Have you? Well, what does your V. S. call it? Darkness, darkness! Some families are not on talking terms with each other. And there is a big court case over Kapil Dev's land. V. S. did try to help them, you know."

A Song for Mr. Biswas

"Umesh, what does the song mean, the one you wanted to keep?"

"It says, 'Only you who me love taught,
'Slept heart to wake up,
'Only you is beauty and adornment my love,' "

"Yes," I said.

※ Chapter Eleven ※

Song of Swans and Snakes

> The male swan is feeding in half of the the pond.
> The female swan is feeding in half of the pond.
> Still, even then the pond is not beautiful without the lotus.
> Oh, even then the pond is not beautiful without the lotus.
>
> Traditional Bhojpurī Song

Moon was a tiny lady, less than five feet, slim, and so named because her pretty face was round like the moon (plate 40). Her enthusiasm for the old wedding songs stirred me, as she explained the melodies, the words, their role in the wedding, and their importance to the Indians of Trinidad. She amazed me with her small crisp voice and her unfailing memory of the long complex texts. I amazed her with my tape recorder and Western music notation.

※ The Swan Song: Moon

"This is a song for Friday of the wedding," she said, "when the sister-in-law has to decorate the *kalasā* [wedding pitcher]." I learned from Moon these Bhojpurī folk songs are like a drama in which a narrator and actors speak the lines.

"The male swan is feeding in half of the pond," Moon said, "and the female is feeding in the other half, yet the pond is not beautiful without the *puraina*, the lotus leaf.

"When the time come for the *nanad*, the sister-in-law, to fix the *kalasā* for the wedding, she was not there. This is between two sister-in-law: the husband sister is called *nanad* and the husband wife is called *bhaujī*. The *nanad* didn't reach in time so the *bhaujī* asking the wife of the barber, 'my *nanad* is not here, but can you do the part for she?' While she was saying that, the *bhaujī* saw the *nanad* and her husband coming. She see the horse with her brother-in-law and the palanquin, so she say, 'well come and do your bidding.' So the *nanad* say, 'well I'm coming to do it, but what you going to give me for doing it?' So the *bhaujī* say, 'Ask.'

"So the *nanad* say, 'I want a very beautiful sari and I want a golden locket for my son, and I want a horse for my husband.' So the *bhaujī* turn to the husband and she said that 'I was telling you not to invite you sister, because we don't have all these things to give!' He say, 'I'm going to give my sister the

Plate 40. Moon Ramnarine, 1975.

sari, and I'm going to give my nephew the golden locket, and I'm going to give my brother-in-law the horse, and they will be happy and return home.' So he say, 'How you don't want me to invite them. She's my own sister from one father and mother. How dare you tell me not to invite her?' He curse her and he say, 'We come from one mother and father. How you don't want me to invite them? I am going to get everything she ask for and she will go back, leave my house pleasing.'"

Moon sang for me (ex. XIX):

Example XIX
Ādhe Talaiyā (Moon's Version)

ādhe talaiyā mẽ hansin chune ādhe mẽ hansā chune ho
are tabahū na talawā sohāwana ekahī puraina bīna ho
are tabahū na talawā sohāwana ekahī puraina bīna ho
ādhe maṛuwā more naihara ādhe sasurāre ke ho
are tabahū na maṛawā sohāwana ekahī nanada bīna ho
are tabahū na maṛawā sohāwana ekahī nanada bīna ho

ālhara basawā kaṭāwe bhaiyā maṛawā chhawāwelā ho
are ūche chaḍhi bhaiyā more chitawe bahinī more āwelā ho
are ūche chaḍhi bhaiyā more chitawe bahinī more āwelā ho
bhītara hauwā ki bāhara e more dhaniyā̃ ho
dhanā āwelā bābā ke dulārī garaba nahī̃ bolabau ho
dhāna āwelā bābā ke dulārī garaba nahī̃ bolabau ho
āwa āwa nanada gosāīnī more ṭhakuraīni ho
nanadī baiṭho more chanana pīḍhaiyā kalasā mora gõṭhau ho
nanadī baiṭho more chanana pīḍhaiyā kalasā mora gõṭhau ho
gõṭhaba e bhaujī kalasā gõṭhaunī kuchha chāhela ho
gõṭhaba e bhaujī kalasā gõṭhaunī kuchha chāhela ho
tohare joge lahara paṭora babula joge hãsulī ho
nanadoiyā joge chaḍhane ke ghorawā hãsata ghare chalī jaibā ho
nanadoiyā joge chaḍhane ke ghorawā hãsata ghare chalī jaibā ho
kahā̃ paibõ lahara paṭora kahā̃ māī paibõ hãsulī ho
are kahā̃ paibõ chaḍhane ke ghorawā kalasā more nāhī̃ goṭha ho
rowata nikare nanadiyā ta susukata bhagīnawā ho
are hãsata ke nikre nanadoiyā bhalere manawā ṭūṭala ho
are hãsata ke nikre nanadoiyā bhalere manawā ṭūṭala ho
chupa rahu ai dhanā chupa rahu awarū se chupa rahu ho
dhanā jaibo māī rājā ke naukariyā sabahe chīza basehaba ho
tohare joge lahara paṭora biṭiwā joge hãsulī ho
are apane joge chaḍhane ke ghorawā ta sāra ke dekhaiba ho
are apane joge chaḍhane ke ghorawā ta sāra ke dekhaiba ho
bajara pare tohare chunarī bajara pare hãsulī ho
are bajara pare tore ghorawā naihara nā bisarāiba ho
are bajara pare tore ghorawā naihara nā bisarāiba ho

76 ☙

The male swan is feeding in half of the pond, the female swan is feeding in half of the pond.
Oh, even then the pond is not beautiful without the one lotus leaf.
Oh, even then the pond is not beautiful without the one lotus leaf.
In half of the wedding tent is my mother's side, and in half is my father-in-law's side.
Oh, even then the tent is not beautiful without the one sister-in-law.
Oh, even then the tent is not beautiful without the one sister-in-law.
My brother is cutting green bamboo to cover the wedding tent.
Oh, my brother climbs to a balcony, watching—is my sister coming?
Are you inside or outside, oh my wife?
Wife, the pet child of my father is coming; don't speak rudely to her.
Wife, the pet child of my father is coming; don't speak rudely to her.
Come on, come on sister-in-law, you are my queen and mistress.
Sister-in-law, come sit down on my sandalwood stool and decorate my pitcher.
Sister-in-law, come sit down on my sandalwood stool and decorate my pitcher.
I will decorate the pitcher oh sister-in-law, but I want something for decorating it.
I will decorate the pitcher oh sister-in-law, but I want something for decorating it.

Example XIX (song 76, CD track 17): Ādhe Talaiyā

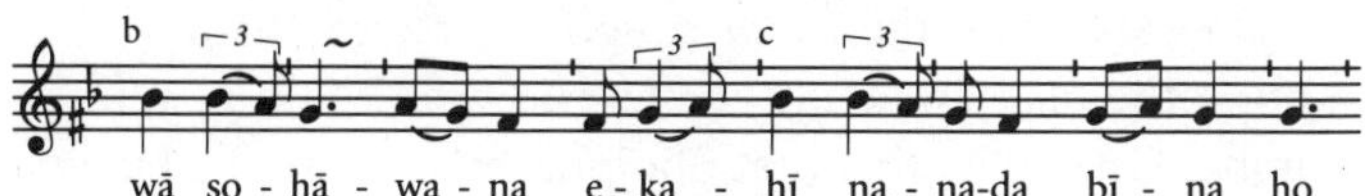

I want a very beautiful sari and a locket for my son.
For the brother-in-law, a horse to ride going laughing back home.
For the brother-in-law, a horse to ride going laughing back home.
Where will I get a silk sari? Where will I get a locket?
Oh, where will I get a horse? Don't decorate my pitcher.
The sister-in-law is coming out crying, and the nephew sobbing.
Oh, the brother-in-law comes out laughing. It is a good thing your pride has perished.
Be quiet my wife, be quiet, be quiet.
Wife, I will go and serve the king and buy everything.
For you, I will buy the silk sari, for the daughter a locket.
Oh, for myself, a horse to ride to show my brother-in-law.
Oh, for myself, a horse to ride to show my brother-in-law.
To hell with your sari, to hell with your locket!
To hell with your horse! I will not forget my mother's house.
To hell with your horse! I will not forget my mother's house.

This song, with its intricate imagery—swans, a pond, gifts, demands of a sister-in-law, reckoned to be just, for performing a small ritual task, and all the variations of these parts—the first Indian folk song I learned on my first visit to Trinidad, has remained my Number One Song. I have searched for it systematically for twenty-five years throughout Trinidad, eastern India, and the old indentureship colony, Mauritius, in the Indian Ocean, and it still presents an inspiring riddle.

Kalawatte and Dhanpatee Sing Number One Song

The sisters had finished but they had not sung Number One Song!

"Do you know the *hardī* song?" I pressed them. "The one about the swans—the male swan and the female swan?" I sang a line or two from my Number One Song, that first Bhojpurī song Moon had taught me. This provided a little surprise.

"That is for the Friday," Dhanpatee said, "When they putting the saffron and the lady is decorating the *kalasā.*" She went out of the room and returned with a *kalasā,* a small earthenware vessel, about six inches high, tapered at the top and with a small lip (see plate 41). Turning to her sister, she whispered, "Are we singing the *hansā hansin* [male swan/female swan]? That is what she sing."

Kalawatee nodded, and they sang Number One Song with a different tune and substituted snakes for swans—indicating the vitality of folksong customs in Trinidad and hinting at the many variations that Bhojpurī songs take in eastern India and throughout the diaspora (ex. XX).

Example XX
Āḍheye Ṭalawā (Permanands' Version)

āḍheye ṭalawā mẽ nāga loṭẽ āḍhe mẽ nāginī loṭẽ ho
āho ṭabahū na ṭalawā chuhila bhailẽ eka re kamala bina ho
āho ṭabahū na ṭalawā chuhila bhailẽ eka re kamala bina ho
āḍhe marauā mẽ gotā baiṭhe āḍhe mẽ goṭinī baiṭhe ho
āho ṭabahū na marawā suhāwana eka re nanada bina ho
āho ṭabahū na marawā suhāwana eka re nanada bina ho
hare hare gā̃wā ke nauniyā̃ nanaḍa hamare lāgahu ho
nāuni baiṭho na mā̃jha marauā kalasā hamare gā̃ṭhahu ho
nāgini baiṭho na mā̃jha marauā kalasā hamare gā̃ṭhahu
iṭanā bachana jaba kahalẽ au kahaū na pawalai ho
āho līlī ghoṛī ābe nanaduiyā ta ḍū̃ḍiyā nanadī hamare ho
āho līlī ghoṛī ābe nanaduiyā ta ḍū̃ḍiyā nanadī hamare
ābahū e nanadī ābahū āike sunābahu ho
nanadī baiṭho na mā̃jha marauā kalasā hamare gõṭhahu ho
gõṭhilā e bhaujī gõṭhilā awarū se gõṭhilā ho

PLATE 41. The earthenware wedding pitcher, *kalasā,* as decorated for a Felicity wedding ceremony, with rows of cow dung embedded with grains of paddy rice; leaves, grain, a ritual cloth, and a *diyā* are placed atop the *kalasā,* 1977.

Example XX (song 77, CD track 18): Āḍheye Ṭalawā

bhaujī kā debo hamara ke dāna rahāsi ghara jāiba ho
mā̃gahu e nanadī mā̃gahu mā̃gi ke sunābahu ho
nanadī jo kachhu haraday samāī soiya saba mā̃gahu ho
apane ke chaṭakī chunariyā bhayanawā̃ ke mohara ho
bhaujī prabhujī ke chaḍhane ke ghuṛawā rahāsi ghara jaibahu ho
āho prabhujī ke chaḍhane ke ghuṛawā rahāsi ghara jaibahu ho
nahī̃ hamẽ choṭkī chunariyā nahī̃ re hamẽ mohara ho
nanadī nahī̃ hammẽ chaḍhane ke ghuṛawā nauji rahāsi ghāre jāu
bolata rahalī̃ hāsa bulanā ke awarū ṭhiṭholanā se ho
prabhu nibatahu tū kula pariwāra bahini jani nibatahu ho
tū tau harwāhe kī beṭī charawāhe kī bahinī̃ tū ho
dhanā ekaī kokhi ke bahiniyā̃ bahini kasanā nibatahu ho
apane māī̃ bahinī̃ ke chunarī basaihau bhayanawā̃ ke mohara ho
āho prabhujī ke chaḍhane ke ghuṛawā rahāsi ghara jaihāhi ho
āho prabhujī ke chaḍhane ke ghuṛawā rahāsi bahinī ghara jaibo ho

77 ☙

The male cobra [*nāgā*] is moving in half of the pond, the female cobra [*nāginī*] is moving in half of the pond.
Oh, even then the pond is not pleasant without the lotus flower [*kamala*].
Oh, even then the pond is not pleasant without the lotus flower.

In half the wedding tent the male relatives are sitting, in half the female relatives are sitting.
Oh, even then the tent is not beautiful without the one sister-in-law.
Oh, even then the tent is not beautiful without the one sister-in-law.
Oh, wife of the barber, sit in the middle of the wedding tent, decorate my pitcher.
Female cobra, sit in the middle of the wedding tent, decorate my pitcher.
Female cobra, sit in the middle of the wedding tent, decorate my pitcher.
As she said all these words, she could not finish.
Oh, my brother-in-law is coming on the mare, my sister-in-law in the palanquin.
Oh, my brother-in-law is coming on the mare, my sister-in-law in the palanquin.
Oh, my sister-in-law, come, tell me your news.
Sister-in-law, sit in the middle of the tent, decorate my pitcher.
I will decorate your pitcher, sister-in-law, I will decorate it, I will decorate it.
Sister-in-law, what gift will you give me so that I will go home happily?
Sister-in-law, ask and let me know your demands.
Sister-in-law, tell what you want.
For myself, I want a deeply colored bride's sari, for my son a golden coin.
Sister-in-law, for my husband I want a horse to ride so that he will go home happily.
Oh, for my husband I want a horse to ride so that he will go home happily.
I do not have a deeply colored bride's sari, I do not have a golden coin.
Sister-in-law, I do not have a horse to ride; I don't care if you go home happily.
Until now she had been talking nicely and joking.
My husband, invite your whole family, but do not invite your sister.
Daughter of the farmer whose plow has broken, sister of a herdsman.
My wife, we are born of the same parents, how can I not invite my sister?
I will buy a sari for my sister and a golden coin.
Oh, I will buy a horse to ride for my brother-in-law, they will go home happily.
Oh, I will buy a horse to ride for my brother-in-law, they will go home happily.

As with many wedding songs from Uttar Pradesh and Bihar, this song is formed from a series of verses and choruses. In Moon's version, the first verse begins "the male swan is feeding in half of the pond, the female swan is feeding in half of the pond," and the first chorus replies "oh, even then the pond is not beautiful without the one lotus leaf, oh, even then the pond is not beautiful without the one lotus leaf." The first verse in Dhanpatee and Kalawatee's version, "the male cobra is moving in half of the pond, the female cobra is moving in half of the pond," is sung to a different melody composed using the higher pitches of the octave—*sol la ti doh* (in Hindi, *pa dha ni sa*) (variations of this tune are given in ex. XXI). The chorus "oh, even then the pond is not pleasant without the lotus flower, oh, even then the pond is not pleasant without the lotus flower," is composed like Moon's, with the lower pitches of the octave—*doh re mi fa (sa re ga ma).* The juxtaposition of a high verse sung once and a lower chorus, sung twice, is a pleasing form that occurs in many

Example XXI: Āḍheye Ṭalawā, verse variants

Bhojpurī songs. The melodies of the verse and chorus in Moon's version are nearly identical. Most Bhojpurī wedding songs follow one of these two patterns: a verse at a higher pitch level followed by a chorus at a lower pitch level, or a simpler form: the same melody at the same pitch for the verse and chorus.

The repetition of verses at a higher pitch level is a musical trait that scholars have been alert to since 1928, when George Herzog identified the "rise" and delineated the Yuman style area of Native America. The common verse–chorus (or question–answer or antecedent–consequence) structure of folk songs, analogous to the *sthāyī* and *antarā* structure of classical Indian music, is so common throughout the world that scholars of an earlier generation called it "natural," not surprisingly, because most communities have both strong as well as weak performers. As one of Laxmi Ganesh Tewari's woman singers told him: "We sing and play the best we can. We are not aware of any specific pitches or rhythms. We are concerned only with imitating the person who knows the song. This is how we learn new songs. . . . Not all of us know the songs, but we try to go along with the lead singer" ("Folk Music," xi).

For some songs, the leader introduces two lines of a couplet and the group sings the second line, thus doubling the line, a routine that continues until the leader decides to introduce another couplet. The leader may repeat some lines of poetry that are pleasing to her, or funny to her; or she may stall while she recalls the next couplet or go on to the next couplet quickly. This style is flexible, and if the song breaks down, the leader can go back and pick up a line, or one of the ladies can shout out "help!" and start the song again.

Fascinated by the possibilities for further variation, I set out to collect as many examples of Number One Song as possible.

❧ More Swans and Snakes

One evening in Felicity, Phakani, Rajeeyah, Ramdaye, Tulsiah, Siewrajiah, and Dhanmati sang Number One Song for me.

78 ❧
In half the pond male swans are pecking, in half female swans are pecking.
Oh, look, the pond is still not pleasing without a single lotus.
[*Shouted*] Oh! Sing! [*Group breaks down*]
Oh, look, the pond is still not pleasing without a single lotus.
Oh, look, the pond is still not pleasing without a single lotus.
In half the wedding tent male relatives are seated, in half female relatives are seated.
Oh, look, the wedding tent is not pleasing without the brother's sister.
Oh, look, the wedding tent is not pleasing without the sister-in-law.
Come on sister-in-law, friend, you are queen.
Sister-in-law, sit in the middle of the wedding tent, decorate my pitcher.
Yes, sister-in-law, sit in the middle of the wedding tent, decorate my pitcher.
Sister-in-law, I want something for decorating the pitcher of this house.
Yes, sister-in-law, I want something to decorate the pitcher of your house.
For me a bright veil [*chatakī chunariyā*], for the nephew a neck ornament [*hānsul*].
For brother-in-law, a horse for riding, to go home happily.
Yes, for brother-in-law, a horse for riding, to go home happily.
Not give, oh sister-in-law, I will not give you a bright veil, a neck ornament for the nephew.
Sister-in-law, I will not give a horse for brother-in-law to return home.
Look, I will not give a horse to brother-in-law whether or not you decorate the pitcher.

That made three versions I had collected in 1974. In 1975, Moon sang the swan song for me a second time. One afternoon Channu's aunt Ramkalia sang it.

Then Solomon's mother, Siewrajiah, sang it, condensing the text into a neat A–B–A form:

79 ❧
Half of . . . [*Interruption*]
In half the pond the male swan Tch! [Siewrajiah hears noise in the background]
In half the wedding tent male relatives are seated, in half the female relatives are seated.
Oh, look, the wedding tent is not pleasing without the sister-in-law.
Come on our great sister-in-law, you are queen.
Sister-in-law, sit in the middle of the wedding tent, decorate my pitcher.

If I decorate the pitcher, I want something for decorating it.
Sister-in-law, I will give a bright veil [*debai chunariyā*], a neck ornament [*hānsul*] for the nephew,
For brother-in-law, a horse for riding, to go home happily.
In half the pond male swans are pecking, in half female swans are pecking.
Oh, look, the pond is still not pleasing without a single lotus.
Oh, look, the pond is still not pleasing without a single lotus.
In half the wedding tent male relatives are seated, in half female relatives are seated.
Oh, look, the wedding tent is not pleasing without the sister-in-law.
Oh, look, the wedding tent is not pleasing without the sister-in-law.

And Mesho's aunts Sahodare Nanan and Bhagmania George sang it, mentioning cobras, not swans:

80 ♫
In half the pond male cobras [*nāgā*] are pecking, in half female cobras [*nāginiyā*] are pecking.
Oh, look, the pond is still not pleasing without the sister-in-law [*sic*].
Oh, look, the pond is still not pleasing without a single lotus [*kewal*].
In half the wedding tent male relatives are seated, in half female relatives are seated.
Oh, look, the tent is not pleasing without the sister-in-law.
Come, come sister-in-law, friend, you are queen.
Sister-in-law, sit in the middle of the wedding tent, decorate my pitcher.
The brother came in from outside, and spoke to the sister-in-law.
Wife! Father's pet daughter has come, don't speak to her in pride.
Come on, sister-in-law, friend, you are queen.
Sister-in-law, sit in the middle of the wedding tent, decorate my pitcher.
Sister-in-law, sit in the middle of the wedding tent, decorate my pitcher.
Ask, oh sister-in-law, ask, ask, make me listen.
Sister-in-law, whatever your heart desires, ask for that.
Take, oh take sister-in-law, I will take everything.
Sister-in-law, I will take a crown to cover the head; I want all three demands.
Sister-in-law, I will take a crown to cover the head; I want all three demands.
For brother-in-law, a horse for riding, for the nephew a neck ornament.
Neither your brother's [meaning obscure].
The sister-in-law came out weeping, then the nephew sobbing.
The brother-in-law came out happily, though he was insulted.
Don't weep, don't weep, don't weep to die.
The wife will go to the king's home to be a servant, she will bring wealth.

By 1977, Moon had died. I went to visit her daughter, Chandroutie Benny, and she sang the swan song. But, she had trouble remembering many of the verses her mother had taught her.

81 ♫
In half the pond the female swan is pecking, in half the pond the male swan is pecking.
Look, pond . . .
In half the pond my female swan is pecking, in half the male swan pecking.
Look, the pond is pleasant [*sic*] without the lotus.
In half the tent my parent's side, in half my father-in-law's side.
In half the tent my parent's side, in half my father-in-law's side.
My father cut green green bamboo to thatch the tent.
My father cut green green bamboo to thatch the tent.
The brother climbed high, look at my sister.
My comes [*sic*]
Wife, my father's pet daughter comes, don't speak with pride.
Wife, my father's pet daughter comes, don't speak with pride.
Come, come sister-in-law, friend, you are my queen.
Come, come sister-in-law my friend, you are my queen.
Sister-in-law, sit on my sandalwood stool, decorate my pitcher.
Sister-in-law, sit on my sandalwood stool, decorate my pitcher.
Oh, sister-in-law I want something to decorate this pitcher.
Oh, sister-in-law I want something to decorate this pitcher.

Chandroutie is one of the few singers to mention the female swan before the male swan. Lines 7–8 are from the song for *kanyādān* (ex. XIV, song 60). Umesh commented, "The singer is under the influence of the English language. While singing she forgets which line is next and she starts to sing the wrong line. Suddenly she reminds she is wrong and stops the line and start to sing the right line. In line 4 she does not mention *tabaho* ('still not'). Then its meaning comes 'Look the pond *is* pleasant.' But in the next line she corrects her mistake."

Rajiah Samooj sang many of the verses her mother had taught her:

82 ♫
In half the pond the female swan is pecking, in half the male swan is pecking.
Look, the pond is still not pleasing without a single lotus.
Look, the pond is still not pleasing without a single lotus.
The male relatives sit in half the tent, the female relatives sit in half the tent, in half the female friends sit.
Look, the tent is still not pleasing without the one sister-in-law.
The brother looks from high, my sister is coming.
Wife [obscure] my father's pet child, don't speak rudely to her.
Wife [obscure] my father's pet child, don't speak rudely to her.
Come, come sister-in-law, you are my friend, mistress.
Sister-in-law, sit in the middle of my tent, decorate my pitcher.
Sister-in-law, sit in the middle of my tent, decorate my pitcher.

If I decorate the pitcher, I want something for decorating it.
Come, sister-in-law, I will give you a bright veil, for the nephew a neck chain.
For the brother-in-law, a horse to go riding happily home.
Yes, for the brother-in-law, a horse to go riding happily home.
The sister-in-law is coming out crying, the sister-in-law is coming out crying.
Be quiet my wife, be quiet.
Wife, I will go to the king's service, I will bring wealth.
Wife, I will go to the king's service, I will bring wealth.
Oh, wife for you a bright veil, for the nephew a gold chain, wife, for myself a horse for riding.
Forget your parent's home [other versions mention not to forget the parent's home].

Just before I left Felicity, Matti invited a group of ladies for a party, and they all sang it for me in the traditional leader-chorus style. That gave me nine versions in all.

83 ♪

LEADER In half the pond the male swan is pecking, in half the female swan is pecking.
Look, the pond is still not pleasing without a single lotus.
CHORUS Look, the pond is still not pleasing without a single lotus.
LEADER Look, the pond is still not pleasing without a single lotus.
CHORUS Look, the pond is still not pleasing without a single lotus.
LEADER In half the tent the family sit, in half the female friends sit.
Look, the tent is not pleasing without the one sister-in-law.
CHORUS Look, the tent is not pleasing without the one sister-in-law.
LEADER Look, the tent is not pleasing without the one sister-in-law.
CHORUS Look, the tent is not pleasing without the one sister-in-law.
LEADER Where the sister-in-law will call from, will you decorate our pitcher?
Sister-in-law, when I decorate your pitcher, I will want something for decorating it.
CHORUS Sister-in-law, when I decorate your pitcher, I will want something for decorating it.
LEADER Sister-in-law, when I decorate your pitcher, I will want something for decorating it.
CHORUS Sister-in-law, when I decorate your pitcher, I will want something for decorating it.
LEADER I want a bright veil, for the nephew a golden chain.
Now, sister-in-law, a horse to go home happily.
CHORUS Sister-in-law, a horse to go home happily.
LEADER Now, sister-in-law, a horse to go home happily.
CHORUS Sister-in-law, a horse to go home happily.
LEADER I will not give you a bright veil, nor a golden chain.
I will not give you a horse for riding, how will you go home?
CHORUS Oh, not give you a horse for riding, how will you go home?
LEADER Look, not give you a horse for riding, how will you go home?

CHORUS Look, not give you a horse for riding, how will you go home?
LEADER Come, you sister-in-law, you are my friend, my queen.
Sister-in-law, sit in the middle of the tent, decorate our pitcher.
CHORUS Sister-in-law, sit in the middle of the tent, decorate our pitcher.
LEADER Sister-in-law, sit in the middle of the tent, decorate our pitcher.
CHORUS Sister-in-law, sit in the middle of the tent, decorate our pitcher.
LEADER The sister-in-law comes out weeping, the nephew sobbing.
Look, brother-in-law my heart is breaking, why are you breaking my heart?
CHORUS Yes, brother-in-law my heart is breaking, why are you breaking my heart?
LEADER Look, brother-in-law my heart is breaking, why are you breaking my heart?
CHORUS Look, brother-in-law my heart is breaking, why are you breaking my heart?
LEADER Wife, I will go to be servant to the king, will bring some wealth.
Yes, I will go to be servant to the king, will bring some wealth.
CHORUS Wife, I will go to be servant to the king, will bring some wealth.
LEADER Wife, I will go to be servant to the king, will bring some wealth.
Wife, I will give a bright veil, for the nephew a golden chain.
CHORUS Look, for the brother-in-law a horse to ride happily home.
LEADER Look, for the brother-in-law a horse to ride happily home.
CHORUS For the brother-in-law a horse to ride happily home.

On a return visit in 1985, Rajiah Sooknanan sang this version:

84

In half the pond the male swan is pecking, in half the female swan is pecking.
Look, the pond is still not pleasing without a single lotus.
The male relatives sit in half the tent, the female relatives sit in half the tent.
Look, the tent is still not pleasing without the one sister-in-law.
The brother climbed and looked from high; my sister is coming.
Wife, my father's pet daughter comes; don't speak with pride.
Come, come sister-in-law you are my friend, mistress.
Sister-in-law, sit in the middle of the tent, decorate the pitcher.
If I decorate the pitcher, I want something for decorating it.
I want a golden bangle for my hand, for the nephew a golden chain.
I will not give you a golden bangle for your hand, nor for the nephew a golden chain.
Sister-in-law, I will not give you a horse for riding.
The sister-in-law is coming out crying, the nephew is coming out crying too.
The brother-in-law is coming out happily, although his heart is breaking.
Be quiet my wife, be quiet.
Wife, I will go to the king's service, I will bring wealth.
I will get a golden bangle for your hand, a golden chain for the nephew.
And for myself a horse to ride happily home.
I will not give you a golden bangle for your hand, nor for the nephew a golden chain.

Sister-in-law, I will not give you a horse for riding.
Forget your parent's home [other versions mention not to forget the parent's home].
I will not give you a golden bangle for your hand, nor for the nephew a golden chain.
Sister-in-law, I will not give you a horse for riding.
Do not decorate the pitcher.

The longer variants, including repetition, have some thirty lines, the shorter about a dozen. In the shorter examples, less of the story is told; some begin with a description of the wedding tent, omitting mention of swans feeding in the pond or snakes moving in the pond. According to different singers, the swan may be a snake, the lake half empty and half full, a tent with two divisions for male or female relatives, the lotus flower a lotus leaf, the sari a skirt and blouse or a veil, and the golden chain a golden coin. But the horse is always the horse. In many versions the *nanad* comes out crying, in some the nephew cries, the wife—the *bhaujī*—cries, and in one version the brother-in-law comes out laughing over the loss of pride for the brother of his wife, and says he will buy the gifts for his family.

The performing style of all the versions is identical. The lady (or chorus) who "carries" (leads) the singing begins with a verse (*antarā*). Then she sings the chorus (*sthāyī*). The ladies who "take up" repeat the chorus. With so many repetitions, the songs are self-teaching, and a lady who is singing on the side that takes up has two chances to learn the words of the chorus before a new verse is introduced. All that is required for this tradition to survive is one strong singer in any generation.

The singers vary the intonation of the third and seventh degrees of the scale, *mi* (or *ga*) and *ti* (*ni*). Some flatten these degrees, and others sing them more nearly natural. Singers differ in their interpretations of the rhythm—"r" on the musical examples—some rendering this motif as a triplet figure, others as two nearly equal eighth notes. Each time I heard another group of women sing Number One Song, I anticipated hearing the high verse melody the Permanand sisters sang, but I never found that tune again. But I heard Moon's tune everywhere. In fact, of the several hundred wedding songs I heard in Felicity, the tune and structure of Moon's version of Number One Song recurred in nearly half of them. Whatever the text, this was certainly the most popular tune in Trinidad.

Interpretation of a Classical Musician

Guru Adesh thought that the elusive high verse melody of the Permanands might have been inspired by a film song.

Example XXII: *Dipchandi Tāl*

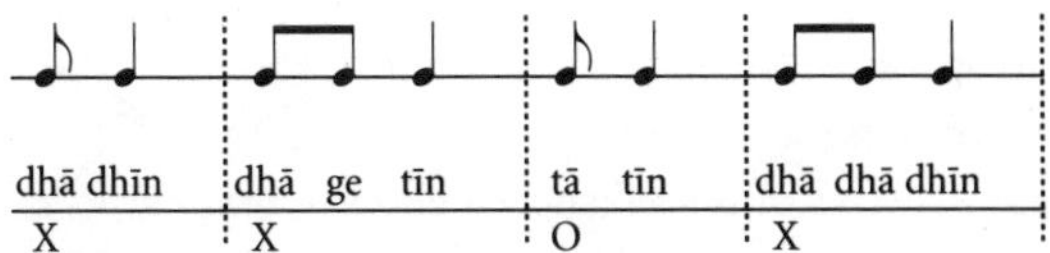

"Most of the wedding songs are from Uttar Pradesh in India," he said, "and many of these tunes are the same. But in India there are plenty more tunes and each with a text. However, certain songs are in the same *tāl.* If the meter is the same, sometimes people start to sing them on the same tune—as people do here. But in India you hardly find this. There the songs are different—different texts and different tunes. In every province, you will find a traditional song; here people sing their own texts on the same tune.

"I haven't heard any wedding songs that were composed in Trinidad," he said. "No doubt some Indian songs have lost their original flavor, but they are carried on. Generally these folk songs go from *sahraj* [first degree] to *pancham* [fifth degree], *sa* [doh] to *pa* [sol]. But some women sing an *antarā* part like a verse and the *sthāyī* like a chorus. They feel it is nice to sing the *antarā* high in order to give improvisations. With the impact of films and film music, folk songs are changing. They put the music director's own version and they carry it towards the high octave now.

"Wedding songs in films are mainly in *kaharwā,* the *tāl* for light music and folk music—eight beats divided four by four. Sometimes wedding songs are in *dīpchandī,* fourteen beats: three, four, three, four (ex. XXII). In Uttar Pradesh, Maharashtra, Gujarat, and Bihar you will find songs in *kaharwā* and *dīpchandī* because this is the rhythm of three and four, three and four. It is also called *chachar,* because the folk singers in the village don't know the term *dīpchandī.* They know *chachar.*"

♮ Marginal Survival in the Diaspora

Perhaps the high verse melody, the *antarā,* as Adesh called it, was not learned from a film but preserved by the sophisticates, Dhanpatee and Kalawatee. Was the high melody a special key to the history of wedding songs in Trinidad, a clue to the changes this repertory had undergone in the New World? According to a theory of marginal survival, people away from their homeland tend to preserve their traditions unchanged, while those at home change their traditions with the times. In a state of suspended animation, away from its original setting, a song repertory might be passed on virtually unchanged from one generation to the next. Did the high melody signal an old song—an original? or the song as it was first composed? or in its most embellished form? or as it was known by hundreds of women in many districts?—an old song that had thrilling musical variety and a text that included every point, pairs of swans and snakes as well, golden chains and golden bangles, golden coins and golden lockets, silk saris, silk skirts, flowing blouses, bright veils, and a horse, a wonderful fat and galloping horse to go riding and laughing home? The notion was magical—that a downtrodden people might have preserved their antique cultural heritage in such detail that one might learn about the United Provinces of the nineteenth century by exploring the diaspora, the lands of the old Coolies—Trinidad, Guyana, Surinam, Mauritius, Fiji, Natal, Malaysia.

The powerful case for marginal survival and conservation is supported by a love of traditional folkways. Although less enchanting, the case for change is alas hard to ignore, taking into account theories such as acculturation (the influence of other racial and cultural groups in Trinidad, particularly the Africans and the English). It is hard to dismiss the pressure for Indians to conform to the norms of plantation life, seen in the breakdown of customs governing the Hindu caste system; hard to rule out forgetfulness, as the passage of the years and the generations overcame memories, however poignant. Finally, the significant loss of contact with the culture of India was crucial, although new recruits continued to arrive in Trinidad up until 1917. This steady influx of indentured labor from India must have affected the wedding song tradition. Do the wedding songs in Trinidad in the 1970s, 1980s, and 1990s reflect the repertory of a typical village in eastern Uttar Pradesh of 1845 or one of 1917? A woman who left India in 1917 may have known different versions of songs from her great-great-grandmother who immigrated in 1845, for we would not expect the musical life of an Indian village to remain static for seventy-five years. Did the newcomer to Trinidad bow to the ways of the established immigrants or did the established immigrants count on her to replenish their repertory? And what happened to the songs of women from non-Bhojpurī–speaking areas—western Uttar Pradesh, Bombay, Madras, Madhya Pradesh? Their traditions seem to have been lost. Inevitably, some of the Bhojpurī wedding song texts must also have been forgotten, even though exceptional singers like Moon remembered a great deal.

Once the text of a song was forgotten in Trinidad, the song was lost forever. Possibly immigrant women remembered some song texts but forgot their tunes. A solution might have been to substitute a well-known tune with an appropriate metric structure. Before visiting India I came to think that is what had happened with Number One Song, that the high verse melody had been forgotten in Felicity and replaced with the chorus melody. In some cases the chorus melody was not well suited to the meter of the text as the verse melody, for example the interpolation of vowels *talaiyā* ("pond") in Moon's version (ex. XIX, line 1) rather than the more usual pronunciation, *talawā,* in the Permanand version (ex. XX, line 1). The popular chorus tune may also have been used to substitute for other forgotten tunes in the Felicity repertory.

❧ Lessons from India

In Trinidad, I could not believe that the sister-in-law *(nanad)* in the swan song (exx. XIX–XXI) could destroy the wedding. How could it be so important that the sister decorate the pitcher with cow dung and paddy rice? In India the song tells exactly what is required, a gift called a *neg,* the minimum a beautiful dress for the woman, a golden chain for the son, and a horse for the man to ride happily home. These are demands, not sentimental requests, to remind the brother of his deep bond to his sister. Indian village women traditionally sacrifice their right to inherit land but claim in return the brother's devotion; she has the right to ask, and he has the duty to give.

As the brother points out to his wife: Don't be proud; my sister and I are of one mother and father and I will go and be a servant of the king in order to buy these things for her. As one moves from village to village in India or in Trinidad the details of the *neg* may change. In Trinidad these rules have relaxed, but no outsider could measure or understand the hurt caused when a brother fails his sister.

These charming old songs from a different time and place have significance in the life of the people who sing them. Although the performance of ritual duties in exchange for gifts and money is part of the marriage ceremony, the visitor to Felicity might not understand the seriousness of this mandatory exchange, for in Trinidad there is a glow of Christian wedding glitz on the Hindu wedding. Many brides take the opportunity to change a third time (yellow sari to red sari to white dress and veil). No one in India understands why an American bride would choose to be married in white, since every image of a Bhojpurī bride involves deep rich colors—red and gold. They do not marry in the color of chastity and mourning, white; they—the betrothed—marry in red, the color of fertility, sacrifice, and consumation:

85 ❧
In all his escort
Is the bridegroom red.
Red is his fringe

Red are its tassels
  Wherever one looks
  He is red
Red is his gold
Red is his earring
Red are his garments
Red is the sash
  Wherever one looks
  He is red
Red are his socks
Red is the paint
Red is his horse
Red is the bridle
  Wherever one looks
  He is red
Red is the litter
Red is the screen
Red is the bride
Red are her features
  In all his escort
  Is the bridegroom red.
(*Songs*, 72–73)

On the one hand, Indian weddings in Trinidad might seem to Western eyes relaxed and happy. But on the other, the bride in Trinidad has lost the unquestioning love or devotion of a brother. The song suggests an older system of reciprocal duties and rights operative in modern India, fading in Felicity. The text of the song may change from version to version but the deeper meaning is constant throughout. One wonders if in Trinidad the deep structure has been undermined as antique Bhojpurī folkways have given way to British, American, and African fashion. The irony is that the song, with a beginning, middle, and end as in Trinidad, is not sung in India. The underlying values are still preserved and cherished in India, though disguised altogether (perhaps new texts, perhaps whatever), whereas many antique variants of the text are remembered and sung in Trinidad over a crumbling value structure (see ex. XXI).

But when you talk to the villagers in Felicity or in districts Ballia, Chapra, Ghazipur, Gorakhpur, Mau, Banaras, Azamgarh, they will all explain the binding relationship between brother and sister.

So it goes. A man will tell you of his duty to his sister where there are no song texts to describe it, no song to tell of this. The man from Felicity tells you of the duty but does not connect it with the women's songs that describe these values.

We have no measure for such abiding feelings as hope, joy, grief, love, devotion, justice, even when objectified in song, frozen in time, noted on paper with text and tune and published in a book. But the tears of the mothers in Felicity village and in Bhojpur villages over the loss of a daughter suggest the kindred feelings of all mothers ("Oh eyes flooded tears, eyes flooded tears"). Yet there is a difference. In Trinidad the women wept when they sang wedding songs for me to tape, less so at the weddings. In India the women wept when they sang the songs for me, with small daughters at hand (whom they would lose someday), and they wept throughout the wedding ceremony. And at the final departure *(vidā)* of their daughter, the mother and her women friends and relatives wailed—*ronā* ("father's home lonely became"). That was a sound I had never heard before. In Trinidad, these older women, the Permanand sisters, sang for me, and as the meaning of the old song welled up in them they cried afresh.

In Trinidad the question: were they weeping for many reasons—the loss of the daughter, the loss of their customs, the loss of their songs, and the remembrance of those old Indian ways ("Wife own scarf tears wipe")?

Rajiah sang:

86

Oh, mother, she weak tear flowing.
Father gives bride.
Look, brother cry, tears flowing.
Sister of others been.
Look, brother cry, tears flowing.
Sister others had been.
One forest went, second forest,
And third forest.
Look, behind turn daughter looks.
Father's home lonely became.
Oh, wife own scarf tears wipe.
Mother forget.
Wife own scarf tears wipe.
Mother forget.
Dawn of day early in the morning,
Bird sings.
Oh, husband, when you sleep, will bitter deep I sleep.
Then who me wake up?
Wife, when you sleep bitter sleep.
Then me only wake you up.
God of love, when I sleep bitter sleep,
Then mother my woke me up.
Wife, when you sleep bitter sleep,
Then me only wake you up.

And Moon sang:

87 ❧
Oh, eyes flooded tears,
Eyes flooded tears.
What we mistook, oh mother?
Oh mistook, oh mother.
Oh, what dripped tears.
Tonight I how will pass?
Oh, how will pass? . . .

Chapter Twelve

Songs of Love and Longing

> Do you not feel a thrill passing through
> the air with the notes of the faraway song
> floating from the other shore?
>
> Rabindranath Tagore, *Gītānjalī*

The search for Number One Song had led me this way and that through the voluminous repertory of Bhojpurī song—from ritual and devotional songs to those of social commentary to humor and jest; from the antique myths to the contemporary; from *bhajan* to *byāh ke gīt* to *birahā, jhūmar, chautāl, lachārī, ghazal, chutney* and so on. Does the repertory of Bhojpurī songs neglect any aspect of village life? Indeed not. Do the songs shed light on the villagers's understanding of their world? Certainly yes. And is there a fundamental theme that all collectors of Bhojpurī songs had found? So it seems!

Separation and Reunion

Number One Song proved elusive, but songs of sensual yearning were in abundance. Songs of love, the absent lover, the union of man and nature, the fire of desire, and the imagery of sensuality in nature—the moist eastern wind that brings aching to the body and sexual longing, the black clouds of the monsoon season arousing the senses, the hovering of the the bee over the lotus flower, the fragrance of blossoming spring trees, the dripping of rain, and the cool breeze that brings relief from the burning summer heat. These themes of passion fulfilled and passion denied run through the Felicity songs as well as through the collection of some 3,000 songs I recorded in eastern Uttar Pradesh. Passion, sensuality in nature, longing for the absent husband—these themes also figure in the published collections of Bhojpurī folk songs, from Sir George Grierson's work in the nineteenth century through William Archer's studies of the 1930s and 1940s to more recent studies including those of K. D. Upadhyaya, Laxmi Tewari, Edward Henry, Nisha Sahai-Achuthan, H. S. Upadhyaya, Oscar Lewis, and Jitka Hertig-Skalická. The cycle of separation and reunion with *saihaya* ("god," "husband") is integral not only to Hinduism and its *sanatan dharma* ("eternal doctrine")—the elusive search for the divine as spun out in the cycle of birth and rebirth. The separation and reunion of lovers is also a part of the social world of the Indian village, so could yearning sparked by absence be the key to excitement as well as loyalty in the Indian system of the arranged marriage?

℘ Love Sickness During the Months of Sāwan and Phāgun

"Krishna left the gopis in his *viraha,*" Umesh explained, "dying of *viraha.* It is the pain of love. We believe that the prohibition of love makes love go higher and higher. *Viraha* is a feeling only for women, and in this condition she is called *viraharni.*"

In Felicity and through Uttar Pradesh, the monsoon month of Sāwan arouses in village women images of fulfillment. Many songs are sung by the *viraharni.* Moon sang:

88 ℘
Came Sāwan most charming.
Forest in begin speak peacock.
Oh, gathering of black clouds, roaring clouds.
Lightning look glow powerfully.
Oh, gathering of black clouds, roaring clouds.
Lightning look glow powerfully.
Nothing is left life in mine.
Nothing is left life in mine.
Came Sāwan most charming.
Forest in speak begin peacock.

Another song of *viraha* is included by Tewari:

89 ℘
Oh dear friend, my husband has gone abroad and I am lying alone in the month of *Sāvana.*
I cannot go to sleep in my bed alone; this separation is tormenting me in the month of *Sāvana.*
Separation is tormenting me in the month of *Sāvana,* no work pleases me in the month of *Sāvana,* for my husband did not come home in the month of *Sāvana.*
Lustful desires are strong in my body; who could satisfy me in the month of *Sāvana?*
("Folk Music," 197)

A song collected by Nisha Sahai-Achuthan describes the restless yearning of the *viraharni* during the monsoon season:

90 ℘
The raindrops are beginning to fall
I am restless since my beloved is away
The four months of the rainy season are over
But my husband has not yet returned.
("Folk Songs of Uttar Pradesh," 401)

The burst of life, the leaping of the river, the murmur of the insects in the Sāwan season only bring fire to the "lotus heart" of the woman whose husband is absent, as in this song from the Archer collection.

91 ❧
Sāwan and the eager river leaps
The water streams
The paths vanish
Swamped are fields and threshing floors,
In the bushes insects murmur
And I tremble at the sound.
Happy is that woman's lot
Whose husband is at home,
Wretched is my fate
Whose husband has gone away.
Absence with its flame
Tortures me each day
And my lotus heart is on fire,
My husband tricked me
And ran to another land.
He cares for me no more.
And his heart is hard,
How my breasts tingle
And burst at their slips!
(*Songs*, 160–61)

The story of Krishna and the longing of the *gopis* in his *viraha* is a theme in Arya's Surinam collection:

92 ❧
Beloved, do not go abroad; the soring (season) has come close.
The mango (trees) have begun to blossom, the bumblebees are seen in the groves.
The trees have become leafy (and the) *ṭesū* flowers are blooming (in their) minds.
The birds are starting out on (their) journeys on the wing—
(And) these days are getting warmer daily.
Oh Kṛṣṇa, listen to just this request; O thou with (a generous) heart, stay home;
Without you (my) sixteen adornments (are futile); who (can) know my suffering?
With whom shall I play (when) in separation?
(My) beloved knows not at all the pains of (my) body.
(*Ritual Songs*, 102)

"A Song of the Twelve Months" from Grierson's 1883 collection from Shāhābād district tells of the particular pain of longing each new season brings. But for this lonely wife, who likens herself to Krishna's favored maid Radha, fulfillment eventually comes with the "wind which howls" in the month of Jeth.

93 ☙

Gladly would I rub sandal paste upon my body and weave a garland of flowers. The parting of my hair would I have rubbed with vermilion in the happy month of *Asāṛh.*

The month of *Sāwan* is a fire of exceeding sorrow, which cannot even be born. May this sorrow be the lot of *Kub'rī* [hunchback girl whom Krishna loved and whom he made straight], who has captivated my love.

In *Bhādāū* the nights are fearful; the clouds thunder and roar and the lightning flashes: so my heart yearns for him. To whom can I go for refuge?

In *Kūār (Āsin)* I get no good news: no one comes or goes. Writing, writing on a letter will I send it. Give it, I pray, into my love's hand.

At the full moon of *Kātik* all my comrades bathe in the Ganges. After the bath their hair hangs down (to dry), while (I) Rādhā alone lament.

In *Ag'han* I put on a cloth of Agra and stand in my court-yard. This cloth was sent me by my husband. May he live ten thousand years.

In *Pūs* snow has fallen, and the cold makes its power known. Even if I filled my quilt with nine *mans* of cotton, the cold will not depart in the absence of my lord.

The thirteenth of *Māgh* is the feast of Siw: may the blessing of Siw be upon thee. Whene'er I turn and gaze upon my dwelling (I see that) without my love my home is full of gloom.

On the full moon of *Phāgun* all my comrades sport in the *holī,* and Rādhā is casting about red water from her syringe.

In *Chait* the *palās*-trees are flowering in the forest and the barley crop is whispering (in the wind); the jasmine and the rose are blooming, but without my love they please me not.

In *Baisākh* I would have cut bamboos and adorned and roofed a bungalow. My husband would have slept in it, while I fanned him with the end of my body-cloth.

In *Jeṭh,* and specially in (the asterism of) Mirag, there is a wind which howls. The hope of her soul is fulfilled, and Bhar'thari sings this song of the twelve months.

(*Seven Grammars,* 116–18)

From Grierson's 1884 collection, we find another a couplet about the "fire of separation as the seasons of the lonely year progress":

94 ☙

In Chait, the Ṭesū tree *(Butea frondosa)* flowers in the forest, and the fair one is sending a message to her beloved.

"As you go, tell him my message also, that the fire of separation can no longer be even endured by me."

("Some Bihārī," 207)

About the dark clouds of July, the great Bengali poet-composer-patriot Rabindranath Tagore (1861–1941) wrote in *Gītānjalī* ("A Song Offering," lit. "songs offered with cupped hands"): "The sky is overcast with clouds and the rain is ceaseless. I know not what this is that stirs in me" (Song 27). Folk poems on this theme are common in Bhojpur as the next song, from the Archer collection:

95 ☙
Often the peacock cries
And the hawk cuckoo calls,
My lover has not come
And the clouds gather.
Often the clouds thunder.
And the lightning glitters,
My lover has not come
And the clouds gather.
My lover has not come
And my heart is scared
And the clouds gather.
(*Songs,* 165)

From my collection in Banpurwā, Uttar Pradesh, women sing of the longing of *viraha,* of the "fire of sex" that burns in the lonely wife during the springtime festive season of Holī (chap. 5, song 10):

Phāgun has come and it is Holī.
Sparrow hawk swears everyday.
Having listened, it shoots my heart like a bullet.
How can I live in my tender age?
Phāgun has come and it is Holī.
The fire of sex gives me pain every day.
Sleep doesn't come to me in the night.
Oh, can't sleep in the bed.
Oh, can't sleep in the bed.
Phāgun has come and it is Holī.
Phāgun has come and it is Holī.

☙ My Husband is Working in a Foreign Land

"We villagers were not just farmers, we were also traders, warriors, pandits, teachers," Umesh explained. "The husband often had to go away to work, and he couldn't take his wife with him because of our strict social system. These songs come from a time when transportation was rare. Men would journey to their jobs on camels, bullock carts, and horses. The way was not safe, and men left their wives behind in care of their parents. A foolish lady can destroy the reputation of the family."

The unhappy fate of the teenage mother whose husband has gone afar to work is described in this song recorded on a 78 r.p.m. disc in Trinidad in the

1940s. Of this song, Umesh writes: "This song explains the pain of a girl who married in teenage and has become mother of a child. Her husband has gone away for work for a long time. She can't go to sleep because of taking care of the child and in memory of her husband. She is searching every direction even ponds and the underworld."

96 ♫
My teenage is lap full [have child],
Ha, lap full.
Me rest not, me sleep not.
Me rest not, me sleep not.
Teenage lap in child.
How pass now not without [my love]?
You without restless become, oh love.
Me rest not, he he he he!
Rest not me, sleep not.
Me teenage is lap full.
Me rest not, me sleep not.
East in searched for, west in also searched for,
North in searched for, south in also searched for.
Ponds in searched for, underworld in searched for.
Is only request, find my love.
Me rest not, he he he he!
Me rest not, me sleep not.
Me teenage is lap full,
Oh, lap full.
Me rest not, me sleep not.
Me rest not, me sleep not.
Me teenage is lap full,
Oh, lap full.
Me rest not, me sleep not.
(Record label: "Hindou Song," *Telana Nath,* sung by Rambarose Pancham, accompanied by the Jit Seeshai's East Indian Orchestra; recorded in Trinidad.)

From Hari S. Upadhyaya's collection also are more songs on this theme—"O my husband, where did you go? I served the meal on a golden plate."

97 ♫
"I served the meal on a golden plate.
Now I feel too lazy to wait on you.
O my husband, where did you go?"

"Hear me, O my wife. I was coming home,
But I overstayed to hear the news from Delhi on the radio."

"The Ganga's water was kept in a goblet.
Now I feel too lazy to wait on you.
O my husband, where did you go?"

"Hear me, O my wife. I was coming home,
But I overstayed to hear the news from Delhi on the radio."

"I prepared betel for you.
Now I feel too lazy to wait on you.
O my husband, where did you go?"

"Hear me, O my wife. I was coming home,
But I overstayed to hear the news from Delhi on the radio."

"I made your bed.
Now I feel too lazy to wait on you.
O my husband, where did you go?"

"Hear me, O my wife. I was coming home,
But I overstayed to hear the news from Delhi on the radio."
("Joint Family," 315–16)

And a further from K. D. Upadhyaya: "I wish your boat sink in the middle of the river . . . because you have left your wife."

98 ❧
Oh, *nanad,* if I knew your brother will go foreign,
I could grind a pitcher full of flour.
I would have tried and handed to him.
Listen, oh tourist, my husband has gone to foreign.
Take my message and explain to my god [husband].
Oh, your wife is of young age.
Explain to God.
Brother-in-law, pedestrian on way, you are brother-in-law to me.
You take my message and explain to my wife.
"Oh, lady [wife], you get stitch the bra of *jājīm* and add strings of *resama.*
Oh, hide breast in it and keep dignity of my family.
[In anger the wife replies:]
[I] wish your boat sink in the middle of the river.
And thief steal your cargo [on returning].
Oh, deceit kill you on the way,
Because you have left your wife.
[Again the man says:]
My boat will go [more] on the side of the river bank,
And my cargo will cross safe.
Oh, lady I will sell you out to some *mogalawa* [Muslims],
And marry some one else.
(K. D. Upadhyaya, *Bhojpurī Lok Gīt [Bhag 2]*, 288, no. 119)

In 1967 Hari S. Upadhyaya contributed:

99 ❧
When I start planting the *mehadi* tree,
My husband goes to a distant land.

When the leaves come out on the *mehadi* tree,
My husband goes to a distant land.
("Joint Family," 325)

The Hari S. Upadhyaya collection includes a song describing how "thin and lean" the wife becomes in the absence of her husband.

100 ☙
My husband is in a distant land.
I become lean and thin day by day.

Day by day I become lean and thin.
I am a beautiful woman.
Who dyed my lower garment?
("Joint Family," 340)

The concept of *viraha* extends beyond Bhojpur. Turning to the west, to the village of Rampur, Delhi State, Oscar Lewis's collection includes a song about a village man leaving his wife for the army. "Where should I sleep?" asks the bride. With my husband's younger brother (a joking and teasing relationship) or my husband's older brother (a strict avoidance relationship).

101 ☙
O Mother-in-law, where should I sleep?
It is so cold.
My man has gone away to the army.
He is the guardian of the country.
O Mother-in-law, where should I sleep?
It is so cold.
My *devar* [husband's younger brother] is very young and innocent.
O Mother-in-law, where should I sleep?
My *jeṭh* [husband's elder brother] has gone to the fields.
He is the guardian of the fields.
O Mother-in-law, where should I sleep?
It is so cold.
(*Village Life,* 192)

☙ The East Wind

Throughout Uttar Pradesh villagers talk about a type of sensual songs for the *viraharni* called *purvī* (literally, songs from the "east"). Tewari's collection includes this *purvī bhajan*:

102 ☙
Both brothers, Rama and Lakshmana, have gone to the forest through the long forest paths. . . .
Without Ram, my Ayodhya is desolate; without Lakshmana there is no lordliness.

In the month of Sāvana and Bhādau, clouds thunder and rain, the easterly wind is blowing hard.
Perhaps both brothers, Rama and Lakshmana, are getting soaking wet under a tree.
Inside, mother Kausalya is crying, outside brother Bharata.
("Folk Songs," 200–201)

"The wind in this song is the eastern wind," Umesh explained. "In every language of the world there is eastern. I am eastern for western people. It never ends. My village is eastern for the people who live in Aligar. But we call those people eastern who live in Kanpur, Lucknow, and Banaras. Those songs which are sung in Gorakhpur, Ballia, Ayodhya these are *purvī* ("east") for us in Karimganj. For Banaras people, Gorakhpur people, and Ballia people eastern songs are Biharī songs. Eastern songs move according to where a person lives. When somebody sings *purvī* from my village it means he is speaking from Bhojpurī area. The blowing wind from the east is cool, makes lazy, and gives ache in the body and reminds of the lover."

In Felicity, Sankey sang (chap. 5, song 17):

Blow eastern breeze, pain comes up!
Oh! pain comes up, oh! pain comes up!
Blow eastern breeze, pain comes up, oh!
What city at search my husband?
Now heart feels city go to, oh!
City go to, oh! city go to, oh!
Blow eastern breeze, pain comes up!
What master to stop my husband?
Master should die, oh! master should die!
Blow eastern breeze, pain comes up, oh!

"We say *pūrav-pachchhim-uttar-dachin*—east-west-north-south, and never north-south-east-west as you people do," Umesh remarked. "Even in school it is taught this way. There is a song for this:

103 ☙
Wherever the sun rises,
Face towards it.
East is in front of you,
And west on your back.
On the left hand side north,
And on right hand side south.

"And we have a saying in the village. 'Even if the sun begins to rise in the west, instead of east, yet I will keep my words of honor.' And in your Felicity song, the mother-in-law asks 'How are you so handsome, what did your mother eat when you were in the womb?' And the bridegroom replies 'My mother rubbed the sandalwood into a paste on the stone and that's why I'm so handsome.' And the mother-in-law asks again 'Can you give me the recipe?' And the bridegroom replies 'Even if the moon rises in the west and not the east, I won't tell you the medicine that my mother ate to make me so handsome.' The concept of getting ache in the body for woman means to be lovesick. *Kasakna* means ache, aching and lazy feelings. *Kasakna* means people want to stretch, and stretching is a kind of sign. If a man stretches in front of an unknown woman, it shows that he is inviting her, and it can create enmity with the woman's family. If she tells her husband, the men will fight. Or it can change into love. If she wants it she will also begin to stretch. And women should never stretch in front of man. When people stretch, the sound of loving ache comes naturally from the body. Our songs tell this."

*

Sir George Grierson's 1886 collection also tells of the longing stirred by the east wind:

104 ☙
The east wind blows, and yawning has come upon me.
As I stand, my poor little body is filled with lassitude.
Who was the gallant swain whose gaze fell upon me?
Neither my home nor the forest pleases me.
("Some Bhoj'pūrī," 226)

In Grierson's transcriptions, one song cautions of the lures of the East and eastern women.

105 ☙
Mahādeb has gone to the East to trade, and four months are passing away. Gaurā sits on a chair and watches the road (saying), "When will my ascetic come?"
Mahādeb returns after twelve years, and stood at the gateway. "Art thou asleep, or awake, O Gaurā? Open the strong fastened door."
"Drink water, and sit, O Mahādeb. Tell me the news of my father's house." "I am quite well, O Gaurā, and all is well in your father's house. But there is one piece of news about me, which is not good—I have married another wife."
("Some Bihārī," 235–37)

The anthology of Hari S. Upadhyaya includes a song expressing an additional thought, the relationship of the eastern wind and longing for a child:

106 ☙
The easterly wind is blowing,
And the southerly wind is moving fast.

Rukumini sleeps in the parlor with the nephew in her lap.
The brother's wife comes out of the room and mocks her.

O, brother's wife takes her son away from Rukumini's lap; . . .

"O Rukumini, another's son is of no use unless it is yours."
("Joint Family," 258–59)

I learned the songs of lovesickness first in Felicity—from Sankey and Moon, and the other village women. Later I heard them in the villages of Bhojpur, and also discovered that they had been noted by fellow scholars who had collected songs across the breadth of north India. And that they had been recognized by the world for their beauty and universal application when, drawing from the ancient folkways of Bengal, Tagore wrote:

107 ꟹ

In the deep shadows of the rainy July, with secret steps, thou walkest, silent as night, eluding all watchers.
To-day the morning has closed its eyes, heedless of the insistent calls of the loud east wind, and a thick veil has been drawn over the ever-wakeful blue sky.
The woodlands have hushed their songs, and doors are all shut at every house. Thou art the solitary wayfarer in this deserted street. Oh my only friend, my best beloved, the gates are open in my house—do not pass by like a dream.
(*Gītānjalī*, 22)

So east is east and west is west, and love and longing persist, while songs tell the story.

Chapter Thirteen

The *Rāmāyaṇ* Tradition

> Those who lovingly sing or hear the story
> of Sītā and Rāmā's marriage shall ever rejoice;
> for Shrī Rāmā's glory is an abode of felicity.
>
> Goswami Tulsī Dās, *Rāmcharitmānas*

From childhood, everyone in Felicity learns the life story of Rām, the prince and hero, who is believed to be the seventh incarnation (avatar) of Lord Vishnu, the "preserver." Everywhere in the village, there are reminders of his presence: statues and pictures in temples, schools, and at the family altar; comic books illustrating his life; and films from India, with English subtitles, dramatizing the legendary events of his career. The story of Rām is as old as the Homeric epics of the Western world, and, like Homer's *Iliad,* is the tale of a ravished bride and her rescue. There are two well-known written versions of the *Rāmāyaṇ*. As far as is known, the earliest was written in Sanskrit some two thousand years ago by the sage, Vālmikī, a shadowy figure in Indian literary history. But it is the later version, the *Rāmcharitmānas* ("Wonderful Lake of the Life of Rām") of Goswami Tulsī Dās (1552–1623), written in the northern Indian Awadhī vernacular (spoken immediately west of Bhojpur), that is known and loved by Hindus throughout north India.

Rām Naumi, the commemoration of Rām's birth, is observed on the ninth day of the second half of the month of Cet (around March). During the ten-day Rāmlīlā festival (in the month of Kūār, around September–October) brahman children reenact each event of his life: his birth; his breaking the great bow of Shiva as a demonstration of his superhuman strength; his betrothal and marriage to Sītā; the jealousy of his stepmother, Kaikeyī; exile in the forest of *ban;* the loyalty of his three brothers, Lakshmaṇ, Bharat, and Shatrughn; the abduction of Sītā by the demon Rāwaṇ and their flight to Lankā; the loyalty of Hanumān, king of the monkey army; the rescue of Sītā; the slaying of the great ten-mouthed Rāwaṇ; Rām's rejection of the faithful Sītā and her trial by fire; Rām's triumphal return to the kingdom of Ayodhya; his noble and righteous ruling of his subjects; Sītā's final return to the lap of Mother Earth; and Rām's ascension to the kingdom of the Gods.

In India, the life of Rām is told in *bārah māsas* ("twelve months"). These songs of separation, characteristically tell the plight of the lover, season to season, as she awaits the return of her love, usually in the twelfth verse, although the metaphor often turns to the devotee longing for God. A well-known poetic form since the earliest times, with examples in Sanskrit and Prākrit, a verse is devoted to each month of the Hindu calendar. In the following *bārah māsas* Rām's mother Kaushalyā bewails her son's banishment and curses her trouble-making co-wife, Kaikeyī. This example begins in the month of Chait, around March–April, and concludes with Rām's return from forest exile, where "thunder rolls," "worms and snakes creep," and "nights are as sharp as the edge of a sword," to the royal palace. "He who sings this song," the performer adds, "will find a place in heaven."

108 ꕥ

Rām is born in Chait in Ajodhyā, and the palace is sprinkled with sandal-wood. The *chauk* is filled with elephant pearls and the *kalas* is made of gold, and within are excellent jars.

Bāisākh is a season (hot) like poison, the earth and sky are writhing under it. As a fish deprived of water writhes, that is the state to which Kekaī has brought me; she has given me dire distress.

In Jeṭh the hot wind affects the body, while Rām, Lakhan, and Sītā are together (in the forest). Rām's feet are tender as lotuses. The earth and sky are writhing, how can he travel on the way.

In Asārh the thunder rolls in all directions, the sparrow-hawk cries, and the peacock screams, Kōsilā laments in her palace in Awadh, Lakhan, Sītā and Rām will be wet as they stand at the foot of a tree.

In Sāwan all the tanks and rivers are filled, Sītā and Raghubīr will be wet. Worms and snakes creep about over the earth with Rām, Lakhan, and Sītā, and the night is dark.

In Bhādo huge rain drops fall, and all the world are mending the roofs of their houses. Sītā and Raghubīr will be wet with the great large drops as they fall, for the rain is loud and sudden.

In Kuār, O friend, is the reign of the God of Virtue, and the whole world is continually arising to do virtuous actions. If, now, Rām were but here, he would have fed Brāhmans and filled dishes with gifts of gold.

Kātik, O friend, has come, and the noose of separation has fallen upon me. In every house women are lighting lamps, but my Ajodhyā is dark, and Kekaī has done it.

In Ag'han virgins adorn themselves, and embroider their garments with golden threads. They wear silk garments, (soft) as woolen ones, and on their heads is the garland of the golden Baijanti.

In Pūs, O friend, falls the frost, and the nights are sharp as the edge of a sword. How will Rām bear a seat of *kus* grass, and how will he rest in the forest? May her (Kekaī's) birth be cursed.

With Māgh, friend, has come the spring, and how will I live without Bhagabant? My mind is fixed upon Rām's feet, while Bharath sits and waves a fan (over Rām's shoes) in the season of spring.

O friend, the jollity of Phāgun has come, and we sprinkle our bodies with perfume and sandal. Bharath sits and pounds *abīr,* but upon whom shall I scatter it, in Rām's absence? With whom shall I sport?
He who sings this song of the twelve months will find a home in heaven. Tul'si sings that Rām and Lachhuman came from the forest to the palace in Awadh, and met Kekaī.
("Some Bihārī," 213–17)

In Felicity, week-long readings of the *Rāmāyaṇ, Rāmāyaṇ yagya,* held throughout the year, are popular. *Bhajan* dedicated to Rām and relating the many episodes of his career are sung at these *yagya,* and at temple services (ex. XXVIII). Six days and twelve days after a birth, women sing *sohar* from the *Rāmāyaṇ,* and at the time of a death, men chant passages from the *Rāmāyaṇ* all through the night. And on Sundays during the summer months—the wedding season in Felicity—the perfect love of Rām and Sītā is renewed and celebrated in the traditional Hindu marriage ceremony: "sweep the way," "bow your head," "offer *ārtī,*" "play the instruments," "bring the golden pitcher," "light the ruby lamp," "auspicious is the lot of the lady Sītā," for "Rām has come to wed."

The Birth of Rām

Rām was the oldest son of King Dasarath of Ayodhya and his first queen, Kaushalyā. Telugu village women of Andhra sing of the birth pangs of Kaushalyā, a topic that might not come up in written accounts of the epic.

109

Now call the midwife, go send for her.
The midwife came in royal dignity.
She saw the woman in labor, patted her on her back.
Don't be afraid, Kaushalyā, don't be afraid, woman!
In an hour you will give birth to a son.
The women there took away the gold ornaments,
They removed the heavy jewels from her body.
They hung ropes of gold and silk from the ceiling.
They tied them to the beams, with great joy.
They made Kaushalyā hold the ropes.
Mother, mother, I cannot bear this pain,
A minute feels like a hundred years.
("A Rāmāyana of their Own," 119)

Moon sang a village *sohar* (childbirth song) for Rām, telling of the happy songs performed at this ceremony, the *havan* fire sacrifice performed to celebrate his birth, and the smoke of the *havan* fire rising to the abode of the gods while flowers rained on the babe.

110 ꕥ
Oh, Shiva Shankar, where was the birth place of Rām?
Where were played happy songs [*badhāī*], listen, Raghunanandan [Rām].
Where were played happy songs, listen, Raghunanandan.
Rām was born in Abaḍhapur, oh, Shiva Shankar.
Janakpur [Sītā's birthplace] being played happy songs, listen, Raghunanandan.
Janakpur being played happy songs, listen, Raghunanandan.
Father, send for the dung of a beautiful cow, send for Shiva Shankar.
Khūte-khūte [vocables] the ritual place [*bediā̃*], listen, Raghunanandan.
Khūte-khūte the ritual place, listen, Raghunanandan.
Father, send the potter for the ritual pot, Shiva Shankar.
Ruby lamp to get plastered, listen, Raghunanandan.
Ruby lamp to get plastered, listen, Raghunanandan.
Father, send to the cattleminder [Ahīr] for ghee, oh, Shiva Shankar.
With that ghee perform the *havan* [ritual fire sacrifice] perform, oh, Raghunanandan.
With that ghee perform the *havan* perform, oh, Raghunanandan.
With that ghee perform the *havan* perform, oh, Raghunanandan.
Smoke go in sky, listen, Shiva Shankar.
Smoke go in sky, listen, Raghunanandan.
Smoke go in sky, listen, Shiva Shankar.
Shimbhū [Shiva] lives Mount Kailas, oh, Raghunanandan.
Shimbhū lives Mount Kailas, oh, Raghunanandan.
Shimbhū lives Mount Kailas, listen, Shiva Shankar.
Flowers rained oh Rām, listen, Raghunanandan.
Flowers rained oh Rām, listen, Raghunanandan.

ꕥ Rām Restrings Shiva's Mighty Bow, Outwits Parsurām, and Wins Sītā's Hand in Marriage

The *Rāmcharitmānas* of Tulsī Dās tells how Sītā's father, King Janaka, declared a contest for her hand in marriage. The winning suitor would be that prince who could string the mighty bow of Lord Shiva. In the presence of the assembled court, Rām, the victor, restrung the bow, and in so doing broke the mighty instrument in half.

Moon sang a Bhojpurī folk song telling of Rām's superhuman strength as he achieved this feat. "The narrator's voice in this song is either Shiva or Kālī," Umesh explained, "the two deities who are depicted wearing a garland of skulls":

111 ꕥ
Oh, Rām lifted up Shiva's bow.
Our neck, garland of skulls.
Rām *sindar* bow lift up.
Our neck, garland of skulls.
Father-in-law builds palace.

Father-in-law builds palace.
Husband builds temple to Shiva.
Our neck, garland of skulls.
Husband builds temple to Shiva.
Our neck, garland of skulls.
Rām lifted up Shiva's bow.
Our neck, garland of skulls.
Rām lifted up Shiva's bow.
Our neck, garland of skulls.
Palace of two stories will break.
Palace of two stories will break.
I will worship in the temple of Shiva.
Our neck, garland of skulls.
Rām lifted up Shiva's bow.
Our neck, garland of skulls.
Head of garland, head of garland.
Rām lifted up Shiva's bow.
Our neck, garland of skulls.

Hearing this news, the jealous Parsurām (believed to be the sixth incarnation of Vishnu) set out to destroy Rām, and challenged him to restring the bow of Vishnu. The debate between Parsurām and Rām is the topic of folk songs. Among the recordings of *Rāmāyaṇ* stories made in Trinidad during the 1940s, is one telling of this contest, the *Parsurām Acamān,* sung (in Hindi and English) by Pandit Kasi Parsad, accompanied by R. S. Narayansingh's Orchestra:

112 ♫
[Sung *dohā,* "couplet" from the *Rāmāyaṇ*]
Rām saw the assembled people and saw Jānakī [Sītā] frightened, and felt in his heart neither happiness nor sorrow. Shrī Raghuvir [Rām] said:
[*Spoken*]
Rāmchandrajī felt neither happiness nor sorrow seeing that all people were frightened to see [Parsurām] and Jānakī was sad. What does he say?
[*Sung*]
Lord who broke Shiva's bow,
Your one servant,
What order do you give to me?
Having listened in anger, the angry *munī* [holy man] spoke:
[*Spoken*]
Oh, Lord who broke Mahādevajī's [Shiva's] bow, your servant has written. Tell me what your order is.
Having listened to this the *munī* began to say. What did he begin to say?
[Sung *chaupāī* (two-line poetic form sung in a different tune and rhythm than a *dohā*)]

Listen ["said Parsurām"]. Rām who broke Shiva's bow is an enemy of Parsurām as is Sahasabahu [enemy of Parsurām in *Rāmāyaṇ*].
Having listened to the *munī*'s words, Lakhan [Lakshmaṇ, Rām's younger brother] smiled [and said]:
[*Spoken*]
Oh, Rām, listen [said Parsurām]. Who ever this Shankar's [Shiva's] bow broke, he is my enemy the same as Sahasabahu. This having listened, Lord of Creation Lakshmaṇ, says, oh, Lord, in childhood we have broken very many small bows like this. But you never had anger like this. This tell, what is the reason this bow at your such affection? This listen.
In anger, Parsurāmjī said:
[*Sung*]
You are in my death trap and you don't have control over your tongue. Are those small bows equal to Tripurārī's [Shiva's] bow, which is famous all over the world?
[*Spoken by Parsurām*]
Oh, death-trapped prince [Lakshmaṇ], having control tongue no speak, that Mahādevjī's [Shiva's] bow is famous in all the world. What are these small bows equal to?
[*Jaykārā*]
Say once King Rāmchand of victory.

Umesh explains: "This is a story from the *Rāmāyaṇ* and this is the way Indian people tell it. We have *Rāmāyaṇ* readings several times a year—house to house. Sometimes a person will decide: If they succeed in whatever they are doing—for example in business or curing illness—they will do *akhand* ("unbreakable") *Rāmāyaṇ*. First the singer sings *dohā* exactly as it is from the *Rāmāyaṇ* and then he explains it in simple spoken Hindi. He picks several good *chaupāī* related to the incident out of the same chapter of the *Rāmāyaṇ* to sing. The Trinidad singer on this old recording also gives a spoken explanation of the *chaupāī.* In my village, usually singers don't explain *chaupāī;* several singers take turns to complete reading of the *Rāmāyaṇ* from beginning to end.

"It is a ritual. Villagers make a stage, beautify with saris, and *Rāmāyaṇ* book is there, also one *diyā*. People come to listen. It begins in the morning around eight or ten o'clock and continues unbreakable nonstop singing for twenty-four hours. As another person comes to sing, he picks up before the first singer ends. Always there are seven or eight singers—people keep coming and going. After each *dohā,* to give a rest to the leading singer, all the other singers chant a *chaupāī.*"

Helen explains: "In Trinidad they do something quite similar, but they explain the *dohā* and *chaupāī* in English. The performance is extended—sometimes to a seven- or eight- or nine-night *Rāmāyaṇ* singing. Trinidadians explain each detail in English, since these sessions aim to familiarize ordinary people with this sacred text. After all, Tulsī Dās composed his version of the *Rāmāyaṇ* in Awadhī, the vernacular, so village people could understand. Trinidadians love to go to *Rāmāyaṇ* sessions, religious and social events with feasting after each night's reading. Villagers want to hear the Hindi verses, know many of them by heart, and admire singers who can give clever and meaningful English explanations. Sometimes the singer will spend three or four hours explaining a few lines of Tulsī Dās. In the 1990s the most popular *Rāmāyaṇ* singer was Suruj Rambachan, also a political leader in the Indian community who served for five years during the 1990s in the Trinidad and Tobago Parliament. Mesho drove to southern Trinidad for me to hear him; we arrived to find an assembly of hundreds. You see, in Trinidad these sessions have political overtones. And they provide a chance for Indians to get together and share their common love of the *Rāmāyaṇ*. I especially remember the night he told the story of Rām and the boatman."

Umesh: "That is the *rām kevat sambād* ['dialogue,' 'argument'], one of the popular *sambād.* All villagers know this story. People discuss many points from the *Rāmāyaṇ* and time to time people hear a *chaupāī* and ask other people to explain the meaning. For example, was Sītā same one who Rāwaṇ has stole from that one who went in exile with Rām? Mostly people don't know. One man might say she was the same Sītā, then another man would say no, she was not, and he gives an example out of the *Rāmāyaṇ.* Once Rām asked to Lakshmaṇ, 'Go and pluck flowers for worship,' and when Lakshmaṇ was gone, then Rām asked Sītā, 'Until I finish these demons, you stay in fire.' And Sītājī went to live in the fire and Rām made a duplicate of Sītā. And this act even Lakshmaṇ couldn't understand. So when someone gives an example from the *chaupāī,* people believe it. Then the question comes, why did Rām put Sītā in fire to test her when he already knew this was the shadow who was stolen? And he punished the real Sītā by sending her in exile. So this is mysterious and people enjoy this and they argue and they dig in the books and they go to some wise man because the answer should be somewhere."

Helen: "In Felicity late one night I heard a big argument about Parsurām. How could he be in the *Māhābhārata* and the *Rāmāyaṇ* at the same time? Was he an avatar? and how could there be two avatars at one time?"

Umesh: "The same type of argument we also have in our villages."

❧ The Wedding of Rām and Sītā

The description of Rām and Sītā's marriage is in the first book of the *Rāmāyaṇ,* "Bālakāṇḍa" (childhood; early section), beginning around the 286th *dohā.* The details are similar to those related in folk songs of Bhojpurī women. Rām arrives in a magnificent wedding procession, Sītā's father greets Rām and bows to him, gifts are exchanged, Rām amazes everyone with his beauty, Sītā's mother greets him and performs *ārtī,* Sītā is given in marriage by her father, and so forth.

Moon taught me a song that celebrates the engagement *(tilak)* of Rām and Sītā:

113 ♫
Where from Bipra [brahman, pandit] arrive?
Where to Bipra reach?
At whose gate Bipra stop,
Asking for good omen?
At whose gate Bipra stop,
Asking for good omen?
Bipra came from Awaḍhaīpura [home of Rām].
Arrive at Janakpur [home of Sītā].
King Janaka gate stop at,
Asking for good omen.
King Janak gate stop at,
Asking for good omen.
Bipra came from Awaḍhaīpura.
Arrive at Janakpur.
King Janaka gate stop at,
Asking for good omen.
Janak Queen came out from inside,
Requesting to Bipra.
Bipra we take *purila* [?obscure] sacred thread [*janeua*].
Present a good omen.
Bipra we take *purila* sacred thread.
Present a good omen.
King Janak came out.
He barber to requesting,
Barber! Take the quilt to spread.
Gentlemen can sit on.
Barber! Take the quilt to spread.
Gentlemen can sit on.
Inside from came out King Janaka.
He barber to requesting,
Barber we take *purila* sacred thread.
Good omen give.
I take the *purila* sacred thread.
Them *mohar* [obscure] change.
Oh, fill cupped hands with pearls.
Then *tilak* will perform.
Oh, I take the *purila* sacred thread.
Give good omen.

The beauty and splendor of Rām at his wedding is the subject of many Felicity songs. His wedding ornaments are so dazzling that even the sun hides his face. "Rām was in a hurry," Umesh pointed out. "He fast grabbed his dhoti from the clothesline! And the crow caws an omen."

Moon sang:

114 ☙

Turmeric who king letter write post [i.e., the husband writes a letter and sends (auspicious) turmeric with it.]
Gives Raghunanadan [Rām] in hand.
Adorn your *ājan* [rhyming vocable: *ājana-bājana*], adorn you band.
Adorn all sixteen ornaments.
Adorn you *ājana,* adorn you band.
Adorn all sixteen ornaments.
Horse of Rām, you like this adorn.
Come to the in-law's home [*sasurār*] Rāmjī.
Horse of Rām, you like this adorn.
Rāmjī come to the in-law's home.
I adorn band, I adorn band.
Had adorned all sixteen ornaments.
Horse of Rām beautifully adorn.
Pearls tied in long hair.
Horse of Rām beautifully adorn.
Pearls tied in long hair.
When King Rāmchandra horse on riding.
Left, right spoke crows.
Crow of speech examine brother Lakshmaṇ.
What omen spoke crow?
Crow of speech examine brother Lakshmaṇ.
What omen spoke crow?
Good gift will get, good dowry will get.
Will get you wise Sītā.
Rām's dhoti slipped away from the clothes line [in haste he grabbed his clothes quickly from the clothes line].
For the same omen spoke crow. [That is why the crow is crying.]
Rām's dhoti slipped away from the clothes line.
For the same omen spoke crow.
Gone groomsmen to Janakpur, got off.
Barber listen to our request.
Oh, barber will give, oh, barber basket full of gold.
Me before Sītā explain.
Oh, barber will give, oh, barber basket full of gold.
Me before Sītā explain.
Did this only work explain of Sītā.
Sītā sun of equal to.

Sītā of forehead in gold of *tikuliyā* [olden word for *bindi,* beauty spot worn in middle of forehead].
Sun disappears.
Sītā of forehead in gold of *tikuliyā.*
Sun disappears.

About the folklore of the crow in Bhojpur, Grierson writes: "Their 'caw' is said by natives to be *ṭhā̃ya, ṭhā̃ya,* meaning 'place, place.' Hence they are supposed to be able to answer any question as to the *place* where any person is, such as, 'where is my beloved?'" (*Seven Grammars,* 126).

Another of Moon's songs describes the rush of Rām's *bārāt* to depart for the wedding ceremony at Sītā's home, Janakpur. The adornment of the men, the elephants, the horses takes time; again the omen of the crow foreshadows Rām's exile.

115 ꩜
Father, getting late to go to Janakpur.
Father, getting late to go to Janakpur.
Who adorn my elephant and horse?
Who adorn my elephant and horse?
Who adorn my groomsmen [*bariāta*] to go to Janakpur?
Who adorn my groomsmen to go to Janakpur?
Father, getting late to go to Janakpur.
Dasarath adorn elephant and horse.
Dasarath adorn elephant and horse.
Lakshmaṇ adorn groomsmen to go to Janakpur.
Father, getting late to go to Janakpur.
Father, getting late to go to Janakpur.
When King Rāmchandar riding on horse.
When King Rāmchandar riding on horse.
Left, right spoke crow, Janakpur to go.
Father, getting late to go to Janakpur.
Father, getting late to go to Janakpur.
Holy men [*rishhia-munīa*] all came to see.
Holy men all came to see.
Brahma, think of Vedas to go to Janakpur.
Father, getting late to go to Janakpur.
Father, getting late to go to Janakpur.
Brahma, think of Vedas to go to Janakpur.
Like these Vedas, think thou Brahma.
Like these Vedas, think thou Brahma.
What omen spoke crow, Janakpur to go.
Father, getting late to go to Janakpur.
[Obscure] of dhoti will not get misty.
[Obscure] of dhoti will not get misty.

For the same omen spoke crow, Janakpur to go.
For going to Janakpur, Rām will be exiled.
For going to Janakpur, Rām will be exiled.
Father, getting late to go to Janakpur.

Ramkallia and Channu sang another Bhojpurī song that tells of the omen of the crow. "Left, right spoke crow."

116 ♫
Skinny Rām, skinny waist.
Stood grocer shop.
Stood grocer shop.
King, either take delicious betel nut.
Or, Oh! ask for bundle of betel leaves.
King, either take delicious betel nut.
Or, Oh! ask for bundle of betel leaves.
Grocer, Oh! neither will take delicious betel leaves.
Nor, Oh! ask for bundle of betel leaves.
Grocer, Oh! I will take small quantity *sindurā* [vermilion].
Sīṭā to marry I go.
In the eastern part of Nepal country, one instrument played.
Sīṭā to marry I go.
Get up brother Latchumaṇ, omen think on.
Left, right spoke crow.
Get up brother Latchumaṇ, omen think on.
Left, right spoke crow.
Married [obscure, rhyming words *dhutiā-dhumila-huhihẽ̃*] dirt will not catch.
Brother for you written exile.
Married [obscure] dirt will not catch.
Get up brother Latchumaṇ, omen think on.
Left, right spoke crow.

A song of the Felicity ladies tells that Rām is the "adornment of the bridegroom's army," listing the important male members of the family in order: mother's father, father's father, father, and the father's younger brother. Presumably the abrupt ending indiates that the song can be extended by listing other male kinfolk. Typical village call-and-response form is illustrated in the following example:

117 ♫
Leader After dressing up the bridegroom stands,
Looks to four sides.
  Who is the adornment of the bridegroom's army,
  Going to a distant country to marry?
Chorus Who is the adornment of the bridegroom's army,
  Going to a distant country to marry.

LEADER Who is the adornment of the bridegroom's army,
Going to a distant country to marry?
CHORUS Who is the adornment of the bridegroom's army,
Going to a distant country to marry?
LEADER Oh, Rām, the mother's father from the assembly speaks,
Grandson I have lost my wisdom.
I am the adornment of the bridegroom's army,
Going to a distant country to marry.
CHORUS Who is the adornment of the bridegroom's army,
Going to a distant country to marry?
LEADER Who is the adornment of the bridegroom's army,
Going to a distant country to marry?
CHORUS Who is the adornment of the bridegroom's army,
Going to a distant country to marry?
LEADER After dressing up the bridegroom stands,
Looks to four sides.
Who is the adornment of the bridegroom's army,
Going to a distant country to marry?
CHORUS Who is the adornment of the bridegroom's army,
Going to a distant country to marry?
LEADER Oh, Rām, the father's father speaks from the assembly,
I have lost my wisdom.
I am the adornment of the bridegroom's army,
Going to a distant country to marry.
CHORUS I am the adornment of the bridegroom's army,
Going to a distant country to marry.
LEADER After dressing up the bridegroom stands,
Looks to four sides.
Who is the adornment of the bridegroom's army,
Going to a distant country to marry?
CHORUS Who is the adornment of the bridegroom's army,
Going to a distant country to marry?
LEADER Oh, Rām, the father speaks from the assembly,
I have lost my wisdom.
I am the adornment of the bridegroom's army,
Going to a distant country to marry.
CHORUS I am the adornment of the bridegroom's army,
Going to a distant country to marry.
LEADER After dressing up the bridegroom stands,
Looks to four sides.
Who is the adornment of the bridegroom's army,
Going to a distant country to marry?
CHORUS Who is the adornment of the bridegroom's army,
Going to a distant country to marry?
LEADER Oh, Rām, the father's younger brother speaks from the assembly,
I have lost my wisdom.

I am the adornment of the bridegroom's army,
Going to a distant country to marry.
CHORUS I am the adornment of the bridegroom's army,
Going to a distant country to marry.
LEADER I am the . . . OK! [song ends abruptly]

The Bhojpurī collection of Hari S. Upadhyaya includes a song describing the splendor of Rām's *bārāt:*

118
Who rides an elephant?
Who rides a horse?
Who comes in a palanquin?

Rama rides an elephant.
Laxuman rides a horse.
Bharat comes in a palanquin.

Over whose head does a diamond umbrella look good?
And who goes to be married?

Over Rama's head a diamond umbrella looks good,
And Rama goes to be married.
("Joint Family," 301)

THE EXILE OF RĀM THE HERO

Rām's fate had been sealed long before his birth. Songs tell how King Dasarath's third wife, Kaikeyī, had ministered to his battle wounds and, for this service, was promised two boons: a jealous wish to have her son Bharat rule the kingdom of Ayodhya, and to have Rām exiled. Fulfilling these demands broke the heart of the great king. Moon sang "King Dasarath is dying . . . Rām and Lakshmaṇ are the pupils of my eyes. How can I exile them?" Umesh explained, "This song shows how tender kings are—tender as well as powerful."

119
Soft bamboo cuts King Dasarath [Rām's father].
Pain of finger, King Dasarath is dying.
Pain of finger, King Dasarath is dying.
Calling for Kaikeyī.
Pain of finger, King Dasarath is dying.
Calling for Kaikeyī.
Go thou to the barber, oh, go thou to the washer of pots.
Calling for Kaikeyī.
Come Queen Kaikeyī, climb and sit on cot.
Take my finger of pain.
Come Queen Kaikeyī, climb and sit on cot.
Take my finger of pain.
Pain of finger, King Dasarath is dying.

Calling for Kaikeyī.
Finger of pain, I will take King Dasarath.
Whatever ask for, present.
Whatever boon we ask of King Dasarath,
That one should be done.
Whatever boon we ask of King Dasarath,
That one should be done.
Whatever boon thou ask for Queen Kaikeyī,
The same boon thou give.
Whatever boon thou ask for Queen Kaikeyī,
The same boon thou give.
Whatever boon we ask of King Dasarath,
The same boon thou give.
Exile Rām and Lakshmaṇ.
Make Bharat and Shatrughan kings.
Exile Rām and Lakshmaṇ.
Make Bharat and Shatrughan kings.
Whatever boon thou hast asked for Queen Kaikeyī.
Shoots my heart like an arrow.
Rām and Lakshmaṇ are the pupils of my eyes.
How can I exile them?
Rām and Lakshmaṇ are the pupils of my eyes.
How can I exile them?

Moon's song about Dasarath and Kaikeyī is popular in India. The version collected in 1965 by Jitka Hertig-Skalická was performed by Kamala Sharma of Chaunhār village, Ballia.

120 ❧

[When] king Dasarath was cutting the green bamboo, he drove a splinter into [his] finger,
And the pain was intense. [In his agony], king Dasarath called out to Kekai:
"Come, come, queen Kekaiya, sit down on the bed [and] take away [this] pain from [my] finger!
O queen Kekaiya, ask for whatever you like, whatever you feel in your heart."
"If [I] am going to ask for something, then [I] am going to ask only for that, king Dasarath, [but] it would be beyond your capacity to give [it].
[I] am going to demand two things: [To give] Bharat the crown [and] to banish Ram to the forest."
"Queen Kekaiya, [you] have asked what [you] had wanted to ask [but you] have broken my heart.
Ram [is] the darling of whole Ajodhya! How is he supposed to be banished to the forest?"
The passers-by were weeping, the travellers were weeping, the water carriers at the well were weeping, and the various betel sellers were weeping: "Who will eat all that betel?"
[Ram:] "Be quiet, passers-by, be quiet travellers, be quiet water carriers at the well,
Be quiet various betel sellers, I shall eat all that betel."

Sita held the bridle of the horse [and] wept: "Thanks to the 'wisdom' of king Dasarath,
Ram left for [his] banishment [while] the king slept undisturbed with the queen."
(*Fifty Bhojpuri*, 43)

The story of Dasarath was also collected by by Hari S. Upadhyaya in 1961, one of the some 450 songs by the prolific performer Devi, of village Sonavaras, Ballia.

121 ☙
King Dasarth goes to cut bamboo in Mathur battlefield.
A small piece of bamboo pierces the finger of Dasarth.
"O barber and *bariya* [a low caste], go and bring Kekai quickly to the Mathur battlefield."

Kekai, by pressing Dasarth's finger, takes out the piece of bamboo,
And the King sleeps pleasantly.

"O Kekai, what do you want?
Ask whatever you want."

Kekai asks exile for Rama and Laxuman
And desires Bharat to be anointed to the throne.

"O Kekai, you shot an arrow and took my soul away.
O barber and *bariya,* go and bring Bharat quickly to the Mathur battlefield."

"Has King Dasarth died?
Or has mother Kausilya died?
Has Sumitra or Kekai died?"

"King Dasarth has not died;
Nor has mother Kausilya.
Sumitra or Kekai has not died.
But Rama and Laxuman have been exiled,
And you will be anointed to the throne."

"O Kekai, you shot an arrow.
You broke my right arm."

"O mother Kausilya, are you inside or outside?"
"Why do you call me, O my son Bharat?
Why don't you call your mother Kekai?"

"O mother Sumitra, are you inside or outside?"
"Why do you call me, O my son Bharat?
Why don't you call your mother, Kekai?"

"O mother Kekai, are you inside or outside?"
"Why have I been called?
O son, eat rice with curd
And enjoy the kingdom of Ayodhya."
("Joint Family," 345–46)

As Rām realizes the implications of his impending exile, he pleads to his father and aunt to protect Sītā, to keep her in their hearts. Ramkallia and Channu, of Felicity, sang:

122 ☙
My son, Sīṭā's food is sweet.
Keep her in heart.
My son, Sīṭā's food is sweet.
Keep her in heart.
Having listened to the bad news, Rāmāchandra,
Then requested of father.
Father, I am exiled to Madhuban forest.
How will keep Sīṭāla?
Father, I am exiled to Madhuban forest.
How will keep Sīṭāla?
Have well in courtyard dug.
My son, Sīṭā's food is sweet.
Keep her in heart.
My son, Sīṭā's food is sweet.
Keep her in heart.
Having listened to the bad news, Rāmāchandra,
Then requested of *phuā* [father's sister; archaic term for *bua*].
Aunt, I am exiled to Madhuban forest.
How will keep Sīṭāla?
Have a well in courtyard dug,
Sīṭāla to give a bath.
My son, Sīṭā's food is sweet.
Keep her in heart.

☙ THE LONGING OF SĪTĀ FOR RĀM

While living in exile in the Panchwatī forest, the demon Rāwaṇ absconds with Sītā to the island kingdom of Lankā. Felicity women sing about Sītā's loneliness and yearning for her husband during her exile:

123 ☙
Rāmā! Without Sīṭā the world is lonely.
Bring Sīṭalā back.
Hey, formerly of horse Vashisṭha Munī.
Following from Lachhiman.
Oh, dear from saint's hut,
Where Sīṭā does devotion.
Oh, son of the saint of the hut,
Where Sīṭā does devotion.
Stood bushes into Sīṭā dried.
Saint now husband, guru is mine.
Oh, saint our *gurujī* is useless.

Debarā Babū Lachhiman is.
Babū useless is *gurujī* of [obscure].
Lashhi . . .
[*Spoken*]
Forgotten.

The Bhojpurī collection of Hari S. Upadhyaya from the 1960s includes several songs that describe Sītā's painful separation from Rām:

124 ☙
Sita's eyes are big, and her hair is long.
Her husband has gone to a distant land,
And she waits for him.
("Joint Family," 350)

125 ☙
O Rama, the husband goes to a distant land.
He plants an orange tree at the gate.

O Rama, the tree bears oranges,
And a parrot eats them.

The parrot tries to defile the wife's chastity.
She goes to threaten the parrot.

But before she can frighten it,
O Rama, her father arrives as a guest.

"O daughter, who planted the thick bushes of oranges
Where you go to drive away the parrot?"

"O father, the person who planted the thick orange bushes
Has gone to a distant land."
("Joint Family," 353)

☙ *Bhajan* Dedicated to Rām

Another recording from the 1940s that celebrates the Tulsī Dās *Rāmāyaṇ* is "Hindou Song," *Kamach Bintee,* sung by Benny Sewnath, accompanied by the Jit Seeshai's East Indian Orchestra, recorded in Trinidad, and sung in Hindi. "This is a *bhajan,*" Umesh explained.

126 ☙
Heart Rām *charan* [feet] in came. ["'I begin to feel about God.' For Hindus the most important part of the body to worship is the feet, the most lowly part," Umesh said.]
Heart Rām feet in came.
Heart Rām feet in came.
Heart Rām feet in came.

Heart Rām feet in came.
Heart Rām feet in came.
Whenever love, love everything is.
Whenever love, love everything is.
God feet in came.
Love attraction when heart of came.
Love attraction when heart of came.
Love is called love.
Heart Rām feet in came.
Heart Rām feet in came.
Heart aah aah aah aah.
Vedas, Purāṇas, Bhagawād Gita,
Your name only chanted.
Heart Rām feet in came.
Heart Rām feet in came.
Tulsī Dās always chanted God.
Love attraction fruit got. ["Because of the attraction of love, I got the fruit, the result, to be in God—to get salvation."]
Victory victory [obscure].
Heart Rām feet in came.
Heart Rām feet in came.
Heart Rām feet in came.

In the 1970s, Guru Adesh composed a simple and powerful *bhajan* to the glories of Rām—"Rām is the sail . . . Rām is the sailor . . . Rām is father . . . mother . . . shelter in trouble . . . Karim and Rahim [for all worshippers, including Muslims] . . . Krishna [of distinction in the Hindu pantheon] . . . creator . . . provider":

127
The Glory of Rām

[*Chorus*]
Rām of grandeur saints world in great is.
World in great is, holy beautiful is.

[*Verses*]
1 Breath of waves in, life of boat.
Rām is sail, Rām sailor.
Drowning of is support, troubled of is shelter.
Only one Rām is, Rām . . .

[*Chorus*]

2 Rām only father is, Rām is mother.
All over world of is Rām only creator,
Sky earth of, sea and land of,
Creator Rām is, Rām . . .

3 Rām is he and he is Rahim.
He Krishna is and he is Karim.
The poet Adesh devotees of, sadhus and saints of,
Provider Rām is, Rām . . .
(*Saptak*, "Rishabh," 13–15)

✧ The *Rāmāyaṇ* Doordarshan Television Serial

"And people kept watching this *Rāmāyaṇ* on television," Umesh was explaining. "Throughout India, they never wanted to miss it. But people had not many televisions that day in the village. It kept going as a serial for one year in the late 1980s."

Helen: "You know that regarding this television series one scholar, Philip Lutgendorf, said, 'The Ramayan serial had become the most popular program ever shown on Indian television—and something more: an event, a phenomenon of such proportions that intellectuals and policy makers struggled to come to terms with its significance and long-range import. Never before had such a large percentage of South Asia's population been united in a single activity; never before had a single message instantaneously reached so enormous a regional audience' ("Rāmāyan," 128). And another Western scholar, Paula Richman, organized a team of researchers to write about the many *Rāmāyaṇ* versions all around India. She was worried that Doordarshan, the government-run television network version, would dominate other versions (see her 1991 *Many Rāmāyaṇas*). Romila Thapur claimed that 'the Doordarshan version had dangerous and unprecedented authority.' ("Syndrome," 74).

Umesh: "First of all, it is something unusual to learn out of this book that people were not so interested in *Rāmāyaṇ* before the TV serial, because most people of northern India have *Rāmcharitmānas* of Tulsī Dās in their home. And almost everywhere in northern India people have Rāmlīlā every year; people go to watch the *līlā* and they know all the story of the *Rāmāyaṇ* except certain details. So the serial was really very helpful to let people learn small details and the concepts as well. It is quite ridiculous that the story is breaking up from place to place. Farmers left their plows, shepherds left their cows, office people left their office, women left their kitchen, whoever was there, everyone wanted to watch TV for one hour on Sunday. People stopped walking on the streets and gathered in front any shop where there was a TV. You remember that when you were ill in Banaras your doctor said was too dangerous to broadcast once in a week for India because Pakistan might attack! And he said his house had been robbed during this hour and he couldn't get the police to come! In Mainpuri, near my village, there was a shortage of power, and the power-cut time was the same as the *Rāmāyaṇ* broadcast. For the first two weeks people tolerated that. On the third week, people assembled and marched toward the power house. Ever since then there was no power cut for the *Rāmāyaṇ* period.

"This is what Tulsī Dās did at the time of Akbar. He combined several versions and composed the *Rāmcharitmānas,* and this brought East, West, North, South together. This was very helpful for India at that time. And today again, to keep united through one story—*Rāmāyaṇ*—taking out and joining things together once again through the TV serial, as in a beautiful *mālā* of so many perfect pearls, East, West, North, South will be together again on the basis of religion. India will never break. Now it is 1998, but the *Rāmāyaṇ* is an evergreen epic."

Chapter Fourteen

Morning at the Temple

> Will you not allow that I have as much of the spirit of prophecy in me as the swans? For they, when they perceive that they must die, having sung all their life long, do then sing more lustily than ever, rejoicing in the thought that they are going to the god they serve.
>
> Plato, *Phaedo*

The most peaceful moments in Felicity were those of early Sunday morning before sunrise, walking to temple in the chill and semidark of dawn to the sounds of cocks crowing and villagers waking to the day. Some of this atmosphere is captured on the recordings I always made: the clock in the Nolan Street temple chiming 6 A.M.; members of the congregation arriving; then, as the service was conducted, the sounds from surrounding houses, of villagers rising, bathing, sweeping their kitchens and preparing breakfast. I always looked forward to the peace of mind that the service brought to me. Perhaps it was a feeling not appropriate to the philosophical complexity of the Vedic mantras whose recitation during the morning services I found so soothing; but as a non-Hindu, I luxuriated in the calm and stillness of these chanted verses.

One Sunday morning, Purnananda, the old Swami from India, was officiating at the Nolan Street temple. His unheralded arrival in Felicity in the early 1950s had been a landmark of local history. Then he had stayed for three years. In 1977, he had returned, invited by local leaders to encourage the congregation in their latest project—building a Hindu secondary school behind the temple. On this Sunday, as he was preparing to conclude his visit, I was astonished to hear him threaten his devotees, in blasting, angry tones, with a curse if they did not complete the building (plate 42).

"You do not know what can happen to you. For billions of years, to be born again, again, and again, like fish and animal and goat and cat and rat. You can be thrown away from all human life if you desert this organization. I give you warning. WARNING! WARNING! WARNING! WARNING! WARNING! Thousands of years you remain as sick man, you remain as poor man, you remain as old and bitter man."

It had been all too easy to forget, during the familiar day-to-day routine of village life, that the villagers were Hindus, who accepted the concept of reincarnation and feared the Swami's warning of being reborn for billions of years, billions of lives as a fish or a dog, just as they accepted the notion of one god who manifests himself in various forms (Brahma, Vishnu, Shiva, Kālī, Ganesh) and in various incarnations (Krishna, Buddha, Jesus Christ, and most prominently Lord Rām).

℘ Hinduism in Felicity: The Missionaries

Some knowledge of Hindu belief is fundamental to an understanding of life in Felicity village, for as the people believe so they live, so they worship, and so they sing, play, and dance. Nine of every ten villagers is a Hindu. Most consider themselves "Sanatanists," that is, members of the Sanatan Dharma Maha Sabha (Eternal Doctrine Great Organization), the largest and most powerful Hindu organization in Trinidad. In the early years of the twentieth century, there were clear divisions among the Sanatanists in Felicity. Most villagers on Pierre Road and Cacandee Road belonged to the Rāmanāndī Panthī, a sect distinguished by the exclusive use of brahman pandits; most in Casacu belonged to the Āghor Panthī; while most in the back streets of Jangli Tola belonged to the Siūnārāynī Panthī. In the Āghor and Siūnārāynī groups, members of lower castes could officiate at services. In recent decades, among Sanatanists, the Rāmanāndī sect predominates. The quarrel, however, between brahmanists (who believe that brahmans alone may be priests) and non-brahmanists remains an active force in village life. Of the three Felicity temples, only the old Siwālā, now called the Shrī Shankar Mandir, represents the brahmanist Sanatan Dharma Maha Sabha.

On 31 December 1950, Swami Purnananda, together with Swami Advaitananda, Swami Mritungaya, and Brahmchārī Rāmakrishna, all missionaries from the Bharat Sevashram Sangha of Calcutta, arrived in Trinidad. Each of the Swamis had a specific duty on their mission. Advaitananda, the leader, was a powerful and outspoken man, said to have aroused large crowds. Purnananda was a teacher, and Rāmakrishna the assistant. Alas for the musicologist, Mritungaya, who was in charge of teaching music, fell ill after a few weeks and returned to India. The three remaining pandits traveled from estate to estate, spending about a week in each. After some months, Advaitananda and Rāmakrishna moved the mission to British Guiana, but Swami Purnananda settled in Felicity in the Siwālā on Cacandee Road, remaining in the village for over three years.

Purnananda did not attack the local religious hierarchy, but he did stimulate something of a religious revival by introducing, in a congregational setting, the most ancient of Hindu services, the Vedic *sanḍhyā* daily prayer and *havan* sacrifice. Both the *sanḍhyā* and *havan* are based on Sanskrit mantras from the Vedas, ancient Indian scriptures. The *sanḍhyā* is a daily worship to be performed at the changes of light—dawn and dusk. The *havan* ceremony

PLATE 42. Trinidad Sevashram Sangha, Nolan Street, Felicity.

is addressed to Agni, god of fire, and a small sacrificial fire is lit during the service and fed with oblations of fruit, camphor, ghee, and spices (plate 43).

Fire sacrifices of this type originated with the Aryan invaders of north India, probably during the second to first millennium B.C. They have had a continuous tradition in India, although the fundamental importance of the oral Sanskrit Vedas (classed as *sruti,* "that which has been heard," "revealed truth") was long overshadowed by the *Purāṇas* and epic literature (*smrti,* "that which is remembered," later written texts). The late nineteenth and early twentieth centuries saw a great revival of Hindu awareness in India, prompting new interest in the Vedic rituals. The renaissance of the *havan* and *sanḍhyā* services in Felicity followed naturally, through the work of Hindu missionaries, from these revival movements, beginning with the "Bengal Awakening" and leading to the Hindu Renaissance: Rām Mohun Roy and the foundation of the Brahmo Samaj (Calcutta, 1828), Justice Ranade and the foundation of the Prarthana Samaj (Bombay, 1867), Swami Dayananda and the Arya Samaj (Bombay, 1875; Lahore, 1877), Madam Blavatsky and the Theosophists (Bombay, 1879), the revelations of Annie Besant (1893–1933), the miracles of Rāmakrishna Pramhansa of Bengal (1836–86), the address of Swami Vivekananda at the first World Parliament of Religions, Chicago (1893), Shrī Aurobindo (1872–1950) and the Pondicherry Mission, and Mahatma Gandhi's policy of *satyāgraha* (nonviolent civil disobedience) which brought nationalism within the sphere of religious revival. The repercussions of these events were many: social reforms (including equality for women, the partial breakdown of the caste system, and the abolition of untouchability); the renewal of interest in Eastern and Hindu ideas, reflected in the Indian nationalist movement; and a return to the ancient Aryan Vedic scriptures, together with a rejection of the later Purāṇas, now considered corrupt. These repercussions were transmitted by Hindu missionaries even to the farthest outposts of the Empire, to the exiled laborers of the West Indies, Mauritius, Fiji, South and East Africa, and Southeast Asia.

In Felicity we witness how one missionary brought to a tiny village in just

PLATE 43. *Havan pūjā,* showing the pandit and celebrants offering camphor, water, ghee, and fruits to the ritual fire, as strings of fragrant blossoms dangle over the ritual space. In the foreground, an earthenware *diyā* is mounted on a *kalasā*, 1974.

a few months a transformation, the revolution against Western values, particularly Christianity (for a revulsion against this faith was at the heart of the Hindu Renaissance)—the changes that occurred in a distant land over an entire century. This, Swami Purnananda accomplished in Felicity in the years from 1951 to 1955. The changes he provoked touched the religious life of every villager. A circle of disciples began to gather, including one young man, Brahmchārī Hari Rām, who later, as Swami Satchidananda, was to become an important figure in the religious life of Felicity, and then, as leader of the Divine Life Society, of Trinidad.

Under Purnananda's leadership, the Siwālā, which had formerly been used only for Rāmlīlā, Shivrātrī, Diwālī, and other Hindu holidays became an important community center where weekly congregational services were held. The congregational *havan* and *sanḍhyā* services became the most frequently performed *pūjā* in Felicity.

Hinduism in Felicity from the late 1950s through the 1960s was fraught with factionalism and doctrinal disputes. After Swami Purnananda left Felicity in 1955, Brahmchārī Hari Rām began to lead the services in the Siwālā. Basraj Bridglal, a devout and learned villager who also had been a close associate of Purnananda, assumed a significant role in running the temple. In 1957, a dispute between the Brahmchārī and Basraj over the issue of brahmanism (the Brahmchārī was a brahman, Basraj was not) led to a split, and a group began meeting in Basraj's home. In the late 1960s, both groups opened new temples—the Trinidad Sevashram Sangha of Basraj (a branch of the Bharat Sevashram Sangha to which Purnananda belonged) on Nolan Street and the Divine Life Society run by the Brahmchārī farther along Cacandee Road near the junction with Peter's Field Road—leaving the Siwālā once again as home for the Sanatan Dharma Maha Sabha.

Despite this history of political differences, services in all three Felicity temples reflect the influence of Swami Purnananda. A typical service consists of one or two hours of singing and reciting mantras, often performed without break or interruption (that is to say, "prayers" with *dhun* and *bhajan* performed in *kīrtan* style). An opening invocation, for example *Aum namo Bhagawate, Vasudeva, Narayana* (*Aum,* followed by the various names of the deity), is sung in call-and-response style as a *dhun.* This may be followed by another *dhun* (also call-and-response), for example, *Hare Rām Hare Rām, Rām Rām Hare Hare; Hare Krishna Hare Krishna, Krishna Krishna Hare Hare,* a mantra valued for the mystic properties of its 16-word structure.

A Sanskrit prayer sung in unison with a harmonium drone usually follows. In the Trinidad Sevashram Sangha they sing: "Thou art peace embodied, Oh, God of Gods. Thou art as vast as sky. Oh, sustainer of the universe thou art fathomless, Oh, embodiment of goodness. Lord of wealth and beauty as Thou art, Thou art the object of meditation for Yogis. I bow to Thee, Oh, Lord of the universe, who removes fear of the world."

ᛟ The *Sanḍhyā* and *Havan* Services

Following the prayer, the mantras of the *sanḍhyā* service are recited, usually accompanied by the harmonium. The Sanskrit text consists of passages from the Vedas and is sung in call-and-response form. The entire recitation occupies some fifteen minutes (Satchidananda, *Divine Life Sandhyaa Bandanaa*).

"Oh, God! Protector and supporter as thou art of the universe, be kind and bestow upon us truth, fame, beauty, and prosperity.

"Omnipresent God, be kind to us and grant the happiness and objects we need.

"Oh, God! Let my words, life, eyes, ears, neck, heart, throat, and head be pure and powerful and arms strong and renowned. Let my palm and back of palm perform religious rites.

"Let the region of Bhuh help us to purify our head. Let the region of Bhubah help us to purify our eyes. Let the region of Swah help us to purify our throat. Let the region of Maha help us to purify our heart. Let the region of Janah help us to purify our navel. Let the region of Satya help us to purify our legs. Let the region of Satya again help us to purify our heads. Let Brahama help us to purify every place.

"Tendency for creation arose in the divine mind of the Absolute God. Then came chaos, then came subtle water, then day and night. The Sun, the Moon, Heaven, world, and the horizon were created as were in the previous creation.

Oh, God! Thou art beyond darkness. The luminous sun represents thy glory. The wise are surprised and illumined by Thine supreme nature. Thou hast given vision to the sun, the sea-god, fire-god. The Heaven, the middle region and the earth are being sustained by Thee. Thou art the soul of the universe.

"Omniscient God, let us see for hundred autumns, let us live for hundred autumns, let us hear for hundred autumns, let us live more than hundred autumns.

"Salvation to Brahma, to preceptor, to sages, to gods, to Vedas.

"Let us be in union with Thine luminous nature who is the creator of the three worlds and giver of our intellect.

"Salutation to the Almighty, the giver of bliss, happiness and peace. May we be blessed with energy, strength, glory, courage, and patience.

"Let there be good to all, let all be free from sickness, let all see good and let none suffer. Let all be happy and fearless, let there be sympathy for each other and success for all work. Let there be prosperity to the King who protects the people every day and also to the people. Let the bipeds and the quadrupeds be prosperous every day. Let there be peace in gods and in the three worlds, let us and all other beings have peace everywhere. Creator and sustainer as thou art of the world, Thou encourageth godliness and establisheth peace amongst the people. Who is my friend today, let him be in peace and who is my enemy let him also be in peace. Peace, peace, peace."

The next section of the *pūjā* is *ārtī,* the ritual offering of fire to the *mūrtī* (icons). In turn, the worshippers circle incense and a *diyā* clockwise before each icon. The devotee also rings a small bell, held in the left hand, to summon the attention of the gods. To accompany the offering, the congregation sings in *kīrtan* style, usually *bhajan* or a series of short *dhun,* performed in call-and-response style, and the pandit or his assistant blows the *shankh* (conch-shell trumpet), also believed to attract the attention of the gods. The service closes with a prayer, which is usually sung to the same chant melody as the opening prayer.

A *sanḍhyā* service performed in many Hindu temples in Trinidad would follow this same pattern: (1) *dhun* or *bhajan,* (2) opening prayer, (3) *sanḍhyā* mantras, (4) *dhun* or *bhajan* (*ārtī* offering), (5) optional address, (6) closing prayer. The *dhun* and *bhajan* are always in Hindi, the prayers and mantras in Sanskrit, and the address in English.

The *sanḍhyā* is the basic service for daily worship. The *havan pūjā* is a more elaborate service, reserved for special occasions: a birthday, wedding anniversary, departure for or return from a long trip, or the commencement or completion of a course of studies. One of the most ancient ceremonies known to man, the *havan* is essentially a ritual sacrifice of foodstuffs and aromatic herbs to Agni, the Vedic god of fire. A fire is prepared and lit during *pūjā* and then fed by the participants with *ghee* (clarified butter), spices, drops of water, and sometimes a green coconut. Naipaul recalls the *havan* ritual from his childhood in Chaguanas: "They required a pundit chanting in Sanskrit (or what in this far-off part of the world passed for Sanskrit), sitting in front of a low, decorated earthen altar, stuck with a young banana tree, and with sugar and clarified butter burning on an aromatic pitch-pine fire: old emblems of fertility and sacrifice" (*A Way,* 241). The smoke thus created is thought to purify the atmosphere, the building, and the people who are enveloped in its fragrance, an essential act, compensating for the pollution of nature that man constantly generates.

The *sanḍhyā* and *havan* are performed in the Felicity temples and homes, either by a group or an individual. Although (like Christian churches) the temples are conspicuous reminders of religious obligations, most devotional services in Felicity take place in homes. Most villagers attend the temple at least once a year at Shivrātrī, but attendance at weekly services (each temple has two per week) is sparse. Of the 6,000 villagers, around 200 to 300 attend temple weekly. But Hinduism is not a congregational religion, and the villagers believe a good Hindu life depends on social customs and family life, not temple attendance. The extent of congregational worship in Felicity is evidence of acculturation—the borrowing by Hindus of an essentially Christian pattern of worship. Were the *sanḍhyā* and *havan* services that Swami Purnananda introduced in the 1950s accepted because villagers were pleased to learn of Hindu congregational services not unlike Christian services? Is this an example of revitalization (refreshment of an immigrant tradition from its source, here India) and syncretism (merging of cultural forms, here Hinduism and Christianity, at points of similarity)? Wouldn't villagers select those new ideas from India that complement their West Indian situation, such as congregational worship, and minimize those teachings, meditation, for instance, that do not address needs posed by their life in Trinidad's plural society?

ঌ The *Bhajan* Repertory

Felicity Hindus practice *bhaktī,* the worship of God through love and devotion, traditionally regarded as the easiest path *(mārg)* to salvation *(moksha),* and more suitable for ordinary individuals than other alternatives suggested in the *Upanishads* such as *karma* yoga (worship through good deeds) and *jnana* yoga (worship through knowledge, the most difficult *mārg*). Although the *bhaktī* theme in Indian literature dates back to the *Vedas,* its philosophy is most clearly expressed in the ninth-century *Bhāgawata Purāṇa,* which teaches devotion to Lord Vishnu, the preserver, through his incarnation, Krishna. The tenth book of this text gives a detailed description of the exploits of Krishna Gopala—the young Krishna, cowherd of Brindāban—as he sports with the *gopīs* (milkmaids); this love-play is a traditional *bhaktī* theme recurring throughout the Hindu scriptures and referred to in many traditional songs.

Bhajan, a term cognate with *bhaktī,* denotes the most popular Hindu religious song type of north and south India. Both words derive from the Sanskrit stem, *bhaj,* "to share," "to give," and the singing of *bhajan* is considered one of the most effective means of practicing *bhaktī. Bhajan* are the most popular temple songs of Felicity. The repertory is large and varied, from songs in Bhojpurī dating from the indenture period to newly composed Hindi *bhajan* learned from recent Indian films.

Bhajan are usually strophic with refrains of one or two lines. The texts deal with the attributes of God in his many manifestations in the Hindu pantheon, with the plight of the devotee (*bhakta*), the sorrows of life, the hope of salvation, "come and quench that thirst."

Yearning for Krishna is the theme in this popular Felicity song:

128 ♫
My Lord, come! Worship Govinda [Krishna].
I am oblivious to everything all around,
My eyes thirst for a vision of Hari [Krishna].
Come and quench that thirst, come now!
Nobody knows you as Lord.
Come and play your flute, come Lord come.

Equally common in the Felicity repertory are *bhajan* dedicated to Lord Shiva, the destroyer, "wearer of snake garlands." It is in these poems that the Hindu acceptance of the dark side of reality is revealed, the acceptance of evil as well as good, of destruction as well as creation:

129 ♫
Salutation to Shiva!
Perform the lamp-worship of Harihara [Vishnu and Shiva combined];
Of the skillful dancer and of Shankara [Shiva];
Of the skillful dancer who in sport
Moves over earth and sky
With a moon-diadem on his head
And star-anklets a-tinkling.
Wearer of snake-garlands
He is Shambhu, protector of the world.
All [things] mobile and immobile and all the world dances;
He held the world aloft on his finger.
Mahādeva! [Shiva] Hail, hail to Shiva Shankara!
Hail to he [from whose locks] the Ganges streams,
He who holds the *damarū* [hourglass drum, often of human skulls]!
Oh, god of gods, remove then
The affliction of every home!

Another type is the *nām kīrtan,* a non-strophic *bhajan* whose text consists solely of the various names and epithets of the deity (local orthography): "Raama Krishna hare, Mukunda Muraare, Seeta Vallabha, Seeta Raama, Brindraabana Govinda, Nanda Nandana"—"Hail Rām Krishna, enemy of Mura, lover of Sītā, cowherd, cowherd of Vrindavana, son of Nanda."

Bhajan texts and the texts of the *sanḍhyā* and *havan* services are printed in several booklets. One is published by the London branch of the Bharat Sevashram Sangha, *Aum Hindutvam: Vedic Prayer, Hindu Catechism* (by Swami Purnananda); another is *Divine Life Bhajans* (by Swami Satchidananda). Most members of the temple congregations have copies of these booklets, but they tend not to bring them to service and prefer to sing from memory. An hour-

and-a-half of continuous singing during a typical *sanḍhyā* or *havan* ceremony is not quite the remarkable feat of recollection it might seem (especially for the Felicity performers who sing in Hindi and chant in Sanskrit—foreign languages). The various response forms of the *bhajan* allow different members of the congregation to specialize in one or two songs, leading those but being led in the rest. Weak singers (I was one) can be led through all the *bhajan:* the strong singers can easily compensate. Nearly all the music of Felicity—*byāh ke gīt, lachārī, chautāl, bhajan, dhun, Rāmāyaṇ* chanting, and so on—has some form of built-in self-teaching feature.

꩜ *Bhajan* Form

The structure of a typical *bhajan* is designed for this tutorial role. "Mere Mana Basigayo Raaghava Raama," "In My Heart Has Settled Rām, Lord of Raghus" (ex. XXIII) opens with a one-line refrain, sung by the leader, repeated by the chorus, sung again by leader, then chorus. The leader follows with two lines of verse echoed by the chorus; two more lines of verse are again echoed by the chorus, followed by a return to the refrain, and so on (see table 5).

Example XXIII
Mere Mana Basigayo (Local Orthography)

[*Chorus*]
mere mana basigayo raaghava raama. . . .
[*Verses*]

1 krita mukuta makaraa krita kundala,
kathina dhanusha liye saaranga paana. . . .

2 jaaya janaka pura dhanusha uthaaye,
saba bhupana ko toryo maana. . . .

3 vishwaa mitra ke yagya suphala kiye,
gowtama naari pathaayo sudhaama. . . .

4 saraju ke teera ayodhyaa nagari,
jahaa bihare seeya, lakshamana, raama. . . .

5 tuma jani bisara jaawo mere mana te,
tuma bina bigara jaaya saba kaama. . . .

6 aashaa ananda kahai kara jori,
chowa satha ghari bhajo aatho yaama. . . .

Table 5 Form of *Mere Mana Basigayo*

Leader	text	R		R		1		2		R		3		4		R		5		6		R		R	
	tune	r		r		a		a		r		a		a		r		a		a		r		r	
Chorus	text		R		R		1		2		R		3		4		R		5		6		R		R
	tune		r		r		a		a		r		a		a		r		a		a		r		r

Key R: refrain text; 1, 2, 3, 4, 5, 6: text, verses 1–6; r: tune, refrain; a: tune, verses.

Example XXIII (song 130, CD track 19): Mere Mana Basigayo

Example XXIII Concluded

130

[*Chorus*]
In my heart has settled Rām, Lord of the Raghus.

[*Verses*]
1 With diadem'd crown and earrings in crocodile's shape,
Sārangapāṇi holds the hard bow in his hand.

2 Going to Janaka's city and lifting the bow,
He broke the pride of all kings.

3 He rendered fruitful Visvamitra's sacrifice,
And liberated the wife of Gautama.

4 On the bank of the Sarayū River in the town of Ayodhya,
Where wandered Sītā, Lakshmaṇ and Rām.

5 Let me not forget you from my mind,
For without you all works flounder.

6 Joyful I express my hopes with hands joined,
Through every minute and every hour of the day.

Many *bhajan* sung in Felicity temples have more complex response forms. In "Hey Jagata Pitaa Bhagawaana" ("Oh Father of the World") (ex. XXIV), each return to the refrain is anticipated by the leader, who sings the last phrase of the refrain after each new verse. This "refrain cue" signals to the chorus group the return of the refrain (table 6).

Similar refrain cues occur in *bhajan* that are composed for Indian films, but their function is different. Often there is no chorus, so the soloist who sings

Table 6 Form of *Hey Jagata Pitaa Bhagawaana*

		refrain		verse 1			
Leader	text	R		i + ii		iii RC	
	tune	rf		a		b f	
Chorus	text		R		i + ii		R
	tune		rf		a		rf
				verse 2			
				i + ii		iii RC	
				a		b f	
					i + ii		R
					a		rf

[as above for verses 3, 4]

Key R: text, refrain; i, ii, iii: text, lines 1, 2, 3; RC: refrain cue; rf: tune, refrain; a: tune, lines 1, 2; b: tune, line 3.

the cue also sings the refrain. In film songs therefore, the refrain cue serves as a signal for the listener, not the performers. While this rather unusual cueing device is not needed by musicians working in a recording studio, it proves extremely useful for Felicity temple congregations trying to memorize new songs.

Example XXIV

Hey Jagata Pitaa Bhagawaana (Local Orthography)

[*Chorus*]
hey jagata pitaa bhagawaana, hame do gyaana,
tu ishwara pyaaraa, duniyaa me eka sahaaraa. . . .

1 bacha pana me hosha na aayaa hai,
jobana me paapa kamaayaa hai,
aba jaawo kahaa vishiyo ne mujha ko maaraa. . . .
. . . duniyaa me eka sahaaraa.
hey jagata pitaa bhagawaana . . . [*repeat chorus*]

2 dila meraa toe yaha kahataa hai,
tu mana mandira me rahataa hai,
dina raata bhatakataa rahaa mai dara dara maaraa. . . .
. . . duniyaa me eka sahaaraa.
hey jagata pitaa bhagawaana . . . [*repeat chorus*]

3 paapo se bhagawana hame bachaa,
vedoe kaa saccha bhakta banaa,
paakhanda jhuta se saba hi kare kinaaraa. . . .
. . . duniyaa me eka sahaaraa.
hey jagata pitaa bhagawaana . . . [*repeat chorus*]

4 majha dhaara me hai bera meraa,
kripaa kara aasrai hai tera,
nandalaala paapa me beeta jiwana saaraa. . . .
. . . duniyaa me eka sahaaraa.
hey jagata pitaa bhagawaana . . . [*repeat chorus*]

131

[*Chorus*]
Oh, father of the world, beloved Lord, give us knowledge,
You are the dear Lord, our only support in the world. . . .

[*Verses*]
1 I did not reach awareness in childhood,
And in youth I stored up sin,
Now where should I go, for my senses have overwhelmed me. . . .

2 My heart maintains
That you live in a temple of my mind,
While day and night I wandered from place to place. . . .

3 Beloved Lord, save me from my sins,
Make me a true devotee of the *Vedas,*
Pushing all pretense and falsehood to one side. . . .

Example XXIV (song 131, CD track 20): Hey Jagata Pitaa Bhagawaana

Example XXIV Concluded

4 My raft is in midstream,
Only in your grace is there refuge,
Nandalāla [Krishna], my whole life has passed in sinfulness. . . .

Many *bhajan* popular in Felicity are learned from Indian religious films—three-hour long Technicolor dramatizations of the *Purāṇas* and the *Rāmāyaṇ* and *Māhābhārata* epics. They always include *bhajan;* some are traditional: for example, the *ārtī bhajan,* "Jai Jagadisha Hare," is sung in many films. Many others are newly composed for films. Indian "playback" singers (so-called because their voices are dubbed in for the actors and actresses, who mime the words for the song) are very popular in Trinidad. Competitions, such as the Trinidad "Lata" (after Lata Mangeshkar) and "Rafi" (after Mohammed Rafi), are sponsored to select the best local imitators of the greatest stars. In Trinidad, *bhajan* popularized by one of these famous singers may become known as a "Lata" or a "Mukesh."

The *bhajan,* "Shiva Shambhu Deeno Ki Bandhu," is a popular Felicity temple song. The original filmī version that the Felicity singers copied was sung by the playback singer Alok (who also composed the arrangement); the lyrics are by Sanam Gorakhpuri. Differences between the filmī version (ex. XXV) and the Felicity version (ex. XXVI) are telling. The filmī version has characteristic film-style instrumental interludes, in which passages sitar, violins, clarinet, flute, and tabla play short phrases, set to Western triadic harmony, usually echoing the *bhajan* melody. The Felicity singers are accompanied by an ensemble of *ḍholak,* harmonium, and *manjīrā* (ex. XXVII). In the film version, instrumental interludes alternate with vocal passages—after each line of the opening Sanskrit mantra and after the choral "refrain tag" at the end of each verse.

Other differences are rhythmic and melodic, as in the film version, repetitions of the refrain tag (by leader, chorus, and instruments) are rhythmically compressed, resulting in an additive rhythm—3/4+3/4+2/4 (ex. XXV, mm 11–13). In the Felicity version this passage is always in 4/4 (ex. XXVI, mm 3–4). The melody of the two versions differs as in the tune used for the first line of the refrain.

The leader–chorus form of the two versions is similar, in the doubling back to the refrain, the insertion of florid passages sung on the vocable "aah," and the use of a short "refrain cue" *(namo namah).* In the Felicity version, however, the florid passages sung on "aah" are sung first by the leader, then by the chorus. In the film version they are sung by the chorus and echoed by the leader. The musical formula in Felicity is leader–chorus, not chorus–leader. In the film version, between each verse, the leader doubles back and sings the second line of the refrain; in the Felicity version, between each verse both leader and chorus sing the entire refrain (see table 7).

EXAMPLES XXV–XXVII
Shiva Shambhu Deeno Ki Bandhu (Local Orthography)

[*Slow improvisatory opening*]
mangalam bhagawaana shambhu,
mangalam vishwa bhakta bhya,
mangalam paarvati naatha,
mangalam bhakta vatsala,
[*Chorus*]
shiva shambhu deeno ki bandhu namo namah,
girijaa pati gangaa dhara hari hara namo namah. . . .

Table 7 Form of *Shiva Shambhu Deeno Ki Bandhu* (Felicity Version)

			refrain									
Leader	text	M X	i		ii		i		ii		X	
	tune	m x	r		f		r		f		x	
Chorus	text	X		RT		RT		RT		RT		X
	tune	x		r'		f'		r'		f'		x

	verse 1								refrain					
Leader	i		ii		iii		RC		i		ii		X	
	a		b		c		f		r		f		x	
Chorus		VT		VT		VT		RT		RT		RT		X
		a'		b'		c'		f'		r'		f'		x

[verses 2, 3 as above]

Key M: Sanskrit mantra text; m: mantra tune; X: florid phrase sung on "aah"; x: tune, florid phrase; i, ii, iii: text, lines 1, 2, 3 of refrain or verse; r, f, a, b, c: tunes, refrain and verse lines; RT: refrain tag; RC: refrain cue; r', f', a', b', c': tune fragment of refrain and verse tags.

[*Verses*]

1 haara chandra tripuraari sukhakar hara daani,
neela kantha saaje trikunda tu hara shaani,
bhawa bhaya haari asuraari shiva namo namah.
shiva shambhu . . . [*repeat chorus*]

2 dama dama dama damaru vinaasha se jaga dole,
nritya kare nat raaj umaa sangha shambhole,
sura saani kalyaani shankara namo namah.
shiva shambhu . . . [*repeat chorus*]

3 mahaa kaali vikraara vrishaba ki asawaari,
shambhu maala aumkaara vishaala ki bali haari,
avi naashi sukha raashi sursari nam namah.
shiva shambhu . . . [*repeat chorus*]

132

[*Slow improvisatory opening*]
Salutations to Shiva as Shambhū,
Salutations to Shiva as Lord of Pārvatī,
Salutations to Shiva as the one who cares for his devotees.

[*Chorus*]
Obeisance to Shiva Shambhū, friend of the wretched,
Obeisance to Harihara, Lord of Girijā [Pārvatī],
[He from whose hair] the Ganges flows. . . .

[*Verses*]

1 Obeisance to Hārachandra [Moon of Hara], Tripurāri, mine of bliss,
Bountiful Hara, Nīlakaṇtha, whose splendor is in the three fires,
Removes the world's fears, enemy of demons, Shiva. . . .

(continued on p. 315)

Example XXV: Shiva Shambhu Deeno Ki Bandhu, Indian Filmī version

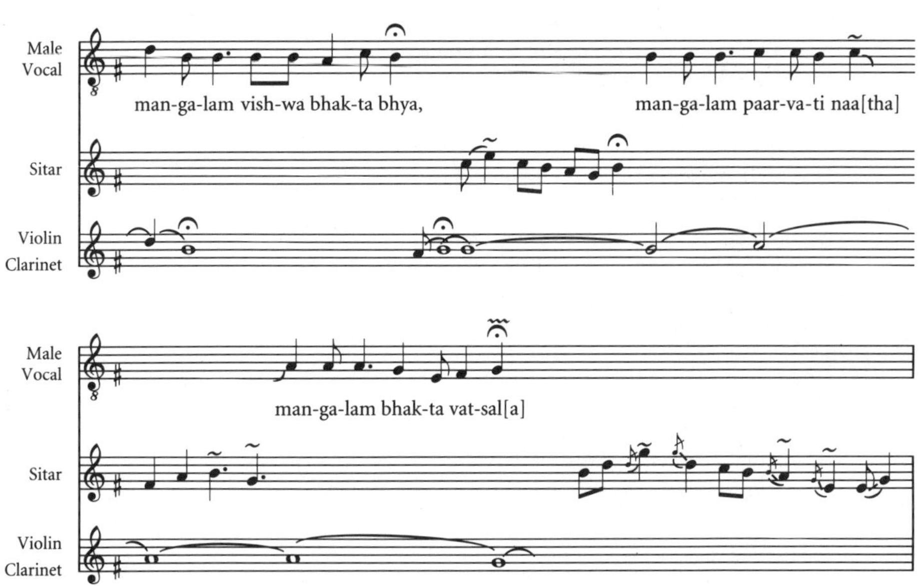

Example XXV Continued

Example XXV Continued

Example XXV Concluded

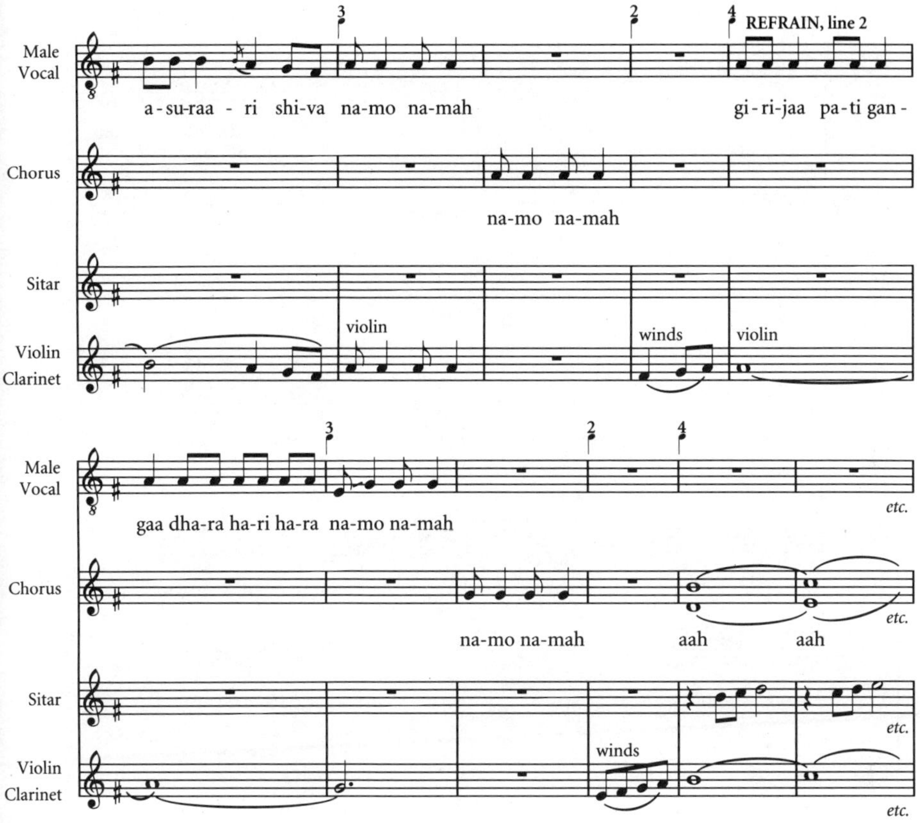

3
2
4
REFRAIN, line 2
Male Vocal
a-su-raa - ri shi-va na-mo na-mah
gi-ri-jaa pa-ti gan-
Chorus
na-mo na-mah
Sitar
violin
winds
violin
Violin Clarinet
Male Vocal
gaa dha-ra ha-ri ha-ra na-mo na-mah
etc.
Chorus
na-mo na-mah
aah
aah
etc.
Sitar
etc.
winds
Violin Clarinet
etc.

Pitch
Range (vocal)

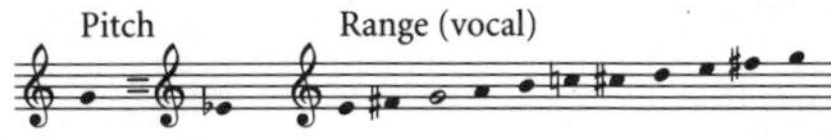

2 Obeisance to he who ever roams the world with the *damarū* drum as destruction,
Lord of the dance, who dances with Umā [Pārvatī],
Shambhū, auspicious like the gods, Shankara. . . .

3 Obeisance to awesome Māhākalī, rider on the bull,
I dedicate myself to Shambhū whose garland bears the *Omkāra,*
Indestructible mass of joy, Ganges.

Example XXVI (song 132, CD track 21): Shiva Shambhu Deeno Ki Bandhu, Felicity version

Example XXVI Continued

Example XXVI Concluded

REFRAIN

r

Leader: shi-va sham-bhu dee - no — ki ban-dhu na-mo na-mah

r'

Chorus: na-mo na-mah

f

Leader: gi-ri-jaa pa-ti gan - gaa dha-ra ha-ri ha-ra na-mo na-mah aah -

Chorus: na-mo na-mah

Leader: - etc.

Chorus: aah - etc.

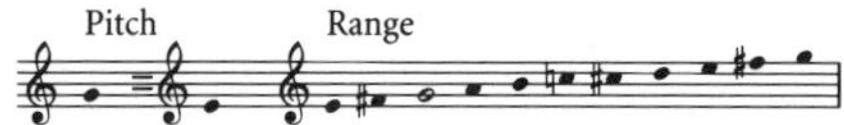

The *bhajan* "Raama Raama Bhaju Raama," known in Trinidad as a "Rafi," opens with a slow improvisatory introduction during which the solo singer can display his artistry. Atmaram Maharajh, a teacher at the Felicity Hindu School, sings this song for me with panache (ex. XXVIII; plates 44, 45).

The response form in "Raama Raama Bhaju Raama" is particularly complex. After each two lines of verse have been sung by the soloist, the chorus echoes with the final four beats of the second line (i.e., half of the line, a "verse tag"; in a later performance, the chorus repeated the entire second line). Following the last line of each verse, the soloist cues the refrain by singing the closing words of the refrain text, *bhaju raama raama seeya raama, bhaju raama raama seeya raama* (a "refrain cue," table 8).

PLATE 44. Divine Life Society, Cacandee Road, Felicity.

PLATE 45. Atmaram Maharajh playing the *ḍhantāl* during the recording of *Raama Raama Bhaju Raama,* 1974.

Example XXVII: Shiva Shambhu Deeno Ki Bandhu, full-score Felicity version

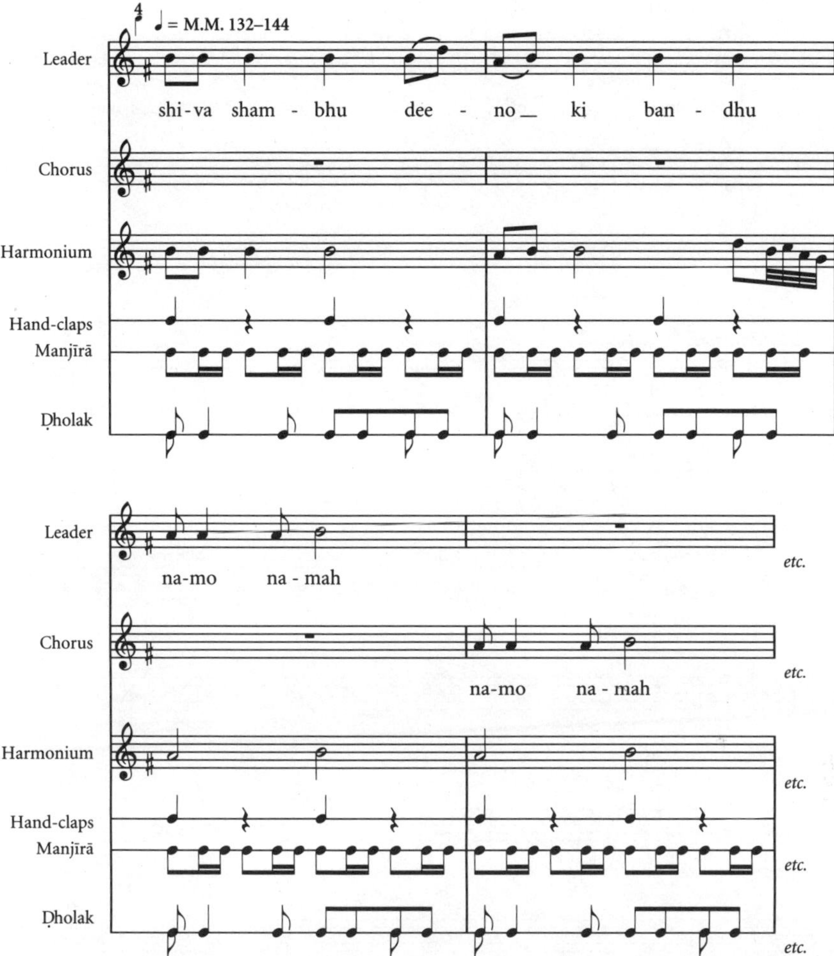

EXAMPLE XXVIII

Raama Raama Bhaju Raama (Local Orthography)

> [*Slow improvisatory opening*]
> raama raama rameti raame raame manorame,
> sahasra naama tat tulyam, raama naama varaanane.
> [*Chorus*]
> raama raama bhaju, raama raama bhaju,
> raama raama bhaju raama.
> raama raama seeya raama bhajale,

(*continued on p. 326*)

Example XXVIII (song 133, CD track 22): Raama Raama Bhaju Raama

Example XXVIII Continued

Example XXVIII Continued

Example XXVIII Concluded

Pitch

Table 8 Form of *Raama Raama Bhaju Raama*

Leader	text	S	R		i + ii		iii + iv		v + vi RC	
	tune	s	rf		a b		a b		c f	
Chorus	text			R		VT		VT		R
	tune			rf		b'		b'		rf
[verses 2, 3 as above]						R' g	R' g		T T	
							R' g	R' g	T T	

Key S: text, solo improvisatory introduction; s: tune, solo improvisatory introduction; R: refrain text; RC: refrain cue; i, ii, iii, iv, v, vi: text, lines 1–6; VT: verse tag; rf: tune, refrain; a, b, c: tunes, lines 1–6; R': text, coda-like concluding phrase; g: tune, coda-like phrase; T: *tihai* (triple cadence).

raama raama seeya raama,
bhaju raama raama seeya raama,
bhaju raama raama seeya raama.
[*Verses*]

1 dharama kaaja prithavi para aaye,
dasarathaji ke putra kahaaye,
janaka puri me shiva dhanu toeraa,
sati seeya sangha naataa joraa,
seeya peeya bana raama prabhu,
kahalaaye seeta raama . . . .

2 pitaa bachana ke paalana haare,
raaja paatha taji bana ko seedhaare,
vishwaa-mintraa yagya rakha waale,
sati Ahilyaa taarana haare,
pancha-watti ko banaadiyaa,
eka raaja dharma kaa dhaama. . . .

3 asuro ko sanhaara maara kara,
senaa sahita charhe Lankaa para,
abhimaanee raavana ko maaraa,
seeta ko sankata se ubaaraa,
raama raaja ho gayaa desha me,
goona gaaya hanumann . . . .

133 ☙
[*Chorus*]
Rām, Rām, worship Rām.
Rām, Rām, worship Sītā and Rām.
[*Verses*]

1 For the sake of *dharma* he came to earth,
He is called the son of Dasaratha,
In Janaka's city he broke the bow of Shiva,
And became betrothed to Sītā, the faithful one,
Lord Rām became Sītā's dear husband,
They are called "Sītā and Rām."

2 In compliance with his father's word,
He gave up the crown and went to the forest,
Sustainer of the sacrifice made by Visvāmitra,
Bestower of salvation to the faithful Ahilyā,
He made the Panchwatī forest
The abode of royal righteousness.

3 He beat and annihilated the demons,
And attacked Lankā with his army,
He overwhelmed proud Rāwaṇ,
And freed Sītā from danger,

TABLE 9 Form of *Bhajale Naama Niranjana Kaa*

		Refrain free tempo							verse 1			
Leader	text	S	R		R		R		i + ii		i + ii	
	tune	s	r		r		r'		a		a	
Chorus	text			R		R		R		i + ii		i + ii
	tune			r		r		r'		a		a

Leader	iii b		iii b		iv c		iv c		R r		R r		R r'		[verse 2 as above]
Chorus		iii b		iii b		iv c		iv c		R r		R r		R r'	

KEY S: solo improvisatory introduction; x: tune, introduction; R: text, refrain; r: tune, refrain; i, ii, iii, iv: text, verse lines 1, 2, 3, 4; a, b, c: tunes, verse lines; r': refrain tune, melodic extension.

Rām rules over the whole land,
And Hanumān sings of his qualities
[Last line ambiguous].

A slow improvisatory opening is typical of many *bhajan.* Another example of this style is "Bhajale Naama Niranjana Kaa" ("Sing in Praise the Name of Niranjana [God free of illusion]"), which opens with a brief florid introduction (ex. XXIX). The response form of this song is straightforward (table 9), and it is easy to compare the performing style of the soloist with that of the chorus. In the setting of the refrain line, *bhajale naama niranjana kaa,* the pitches for the syllables "le," "naama," and "kaa" are highly ornamental, given more inflection. These ornaments are known in the Indian classical tradition as *gamak,* a generic term for ornament or embellishment. Usually these are movements around a single pitch, but the term may also indicate slides between pitches (also called *mīnd*), and other types of embellishment. To translate *gamak* as "ornament" or "embellishment" is somewhat misleading as these pitch movements are essential to the performing style of the *rāg* in the Indian classical tradition: no vocal or instrumental performance is complete without them. *Gamak* occur in both the solo and choral renditions of "Bhajale Naama Niranjana Kaa" although the solo *gamak* are not identical with the choral ones (ex. XXIX).

Pitch inflections of less than a semitone are impossible to represent precisely in Western notation; a more accurate picture of the slides and turns in this example (shown in these transcriptions with grace notes, mordents, inverted mordents, straight lines indicating glides, curved lines indicating glides

Example XXIX (song 134, CD track 23): Bhajale Naama Niranjana Kaa

Example XXIX Continued

Example XXIX Continued

Example XXIX Concluded

into a pitch, and so on) could be drawn by a computer. *Gamak* occur in the *bhajan* of the Felicity repertory, often on a syllable with important meaning, for example, the mantra, "aum" ("Jai Jagadisha Hare," ex. XXXI) and the syllable "Raa" of *Raama* ("Raama Raama Bhaju Raama," ex. XXVIII), in which the rhythm long–short, long–short, short–short exactly matches the text rhythm, *Raa-ma Raa-ma bha-ju.*

EXAMPLE XXIX
Bhajale Naama Niranjana Kaa (Local Orthography)

[*Chorus*]
bhajale naama niranjana kaa. . . .

1 ye sanasaara saraaya chala aachala
eka aataa eka jaataa hai,
koi bastu nahi sthira jaga me,
brithaa mamataa dhana jobana kaa. . . .

2 yonee anekan me phirate phirate,
dhanya manusha deha milaa,
karale bhaaeeyo kaama kachu aba,
taja yaha duniyaa maayaa kaa. . . .

134 ❧

[*Chorus*]
Sing in praise the name of Niranjana [God free of illusion].

[*Verses*]
1 This world is an inn for all kinds of beings,
One comes, another goes,
Nothing is permanent in the world,
And vain is the attachment of wealth and youthfulness.

2 Wandering from birth to birth,
Blessed is he who gains a human form,
Now brother, achieve something,
And abandon this world of illusion.

Nearly all *bhajan* singing in Felicity temples is accompanied by harmonium. The leader may accompany himself, or he may be accompanied by another musician. Singers usually accompany themselves with a drone at the unison and fifth, or by echoing the melody. When the singer is accompanied by another musician, the accompaniment is often more complex, with many rhythmic and melodic variations of the melody, as shown in the two solo passages from "Bhajale Naama Niranjana Kaa," verse 2, transcribed in Example XXX.

The Felicity *bhajan* repertory is interesting not so much for metric complexity (most of the *bhajan* are in 4/4 time) or modality (most are in the diatonic major or minor), but for performing style. Many pitches are highly

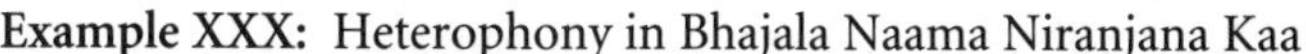

Example XXX: Heterophony in Bhajala Naama Niranjana Kaa

inflected, and at times the pitch that we think we hear may not actually be present, or at any rate not sustained, but defined by upper and lower neighbors. Felicity singers show rhythmic discretion in approaching the first beat of a bar. They tend to disguise beat one, either by tying into the bar (as in "Bhajale Naama Niranjana Kaa," verse 1, line 2), by leaving an eighth rest on beat one ("Mere Mana Basigayo," throughout), by gliding into the principal pitch in beat one from below ("Raama Raama Bhaju Raama," throughout), or through syncopation (usually eighth, quarter, eighth in many of the examples). This careful approach to the first beat can be heard in some form in nearly all of the Felicity examples.

These features of style can be studied by comparing performances of the same song by different groups. Example XXXI displays three versions of "Jai Jagadisha Hare," an *ārtī bhajan* sung in all the village temples many times throughout the year. For comparison, two of the variants were recorded outside Felicity: version 1 was recorded at an Arya Samaj service in Carolina, a small village in the cane lands of central Trinidad; version 2 in the Trinidad Sevashram Sangha on Nolan Street in Felicity; and version 3 in the Divine Life

Society (Unit 24), in the village of Enterprise, a few miles east of Felicity. For the Carolina village version, the harmonium part is also shown.

EXAMPLE XXXI
Jai Jagadisha Hare (Local Orthography)

[*Chorus*]
jai jagadisha hare, swaami jai jagadisha hare,
bhakata jano [janana] ke sankata, kshana me dura kare. . . .

1 jo dhyaawe phala paawe, dukha bina se mana kaa,
swaami dukha bina se mana kaa,
sukha sampati ghara aawe, kashta mite tana kaa. aum jai jagadisha hare. jai jagadisha hare . . . [*repeat chorus*]

2 maata pitaa tuma mere, sharana gahu kis ki,
swaami sharana gahu kis ki,
tuma bina owra naa dujaa, aasha karu kis ki. aum jai jagadisha hare. jai jagadisha hare . . . [*repeat chorus*]

3 tuma purana paramaatma, tuma antarayaami,
swaami tuma antarayaami,
parama brahma prameshwara, tuma saba ke swaami. aum jai jagadisha hare. jai jagadisha hare . . . [*repeat chorus*]

4 tuma karunaa ke saagara, tuma paalana karata,
swaami tuma paalana karata,
deena dayaalu kirpaalu, kripaa karo bhartaa. aum jai jagadisha hare. jai jagadisha hare . . . [*repeat chorus*]

5 tuma ho eka angochara, saba ke praana pati,
swaami saba ke praana pati,
kisa bidhee milu dayaamai, tuma ko mai kumatee. aum jai jagadisha hare. jai jagadisha hare . . . [*repeat chorus*]

6 deena bandhu dukha haratаа, tuma rakshaka mere,
swaami tuma rakshaka mere,
karunaa hasta barhaawo, sharana paraa tere. aum jai jagadisha hare. jai jagadisha hare . . . [*repeat chorus*]

7 vishaya vikaara mitaawo, paapa haro devaa,
swaami paapa haro devaa,
sraddhaa bhakti barhaawo, santana ki sewaa. aum jai jagadisha hare. jai jagadisha hare . . . [*repeat chorus*]

135

[*Chorus*]
May the supreme being, lord of the world, be ever victorious.
May he remove in an instant the misfortunes of the pious ones.
[*Verses*]

1 Who prays to you receives good fruit and avoids mental distress. Happiness and worldly riches come to the home, bodily trouble is avoided.

2 Oh, supreme one! You are our mother and our father, whose shelter and protection we seek. There is no other but you, on whom we may place our hope.

3 You are the perfect one, the all-everlasting one, the supreme soul, the supreme being. You are the protector of all.

4 You are the ocean of mercy. You are the preserver of all. Have mercy on us oh supreme being and destroy our sensuality and defects.

5 You are invisible, you are aspiration. Oh merciful God, how can I meet you when I am foolish?

6 You are brother of the poor, remover of all hindrance and my protector. Oh God, increase mercy in me, I kneel to you.

7 And may you increase the sum of good will and devotion for the benefit of pious people.

The *gamak* in the three versions correspond: on the syllable "jai" (measure 4), "di" (measure 5), "re" (measure 6), "san" (measures 9, 12), "Aum" (measures 15, 18, 36), "ow" (measures 29, 32), and so on. This agreement between the versions suggests that *gamak* are not casual "ornaments" but fixed features of performing style as indeed they are in the Indian classical system. For example, if the underlying melodic movement of the song is from A to G, singers from Felicity, Enterprise, or Carolina are likely to add the upper neighbor, hence A B A G (ex. XXXI, measures 9, 12); if the melodic movement is a leap from B to D, these singers are likely to bridge the gap (B C D; ex. XXXI, measures 3–4), and so on.

The *gamak* in versions of "Jai Jagadisha Hare" in Indian films are much bolder, and in many cases so pronounced that the transcriber might better show them as main melody notes rather than as subsidiary notes as in the Trinidad examples.

Vocal *gamak* occur in the older Bhojpurī repertory but the intensification of this practice in the more recent temple *bhajan* suggests that this style has been reinforced since the importation of Indian films and records after World War II.

ஐ

A morning in the Felicity temple left one with much to ponder: about religion and history; about music repertory and performing style; about the purification rites of ancient Aryans, introduced to a Trinidad village of the twentieth century, embraced by local Hindus, and now faithfully performed

Example XXXI (song 135, CD tracks 24, 25 and 26): Jai Jagadisha Hare

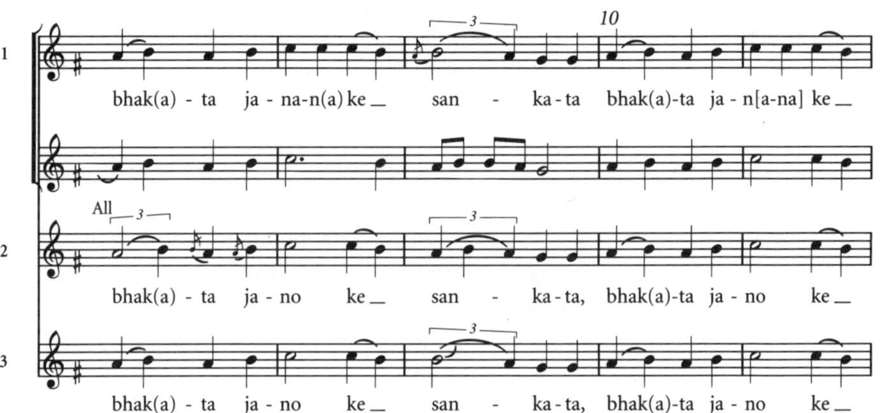

Example XXXI Continued

Example XXXI Continued

Example XXXI Concluded

each Sunday at the break of day; about new *bhajan* from Indian films, purchased on record or pirated with cassette recorders at the cinema, then carefully memorized by temple congregations; and about the vocal mannerisms of an old generation of vocalists from the Bombay studios, the Rafi's and the Lata's, Mukesh, and Hemant Kumar, inspiring a new generation of Indian singers half a world away.

Chapter Fifteen

Music and Miracles

> The Miracles of the Church seem to me to rest not so much upon faces or voices or healing power coming suddenly near to us from afar off, but upon our perceptions being made finer, so that for a moment our eyes can see and our ears can hear what is there about us always.
>
> Willa Cather, *Death Comes for the Archbishop*

"I was wondering about these amazing things that happened to you," I said.

"Ah, well," Dhun replied. "It started about four years ago. We lived as anybody else in Felicity. We had a small altar right across here and the children did *pūjā* there. One night the neighbor next door had prayers and we went across to them. When I came back, I saw on the pictures—there were about four or five different pictures, we had Shiva, Sai Baba, Māhā Lakshmī, Hanumānjī, Shrī Ganesh—I see from the forehead of all the picture three streams of things start leaking. It's like water but it's thicker than water. Before, I heard they say honey from Sai Baba's picture does be flowing. So when I look at it, I show the wife. I wake the neighbors and I call the children and I show them. In the space of half an hour, we had over a thousand of people here. And this keep flowing. This continue for about six or seven months, coming and leaking, and we doesn't know where it coming from. We look around, right around. There was nothing. They say it is *amrit* ['nectar'].

"As the news went around, people started coming with groups, and chanting the name of the Lord. We had prayers and *sanḍhyā*. Night upon night, night after night, we had a different group come and every group come they offer flowers, and they went and bowed to Lord Shiva and Sai Baba. This went for a few months.

"A lady from Assam in India was here. She ask if she could offer her flowers. I say, 'Sure,' so she made flowers and she bring and offer it to the pictures. When she offer the flowers to Lord Shiva picture, we see some smoke come right across, and the whole Sai Baba picture get wet. And she saw it, so she asked me if this was so. 'No, when you started it wasn't so,' I said. Then she say she left home in the intention to see what we speak about and she see and she is very happy. She say she were expecting that.

"We had three Swamis from Venezuela here. They said, 'I heard about honey coming from your picture.' I say, 'Well, I really don't know if it's honey or what it is, but I believe on Sai Baba.' They sit down and they start looking at the picture, and while looking at the picture, the honey start flowing again and it start dripping down by the drop. These is some of the things that happen. God himself came into me, into this house."

"How did you feel?" I asked.

"Well," he said, "you get vibration. When you get vibration you get strength twice the amount you got."

"You're not afraid?" I asked.

"No," he said. "These things I expect."

Sai Baba

Bhagwān Shrī Sathya Sai Baba was born on 23 November 1926, in Puttaparthi, a small village in Andhra Pradesh in southeastern India. The third child of a pious but otherwise unremarkable family, he was given the name of Sathyanarayana Raju. It is said that he performed his first miracle as a schoolboy at the age of eight, and that he subsequently developed quite a reputation for materializing sweets, fruits, pencils, and toys, for tracing lost property, and for reading far into the future and deep into the past. On 23 May 1940, he declared himself to be "Sai Baba," the reincarnation of the Shaivite, Sai Baba of Shirdi (?1850–1918), and an avatar, come to save humanity from downfall. "I have come in order to repair the ancient highway leading man to God. Become skillful, sincere engineers, overseers and workmen, and join me. The *Vedas, Upanishads* and *Shastras* are the roads I refer to. I have come to reveal them and revive them. I have come to sow the seeds of faith in religion and God. I come in response to the prayers of sages, saints and seekers for the restoration of *dharma* [duty, righteousness]" (Kasturi, *Sathyam,* 1–15).

Baba said that his first sixteen years would be devoted to "sportive pursuits" and that he would then draw people to him and his mission by means of miracles, up to the age of 32. His *upadesh,* or teaching, would begin after 32. He requested that his devotees should worship him on Thursdays.

The teachings of Sai Baba fall within the scope of conventional Hindu thought. He maintains that each man is linked to God through the *ātmān* ("soul," "spirit") which, like God, is formless and eternal. At death, the *ātmān* survives the physical body and, because of man's earthly desires, reincorporates itself into another creature. The goal for Hindus is *moksha,* liberation of the *ātmān* from the cycle of birth and rebirth. To achieve *moksha,* a man must eliminate all his worldly attachments and train himself to distinguish between the permanent *(brahman)* and the transitory *(māyā)* through spiritual practices *(sādhanā).* Yoga is an effective means of spiritual self-discipline. Of the three principal types of yoga, *karma* ("action"), *jnana* ("knowledge"), and *bhaktī* ("devotion"), Sai Baba teaches that *bhaktī* is the surest and easiest path for most people to follow.

Among Hindus, there is much less skepticism over Baba's divinity than a Christian might expect, for Hindus do not find it surprising that God would manifest himself on earth in human form more than once. Although there is much disagreement about who the modern-day avatars are, the principle of divine incarnation is practically unchallenged. In Felicity, any villager will point out that God has visited man on a number of occasions, for example, the avatars Rām, Krishna, the Buddha, and Jesus Christ. The scriptural justification for divine incarnation is found in the *Bhāgawad Gītā,* best-loved of the Hindu texts, in the passage where Krishna reveals himself to the warrior, Arjuna.

> For the protection of the good,
> And for the destruction of evil-doers,
> To make a firm footing for the right,
> I come into being in age after age.

It is the miracles of Sai Baba that have attracted attention. Hindus expect great yogis to possess superhuman powers, and Baba's attributes do seem extraordinary even to very devout Hindus. His best-known claim to power is the materialization of *vibhūtī,* a sweet-smelling sacred ash. He is also said to materialize other items including gold chains, coins, gems, and religious statuettes. He is attributed with miraculous powers of healing, and, it is claimed, raised the dead to life. He has also been reported to be in different places at the same time.

Baba in Trinidad

In April 1974, a group of Trinidadians returned from a visit to Guyana and Surinam with news of Sai Baba and his miraculous feats. The first devotional session in Trinidad was held in May, and frequently thereafter. Before long miracles were reported in the Trinidad "Sai Bulletin":

> We in Trinidad believe that Sai Baba is acknowledging our faith in him by adding fuel to our fires of devotion. This is in the form of certain esoteric, phenomenal occurrences which are beginning to happen almost weekly to certain devotees. Also, I feel very fortunate, and humbly so, that he has tangibly satisfied my faith by allowing *vibhūtī* to appear on the surface of the big picture I have of Him. On Friday 28th June, Miss Vidya Roopnarinesingh and the family of Dr. H. Sukhbin were blessed with similar experiences. *Vibhūtī* appeared on a small picture of Sai Baba given to Miss Roopnarinesingh by Mrs. Rooplalsingh whilst *vibhūtī* appeared on a dressing table belonging to the Sukhbins. How wonderful and reassuring it is to know that Baba's divine presence is always

with his devotees and what more can one expect from God? (Bahadoorsingh and Noel)

During the crop time in 1974, Parsuram and Sulin Ramsundar held the first Sai Baba *satsangh* in Felicity, an event that attracted a crowd so large it spilled out of their spacious yard and into the neighboring school and temple grounds. In August 1975, a group of villagers took a charter flight to the Baba *āshram* in India. Among the pilgrims was Swami Satchidananda of the Divine Life Society, who brought back a remarkable vial of *vibhūtī* to distribute among his devotees, remarkable because, as the villagers told me, as much as he doled out to his congregation, that amount was replenished by the following Sunday.

Until the August visit, no one in Felicity had seen Sai Baba. What they knew they had learned through discussion, reading, and films distributed by his international organization. By 1975, seven 20-minute films with English sound tracks were in circulation around Trinidad, giving Baba's life story, facts about his mission, and documentation of his feats, particularly the materialization of *vibhūtī.* The Baba is pictured giving *darshan* ("viewing" of himself in long, salmon-colored robes) to crowds of thousands at his *āshram.*

Trinidad devotees long for *darshan* of Sai Baba, and many undergo the expensive and arduous trip to Bangalore, India (far south of the region of their origin). The belief has grown that even the poorest follower may miraculously find the money to go. As a visit to India is a shock for any traveler, it is more so for these East Indians, who anticipate something of a spiritual homecoming. But the Sai pilgrimage subjects these devotees to jet lag, overcrowded hotels, strange food, and exotic South Indian customs. Truth to tell, some Asian Indians told me they don't like these Caribbean pseudo cousins.

Ironically, Sai sports a 1970s Afro hairstyle. This full halo of tight black curls bewilders some of the Hindu members of Trinidad's plural society, in which animosity between blacks and Indians is commonplace and well-documented. "I felt guilty, of disowning the picture: Dear Lord, I am sorry because the hair on your head really baffled me," one young lady said (Klass, *Singing with Sai Baba,* 145).

Bhaktī: The Sai Song Repertory

Singing is believed to be one of the most effective forms of *bhaktī* yoga, and all of the Sai films include several *dhun* composed by Baba and his followers. The songs have short and rather simple nonstrophic texts, referred to in Trinidad as "chants" or "Sai Baba" songs. Around 1975, a song book *Bhajans and Chants of Shri Satya Sai Baba* was printed in Trinidad; it includes 80 Hindi texts (113 in the second edition) in Roman transliteration.

The performance of a Sai Baba song starts slowly and softly and gains speed and volume with each of the many repetitions of the text. The melody usually begins on a low pitch level and progresses to a higher one. In Trinidad, as the excitement builds and the momentum of the singing increases, loud clapping on the beat is added. By contrast, a uniform volume and tempo are maintained in *bhajan* singing, and hand clapping is avoided.

"Ganesha Sharanam" is a popular Sai song in Felicity. An LP record from India illustrates many typical features of the style: simple duple meter with syncopation producing rhythmic interest; an uncomplicated melody that starts in a medium register and moves higher; a short nonstrophic text; leader–chorus response form; accompaniment by tabla, flutes, cymbals, and clappers; accelerando and crescendo; and pronounced *gamak,* particularly on the syllables "nam" (of *sharanam*) and "e" (of *Ganesha* and *Sayesha*) (ex. XXXII). The Felicity version (ex. XXXIII) retains simple duple meter but lacks the syncopations; the melody is pentatonic and moves from a medium to a high register and back again. Some pitches differ from those in the Indian model. The text follows the Indian version, with most of the *gamak* omitted. The form is responsorial. The accompaniments are by harmonium, *ḍholak,* and idiophones. Altogether lacking in the Felicity version are the undulations and irregularities of pitch and rhythm that give the Indian version its distinctive character (ex. XXXII).

136
Surrender to Lord Ganesh.
Surrender to Lord Ganesh.
Surrender to Lord Sai.
Surrender to Lord Sai.

In "Aum Bhagawān," another popular Sai song, both the harmonium drone and the modality (diatonic major with lowered 7th degree) are somewhat unusual for the village style (ex. XXXIV). This example also illustrates the typical leader–chorus response form of Sai songs, crescendo and accelerando, the repeated use of a short simple text, *gamak* (on syllables "Aum," "wān"—*Bhagawān,* "Sai," and so on), and the preferred overall timbre, distorted by the overly close miking and the use of a public address system.

137
Oh Lord, grant me a vision of you.
Lord of Patri,
Mother of all,
Lord of my soul.

Have mercy, Baba.
Grant me your blessings.
Sai, the blue-complexioned Lord [Krishna], Rāma.
Sai, the blue-complexioned Lord, Rāma.
Sai Baba, Satya Sai Baba.
Sai Baba, Satya Sai Baba.

During my third visit, I had three opportunities every week to hear Sai Baba songs. On Thursdays, Matti, her aunt Kowsil, and I would go to the Sai Baba *satsangh* (prayer meeting) in the market town of Chaguanas, a few miles east of Felicity. The session was held in a new building on the main street, in a large room that could have seated some five hundred. Our weekly gathering usually numbered less than one hundred, leaving plenty of space for the small children to run and play during the service. At the altar were many pictures of Baba—standing, seated, hands raised, serious, smiling. There were also the usual colored pictures of the other deities such as Hanumān, Ganesh, and Shiva. All the images were adorned with garlands of fresh flowers, and incense was burning. An empty armchair draped with a saffron-colored bedspread was in the center of the altar, and on the floor, propped up against this chair, was a photograph of the saint's feet and hem of his robe for the devotees to touch and worship.

The Chaguanas service always began with the chanting of an opening prayer, then an hour or more of Sai Baba songs sung by the congregation. Different members would take turns leading the singing—sometimes a woman, sometimes a man, and sometimes a child. All the songs were accompanied by an instrumental group—harmonium, *ḍholak, kartāl,* and *ḍhantāl.* Many pairs of tiny *manjīrā* finger cymbals were passed among the congregation and their jingling accompanied all the songs. During the singing, members of the congregation would rise, one by one, and perform *ārtī,* the offering of fire, to the images at the altar. On special occasions like Sai Baba's birthday in November, a short address might be given after the *ārtī,* but normally the service ended with prayers and meditation, the distribution of *vibhūtī* from India and *prasād* (sweets) and the closing prayers.

On Wednesday nights, I went to the Sai Baba *satsangh* at the home of Mr. and Mrs. Dhun on Pierre Road. They began holding services in their home in 1974, following the miraculous occurrences at their family altar—the honey "leaking" from the icons, and the dreams and visions of Baba. The usual order of this service was opening prayer, Sai Baba songs and other *bhajan, sanḍhyā,* distribution of *vibhūtī,* perhaps more Sai Baba songs, and closing prayer.

Example XXXII: Ganesha Sharanam, Indian and Felicity versions compared

Example XXXII Concluded

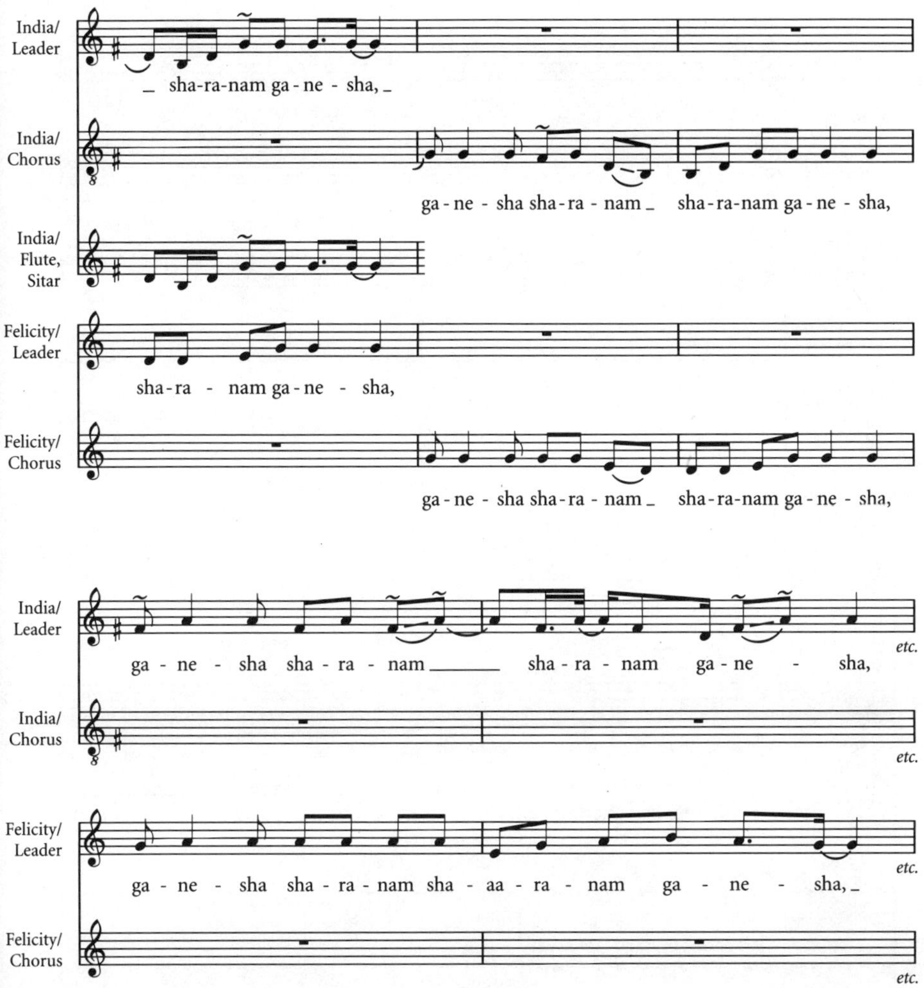

India/ Leader
_ sha-ra-nam ga - ne - sha, _
India/ Chorus
ga - ne - sha sha-ra - nam _ sha-ra-nam ga - ne - sha,
India/ Flute, Sitar
Felicity/ Leader
sha-ra - nam ga-ne - sha,
Felicity/ Chorus
ga - ne - sha sha-ra - nam _ sha-ra-nam ga-ne - sha,
India/ Leader
ga - ne - sha sha - ra - nam ______ sha - ra - nam ga - ne - sha,
etc.
India/ Chorus
etc.
Felicity/ Leader
ga - ne - sha sha - ra - nam sha - aa - ra - nam ga - ne - sha, _
etc.
Felicity/ Chorus
etc.

Pitch (India)
Range (India)
~ = *Gamaka*

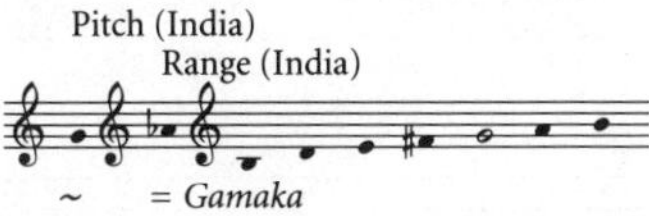

Example XXXIII (song 136, CD track 27): Ganesha Sharanam, Felicity version

Example XXXIII Concluded

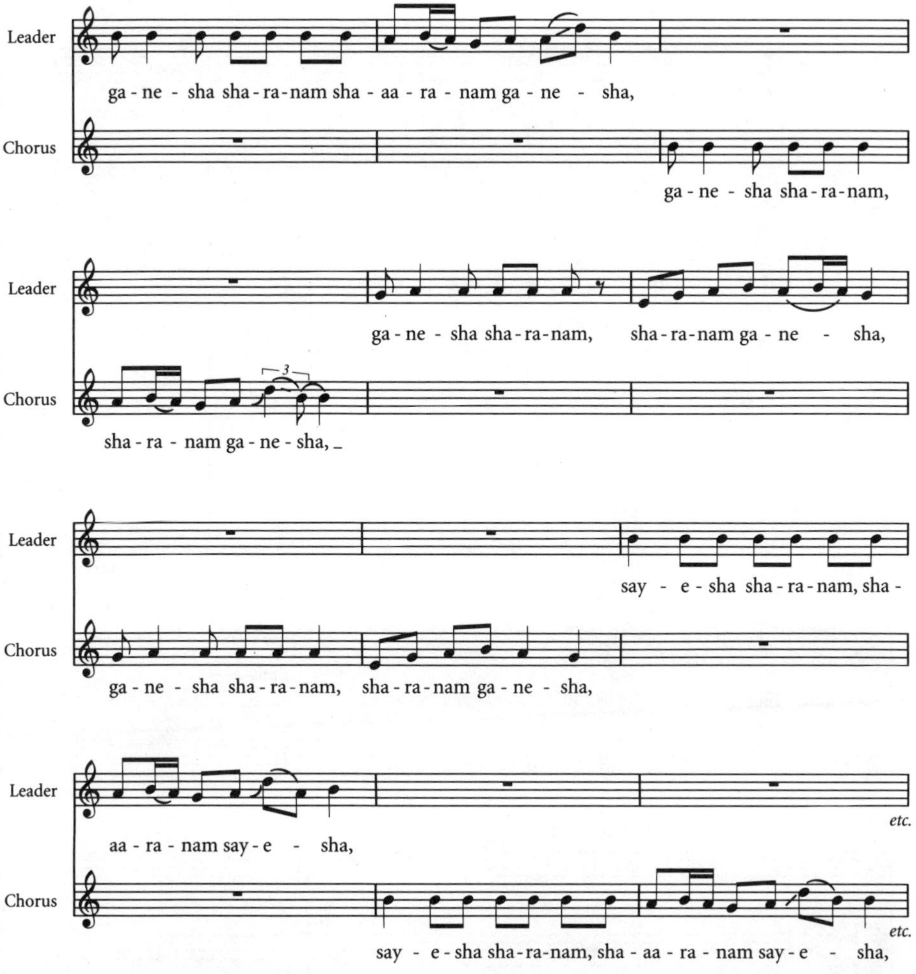
Leader
ga - ne - sha sha - ra - nam sha - aa - ra - nam ga - ne - sha,
Chorus
ga - ne - sha sha - ra - nam,
Leader
ga - ne - sha sha - ra - nam, sha - ra - nam ga - ne - sha,
Chorus
3
sha - ra - nam ga - ne - sha, _
Leader
say - e - sha sha - ra - nam, sha -
Chorus
ga - ne - sha sha - ra - nam, sha - ra - nam ga - ne - sha,
Leader
aa - ra - nam say - e - sha,
etc.
Chorus
etc.
say - e - sha sha - ra - nam, sha - aa - ra - nam say - e - sha,

Pitch
Range (Pentatonic)

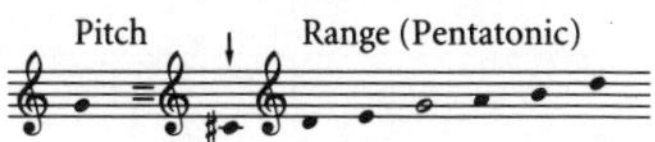

Example XXXIV (song 137, CD track 28): Aum Bhagawān

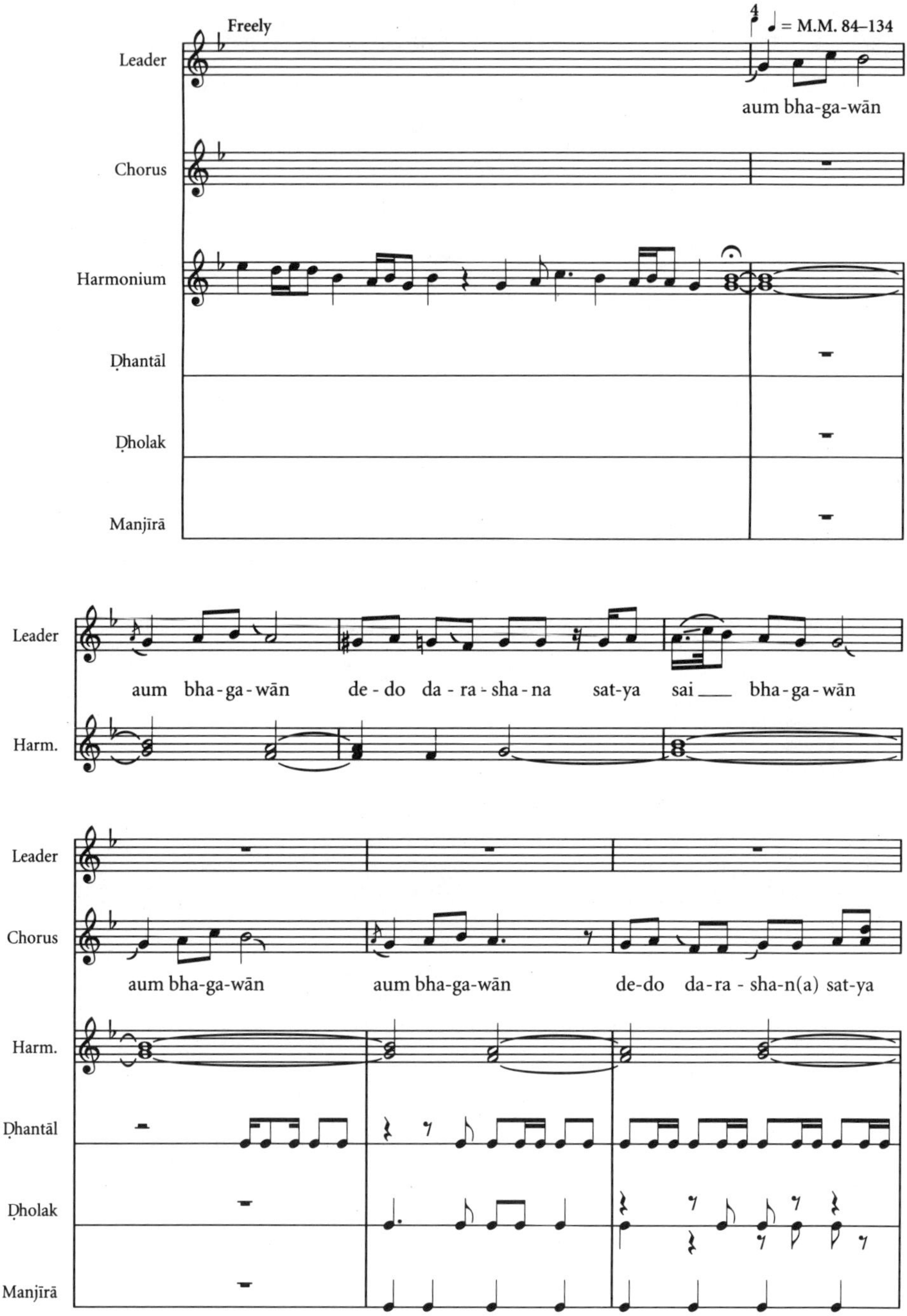

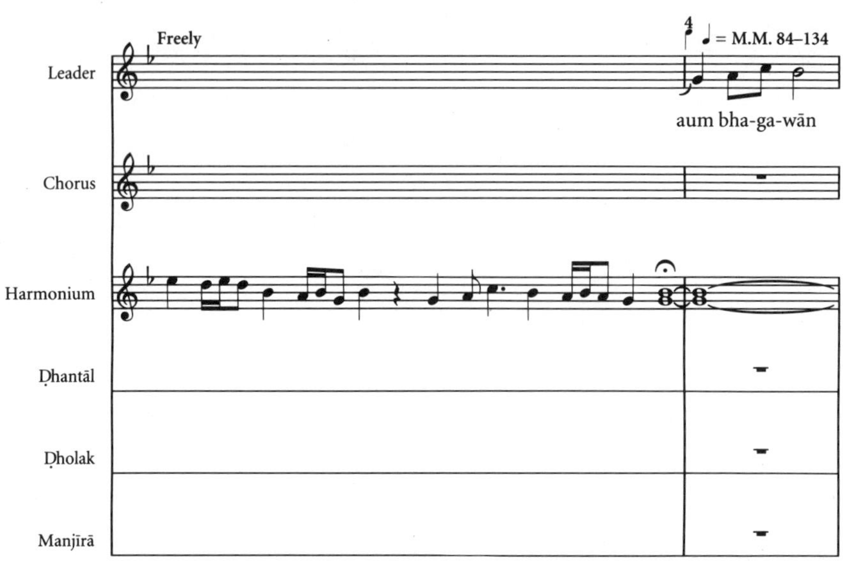

Leader

aum bha-ga-wān de-do da-ra-sha-na sat-ya sai ___ bha-ga-wān

Harm.

Leader

Chorus

aum bha-ga-wān aum bha-ga-wān de-do da-ra-sha-n(a) sat-ya

Harm.

Ḍhantāl

Ḍholak

Manjīrā

Example XXXIV Continued

Example XXXIV Continued

Example XXXIV Continued

Example XXXIV Concluded

Sai Baba songs were sung also at the Divine Life Society. On Friday nights, Mesho, Matti, their children, and I went to the Unit 1 temple on Cacandee Road. The simple service lasted only an hour. It began with an opening prayer, then continued with half an hour of *bhajan* singing and then *ārtī.* Sometimes a *sanḍhyā* service followed, but often the evening ended with meditation, a few more songs, and the closing prayer.

Mesho usually played the *ḍholak,* and he often led the singing. In 1974, the first year I visited Felicity, nearly all the songs at the Friday evening service were traditional *bhajan* from *Divine Life Bhajans* (the "yellow book"). On my second visit, in 1975, I was surprised to learn how many new songs the group had added to their repertory from *Bhajans and Chants of Shri Satya Sai Baba.* They sang the Baba songs in the characteristic style, starting softly and slowly and ending loud and fast with enthusiastic hand clapping. During 1974, I had never heard any clapping in the Divine Life Society temple, but in 1975 they occasionally added clapping and accelerando to the older *bhajan.*

In 1977, on another visit to Felicity, both songbooks were still being used in the Friday night service, but the traditional *bhajan* were regaining some of their former popularity. Most evenings, about half the songs were taken from one book and half from the other. The familiar *bhajan* were too well loved to be forgotten, but the villagers really enjoyed singing the Sai Baba songs, with their short catchy texts and lively style.

Mesho's group from the Divine Life Society temple often went out to sing *bhajan* at *havan* blessing services around Felicity and in other villages. They always sang a few Sai Baba songs at these functions, before the *havan* and after. Several members of the temple group taught at the Felicity Hindu School, and, during 1975, they began teaching the Baba songs to the children during the morning devotional period. The songs caught on quickly, even though the children are not allowed to clap while they are singing in school.

❧ Felicity Temple Repertories: Fast or Slow?

I never heard the Sai Baba songs performed at the Shrī Shankar Mandir on Cacandee Road or the Trinidad Sevashram Sangha on Nolan Street. Chandra was a member of the Nolan Street group. When I played a Sai song for her, she said, "Well, you see I would say it's too fast, right? Probably different groups sing it different way."

"But what is your opinion?" I asked.

"Well, I think it's too fast, because in our temple we didn't learn it so. We learn it as slow and easy way. We don't go rushing down, and probably at the end of the song we sing it a little fast and cut it off with that. When you sing anything too fast, people get sort of stupid and they start dancing, and the temple isn't the thing for that, right? They start making unnecessary noise. If we have to sing one, we sing it very slow."

"Are they normally fast?" I asked.

"Yes," she said. "Well, anywhere I hear them, I hear them fast."

"And loud or soft?" I asked.

"Very loud," she replied. "There's a lot of clapping in it. Probably the songs that he [Sai Baba] made, he sang them like that and they tape them just like that. And the records were sent out and the people learned it just like that."

Channu, a member of the Shrī Shankar Mandir, explained that the Sai Baba songs had "more speed and more action" than traditional *bhajan.* But she added that the fast tempo and hand clapping made it hard for her to meditate.

One afternoon we listened to one of my recordings:

"That's a Sai Baba song," she said. "It's a song that one can concentrate when giving devotion to Sai Baba. Some of the devotees now do more prayer to Sai Baba. They consider Sai Baba as a lord that they achieve lately, a re-incarnation, an avatar of Lord Shiva."

"Do you believe that?" I asked.

"Well, no," she said. "I don't believe in Sai Baba. Well, I say he is just a disciple, he is not the Lord himself. He is just a follower of the Lord. Maybe his standard is higher than ours, but I don't believe that he is the Lord. I too, myself, can sit down and concentrate on Mātā Lakshmī and I can feel the difference. And I can concentrate on Hanumān and I feel the difference, but I don't have that amount of belief in him."

"What about the songs? Are they the same as *bhajan?*"

"Yes, it's just that, to my knowledge, I know the *dhun* in Sai Baba is a little bit different from the *dhun* in the ordinary *bhajan* that we sing. They use a lot of clapping and meditating and more tempo, like. They put some more action in them. They take on more speed like to concentrate when they do it. But most of our *bhajan* now, we sit down relax and quiet and, now like them, they will sing fast fast fast. But if we have to sing, we will sing slowly and soft, in a smoothing kind of way. We get accustomed to that from ever since, so we like it that way. But probably if we was together with them, and in that tempo kind of way, we might value it."

Many people who don't believe in Sai Baba or his miracles like the songs. "To be honest," Kedar Pandit said, "my personal opinion is that I really don't believe that Sai Baba could perform those miracles that we read about and we hear about. Some of these miracles are so great that I believe it only could be performed by the Almighty God. There are lots of people in India today who can do a lot of things with their hand which you call the black part of magic."

"What about the songs?" I asked.

"The sound is very very enchanting. There is nothing wrong with the songs. They are well worthy and I believe it gives you a certain amount of integration, vigor. They really stir you up and it put you in mood to be near the Lord. If music has got in it what Shakespeare said, if music be the food of love, then play on, right? And any one of these deities that we serve, you will notice that Saraswatī Mātā, she has the *vīṇā* right? Lord Krishna was playing the flute, right? And so music is one of the ways whereby you could really take your mind off the material things."

Suruj Pandit agreed with Kedar that Sai Baba was not an avatar. But he too liked the songs. He explained to me that the performance style gave these pieces their characteristic sound, not the songs themselves.

"Sai Baba is a devotee of the Lord," Suruj said, "and he's got some powers. He's a devotee as I and you. He's not no avatar. But often we worship the Lord for a certain period of time and the Lord is pleased with our devotion. Then he give us a gift. It is a gift given unto you whatever you are praying for, and with that gift you can perform miracles. You can heal people, but it is through His power, not through your power."

"What do you think about the songs?" I asked.

"The songs are wonderful," he said. "They teaching people to pray to God, not to Sai Baba."

"What is different about these songs?" I asked.

"The songs not different, but the method in which they sing it. It brings a certain amount of force into you, compelling you to worship, to sing it. You see, the tune they sing the *bhajan* then, it is very nice to listen to. Yes, very pleasing to the ears, and it at least interests you a lot to take part in singing it."

"They use a lot of clapping," I said.

"Nothing wrong with that," he said. "You are just joyful in mind. You feel happy when you sing these things. It does not mean to say that when you are singing the other *bhajan* you can't clap, you can't dance, you can't play all music. No harm in that—that is very good, when the amount of joy come in you."

"When I'm listening to them, they seem to go in a more . . ."

"A faster way," he said. "They start slow and then they move up a little higher, and then they go a little faster again. They start slow and then get faster. It is a sort of a chant."

"Is it a *dhun?*"

"Yes, yes, it is a *dhun.* Well, the chant is the *dhun.*"

Brahmchārī Karma of the Divine Life Society also liked the songs. One morning, we were discussing the change in repertory of the Unit 1 Temple since 1974.

"What is the difference between the Sai Baba songs and the other *bhajan?*" I asked.

"Well," he replied, "the Sai Baba songs, they are very short chants. They calling the name of God in different ways. Very short, so that someone could grasp it very quickly whether they do not know the song, they can grasp the words very quickly. Just two lines or three lines, very easy. And they feel different. Slow beginning, slow start, then goes faster."

"And I noticed they had clapping."

"Clapping, yes. More to be happy. They say that when you sing and you clap you destroy all the past karmas. You beat them off."

"What happens to the devotee when he's singing these songs?" I asked.

"Well, you see, now he is so inspired that he gets in a mood. He becomes emotional."

"What sort of feelings would he have after a long session of these songs?"

"Well, he would have a divine or serene."

"If they start slow and go fast, why wouldn't he become very excited. Why would he become serene?"

"Well," he said, "this is more emotional. You know, *feeling.* You know, this amount of joy, it begins to expand. From small it begins to expand."

"Do the Sai Baba songs make people feel in a different way than the other *bhajan,* the ones that are in the yellow book?"

"Well, this is more so with the individual. The individual can sing other songs. He will get the same amount of inspiration, whether it is a Sai Baba or a *bhajan,* the same amount of inspiration, or even more. That is dependent on the individual."

"Do you prefer songs to be sung fast or slow?" I asked.

"Now some have to be sung faster, some have to be slower," he said.

"What about 'Jai Jagadisha Hare'?" I asked, picking a well-known *bhajan.*

"Yes, well, that is done in a medium beat."

I began to sing "Jai Jagadisha Hare" in what seemed to me to be a medium beat.

"Is that too fast or too slow?" I asked.

"Well, this is dependent on the individual taste. So some singers prefer it slow, some little faster, some fast."

"Is one way better than the other?" I asked.

"Ah, no," he said. "I didn't say one way is better."

Was it just a question of taste? Chandra, Channu, Suruj, Kedar, and Karma, all were saying that there were two styles of singing in Felicity. Chandra had summed it up when she said, "Well, different groups sing it different way. I think it's too fast. We learn it as slow and easy way. We don't go rushing down." Channu had explained it in a similar way. "You see, they use a lot of clapping and meditating and more tempo, like. They put more action. They take on more speed. But if we have to sing, we will sing slowly and soft, in a smoothing kind of way." Some villagers preferred the one style, the "rushing," the "action," and some the other, the "slow," the "smoothing." But why did the Sai Baba movement and the Sai Baba songs catch on in the Divine Life Society and not in the Shrī Shankar Mandir and the Trinidad Sevashram Sangha? Perhaps it was indeed a question of taste. Mesho and the other musicians at the Divine Life Society were bold, and liked to experiment with different styles including the Sai Baba songs. But Mesho also appreciated many features of Sai Baba's teachings, especially the antibrahmanical ideals. Whether he and the others were more influenced by musical style, by theology, or by local political currents that affected the three temples, I cannot say.

It is easier to explain why the Sai Baba songs caught on in the Divine Life Society than why they didn't in the other two temples. Their musical style is well suited to group worship. Short and simple, their tunes are easily learned. The repeated verses in leader–chorus style are ideal for singing at large gatherings, and a villager could easily learn four or five new songs during one evening *satsangh.*

Do villagers feel they are better able to assert their Asian ethnicity with the loud and fast Sai style than with older soothing styles? Do they feel that Sai songs, with their drones and unusual modalities, are an "acceptable speciality," "alternative," "distinctive cultural equipment . . . to serve as a rallying point for sentiments of group solidarity?" (Wagley, *Minorities,* 287).

Is the Sai style a more effective enculturative medium than older *bhajan* and traditional folk songs? Felicity children don't sing wedding songs, *sohar,* or *chautāl,* but they love the Sai songs. Village children of the 1990s cannot speak or sing in Bhojpurī, and even the much-loved *bhajan* (from *Divine Life Bhajans*) have challenging Hindi texts.

Contrary to Merriam's theory of 1964 that "less change can be expected in religious than in social or recreational music" (*Anthropology,* 307–8), in Felicity, religion and religious music have been flexible cultural forms. The experimentation in religious life and fluctuation of issues Morton Klass observed in the 1950s are still important in Felicity today: defiance against the power of brahmans, weekly congregational prayers, and even an every-man-as-his-own-priest rebellion against the monopoly of the brahman pandits (*East Indians,* 237).

The Westernization, congregationalism, and antibrahmanism that Klass noted in the 1950s typify the Baba movement of the 1970s and '80s. That Baba's teachings suited theological requirements of some villagers surely contributed to the sudden popularity of the movement and its songs.

In the mid-1980s fifteen Sai Centers flourished with an estimated six to eight thousand devotees, mostly Trinidadians of Indian descent. Returning in 1985, Klass found:

> On the one hand, the movement provides a way in which devotees can evade the control of the Indian community by the village pandits and the Sanatan Dharma Maha Sabha—without themselves leaving Hinduism and the Indian community. Potentially, it is an avenue through which they may achieve the leadership of that community, and perhaps even of the Sanatan Dharma Maha Sabha. And, on the other hand, it provides the devotees with what they perceive as an intellectually valid and respectable basis for maintaining Indian culture and ethnic separation. Even further, it has the potential to provide a source of political strength and even ideological strength, when viewed as a Hindu alternative to Western-derived philosophy and religion. (*Singing with Sai Baba,* 170–71)

❦

The Baba movement in Felicity exemplifies many features of revitalization, as in the messianic message (Sai Baba as divine avatar) and in the nativistic and revivalistic thrust (Felicity Hindus wishing to alter their culture to correspond more nearly to the culture of India).

From 1974 to 1977, the first three years of the Sai Baba movement in Felicity, I witnessed the dynamic nature of village religious life and documented the rapidly changing musical repertory of the temples. But the Baba movement is not a unique example of sudden musical change. Morton Klass witnessed a similar transformation following Swami Purnananda's stay in Felicity in the 1950s.

Certainly there have been other such periods of cultural flux, some unrecorded by outsiders: during the indenture years when shiploads of new immigrants were brought to work on Felicité Estate (including perhaps a few skilled singers and instrumentalists); when the Arya Samaj missionaries came to Chaguanas in the 1920s; when films from India were imported in the 1930s; when recordings from India became available later in the 1930s; and in the 1990s when records made by Trinidadians gave a special West Indian color to music with an East Indian tinge.

I believe that future generations will be equally concerned with change. If the patterns of the past can help us predict the future, it seems likely that the villagers of Felicity will continue to look for inspiration to their mother India, revitalization; but it seems inevitable too that the generations born in Trinidad since Independence will also look about them for insights, back to the local home-made music of the old Trinidadian songsters, revival. Then, to make an even more exciting prediction, we can look to the new cultural influences of the island that surrounds them, and to the world, modernization.

ꕤ Chapter Sixteen ꕤ
The Death of Rani

> Let all my songs gather together their diverse strains into a single current and flow to a sea of silence in one salutation to thee.
>
> Rabindranath Tagore, *Gītāñjalī,* 103

"You see," Moon had been explaining, "from Sunday we calling people to sing here."

"For the wedding?" I asked.

"For the wedding. Yes. So you could come Sunday or Monday?"

"You will be singing?"

"At night," she said, "with drum and thing."

"Yes," I said. "I'll come."

Moon lived two miles away in Charlieville, Felicity's nearest neighbor to the east. On Monday night, Matti didn't want me to walk over in the dark. Mesho packed my gear into the car, and their son Choko decided to come along for the ride. Matti opened the gate and held the dogs while Mesho reversed out of the yard onto Cacandee Road. Dabin swung on the gate till it closed and then climbed up two rungs of the railing to fasten the latch at the top. We drove past the Chinese shop on the corner and turned onto Pierre Road, past Popo's house, past Mona's house, past the Dhun's, then a marshy stretch with rice fields, over the culvert, the official post office boundary between Felicity and Charlieville, and then right again at the filling station onto Caroni Savannah Road. Moon's house was on the left, and we began to hunt for hers among the row of upstairs houses, all looking alike, silhouetted against the night sky.

As always, the car windows were wound down and we listened for the singing and the sound of the drum.

"I think that's it," I said.

"House is dark," Mesho said, "and neighbor's house is dark." And there was silence. He pulled over to the side of the road.

"You wait in the car," he said. "I'll go."

I saw Moon and another person coming down the outside steps of the neighbor's house. Mesho went up to them and they spoke quietly.

Mesho came back to the car and got in.

"There is a dead there," he said. And we drove away.

Tomorrow, I thought, the "mike" truck will drive slowly by our house, blaring out the details from the big horn speaker mounted on its roof:

"Beloved so and so, cherished mother (or father) of him and her, bereaved by family and friends, died at thus and so time, on this or that day, the service on Wednesday, No. 3 Caroni Savannah Road, at thus and so time, then burial (or cremation) at the cemetery (or by the river); beloved so and so, cherished mother of him and her, bereaved by family and friends, died. . . ." Just as they did for Rani, I remembered.

Ritual at Home

A young beautiful woman, only 24 years old, Rani had succumbed to fever, leaving two small children. Matti and Mesho went over to the family's home with Matti's brother to attend the wake, which lasted for three nights, as they waited for Patsy, Rani's sister, to arrive from Canada for the cremation.

Mesho explained: "In Trinidad, when someone dies, not just the immediate family, the whole village is involved, and goes to the home of the grieving family."

On the day of the cremation, the ceremony began at one o'clock in the afternoon at the home of Rani's mother, on Cacandee Road. As we entered, men were starting to gather outside the house under the "tent" of bamboo and galvanized tin that had been erected the day before for the funeral. Card games were starting.

Rani's mother was seated inside the house. She spoke occasionally, especially to close relatives, but did not go into the next room, where groups of women were chatting in hushed tones. Patsy had arrived from Canada, and was surrounded by friends, young and old, who were relieved she had made it back to Felicity: now the cremation could go ahead.

People kept drifting in, the men outside in front, playing cards, the ladies chatting in the rear room. In the center room, a group of men and women had assembled, and Solomon, with the Brahmchārī, chanted Hindi verses from the Tulsī Dās *Rāmāyaṇ.* After the reading, Siewrajiah, his mother, sang a *bhajan,* but no one joined in.

Matti said: "If you would like to go to the funeral, your white dress would be good" (I was wearing a yellow dress just then). "No colors are permitted; black is okay and also mauve. You will need a black *oḍhanī.*" She lent me one.

"Sugar and ghee." There was a great deal of discussion about "good" burning. (A fantastic story was told by one of the older ladies about a cremation in which the body burned to ashes in the perfect shape of the body—"you could see the nose, the limbs, all in ash.") After the burning, the ashes are spread on the river. The greatest worry is that a body may might not burn completely. So sugar is put under and over the body, and ghee as well, to assure that it will burn. A great deal of advice was offered about just how this was to be done.

As the evening wore on, the mother, sweating, looked faint, but never moved from her armchair. Finally she called her son, Vishram, to put Limacol astringent over her hair and have a cloth bound tight around her forehead, turban-like.

The chanting of the *Rāmāyaṇ* lasted an hour and a half until Solomon grew tired and hoarse. The card games outside were boisterous, and rum was flowing. The women complained mildly, but in truth they wanted the men to make noise and "wake."

By dawn, more than a hundred people had crowded into the house; chairs had been rented, and benches brought from the temple.

I was told that at the cremation, there would be no food—so unusual for any Indian gathering—but that ten days after the cremation, the group would reassemble for the shaving ceremony and have a meal at the mother's home. Thirteen days after the cremation, the *bhandara* feast would be held and again at the first anniversary the final *bhandara* feast. For the first thirteen days after the cremation, people attend night waking, but conversation is sparse and many sit for hours saying nothing.

Mesho explained: "At the shaving ceremony after ten days, a close male relative must be shaved by the river—all facial hair including his head. On this day we pray that even if the physical body was bad, that it returns to earth in a form that has the five senses—sight, taste, hearing, touch, smell—and also that the new being that returns can perceive and act according to these five senses. This we call the *das indriya,* the ten sensations.

"Thirteen days after the cremation marks an important moment for us. This period has the same symbolism, the same meaning as the forty days of waiting in Christianity. We are taught that the physical body is controlled by three *gunas,* three qualities that form our nature and control our actions. The first is the *satu gun,* equipoise, what causes us not to take sides. The second is the *tamo gun,* our lazy qualities. And third is the *rāju gun,* our aggressive qualities. All human actions are based on these three, and we act on them. The *bhandara* ceremony pacifies these qualities that were in the physical body of the deceased. Until these qualities are pacified, we believe they linger on earth. A proper *bhandara* ceremony should be performed by the river, but people find it inconvenient to cook there, so normally in Felicity they are performed in the home. In the ceremony we ask Mother Ganga to take the soul. We pray to Lord Krishna through the medium of Pitri Devas. The Lord should be pacified. After one year we hold the final *bhandara* feast because we believe that it takes the soul one year to reach its final destination."

The cremation ceremony had started at the home of Rani's mother, and it ended at the Cunupia River. At first not many people were at the house, except the mother, still with her headband on, in an old blue dress with some of the buttons broken, and the grandmother, in a cotton blouse and skirt pinned on. Other guests arrived, many in blue and mauve, some in white, and a few in black. Most of the men wore the white, Spanish-style shirts, loose-fitting, and dark trousers. Each woman carried her *oḍhanī* and covered her head upon arriving, and at all important moments of the ceremony.

Sighs and gasps erupted as the black hearse drew up to the house. Rani's mother began to wail.

"Let her cry!"

"Make her stop."

"No! leave her, she needs to cry."

"Make her stop!"

Matti took the bottle of Limacol and poured some on the ground before the hearse. Then she poured some on the head of Rani's mother. The funeral director hauled out a metal stand for the coffin and asked in a matter-of-fact way where it should it be placed. Rani was shrouded in a pink sari, on her hands lace gloves, and she lightly held a white handkerchief. The *ānchal* of her sari was drawn up around the back of her head, framing her face as was proper for a bride. Only a glimpse of the part in her hair showed, her eyes closed, her lips colored slightly red. Heavy, inexpensive perfume masked the chemical odor of the embalming fluids.

The grandmother, poised, hair streaming to both sides, calmed the mother and brought her to the head of the white coffin. The grandmother began her soliloquy:

"Rani, hear me. Rani, be good. Rani, hear me. Rani, hear me." Talking softly and assuredly, she soothed the gathering.

Chairs were brought up for the mother and grandmother. Matti sat at the foot of the coffin; but Rani's sisters and brothers held back, still preparing the house, turning images, framed pictures, and the TV to the wall, and covering the radio. No cooking, no fire, no cleaning, no sweeping had been done since the hour of Rani's death.

"Rani, hear me. Rani be good."

The family sat, the friends, neighbors sat in silence.

Guests continued to arrive, approach the body, stop for a long look, then move to their seats. The father's sister approached the coffin, shouting "Rani! Rani!" Although the litany of consolation was repeated again and again, how could these family women be consoled? "But, she had two young children," the women cried. "They will never know their mother." Rani's husband could be seen, waiting inside.

Rani's children were brought in, sleeping in the arms of relatives. They were carried to the front, and as they awoke, they did not recognize their mother; the small boy gazed long at the body lying so still.

"Rani, hear me. Rani be good."

At one o'clock, "Cookie" Pandit, dressed in white, began the ceremony with prayers and oblations, dipping with *tulsī* leaves into the *lotā.* The eldest brother, Vishram, made a *tīkā* (mark) on Rani's forehead, and the brothers and sisters performed *ārtī* describing a circle around Rani's body with the lit *diyā.* The mother and father did not take part in the ceremony, for it is believed that "the parent who burns one child must burn all." They did not go down to the river, staying behind while family women swept and mopped. After *ārtī,* performed in silence, the Pandit said a few words about death, which comes to all. Two *bhajan* from the *Divine Life Bhajans, Book 1* concluded the ceremony.

138 ❧
One day this world will be left behind.
Even those who have lit thousands of devotional lights,
Even those who are rich, they go with empty hands.
Rich or poor, nobody is left,
Everyone is taken [lit. "eaten"].
Nobody knows everything about it [lit. even in the *Vedas, Purāṇas*].
The boat of life is shaking in the ocean of trouble;
Oh, Lord Rām will carry me.

139 ❧
[*Refrain*]
Oh, my Lord, do this for me.
When the soul is about to leave the body,
Govinda's [Krishna's] name should be on my lips.

[*Verses*]
1 At the bank of the Holy River Ganges.
At the bank of the Holy River Jamuna.
My Lord Shāmla [the blue Krishna] beside me.

2 The great earth of Brindābana [forest of *tulsī* plants, where Krishna played],
Tulsī leaf in my mouth,
Holy water of Lord Vishnu's feet [the Ganges came out of the toe of Vishnu].

3 My Shāmala [Krishna] stood [in front of me],
Full of music of flute.
His dancing feet on the ground intertwined.

4 Crown beautifying head,
Black dot [*tīkā*] on forehead,
Only meditation in my heart.

5 Make haste to come the moment,
Do not forget me.
Let me listen to the jingling of the anklet bell [of Krishna as child].

6 When life comes to the throat,
No illness will trouble me.
I will not see Yama [messenger of the god of death].

The singing was unaccompanied, subdued, quiet. This solemn ceremony, with singing, prayers, and oblations lasted about 45 minutes, after which people began to walk to the river.

I did not witness the last goodbye of the parents. Just before I left for the river, the husband came forward, bent down to his wife's face, as women covered him and the coffin entirely with a bedsheet. Under this shroud, he traced the *sindūr* in the part of Rani's hair, as is done during the Hindu wedding rite.

"Did Rani have a large wedding?" I asked Matti.

"No," she said. "They only went and registered their marriage. But today was Rani's wedding. There at the home, dressed in a wedding sari, pink and flowered, looking so nice, with all the flowers, the family, the friends, the whole village. Today was Rani's wedding."

"In India, we say this is the last *bārāt,* the last procession of the groomsmen," Umesh later commented. "And if a village wife dreams she is wearing pink or red, it means the death for that lady is very near."

The Cremation at the River

Crowds gathered on both banks of the Cunupia River. The hearse backed up to the footbridge, and six men carried the white box across to the funeral pyre *(chitā)*—boards stacked according to antique design with a space in the center for the coffin. As the body passed, I saw her young face, the *tulsī* leaves placed between her lips, the *tīkā* on her forehead, the red *sindūr* from her husband.

Prayers were said as Vishram circled the pyre. The fire was lit, and the crowd stood back as flames leapt out from the ghee and the sugar.

Afterward

At the mother's house, the floors had been mopped and the rented chairs stacked ready to return. Rani's mother had changed her dress and looked fresh. The women chatted and Siewrajiah announced a death song and sang it.

After a few days, I asked Siewrajiah if she would sing the death song again, and she said "there is no song for death. I can't remember what I sang the day of Rani's funeral."

Later I spoke with Rani's mother, Kowsil.

"What about the sari?" I asked. "Matti said Rani dreamt about a pink sari."

"That was when she got sick, when she died. She had this brain 'sephalitis and she was getting attack of it. So she started to talk. I don't know is Sai Baba power or whose power or what. When we bring her out in the hall to sit down she say, 'No, I'm not going to change my clothes. Baba will bring a pink sari for me, and he will change it for himself. You won't have to change my clothes.' And she say 'he will come twelve o'clock,' and it will have three of them in the car, and they will come and stop just in front my door."

"And what happened?"

"She happens to die. Maybe Baba came and she have to go.

"But she saw Baba?"

"Baba, yes, protecting her. And, you know, all really come to pass. And when she died, I really buy the pink sari for her. I say, well she tell me Baba was going to put on that for her. And I buy the pink sari. Two days after, two or three days, my Vishram dream that he see Baba and Jesus Christ taking Rani up to heaven. That Jesus Christ on one side and Baba on the next side, and have her in the middle and they going up."

"After?"

"Three days."

Rani's story, vital ethnographic data, does not touch upon music. Yet this account of tragic death, of waiting and wailing, of ritual and fire tells us much. There was no music.

ꕤ

ek din ure tāl ke hansā
pheri nahi āvenge
mātī mātī me mili jābe
ūpar harī ghās jami ābe
āi nagar ke pasū bāhi chari jābenge.

"One day the swan will fly off the pond and will not come back again. The soul will go in the soil and green grass will grow on it and the cattle of the village will come and graze on it."

Chapter Seventeen
Chutney

> Give me *paisā!* Give me money!
> Give me give me *paisā!*
> Give me give me dollar!
> Money! Money! Money!
> *Paisā! Paisā! Paisā!*
>
> Kanchan, "Give Me *Paisā!*"

"It's not a form to be proud of," Amar explained as we exchanged greetings on New Year's Day, 1995. "But it is sweeping across Trinidad these days. I would hate to see a book written about this topic alone. What would people think of us—our heritage, our religious beliefs, and our ancient culture? Listen to this! Pure English."

140
[*Refrain*]
I drinking to die, so I drinking to die,
And I drinking to die.
I know nobody loves me, so that's the reason why.
Drinking to die, so I drinking to die,
And I drinking to die.
I know nobody loves me, so that's the reason why.
[*Verse 1*]
You must not clear the table, I'm singing this song.
There was tears in his eyes, and a bottle of rum.
You must not clear the table, I'm singing this song.
There was tears in his eyes, and a bottle of rum.
I went to his table, to ask him his name,
And this is what he told me, he feeling so.
[*Refrain*]
I drinking to die, so I drinking to die,
And I drinking to die.
I know nobody loves me, so that's the reason why.
[*Verse 2*]
He said he was my friend boy, a friend he will be,
So I took him home with me to meet my family.
He said he was my friend boy, a friend he will be,
So I took him home with me to meet my family.
I made a mistake and now I must pay,
So that is why I'm drinking to kill myself today.

[*Refrain*]
I drinking to die, so I drinking to die,
And I drinking to die.
I know nobody loves me, so that's the reason why.
[*Instrumental interlude*]
[*Verse 3*]
I tried to be honest, I tried to be true.
I love her so much that I don't know what to do.
I tried to be honest, I tried to be true.
Love her so much that I don't know what to do.
[*Verse 4*]
She leave me and come to have someone else,
So that is why I'm drinking, to kill myself.
[*Refrain*]
I drinking to die, so I drinking to die,
And I drinking to die.
I know nobody loves me, so that's the reason why.
I drinking to die, so I drinking to die,
And I drinking to die.
I know nobody loves me, so that's the reason why.
[*Instrumental closing*]
(Transcribed from recording; original in English)

A New Commercial Form

"Sure is easy fieldwork," I said, laughing, "sitting in clubs, and five-star hotels, drinking beer and recording spicy songs!"

"No, I wouldn't be taking you there!" Amar said. "Better like you did—go to India and get the depth of our old songs. You know, there is a motivating force behind everything. And the motivation for *chutney* is money. You could hear that with the older Kanchan songs—remember the cassette you bought from the Chaguanas market in 1990? 'Give me Paisā!'"

141
Give Me Paisā!
Kanchan
[*Verse 1*]
You buy me the wedding ring, you buy me the wedding ring.
Jewelry and sari, necklace and thing, jewelry and sari, necklace and thing.
[*Refrain*]
Give me *paisā* ["money"]! And give me dollar!
Give me *paisā!* And give me dollar!
No matter what you do, I will marry you.
For my love is true, so I will marry you.
Give me *paisā!* Give me *kaparā* ["clothes"]!

Give me *makān* ["house"]! Give me *kangan* ["golden bangle"]!
Give me give me *paisā!* Hey, give me give me *paisā!*
Hey, give me give me *paisā!* Hey, give me give me *paisā!*
[*Instrumental interlude*]
[*Verse 2*]
See how *bhaiyā maī ginatī* ["my brother is counting"] cent. See how *bhaiyā maī ginatī* cent.
And Papa keep spending every cent. And Papa keep spending every cent.
And *bhaiyā* ["brother"] quarreling. And duty sharing.
And *bhaiyā* quarreling. And duty sharing.
[*Refrain*]
No matter what you do, I will marry you.
For my love is true, so I will marry you.
Give me *paisā!* Give me *kaparā!*
Give me *makān!* Give me *kangan!*
Give me give me *paisā!* Give me give me *paisā!*
Oh, give me give me *paisā!* Oh, give me give me *paisā!*
[*Percussion interlude; then chorus, double track*]
Hai! Hai! Hai! Hai!
[*Instrumental interlude*]
[*Verse 3*]
Comes with the father before twelve noon. Comes with the father before twelve noon.
Friendship and marry me, come for honeymoon.
Friendship and marry me, come for honeymoon!
Point to London! At the Hilton!
Point to Venice! And to Paris!
[*Refrain*]
No matter what you do, I will marry you.
For my love is true, so I will marry you.
Give me *paisā!*
Give me *kaparā!*
Give me *makān!*
Give me *kangan!*
[*Repetition with fragmentation*]
Give me give me *paisā!* Give me give me *makān!*
Give me give me *kangan!* Plenty plenty dollar!
Give me give me *paisā!* More more money!
Give me give me *paisā!* Give me give me dollar!
Give me give me! Hey, give me give me!
Eh, give me give me! Hey, give me give me!
[*Add reverb; shouted*]
PAISĀ! PAISĀ! PAISĀ!
Give me give me! Give me give me!
Give me give me *paisā!* Give me give me!
Paisā! Paisā! Give me give me!

[*Fade; shouted with reverb*]
Paisā! Paisā! Paisā!
[*Final fade*]
Give me give me money!

The studio mix renders the percussion and brass in "*Paisā*" very forward, and they tend to overwhelm the singer, who is set in a fairly natural acoustic. The brass section is somewhat more distant, but without reverb appropriate to this apparent distance.

"This is like 'Indian soca,'" Amar explained. "But *chutney*," Amar continued, "*chutney* in the '90s is different. It is for money, but it comes together with tourism, alcohol, and lewd dancing. Although it's a kind of Indian soca, the words, if you listen to the words of some of these newer *chutney*, you will like them. They are very old folk songs. Take this one for example, from around 1990. It comes in the form of a love song but nevertheless it is an old folk song, something like a *lachārī*" (English translation from Hindi original):

142 ♫
[*Refrain*]
My heart linked to you,
My heart linked to you.
Your unworthy lover, your unworthy lover,
My heart linked to you.
Your unworthy lover, your unworthy lover,
My heart linked to you.
[*Verse 1*]
Where is voice cuckoo cuckoo?
Where is voice cuckoo cuckoo?
Where voice peacock, where voice peacock?
[*Refrain*]
My heart linked to you.
Your unworthy lover, your unworthy lover,
My heart linked to you.
[*Verse 2*]
Where is voice sparrow hawk, where is voice sparrow hawk?
Where cuckoo, peacock? Where cuckoo, peacock?
[*Refrain*]
My heart linked to you.
Your unworthy lover, your unworthy lover,
My heart linked to you.
[*Verse 3*]
Mango of branch cuckoo sang.
Jungle in spoke peacock. Jungle in spoke peacock.

[*Refrain*]
My heart linked to you.
Your unworthy lover, your unworthy lover,
My heart linked to you.
[*Verse 4*]
River bank sparrow hawk, river bank sparrow hawk.
River bank sparrow hawk, river bank sparrow hawk.
Bed of love peacock, bed of love peacock.
[*Extended refrain*]
My heart linked to you.
Your unworthy lover, your unworthy lover,
My heart linked to you.
My heart linked to you.
Your unworthy lover, your unworthy lover,
My heart linked to you.
Your unworthy lover, your unworthy lover,
My heart linked to you.

"This song comes in the form of a *lachārī*," Umesh remarked, "these songs end by the bed and the conclusion is always end with love. In Uttar Pradesh, in our villages, cuckoo does not come often. We hear her when the green mango comes. Cuckoo loves mango. Sometimes green mango gets dark spot—we call *koiliyā*. These scarred mangoes do not grow all the way. They fall early. But when we eat, although it is green—sour—surprisingly is sweet inside. We believe cuckoo make these darker spots, like a dark scar, that cuckoo make it sweet. And we love cuckoo because her voice is very sweet. A village song of ours tells:

143
Kagā kau koo letu hai
Koyal kau doo dei
Mīṭhe bachan sunāi kẽ
Jag wash mẽ karilei

"This means, 'What does crow take from others? What does cuckoo give to others? To cause to hear sweet voice controls whole the world.'

"And in this Trinidad song, this *chutney*, these are beautiful and sweet birds. Cuckoo is a song bird. Sparrow hawk, *papīhā*, calls 'piyu piyu'—that means 'love, love.' Peacock is beautiful bird, a male bird. In this song the line 'peacock by my bed,' it means lover is by my bed. The voice of the peacock is the man's voice. He pleases on the bed and in the jungle both. It shows that man is wild. But I never heard this song in India. We usually feel bird has one place, either on the bed or in the jungle. For us, main thing, peacock wants to find a separate place to dance. The peacock dances to call peahens and wherever he dances one or two peahens are around him."

William Archer collected a wedding song in the mid-1930s that combines imagery of the cuckoo with the dance of the peacock and the jungle:

144 ꕤ
O Cuckoo, where is the jungle
Where you lived?
And where is the jungle
Where you've gone?
Where is the door
Where you dance with joy?
(*Songs for the Bride,* 23)

ꕤ Indo-Afro Relations in Song: Pre-Independence

"Actually nothing is really new here," Amar explained. "Afros and Indians have been mixing their songs—words and melodies—long before I was born!"

Gordon Rohlehr (1990), dates a calypso recounting an interracial affair back to 1930, when the famous Afro singer, Duke of Normandy, sang: "After she give me parata ['fried bread'], She had me cooraja" about an Indian woman. In 1939, the great calypsonian Attila the Hun describes an Indian woman in "Dookanii" (English original):

145 ꕤ
She was the prettiest thing I'd ever met
Her resplendent beauty I can't forget
With her wonderful, dark bewitching eyes
I used to gaze in them hypnotized
Then she had the kind of personality
That tempted one to behave ungentlemanly.

She was exotic, kind and loving too
All her charms I could never describe to you
When she smiled her face lit up rapturously
Radiating joy, life and vitality
The most reserved was bound to feel
The power and force of her sex appeal.
[*English original*]
(Rohlehr, *Calypso and Society,* 251)

Also in 1939, the calypsonian Lord Executor described a "gala Indian fête" where:

146 ꕤ
An Indian man was holding a piece of wire
One passing right through the fire
One had a ram goat he was killing
With rum their bodies they filling.
[*English original*]

And he parodied Hindi words in a joking fashion:

Mahabir, mahhaba, puja koray . . .
Cobanay talkarie
(252, 256)

This kind of ridicule, with a mixture of Hindi and English, is in Tiger's "Gi Sita Ram Gi" (1939):

147 ♫
Me work for me money, me go back to me country
Gi Sita Ram Gi
Cook am choti [small] bigan [eggplant] talcarry [casserole]
Gi Sita Ram Gi
Me tell you me go me going home tomorrow
Gi Sita Ram Gi
Me have the privilege to live Rambat village
Gi Sita Ram Gi.
[*English/Hindi original*]
(256)

This type of song characterized much calypso of the late 1930s and prefigured the later Indian soca of the popular East Indian singer Sundar Popo.

Rohlehr also cites interracial calypso back to Executor's "Tobago Scandal" of 1938, and to 1945, when The Mighty Killer, who was said to know Bhojpurī, was singing about Indo-Trinidadians. In 1947, Killer in "Grinin' Massala" gives his news of a Hindu wedding:

148 ♫
[*Verse 1*]
This is really true
Ah decide this year to marry a Hindu . . .
So is hundreds of Indians gather
Yes . . . up in Marabella
Man, Pooran get crazy
When they start with this sweet melody
[*Refrain*]
Singing: Shago shago shilom, shago shago shilom
Updika dingaka dangika dangika dum
[*Verse 2*]
Things now getting sweet
They bring a set of dhal bhaat for me to eat
Lahd! Is pepper like fire
Ah cyan stan de bunnin I bawling fuh waataa
So big belly Ramlal
Come wid a coolie drum an' a dhantal

[*Refrain*]
Singing: Every time ah passin gal yuh grinin' massala
Every time ah passin gal yuh grinin' massala
Grinin' massala, grinin' massala
An every time ah passin well she grinin' massala.
[*English original*]
(493)

This reference to Indian food, which the singer always finds strange and unpleasant, is one example of many such denigrations. During the 1950s, "race" calypsos included The Mighty Terror's "Civilised Indians" (1950); Killer's "Indians Adopting Creole Names" (1950–51; "Long ago was Sumintra, Ramnalawia . . . / But now is Emily, Jean and Dinah"); Mighty Dictator's "Mooniyah" (1955; "Moon," common Hindu name in Trinidad; "Bap [father] na likeam kilwalni [Creole man], Mooniya / Ow mi gyal! . . . / So you likeam dat nigger breed"); Cobra's "The Changes of the Indians" (1954); Lord Eisenhower's "Creolised Indians" (1955; "It's no more pumpkin talkarie . . . / They now eating stew beef, pork and salad"); King Fighter's "Indian Wedding" and "Dhalpourie" (1957) and "Indian Party" (1958; "They examine the hair on top me head / Saying 'Aray ada we goh killam dead!' "); Lord Melody's "Apan Jhaat" (1958; "And who isn't entitled to the vote / But in the end the Indian cut dey throat . . . / Apan Jhaat! Chutna Kilwili ['Our own race! Fuck the Creoles!']"); and The Mighty Striker's the "The United Indian" (1959; "Every election / Negro can't get a vote from Indian") (498–508).

Post-Independence Indian Calypsos

In 1972, the famous Afro-calypsonian, Lord Shorty, scandalized Trinidad Indians by wearing on stage an Indian woman's garment, the *oḍhanī,* which has special significance as a protector of female privacy—a gambit that could hardly help to achieve rapprochement between the races.

In 1982, '83, and '84, Mighty Sparrow produced a trilogy "Marajhin," "Marajhin Sister," and "Marajhin Cousin," with vocabulary that Keith Warner characterizes as "the now classic references to Indian foods and their preparation, to the supposed strictness of the Indian parents, to Indians' purported penchant for violence, to their clothing, and even to their supposed inability to keep the same time as 'real' Trinidadians ('And jump out of time to sweet pan for carnival')" (1993, 287). Sarcastically, Sparrow claimed in these love songs between a Hindu woman and an African man, that he even would 'Gladly trade my toilet paper for some water [in a *lotā*].' "

149 ☙
Om Shanti ("Om Peace")
Shorty (1979)
This song you hear
Is an Indian prayer
From ancient times
Created to soothe your mind
In danger, in anger, remember
Sing this mantra
This golden mantra from the master
This song is to enable people
To struggle against the devil
In this human jungle
Is plenty people, yes plenty people.
[*English original*]
(Warner, 287)

But despite the calypsos showing differences between the races, in 1989 Drupatee, an East Indian singer, came up with "Indian Soca," which stressed Afro-Indian ethnicity:

150 ☙
Indian Soca
Drupatee
They give me blows
Last year for doing soca
But it shows
How much they know 'bout culture
For the music of the steeldrums from Laventille
Cannot help but mix with rhythm from Caroni
For it's a symbol of how much we've come of age
Is a brand new stage
[*Chorus*]
Indian soca, sounding sweeter
Hotter than a chula [oven]
Rhythm from Africa and India
Blend together is a perfect mixture
All we do is add new flavour
Leh we get down to Indian soca.
[*English original*]
(Warner, 287–88)

☙ CHUTNEY

The new Indian music in Trinidad of the 1980s and '90s is *chutney.* The older hot songs had come into their own, now used to mix music of the different races of Trinidad in every imaginable way. I had wondered how the

Felicity villagers would solve their predicament—the development of new Indian music despite the demise of spoken Bhojpurī. I had not been able to imagine how they could create a non-Bhojpurī, but Indian, repertory. By the mid-1980s, the answers to this question were arising from the popular repertory of the village and by the mid-1990s the villagers had produced a bouquet of acculturated, syncretized forms. I had not understood that reinventing their culture had always been their problem and likewise never their problem. New music—hot and spicy, sober and devotional—had been composed year to year since the indentureship period.

"Kanchan, Sundar Popo, well you could say this was the beginning of modern *chutney,*" Amar explained. "But it really grew out of the 'tent singing,' recordings from Windsor Records in the late '70s, for example the record series *Tent Singing—Tent Singing by Abdool "Kush" Razack, Tent Singing by Yusuf Khan, Tent Singing by Sharm Yankarran, Tent Singing by Sookdeo Sookhraj.* Later they became like a kind of Indian soca. If you listen to the words of the *chutney,* Helen, you will like them. They are old folk songs. But they have added rhythm, spice it up, pepped it up, given it fast speed. Also you will not hear electronic instruments and synthesizers from the Indian orchestras. Naya Zamana [New Era], our first Indian orchestra, is still going strong. But they do not perform *chutney.*"

"Where do you hear *chutney?*" I asked.

"Mostly paid programs. On the radio, 103 FM plays only Indian music, and on Friday and Saturday nights they have *chutney* programs. You can hear them on TV. And they have paid *chutney* programs in clubs like the Himalaya Club in San Juan, The Triangle in Aranguez, The Highway Inn, one down south at the complex in Penal, one club in Gulf City—all around here are clubs everywhere.

"Both men and women go to the clubs, mainly on weekends. There is a show on the stage featuring four or five local artists. Each one sings three or four songs. For accompaniment they only use the old instruments—*ḍholak, ḍhantāl,* and harmonium. This *chutney,* Indian soca they call it, comes in these clubs with drinking and lewd dancing. Tickets cost between TT 5 dollars and TT 10 dollars. The motivation for *chutney* is money. But the words, the instruments, they are very old. Even at weddings, time to time you might hear one *chutney.*"

"Is *chutney* bringing the Indian community together," I asked?

"Well not really. I say it is dividing East Indians into those who like it and those who don't. We have new artists on the scene, Boodram Holas from Cedras, Anand Yankarran, brother of Sharm, and the lady Ramrajie. And the songs are local composed. There is even one Guyana ke Baba! For *chutney,* they took something sober, and for the sake of rhythm, drink, and lewd dancing—it is not something to be proud of."

ঌ Indian, East Indian, and West Indian Music: Sundar Popo and Kanchan

Beginning in 1969, 1974, continuing to 1984 and 1985, and up until 1994, the popular Indian vocalist Kanchan and her husband, Bombay arranger Babla, made concert tours of Trinidad. Kanchan's first hit was "Kayse Banie," a *chutney* composed by Sundar Popo, a popular local Indian singer from Monkey Town in southern Trinidad near Débé.

Sundar tells: "My father was Popo Bahora and my mother Etawaria Popo. I happened to be born in Lengua, in my mother's father's village, but they brought me home quick. From my early life my parents encouraged me in music. They never wanted to leave me home alone, so they took me to *chatī* and *barahī* and cooking night at the weddings, and by age eight or nine I had learned the hot songs. My first album was in 1969—*Nani Nana.* And it went from there. I met Kanchan and Babla in 1969 when they came to perform at Presentation College in San Fernando. They heard me sing 'Nani Nana' on the same program. When they returned in 1974, they rereleased their own version of my songs. They appreciate the world-wide scope of Trinidad music. I've made sixty or seventy albums. But so much depends on the promoters. Of my four children, my third son, Hemant Sundar, can sing. He may carry it on."

Sundar's "hot and spicy" songs had been popular in Felicity for some years, and he had made several best-selling LP records. And Kanchan's rerelease of "Kayse Banie" was a breakthrough. Without changing a word of the Hindi text, she altered the style of the song, adding the typically Indian filmī sound with the characteristic style of attack and light, little-girlish vocal quality. The song was transformed, and every villager knew it. Sundar's "local composed" took on a fresh sound and found a new validity, since Kanchan was herself authentic, that is India-born, "from away." For the Felicity villagers, she made the song truly Indian.

Sundar Popo's hit, "Chaadar Beechawo Baalma" appeared shortly thereafter on his new album of "sure shot chartbusters." The liner notes by Moean Mohammed, of the prominent Muslim family and the leading music producer in Trinidad, tell us about the recording:

> From the Desk of: The Producer
> Dedicated to: Music lovers the world over
>
> It is my sincerest wish that all who listen to the selections on this album will appreciate each one for what it is.

Presented here is a style, and type of music and song which is fast becoming extinct in our fast moving world and which our forefathers brought with them almost 135 years ago. These selections are as old (in style) and precious as our cultural heritage and day to day living.

Here, I attempt to rejuvenate and present to our up and coming generation the music and songs that is traditionally ours, with an artiste who needs no introduction. Sundar Popo is certainly one of the finest in our talented land, and he is accompanied, musically, on this album by India's famous Anup Jalota and his group. It is the first major attempt to blend the talent of India (the East) and Trinidad and Tobago (the West).

May each and every one of you find complete enjoyment in these renditions.

151 ☙
Chaadar Beechawo Baalma
Sundar Popo
[*Slow ālāp-like introduction; original in Hindi*]
Oh sweetheart, oh sweetheart, oh sweetheart, oh sweetheart.
Oh sweetheart, kill not with loving look, oh sweetheart, heart begins to pump hard.
Oh sweetheart, kill not with loving look, oh sweetheart, heart begins to pump hard.
Heart begins to pump hard, heart begins to pump hard.
Sweetheart, kill not by loving look, oh heart begins to pump hard.
Sweetheart, kill not by loving look, oh heart begins to pump hard.
[*Original in English; Spoken in the form of an announcement with reverb*]
My dear brothers and sisters. This is Anup Jalota of India, presenting you very popular singer of Trinidad, West Indies: [*add extreme ping-pong bounce*] SUNDAR POPO!
[*Original in Hindi; Refrain*]
Sheet spread sweetheart, little sheet spread sweetheart.
Sleep feel comfortable, sleep remain.
Sleep feel comfortable, sleep remain.
Sheet spread sweetheart, spread little sheet sweetheart.
Sleep feel comfortable, sleep remain.
Sleep feel comfortable, sleep remain.
[*Verse 1*]
My father-in-law has two two palaces.
My father-in-law has two two palaces.
The most beautiful our palace.
[*Refrain*]
Little sheet spread sweetheart.
Sleep feel comfortable, sleep remain.
Sleep feel comfortable, sleep remain.
[*Verse 2*]
My father-in-law has two two beds.
My father-in-law has two two beds.
The most beautiful our bed.

[*Refrain*]
Little sheet spread sweetheart.
Sleep feel comfortable, sleep remain.
Sleep feel comfortable, sleep remain.
[*Verse 3*]
My father-in-law has two two sons.
My father-in-law has two two sons.
The most handsome my husband.
[*Refrain*]
Little sheet spread sweetheart.
Sleep feel comfortable, sleep remain.
Sleep feel comfortable, sleep remain.
[*Verse 4*]
My father-in-law has two two daughters-in-law.
My father-in-law has two two daughters-in-law.
The most beautiful my body [soul].
[*Extended refrain with fade to silence*]
Little sheet spread sweetheart.
Sleep feel comfortable, sleep remain.
Sleep feel comfortable, sleep remain.
Sleep feel comfortable, sleep remain.
Sleep feel comfortable, sleep remain.
Sleep feel comfortable, sleep remain.
Sleep feel comfortable, sleep remain.

"These songs are like *khicharī*—rice and *dāl* mixed together," Umesh commented as he first heard Sundar Popo's recordings. "Little bit salt. Little bit hot. Indian and English mixed. According to my point of view this is a woman's song, a *lachārī* type, with gentle teasing and loving. Of course Anup Jalota is great great modern folksinger. He makes cassettes, he sings, he is invited to sing for money at functions. We have folksinging concerts all over India, and people pay them to arrange this concert, and people also make money out of that and pay him. Tickets are sold for such kind of shows. Every year we have such kind of programs at the exhibition in Mainpuri when some important star comes to participate these concerts. The tickets cost about 25, 50, 100 rupees [$1.00 to $4.00]—first-class ticket maybe 100 rupees. Tickets are advance sold. Anup Jalota came to Mainpuri once. He is most famous in Madhya Pradesh, but he sings in Hindi."

℘ SOCA

Calypso underwent changes in the mid-1970s under the influence of new disco dance rhythms and soul music as well as a new generation of sophisticated studio technology. Soca (soul plus calypso) became the music of the new party culture of Trinidad, spawned by the oil boom and prosperity in the mid-1970s. Increasingly, Trinidadian calypsonians recorded in the modern Brooklyn studios. Lord Shorty's (Garfield Blackman, later Ras Shorty I) hit, of the mid-1970s, "Soul Calypso," is generally held to be the song that gave name to a new genre. A style influenced by many artists, soca came to include stylistic features of funk, ska, salsa, meringue, as well as calypso—usually set to a disco beat, often incorporating syncopation. The topical lyrics of traditional calypso give way in soca to a new lively rhythmic accompaniment influenced by disco beat. Critics bemoaned how soca transformed the sharp social commentary of the classic calypsos to commercial party music, as in Arrow's party soca "Hot Hot Hot." In the 1990s important soca artists include the old-timers Mighty Sparrow (Francisco Slinger), Lord Kitchener (Aldwyn Roberts), Baron "Lovers' Soca" Arrow, Rasta calypsonian Black Stalin (Leroy Calliste), Super Blue, Crazy, and Tambu (Chris Herbert), who won the Carnival Road March in 1988 with the soca "This Party Is It" and in 1990, with "No, No We Eh Going Home." This repertory has rapidly circulated through the expatriate Trinidadian communities in London, Toronto, Miami, and Brooklyn.

On the 1985 tour, the Indian artist, Kanchan, sang arrangements of three prize-winning West Indian socas from the 1985 Carnival: "Tiny Winy," "Bust up Shot," and "Rock. .It." "Rock. .It" by Merchant (Denis Williams) appeared with "Pan in Danger," "Caribbean Connection," and "Be Careful" in 1985, recorded at KH Studios, Sea Lots, Port of Spain, Trinidad.

Its English text is pure soca:

152 ⯐

[*Chorus, Refrain*]
Would you like to rock it with me baby?
Would you like to jam it with me honey?
Would you like to rock it with me baby?
Would you like to jam it with me honey?
[*Solo, Verse 1*]
Music jamming hard in the party,
People socanizing their body.
And there she was standing in a corner,
Looking so sweet and without her partner.
So I went to her, I spoke to her,
She smiled, and I said to her,
[*Chorus, Refrain*]
Would you like to rock it with me baby?
Would you like to jam it with me honey?
[*Solo, Refrain*]
Sweet calypso, music jamming for soul.

Come and rock it with me baby.
Come and jam it with me honey.
Mumm mumm mumm mumm mumm mumm mumm . . .
[*Solo, Verse 2*]
She say I'm expecting somebody,
He say he be here seven-thirty.
I say well darling it's ten o'clock now,
And I have a feeling that somehow,
You shouldn't be alone this way,
If there's no objection, I say,
[*Chorus, Refrain*]
Come and rock it with me baby!
Come and jam it with me honey!
[*Solo, Refrain*]
Sweet calypso, music jamming for soul.
Come and rock it with me baby!
Come and jam it with me honey!
[*Solo, Verse 3*]
Listen to the music they playing,
The identical thing for rocking.
With all the jamming and all the hustle,
How could you stand and not move a muscle?
Well let me brighten up your night,
Come on—I could make you feel right.
[*Chorus, Refrain*]
Come and rock it with me baby!
Come and jam it with me honey!
[*Solo, Refrain*]
Sweet calypso, music jamming for soul I tell you,
[*Chorus, Refrain*]
Come and rock it with me baby!
Come and jam it with me honey!
[*Solo, Vocables: mellow*]
Oh oh oh oh oh oh oh oh oh . . .
[*Chorus, Refrain tag*]
Come and rock it with me baby.
[*Solo, Refrain variation fragment*]
I would like to rock it with you.
[*Chorus, Refrain tag*]
Come and jam it with me honey.
[*Solo, Refrain variation fragment: mellowing to the song end*]
Say yes you gonna rock it with me too.
[*Chorus, Refrain tag*]
Come and rock it with me baby.
[*Solo, Verse fragment*]
Who knows what the night might offer.

[*Chorus, Refrain tag*]
Come and jam it with me honey.
[*Solo, New verse fragment, vocables*]
If we can rock it with some soca, eh eh . . .
Oh oh oh oh oh oh oh oh, um um . . .
[*Chorus, Refrain tag*]
Come and rock it with me baby.
[*Solo, New verse fragment*]
Look how everybody moving.
[*Chorus, Refrain tag*]
Come and jam it with me honey.
[*Solo, New verse fragment*]
Come on let me do some grooving.
[*Chorus, Refrain tag*]
Come and rock it with me baby.
[*Solo, New verse fragment*]
I would like to rock it with you.
[*Chorus, Refrain tag*]
Come and jam it with me honey.
[*Solo, New verse fragment, vocables*]
Say yes you gonna rock with me too.
Oh no, eh . . .
Umm umm umm umm umm . . .
[*Begin fade*]
[*Chorus, Refrain tag*]
Come and rock it with me baby.
[*Solo, New verse fragment*]
Who knows what the night might offer?
[*Chorus, Refrain tag*]
Come and jam it with me honey.
[*Solo, New verse fragment*]
If we rock it with some soca.
[*Fade further*]
[*Chorus, Refrain tag*]
Come and rock it with me baby.
[*Solo, New verse fragment*]
Look how everybody moving.
[*Chorus, Refrain tag*]
Come and jam it with me honey.
[*Solo, New verse fragment*]
Come and let me do . . . [*fade to silence*]

Kanchan's version of "Rock. .It" was released under the title "Kuch Kuch Baby," literally "some-some" or "little-little" baby, indicating a charming doll—a term often used for an infant girl in Uttar Pradesh. The text, in Hindi, is not sexually explicit. These Creole compositions, such as "Rock. .It" had no place in Felicity until Kanchan transformed them into hits through changes in language (English to Hindi), modality (diatonic to pentatonic), and vocal style including ornamentation, nasal resonance, and style of attack and decay.

153
[*Refrain*]
A party in girl came,
Her name was little little baby,
Her name was little little baby.
A party in girl came,
Her name was little little baby.
A party in girl came,
Her name was little little baby.
She dances, she sings "ho ho ho ho ho ho."
A party in girl came,
Her name was little little baby.
She dances, she sings "ho ho ho ho ho ho."
Little little baby.
Little little baby.
[*Verse 1*]
People when saw her moon-like face,
Looked she sweet.
Each heart of had eye on,
She beauty was, she cutie-pie was.
Became all insane.
[*Refrain*]
A party in girl came,
Her name was little little baby.
She dances, she sings "ho ho ho ho ho ho."
Little little baby.
Little little baby.
[*Verse 2*]
Forehead at *bindiyā* [beauty spot] was,
Wrists on were bangles.
She dressed was in sari,
Seemed she India of.
She beauty was, she cutie-pie was.
Became all insane.
[*Refrain*]
A party in girl came,
Her name was little little baby.
She dances, she sings "ho ho ho ho ho ho."
Little little baby,
Little little baby.

[*Verse 3*]
Somebody say [*Hindi in original*] "Hi, darling," [*English in original*]
How you look so charming. [*English*]
Look soon don't go,
Sing you any song.
She beauty was, she cutie-pie was.
Became all insane.
[*Refrain*]
A party in girl came,
Her name was little little baby.
She dances, she sings "ho ho ho ho ho ho."
A party in girl came,
Her name was little little baby.
Happiness of this gathering,
Happiness of all sort,
Fragrant fragrant days those,
Uncontrolled uncontrolled nights.
She beauty was, she cutie-pie was.
Became all insane.
[*Refrain with fragmentation and slow fade*]
A party in girl came.
Her name was little little baby.
She dances, she sings "ho ho ho ho ho ho,"
"He he hay hay hay,"
Little little baby.
"Hu hu ho ho ho,"
Little little baby.
"He he hay hay hay,"
Little little baby.
"Hu hu ho ho ho,"
Little little baby.
"He he hay hay hay,"
Little little baby.
"Hu hu ho ho ho,"
Little little baby.
[*Fade to silence*]

The most stunning difference between Merchant's West Indian recording of "Rock. .It" and Kanchan's "Kuch Kuch Baby" is the sound field created in the recording studio. "Rock. .It" presents an artificial anechoic sound field, achieved by direct injection of the electronic instruments into the mixing console, by very close miking of the acoustic instruments and loudspeakers, and by reducing the dynamic range to almost nil through electronic limiting and compressing. Kanchan's "Kuch Kuch Baby" presents an equally artificial, but highly echoic sound field created by studio techniques associated with Indian film songs. These include reverb, double-tracking of the vocal line with a right-left bounce ("ping-ponging"), and a more extended dynamic range, with the limiter and compressor used only to avoid distortion. These studio techniques had reached Trinidad and many other developing nations in the 1980s, allowing local musicians to expand their repertory of possible sounds.

So during the '90s a telling turnabout occurred.

West Indian artists have made use of Indian themes in calypso and soca for over twenty years, and Bombay artist Kanchan supplied the villagers of Felicity with new musical material from India. With the Kanchan arrangements, India began to draw musical inspiration from Trinidad—from both its East Indian and its West Indian populations. I heard Kanchan's "Kayse Banie" playing on the in-house audio system of a cheap hotel in Gorakhpur, only a few miles from the village of Naipaul's grandfather.

I played another cassette for Umesh. "Here is a *chutney* from Trinidad."

After listening for a while he said: "This is a kind of *bhajan* sung at Holī, a song from my grandmother. The brave young Kanhaiyā [Krishna] came to play at the bank of Kālī—the Jamuna River. Women sing at the time of Holī, and my grandmother learned these songs from her parent's home. This song must be at least a hundred years old, probably more. All of the sudden hearing it just gave me a glimpse that this idea was around the area of U.P. and Bihar. This is Krishna's childhood and he is playing with the ball and bat." (Translated from Hindi original):

> 154
> Nand Bābāji of son,
> Ho oo oo oo oo keep Rām Kanhaiyā.
> Ho oo oo oo oo oo.
> Ho oo oo oo oo oo.
> Keep Rām Kanhaiyā,
> Oh, Nand Bābāji of son,
> His name is Kanhaiyā [as son], Kanhaiyā, Kanhaiyā re.
> Oh, Nand Bābāji of son,
> His name is Kanhaiyā, Kanhaiyā, Kanhaiyā re.

"Nand Bābāji was a rich man who brought up Krishna," Umesh explained. "And he called Krishna 'Kanhaiyā'—a loving son is Kanhaiyā."

> What made of ball, what made of bat?
> Ball in what of around ring? [What is the ring of the ball made of?]
> Ho ho hu hu ho oo oo oo,
> What made of ball, what made of bat?

"Here the composer asks questions," Umesh interrupted. "Krishna is playing bat and ball. What are they made of? The ring around the ball, what is it made of?"

> Ball in what of around ring?
> Shepherds and their children these play came.
> Dressed like Radhā's lover, Krishna.
> Oh, Gora [wife of Shiva], Kanhaiyā, Kanhaiyā, Kanhaiyā.
> Ho, Nand Bābāji of son.
> His name is Kanhaiyā, Kanhaiyā, Kanhaiyā re.
> Gold made of ball is, gold made of bat.
> Ball around gold made a ring. [The ring around the ball is made of gold.]
> Oh, gold made of ball is, gold made of bat.
> Ball around gold made a ring.
> Gold made of ball is, gold made of bat.
> Ball around gold made a ring.

"There are the answers to these questions," Umesh explained. "The ball, the bat, and the ring are all made of gold. In our custom, Krishna was a naughty and lovable and playful child."

> Now shepherd children these play came,
> Shepherd's children these play came.
> Being of Radhā love Kanhaiyā.
> Ho, Gora ho, Kanhaiyā Kanhaiyā re.
> Ho, Nand Bābāji of son.
> His name is Kanhaiyā, Kanhaiyā, Kanhaiyā.
> Blue the Jamuna, blue the sky is, blue the sky is.
> Blue Kanhaiyā, blue the sky is.
> Blue the Jamuna, blue the sky is, blue the sky is.
> Blue Kanhaiyā, blue the sky is.
> Handsome blue play come,
> Being of Radhā sweetheart Kanhaiyā.
> Oh, Gora oh, Kanhaiyā Kanhaiyā re.
> Ho, Nand Bābāji of son.
> His name is Kanhaiyā, Kanhaiyā, Kanhaiyā re.
> Ho oo oo oo oo.
> Ho, re Kanhaiyā, Kanhaiyā re.
> Ho, ho Kanhaiyā, Kanhaiyā re.
> Ho, re Kanhaiyā, Kanhaiyā re.

"How do you feel when you hear these religious thoughts in the form of a dancing and drinking song?" I asked.

"You know," Umesh replied, "when the thief goes to steal, he promises 'I will donate this much in the name of God if I come back successfully.' I mean that any person, whether he drinks or not, he needs God, and he worships in his way. And I like this song, I like the tune, I like the music. This is *bhajan.* It is out of the *Rāmāyaṇ.* Any religious person will accept this *chutney.* On the other hand, 'My heart is attached to you'—it is not acceptable in the family, in the social system, this kind of love arrangement."

"Well, people really get bent out of shape when something they know comes back in a new form," John Storm Roberts commented as he and I bemoaned the difficulty of getting Trinidad records imported into the United States. "And," he added, "Remember the old hymn, 'Change and decay in all around I see; Oh Thou that changest not, abide with me.'"

"*Chutney* will just come and go like a fashion," Umesh went on. "I promise you it won't remain forever. Some music always has depth. Just like some clothes always have depth. Suit and tie—they have depth.

"But these *chutney* programs in Trinidad sound like our *jawābī kīrtan* cultural shows. They are well-known around U.P. State. But *jawābī kīrtan* does not produce dance or drink! For our shows, groups appear in cities from time to time. *Jawābī kīrtan* means some person sings and leaves questions in his song and the other singer has to reply—compose same tune other singer is singing. In reply he has to sing the same rhythm, tune, and *alankār* (characteristic phrases). A question might have been put out of deep *Rāmāyaṇ* or *Māhābhārata* which normally people don't know. These people have copies of the *Rāmāyaṇ* and *Māhābhārata* with them to say all of the sudden, 'This is it!' These groups call a wise man who have deep knowledge of religion and this man tells what the true answers are."

"Does he tell the winner?" I asked.

"No need," Umesh said. "When they sing it is just like fighting with each other on a battlefield.

"In life, winner always realize he is winner. And loser, well they are loser."

☙ The Mid 1990s: Chutney Lambada, Chutney Rap, and Screwdriver

"Indra? Is that Indra?" I asked. "Charlie gave me your number."

"You know Charlie?" a Trinidadian voice asked.

"I do now! He talked for nearly an hour, about soca and *chutney* and Fulton Street and Brooklyn and all. But when he understood that I actually wanted *chutney* he said to phone you because he gets his *chutney* from you."

"Yeah, that's true."

"So you *are* Indra. I'd like to get some of this season's *chutney.* What do you have?"

"What do you want? We can get anything from the island you like. We have *chutney* soca, *chutney jhūmar, parang jhūmar,* film soca, *punjabee chutney, chutney* rap, *chutney lambada,* and 'Screwdriver.' And many of the Trinidad artists come here to Brooklyn studios to record because we have more sophisticated studios up here."

"Well, I've got about $50. What can I get?"

"A lot for that. But why don't you come down and meet the artists here in Brooklyn."

"Well, I usually go to the island. I go to Felicity. Do you know Felicity?"

"Yeah. Central. But you know there's no real need to go any more. The popular artists come here and do big concerts for the Indo-Caribbean community. It be popular in Brooklyn you know. I can introduce you."

"Well, I'll come, but I can't wait for the records. How do I pay?"

"We do all COD, around the world—to Toronto and Miami—all over the USA—and London—everywhere there is East Indians there is *chutney* these days. You'll get a lot for $50. I'll send a mix."

And a Pan-Caribbean mix it was!

"*Chutney Lambada,*" sung by Geeta Kawalsingh (keyboards/guitar, Ricky Rampersad; bass, Rodney John; *ḍholak,* Sunil Ramsook; drum machine, Vijay Mohan), was recorded in Jamaica, N.Y., in 1994. It presents an imitation of the typical Indian film orchestra with synthesized violin sound and drum machine, and words in Hindi. The singer is in her own muddy acoustic, somewhat swamped by the instrumentals around her.

155
[*Refrain*]
You, you, you! [*tūtū tārā*]
Break not heart mine.
Ho, you, you, you!
Break not heart mine.
True story you to tell,
Has come me you appease.
Grant me pardon you.
[*Refrain repeated*]
Hey, you, you, you!
Break not heart mine.
Hey, you, you, you!
Oh, break not heart mine.
[*Verse 1*]
Let come, let come, me let come na,
Speak na! Speak why confused are?
Ho, let come, let come, me let come na.

Speak na! Speak na why confused are?
Virgin beauty spot [*bindiyā*], virgin golden bangles,
You my love call.
Virgin beauty spot, virgin golden bangles,
You my love call.
Close come look into eyes.
Grant me pardon you.
[*Refrain*]
You, you, you! Come on do!
Break not heart mine.
Hey, you, you, you!
Hey break not heart mine.
True story you to tell,
Have come me you oppose.
Grant me pardon you.
[*Refrain*]
Hey, you, you, you!
Oh, break not heart mine.
Hey, you, you, you!
Hey! break not heart mine.
[*Verse 2*]
Displeased do not be, displeased do not be now displeased in this way.
Gentleman, come on why confused are?
Displeased do not be, displeased do not be now displeased in this way.
Gentleman, gentleman, oh confused are?
Does accept, does not accept what I have said.
How head shaking [*nachāī,* meaning ambiguous, either bending head downward or turning head side to side indicating no] is,
Does accept, does not accept what I have said.
How head shaking is.
Oh, you *bābā:* [*bābā* does not refer to father here but used more in the sense of 'go man go!'] go you *bābā!*
Grant me pardon you.
[*Refrain*]
You, you, you!
Break not heart mine.
Hey, you, you, you!
Oh, break not heart mine.
True story you to tell,
Have come I you appease.
Grant me pardon you.
[*Refrain, fragmented, fade to silence*]
Ho, you, you, you!
Oh, break not heart mine.
Hey, you, you, you.
Break not heart mine.
You, you, you!

Break not heart mine.
Yes, you, you, you!
Oh, break not heart mine.

Sharlene Boodram hit the new season with *'94 Summer Chutney Time.* (Parrot Records, Caribbean–Miami–New York; lyrics, Rankie Boodram; arranged, Pelham Goddard; drummers, Balma *tāssā* drummers; *ḍholak* and *ḍhantāl,* Aaron Jeewansingh; back vocalists, Juslyn Jones, Adrian Philbert, and Natalie Yorke). The '90s reggae style is unmistakable in this fast-action song with its dense lyrics, aggressive monotone style of vocal delivery, and relentless duple meter. The lyrics are English, peppered with those Bhojpurī terms that are still in common use. The song appeals to young and old in Trinidad to "*chutney* down," for the grandparents to "show them young girl how to *chutney* man," referring to the traditional wedding dances of Bhojpurī ladies. It invites abandon of older Indian customs ("No more sari man, no more dhoti man") in favor of freedom ("Time to free up in the party—wind down!").

156 ♫
[*Fast; with driving intensity*]
[*Chorus*]
[*Hindi*] *Ek, do, ek, do, tīn, chār* ["One, two, one, two, three, four"].
[*Solo; Verse 1*]
[*English*] Come hear me *nānī* [archaic in India; mother's mother] man, come hear me girl we say,
Come hear me *ājī* [archaic in India; father's mother] man, come hear me girl we say—come come!
Come hear me *kākī* [father's younger brother's wife] man, come hear me girl we say,
Come hear me *mausī* [mother's sister] man, come hear me girl we say—come come!
Pull your *oḍhanī* girl, take it down we say,
Rest it on our shoulder, *chutney* down we say—come down!
Pull up your gown up way to your knee man,
Show them young girl how to *chutney* man—come down!
CHUTNEY TIME!
[*Refrain*]
Form a little ring man and I do a little thing man,
And a wiggle of your body and I make your waist thin.
Spin spin spin and I spin the tape you see,
A wiggle of your body and I make your waist thin.
[*Hindi*] *bol!* ["say"] *bol! bol! bol! are!* [*ā-re,* "oh"] *bap re bap!*
[*Hindi*] *are! are! are! are! are bap re bap!*
[*Hindi*] *are bap!* ["Oh God!"] *are bap! are bap! bap! bap!*
are! are! are! are! are bap re bap!
bol! bol! bol! bol! are bap re bap!

are! are! are! are! are bap re bap!
are bap! are bap! are bap! bap! bap!
are! are! are! are! are bap re bap!
[*Chorus*]
Ek, do, ek, do, tīn, chār.
[*Solo*]
[*English; Verse 2*] Come hear me *nānā* [archaic in India; mother's father] man, come hear me boy we say,
Come hear me *ājā* [archaic in India; father's father] man, come hear me boy we say—come come!
Come hear me *kākā* [archaic in India; father's younger brother] man, a come hear me boy we say,
Come hear me *mausā* [mother's sister's husband] man, a come hear me boy we say—come come!
Tie your dhoti man, tie it up cause,
Chutney down it extremely hot we say—come down!
Pull your *kaprā* ["clothes"] now, take it down we say,
Rest it on the ground and *chutney* down we say—come down!
CHUTNEY TIME!
[*Refrain*]
Form a little ring man and I do a little thing man,
And a wiggle of your body and I make your waist thin.
Spin spin spin and I spin the tape you see,
A wiggle of your body and I make your waist thin.
bol! bol! bol! bol! are bap re bap!
are bap! are bap! are bap! bap! bap!
are! are! are! are! are bap re bap!
bol! bol! bol! bol! are bap re bap!
are! are! are! are! are bap re bap!
are bap! are bap! are bap! bap! bap!
are! are! are! are! are bap re bap!
[*Chorus*]
Ek, do, ek, do, tīn, chār.
[*Solo*]
[*English; Verse 3*] Come now *betī* ["daughter"] man, come here girl we say,
Come now *betā* ["son"] man, come here boy we say—come come!
Come now *dulahin* ["bride"], come here girl we say,
Come now *dulahā* ["bridegroom"], come here boy we say—come come!
No more *oḍhanī* man, no more *gharī* ["watch"] man,
Not take hold and we back in the *chutney* man—wind down!
No more sari man, no more dhoti man,
Time to free up in the party—wind down!
CHUTNEY TIME!
[*Refrain*]
Form a little ring man and I do a little thing man,
And a wiggle of your body and I make your waist thin.

Spin spin spin and I spin the tape you see,
A wiggle of your body and I make your waist thin.
bol! bol! bol! bol! are bap re bap!
are! are! are! are! are bap re bap!
are bap! are bap! are bap! bap! bap!
are! are! are! are! are bap re bap!
bol! bol! bol! bol! are bap re bap!
are! are! are! are! are bap re bap!
are bap! are bap! are bap! bap! bap!
are! are! are! are! are bap re bap!
[etc.]

Boodram's rap-style number is to a degree layered front to back acoustically with percussion and bass fully forward. The singer is given a natural, broad acoustic by the use of a microphone at a reasonable distance, so achieving the feel of a real room setting around her with the close-miked *tāssā* drum, *ḍholak,* and *ḍhantāl* reminiscent of the old local instruments, together with distant muted, synthesized brass and wind. The song is sung in Creole (often called "home English" or "broken English," the English vernacular of Felicity) with Hindi interpolations, mainly iterative text phrases such as "Oh God! God! God! God!"

Sundar Popo, by the mid-1990s, had lost some of his following, and his earlier favorites, such as "Chaadar," were thought of as "oldies" and "classics." Boodram's "Chutney Time" took first place over his *chutney* in the Caribbean Music Award, 31 March 1995. Two weeks later, Popo said: "The reggae style should not be favored over our local Trinidad *chutney.*" The text of his newer release, "Screwdriver," presented the mid-90s *chutney* audience with a more raw, simple, vivid sexual message in English ("For he gonna screw and she gonna screw and screw upon another") than the mid-80s suggestive Hindi lyric "spread the little sheet, sweetheart." Even so, the "Screwdriver" lyrics alternate between Hindi and English and are rather more demanding on Hindi fluency than other contemporary hits. Surely the album cover, with its close-up shot of a woman's breasts nearly concealed by a working man's undershirt, sold some of the albums.

"Screwdriver" has a bright, forward sound, instruments and vocalists, each and every one appearing to have been mixed for a center-stage position, appropriate given the text and the album cover.

157
[*Instrumental introduction*]
[*Refrain*]
[*Hindi*] Mother-in-law is to me *ghachuriya re* ["careless, very careless"].

[*Hindi*] Husband without [*English*] look me [*Hindi*] *ghachuriya re.*
[*Hindi*] So having fell in love and then separated [i.e., first eyes met and later they separated]
[*Hindi*] Having fell in love and then separated, oh Rām.
[*Solo, English, Verse 1*]
She says she was a virgin and wanted to get married,
She says she was a virgin and wanted to get married,
She never married a taxi driver.
For he got drive and she got drive and drive upon another.
[*Refrain*]
[*Hindi*] Mother-in-law is to me *ghachuriya re.*
[*Hindi*] Husband without [*English*] look me [*Hindi*] *ghachuriya re.*
[*Hindi*] So having fell in love and then separated,
[*Hindi*] Having fell in love and then separated, oh Rām.
[*Solo, English, Verse 2*]
She says she was a virgin and wanted to get married,
She says she was a virgin and wanted to get married,
She'll never married an electrician.
For he gonna screw and she gonna screw and screw upon another.
[*Refrain*]
[*Hindi*] Mother-in-law is to me *ghachuriya re.*
[*Hindi*] Husband without [*English*] look me [*Hindi*] *ghachuriya re.*
[*Hindi*] So having fell in love and then separated,
[*Hindi*] Having fell in love and then separated, oh Rām.
[*Solo, English, Verse 3*]
She says she was a virgin and wanted to get married,
She says she was a virgin and wanted to get married,
She'll never married a gardener.
For he gonna fork and she gonna fork and fork upon another.
[*Refrain*]
[*Hindi*] Mother-in-law is to me *ghachuriya re.*
[etc.]

"Scorpion Gyul [girl]," recorded by Sundar Popo in 1994 (JMC Triveni Classic), has opening instrumentals that imitate an Indian filmī orchestra, with prominent bells, sax, brass, accordion, bass, and string section. This song has a multi-layered acoustic with the various instrumental sections apparently occupying differing front to back positions. Sundar Popo is placed in a muddy acoustic at mid-point, with prominent percussion and bass sections.

158 ♫
[*Refrain 1*]
[*Hindi*] *Jaldī na mārio prem* ["Quick not kill love"], [*English*] my darling.
[*English*] When we gonna meet up again, my darling?
When we meet up again?
[*Hindi*] Quick not kill love, [*English*] my darling.

[*English*] When we gonna meet up again, my darling?
When we meet up again?
[*Refrain 2*]
[*English*] A scorpion sting me, I feeling I gonna dead,
Darling if you love me come lie down in my bed.
[*Refrain 1*]
[*Hindi*] Quick not kill love, [*English*] my darling
[*English*] When we gonna meet up again, my darling?
When we meet up again?
[*Instrumental*]
[*Verse 1*]
[*English*] You leaving in a plane girl, you leaving me alone.
I wish I got someone just to call me call to call.
I love you very much girl, I love you with my heart,
And it is very sad now for us to depart.
[*Refrain 2*]
A scorpion sting me, I feeling I gonna dead,
Darling if you love me come lie down in my bed.
[*Refrain 1*]
[*Hindi*] Quick not kill love, [*English*] my darling.
[*English*] When we gonna meet up again, my darling?
When we meet up again?
[*Instrumental*]
[*Verse 2*]
[*English*] Every night I go to sleep, my ears begin to ring,
And when I think I kiss you, I kiss my wedding ring.
To love is a pain, it pain that way,
But the greatest pain of man boy is to live in vain.
[*Refrain 2*]
[*English*] A scorpion sting me, I feeling I gonna dead.
Darling if you love me come lie down in my bed.
[*Refrain 1*]
[*Hindi*] Quick not kill love, [*English*] my darling.
[*English*] When we gonna meet up again, my darling?
When we meet up again?
[*Instrumental*]
[*Verse 3*]
[*English*] Darling I can roam from place to place,
Singing a song just for your special face.
Do I could miss you, I want you to know,
So come with me my lover I need you wherever I go.
[*Refrain 2*]
A scorpion sting me, I feeling I gonna dead.
Darling if you love me come lie down in my bed.
[*Refrain 1*]
[*Hindi*] Quick not kill love, [*English*] my darling.

[*English*] When we gonna meet up again, my darling?
When we meet up again?
[*Refrain 2*]
A scorpion sting me, I feeling I gonna dead.
Darling if you love me come lie down in my bed.
Darling if you love me come lie down in my bed.
Darling if you love me come lie down in my bed.
[*Begin fade*]
Darling if you love me come lie down in my bed.
[*Continue fade*]
Darling if you love me come lie down in my bed.
[*Final fade*]
Darling if you love me come lie down in my bed.

Spice

"Well, what do you think about *chutney,*" I asked Umesh. "Amar said it is nothing to be proud of."

"*Chutney* is really village stuff, deep village stuff. It is not considered cultured. Cultured people *do* filth but they don't sing; village people *sing* filth but they don't do."

"Well, what about "Give Me *Paisā*?" I asked.

"That is a kind of sexual *chutney*—to burn your mouth. Amar won't like it, but some people like to burn their mouth. It is how people use spice—to feel taste better, to burn the mouth, or, or get diarrhea. Spice, if you take it in the way which give you pleasure, that is great. But if you eat too much and burn your mouth, get diarrhea, you spoil the physical body."

"Do Indian villagers use the term *chutney?*"

"No, in our area *chutney* is *chatpatī*—'spicy,' 'hot'—sour, salty, food with little bit chili in it. We say let us sing some sour and salt and spicy songs—*chatpatī.* In India, dancing songs are considered little bit *chatpatī,* little bit *chutney,* because dancing song is a kind of rhythm. Or we can say 'she is very *chatpatī.*' Or we can say 'get some *chatpatī* thing to eat with liquor.' Or we can say 'have spicy talk' '*chatpatī bāt hai.*' Or we say 'do this *chatpat*'—fast fast.

"Spice gives pleasure, rhythm, and taste. If you want real pleasure you must have a spicy life, means taste of every side of life. With much knowledge and better taste you can understand everything. Our poet, Tulsī Dās, has written in the *Rāmāyaṇ* about politics; he has written on the nature of women on every side—wicked, fair, trustworthy; he has written on behavior of brother to brother; on behavior and duty of king to subject; and he also compose about nature—flowers, trees, branches. This *Rāmāyaṇ* is spicy to love God, created with every kind of worldly spice to put the mind toward God.

"Spice is not some cursing words. It is natural. Some people get pleasure of singing, some get pleasure of listening, some get pleasure to achieve the last goal—to reach to God. What makes better the way to achieve the last goal? The way is not easy if it is dried. It must be spicy, and spice comes from music. The main way to God is by music, by singing."

"Is that *bhaktī?*" I asked.

"Yes, certainly it is *bhaktī.* In real life spice is the most important. Even to achieve *moksha.* The definition of spice is not only for one thing, not only for talk, sex, music. Spicy means that thing which pleasurely puts us toward that goal. When we sing for God we fill with spice those songs so we can appease our God to get him. Does God not like great singing?

"And what is in the music? What had Mozart composed? It is spice. Rhythm to excite people—that is spice. To make mouth tingle—that is spice. To make mind run—that is spice. To make feeling in body—that is spice. Mozart found the real recipe. He put the right amount of spice to make music great. Even when *I* listen (it is composed, not for Germany, I think—it is composed for the world) Mozart gives me great spicy pleasure. Spice to attain salvation."

Chapter Eighteen
Sweet Memory

I know how men in exile feed on dreams.

Aeschylus, *Agamemnon*

As the time drew near for me to leave Felicity, I watched the planes flying over the village, away from Trinidad, with an ever increasing sense of sadness. The villagers and I joked about the possibility of my returning in a few months to record the *chautāl* at Phāguā and the all-night *bhajan* singing at Shivrātrī. But they surmised and I felt that, in all likelihood, we would not meet again for a very long time. So I reasoned then, not being able to foresee at that moment the extended research to come—research that continues and may reach out for a lifetime.

Saying goodbye to Felicity was not easy. Ever since I was a child, I had been fascinated by stories of other people in other lands, but it was from these villagers and in this village that I had first experienced the "otherness" of another people and another culture. And they had made the discipline of musicology come alive for me. These were debts that I could never repay.

I had come to love the music of Felicity—the traditional folk songs, temple songs, film songs, Sai Baba chants, *chutney.* I had enjoyed the hours spent sitting with groups of women as they recalled one wedding song after another, or relaxing in the evenings with Mesho's mother who would play the *ḍholak* and sing *lachārī,* or walking down Cacandee Road to see Sankey or Channu or Dolan to chat about music, or going out of the village with Mesho's group to sing at a *pūjā.* I would miss those times I myself joined in the singing—so much singing. I knew I would especially miss the quiet of the temple services at dawn and dusk (since the *sanḍhyā* is always performed at the change of light) and the special mood of repose that those services invoked in me. Even before I had left the village I could see that my memories of Felicity would be good.

But I had many regrets. The old traditional songs could easily have been the subject of my entire study. I was sad to think that songs of this repertory that I had failed to collect might never be recorded. I wished that I had collected more variants, done more work on the song texts, delved more deeply into the genres associated with rice cultivation—pursued these and many other lines of inquiry. I also regretted that I had not had time to learn to play the *ḍholak* or the harmonium well enough to perform in the temple songs.

Village drumming could easily have been the subject for yet another major study; Dhanlal, the village drummer, and I had only just begun to discuss the more important techniques when it was time to return home. My goal had been a portrait of the musical life of Felicity, and although that story was not complete it was well begun; much of the picture was still buried in the many reels of tape recordings I was busy packing during my last few days. Looking ahead to the hours of transcription to come, I knew the memories of these musicians and this music would all be very good indeed.

About the musical life of Felicity I had come to a number of conclusions. Singing, especially of religious songs, was the most important musical activity for the villagers. Most people I met liked to sing *bhajan;* some of the women were noted for their proficiency at wedding songs and some of the men for *chautāl, jhūmar,* and *ulārā.* Nearly everyone who could sing was able to accompany themselves on the *manjīrā* (finger cymbals) and *kartāl* (clappers with jingles). The *ḍhantāl* (stick idiophone) is much more difficult, but many villagers played it. Many were also able to perform simple drone or heterophonic accompaniments on the harmonium. Drumming on the *ḍholak, tāssā,* or *nagārā* is thought to be more of a speciality, and there are relatively few experts.

Nearly all the music I heard in Felicity was in call-and-response form, an important self-teaching feature crucial in a musical culture in which the song texts are in a foreign language and difficult to master. But the varieties of response styles in Felicity seemed endless, from the simple leader–chorus form of the *kīrtan, chautāl, Rāmāyaṇ* recitation, and Sai Baba songs (in which the answer duplicates the call), to the many complex verse and refrain patterns of the *bhajan* and wedding songs.

Most dear to the villagers was what they called "Indian music." Indian music meant different things to different people. For the younger generation it referred especially to *chutney* and film songs, for the older, to the traditional folk songs, and for practically everybody, to temple songs. But for all, it meant a repertory with some texts in an Indian language, be it Bhojpurī or Hindi, Bengalī or Sanskrit. This special relationship with Hindi and Bhojpurī—what is for a few older villagers their mother tongue and for others a foreign language—dominates the culture of Felicity and the music of Felicity. I cannot imagine songs with English words ever replacing the much-loved Indian genres. Bhojpurī is little spoken by the younger generation. The songs are still sung by older women, but how the villagers will continue singing them if the spoken language finally dies (as it seems it surely must) is an imponderable question. Newly introduced songs in Hindi will perhaps replace the traditional Bhojpurī repertory; this process is already well under way, as for example, in the wedding ceremony, where the *byāh ke gīt* are often enough drowned out by recorded music or songs played by a hired Indian orchestra.

Another way of maintaining an Indian repertory I saw exemplified with the Sai Baba songs—substituting short catchy Hindi songs for longer, structurally complex strophic Hindi *bhajan.* Songs learned from Indian films offer yet another solution. Villagers find it easy enough to learn the tunes from the cinema, the radio, or records. The texts and translations for recently imported film songs are available in *Filmindia,* a monthly magazine published in Trinidad. *Chutney* reduces the knowledge of Hindi to a minimum, as—in Sharleen Boodram's "Chutney Time"—to those archaic Bhojpurī kinship terms that still are used on a daily basis along with other words that linger in the active vocabulary: *makān* ("house"), *kaparā* ("clothes"), sari, dhoti ("man's wear"), *oḍhanī* ("veil"). Another strategy is for the villagers to turn more toward instrumental music—*tāssā* drumming is already very popular as are the island's many Indian orchestras. Also studio recordings that use Indian film-music techniques orchestration, voice quality, and the preferred Indian reverberant acoustic maintain the authentic flavor of acculturated music. Changing social mores and new social settings—clubs—have provided the opportunity for dating and dancing that have given life to the *chutney* movement. No doubt the villagers will devise other solutions for retaining "Indian music" without fluency in an Indian language, looking all the while to India for new musical inspiration.

This process of musical revitalization, rejuvenation, and revival is the great fascination of musical history in Felicity. For over a hundred years India has been the source of new musical ideas for these immigrants. Some of the styles to reach Trinidad were new in India (film songs, for example); others (such as Indian classical music) were not. During the indentureship period, with immigrants arriving by the thousands each year, established settlers must have been glad to learn new folk songs from the recruits. The core repertory known to both the settled immigrants and the recruits was reinforced, and minority views (the south Indian repertory, for example) seem to have been rejected. But for the original village ladies, every new ship arriving in the harbor of Port of Spain brought more women to sing the many songs of the life cycle and the agricultural calendar.

From 1917, the Trinidad Indian's repertory was enhanced by the songs and chants of missionaries from the Bombay-based Arya Samaj (Society of Aryans), including Pandit Mehta Jaiman and Pandit Ayodhya Prasad. In 1935, *Bala Joban,* the first Indian talkie, opened in San Fernando, inaugurating a new period of musical history in Felicity—that of the film song. In 1936, the first shipment of Indian records reached Trinidad, providing more material from which the Felicity villagers might replenish their repertory, particularly that of "local classical" songs like the *ghazal* and *ṭhumrī*. In 1951, Swami Purnananda of the Bharat Sevashram Sangha arrived in Felicity, introducing new forms of temple worship and new songs, still performed in the Nolan Street temple. In the 1960s Professor Adesh introduced Indian classical music to Trinidad. In 1974, the Sai Baba movement brought yet another style of worship and another song repertory to Felicity. Then in the 1970s "tent singing" and by the 1980s *chutney* revival caught hold. These influences both still persist. This pattern of revitalization from Indian sources has been continuous in the village since the early years of this century, and is a force for change in the musical history of Felicity.

Until recent decades, acculturation was inconspicuous in Felicity music. Certain features of musical style may be Westernized, but this is often difficult to pinpoint. For example, musical pitch in Felicity appears to be much influenced by the fixed equal-tempered pitch of the harmonium, a product of the West—via India, to be sure. Rhythmic organization tends to be in groupings of twos and fours. In general, the grouping of three and four of the song texts of the Bhojpurī repertory has been abandoned in the more recent song forms. This simplification of rhythmic forms may also result from Westernization, although this is difficult to say with certainty as *kaharwā tāl* (eight beats) is also typical of north Indian folk and devotional music.

Villagers sing the occasional Hindi calypso, but these songs tend to be regarded as curiosities. Locally composed Indian film-type songs are popular on the long-lived weekly television program, *Mastana Bahaar,* and on the various radio programs devoted to Indian music; these items often find their way to village jukeboxes in rum shops. Apart from hymns, I never saw a villager perform any of the English or Afro-Caribbean genres popular in Trinidad, such as calypso, steel band, and cult forms. But the social role of music has certainly been influenced by its West Indian setting. *Bhajan* singing in temple services is analogous to English hymns; *Rāmāyaṇ* chanting during the night after a death is analogous to the Christian singing at Creole wakes. *Chautāl* competitions compare with calypso competitions, tent singing with pan yards. And so on.

AFTERTHOUGHTS

In the past, Felicity villagers have tended to select Indian models for their temple repertory and for other religious contexts. They have selected Western models, including calypso, soca, and disco, for dance and other entertainment music. Indian-inspired pieces are described as "classical," "from books," "deep" (profound, meaningful), or "from away" (the opposite of local).

Western-inspired pieces are described as "make up," "composed," "local." In the 1980s, Kanchan and other visiting artists began to draw on Trinidad Indian sources for pop and entertainment music. In composing new items in the musical repertory, villagers now have a wide selection of models: Indian, Western, local East Indian as interpreted by an Indian performer, and local West Indian as interpreted by an Indian performer. This rich and interesting situation cannot be properly explained in older terms of conventional concepts of acculturation. An ethnomusicologist might opt to label new compositions influenced by West Indian music "acculturated" and all three varieties of Indianized music "revitalized." Whatever happened to the notion of "authenticity" (what I felt I had found in Number One Song and came to love), so important in folk music studies only a few decades ago? It is not lost, for the villagers would happily apply the term authentic to their Indianized repertory, including the Kanchan songs. And in the *chutney* craze, Trinidadians see a revival of the authentic local classic oldies. But the observer, the ethnomusicologist, might hesitate before concurring with the villagers that these Indianized pieces, borrowed from a twentieth-century urban Hindi culture, are more authentic than the local Westernized repertory, a reflection of their New World heritage.

The modern musical history of Felicity illustrates a number of fundamental issues in ethnomusicology.

First, the deliberateness of musical change and exchange. We sometimes fall into the habit of describing musical change as something that happens to people as opposed to something that people cause to happen. In Felicity, musical change is conscious and deliberate. And villagers like to discuss the musical decisions they have made.

Second, the differential nature of change. Different repertories in a musical tradition often change in different ways. Felicity villagers have tended to Indianize their religious repertory and to Westernize their popular repertory.

Third, the speed of change. In Felicity, new styles and repertories can gain acceptance in a single season.

Fourth, terms. The ethnomusicologist might describe the Kanchan songs as acculturated while the villagers might call them authentic. The ethnomusicologist might categorize the local East Indian *chutney* of Sundar Popo as genuinely Trinidadian, while the villagers think it is "broken," "local," and "make-up," or as a classical revival.

Fifth, the musical grey-out. Let this account of music in a Trinidad village be added to the mounting evidence demonstrating that a worldwide grey-out, the universal Westernization of the world's music (much feared by ethnomusicologists in the 1970s), is not taking place. Musical change is moving in directions we did not anticipate.

Sixth, the essential vitality of traditions in flux. Our descriptive terms, such as acculturation and revitalization, refer not so much to the winding down of traditional styles as to the unleashing of enormous expressive and creative forces. The music history of Felicity shows that living traditions are continuously being reformed. As we witness over and again the pervasiveness of musical change and exchange around the world, we must acknowledge that, with such creative acts, the bearers of tradition reinvoke their culture.

Conclusions. Yet an intuition persists: India remains forever India, but Trinidad is of the New World.

ꕤ Chapter Nineteen ꕤ

Passage to India

Singing my days.

Walt Whitman, *Passage to India*

"Is that when you lost your diamond?" she asked.

"Yes, and found it," I replied.

"I can't even remember what year that was," Mom said.

"1986."

"1986, really. Where did I say goodbye to you?"

"At the airport."

"Was that when you carried your Trinidad tapes to India?"

"Yes," I replied, "for the archive in Delhi. But really I went to find Number One Song."

Then Mom said in a special voice, "Everybody should have a daughter like you."

"I don't," I had to say.

"But you have three sons like you," she said.

Years later I asked her "How did you know what to say?" and she thought a moment and replied, "Well, you focus on the situation. What I said was true."

Arrival

I had been on my way to India to study Bhojpurī music and to visit the ancestral villages of my friends in Trinidad. I had tapes of Felicity music to play for the Indian villagers and I was eager to hear their comments. I also had an invitation to lecture in Bombay. After living in an Indian village in Trinidad, I figured I knew something about India. What I learned when I arrived in India was that I was not prepared for India.

In Trinidad I had been a student with meager funds. The Trinidadians were almost prosperous; on my first trip they used an outdoor toilet, later they put in an indoor bathroom, and on my last visit showed me to a second bathroom, a powder room, in avocado and maroon. They had a second car and a color television set in a new upstairs living room.

But when I arrived in India with modest grant funds, I found I was a "millionaire" surrounded by grotesque poverty. No colleague had taught me how to resolve the inner conflict of being a "rich" American scholar in a desperately poor country. My first thought was to go native and suffer with the sufferers. But my friends at the archive and later the villagers dissuaded me and kept me healthy.

❧ THE FIRST VILLAGE

Once there I was puzzled how to go about my research, even how to find a village, as my arrangements for a field assistant apparently had fallen through. But as I was about to leave Delhi for Banaras a telegram arrived: Umesh was coming to help out (plate 46).

He had never been on a plane before. We took off for Banaras on the night of Diwālī. "Just like an Indian bus," Umesh commented as we were airborne. Then looking below at the Diwālī lights, "but look, stars on earth!"

After three days in the city, I cried out in exasperation: "Just find a village, any village—567,000 villages and you can't find one!"

"We could hire a rickshaw," he said.

"Then I'll begin in the first village we find."

Banpurwā is not on any map, but eventually we found it, farther from Banaras than expected.

"I'll just go and sing one of these songs," I proposed.

"No, we must find the *pradhān* (headman)," Umesh said. "We need permission."

"I don't need permission to sing," I said. "You watch me. Just let me out of this rickshaw."

So it was through music, not through negotiation, that I made my way to the Bhojpurī villages of eastern Uttar Pradesh. I would take my handwritten song book, find an old woman (there was always one resting in the shade), present myself with "Namaste," and sing a village song from Trinidad. "*Sānkara koriyā baharo ho pandita rāmā baharo. . . .*" More women arrived, and some young girls leaned on me. The old lady knew the song. "Sweep the way for Lord Rām," she told her friends. "This white is singing for some wedding." She corrected my tune, and took over just as I came to the end of the Felicity song. A crowd was gathering but we were involved with each other and with the song which we were now singing together.

Off to the side with a gathering of men, Umesh was answering questions: "Who is Memsahib who sings but doesn't talk much?" Umesh: "She is a distinguished professor from the United States. You'll be surprised to know that she learned these songs in South America."

Meanwhile I was trying to look distinguished while sitting on the ground.

"*Bābā bābā pukare* (Father! Father!)," I sang.

"That is when they put the *sindūr*," the old lady told her friends.

"Mother! Mother!" I sang.

Plate 46. Umesh Pandey and his daughter Alaka, Karimganj, U.P., 1986.

A small boy arrived with tea for the singers.

Umesh came over and had tea. "They have two widows here in Banpurwā," he said. "They are the best singers and you can record them tomorrow morning. I told them you were kind, so you should bring saris for them. They say this lady here doesn't know anything about wedding songs."

⅋ Marriages in India

Conversations often turned to the marriage ceremony itself, the many difficulties in arranging a wedding in village India. The couples in Felicity had married for love, a practice that the Bhojpurī women found extremely foolish: no momentous decision should be left in the hands of a teenager, particularly the choice of a life partner. (They were doubly shocked to learn that Americans married in a ceremony lasting less than one hour.) "Our success in life can be measured by counting how many daughters we have married, how many *bahū* (wives) we brought into our house, and how many *tervī,* funeral feasts, we have performed." "This is the way of the world," Grierson recorded in 1883 in Shāhābād District.

159 ⅋
A Song of Consolation
My husband, on the day when my daughter was born I became sad.
Had it been a son, he would have served you (in your old age), but a daughter is but a four-days' guest.
When, love, you will give her in marriage, she will go to live in her father-in-law's house.
This our daughter they will call "the bride" in her husband's house, but a guest in ours.
She will enjoy life and sit with her husband: with him she will sing songs.
Four men will together lift her litter, and the wedding party will follow her.
Ambikā saith, "O mother! have patience: this is the way of the world."
(*Seven Grammars,* 140–41)

In northeastern India the village system of arranged marriage is caste endogamous and village exogamous, that is to say, a woman always marries a man of the same caste but from a different village. Hence the women of any village comprise two groups, the daughters of the village *(betī)* and the brides of the village *(bahū).* The many folk songs that describe marriage tell of the sadness of parents at the birth of a daughter, realizing she has come to them for a short time and must leave after her marriage. The marriage of one daughter can cost a life's savings, of several daughters can place the family in debt for generations. When I talked to villagers about the reality of marriage, I began to understand Indian discrimination against women in a new light. Ironically, daughters are believed to be *devī* (goddesses), but how many goddesses can one family serve? Jitka Hertig-Skalická's song collected in Ballia district described the pain of the mother at the birth of her daughter, the wish that she had lost her unborn child rather than given birth to a child who would bring her so much pain of loss:

160 ꕥ
A beautiful girl stepped near the canopy;
[Her] mother was standing in a corner.
[When] the beautiful girl came to the cauk [and] sat down,
[Her mother's] eyes filled with tears:
"If I had known that a daughter would be born in [my] womb,
[I] should have drunk hot pepper."
In the heat of the pepper, [my] daughter would have died,
[And I] should have been spared from the big trouble [of her marriage].
[I] should rather have put out the burning lamp
[And] remained hidden from [my] husband.
[I] should rather have put away the bed that was prepared
[And] remained hidden from [my] husband."
(*Fifty Bhojpuri*, 63)

At marriage, the new bride carries with her the songs of her mother's home to her husband's home. This custom became truly fascinating when I learned that, in each village, families more or less search for husbands in a particular direction, say east. Families expect to find brides in another direction, say north.

"In my village brahmans are supposed to marry wives from the west," Umesh explained. "Lower caste people are supposed to marry from the east. *Teli,* the oil pressers, get their wives from the east. This is a rule we made to keep marriage and to keep respect. I must get respect from my *sasurāl* (father-in-law's home) which is in the west. And I must pay respect to my sister's husband's family which is in the east. My sister's family will never accept a bride from my *sasurāl.* It would disgrace my reputation and I wouldn't let it happen. It would make my *sasurāl* people equal to me. And there would be much difficulty arranging marriages. Also blood would be close. Brahmans pay respect to eastern people because of the marriage system. But the *Teli* respect western people. My bride bring songs to our village from the west, but in other castes those brides brings songs to our village from the east."

Thus it could be thought that folk songs might circulate in particular directions around Uttar Pradesh, and I could picture a map with swirling patterns and arrows. The ethnomusicologist as humanist is tempted to become scientist and to chart the flow of song texts and song tunes.

In interviewing young brides, I learned from some that they were too shy to introduce songs from their *naihar* (mother's home), into the *sasurāl* (husband's home). Other brides felt the quality of singing in their *sasurāl* was inferior to their *naihar* and were eager to introduce their new songs. The most forthright brides were sometimes criticized by their *sas* (mothers-in-law) for doing this. Having discovered an opportunity for applying a scientific theory to the study of music, my travels through the villages seemed to indicate that something more universal and much simpler was happening. Had I spent thousands of dollars only to discover that the bossiest woman with the loudest voice was the one who controlled musical life in the extended family? In part, yes.

℘ Felicity Songs in India

My researches in India helped me to understand and interpret what I had seen and heard in Trinidad, for I found the districts of eastern Uttar Pradesh and western Bihar (Banpurwā, Chapra, Ballia, Mahadewā Dube, Ghazipur, Gorakhpur, Azamgarh, and Mau) which many Trinidadians identify as their ancient homeland. Moon's people were from Ghazipur; the Permanand sisters were from the village of the Dubes east of Anandnagar. I began to see how past traditions could be transmitted from one generation to the next. The village girls hung around me every hour of the day, observing my special interest in *dehatī gīt* (country song), and they listened to the older women singing traditional songs for me to record. They asked me to record them singing filmī songs.

Almost without exception, the Indian women for whom I played the songs from Trinidad easily identified each example, explained its meaning, and in many cases sang the same song for me. Usually the text of the song was similar to that from the West Indies, but often the tune was different. They were insistent that the meaning of the song derives from the words, not the tune (plate 47).

When I sang Felicity tunes for them substituting "la-la-la" for the words, they all laughed; "la-la-la" was no substitute for the important ideas embodied in wedding songs. Thus it was difficult to search for tunes, and women in every village reminded me that the tune, the *tarz,* varied from area to area and wasn't important. It was startling to learn through the slow and painstaking process of recording and interviewing in many Uttar Pradesh villages that the most poignant song texts were identical in every site and identical to those from Felicity ("Father! Father! . . . Mother! Mother! . . ." as the groom applies the *sindūr* to the part of her hair; "How can I give my virgin daughter?" her father cries as he sets her on his knee and gives her to the groom's family).

The mystery of Number One Song persisted throughout my travels, and remains even after eight research visits to India. As our discussions continued over the years, I learned that the metaphors of Number One Song drew on central themes of Indian thought: the pitcher of fertility, the lotus of the heart and of sensuality, the swan of purity and justice. I was gratified that the first song Felicity women taught me proved to be of abiding importance in their lives and also in mine, that its meaning had come from the ages and had persisted in the Old World and the New.

Plate 47. Bhojpurī village women of Banpurwā, U.P., listen to wedding songs from Felicity, 1986.

Archer offers a description of the "wedding pitcher": "brought in by the potter's wife . . . girl's mother takes it into the bridal chamber . . . women smear it with fresh cow dung . . . formally brought out by the barber's wife," but reports no song to accompany its decoration (*Songs*, 26). And a song from Hari S. Upadhyaya's tells the symbolism of the *kalasā* in Bhojpurī song:

161

O daughter-in-law, the pitcher symbolizes your married life and the mangoes symbolize children.
The mangoes symbolize children.
("Joint Family," 267)

For the lotus in Number One Song, Upadhyaya's collection tells:

162

Rama says, "I am like a lotus flower.
Sita and I will enjoy each other."
("Joint Family," 283)

The ritual role of the wedding pitcher and the importance of its decoration is described by Barua for Bihar, from which he cites the following verse:

163 ꩜

Who will tattoo the *kalsa?*
The seven suasins are asleep in the booth.
Who will tattoo the *kalsa?*
The bridegroom's sister is the sugar of love,
She will tattoo the *kalsa.*
(*Folksongs,* 36)

And the *Chāndogya Upanishad* tells: "If someone says to you: 'In the fortified city of the imperishable, our body, there is a lotus and in this lotus a tiny space: what does it contain that one should desire to know it?' You must reply: 'As vast as this space without is the tiny space within your heart: heaven and earth are found in it, fire and air, sun and moon, lightning and the constellations, whatever belongs to you here below and all that doesn't, all this is gathered in that tiny space within your heart'" (VIII, 1, 2–3; plate 48).

That a version of Number One Song was sung in Surinam in the 1960s proves that it was not composed in Felicity. If proof were needed, I had it, since those West Indian variants had to come from a common Indian source, in particular, a song with all these features—the metaphor of a pond and a wedding tent, combined with a story of a sister-in-law's demands for special *neg* gifts to decorate the ritual pitcher (exx. XIX–XX). Arya's 1965 version from Paramaribo, Surinam, had items similar to the ones in my Felicity collection:

Ādhe Marauvā Me

ādhe maṛauvā mē̃ naga cune ādhe me nagini cune re
tabahū̃ na maṛavā suhāvana ek re nanada binā re
ādhe maṛauvā mē̃ gota bāiṭhe ādhe mē̃ gotini bāiṭhe re
are tabahū̃ na maṛavā suhāvana eka re nanada binā re
bāhar se bhaiyā bhītar bhaile bhaujī se mati karē̃ re
dhana āvata bāṭī̃ bābā de dulārī ghara bhajini boleo re
āvo na nanadī gotāina more ṭhakurāin re
nanada bāiṭho na mā̃jhe maṛauvā kalasa hamare goṭhāu re
bhāuji kalasa gothāunī kāhū dehihau kalasa tohare gū̃ṭhaba re
devai maī̃ hāthe ke munariyā are gale bhara tilariyā ho re
nanadoiyā ke caṛhane ke ghuṛavā caṛha usi gharavā jāiho re
(*Ritual,* 74–75)

164 ꩜

Under half the wedding tent jewels are inlaid [perhaps male cobra pecking] and under the other half semi-precious stones are inlaid [perhaps female cobra pecking];

Plate 48. Rādhā gathering *purain* (lotus) flowers. Rāgamāla miniature, detail. (Bundi Rajasthani, 18th century. Prince of Wales Museum, Bombay)

Even then, without (that) one, the *nanad,* the *māṛo* does not appear attractive.
Under half the wedding tent are sitting the kinsmen and under the other half are sitting the kinswomen;
Even then without (that) one, the *nanad,* the *māṛo* does not appear attractive.
The brother (of the bride) went inside from outside and is discussing with the *bhāujī.*
The precious darling of (her) father is just coming—said the *bhāujī* in the house.
Come (won't you?), oh *nanad,* (my) kinswoman, my duchess!
Nanad, sit (won't you?), in the centre of the *māṛo* and tie up my pitcher.
Bhāujī, what would you pay me (as the fees) for the *kalasa guṭhaunī*?
(Tell me and) I will tie your pitcher.
I shall give (you) a finger-ring (for your) hand and a three-string necklace to (adorn your) neck.
For the *nanadōī* I will give a horse to ride which you will mount (with him and) go to his home.
(*Ritual,* 74–75)

As I worked on and on in India, season after season, I hoped to hear the familiar lines of my Number One Song. The harder I searched for this single item, the more I learned about Bhojpurī music. Men volunteered to sing *birahā* (lively topical songs, lasting up to an hour), long since vanished from Trinidad. In other villages, men organized sessions to perform improvised compositions based on passages from the *Rāmāyaṇ.* Umesh arranged for me to take lessons on the *ḍholak* to help me understand *chachar* and *dīpchandī tāl* as they are rendered in the folk songs I had collected in Felicity. Still I was waiting for my song, and even Umesh started pestering villagers about swan songs and snake songs. "Swans swallow pearls," he said. "You people should sing about them."

"I haven't seen any swans here," I said.

"We don't get swans in U.P.," Umesh answered.

After my fourth visit to India, I announced to my family that I would die from happiness if I could find Number One Song. "You'll see. Like Shakespeare, 'I will play the swan and die in the music.'" Several more visits passed.

In 1988, the Bombay *Sunday Mid-Day* newspaper (18 September) offered the following description of me: "One Bhojpurī song about a pond that is half full of lotus brought Dr. Helen Myers, an ethnomusicologist, halfway around the world, to India. And took her to the villages of eastern Uttar Pradesh and western Bihar where she had to give up her jeans and shirt, don a sari, *bindī,* bangles, and *jūdā* before she could vibe with the residents on the origins of their music." This was the introduction of a report by Veena Gokhale on a lecture I had given at the National Centre for the Performing Arts in Bombay. She went on to quote me: "As the train sped through north India, I saw lotus

Plate 49. Pond alongside the road from Mahadewā Dube to Anandnagar, half with flowering *purain,* and half without, 1986.

ponds just like the one mentioned in this song sung during the *hardī* ceremony, which had so aroused my curiosity in Trinidad" (plate 49).

By the summer of 1990 I had reached the remote interior town of Mau. My fever had begun on the journey and with it a lightheadedness and giddy abandon. As we passed through the lanes of the town I began to see ladies dressed in the antique *lahar pator* skirts and heavy blouses mentioned in Number One Song. They wore the heavy ornaments I had seen in pictures of the original Felicity Coolie women. Wasn't that the *ghorā,* the horse for *nanad's* husband to ride happily home?

The ladies of Mau were particularly shy, particularly "backward." As if we had stepped back into time, Umesh and I began work afresh. I sat on the curb, at one with the heat of midday, and sang to a lady wearing olden dress. "*Sānkara koriyā baharo ho pandita rāmā.*" And the crowds gathered again. . . .

After five days in Mau, the fever rose, and the ladies crowded round and rubbed oil into my hair. I fell seriously ill and had to try to get back to Delhi.

And I had to go home. "After many a summer dies the swan." It seemed as if the search for Number One Song was finally over.

ꙮ

"In India I know I am a stranger; but increasingly I understand that my Indian memories, the memories of that India which lived on into my childhood in Trinidad, are like trapdoors into a bottomless past" (Naipaul, *India,* xi).

Trapdoors

Upon reflection, I questioned whether Number One Song could be engulfed unrecognized in a transformed state in my collection. In fact I had found a whole world of music that spoke to the question of Number One Song. In Gorakhpur, one family of the Dubes sang a song which described a pond that is half lotus and half cobras (ex. XXXV). The women of one Dube family told me that Moon's song and the Permanands's song and their song were all the same, but sung to different *tarz* ("tunes"). The text of each version deals with a pond, with either a male and female swan, or with a male and female snake. One family of Dube women sang:

165
Wedding tent full all people and all female relatives.
Wedding tent full all people and all female relatives.
Wedding tent full all people and all female relatives.
Wedding tent full all people and all female relatives.
Even then not wedding tent beautiful look one brother-in-law without.
Even then not wedding tent beautiful look one brother-in-law without.
Even then not wedding tent beautiful look one brother-in-law without.
Even then not wedding tent beautiful look one brother-in-law without.
Pond full of male cobras and all female cobras.
Pond full of male cobras and all female cobras.
Even then pond not beautiful look one female swan without.
Even then pond not beautiful look one female swan without.
Even then pond not beautiful look one female swan without.
Even then pond not beautiful look one female swan without.
Even then pond not beautiful look one female swan without.
At river bank broken bridegroom calls.
At river bank broken bridegroom calls.
What father not father not cry to feel?
What father not father not cry to feel?
Neither home boat nor home boatman.
Neither home boat nor home boatman.
To whom sacred thread of wish give?
To whom sacred thread of wish give?

Example XXXV (song 166, CD track 29): Talawā Bharla Saba Nāga

Get wet body of parts heart of sandalwood.
Get wet body of parts heart of sandalwood.
Get wet all sixteen ornaments sacred thread of.
Get wet all sixteen ornaments sacred thread of.

This song, including a metaphor with both snakes and swans and the wedding tent, suggested that an old and original Number One Song had included all the details I had heard in the modern versions. The women of another Dube family, sang this version of Number One Song:

Example XXXV
Talawā Bharla Saba Nāga

talawā bharla saba nāga ta abaru nāginī saba
talawā bharla saba nāga ta abaru nāginī saba
tabahū na talawā sohāwana eka kare kewala bina
tabahū na talawā sohāwana eka kare kewala bina
tabahū na talawā sohāwana eka kare kewala bina
tabahū na talawā sohāwana eka kare kewala bina
maṛawā bharatā sabhagowa ta abaru gotinī saba
maṛawā bharatā sabhagowa ta abaru gotinī saba
tabahū na maṛawā sohāwana ekare bahinī bina
tabahū na maṛawā sohāwana ekare bahinī bina
tabahū na maṛawā sohāwana ekare bahanoiyā bina
tabahū na maṛawā sohāwana ekare bahanoiyā bina
ghuṛawana ayelẽ kawana rāma, ṛaḍhiyā kawanī deī
ghuṛawana ayelẽ kawana rāma, ṛaḍhiyā kawanī deī
chote ghoṛa ayelẽ horilawā maṛauā roshiāwana
chote ghoṛa ayelẽ horilawā maṛauā roshiāwana

chote ghoṛa ayelẽ horilawā maṛauā roshiāwana
chote ghoṛa ayelẽ horilawā maṛauā roshiāwana

166 ♫
Pond full all male cobra and female cobra all.
Pond full all male cobra and female cobra all.
Even then not pond beautiful one of the lotus without.
Even then not pond beautiful one of the lotus without.
Even then not pond beautiful one of the lotus without.
Even then not pond beautiful one of the lotus without.
Tent full all family and female friends all.
Tent full all family and female friends all.
Even then not tent beautiful one of sister without.
Even then not tent beautiful one of sister without.
Even then tent not beautiful one of brother-in-law without.
Even then assembly not beautiful one of brother-in-law without.
Horse on comes Rām, on palanquin bride.
Horse on comes Rām, on palanquin bride.
On small horse comes son, tent looks pleasant.
On small horse comes son, tent looks pleasant.
On small horse comes son, tent looks pleasant.
On small horse comes son, tent looks pleasant.

Each described the beautiful flowers of the lotus, and each draws an analogy between the halves of the pond and the two sides of the wedding—the *naihar* and the *sasurāl.* The narrative of the Dube version ends with the arrival of the groom's party, whereas the narrative of the Felicity songs continue and describe conflict between the two sisters-in-law.

The melodies of the Dube examples pose other questions. The simple melody of the Dube example (ex. XXXV) appears to be based on the opening melodic motif of the *antarā* phrase of the Permanand version, followed by a descending line. However, this smooth undulating melodic quality is common in most Bhojpurī women's songs.

The collection of Bhojpurī folk songs from Ballia district by Jitka Hertig-Skalická held a clue, an item with the opening metaphor of a pond and lotus flowers trembling as the bridegroom washed his clothes. "To whom are you near and dear, the bride asks?":

167 ♫
In [my] father's pond behind [my] house,
Lotus [*puraini*] flowers are trembling
[And] bridegroom is there washing [his] dhoti.
Bride asks [him]:
"To whom are [you] near and dear?

To what sister [are you] the brother?
For what purpose have [you] come, beautiful boy?
In whose pond have [you just] bathed?"
"I am near and dear to [my] father,
[I am] the brother of. . . .
Beautiful girl, I have come [here] for the purpose of marriage.
[I] have [just] bathed in [my] father-in-law's pond."
When bride heard these words,
She calls: "Sister-in-law, sister-in-law!
Are [you] outdoors or inside, o sister-in-law?
Listen to my words, sister-in-law!
The bridegroom [my] father was looking for in the country has just bathed in [our] pond."
"Come in, brother-in-law, sit down on the bed [and] eat [this] bundle of Magahi betel!
[Then] get a palanquin ready outside the town [and] take my enemy away [from here]!"
"Sister-in-law, do not [ever] call her [your] enemy!
[This] enemy is the dearest one of [my] life.
[It is] only because of this enemy [that] I have come to your town."
(*Fifty Bhojpuri*, 48–49)

In villages around Banaras women told me that the song with swans was a *sohar* (childbirth song) and not a wedding song. I recalled the swan *sohar* that Moon had sung for me in Trinidad:

168 ♫
Male swan female swan both of them pond at trouble in.
Son scarce water fish, scarce shrimp fish.
Oh, son scarce pond fish, scarce shrimp fish.
Son scarce water fish, scarce shrimp fish.
White blue both sisters, both ladies sad are.
Son scarce lady to son, scarce *sohar* are.
Son scarce lady to son, scarce *sohar* are.
Drizzling clouds rain.
Son jumping water fish, spread all around shrimp.
Oh, son jumping pond fish, spread all around shrimp.
Early morning a ray of light, son born.
Son, husband my gone flower garden, *sohar* who will listen?
Son, husband my gone flower garden, *sohar* who will listen?

In Ballia and adjacent areas, they sang about a greedy *nanad,* her ceremonial function in a wedding, and the angry wife. None of these songs in Uttar Pradesh used the tune from Felicity. But in Azamgarh, a hermaphrodite singer with unusual musical talent remembered this tune. He sang it to "la-la-la" and drifted in and out of snatches of text. He wept and told me that old tune came from a bygone and happier time when people had been kind to him. Even after many weeks, though, he was unable to relate this tune to a text.

This simple example (a single song) poses for ethnomusicologists many questions. I believe that the Trinidad version is very old and has been faithfully passed down in oral tradition to modern times, what we call a marginal survival. In India it seems that the metaphor of swans, lotus, and the wedding tent has been truncated and detached from the body of the narrative. The popular tune from Felicity does not go with this text in the villages I happened to visit. But in all the villages men told me about the difficult relationship of *nanad* and *bhaujī*.

A tune here, lines of text there. Had Number One Song been caught up in the swirls and arrows of my map and been scattered around the Bhojpurī region? And wasn't this, after all, the classic definition of a true folk song—that it exists only in a state of continual transformation? Focusing thus on a single song had been a method for formulating theory about the powerful role of music.

ঌ

"On the day when the lotus bloomed, alas, my mind was straying, and I knew it not. My basket was empty and the flower remained unheeded. . . . / I knew not then that it was so near, that it was mine, and that this perfect sweetness had blossomed in the depth of my own heart" (Tagore, *Gītāñjalī*, 20).

ঌ UMESH

"And Umesh," I asked, "after hearing the songs of Felicity what do you think about your West Indian cousins?"

"I feel hearing their music they are happy. Slowly slowly they are losing their own language, but certainly they're becoming more Indian because they are more religious than people in India usually are."

"Why do you think they remembered so many old songs?"

"Songs are a treasure for them. They had those songs with them and they wanted to keep what they had. They feared they might be changed if they forgot their songs. Far away from the country of their origin, they kept the old songs alive to support their wedding and religious traditions. For me they are wise and brave people, living in different circumstances on the other side of the world. Yet they kept their thoughts and their being. It was not possible. And they did it."

"And now since you have heard all these songs from Felicity," I asked, "and also traveled with me through eastern Uttar Pradesh, searching for Number One Song from place to place, and now that you have visited great countries of the West—England, Sweden, and the United States, and now on the eve of your departure for India, what can you tell me about music?"

"Helen, I have been prepared for your final question. Here is your farewell gift, the eleven truths of music. If you believe in God, they are true."

The Eleven Truths of Music
Umesh Pandey

1. Music and dance are the sixteenth and last art of God; their practice is the philosophy of love and God.
2. The world was born with the sound of music.
3. People believe that music is the language of the world.
4. Music is life.
5. The world is lonely without music.
6. Music provides peace and power to our mind and our soul.
7. Music purifies our mind and our soul.
8. There is an unbreakable relationship between music and love.
9. History bears witness that in any age whenever music receives the proper place in society and in the nation, man receives unexpected progress and social welfare.
10. It is easy and quick to learn any subject through music.
11. The notes of music play on the strings of the mind and, revealing new thoughts, they give the actual feelings of sadness and pleasure, and continuously light our life.

Return to Felicity

While I had been searching for the roots of Felicity tradition in India—preoccupied with the past—my Felicity friends were pressing on with new musical developments. I hardly recognized the changing scene when my son Ian and I arrived in 1990.

On the plane we talked about Trinidad. "Felicity is unusual," I explained, "in that it is inhabited not by West Indians—the African derived peoples of the Caribbean—but by a group that calls itself 'East Indian.'"

"Indonesian?" Ian asked.

"No," I replied. "I hate Columbus for that mix up!"

"These Indians were originally known as the 'Gladstone Coolies,'" I said. "They served as indentured laborers on the island's sugar plantations. You're going to be surrounded by the cane. Felicity lies midway along the road leading west from the market town of Chaguanas to the cane fields and the sea. In this village you will find sights and sounds that transport you to an Asian world. But you will understand Felicity since you have been raised in England. Theirs is the world of the BBC external services and of relaxed afternoons in the shade, listening to the cricket test match from Islamabad or Melbourne or

Lord's, the world that hears the Queen's Christmas message and watches Commonwealth Games, the world of Paddington Bear."

"I thought everyone knew about Paddington Bear."

"Not in the States."

"Oh."

During his stay, Ian read Mesho's entire *World Book Encyclopedia,* dozens of Enid Blyton children's classics, and my doctoral thesis—on display in the new study Mesho had built in his house. Ian learned that the oldest music was the Bhojpurī repertory—songs that originated in northeastern India and have been passed on in oral tradition. He read two versions of my Number One Song and hoped to find a snake—or a swan.

Matti and I took Ian to Chaguanas, where we bought him two school uniforms—khaki shorts and sky-blue shirts. From the first day of school onward he was known as "White Boy" (plate 50).

One afternoon Mesho asked me to set up my Stellavox tape recorder and

Plate 50. "White Boy" Ian begins the day in the back row of the fourth form, Felicity Hindu School, 1990.

good microphones for a special surprise. After school his living room filled with girls from the primary school and they sang for me a series of the old Bhojpurī wedding songs. They illustrated the meanings with hand gestures the older women had taught them. They had just won the island-wide competition for "village folk song." I do not believe that this revival was influenced by my intensive study of this material over the last twenty years, but Mesho knew I would be pleased, and I was.

After Easter, Ian returned home, suntanned and effervescent. His handwriting had improved enormously, and he was ahead in math. He had learned the Hindi vowels in Devanagari script and could sing over a dozen *bhajan.* He had seen the scarlet ibis in their mangrove nesting ground, gone swimming at Mayaro, and eaten lunch most days with the shopkeeper's daughter Michelle, the "Chīnī" girl.

He held the drake for Matti, before she slaughtered it for dinner that night (Ian told me, "I stroked him, and that night I didn't eat him."). He had been in line for "licks" from the teacher for talking in class, but White Boy got off at the very last moment: "We don't want to send you back with red skin!"

Indeed all the girls at the Hindu school fancied Ian, and gave him Valentines in February and, when he was about to leave, cards and presents including a home-made plaster-of-Paris map of Trinidad rendered to show his horoscope sign, Gemini. On his last day they danced in school and later the shy girl wrote him a note asking for a dance next time.

"By the way," Mesho asked me, "did you find that favorite song of yours in India?"

"Well, not really," I replied. "That's what I've been saying. You Felicity people have some very rare songs."

"Well you will need to buy some new *chutney* this time," he replied. And we headed off for the Chaguanas market.

ꕤ Mesho

January 1995: "Maa, Maa, it's me!" Ian shouted down the phone.

"So how is you? You've gone low in the voice."

"I'm in high school Maa, and we went to London. Our house burnt down in London. And Adam broke his arm in London and it was serious. And Sean broke his arm last month. But that was not serious. Mummy has been sick, but she is okay."

"So really you all well then. That is okay."

"Mummy is here too. She wants to talk to you and Mesho and everybody."

"Is everybody okay there?"

"We all well here."

"So, old man how is it?" I asked. "We made our twenty-one years now you know. I saw you first twenty-one years ago in July."

"Twenty-one years. Hard to believe. I retired, but not old you know. Four miles per day I does walk and Maa one-and-a-half."

"So how are the children?"

"Choko, he has a baby boy, and Daughter she took training and is in hospital administration, and Boyee, well he still have the same bank job, and Dabin, he is a dentist now. He made it to doctor."

"Hard to believe. We got old together."

"I tell you I ain old now yet."

"I feel old. I got really sick in India. You recover from India fever but never your full health. You people, I mean your ancestors, they really had the right idea to come out and stay out. They were courageous. I've seen all those places in Bhojpur, those little thatched mud houses. It's impossible to get pure water, hard to get vegetables or fruit."

"I'm working on the kitchen garden these days."

"Vegetables, that's good for you. Indian families don't always get them every day you know. And they're vegetarians."

"Did you get to see Sai Baba yet, Helen?"

"No, I didn't go there yet."

"Well, now my friend here, he went to Mysore, to Datta Treya."

"What about Kanchan? She still coming?" I asked.

Mesho laughed when I asked him about the 1994 *chutney* season. "These are for the younger boys. I can't stay with all this *chutney* any more, Helen. You know I am more on the devotional side, the *Rāmāyaṇ*. As time passes this is what there is—worship. We are talking about Datta Treya."

"And now since Choko had his first son, you are an *ājā* [grandfather]. What is that like?"

"Well, there is something really charming about it, you know. He is Kaveer, two years now. But since I retired I want to tell my story, from birth, boyhood, and married life, about my years living behind the temple with the Swami. There's some difficult and complicated episodes, but I want to tell them."

"We always agreed that we would do this. You tell and I will write. I didn't forget anything that happened to us—all of us these last years. I'll get it down on paper for you.

"You know most of those older heads have passed away now," I said. "Moon, she died in '75. And Popo is gone, and Rajiah as well. And Charran and Bridglal. And Siewrajiah?" I asked.

"Passed away."

"And the Permanand sisters, I'm afraid they are gone."

"Dhanpatee and Kalawatee gone as well you know."

"So are any of them left who can sing those old songs?"

"There be a few."

"And the Swami?"

"Well he did pass away since one year, you know."

"And his Divine Life Society Ashram?"

"Well, they still keep it there, but nothing going on so much any more. Seem to me like you old and me young. Here, Sailor want to say greetings."

"Is that you?" I hollered. "How you doing Sailor! Old man doesn't want to tell me about Kanchan."

"Can't complain. Going good girl."

"So Mesho can't say anything about *chutney.* What do you say? Is Sundar Popo still the main man?"

"We don't hear him so much these days. But local is in. We have quite a few. You know Christmas is *chutney* time, and this year we just had Surindra from St. Augustine. Top song in the charts is "Bombay Ka Dolahin" ["Bombay Bride"]. In the song he in Trinidad and he want she to come from India to Trinidad. You know Bombay?"

"Yeah," I said [I was remembering the hutments]. "I taught there."

The journey to the interior of Bhojpur had taken me back and as far away from their present lives as they themselves were from their heritage and they, they had moved forward. Now I had more information about Number One Song than the Felicity singers did, but it didn't matter. It was theirs; it had never belonged to me.

Mesho came back on the phone.

"I'm coming to see you in Connecticut."

"That's great Mesho. I'll be happy to see you here."

❦

"Shall I say it again? In order to arrive there, / To arrive where you are, to get from where you are not, / You must go by a way wherein there is no ecstasy. / In order to arrive at what you do not know / You must go by a way which is the way of ignorance. / In order to possess what you do not possess / You must go by the way of dispossession. / In order to arrive at what you are not / You must go through the way in which you are not. / And what you do not know is the only thing you know / And what you own is what you do not own / And where you are is where you are not." (Eliot)

ஜ

When we met, I had set my goal to discover Number One Song in its original home, and I had suffered much in the search. Mesho, the humanitarian, now set for himself a kinder, simpler goal, to discover Number One Ethnomusicologist in her original home. I wanted to say to him:

"I left you people to discover your past. I wish some days I had not made that journey backward in time. And all the while, you people were moving forward, with jump-up and soca, *chutney,* Sundar Popo and Kanchan—new things from the New World. And you sent your children off for schooling in Canada and England and Florida. I sank in the depths of the caste system and met brahmans who could not escape from the darkness of their dreams, from the inevitability of the *Gītā*'s lessons of duty, to save your brother or destroy your brother as it is foretold, on the battlefield of Kurūchhetra, and will unfold in the future according to your actions. *Dharma,* belief, and *karma,* fate.

"I left you people for a while in order to understand you. But now you must pull me back from your own veiled past that I had longed to see. The price of understanding your history has proved a heavy burden: I did not know this in the beginning when Number One Song caught my ear.

"Now we can work on your book up here, I thought. Maybe that will cure me from this Indian burden. You folks have hope. I passed too many days in the villages of your cousins. Well, they are not progressing there in the sense that we understand. The rules of Hinduism have trapped them in an ancient time and place, but ironically the rules of Hinduism are the only salvation from the punishment of Indian clime and time.

"Yet certain Indians were able to become and remain Coolies in the New World. I had thought it was their bad luck, but now I see that it was their good fortune, but a fate that could only be realized after generations. In order to learn of your past, I had to leave you folks for a while. I missed Daughter's and Choko's weddings, Dabin's graduation. I'm sorry for missing those happy days with you and Maa. I was deep in India, lost in India at the time.

"And I have learned that the social messages buried in those lovely old wedding songs do not belong in the life of Trinidad today; the instructions given in these songs must go. You have preserved the important religious feelings and symbolism, but those prescriptions, that still hold in the Indian villages of your ancestors, are not for Trinidad today. 'A hundred years had been enough to wash me clean of many Indian religious attitudes; and without these attitudes the distress of India was—and is—almost insupportable' (Naipaul, *India,* ix).

"And what for you, Mesho, was this 'Chīnītāt,' this Trinidad? After crossing the seven seas, your ancestors arrived at a beautiful place, according to your wish, your imagination. I have learned that for you this 'Chīnītāt,' this Trinidad, has been the land of opportunity."

ꕥ

"If thou didst ever hold me in thy heart, / Absent thee from Felicity a while, / And in this harsh world draw thy breath in pain, To tell my story."

ꕥ SINGING MY DAYS

The essential question I had hoped to answer, was why? Why was music important in Felicity village? I could see that music was essential for their religious rites, for events of the life cycle, and for entertainment. It was also an effective way of teaching children Indian language and religion. It was a symbol of Indian life, to hold up to the Creole population of Trinidad and to the world. But these were not the answers the villagers gave me.

"Why sing?" I had asked Brahmchārī Karma.

"They say that, you know, when you sing and you clap, you destroy all the past *karmas.* You beat them off."

"Why sing?" I had asked Kedar Pandit.

"If music has got in it what Shakespeare said, 'if music be the food of love, then play on,' right?"

"Why sing?" I had asked Kalawatee.

"The feeling is there," she replied. "I sing to my feelings—if I was in the person's place how I would feel."

"Why sing?" I had asked Dhanpatee.

"Well this is the world. This is nature. This is what really is."

"Why sing?" I had asked Popo.

"Like to sing," she replied, "and fête naa. I like to sing and fête. Enjoy yourself to live. Nice, I feel nice."

"Why sing?" I had asked Siewrajiah.

"Who could afford to have music make it more beautiful, more pleasure, more happiness."

"Why sing?" I had asked Moon.

"You know how she like singing?" her daughter replied. "If it have a wedding anywhere, she want to go and sing, you know."

"I feel I should get more young," Moon said, "only just for singing's sake."

Glossary, Biographical Dictionary, and Gazetteer

abīr Red-colored liquid, also powder, thrown in abandonment during the springtime Hindu Phāgwā (Holī) festival.
ãchara [Bhoj., ãncharwā] Breast.
Agni Vedic god of fire.
amrit Sacred nectar.
ãnchal [Bhoj., ãchalwā] End of the sari, veil.
antarā In Indian classical music, the consequent phrase of a melody.
arkatiā [arkati, arkattie, arkat] Agent, middleman.
ārtī In Hinduism, the offering of a flame to an icon or honored person.
Arya Samaj Hindu reformist organization. Believers reject the modern caste system and religious works written after the ancient Sanskrit Vedas.
ashram Hindu religious school, community.
aum [om] For Hindus, a holy syllable encompassing all sounds of the universe.
bābā Father, old man, priest or holy man, powerful and possibly dangerous man.
Ballia District and district town of eastern Uttar Pradesh.
Ban From the *Rāmāyaṇ,* the forest into which Rām and Sītā were exiled.
Banaras [Benares, Varanasi; archaic Kashi] In Uttar Pradesh, crowded city of considerable culture and antiquity on the banks of the River Ganges. Considered holy by Hindu faithful.
barahī Women's celebration, twelve days after the birth of a child.
bass Large double-headed cylindrical drum played in Trinidad with *tāssā* drums.
Bhādõ Month of the Hindu calendar, usually in August.
bhagwān [Trinidad, bhagawaana] For Hindus, a term for God.
bhāgwat [Trinidad, bhaagawata, bhagawān] Hindu religious observance lasting several days.
bhajan Hindu devotional song.
bhaktī In Hinduism, the worship of God through music, love, and ecstasy.
bhāng Festival drink made of *cannabis,* shared by men in the springtime Phāguā celebration.
Bhārat Hindi name for India.
Bharat Sevashram Sangha Hindu missionary organization based in Calcutta.
Bhojpurī A vernacular language of northeastern India, spoken by some eight million and extending approximately from Banaras to the west and Patna to the east.
Bihar Poor and arid state of western India, situated between Uttar Pradesh and Bengal.
birahā Long topical men's songs of Uttar Pradesh and Trinidad.
byāh ke gīt [Trinidad Bhoj.] Wedding song.
Cacandee The main road through Felicity, also the most fashionable district of the village. *See also* Kakandi
Caroni County of central Trinidad in which Felicity is located.

Casacu Felicity district near the Cunupia River. Considered unfashionable.
Chaguanas Market town east of Felicity.
Chamār [Hindi, Bhoj.] Lowest of the four Hindu *varna* (social and occupational categories, castes or, as they are known as in Trinidad "nations").
chatī Celebration held six days after the birth of a child.
chautāl [Trinidad, chowtal] Men's festive songs for the springtime Holī season.
Chīnītāt [Bhoj.] Nineteenth-century Coolie name for Trinidad.
chutney Hot sauce. Hot, spicy songs in traditional Bhojpurī culture. Since the 1980s in Trinidad, lively sexy dance songs, "Indian soca."
darshan A view, sight of a venerated saint; a vision.
dev A god.
ḍhantāl Obsolete in India, an instrument once used to accompany *birahā*. In Felicity, this meter-long iron rod (struck rhythmically with a U-shaped beater) is used to accompany many types of songs. Fine example of a marginal survival in Felicity Bhojpurī culture.
ḍholak Double-headed barrel drum used to accompany folk song in Trinidad and north Indian villages.
dhoti In north India, five yards of cotton wrapped and tied so as to fashion trousers for men. Also, the term for a simple cotton sari worn by village women.
dhun Repetitive Hindu devotional song or chant. Also tune.
Divine Life Society Hindu reformist organization founded in Trinidad in the 1960s by Swami Satchidananda.
Diwālī [Divālī] The Hindu festival of lights, held around November.
diyā [Trinidad Bhoj., deya] Miniature primitive clay lamp with twisted cotton wick.
filmī gīt Popular Indian film songs.
gamak In Indian classical music, ornaments, embellishments to the main melody notes.
Ganesh The Hindu elephant-headed god of wisdom and luck.
Ganges [Ganga, Gangamai, Gangaji] The most holy of India's rivers, flowing from her source in the Himalayan Mountains to Allahabad where she joins the Jamuna River and they continue eastward as the Ganges to the delta surrounding Calcutta. The Gangeatic plain is the bread basket of north India and was the source of indentured Coolie labor in the nineteenth century.
Ghazipur District, also district town, in eastern Uttar Pradesh, India.
ghee Clarified butter.
gopī Milkmaids, lovers of Lord Krishna.
Gorakhpur District, also district town, in northeastern Uttar Pradesh, near the Nepal border.
Grierson, Sir George (1851-1941) Irish civil servant in India. Linguist of distinction.
gudanā Song to accompanying tattooing.
hand In Trinidad, term for drum pattern for the *tāssā* or *ḍholak*.
hansā/hansin Male swan/female swan.
Hanumān From the *Rāmāyaṇ*, a devotee of Rām, the monkey leader of the monkey army that rescued Sītā from Lankā.
hardī [haldī] Vermilion, used as a cooking spice; also for ceremonial purposes in the Hindu wedding.

harmonium Portable keyboard instrument controversial in India because it produces inflexible pitches of equal temperament. Popular in Trinidad to accompany both *bhajan,* classical, and popular songs.

havan [hawan] Ancient Vedic ceremony centered on a sacrificial fire.

Hindi calypso In Trinidad, song using calypso style but incorporating Hindi words.

Holikā Demon after which the the Hindu springtime Holī or Phāguā festival takes its name.

honkie Derogatory term for a white person.

idiophone Musical instrument whose sound is produced by the vibrations of the body of the instrument; a "self-sounder"; the most common type of instrument around the world. Examples from Trinidad include the *ḍhantāl, jhāl, manjīrā,* and *kartāl.*

jahāj Ship.

jal Holy water.

jal tarang ["water wave," "vibration"] In Indian classical music, a set of more than a dozen china bowls each filled with exact amounts of water, so as to be tuned to a *rāg.*

Janamāshhtāmī The birthday of Lord Krishna, celebrated on the 8th day of the first half of the Hindu month of Bhādõ, usually in August.

Jangli Tola ["jungle district"] Westernmost district of Felicity, "in the back"; less fashionable than Cacandee.

jhāl Brass cymbals approximately 10 inches in diameter. Played with the *tāssā* and bass.

jhanḍī Hindu prayer flag.

jhīl Lake.

-ji An honorific suffix.

kaharwā North Indian *tāl* with eight beats.

kajarī [kajalī, "dark eyes"] Romantic women's songs for the rainy season, Sāwan (July–August), north India.

Kakandi First settler of Felicity. Now spelled "Cacandee."

kālāpānī ["black water"] Sea crossing resulting in banishment, loss of caste.

kāmdev God of love and sex.

Kanchan Popular singer from Bombay, India, well known in Felicity for her concert tours beginning in 1969, and particularly for her arrangements of local African and East Indian compositions.

Karimganj [Karimpur] Village in western Uttar Pradesh near Agra. Home of Umesh.

karma Action, work, also consequences of action, fate.

kartāl ["hand tune"] In Felicity, clappers with disk-shaped jingles.

kathā ["story," "narration"] Religous celebration *(pūjā)* including scriptural exposition by the officiating pandit.

khyāl In Indian classical music, an important classical vocal form.

Kingsley, Charles (1819–75) Anglican clergyman and novelist. Nineteenth-century visitor to Trinidad and author of *At Last, Christmas in the West Indies.*

kīrtan Hindu devotional song or song session.

lachārī Saucy women's songs for weddings and childbirth celebrations, sung both in Felicity and in Bhojpur.

Lakshmaṇ From the *Rāmāyaṇ,* younger brother to Rām, son of King Dasarath.
lāwā [lāvā] Popped rice. Also Bhojpurī wedding ritual involving popped rice.
lime [Creole] Chat, gossip, pass time.
lotā Brass or steel pot (approx. one pint capacity) with a waisted neck.
Māhābhārata Ancient epic of north India.
Mahadewā Dube In Gorakhpur district, west of Anandnagar, the ancestral Bhojpurī village of V. S. Naipaul.
Maharajh [Maharaj, "great king"] In Felicity, a surname indicating a member of the brahman nation (caste).
manjīrā [Trinidad Bhoj., manjeera, majera, majira] Finger cymbals used for song accompaniment.
Marīch Mythical king of Mauritius, told of in the *Rāmāyaṇ* epic. *See also* Mauritius.
Mastana Bahaar Weekly Trinidad television program featuring local East Indian talent.
Mauritius [19th century, also Mirich, Morisu, Marīch] Island of the Indian Ocean, 500 miles east of Madagascar. The first indentured Coolie laborers were taken there by the British beginning in 1835.
Merchant Soca artist Denis Williams.
Mukesh Popular Indian filmī playback singer.
nāg/nāginī Male cobra/female cobra.
nagārā Kettledrum of Trinidad. Derived from India and cognate with kindred Islamic instruments played from Spain to Indonesia.
naihar [archaic Bhoj.; in Hindi, *maica,* "of the mother"] The home and the village of one's birth.
Naipaul, Vidiadhar Surajprasad (b. 1932) Renowned East Indian novelist from Trinidad. Educated in England. Grandson of Kapil Dev and nephew of Dhanpatee and Kalawatee Permanand.
nation In Trinidad, term for Hindu caste and *varna.*
Number One Song Antique Bhojpurī wedding song, the object of Helen's search.
pan Steel drum.
Panchwatī [Panchvatī; "five trees"] From the *Rāmāyaṇ,* the forest in which Rām and Sītā were exiled.
Peter's Field Southernmost district of Felicity near the junction with the main road to Chaguanas. A few Afro-Trinidadian families live in Peter's Field.
Phāguā [Phaguwa; Trinidad, Phagwa] In Felicity, a springtime festival celebrated in the month of Phāgun. In India this festival is usually referred to as Holī.
Phāgun In the Hindu lunar calendar, springtime month, usually around March.
pitch In Trinidad, term for game of marbles.
play [English; Hindi, Bhoj., līlā] A drama or story such as *Rāmlīlā,* the story of Rām enacted by villagers every year. Also **playful** such as the tradition of throwing colored powders, *abīr,* during the springtime Holī, or Phāguā, festival. Also metaphoric as in "All the world's a play."
pot hound Common village mongrel dog. "Bawling" pot hounds can be heard on CD tracks 14 and 21.
prasād Blessed sweet food offered to the deity and then distributed to the congregation after *pūjā.* In Felicity, a sweet, mushy combination of *ghee,* flour, sugar, and raisins fried in an enormous iron pot.

pūjā Hindu worship service.
Purāṇa [“ancient”] Hindu scriptures telling of the creation and destruction of the universe, the genealogy of gods, sages, and earthly kings. The ninth-century *Bhāgawata Pūraṇa* tells the often-sung love expoits of Lord Krishna.
Pushhpakvimān From the *Rāmāyaṇ,* the mythical swan plane of the ten-mouthed demon Rāwaṇ.
rāg [Sanskrit rāgā; English, raga; Trinidad, raaga, raag, raga] Indian modal system.
Rām [Trinidad, Raama, Rama] Believed by Hindus to be the incarnation of Lord Vishnu.
Rāmāyaṇ The story of Rām, one of the two great epics of India.
Rāmcharitmānas [“The Lake of the Acts of Rām”] The life of Rām as written in the vernacular Awadhī by the seventeenth-century poet, Goswami Tulsī Dās, ca. 1574–77. Much influenced by the *Bhāgawata Pūraṇa,* most beloved of the *Rāmāyaṇ* versions, and well known in Trinidad, it expresses with eloquence the Hindu sentiment of *bhaktī* (devotion through love).
Rāmlīlā A play held to celebrate the birth of Rām.
Rāwaṇ [Rāvaṇ] From the *Rāmāyaṇ,* demon king of Lankā.
rupee [rupai] Currency unit of India, also generic term for money.
Sai Baba Twentieth-century Hindu saint believed to be an incarnation of Shiva.
sanḍhyā Period of worship at the change of light—dawn, noon, and dusk. In Trinidad, ceremony based on Vedic mantras and published in several prayer books.
saptak In Indian classical music, an octave.
sāraṇgī Bowed fiddle of Indian folk and classical music. Played in the nineteenth century in Trinidad, but rarely heard in the 1990s.
Saraswatī Goddess of wisdom and music, typically portrayed playing a *vīṇā* and riding a swan.
sasurāl The home and the village of one's spouse and in-laws.
sāt samundar pār [“across seven seas”] Mythical journey to paradise.
satsangh Hindu religious gathering.
Sāwan The Hindu month of the monsoon rains, around July.
shanti Peace.
Shiva In Hinduism, the god of destruction, the cosmic dancer in a circle of fire.
Shivrātrī Hindu festival celebrating the birth of Lord Shiva.
Siwālā [“home of Shiva”] Type of Hindu temple. The oldest temple of Felicity, on Cacandee Road (the Shrī Shankar Mandir).
soca [soul + calypso] Afro-Trinidadian popular song form of the 1980s and 1990s.
sohar A genre of songs for childbirth, in India especially for boys, sung at *chatī* (six days after birth) or *barahī* (twelve days).
sthāyī In Indian classical music, the antecedent phrase of a melody.
Sundar Popo East Indian star singer, popular in Trinidad since 1969.
swami [Trinidad, swaami] Priest, holy man.
tabla Drum pair used in north Indian classical music.
tāl Large pond.
tāla [Sanskrit; Hindi, Bhoj., tāl; Trinidad, taal, taala, tala] Indian rhythmic system.
talaiyā Small pond.
tamburā Plucked chordophone played as a drone to accompany Indian classical music.

tāpū Island.

tāssā Earthenware kettledrum with laced goatskin head, of Trinidad and India.

Trinbago Trinidad and Tobago.

Trinidad Sevashram Sangha Felicity branch of the India-based Bharat Sevashram Sangha. The Nolan Street Temple.

Tulsī Dās (?1543–1623) Author-poet of the Awadhī vernacular *Rāmcharitmānas* and eleven other collections of songs and poems.

Union Village Newer district of Felicity, "in the back." Less fashionable than Cacandee.

uṛan kharāmūn In north India, mythical flying wooden sandals.

uṛan khatolā In north India, mythical flying cot.

Uttar Pradesh Large state in north India, extending from the Himalayan foothills to the Gangeatic plain, formerly the North-Western Provinces, then Oudh, then the United Provinces. Region from which the majority of Trinidad-bound East Indian Coolies were recruited.

Vedas Earliest Aryan texts of India, ca. 3,000 years old.

vīṇā In India, a generic term for plucked lute. Different instruments are named *vīṇā* in north and south Indian classical music. In Hinduism, the instrument played by the goddess of music, Saraswatī.

yagya In India, ancient Vedic sacrifice. In Trinidad, religious observance held on seven to nine successive nights. *Yagya* are based on various sacred texts, including the *Māhābhārata.*

Selections on the Compact Disc

The musical examples on the compact disc that accompanies this book were recorded in Trinidad and India by the author, 1974–91.

1. **Boliye Rājā Rāmachandra Kī Jay,** "Shout Victory to King Rāmachandra! Sītā Rāma name day and night speak keep loving," *chautāl,* Felicity Chautāl Group, Ramnarine, leader. Excerpt, 3′22″

A loud, lively men's song, with *ḍholak* and *manjīrā* accompaniment, popular with villagers at the springtime Phāgūa festival. Each verse is introduced slowly by the leader and then repeated by the group, gradually accelerating until, cued by the *ḍholak,* the ensemble swings with full voice, clanging cymbals, and a burst from the *ḍholak* into an ecstatic double-tempo *dugun* section. Island-wide *chautāl* competitions are held every March.

A discussion of this *chautāl* and other Phāgūa songs is on pp. 74–83. The musical transcription (ex. II) is on p. 76, the romanized Awadhī text and English translation on pp. 77–78 (song 5), and the Awadhī text in Devanagari script on p. 441.

2. **Saraswatī Vandanā,** "Prayer to Mother Saraswatī," students of the āshram of Guru H. S. Adesh; music, text, and arrangement by H. S. Adesh. Excerpt, 2′42″

This beautiful song by Guru H. S. Adesh is sung at the beginning of each meeting at the Adesh Ashram. The text appeals to Mother Saraswatī, the Hindu goddess of knowledge and music, to "grant me a boon of a new awakening, a boon of limitless knowledge . . . a new phrase, rhythm, and melody . . . that we may live a hundred years drinking the nectar of happiness . . . that this universe be one family." The singing is accompanied by sitar, harmonium, tabla, and *manjīrā.* Before the song proper, the singers chant the Sanskrit mantra, "Lead us from untruth to truth, lead us from darkness to light" etc.

The musical transcription (ex. III) in the traditional Hindi *sargam* solfeggio system developed by V. N. Bhatkhande is on p. 141, and the English translation of the text on pp. 142 (song 30). The *tāl* is *rupak* (seven beats).

3. **Karnivāl Kā Desh,** "The Country of Carnival," students of the ashram of Guru H. S. Adesh, music, text, and arrangement by H. S. Adesh. Excerpt, 2′18″

This lively song by H. S. Adesh tells of a country where people of many races and religions live in harmony, "the heart's pride in the chain of the Western continent . . . the land of chirping birds . . . flourishing rice . . . engulfed in the net of the sea, loaded with fruits in every branch." The singing is accompanied by sitar, harmonium, tabla, and *manjīrā.*

The musical transcription (ex. IV) in traditional *sargam* notation in Devanagari script is on p. 143, and the English translation of the text on pp. 142 (song 32). The *tāl* is *dādrā* (six beats).

4. **Tāssā Drumming,** Wedding Hands, Felicity Tāssā Group, Dhanlal Samooj, leader. Excerpt, 2′58″
   The high crisp sound of the *tāssā* drum is important throughout the three-day Hindu wedding celebration. Accompanied by the cumbersome bass drum and *jhāl* cymbals, the *tāssā* plays a variety of patterns known as "hands," two of which are illustrated in this excerpt.
   This item (ex. V) and *tāssā* drumming for the Hindu wedding are discussed on pp. 155–62, and the role of *tāssā* in the Muslim Hosay festival is covered on p. 65.
5. **Āre Nadiyā Kināre,** "On the bank of a river there is a bungalow," *lachārī,* Sankey Ramroop, vocal, Rukmin Bhagaloo, *ḍholak,* Saffarin Pagie, *ḍhantāl.* Excerpt, 2′59″
   During the afternoons and evenings of the wedding, family women gather, chat, dance, drink, and sing their favorite *lachārī.* This number is a popular choice for weddings and childbirth celebrations in Felicity. Women prefer a loud raspy excited vocal quality for these bawdy teasing songs. The references to a hankie and a Panama hat help to date this item to 1900–1910. The idea of such a well-dressed husband walking happily down the road with his balls swinging is the punch line that ends the song.
   A discussion of this *lachārī* and other wedding songs for the groom's home is on pp. 162–72. The musical transcription (ex. VI) is on pp. 166–67, the romanized Bhojpurī text and English translation on pp. 168–70 (song 36), and the Bhojpurī text in Devanagari script on pp. 442–43. Song 37 gives Rajiah's abbreviated version.
6. **Sānkara Koriyā Bahāro,** "Sweep the way, Pandit Rāma," *byāh ke gīt,* Dhanpatee and Kalawatee Permanand. Complete, 1′15″
   "Sweep the way . . . they bring the elephant in . . . The wedding party will come only to the door of the house where there is a maiden to be married." Many singers in Trinidad and India know such a song for greeting the bridegroom. The three-stanza Permanand version is short and succinct, sung with a low vocal tessitura and sober tempo characteristic of this genre.
   A discussion of this *byāh ke gīt* and those for greeting the bridegroom collected by William Archer, Laxmi Tewari, and Hari S. Upadhyaya is on pp. 174–78. The musical transcription (ex. VII) is on p. 175, the romanized Bhojpurī text and English translation (song 39) on pp. 174–76, and the Bhojpurī text in Devanagari script on p. 444. Songs 40 and 42 give Moon's versions for the arrival of the *bārāt.*
7. **Leu Na Paṇḍiṭa Rāma,** "Pandit Rāma, take a jug of water in your hand," *byāh ke gīt,* Dhanpatee and Kalawatee Permanand. Complete, 1′06″
   As often happens, in this performance the sisters take a few moments to settle on a starting pitch and tempo. This short example illustrates the antecedent ("Pandit Rāmā take a jug of water in your hand")/consequent ("Wherever I went I never bowed to anyone") *sthāyī/antarā* phrases characteristic of many wedding songs as well as the typical alternation of rhythmic groups of three's and fours's of *dīpchandī tāl* (set out in ex. XXII). The most significant social message of the Hindu wedding is given in the final verse when the father of the bride confesses that "Because of my daughter, today I bowed."
   A discussion of this *byāh ke gīt* is on p. 180. The musical transcription (ex. VIII) is on p. 182, the romanized Bhojpurī text and English translation on p. 180 (song 43), and the Bhojpurī text in Devanagari script on p. 445.

8. **Dasa Sakhī,** "Ten female friends are in front," *byāh ke gīt,* Dhanpatee and Kalawatee Permanand. Complete, 1′47″

The Hindu bride is escorted like a fragile never-before-displayed porcelain figurine from location to location on her wedding day, both by her maiden and matron family and friends. Women in groups of five arrange her arms and hands, legs and feet, head and veil, as prescribed according to tradition to insure the perfection of the ritual. Delicate as a china doll, limp as a rag doll, the wedding marks her transposition from her father's lineage to that of her groom.

A discussion of the *byāh ke gīt* "Dasa Sakhī" is on pp. 183–87. The musical transcription (ex. IX) is on p. 183, the romanized Bhojpurī text and English translation on pp. 183–85 (song 44), and the Bhojpurī text in Devanagari script on p. 446. Song 45 gives Moon's version of this important item ("Ten female friends walk ahead and ten female friends behind her") and song 46 George Grierson's from 1883 ("Five matrons arranged the lamp with four wicks"). Plate 33 shows the mother of a Felicity bride greeting the bridegroom with a *lotā* of water as described in the song, "offer ārtī to Rāma . . . I will do the *parachhan* of the bridegroom myself."

9. **Sā̃jhe Chha Sukawā,** "In the evening six stars come out," *byāh ke gīt,* Dhanpatee and Kalawatee Permanand. Complete, 2′16″

"In the evening six stars come out; in the evening the moon comes out; the evening star comes out in the middle of the night. Rām has come to wed, his friends and four brothers." This longer song describes the splendor of Rām, the bridegroom, as the night of the wedding is at hand. The song's clear verse and refrain structure is notable.

A discussion of this *byāh ke gīt* is on pp. 187–91. The musical transcription (ex. X) is on p. 190, the romanized Bhojpurī text and English translation on pp. 189–91 (song 47), and the Bhojpurī text in Devanagari script on pp. 447–48. Archer's version from 1930 (song 48) describes the splendor of Rām ("Fine his pearl, grand his sash").

10. **Hare Hare Bhaiyā,** "Oh, oh, brother who plays the musical instruments, play," *byāh ke gīt,* Dhanpatee and Kalawatee Permanand. Complete, 1′04″

"Come on drummers, our brother, beat the drum!" This song has a clear antecedent/consequent *sthāyī/antarā* melodic structure and rhythmic alternation of three's and four's of *dīpchandī tāl* (ex. XXII).

A discussion of this *byāh ke gīt* is on pp. 191–94. The musical transcription (ex. XI) is on p. 192, the romanized Bhojpurī text and English translation on pp. 193 (song 49), and the Bhojpurī text in Devanagari script on p. 449. Song 50 gives Moon's version of a song encouraging wedding drummers ("My father's gate drum is being played"), and song 52 is Rajiah's song of wedding musicians ("Look, my people will listen"). Song 51 is Barura's song for drummers from Tripura ("Beat the drum to such a rhythm. Beat, it may please the ears"). Wedding drumming may be heard on track 4 of this disc (ex. V).

11. **Surāiyā Gaiyā Ke Gobara,** "Get the dung of a beautiful cow," *byāh ke gīt,* Dhanpatee and Kalawatee Permanand. Complete, 3′07″

The preparation of the wedding altar is the topic of this song. Even though only four or five cows are owned by Felicity villagers, the ritual importance of the cow is invoked in this traditional Bhojpurī text. The song has a *sthāyī/antarā* structure in *dīpchandī tāl* (ex. XXII).

A discussion of this *byāh ke gīt* is on p. 194. The musical transcription (ex. XII) is on p. 195, the romanized Bhojpurī text and English translation on pp. 194–97 (song 53), and the Bhojpurī text in Devanagari script on p. 450.

12. **Āī Gailẽ Ḍala,** "The wedding party has come," *byāh ke gīt,* Dhanpatee and Kalawatee Permanand. Complete, 0′52″

A particularly pleasing tune. "They bring gold and silver in the big cane basket. Now my daughter belongs to somebody else." The exchange of gifts and offering of a large dowry remains an important custom in traditional Hindu weddings, essential in village India and vestigial in Felicity, where the burden of wedding expenses is shared between the families of the bride and groom, much as in a typical American ceremony of the 1990s. In modern India the archaic dowry system has come under attack by urban sophisticates and social reformers who cite the treachery and abuse this antiquated custom has fostered. Nevertheless, gifts are exchanged at Felicity weddings and songs sung to mark this tradition, as here with ex. XIII, song 57, discussed on p. 199.

"Āī Gailẽ Ḍala" is another example of a *byāh ke gīt* with *sthāyī/antarā* structure in *dīpchandī tāl* (ex. XXII). The romanized Bhojpurī text and English translation are on pp. 199–200 and the Bhojpurī text in Devanagari script on p. 451. Song 58 gives Moon's text of wedding gifts, rings, money, and precious stones presented in the winnowing basket; in song 59 Moon's text describes the presentation of the sixteen traditional ornaments of the Hindu woman. "Then my daughter is partnered to another."

13. **Harīhara Bāsawā,** "My father has cut green bamboo," *byāh ke gīt,* the *kanyādān* song Dhanpatee and Kalawatee Permanand. Complete, 1′52″

The setting for this song is the wedding tent made of green bamboo thatched with *tulsī* leaves. The giving of the virgin daughter by the father to the groom *(kanyādān)* is the centerpiece of the wedding. Many songs describe the pure innocence of the maiden bride, in olden days under the age of thirteen, and the trembling of the father as he performs his painful duty. *Kanyādān* songs are sung throughout the villages of Uttar Pradesh and are well known in Felicity. The Permanand melody is unusual, especially the *antarā* phrase with which the song opens; the listener will note the importance of so-called ornamental notes to the main melody skeleton.

Song 61 gives Moon's text for the *kanyādān* ritual and song 52 another version sung by an ensemble of Felicity women in call-and-response form. Song 65 gives Rajiah's *kanyādān* text, and song 66 a *kanyādān* text collected by Archer in the 1930s. A discussion of these versions is on pp. 201–6. The musical transcription for the Permanand song (ex. XIV) is on p. 202, the romanized Bhojpurī text and English translation on pp. 201–3 (song 60), and the Bhojpurī text in Devanagari script on p. 452.

14. **Lauwā Na Parichho,** "Brother, welcome the popped rice," *byāh ke gīt,* Dhanpatee and Kalawatee Permanand. Complete, 1′08″

This simple six-phrase song in *dīpchandī tāl* is sung softly and at a remarkably low pitch. *Lāwā* or popped rice is a popular food in Uttar Pradesh, less so in Felicity, though for the Trinidad wedding the *lāwā* ceremony on Sunday morning is crucial. The text praises the bride ("delicate," "the daughter of a king") and hurls typical insults at the groom ("clumsy," "the son of a plowman"), a song custom which is always described as "loving" but which must surely bolster the pride of the bride's family and lift a measure of sorrow as they surrender their daughter and her dowry to another family. Song 73 by Felicity women also proclaims the innocence of the bride but goes on to describe the groom as "a lotus flower."

A discussion of this *byāh ke gīt* is on pp. 206–8. The musical transcription (ex. XV) is on p. 207, the romanized Bhojpurī text and English translation on pp. 207–8 (song 67), and the Bhojpurī text in Devanagari script on p. 453. Song 68, Archer's *lāwā* song from the 1930s, also includes a small *gālī* ("insult"; "touch the girl's toes, you little bastard"), likewise Henry's more recent version from Ghazipur district ("have our father and your mother sleep together").

15. **Bābā Bābā,** "She is calling 'father, father,' but the father does not speak," *byāh ke gīt,* Dhanpatee and Kalawatee Permanand. Complete, 1′00″

This song is well known in Trinidad and India. With only six phrases, it signals the culmination of the wedding ritual, the point of no return, when the bridegroom places the blood-red vermilion in the parting of the bride's hair. As this ritual is performed the song depicts the bride pleading for help from each of her kin folk ("She is calling 'father, father,' but the father does not speak . . . she is calling 'mother, mother' . . ."), though in fact brides are tearful (India) or silent (Felicity) at this signal moment.

A discussion of this *byāh ke gīt* is on p. 208. The musical transcription (ex. XVI) is on p. 209, the romanized Bhojpurī text and English translation on pp. 209–10 (song 69), and the Bhojpurī text in Devanagari script on p. 453. Song 70 gives Moon's version of this item. Song 71 is a Ballia text from the collection of Hari S. Upadhyaya ("after accepting a pinchful of vermilion, you belong to others").

16. **Sā̃jhai,** "In the evening the clouds come in the sky, and at midnight it starts to rain," *byāh ke gīt,* Dhanpatee and Kalawatee Permanand. Complete, 0′29″

This short song marks the end of the wedding as the bride and groom are led into the ritual *kohabar* chamber where they will pass the night.

A discussion of this *byāh ke gīt* is on p. 210. The musical transcription (ex. XVII) is on p. 211, the romanized Bhojpurī text and English translation on pp. 210–11 (song 72), and the Bhojpurī text in Devanagari script on p. 454.

17. **Ādhe Talaiyā** (Number One Song), "The male swan is feeding in half of the pond, the female swan is feeding in half of the pond," *byāh ke gīt,* Moon Ramnarine. Complete, 6′11″

This special song, the first song Moon taught me, became my Number One Song. It opens with a metaphor—an analogy between a pond half empty and half covered with flowering lotus or half with a male swan and half with a female swan—and the ceremonial wedding tent, half full of relatives from one side of the family, and half from the other side, or half empty. The body of the song describes the problem the man of the house has mediating a quarrel between his wife and his sister, who demands payment for decorating the ritual wedding pitcher.

Moon's voice is clear and crisp, and the simple melody is the most frequently sung wedding tune in Felicity. In this rendition, Moon mistakenly sings "the pond is not beautiful without the one sister-in-law," later explaining to me it should be "without the one lotus leaf." Quite a few singers muddled this metaphor.

A discussion of this *byāh ke gīt* is on pp. 242–46 and pp. 249–51. The musical transcription (ex. XIX) is on p. 245, the romanized Bhojpurī text and English translation on pp. 243–45 (song 76), and the Bhojpurī text in Devanagari script on pp. 455–56.

Songs 77–84 offer variants of my Number One Song from Trinidad. Song 164, Arya's version of this song collected in Surinam in 1965, is remarkably similar to the texts sung in Felicity. Further documention for my Number One Song, in Trinidad and India, is given in the notes for tracks 18 and 29. Plate 41 shows a *kalasā* decorated for a Felicity wedding.

18. **Āḍheye Ṭalawā** (Number One Song), "The male cobra is moving in half of the pond, the female cobra is moving in half of the pond," *byāh ke gīt,* Dhanpatee and Kalawatee Permanand. Complete, 5′16″

In the Permanands' version of Number One Song cobras are moving in the pond, not swans feeding. The melody of the Permanand sisters' version of my Number One Song is different from that of Moon (track 17) and other Felicity singers. In addition, the Permanand text has a startling image of the female cobra in the middle of the wedding tent, and it is the wife of the barber, not the sister-in-law, who is asked to decorate the pitcher. The Permanand sisters include a mild insult, "Daughter of the farmer whose plow has broken, sister of a herdsman."

A discussion of this *byāh ke gīt* is on p. 246. The musical transcription (ex. XX) is on p. 248, the romanized Bhojpurī text and English translation on pp. 246 and 248–49 (song 77), and the Bhojpurī text in Devanagari script on p. 457. Musical example XXI compares verses 1, 4, 7, and 13 of this song, showing the minor melodic and rhythmic variety through the performance.

19. **Mere Mana Basigayo,** "In my heart has settled Rām, Lord of the Raghus," *bhajan,* Divine Life Society, Unit 1, Felicity. Excerpt, 1′35″

This *bhajan* celebrates the bravery and splendor of Rām "with diadem'd crown and earrings in crocodile's shape . . . he broke the pride of all kings." In this number and in those on tracks 20–23 following, the singers accompany themselves on harmonium, *ḍholak, ḍhantāl, kartāl,* and *manjīrā.*

A discussion of this *bhajan* is on p. 303. The musical transcription (ex. XXIII) is on pp. 304–5, and the romanized Hindi text and English translation on pp. 303 and 306 (song 130). The leader-chorus structure is analyzed in table 5, p. 303.

20. **Hey Jagata Pitaa Bhagawaana,** "Oh, father of the world, give us knowledge," *bhajan,* Divine Life Society, Unit 1, Felicity. Excerpt, 1′20″

A popular song in Felicity, this *bhajan* is a confession of human frailty and a plea for God's aid: "where should I go for my senses have overwhelmed me . . . day and night I wandered from place to place . . . only in your grace is there refuge."

A discussion of this *bhajan* is on pp. 306–7. The musical transcription (ex. XXIV) is on pp. 308–9, and the romanized Hindi text and English translation on pp. 307 and 309 (song 131). The leader-chorus structure is analyzed in table 6, p. 306.

21. **Shiva Shambhu Deeno Ki Bandhu,** "Salutation to Shiva as Shambhu," *bhajan,* Divine Life Society, Unit 1, Felicity. Excerpt, 2′21″

A popular song in India and Trinidad, this *bhajan* to Lord Shiva opens with a slow solo improvisatory section in Sanskrit reminiscent of the opening *ālāp* section of north Indian classical music.

A discussion of this *bhajan* is on p. 310. The musical transcription (ex. XXVI) is on pp. 316–18, and the romanized Hindi text and English translation on pp. 310–11 and 315 (song 132). The leader-chorus structure of this *bhajan* is analyzed in table 7, p. 311.

Ex. XXVII gives a transcription in full score of this *bhajan* with the accompaniment of harmonium, *manjīrā, ḍholak,* and hand claps. Ex. XXVI shows the song arranged and performed by playback singer Alok for an Indian film soundtrack with the accompaniment of sitar, violin, clarinet, and tabla.

22. **Raama Raama Bhaju Raama,** "Rām, Rām, worship Rām," *bhajan,* Divine Life Society, Unit 1, Felicity. Excerpt, 2′29″

Atmaram Maharajh sings this beautiful *bhajan* for me every time I visit Felicity. The text tells the life story of Rām "son of Dasarath . . . betrothed to Sītā . . . went to the forest . . . beat and annihilated the demons . . . rules over the whole land." As with many *bhajan* it opens with a slow solo improvisatory section comparable with the classical *ālāp.*

A discussion of this *bhajan* is on p. 318. The musical transcription (ex. XXVIII) is on pp. 322–25, and the romanized Hindi text and English translation on pp. 319 and 326–27 (song 133). The leader-chorus structure is analyzed in table 8, p. 325.

23. **Bhajale Naama Niranjana Kaa,** "Sing in praise the name of Niranjana [God free of illusion]," *bhajan,* Divine Life Society, Unit 1, Felicity. Excerpt, 3′03″

This well-known *bhajan* describes the transitory nature of earthy life—"one comes, another goes, nothing is permanent in the world . . . abandon this world of illusion."

A discussion of this *bhajan* is on p. 327. The musical transcription (ex. XXIX) is on pp. 328–31, and the romanized Hindi text and English translation on p. 332 (song 134). The leader-chorus structure is analyzed in table 9, p. 327. Musical example XXX, p. 333, highlights the heterophony of the performance, characteristic of singing in Felicity—small rhythmic and melodic variations between the vocal line and the accompaniment of the harmonium.

24. **Jai Jagadisha Hare,** "May the supreme being, lord of the world, be ever victorious," *ārtī bhajan,* Arya Sabha, Carolina village. Excerpt, 1′11″

This song describes the attributes of the deity: "Oh Supreme One! You are our mother and our father . . . you are the ocean of mercy . . . how can I meet you when I am foolish?" It is the most familiar *bhajan* in Trinidad, here sung by the small branch of the Arya Sabha of Carolina village, deep in the cane lands of central Trinidad. Usually "Jai Jagadisha Hare" is sung at the end of a *sandhya* or *havan* service, during the offering of *ārtī* and *prasad.* The refrain text "Be triumphant, Hare, lord of the world" is from the 12th century *Gītā Govinda* of Jayadeva.

A discussion of this *bhajan* is on pp. 333–34. The musical transcription (ex. XXXI) is on pp. 336–39 and the romanized Hindi text and English translation on pp. 334–35 (song 135).

Tracks 24, 25, and 26 are three different versions of "Jai Jagadisha Hare," performed by different religious groups; in example XXXI the versions are aligned vertically so the listener can compare differences in melody, tempo, ornamentation, rhythm, and text. The harmonium part of version 24 has been transcribed in ex. XXXI, so the listener can evaluate the particularly pleasing melodic interplay between voice and harmonium.

25. **Jai Jagadisha Hare,** *ārtī bhajan,* Trinidad Sevashram Sangha, Felicity. Documentation is under track 24. Plate 42 shows the Trinidad Sevashram Sangha where this recording was made. Excerpt, 2′26″

26. **Jai Jagadisha Hare,** *ārtī bhajan,* Divine Life Society, Unit 24, Enterprise. Documentation is under track 24. Excerpt, 2′21″

27. **Ganesh Sharanam,** "Surrender to Lord Ganesh," Sai Baba song, Divine Life Society, Unit 1, Felicity. Excerpt, 1′28″

Sai Baba songs became popular in Felicity in 1974. The short repetitive Hindi texts are easy to learn and the singing style exciting with accelerando, crescendo, and hand clapping. The opening lines of the song praise Lord Ganesh, but later the text changes to praise Lord Sai.

A discussion of this song is on p. 344. The musical transcription (ex. XXXIII) is on pp. 348–49, and the English translation of the Hindi text is on p. 344 (song 136). Example XXXII, pp. 346–47, compares the singing of "Ganesh Sharanam" in Felicity with a version from India.

28. **Aum Bhagawān,** "Oh Lord, grant me a vision of you," Sai Baba song, Sai Baba Devotees, Tunapuna. Excerpt 3′13″

This well-known popular song has a short simple Hindi text with accelerando and hand clapping. The melody shows the *sthāyī/antarā* and leader-chorus structure. The listener will note the large group of some 200 singers, with an in-house public address system, at this gathering of devotees from all over Trinidad.

A discussion of this song is on p. 344. The musical transcription (ex. XXXIV) is on pp. 350–54, and the English translation of the Hindi text is on pp. 344–45 (song 137).

29. **Talawā Bharla Saba Nāga** (Number One Song), "Pond full all male cobra and female cobra all," *byāh ke gīt,* Mahadewā Dube, Gorakhpur District, U.P., India. Complete, 3′44″

This version of my Number One Song was sung in V. S. Naipaul's ancestral village of Mahadewā Dube in 1986. The performing style of these village women is similar to that of Felicity women, but the melody and the text of the song are considerably different. Each describes the beautiful flowers of the lotus, and each draws an analogy between the halves of the pond and the two families of the wedding. The narrative of this Dube version ends with the arrival of the groom's party, whereas the narrative of Moon's version (track 17, ex. XIX, song 76) and the Permanands' version (track 18, ex. XX, song 77) go on to describe a fraught relationship between the sisters-in-law, the demanding of gifts, and the decoration of the wedding pitcher.

A discussion of this *byāh ke gīt* is on pp. 415–17. The musical transcription (ex. XXXV) is on p. 416, English translation on p. 417 (song 166), and the Bhojpurī text in Devanagari script on p. 458. Songs 161, 162, and 163, from India, include the imagery of Number One Song such as the wedding pitcher and the lotus flower.

Songs 165 and 167 are variants from India of my Number One Song. Song 164, Arya's version collected in Surinam in 1965, is remarkably similar to the texts sung in Felicity. The passage of the *Chāndogya Upanishad* on p. 411 reveals the depth and antiquity of the metaphor of the lotus in Indian thought, describing the lotus within the human heart, embracing a tiny space that contains heaven and earth, fire, air, sun, moon, lightning, and the constellations.

Bhojpurī Texts in Devanagari Script

1. Boliye Rājā Rāmachandra Kī Jay, "Shout Victory to King Rāmachandra! Sītā Rāma name day and night speak keep loving," *chautāl,* Felicity Chautāl Group, Ramnarine, leader.

बोलिये राजा रामचन्द्र की जय

[जयकारा]
बोलिये राजा रामचन्द्र की जय!
[गीत]
सिया राम नाम दिन रहन कहत चलो प्यारे
ए ग्रीद्ध अजामिल गनिका तारी सेवरी कीन्ह सुखारी
देखहु ध्रुप प्रहलाद नयन भये
आहे गज के जब गाह पकारे कहत चलो प्यार
ए द्रुपद सुता के चीर बढाये गणिक सुता तनहाये
भारत में बरदोर मंचाओ
अहे गन्टा तेरे से कृष्ण मुरारे कहत चलो प्यारे
ओ जब-जब गाड परे भकतन पर तब-तब हरी अवतारे
कहन लगे करहु बयान एक मुख
आहे सारद पावक नाहिं पारये कहत चलो प्यारे
ए सेश महेश गनेष अदि सब बरनहिं बारहि बारे
सुन्दर ब्रजहि अमाहि बसबहु
अये दसरथ सुत राम उदारे कहत चलो प्यारे
सुमिरों मन राम सहित सीता
हे दसमुख येसा भूप महाबल
हे इन्द्र कुबेर वरुण से कांपें
सुमिरों मै राम-सहित सीता
[जयकारा]
बोलिये-बोलिये अजोध्यानाथ सिया बर रामचन्द्र की जय!

॥

2. Āre Nadiyā Kināre, "On the bank of a river there is a bungalow," *lachārī*, Sankey Ramroop, vocal, Rukmin Bhagaloo, *ḍholak*, Saffarin Pagie, *ḍhantāl*.

आरे नदिया किनारे

आरे नदिया किनारे छाये बँगला
ओपर बइठे नबाब, ओपर बइठे नबाब
आरे कइसे के मारों नजरिया, ओ कइसे के मारों नज़रिया
सइयाँ लागे हमार
कइसे के मारों नजरिया
बाके [?गलती, लागे] हमार, जिया लागे हमार, जिया लागे हमार
कइसे के मारों नजरिया, ओ कइसे के मारों नज़रिया
हाय हमार कइसे के चरइया
ननदी के भतार [?बुखार], ननदी के भतार [?बुखार]
आरे सइयाँ के आवे रतौनी, ओ सइयाँ के आवे रतौनी
हाय दिना टूटे [?सूझे] न रार [?रात]
सइयाँ के आवे रतौनी
टूटे [?सूझे] न रार [?रात], दिना टूटे [?सूझे] न रार [?रात],
दिना टूटे [?सूझे] न रार [?रात]
सइयाँ के आवे रतौनी, ओ सइयाँ के आवे रतैनी
काहे क झारों जगहिया
कइसे के बोखार, कइसे के बोखार
आरे कइसे के झारों रतैनी, ओ कइसे के झारों रतौनी
हाय दिना टूटे [?सूझे] न रार [?रात]
कइसे के झारों रतौनी
आरे बाहों [बारो] से झारे जगहिया
मंत्र से बोखार, मंत्र से बोखार
आरे अँचरा से झारों रतैनी, ओ अँचरा से झारों रतौनी
हाय दिना टूटे [?सूझे] न रार [?रात]
अँचरा से झारों रतौनी
दिना सूझे न रात
अँचरा से झारों रतौनी
दिना सूझे न रात, दिना सूझे न रात, दिना सूझे न रात,
दिना सूझे न रात
अँचरा से झारों रतौनी, ओ अँचरा से झारों रतौनी

2. *Continued*

दिना सूझे न रात, सासु के थोरे जगइया, ननदी के बोखार,
ननदी के बोखार
सइयाँ के छोरे रतौनी, ओ सइयाँ के छोरे रतौनी
हाय दिना सूझे न रात
सइयाँ के छोरे रतौनी
हाय मन लागे हमार
सइयाँ के छोरे रतौनी
आरे बोके पलांवां [?पनामा] के तोपी
गल बाँधे रूमाल, गल बाँधे रूमाल
आरे लटकत [लचकत] आवे गलिन में
ओ लटकत [लचकत] आवे गलिन में
हाय मन लागे हमार
लटकत आवे गलिन में
मन लागे हमार
लटकत आवे गलिन में
[हँसी]

॥

3. Sānkara Koriyā Bahāro, "Sweep the way, Pandit Rāma," *byāh ke gīt,* Dhanpatee and Kalawatee Permanand.

सांकर कोरिया बहारो

सांकर कोरिया बहारो हो पंडिट राम
बहारो हो पंडिट राम
हठियाँ लीन पइठारि हो
हठियाँ लीन पइठार

कि डल उटरेले आम अमिली टरे
आम अमिली टरे
किय रे कदम जूरी छाँह
आहो किय रे कदम जूरी छाँह

ओही डल उटरे पंडिट राम डूअरवा
पंडिट राम डूअरवा हो
जिन्हि घर कन्या कुआँरी हो
जिन्हि घर कन्या कुआँरी हो

॥

4. Leu Na Panḍiṭa Rāma, "Pandit Rāma, take a jug of water in your hand," *byāh ke gīt,* Dhanpatee and Kalawatee Permanand.

लेउ न पंडिट राम

लेउ न पंडिट राम गेरूवा
हाँठे पान के बीरा
हाँठे पान के बीरा

करहु न बिनटी समढी राम से
सीर पाग झुकाये

करहु न बिनटी समढी राम से
सीर पाग झुकाये

डिल्ली न ए पर्बत न ए
हम्त कबहूँ न निवली
हम्त कबहूँ न निवली

बेती कवन डेई के कारना
अजु शीश निवायो

बेती कवन डेई के कारना
अजु शीश निवायो

॥

5. Dasa Sakhī, "Ten female friends are in front," *byāh ke gīt,* Dhanpatee and Kalawatee Permanand.

दस सखी

दस सखी अगवाँ दसही सखी पछवाँ
दसही सखी पछवाँ हो
दस सखी गोहनें लगाई
ओ दस सखी गोहनें लगाई

कंचन ठार कपूर के बाती
कपूर के बाती
हो रामजी के आरती उतारे
ओ रामजी के आरती उता

परिछन चलले हो सासु कवन देई
सासु कवन देई
परछत बर के लिलार
हो परछत बर के लिलार

पहिले मैं परछहु मांठे के माउर
मांठे के माउर
पीछे से बर के लिलार हो

अपन राम मइ अपने परिछिबों
मइ अपने परिछिबों
हो जनि कोइ परिछे मोरे राम [हो]
जनि कोइ परिछे मोरे राम हो

॥

6. Sā̃jhe Chha Sukawā, "In the evening six stars come out," *byāh ke gīt,* Dhanpatee and Kalawatee Permanand.

साँझे छ सुकवा

साँझे छ सुकवा उदये भये
साँझे चंद्र उदये भये
सुकवा उगे आधी राट

राम आये बिआहन
राम आये बिआहन
सजन सहिट चारो भाइ री

राम आये बिआहन
राम आये बिआहन
सजन सहिट चारो भाइ री

मांठे मउर जो सोहै
मांठे मवर जो सोहै
गल बइजन्ती के माला जी

मांठे मवर जो सोहै
मांठे मवर जो सोहै
गले बइजन्ती के माला जी

काने कुण्डल झलके
काने कुण्डल झलके
चंदन खोर ललाट लसी

राम आये बिआहन
राम आये बिआहन
सजन सहिट चारो भाइ री

6. *Continued*

दाँते झलके बतिसिया
दाँते झलके बतिसिया
पानन ओठ के लाली जी

राम आये बिआहन
राम आये बिआहन
सजन सहित चारो भाइ री

हाठे धनुष जो सोहै
हाठे धनुष जो सोहै
पीटाम्बर से कमर कसी

राम आये बिआहन
राम आये बिआहन
सजन सहित चारो भाइ री

॥

7. Hare Hare Bhaiyā, "Oh, oh, brother who plays the musical instruments, play," *byāh ke gīt,* Dhanpatee and Kalawatee Permanand.

हरे हरे भइया

हरे हरे भइया बजनियाँ
टो बजना बजाबहु हो

भइया आइ गइले राजा के कुव
ट बजना बजाबहु हो

हरे हरे बाबा कवन राम टमुआ टनाबहु हो
बाबा भीजे न राजा के कुवर टमुआ टनाबहु हो

हरे हरे मा कवन देइ अँचरवा टूं टानहु हो
मइया भीजें न राजा के कूँवर अँचरवा टूं टानि देउ हो

॥

8. Surāiyā Gaiyā Ke Gobara, "Get the dung of a beautiful cow," *byāh ke gīt,* Dhanpatee and Kalawatee Permanand.

सुराइया गइया के गोबर

सुराइया गइया के गोबर मंगायो
चारो खोटा बेडेंइया लिपाये हो
सोने के कलसा ढराये मोरे बाबा
सुरुज छकित होइ जाय
सोने के कलसा ढराये मोरे बाबा
सुरुज छकिट होइ जाय
जइसे बजारे के मोटी जो झलके
अवरू दखिनवाँ के चीर हो
राम लछन डौनो मरये में झलके
सुरुज छकित होइ जाय
राम लछन डौनो मरये में झलके
सुरुज छकित होइ जाय
देखन आये रे सखिया सहेलरि
नयनन गइले मुरझाइ हो
कवन-कवन टप किहलो सीतल देई
राम से होबेला बिआह
कवन-कवन टप किहलो सीतल देई
राम से होबेला बिआह
गंगा नहायो सुरुज मांठा लागौ
बिधि से रहउ इटवार हो
निबुला सराफल ब्राह्मन के दिहलऊ
ओही से मोरे राम से बिआह
निबुला सराफल ब्राह्मन के दिहलऊ
ओही से मोरे राम से बिआह
निबुला सराफ . . .
भुखल-डुखल हम बिप्र जिंबइलौ
ओही से मोरे राम से बिआह
उरखे टे बाबा मोरे बछिया सँकलपै
ओही से मोरे राम से बिआह
उरखे टे बाबा मोरे बछिया सँकलपै
ओही से मोरे राम से बिआह

॥

9. Āī Gailẽ Ḍala, "The wedding party has come," *byāh ke gīt,* Dhanpatee and Kalawatee Permanand.

आई गइलें डल

आई गइलें डल मउनी
आई गइलें सिर मउरी

आई गइलें बेटी के सिंगार ट
बेटी मोरी पराई भइलें

आई गइलें बेटी के सिंगार ट
बेटी मोरी पराई भइलें

सोने डलवा सोन अइलें
रूपे डलवा रूपे अइलें

बाँसे डलवा ढिया के सिंगार ट
ढिया मोरी पराई भइलें

बाँसे डलवा ढिया के सिंगार ट
ढिया मोरी पराई भइलें

॥

10. Harīhara Bāsawā, "My father has cut green bamboo," *byāh ke gīt,* the *kanyādān* song, Dhanpatee and Kalawatee Permanand.

हरीहर बंसवा

हरीहर बंसवा कटाये मोरे बाबा
पानन मरवा छवायेला हो
टेही टरे बइठेले बेटी के बाबा
आई गये ढरमवाँ के जून
टेही टरे बइठेले बेटी के बाबा
आई गये ढरमवाँ के जून
काँपेला ढोतिया अउ काँपेला लोटिया
काँपेला कुसवा के डाभ हो
मरये में काँपेला बेटी के बाबा
कइसे-कइसे डेबो कन्याडान
मरये में काँपेल बेटी के बाबा
कइसे-कइसे डेबो कन्यादान
सोनवाँ अउ रूपली के गुप्ट संकलपौ
डेओ गउरा देई के दान हो
हमके टू मोरे बाबा जंघा बइठाओ
वइसे-वइसे देओ कन्यादान
हमके टू मोरे बाबा जंघा बइठाओ
वइसे-वइसे देओ कन्यादान

॥

11. Lauwā Na Parichho, "Brother, welcome the popped rice," *byāh ke gīt,* Dhanpatee and Kalawatee Permanand.

लउवा न परिछो

लउवा न परिछो कवन भइया हो
ओटो बहिनी टोहारइ हो
लउवा न परिछो कवन भइया हो
ओटो बहिनी टोहारइ हो
हल-बल हल-बल दुलहा चले
हरबाहे के पुतउ हो
ठुमुकि-ठुमुकि मोरि धीया चले
रजबारे के धीयाउ हो
अँगुठ न मारो दुल्हे रामा हो
उटो बहिनी टोहारइ हो
अँगुठ न मारो दुल्हे रामा हो
उटो धनियाँ टोहारइ हो

॥

12. Bābā Bābā, "She is calling 'father, father,' but the father does not speak," *byāh ke gīt,* Dhanpatee and Kalawatee Permanand.

बाबा बाबा

बाबा बाबा पुकारे त बाबा ना बोलेला हो
आहो बाबाइ के बरियाई सिंदुर बर डारेइ हो
माई माई पुकारे त माई ना बोलेला हो
आहो माईय के बरियाइ सिंदुर बर डारेला हो
भाई भाई पुकारे त भाई न बोलेला हो
आहो भाईय के बरियाई सिंदुर बर डारेला हो

॥

13. Sā̃jhai, "In the evening the clouds come in the sky, and at midnight it starts to rain," *byāh ke gīt,* Dhanpatee and Kalawatee Permanand.

सांझइ

सांझइ बढरा उमरि अइले
आधी राति बरसइ हो

मइया खोलि देउ चनन केंवरिया
रमइया जइहंइ कोहबर हो

मइया खोलि देउ चनन केंवरिया
सीतला जइहंइ कोहबर हो

॥

14. Ādhe Talaiyā (Number One Song), "The male swan is feeding in half of the pond, the female swan is feeding in half of the pond," *byāh ke gīt,* Moon Ramnarine.

आधे तलइया

आधे तलइया में हंसिन चुने आधे में हंसा चुने हो
अरे तबहू न तलवा सोहावन एकही ननद [पुरइन] बीन हो
अरे तबहू न तलवा सोहावन एकही ननद [पुरइन] बीन हो
आधे मड़उवा मोरे नइहर आधे ससुरारे के हो
अरे तबहू न मड़वा सोहावन एक ही ननद बीन हो
अरे तबहू न मड़वा सोहावन एक ही ननद बीन हो
आल्हर बसवा कटावे भइया मड़वा छवावेला हो
अरे ऊचे चढ़ि भइया मोरे चितवे बहिनी मोरे आवेला हो
अरे ऊचे चढ़ि भइया मोरे चितवे बहिनी मोरे आवेला हो
भीतर हउवा कि बाहर ए मोरे धनियाँ हो
धना आवेला बाबा के दुलारी गरब नहीं बोलबउ हो
धाना आवेला बाबा के दुलारी गरब नाहीं बोलबउ हो
आव आव ननद गोसाईनी मोरे ठकुरईनि हो
ननदी बइठो मोरे चनन पीढ़इया कलसा मोर गोंठउ हो
ननदी बइठो मोरे चनन पीढ़इया कलसा मोर गोंठउ हो
गोंठब ए भउजी कलसा गोंठउनी कुछ चाहेल हो
गोंठब ए भउजी कलसा गोंठउनी कुछ चाहेल हो
तोहरे जोगे लहर पटोर बबुल जोगे हँसुली हो
ननदोइया जोगे चढ़ने के घोरवा हँसत घरे चली जइबा हो
ननदोइया जोगे चढ़ने के घोरवा हँसत घरे चली जइबा हो
कहाँ पइवों लहर पटोर कहाँ मैं पइबों हँसुली हो
अरे कहाँ पइबों चढ़ने के घोरवा कलसा मोरे नाहीं गोठ हो
रोवत निकरे ननदिया त सुसुकत भगीनवा हो
अरे हँसत के निकरे ननदोइया भलेरे मनवा टूटल हो
अरे हँसत के निकरे ननदोइया भलेरे मनवा टूटल हो
चुप रहु ऐ धना चुप रहु अवरू से चुप रहु हो
धना जइबो मैं राजा के नौकरिया सबहे चीज बसेहब हो
तोहरे जोगे लहर पटोर बिटिवा जोगे हँसुली हो

14. *Continued*

अरे अपने जोगे चढ़ने के घोरवा त सार के देखइब हो
अरे अपने जोगे चढ़ने के घोरवा त सार के देखइब हो
बजर परे तोहरे चुनरी बजर परे हँासुली हो
अरे बजर परे तोरे घोरवा नइहर ना बिसराइब हो
अरे बजर परे तोरे घोरवा नइहर ना बिसराइब हो

॥

15. Āḍheye Ṭalawā (Number One Song), "The male cobra is moving in half of the pond, the female cobra is moving in half of the pond," *byāh ke gīt,* Dhanpatee and Kalawatee Permanand.

आढेये टलवा

आढेये टलवा में नाग लोटें आढे में नागिनी लोटें हो
आहो टबहू न टलवा चुहिल भइलें एक रे कमल बिन हो
आहो टबहू न टलवा चुहिल भइलें एक रे कमल बिन हो
आढे मरउआ में गोता बइठे आढे में गोटिनी बइठे हो
आहो टबहू न मरवा सुहावन एक रे ननद बिन हो
आहो टबहू न मरवा सुहावन एक रे ननद बिन हो
हरे हरे गाँवा के नउनियां ननड हमरे लागहु हो
नाउनि बइठो न माँझ मरउआ कलसा हमरे गांठहु हो
नागिनि बइठो न माँझ मरउआ कलसा हमरे गांठहु
इटना बचन जब कहलें अउ कहऊ न पवलइ हो
आहो लीली घोड़ी आबे ननदुइया त डुंडिया ननदी हमरे हो
आहो लीली घोड़ी आबे ननदुइया त डुंडिया ननदी हमरे
आबहू ए ननदी आबहू आइके सुनाबहु हो
ननदी बइठो न माँझ मरउआ कलसा हमरे गोंठहु हो
गोंठिला ए भउजी गोंठिला अवरू से गोंठिला हो
भउजी का देबो हमर के दान रहंसि घर जाइब हो
मांगहु ए ननदी मांगहु मांगि के सुनाबहु हो
ननदी जो कछु हृदय समाइ सोइय सब मांगहु हो
अपने के चटकी चुनरिया भयनवाँ के मोहर हो
भउजी प्रभुजी के चढने के घुड़वा रहंसि घर जइबहु हो
आहो प्रभुजी के चढने के घुड़वा रहंसि घर जइबहु हो
नहीं हमें चोटकी चुनरिया नहीं रे हमें मोहर हो
ननदी नहीं हम्में चढने के घुड़वा नउजि रहँसि घरे जाउ
बोलत रहलीं हँस बुलना के अवरू ठिठोलना से हो
प्रभु निबतहु तू कुल परिवार बहिनि जनि निबतहु हो
तू तौ हरवाहे की बेटी चरवाहे की बहिनीं तू हो
धना एकई कोखि के बहिनियाँ बहिनि कसना निबतहु हो
अपने मैं बहिनीं के चुनरी बसइहौ भयनवाँ के मोहर हो
आहो प्रभुजी के चढने के घुड़वा रहँसि घर जइहंहि हो
आहो प्रभुजी के चढने के घुड़वा रहँसि बहिनी घर जइबो हो

॥

16. Talawā Bharla Saba Nāga (Number One Song), "Pond full all male cobra and female cobra all," *byāh ke gīt,* Mahadewā Dube, Gorakhpur District, U.P., India.

तलवा भरल सब नाग

तलवा भरल सब नाग त अबरु नागिनीं सभ
तलवा भरल सब नाग त अबरु नागिनीं सभ
तबहू न तलवा सोहावन एक करे केवल बिन
तबहू न तलवा सोहावन एक करे केवल बिन
तबहू न तलवा सोहावन एक करे केवल बिन
तबहू न तलवा सोहावन एक करे केवल बिन
मड़वा भरता सभगोव त अबरु गोतिनीं सभ
मड़वा भरता सभगोव त अबरु गोतिनीं सभ
तबहू न मड़वा सोहावन एकरे बहिनीं बिन
तबहू न मड़वा सोहावन एकरे बहिनीं बिन
तबहू न मड़वा सोहावन एकरे बहनोइया बिन
तबहू न सभवा सोहावन एकरे बहनोइया बिन
घुड़वन अयेलें कवन राम, ड़ढिया कवनीं देई
घुड़वन अयेलें कवन राम, ड़ढिया कवनीं देई
छोटे घोड़ अयेलें होरिलवा मड़उआ रोशिआवन
छोटे घोड़ अयेलें होरिलवा मड़उआ रोशिआवन
छोटे घोड़ अयेलें होरिलवा मड़उआ रोशिआवन
छोटे घोड़ अयेलें होरिलवा मड़उआ रोशिआवन

॥

Notes

1. Alan P. Merriam, "Definitions of 'Comparative Musicology' and 'Ethnomusicology': An Historical-Theoretical Perspective," *Ethnomusicology* 21 (May 1977): 204; idem, "Ethnomusicology Today," *Current Musicology* 20 (1975): 57; and idem, *The Anthropology of Music* (Evanston: Northwestern University Press, 1974), 27; A. L. Kroeber and Clyde Kluckhohn, *Culture: A Critical Review of Concepts and Definitions* (New York: Vintage Books, 1952).

2. Karl Popper, *Conjectures and Refutations: The Growth of Scientific Knowledge* (London: Routledge and Kegan Paul, 1963); idem, *Objective Knowledge: An Evolutionary Approach* (London: Oxford University Press, 1972); and idem, *Unended Quest: An Intellectual Autobiography* (Glasgow: William Collins Sons, 1974). See also Ernest Gellner, *Cause and Meaning in the Social Sciences* (London: Routledge and Kegan Paul, 1973); and idem, *Legitimation of Belief* (London: Cambridge University Press, 1974); Thomas Kuhn, *The Structure of Scientific Revolutions,* 2d ed., enlarged (Chicago: University of Chicago Press, 1970); Bryan Magee, *Modern British Philosophy* (London: Secker and Warburg, 1971).

3. Merriam, *The Anthropology of Music,* 32; John Blacking, *How Musical is Man?* (Seattle: University of Washington Press, 1973).

4. This term is of disputed origin. *The Oxford English Dictionary* gives "Coolie" (Urdu *qulī, qūlī,* Bengalī *kūlī,* Tamil, Telugu, Canarese, Malayalam, *kūli*), "by some considered to be originally Tamil, and identical with the word *kūli,* "hire, payment, for occasional menial work." . . . The objection to this is that the first known mention of Coolies early in the 17th c. refers not to the Tamil country, in the south, but to the region of Guzerat, in the west of India." The word was used in 1680 according to J. T. Wheeler, *Madras* (1861), 1, 129: "That the drum be beat to call all coolies."

5. Statistics on the social, religious, and economic profile of the indentured laborers can be found in Louis Aimé Gastons de Verteuil, *Trinidad: Its Geography, . . . and Prospects* (London: Cassell, 1884); Surgeon-Major D. W. D. Comins, *Notes on Emigration from India to Trinidad* (Calcutta: Bengal Secretariat Press, 1893); N. P. Bowen and B. G. Montserin, eds., *Colony of Trinidad and Tobago Census Album* (Port of Spain: Government Press, 1948); V. Richards, *Annual Report on Emigration from the Port of Calcutta to British and Foreign Colonies in 1877–78* (1878), in *Notes on Indian Immigration 1878–1893;* George Grierson, *Report on Colonial Emigration* (Calcutta: Government of India, 1883); Morton Klass, *East Indians in Trinidad: A Study of Cultural Persistence* (New York: Columbia University Press, 1961); Hugh Tinker, *A New System of Slavery: The Export of Indian Labour Overseas, 1830–1920* (London: Oxford University Press, 1974); Nagendranath Gangulee, *Indians in the Empire Overseas* (London: New India Publishing House, 1947); Caird to Hope, 19 September, 16 October, 23 December 1844, Public Record Office MSS, Colonial Office, 318: 162 (Coolie Emigration 2058, 2300, 188); *Parliamentary Papers,* 1846, XXIV [c. 708], 32–33, and 1847, XXXIII [c. 809], 158–63; Edgar L. Erickson, "The Introduction of East Indian Coolies into the British West Indies" (*The Journal of Modern History* 6, no. 2 [June 1934]); Arthur and Juanita Niehoff, *East Indians in the West Indies* (Milwaukee, Wisc.: Milwaukee Public Museum, 1960); Eric Williams, *History of the People of Trinidad and Tobago* (London: André Deutsch, 1962); Bridget Brereton, "The Experience of Indentureship, 1845–1917," in John Gaffar La Guerre, ed., *Calcutta to Caroni: The East Indians of Trinidad* (Trinidad: Longman Caribbean, 1974).

6. Further information about the Indian diaspora, including distribution and population statistics, can be found in Colin Clarke, Ceri Peach, and Steven Vertovec, *South Asians Overseas: Migration and Ethnicity* (Cambridge: Cambridge University Press, 1990); George Kurian and Ram P. Srivastava, *Overseas Indians: A Study in Adaptation* (New Delhi: Vikas, 1983); I. M. Cumpston, *Indians Overseas in British Territories, 1834–1854* (London: Oxford University Press, 1953); Noel Deerr, "Indian Labour in the Sugar Industry" (*International Sugar Journal* 40 [1938]: 94–98); Kingsley Davis, *The Population of India and Pakistan* (Princeton: Princeton University Press, 1951); Raymond Firth, David Pocock, H. S. Morris, Afrian Mayer, and Burton Benedict, "Factions in Indian and Overseas Indian Societies" (*British Journal of Sociology* 8 [1957]: 291–342); N. Gangulee, *Indians in the Empire Overseas* (London: New India Publishing House, 1947); Chandra Jayawardena, "Migration and Social Change: A Survey of Indian Communities Overseas" (*Geographical Review* 58 [1963]: 426–49) and "Migrants, Networks and Identities" (*New Community* 2 [1973]: 430–50); A. Lemon and N. Pollock, eds., *Studies in Overseas Settlement and Population* (London: Longman, 1980); G. W. Roberts and J. Byrne, "Summary Statistics on Indenture and Associated Migration Affecting the West Indies, 1834–1918" (*Population Studies* 20 [1966]: 125–34); Panchanan Saha, *Emigration of Indian Labour, 1834–1900* (Delhi: People's Publishers, 1970); Hugh Tinker, *A New System of Slavery: The Export of Indian Labour Overseas, 1830–1920* (London: Oxford University Press, 1974); Michael Twaddle, ed., *Expulsion of a Minority* (London: Athlone, 1975); Steven Vertovec, *Hindu Trinidad: Religion, Ethnicity, and Socio-Economic Change* (London: Macmillan; Warwick University Press, 1992); James L. Watson, ed., *Between Two Cultures* (Oxford: Blackwell, 1977).

7. *John Morton of Trinidad: Pioneer Missionary of the Presbyterian Church in Canada to the East Indians in the British West Indies. Journals, Letters and Papers,* ed. Sarah Morton (Toronto: Westminster, 1916), 321. The village described in this passage is Charlieville, Felicity's neighbor to the east. The following year, Morton visited Felicity: "Sabbath, Sept. 16, 1891, I spent in Chaguanas. In the morning I went to Kakandi settlement, on the margin of the Grande Savanna; for two miles the road was a mere track through tall grass. I had to dismount several times to get my mule over deep ravines with only a log across them. At length I came to rice fields all under water, and a stream that had carried away the passengers' log. John Ganesh, my catechist [at Chaguanas], here fortunately met me. He wears the native clothing and no shoes, so with his kapra [i.e., loin-cloth] tucked up to his thighs he fears neither mud nor water. He was a soldier in India, is over six feet high, and fertile in resources; so he carries me over on his back. . . . We met in a shed thatched with palm leaves, and without walls. Into this shelter seventy-five persons were packed. To one of the posts a cock was tied which plumed its feathers close to my feet during the service, while several dogs lay at their masters' feet" (324). Ellipsis in original.

8. Many words now obsolete in England are preserved in the everyday language of Trinidad. *Crapaud,* now obsolete according to *The Oxford English Dictionary,* is an example of these marginal survivals. In the fifteenth century, it took the forms *crapault, -pauld, -pault, -pald, crepaud(e), -pawd;* in the sixteenth century, *crapaude, -pawd (crapeaux, cropolte, crapal);* and, in the seventeenth century, *crapaud,* from the French *crapaud,* in Old French *crapaut, -ot,* for earlier *-ault.* It was used by William Caxton in 1481: "Yf the tode, Crapault, or spyncop, byte a man or woman, they be in daunger for to dye"; and by him again in 1485: "Serpentes, crapauldes, and other beestes."

9. The word *ramage* (pronounced in Trinidad as *ramagé*), the song or cry of birds, also is obsolete, but persists in Trinidad as a marginal survival. *The Oxford English Dictionary* says that it is derived from the French *ramage* = Provencal *ramatge.* In the seventeenth century, it was also spelled *rammage.* In 1616, William Drummond of Hawthornden used it in one of his poems: "My Lute bee as thou wast when thou didst grow . . . in some shadie Groue. . . . And Birds on thee their Ramage did bestow." Before 1693, Sir Thomas Urquhart used it in *The Works of Mr. Francis Rabelais:* "The barking of currs, bawling of mastiffs . . . rammage of Hawks."

10. *Bawling* is another unusual Trinidadian word. Unlike *crapaud* and *ramage,* it is not obsolete, but is commonly used in Trinidad, especially informally, in a sense that has long been obsolete elsewhere. The Trinidadian meaning follows the earliest use in English (in the fifteenth century), referring to the howling or yelping of dogs, and later to other animals. *The Oxford English Dictionary* says the word was probably adapted from the medieval Latin *baula-re* (unlike *crapaud* and *ramage,* which are derived from the French). The *Promptorium parvulorum* of 1440 mentions "Baffynge or bawlynge of howndys" and the *Fardle of Facions Conteining the Auncinte Maners of Affrike and Asia* of 1555 says: "Their singing is like the bawlynge of woulues." "Bawling" is mentioned in song 148.

11. The Hindu lunar calendar used in Felicity has months of 30 days, each divided into halves *(paksh)* of 15 days. The first half is called *sukr-paksh* and the second *krishn-paksh.* The days of each half are numbered 1 to 15.

12. A. C. Burnell, "Saman Chants from 'The Arsheyabrahmana,'" *Hindu Music from Various Authors,* 3d ed., comp. Sourindro Mohun Tagore (Varanasi: Chowkhamba Sanskrit Series Office, 1965), 407–12; Alain Daniélou, "Vedic Recitation and Chant," *The Music of India* 1 (Barenreiter Unesco Series, 1965–68), disc notes; A. H. Fox Strangways, *The Music of Hindostan* (Oxford: Clarendon Press, 1914); J. E. B. Gray, "An Analysis of Nambudiri Rgvedic Recitations and the Nature of the Vedic Accent," *Bulletin of the School of Oriental and African Studies* (University of London), 22 (1959): 500-530; J. M. Van Der Hoogt, *The Vedic Chant Studied in its Textual and Melodic Form* (Wageningen, Holland: H. Veenman and Sons, 1929); V. Raghavan, "Sama Veda and Music," *Journal of the Music Academy, Madras* 33 (1962): 127–33; T. S. Ramakrishnan, "The Music in the Chant of Sama Veda Hymns," *Journal of the Music Academy, Madras* 38 (1967): 59–62; F. J. Staal, *Nambudiri Veda Recitation* (The Hague: Mouton, 1961).

13. An insightful discussion of the evolution of *parang* is in Krister Malm, "The Parang of Trinidad: A Case of Transformation through Exploitation" (*Anthropologiska Studier,* nos. 25–26 [1978]: 42–44).

14. The connection between this repertory and the north Indian *tāl, chautāl,* a rhythmic cycle of 12 beats, is not clear, as most of the Trinidad examples have a rhythmical cycle of four, seven, or eight beats (as in Example II).

15. Religious ecstasy during Holī is described in Henry, "The Meanings of Music in a North Indian Village," 119–142: "The music of holi is an important agent in the infusion of *mastī,* which is the valued sensual, intoxicating experience of the participants in the rites of holi' (142). When I played my Trinidad recordings for S. M. Pandey of Ballia, Professor of Hindi and Bhojpurī and authority on Indian oral epic, he told me that they exemplified the *nāradi* singing style as he remembered it from Uttar Pradesh over thirty years ago. This style of group singing of the *Rāmāyaṇ* with crescendo and accelerando, is dying out in the regions of Uttar Pradesh with which he is familiar. In the more remote rural areas of Uttar Pradesh I recorded examples similar to those here presented from Trinidad. The Holī repertory is changing with the times, no surprise since this festival is so popular and so lively. The texts of Holī songs from Surinam are given in U. Arya, *Ritual Songs and Folksongs of the Hindus of Surinam* (Leiden: E. J. Brill, 1968). The reversal of social roles during Holī festivities in western Uttar Pradesh is discussed in McKim Marriott, "The Feast of Love," in *Krishna: Myths, Rites, and Attitudes,* ed. Milton B. Singer (Chicago: University of Chicago Press, 1966). Further information on Trinidadian customs for Holī is offered in *The Phagwa Annual '74,* ed. Harry Amarsingh (1974).

16. In *Caribbean Currents: Caribbean Music from Rumba to Reggae* (1995), Peter Manuel described local Indo-Caribbean classical music as incorporating "somewhat garbled elements of North Indian classical music," assuming perhaps a historical relationship that never existed between India's urban elite and Uttar Pradesh peasants.

Bibliography

Adams, Harriet Chalmers. "The East Indians in the New World." *National Geographic Magazine* 18, no. 7 (July 1907): 485–91.

Adesh, H. S. *Aayaa Sharan Tumharee.* Vol. 5. Aranguez, Trinidad: Bharatiya Vidya Sansthhaan, n.d. Mimeo.

———. "Bharatiya Vidya Sansthhaan of Trinidad and Tobago: Syllabus and Rules and Regulations from Sargam to Seventh Year—Sangeet Kalanidhi—Vocal and Instrumental and Fourth Year—Sangeet Prasson—Dance," *Saptak* ("Octave"), comp. Kumar Satyaketu. 34 pp. Aranguez, Trinidad: Bharatiya Vidya Sansthhaan, n.d. Mimeo.

———. *Collection of a Few Articles on Diwali,* comp. Rajendra Gajadarsingh. Aranguez, Trinidad: Bharatiya Vidya Sansthhaan, n.d. Mimeo.

———. "Contribution of Antarraashtreeyaa Bharatiya Vidya Sansthhaan in the All-Round Development of the Hindu Society of Trinidad by Prof. H. S. Adesh, Director General of B.V.S. on the Occasion of the Second World Hindu Conference to be Held in Pyayag India, from the 25th to 27th January, 1979." *Jyoti* 11, no. 9 (March 1979): 4–9. Mimeo.

———. *Deshbhakti* ("Patriotism"): *One Act Play.* Aranguez, Trinidad: Bharatiya Vidya Sansthhaan, n.d. Mimeo.

———. *Jeewan Deepak: Selected Divali Songs,* comp. Kumar Satyaketu. Aranguez, Trinidad: Bharatiya Vidya Sansthhaan, n.d. Mimeo.

———. *Jyoti. Monthly Magazine of the Bharatiya Vidya Sansthhaan, Trinidad and Tobago.* Vol. 1 (1968). Mimeo.

———. *Koti Koti Deep Jale: Diwali Songs by Prof. H. S. Adesh, M.A.B.T.* Aranguez, Trinidad: Bharatiya Vidya Sansthhaan, 1978. Mimeo.

———. *Lagan Lagee Tere Charano Men.* Vol. 4. Aranguez, Trinidad: Bharatiya Vidya Sansthhaan, n.d. Mimeo.

———. *Light of Divali (Excerpts from the Speeches of Gurudev Prof. H. S. Adesh),* ed. Shri Doechan Das. 2 Vols. Aranguez, Trinidad: Bharatiya Vidya Sansthhaan, 1977–78. Mimeo.

———. *Mat Ho Niraash,* Vol. 3. Aranguez, Trinidad: Bharatiya Vidya Sansthhaan, n.d. Mimeo.

———. *Nishkaam Raho.* Aranguez, Trinidad: Bharatiya Vidya Sansthhaan, n.d. Mimeo.

———. *Raaga Vivek.* 2 vols. Aranguez, Trinidad: Bharatiya Vidya Sansthhaan, n.d. Mimeo.

———. *Ramzan: Selected Eid Songs of Prof. H. S. Adesh,* comp. Kumar Satyaketu. Aranguez, Trinidad: Bharatiya Vidya Sansthhaan, n.d. Mimeo.

———. *Saagar-Suttaa Lakshmi: Divali Songs of Prof. H. S. Adesh, M.A.B.T.* Aranguez, Trinidad: Bharatiya Vidya Sansthhaan, 1978. Mimeo.

———. *Saptak* ("Octave"), comp. Kumar Satyaketu. Tunapuna, Trinidad: Bharatiya Vidya Sansthhaan, n.d. Mimeo.

———. *Taal Vivek.* Aranguez, Trinidad: Bharatiya Vidya Sansthhaan, n.d. Mimeo.

———. *Trinidad Men Prathhana Hindi Sahitya Sādhaka,* ed. Smt. Nirmala Adesh. Aranguez, Trinidad: Bharatiya Vidya Sansthhaan, n.d. Mimeo.

Ahye, Molly. "Carnival, the Manipulative Polymorph: An Interplay of Social Stratification." Pp. 399–416 in *Social and Occupational Stratification in Contemporary Trinidad and Tobago,* ed. Selwyn Ryan. St. Augustine, Trinidad: Institute of Social and Economic Research, University of the West Indies, 1991.

———. *Golden Heritage: The Dance in Trinidad and Tobago.* Port of Spain: Heritage Cultures Ltd., 1978.

Alladin, M. P. "Artists and Craftsmen." Pp. 136–46 in *David Frost Introduces Trinidad and Tobago,* ed. Michael Anthony and Andrew Carr. London: André Deutsch, 1975.

———. "Festivals of Trinidad and Tobago." *New Vision* 1, no. 1 (March 1974): 3–10.

———. *The Folk Arts of Trinidad and Tobago.* Port of Spain: Ministry of Education and Culture, Trinidad and Tobago, n.d.

Allmon, Charles. "Happy-go-Lucky Trinidad and Tobago." *National Geographic Magazine* 102, no. 1 (January 1953): 35–75.

Amarsingh, Harry, ed. *The Phagwa Annual '74.* San Fernando: By the author, 1974.

Anthony, Michael. *First in Trinidad.* Port of Spain: Circle Press, 1985.

———. *Parade of Carnivals of Trinidad, 1839–1939.* Port of Spain: Circle Press, 1989.

Anthony, Michael, and Andrew Carr, eds. *David Frost Introduces Trinidad and Tobago.* London: André Deutsch, 1975.

Archer, William George. *Songs for the Bride: Wedding Rites of Rural India,* ed. Barbara Stoler Miller and Mildred Archer. New York: Columbia University Press, 1985.

Archer, William George, and Sankatha Prasad. "Bhojpurī Village Songs." *The Journal of Bihar and Orissa Research Society* (1948): 1–48.

Arensberg, Conrad M. "The Community Study Method." *The American Journal of Sociology* 60, no. 2 (1954): 109–24.

Arya Pratinidhi Sabha of Trinidad (Inc.). *Arya Vir Dal, Youth Arm of the Arya Pratinidhi Sabha of Trinidad (Inc.), 3d Annual Shikshan Shivir (Training Camp).* Trinidad: Barrackpore Vedic School, 1977. Mimeo.

The Arya Sandesh 1, no. 3 (July 1947). Port of Spain: Arya Samaj.

Arya, Usharbudh. *Ritual Songs and Folksongs of the Hindus of Surinam.* Leiden: E. J. Brill, 1968.

Asja Qaseeda Book. Rev. ed. Port of Spain: Anjuman Sunnat ul-Jamaat Assoc. Inc. of Trinidad and Tobago, 1962; 2d rev. ed., 1967.

"A Tribute—The Late Nazir Mohammed." *Filmindia* (March 1967).

Baba, Bhagawan Sri Sathya Sai. *Why I Incarnate.* Anantapur, Andhra Pradesh: By the author, n.d.

———. *Bhajans and Chants of Shri Satya Sai Baba.* [Trinidad, ?1975].

———. *Bhajan Songbook: Coordinated with Bhajan Learning Tapes No. 1 & 2.* Los Angeles: S.A.I. Foundation, n.d.

Bahadoorsingh, Ganesh, and Roderick Noel. *Sai Bulletin* 1, no. 1 (July 1974).

Banks, C. *Report on the Emigration from the Port of Calcutta to British and Foreign Colonies.* Calcutta: The Bengal Secretariat Book Depot, 1905, 1906, 1907.

Barth, Fredrik, ed. *Ethnic Groups and Boundaries: The Social Organization of Culture Difference.* Boston: Little, Brown, 1969.

Barua, Hem. *Folksongs of India.* Delhi: Indian Council for Cultural Relations, 1963.

Beames, John. "Notes on the Bhojpurī Dialect of Hindi Spoken in Western Bihār." *Journal of the Royal Asiatic Society* 3 (1868): 483–508.

Belcher, E. A., and J. A. Williamson. *Migration within the British Empire.* London: W. Collins Sons and Co., Ltd, 1924.

Bell, J. H. "Field Techniques in Anthropology." *Mankind* 5, no. 1 (November 1954): 3–8.

———. "Observation in Anthropology." *Mankind* 5, no. 2 (September 1955): 55–60.

Benedict, Burton. *Indians in a Plural Society: A Report on Mauritius.* London: HMSO, 1961.

———. "Stratification in Plural Societies." *American Anthropologist* 64 (1962): 1235–46.

Besson, Gérard. *A Photograph Album of Trinidad at the turn of the Nineteenth Century.* Port of Spain: Paria Publishing Co., 1985.

Bhajanavali. Prasanthinilayam, India: Sri Sathya Sai Books and Publications, Sri Sathya Sai Central Trust, 1983.

Bharat Sevashram Sangha. *Statements of Accounts for 1973–74 & 74–75 Corresponding to 1380 & 1381 B.S. & General Report.* Bharat Sevashram Sangha, Calcutta, [?1975].

Bhatkhande, Vishnu Narayan. *Hindustānī-Sangīta-Paddhati.* 4 vols. Poona: B. S. Skuthankar, 1914–32.

———. *Kramik-Pustak-Mālikā.* 6 vols. Bombay, 1913–37.

Bisson, S. Ganga. *The Ramayana: A Way of Life.* Chase Village, Trinidad: By the author, 1973.

Bissoondath, Neil. *Digging Up the Mountains.* London: Penguin, 1987.

Bissoondialsingh, Smt. Usha Tara. "Dhrupad Singing in Trinidad." B.I. Mus. thesis. Aranguez, Trinidad: Bharatiya Vidya Sansthhaan, 1973. Mimeo.

———. "Indian Music in Trinidad." *Jyoti* 9, nos. 1–5 (July–November 1976).

Blacking, John. *How Musical is Man?* Seattle: University of Washington Press, 1973.

Blank, Jonah. *Arrow of the Blue-Skinned God: Retracing the Ramayana Through India.* New York: Doubleday, 1993.

Bowen, N. P., and B. G. Montserin, eds. *Colony of Trinidad and Tobago Census Album.* Port of Spain: Government Press, 1948.

Boyke, Roy, ed. *Patterns of Progress: Trinidad and Tobago 10 Years of Independence.* Port of Spain: Key Caribbean Publications (Trinidad) Ltd., 1972.

Braithwaite, Lloyd. "The Present Status of Social Sciences in the British Caribbean." Pp. 99–109 in *Caribbean Studies: A Symposium,* ed. Vera Rubin. Seattle: University of Washington Press, 1960.

———. "Social Stratification and Cultural Pluralism." *Annals of the New York Academy of Sciences* 83, art. 5: "Social and Cultural Pluralism in the Caribbean" (20 January 1960): 816–36.

———. "Social Stratification in Trinidad: A Preliminary Analysis." *Social and Economic Studies* 2 (October 1953): 5–175.

———. "Stratification in Trinidad." *Slaves, Free Men, Citizens: West Indian Perspectives,* ed. Lambros Comitas and David Lowenthal. Garden City, N.Y.: Anchor Books, 1973.

Brenneis, Donald. "About Those Scoundrels I'll Let Everyone Know: Challenge Singing in a Fiji Indian Community." *Journal of American Folklore* 88 (1983): 283–91.

———. "The Emerging Soloist: Kavvali in Bhatagaon." *Asian Folklore Studies* 42 (1983): 63–76.

Brereton, Bridget. "The Experience of Indentureship, 1845–1917." Pp. 25–38 in *Calcutta to Caroni: The East Indians of Trinidad,* ed. John Gaffar La Guerre. Trinidad: Longman Caribbean, 1974.

———. *Race Relations in Colonial Trinidad 1870–1900.* Cambridge: Cambridge University Press, 1979.

———. "Social Organisation and Class, Racial and Cultural Conflict in Nineteenth-Century Trinidad. Pp. 33–59 in *Trinidad Ethnicity,* ed. Kevin A. Yelvington. Knoxville: University of Tennessee Press, 1993.

British Consul, Surinam. "Account of Dr De Wolfe." Foreign Office, London, 2 March 1883.

Brooke, Tal. *Sai Baba: Lord of the Air.* New Delhi: Vikas Publishing House, 1979.

Budram, Km. Uma. "Raag-Raaginee Paddhati" (Classification of Ragas and Raginees in Indian Music). B.I. Mus. thesis, Bharatiya Vidya Sansthhaan, Aranguez, Trinidad, 1972.

Burnley, William Hardin. *Description of the Island of Trinidad and of the Advantages To Be Derived from Emigration to that Colony.* New York: J. Van Norden, 1839.

———. *Observation on the Present Condition of the Island of Trinidad, and the Actual State of the Experiment of Negro Emancipation.* London: Longman, Brown, Green and Longmans, 1842.

Canadian Mission Council, Trinidad. *The Canadian Presbyterian Mission to East Indians.* Port of Spain: B. W. I. Franklin's Electric Printery, 1911.

Carmichael, Mrs. A. C. *Five Years in Trinidad and St. Vincent: A View of the Social Conditions of the White, Colored, and Negro Population of the West Indies.* 2 vols. London: Whittaker, 1834.

Chandrasekhar, S. "The Emigration and Status of Indians in the British Empire." *Social Forces* 24, no. 2 (Dec. 1945): 152–60.

Chaudhuri, Shubha. "Sohar, Kajri, and Steel Bands: Helen Myers' Collection of Bhojpuri Songs from Felicity, Trinidad." *Samvadi,* Newsletter of the Archive and Research Center for Ethnomusicology, New Delhi (Summer–Fall, 1989).

Clark, Henry James. *"Iere," the Land of the Humming Bird, Being a Sketch of the Island of Trinidad. Specially Written for the Trinidad Court of the World's Fair, Chicago, by Henry James Clark, F.S.S.* Port of Spain: Government Printing Office, 1893.

———. *Trinidad: A Field for Emigration, A Sketch.* Port of Spain: Government Printing Office, 1886.

Clarke, Colin G. "Caste Among Hindus in a Town in Trinidad: San Fernando." Pp. 165–99 in *Caste in Overseas Indian Communities,* ed. Barton M. Schwartz. San Francisco: Chandler Publishing Co., 1967.

———. *East Indians in a West Indian Town: San Fernando, Trinidad, 1930–1970.* London: Allen and Unwin, 1986.

———. "Spatial Pattern and Social Interaction Among Creoles and Indians in Trinidad and Tobago." Pp. 116–135 in *Trinidad Ethnicity,* ed. Kevin A. Yelvington. Knoxville: University of Tennessee Press, 1993.

Clarke, Colin, Ceri Peach, and Steven Vertovec. *South Asians Overseas: Migration and Ethnicity.* Cambridge: Cambridge University Press, 1990.

Collens, J. H. *A Guide to Trinidad.* London: Elliott Stock, 1888.

———. *Handbook of Trinidad and Tobago for the Use of Settlers.* Board of Agriculture. Port of Spain: Government Printing Office, 1912.

Comins, D. W. D. "Letter to the Secretary to the Government of Bengal General, Dept., Calcutta." *Notes on Indian Immigration, 1878–1893.* Bengal, Calcutta: Secretariat Press, 1893.

———. "Note on the Abolition of Return Passages to East Indian Immigrants from the Colonies of Trinidad and British Guiana." Pp. 41–60 in *Notes on Indian Immigration, 1878–1893.* Calcutta: Bengal Secretariat Press, 1893.

———. *Notes on Emigration from India to Trinidad.* Calcutta: Bengal Secretariat Press, 1893.

Comitas, Lambros. *Caribbeana 1900–1965: A Topical Bibliography.* Seattle: University of Washington Press for the Research Institute for the Study of Man, 1968.

Comitas, Lambros, and David Lowenthal. *Slaves, Free Men, Citizens: West Indian Perspectives.* Garden City, N.Y.: Anchor Books, 1973.

———. *Work and Family Life: West Indian Perspectives.* Garden City, N.Y.: Anchor Books, 1973.

Correspondence Respecting the Coolie Disturbances in Trinidad at the Mohurrum Festival and the Report of H. W. Norman. London: Eyer and Spottiswoode, 1885.

Cross, Malcolm. *The East Indians of Guyana and Trinidad.* London: Minority Rights Group, 1972.

Crowley, Daniel J. "Cultural Assimilation in a Multiracial Society." *Annals of the New York Academy of Sciences* 83 (20 January 1960): 850–54; art. 5: "Social and Cultural Pluralism in the Caribbean."

———. "East Indian Festivals in Trinidad Life." *Caribbean Commission Monthly Bulletin* 7, no. 9 (April 1954): 202–4, 208.

———. "Plural and Differential Acculturation in Trinidad." *American Anthropologist* 59, no. 5 (1957): 817–24.

Cudjoe, S. *V. S. Naipaul: A Materialistic Reading.* Amherst: University of Massachusetts Press, 1988.

Cumpston, I. M. *Indians Overseas in British Territories, 1834–1854.* London: Oxford University Press, 1953.

———. "A Survey of Indian Immigration to British Tropical Colonies to 1910." *Population Studies* 10 (1956): 158–65.

Daniélou, Alain. *Northern Indian Music.* New York: Frederick A. Praeger, 1969.

Dauxion-Lavaysse, Jean François. *A Statistical, Commercial and Political Description of Venezuela, Trinidad, Margarita, and Tobago: Containing Various Anecdotes and Observations, Illustrative of the Past and Present State of these Interesting Countries.* Reprint. Westport, Conn.: Negro Universities Press, 1969. (Eng. trans. of *Voyage aux îles de Trinidad, de Tobago, de la Marguerite, et dans diverses parties de Venezuela dans l'Amérique Méridional.* Paris: F. Schoell, 1813.)

Davids, Leo. "The East Indian Family Overseas." *Social and Economic Studies* 13, no. 3 (September 1964): 383–96.

Davis, J. M. *The East Indian Church in Trinidad: Report of a Survey of the Economic and Social Position of the East Indian Churches in Trinidad made for the Board of Foreign Missions of the United Church of Canada by the Dept. of Social and Economic Research of the International Missionary Council.* New York: International Missionary Council, 1942.

Deerr, Noel. "Indian Labour in the Sugar Industry." *International Sugar Journal* 40 (1938): 94–98.

Despres, Leo. A. *Cultural Pluralism and Nationalist Politics in British Guiana.* Chicago: Rand McNally, 1967.

Domingue, Nicole Zuber. "Bhojpuri and Creole in Mauritius: A Study of Linguistic Interferences and its Consequences in Regard to Synchronic Variation and Language Change." Ph.D. diss., University of Texas at Austin, 1971.

Dookeran, Winston. "East Indians and the Economy of Trinidad and Tobago." Pp. 69–83 in *Calcutta to Caroni: The East Indians of Trinidad,* ed. John Gaffar La Guerre. Trinidad: Longman Caribbean, 1974.

Durbin, Mridula Adenwala. "Formal Changes in Trinidad Hindi as a Result of Language Adaptation." *American Anthropologist* 75 (1973): 1290–1304.

Ehrlich, Allen S. "History, Ecology, and Demography in the British Caribbean: An Analysis of East Indian Ethnicity." *Southwestern Journal of Anthropology* 27 (1971): 166–88.

Elder, J. D. "Color, Music and Conflict: A Study of Aggression in Trinidad with Reference to the Role of Traditional Music." *Ethnomusicology* 8, no. 2 (May 1964): 128–36.

———. "Evolution of the Traditional Calypso of Trinidad and Tobago: A Socio-Historical Analysis of Song-Change." Ph.D. diss., University of Pennsylvania, 1966.

———. "The People and their Culture." Pp. 80–84 in *Patterns of Progress,* ed. Roy Boyke. Port of Spain: Key Caribbean Publications, Trinidad, 1972.

———. *Song Games from Trinidad and Tobago.* Philadelphia: American Folklore Society, 1965. Rev. ed. Port of Spain: National Cultural Council Publications, 1973.

Eliot, T. S. *Four Quartets.* London: Faber and Faber, 1944.

Erickson, Edgar L. "East Indian Coolies in the West Indies." Ph.D. diss., Indiana University, 1930.

———. "The Introduction of East Indian Coolies into the British West Indies." *The Journal of Modern History* 6, no. 2 (June 1934): 127–46.

Faigen, Sandra. "Women's Music in Rituals in the Bhojpurī Region of North India." M.A. thesis, Monash University, 1982.

Fairbanks, Gordon H., and Bal Govind Misra. *Spoken and Written Hindi.* Ithaca, N.Y.: Cornell University Press, 1966.

Fanibunda, Eruch B. *Vision of the Divine.* Prashanti Nilayam: Shri Satya Sai Books and Publications, 1976.

Farquhar, J. N. *Modern Religious Movements in India.* London: Macmillan, 1929.

Forbes, Richard Huntington. "Arya Samaj as Catalyst: The Impact of a Modern Hindu Reform

Movement on the Indian Community of Trinidad between 1917 and 1939." *The East Indians in the Caribbean: A Symposium on Contemporary Economics and Political Issues,* ed. Faculty of Social Sciences and Institute of African and Asian Studies. St. Augustine, Trinidad: University of the West Indies, 1979.

Fox Strangways, A. H. *The Music of Hindostan.* Oxford: Clarendon Press, 1914.

Fraser, H. "Folklore from Eastern Gorakhpur." *Journal of the Indian Society of Bengal* 52, pt. 1 (1883): 1–32.

Freilich, Morris. "Cultural Diversity Among Trinidadian Peasants." Ph.D. diss., Columbia University, New York, 1960.

Freilich, Morris, ed. *Marginal Natives: Anthropologists At Work.* New York: Harper and Row, 1970.

Furnivall, J. S. *Colonial Policy and Practice.* London: Cambridge University Press, 1948.

Gambhir, Surendre. "Mauritian Bhojpuri." *Indian Labour Immigration,* ed. U. Bissoondoyal and S. B. C. Sevansing. Mauritius: Mahatma Gandhi Institute, 1986.

Gamble, Rev. W. H. *Trinidad: Historical and Descriptive Being a Narrative of Nine Years in the Island with Special Reference to Christian Missions.* London: Yates and Alexander, 1866.

Gangulee, Nagendranath. *Indians in the Empire Overseas: A Survey.* London: New India Publishing House, 1947.

Gellner, Ernest. *Legitimation of Belief.* London: Cambridge University Press, 1974.

Geoghegan, John. *Note on Emigration from the East Indies to Trinidad.* Calcutta, 1893.

———. "Report on Coolie Emigration from India." *Parliamentary Papers* 47 (1874), 314.

Gokhale, Veena. "Speaking in (Musical) Tongues," *Sunday Mid-Day,* Bombay, 18 September 1988.

Gosine, M. *East Indians and Black Power in the Caribbean: The Case of Trinidad.* New York: African Research Publication, 1986.

Great Britain Colonial Office. *Report on Trinidad and Tobago.* Annual. Suspended 1939–45. London: H.M. Stationary Office.

Green, Helen Bagenstose. "Values of Negroes and East Indian School Children in Trinidad." *Social and Economic Studies* 14, no. 2 (June 1965): 204–16.

Grierson, George Abraham. *Linguistic Survey of India.* 11 vols. Calcutta: Government Printing Office, 1903–27. 2d ed. Bombay: Motilal Banarsidas.

———. *Report on Colonial Emigration from the Bengal Presidency.* Calcutta: Government of India, 1883.

———. *Seven Grammars of the Dialects and Subdialects of the Bihārī Language: Spoken in the Province of Bihār, in the Eastern Portion of North-Western Provinces, and in the Northern Portion of the Central Provinces.* Part 3, *Magadhī Dialect of South Patna and Gaya.* Calcutta: Bengal Secretariat Press, 1883.

———. "Some Biharī Folksongs." *Journal of the Royal Asian Society* 16 (1884): 196–246.

———. "Some Bhoj'pūrī Folksongs." *Journal of the Royal Asian Society* 18 (1886): 207–267.

Gumperz, John J. "Phonological Differences in Three Western Hindi Dialects." *Language* 34 (1958): 212–24.

Gumperz, John J., and C. M. Naim. *Formal and Informal Standards in Hindi Regional Language Area.* Indiana University Publications in Anthropology, Folklore, and Linguistics, 13 (1960): 92–118.

Haley, Alex. *Roots.* Garden City, N.Y.: Doubleday, 1976.

"Half a Century of Indian Film Music." *Filmindia* (May, June, July, 1970).

Handbook of Trinidad and Tobago Published by the Government of Trinidad and Tobago for the use of those who Wish to Know Something About the Colony and its Institutions. Port of Spain: Government Printing Office, 1924.

Haraksingh, Kusha R. "Control and Resistance among Overseas Indian Workers: A Study of Labour on the Sugar Plantations of Trinidad, 1875–1917." *Journal of Caribbean History* 14 (1981): 1–17.

———. "The Hindu Experience in Trinidad." *Collected Papers, Third Conference on East Indians in the Caribbean, August 28–September 5, 1984.* University of the West Indies, 1984.

———. "Structure, Process and Indian Culture in Trinidad." *Immigrants and Minorities* 7, no. 1 (1988): 113–22.

Harris, Marvin. *The Rise of Anthropological Theory: A History of Theories of Culture.* New York: Thomas Y. Crowell, 1968.

Hart, Daniel. *Trinidad and the other West Indian Islands and Colonies.* 2d ed. Port of Spain: The "Chronicle" Publishing Office, 1866.

Henry, Edward O. *Chant the Names of God: Musical Culture in Bhojpuri-speaking India.* San Diego: San Diego State University Press, 1988.

———. "The Meanings of Music in a North Indian Village." Ph.D. diss., Michigan State University, 1973.

———. "Music in the Thinking of North Indian Villagers." *Asian Music* 9, no. 1 (1977): 1–12.

———. "The Variety of Music in a North Indian Village: Reassessing Cantometrics." *Ethnomusicology* 20 (January 1976): 49–66.

Henry, Ralph M. "Notes on the Evolution of Inequality in Trinidad and Tobago." Pp. 56–80 in *Trinidad Ethnicity,* ed. Kevin A. Yelvington. Knoxville: University of Tennessee Press, 1993.

Herskovits, Melville J. *Acculturation: The Study of Culture Contact.* New York: J. J. Augustine, 1938.

———. *Man and His Works.* New York: Alfred A. Knopf, 1948.

———. *The Myth of the Negro Past.* Boston: Beacon Press, 1958.

———. "Problem, Method and Theory in Afroamerican Studies." Pp. 247–70 in *Work and Family Life: West Indian Perspectives,* ed. Lambros Comitas and David Lowenthal. Garden City, N.Y.: Anchor Books, 1973.

Herskovits, Melville J., and Frances S. Herskovits. *Trinidad Village.* New York: Alfred A. Knopf, 1947.

Hertig-Skalická, Jitka. "Fifty Bhojpuri Folksongs from Ballia District: Text, Translation, Commentary, Skeleton-Grammar and Index." Ph.D. diss, University of Basle, 1974.

Hintzen, P. C. *The Costs of Regime Survival: Racial Mobilization, Elite Domination and Control of the State in Guyana and Trinidad.* Cambridge: Cambridge University Press, 1989.

Hood, Mantle. *The Ethnomusicologist.* New York: McGraw-Hill, 1971.

Horowitz, Michael M., ed. *Peoples and Cultures of the Caribbean.* Garden City, N.Y.: Natural History Press, 1971.

India Office Records. *Annual Report on Emigration from the Port of Calcutta to British and Foreign Colonies,* by the Protector of Emigrants. Calcutta: Bengal Government, 1871–1917.

———. Immigration Agent-General, *Trinidad Immigration Report for 1871.*

———. Reports by the Protector of Emigrants, Madras. Annual, 1874–.

Jairazbhoy, Nazir A. *The Rāgs of North Indian Music: Their Structure and Evolution.* Middletown, Conn.: Wesleyan University Press, 1971.

Jayawardena, Chandra. "Migration and Social Change: A Survey of Indian Communities Overseas." *The Geographical Review* 58, no. 3 (July 1968): 437–49.

[Jenkins, John.] *The Coolie, His Rights and Wrongs. Notes of a Journey to British Guiana, with a Review of the System and of the Recent Commission of Inquiry.* London: Strahan and Co., 1871.

Jha, J. C. "The Indian Heritage in Trinidad." Pp. 1–24 in *Calcutta to Caroni: The East Indians of Trinidad,* ed. John Gaffar LaGuerre. Trinidad: Longman Caribbean, 1974.

Kasturi, N. *The Life of Bhagavan Sri Sathya Sai Baba.* Bombay: Dolton Printers, 1969.

———. *Sathya Sai Speaks: Discourses of Bhagavan Sri Sathya Sai Baba.* Vol. 4. Bangalore: Sri Sathya Sai Books and Publications, 1981.

———. *Sathya Sai Baba Speaks: More Discourses Given by Bhagavan Sri Sathya Sai Baba.* Vol. 10. Prashanti Nilayam: Sri Sathya Sai Books and Publications, 1981.

———. *Sathyam, Shivam, Sundaram: The Life of Bhagavan Sri Sathya Sai Baba,* part 2. 2d ed. Sri Sathya Sai Education Foundation, Dharmakshetra, Bombay, 1973.

Kaufmann, Walter. *The Ragas of North India.* Bloomington: Indiana University Press, 1968.

Khan, Aisha. "*Juthaa* in Trinidad: Food, Pollution, and Hierarchy in a Caribbean Diaspora Community." *American Ethnologist* 21, no. 2 (1994): 245–69.

———. "Sipari Mai." *Hemisphere* 2, no. 22 (1990): 40–41.

———. "Survey of Indo-Trinidadian Musical Forms." Report for Smithsonian Institution Folklife Programs, Smithsonian Archives, Washington, D.C. N.d.

———."What is 'a Spanish'?: Ambiguity and 'Mixed' Ethnicity in Trinidad." Pp. 180–207 in *Trinidad Ethnicity,* ed. Kevin A. Yelvington. Knoxville: University of Tennessee Press, 1993.

Kingsley, Charles. *At Last, A Christmas in the West Indies* [1871]. 3d ed. London: Macmillan, 1900.

Kirpalani, Murli J., Mitra G. Sinanan, S. M. Rameshwar, and L. F. Seukeran. *Indian Centenary Review: One Hundred Years of Progress.* Port of Spain: Guardian Commercial Printery, 1945.

Klass, Morton. "Cultural Persistence in a Trinidad East Indian Community." Ph.D. diss., Columbia University, New York, 1959.

———. "East and West Indian: Cultural Complexity in Trinidad." *Annals of the New York Academy of Sciences* 83 (20 January 1960): 855–61; art. 5: "Social and Cultural Pluralism in the Caribbean."

———. *East Indians in Trinidad: A Study of Cultural Persistence.* New York: Columbia University Press, 1961. Reissued by Waveland Press, 1988.

———. *Singing with Sai Baba: The Politics of Revitalization in Trinidad.* Boulder, Colo.: Westview Press, 1991.

Klass, Sheila Solomon. *Everyone in This House Makes Babies.* Garden City, N.Y.: Doubleday, 1964.

Kondapi, C. *Indians Overseas, 1838–1949.* Bombay: Oxford University Press, 1951.

Kroeber, A. L., and Clyde Kluckhohn. *Culture: A Critical Review of Concepts and Definitions.* New York: Vintage Books, 1952.

Kurian, George, and Ram P. Srivastava. *Overseas Indians: A Study in Adaptation.* New Delhi: Vikas Publishing House, 1983.

La Guerre, John Gaffar. "The East Indian Middle Class Today." Pp. 98–107 in *Calcutta to Caroni: The East Indians of Trinidad,* ed. John Gaffar La Guerre. Trinidad: Longman Caribbean, 1974.

———. "Leadership in a Plural Society: The Case of the Indians in Trinidad and Tobago." Pp. 83–112 in *Social and Occupational Stratification in Contemporary Trinidad and Tobago,* ed. Selyn Ryan. St. Augustine: Institute of Social and Economic Research, University of the West Indies, 1991.

La Guerre, John Gaffar, ed. *Calcutta to Caroni: The East Indians of Trinidad.* Trinidad: Longman Caribbean, 1974. 2d ed. 1985.

Lakheeram, Shri R. L. "Importance of Hindi in Trinidad." *Jyoti* 11, no. 6 (December 1978): 7–8.

Lall, G. B. "A Brief Survey of the Arya Samaj Movement in Trinidad." *The Arya-Samaj Brochure* 1, no. 1 (February 1945).

———. [Hindu Marriage Ordinance in Trinidad.] *The Arya Sandesh* 1, no. 3 (July 1947).

"Lata Mangeshkar Imitation Singing Contest." *Filmindia,* 1968.

Lemon, Anthony. "The Indian Communities of East Africa and the Caribbean." Pp. 225–41 in *Studies in Overseas Settlement and Population,* ed. A. Lemon and N. C. Pollock. London: Longman, 1980.

Lesser, Alexander. "Problem Versus Subject Matter as Directives of Research." *American Anthropologist* 41 (1939): 547–82.

Lewis, Oscar. "Controls and Experiments in Field Work." *Anthropology Today,* ed. A. L. Kroeber. Chicago: University of Chicago Press, 1953.

———. *Village Life in Northern India: Studies in a Delhi Village.* Urbana: University of Illinois Press, 1958.

"Local Talent on Parade." *Filmindia,* April–May, 1967.

Lowenthal, David. "The Range and Variation of Caribbean Societies." *Annals of the New York Academy of Sciences* 83 (20 January 1960), art. 5: "Social and Cultural Pluralism in the Caribbean," 786–95.

———. *West Indian Societies.* London: Oxford University Press, 1972.

Lowenthal, David, and Lambros Comitas. *The Aftermath of Sovereignty: West Indian Perspectives.* Garden City, N.Y.: Anchor Books, 1973.

———. *Consequences of Class and Color: West Indian Perspectives.* Garden City, N.Y.: Anchor Books, 1973.

Lubbock, Basil. *Coolie Ships and Oil Sailers.* Glasgow: Brown, Son and Ferguson, 1935.

Lutgendorf, Philip. "Ramayan: The Video." *The Drama Review* 34, no. 2 (Summer 1990): 127–76.

———. "Ram's Story in Shiva's City: Public Arenas and Private Patronage." Pp. 34–61 in *Culture and Power in Banaras: Community, Performance, and Environment, 1800–1980,* ed. Sandria B. Freitag. Berkeley and Los Angeles: University of California Press, 1989.

M'Callum, Pierre Franc. *Travels in Trinidad During the Months of February, March and April, 1803, in a Series of Letters Addressed to a Member of the Imperial Parliament of Great Britain.* Liverpool: W. Jones, 1805.

McKenzie, H. L. "The Plural Society: Some Comments on a Recent Contribution." *Social and Economic Studies* 15, no. 1 (March 1966): 53–60.

McMartin, Grace J., ed. *A Recapitulation of Satya Sai Baba's Divine Teaching.* Hyderabad: Avon Printing Works, 1982.

Mahabir, Kamla. "Satya Sai Movement in Trinidad." M.A. thesis, University of the West Indies, St. Augustine, Trinidad, 1976.

Mahabir, N., and A. Maharaj. "Hindu Elements in the Shango/Orisha Cult of Trinidad." *Indenture and Exile: The Indo-Caribbean Experience,* ed. F. Birbalsingh. *Toronto South Asian Review* (1989): 191–201.

Maharaj, Aknath, ed. *New Vision: A Quarterly Publication* 1, no. 1 (March 1974).

Maharaj, Grace. "To the Black People in T'dad." *Embryo* 2, no. 19 (24 March 1970).

Malik, Yogendra K. *East Indians in Trinidad: A Study in Minority Politics.* London: Oxford University Press, 1971.

Malinowski, Bronislaw. *Argonauts of the Western Pacific.* New York: E. P. Dutton, 1922.

Malm, Krister. "The Parang of Trinidad: A Case of Transformation through Exploitation." *Anthropologiska Studier,* nos. 25–26 (1978): 42–49.

———. "Writings on Ethnic Music and Mesomusic in The Lesser Antilles: A Bibliography." Institute of Musicology, University of Uppsala, Sweden, 1969. Mimeo.

Manuel, Peter. *Caribbean Currents: Caribbean Music from Rumba to Reggae.* Philadelphia: Temple University Press, 1995.

Marriott, McKim. "The Feast of Love." *Krishna: Myths, Rites, and Attitudes,* ed. Milton B. Singer. Chicago: University of Chicago Press, 1966.

———. "Social Structure and Change in a U.P. Village." Pp. 106–21 in *India's Villages*, ed. M. N. Srinivas. London: Asia Publishing House, 1955. 2d rev. ed. 1960.

Merriam, Alan P. *The Anthropology of Music.* Evanston: Northwestern University Press, 1964.

Mesthrie, Rajend. *Language in Indenture: A Sociolinguistic History of Bhojpuri-Hindi in South Africa.* Witwatersrand: Witwatersrand University Press, 1991.

Michaud, Roland, and Sabrina Michaud. *Mirror of India.* Paris: Editions Nathan, 1990.

Mills, George. "Art and the Anthropological Lens." *The Traditional Artist in African Societies,* ed. Warren d'Azevedo. Bloomington: Indiana University Press, 1973.

Mohammed, Patricia. "The 'Creolization' of Indian Women in Trinidad." Pp. 381–97 in *Trinidad and Tobago: The Independence Experience 1962–1987,* ed. Selwyn Ryan. St. Augustine: Institute of Social and Economic Research, University of the West Indies, 1988.

———. "Structures of Experience: Gender, Ethnicity and Class in the Lives of Two East Indian Women." Pp. 208–34 in *Trinidad Ethnicity,* ed. Kevin A. Yelvington. Knoxville: University of Tennessee Press, 1993.

Mohammed, Sham S. *Nur-E-Islam Souvenir Brochure.* San Juan, Trinidad: Nur-E-Islam Mosque Board, [1967].

Mohammed, Sham S., ed. *Tackveeyatul Islamic Association of Trinidad and Tobago Inc. Silver Anniversary Souvenir Brochure.* Port of Spain: Tackveeyatul Islamic Association of Trinidad and Tobago, Inc. [1974].

Mohan, Peggy Ramesar. "Trinidad Bhojpuri: A Morphological Study." Ph.D. diss., University of Michigan, Ann Arbor, 1978.

———. "Two Faces of a Language Death." *India International Centre Quarterly* 2, no. 2 (1984): 133–44.

Mohan, Peggy Ramesar, and P. Zador. "Discontinuity in a Life Cycle: The Death of Trinidad Bhojpuri." *Language* 62 (1986): 291–319.

Morris, H. S. "Indians in East Africa: A Study in a Plural Society." *British Journal of Sociology* 7 (1956): 194–211.

———. *The Indians in Uganda: Caste and Sect in a Plural Society.* London: Weidenfeld and Nicolson, 1968.

Morton, John. *John Morton of Trinidad. Pioneer Missionary of the Presbyterian Church in Canada to the East Indians in the British West Indies. Journals, Letters and Papers,* ed. Sarah E. Morton. Toronto: Westminster Co., 1916.

Mouat, F. J. *Report on the Mortality of Emigrant Coolies on the Voyages to the West Indies in 1856–57. Public Consultations.* Governor-General's Council, September–December, 1858.

Murphet, Howard. *Sai Baba: Man of Miracles.* Delhi: Macmillan of India, 1971.

Myers, Helen. "Felicity, Trinidad: The Musical Portrait of a Hindu Village." Ph.D. diss., University of Edinburgh, 1984.

———. "Folk Music." *The New Oxford Companion to Music.* Oxford: Oxford University Press, 1983.

———. "Indian, East Indian, and West Indian Music in Felicity, Trinidad." Pp. 231–41 in *Ethnomusicology and Modern Music History,* ed. Stephen Blum, Philip V. Bohlman, and Daniel M. Neuman. Urbana: University of Illinois Press, 1991.

———. "The Process of Change in Trinidad East Indian Music." *Journal of the Indian Musicological Society* 9, no. 3 (September 1978): 11–16.

———. "Trinidad and Tobago." *The New Grove Dictionary of Music and Musicians,* 6th ed. London: Macmillan, 1980.

Myers, Helen, ed. *Ethnomusicology: An Introduction.* New York: W. W. Norton, 1992.

———. *Ethnomusicology: Historical and Regional Studies.* New York: W. W. Norton, 1993.

Naipaul, Seepersad. *Gurudeva and Other Indian Tales.* Trinidad: Privately printed 1943; reprinted London: André Deutsch, 1976.

Naipaul, Shiva. *Beyond the Dragon's Mouth.* New York: Viking, 1985.

———. *The Chip-Chip Gatherers.* London: André Deutsch, 1973.

Naipaul, V[idiadhar] S[urajprasad]. *An Area of Darkness.* London: Penguin, 1968.

———. *A House for Mr Biswas.* Harmondsworth: Penguin, 1969.

———. *India: A Wounded Civilization.* New York: Alfred A. Knopf, 1977.

———. *The Loss of El Dorado: A History.* London: André Deutsch, 1969.

———. *The Middle Passage: Impressions of Five Societies—British, French and Dutch—in the West Indies and South America.* Harmondsworth: Penguin, 1969.

———. "Power to the Caribbean People." *The Aftermath of Sovereignty: West Indian Perspectives,* ed. David Lowenthal and Lambros Comitas. Garden City, N.Y.: Anchor Books, 1973.

Narayan, K. "Birds on a Branch: Girl Friends and Wedding Songs in Kangra." *Ethos* 14 (1986): 47–75.

Neehal, R. G. "Presbyterianism in Trinidad: A Study of the Impact of Presbyterianism in the Island of Trinidad in the Nineteenth Century." M.A. thesis, Union Theological Seminary, New York City, 1958.

Nettl, Bruno. *The Study of Ethnomusicology: Twenty-nine Issues and Concepts.* Urbana: University of Illinois Press, 1983.

Nettl, Bruno, and Helen Myers. *Folk Music in the United States: An Introduction.* Detroit: Wayne State University Press, 1976.

Nevadomsky, Joseph John. "Changes in Hindu Institutions in an Alien Environment." *Eastern Anthropologist* 33 (1980): 39–53.

———. "Changing Conceptions of Family Regulation among the Hindu East Indians in Rural Trinidad." *Anthropological Quarterly* 55, no. 4 (1982): 189–96.

———. "The Changing Family Structure of the East Indians in Rural Trinidad." Ph.D. diss., University of California at Berkeley, 1977.

———. "Cultural and Structural Dimensions of Occupational Prestige in an East Indian Community in Trinidad." *Journal of Anthropological Research* 37 (1981): 343–59.

———. "Economic Organization, Social Mobility and Changing Social Status Among the East Indians in Rural Trinidad." *Social and Economic Studies* 33, no. 3 (1984): 31–62.

———. "Social Change and the East Indians in Rural Trinidad: A Critique of Methodologies." *Social and Economic Studies* 31, no. 1 (1982): 90–126.

Nevill, H. R. *Gorakhpur: A Gazetteer, Being Volume XXXI of the District Gazetteers of the United Provinces of Agra and Oudh.* Allahabad: Superintendent, Government Press, United Provinces, 1909.

Niehoff, Arthur. "The Function of Caste among the Indians of the Oropuche Lagoon, Trinidad." Pp. 149–64 in *Caste in Overseas Indian Communities,* ed. Barton M. Schwartz. San Francisco: Chandler Publishing Co., 1967.

———. "The Survival of Hindu Institutions in an Alien Environment." *Eastern Anthropologist* 12, no. 3 (March–May 1959): 171–87.

Niehoff, Arthur, and Juanita Niehoff. *East Indians in the West Indies.* Milwaukee, Wisc.: Milwaukee Public Museum, 1960.

Olmstead, Michael P. *The Small Group.* New York: Random House, 1959.

Osborne, Arthur. *The Incredible Sai Baba: The Life and Miracles of a Modern-day Saint.* Bombay: Orient Longman, 1957.

Pande, T. "Bhojpuri Folklore and Folk Music." *Folkmusic and Folklore: An Anthology,* ed. Hemango Biswas. Vol. 1. Calcutta: Folkmusic and Folklore Research Institute, 1967.

Pareek, Radhey Shyam. *Contribution of the Arya Samaj in the Making of Modern India 1845–1947.* New Delhi: Arya Samaj Foundation Centenary Publications, Sarvadeshik Arya Pratinidhi Sabha, Dayanand Bhawan, Ramlila Ground, 1973.

Parmasad, K. V. "By the Light of a Deya." Pp. 283–91 in *The Aftermath of Sovereignty: West Indian Perspectives,* ed. David Lowenthal and Lambros Comitas. Garden City, N.Y.: Anchor Books, 1973.

Parsons, Talcott. *The Social System.* Glencoe, Ill.: The Free Press, 1951.

Paul, Benjamin D. "Interview Techniques and Field Relationships." *Anthropology Today,* ed. Alfred L. Kroeber. Chicago: University of Chicago Press, 1953.

Pearse, Andrew C. "Aspects of Change in Caribbean Folk Music." *Journal of the International Folk Music Council* 7 (1955): 29–36.

———. "Carnival in Nineteenth Century Trinidad." *Caribbean Quarterly* 4, nos. 3, 4 (March–June 1956): 176–93.

Pelto, Perti J. *Anthropological Research: The Structure of Inquiry.* New York: Harper and Row, 1970.

Polak, Henry S. L. "Indian Labour Emigration Within the Empire." *Asiatic Review* 14 (1918): 140–56.

Popper, Karl R. *Conjectures and Refutations: The Growth of Scientific Knowledge.* 4th ed. London: Routledge and Kegan Paul, 1972.

———. *The Logic of Scientific Discovery.* London: Hutchinson, 1959.

———. *Objective Knowledge: An Evolutionary Approach.* London: Oxford University Press, 1972.

———. *Unended Quest: An Intellectual Autobiography.* Glasgow: William Collins Sons, 1974.

Poynting, J. "East Indian Women in the Caribbean: Experience and Voice." Pp. 231–63 in *India in the Caribbean,* ed. D. Dabydeen and B. Samaroo. London: Hansib, 1987.

Prasad, Hari. "Vedic Organizations in North America and South America." Vedic Research Council, Guyana Arya Pratinidhi Sabha, n.d. Manuscript.

Premdas, Ralph. "Ethnic Conflict in Trinidad and Tobago: Domination and Reconciliation." Pp. 136–60 in *Trinidad Ethnicity,* ed. Kevin A. Yelvington. Knoxville: University of Tennessee Press, 1993.

Purnananda, Swami. *Aum Hindutvam: Vedic Prayer, Hindu Catechism.* London: By the author, n.d.

———. *The Hindu Catechism.* Hindu Cultural Association, Siparia, Trinidad, n.d.

Purnananda, Swami, ed. *Hinduism: Journal of the Bharat Sevashram Sangha, London Branch,* n.d.

Raghubar, Mona. "Is Indian Music a Nuisance?" *Filmindia,* July 1968.

Ramaya, Narsaloo. "Classical Period of Indian Music." *Trinidad Guardian,* September 1973.

———. "How 'Bala Joban' Changed the Song in Our Hearts." *Trinidad Guardian,* 22 January 1974, p. 4.

———. "Indian Dance in Trinidad." *Filmindia,* 1968.

———. "Indian Music and Western Music: A Comparison." *New Vision* 1, no. 1 (March 1974): 30–32.

———. "Indian Music in Trinidad." Port of Spain, 1965. Manuscript.

———. *Naya Zamana 25th Anniversary 1944–1969: A Record of Progress and Achievement in Indian Music by the Oldest Indian Music Band in Trinidad and Tobago.* Port of Spain: Naya Zamana, 1969.

———. "Songs of Tears and Laughter that Lightened the Burden of Barrack Life and Cane-Field Work." *Trinidad Guardian,* n.d.

Ramchand, Kenneth. "Indian-African Relations in Caribbean Fiction." *Wasafiri,* no. 2 (Spring 1985): 18–23.

———. *The West Indian Novel and Its Background.* 2d ed. London: Faber and Faber, 1970; 2d rev. ed. 1983.

Ramdeen, Ramadhar, ed. *Sai News Letter.* Published by the Co-ordinating Committee, West Indies, 27 Grove Road, Valsayn, Trinidad. N.d.

Ramesar, Marianne Diana. "Indian Immigration into Trinidad: 1897–1917." M.A. Thesis, University of the West Indies, St. Augustine, Trinidad, 1973.

Rao, Velcheru Narayana. "A Rāmāyaṇa of Their Own: Women's Oral Tradition in Telugu." Pp. 114–36 in *Many Rāmāyaṇas: The Diversity of a Narrative Tradition in South Asia,* ed. Paula Richman. Berkeley and Los Angeles: University of California Press, 1991.

Redemption Songs: A Choice Collection of One Thousand Hymns and Choruses for Evangelistic Meetings, Soloists, Choirs, the Home. London: Pickering & Inglis, n.d.

Redfield, Robert, Ralph Linton, and Melville J. Herskovits. "Memorandum for the Study of Acculturation." *American Anthropologist* 38 (1936): 149–52.

Richards, V. "Annual Report on Emigration from the Port of Calcutta to British and Foreign Colonies in 1877–78." Pp. 3–18 in *Notes on Indian Immigration 1878–1893.* Calcutta: Bengal Secretariat Press, 1878–93.

Richman, Paula, ed. *Many Rāmāyanas: The Diversity of a Narrative Tradition in South Asia.* Berkeley and Los Angeles: University of California Press, 1991.

Roberts, Helen. "Suggestions to Field-Workers in Collecting Folk Music and Data about Instruments." *Journal of the Polynesian Society* 40 (1931): 103–28.

Rohlehr, Gordon. *Calypso and Society in Pre-Independence Trinidad.* Port of Spain: By the author, 1990.

Rubin, Vera. "Cultural Perspectives in Caribbean Research." Pp. 110–22 in *Caribbean Studies: A Symposium,* ed. Vera Rubin. 2d ed. Seattle: University of Washington Press, 1960.

Ryan, Alan. *The Philosophy of the Social Sciences.* London: Macmillan, 1970.

Ryan, Selwyn D. *Race and Nationalism in Trinidad and Tobago: A Study of Decolonization in a Multiracial Society.* Toronto: University of Toronto Press, 1972.

Saha, Panchanan. *Emigration of Indian Labour, 1834–1900.* Delhi: People's Publishers, 1970.

Sahai-Achuthan, Nisha. "Folk Songs of Uttar Pradesh." *Ethnomusicology* 31, no. 3 (1987): 395–406.

Samaroo, Brinsley. "East Indian Life and Culture." Pp. 119–126 in *David Frost Introduces Trinidad and Tobago,* ed. Michael Anthony and Andrew Carr. London: André Deutsch, 1975.

———. "Hindu Marriage in the Caribbean." *New Vision* 1, no. 1 (March 1974): 11–15.

———. "The Indian Connection: The Influence of Indian Thought and Ideas on East Indians in the Caribbean." Pp. 43–59 in *India in the Caribbean,* ed. D. Dabydeen and B. Samaroo. London: Hansib, University of Warwick, 1987.

———. "Politics and Afro-Indian Relations in Trinidad." Pp. 84–97 in *Calcutta to Caroni: The East Indians of Trinidad,* ed. John Gaffar La Guerre. Trinidad: Longman Caribbean, 1974.

———. "Two Abolutions: African Slavery and East Indian Indentureship." Pp. 25–41 in *India in the Caribbean,* ed. D. Dabydeen and B. Samaroo. London: Hansib, University of Warwick, 1987.

Samlal, Shri Mohan. "Indian Folk Songs in Trinidad." B.I. Mus. thesis, Bharatiya Vidya Sansthhaan, Aranguez, Trinidad, 1972.

Samlal, Shri Mookoonlal. "Pt. V. N. Bhatkhande and His Contribution." B.I. Mus. thesis, Bharatiya Vidya Sansthhaan, Aranguez, Trinidad, 1974.

Sampath, Hugh. "An Outline of the Social History of the Indians in Trinidad." M.A. thesis, Columbia University, New York, 1951.

Sampath, Niels M. "An Evaluation of the 'Creolisation' of Trinidad East Indian Adolescent Masculinity." Pp. 235–53 in *Trinidad Ethnicity,* ed. Kevin A. Yelvington. Knoxville: University of Tennessee Press, 1993.

Sanatan Dharma Maha Sabha of Trinidad and Tobago. *My Prayer Book.* Port of Spain: By the author, n.d.

Sankey, Ira D. *New Hymns and Solos.* London: Morgan and Scott, n.d. Bound in one volume with *Sacred Songs and Solos.*

———. *Sacred Songs and Solos: With Standard Hymns Combined, 750 Pieces.* London: Morgan and Scott, n.d.

Sankey, Ira D., and James McGrananan. *The Christian Choir.* London: Morgan and Scott, n.d. Bound in one volume with *Sacred Songs and Solos.*

Sarma, D. S. *Hinduism through the Ages.* 3d ed. Bombay: Bharatiya Vidya Bhavan, 1967.

Satchidananda, H. H. Sri Swami, comp. *Divine Life Bhajans, Book 1.* Enterprise, Trinidad: Divine Life Society of Trinidad and Tobago, n.d.

———. *Divine Life Havan Yagya Prayer Book.* International Sivananda Yoga Vedanta Academy, Enterprise, Trinidad, n.d.

———. *Divine Life Hindi Text, Book 1.* International Sivananda Yoga Vedanta Academy, Enterprise, Trinidad, n.d.

———. *Divine Life Sandhyaa Bandanaa.* International Sivananda Yoga Vedanta Academy, Enterprise, Trinidad, n.d.

———. *Know Your Ramayan: Lesson 1, Pratham Visraam-Baalkaand.* International Sivananda Yoga Vedanta Academy, Enterprise, Trinidad, n.d.

Schwartz, Barton M. "Caste and Endogamy in Trinidad." *Southwestern Journal of Anthropology* 20, no. 1 (1964): 58–66.

———. "The Dissolution of Caste in Trinidad." Ph.D. diss., University of California at Los Angeles, 1963.

———. "The Failure of Caste in Trinidad." Pp. 117–47 in *Caste in Overseas Indian Communities,* ed. Barton M. Schwartz. San Francisco: Chandler Publishing Co., 1967.

———. "Patterns of East Indian Family Organization in Trinidad." *Caribbean Studies* 5, no. 1 (April 1965): 23–36.

[Scoble, John.] *Hill Coolies: A Brief Exposure of the Deplorable Condition of the Hill Coolies, in British Guiana and Mauritius.* London: Harvey and Darton, 1840.

Seapaul, O. "Hindu Women in Today's Society." *Caribbean Affairs* 3, no. 1 (1988): 90–95.

Segal, Daniel A. "'Race' and 'Colour' in Pre-Independence Trinidad and Tobago." Pp. 81–115 in *Trinidad Ethnicity,* ed. Keven Yelvington. Knoxville: University of Tennessee Press, 1993.

Selvon, S. "Three into One Can't Go: East-Indian, Trinidadian, West Indian." Pp. 13–24 in *India in the Caribbean,* ed. D. Dabydeen and B. Samaroo. London: Hansib, University of Warwick, 1987.

Shils, Edward. *Tradition.* London: Faber and Faber, 1981.

Shirreff, A. G. *Hindi Folk Songs.* Allahabad: Hindi Mandir, 1936.

Shivaprasad, Pandit L., and H. Seereeram. *Vedic Upaasnaa (Vedic Devotions).* Port of Spain: Arya Pratinidhi Sabha of Trinidad, n.d.

Shukla, Shaligram. *Bhojpuri Grammar.* Washington, D.C.: Georgetown University Press, 1981.

Singer, Milton B., ed. *Krishna: Myths, Rites and Attitudes.* Chicago: University of Chicago Press, 1966.

Singh, Chandramani, with Ronald Amend. *Marriage Songs from Bhojpuri Region.* Jaipur: Champa Lal Ranka, 1979.

Singh, Durga Shankar. *Bhojpurī Lok-gīt mẽ Karun Ras.* Allahabad: Hindi Sahitya Sammelan, 1965.

Singh, Kelvin. "East Indians and the Larger Society." Pp. 39–68 in *Calcutta to Caroni: The East Indians of Trinidad,* ed. John Gaffar La Guerre. Trinidad: Longman Caribbean, 1974.

Singh, V. "The Indian in the Trinidadian Novel." *Indenture and Exile: The Indo-Caribbean Experience,* ed. F. Birbalsingh. *Toronto South Asian Review* (1989): 148–58.

Sivananda, Sri Swami, ed. *The Bhagavad Gita: Text, Word-to-Word Meaning, Translation and Commentary.* Sivanandanagar, U.P., India: The Divine Life Society, 1969.

Skinner, E. P. "Ethnic Interaction in a British Guiana Rural Community: A Study in Secondary Acculturation and Group Dynamics." Ph.D. diss., Columbia University, New York, 1955.

Smith, M. G. *A Framework for Caribbean Studies.* Extra-Mural Department, University College of the West Indies, Mona, Jamaica, 1955.

———. "Pluralism and Social Stratification." Pp. 3–35 in *Social and Occupational Stratification in Contemporary Trinidad and Tobago*, ed. Selwyn Ryan. St. Augustine: Institute of Social and Economic Research, University of the West Indies, 1991.

———. *The Plural Society in the British West Indies.* Berkeley and Los Angeles: University of California Press, 1965.

———. "Social and Cultural Pluralism." *Annals of the New York Academy of Sciences* 83 (20 January 1960), art. 5: "Social and Cultural Pluralism in the Caribbean," 763–85.

Smith, Raymond T., and Chandra Jayawardena. "Hindu Marriage Customs in British Guiana." *Social and Economic Studies* 7, no. 2 (June 1958): 178–94.

———. "Marriage and the Family Amongst East Indians in British Guiana." *Social and Economic Studies* 8, no. 4 (December 1959): 321–76.

Smith, Robert Jack. "Muslim East Indians in Trinidad: Retention of Ethnic Identity Under Acculturative Conditions." Ph.D. diss., University of Pennsylvania, 1963.

[Song Sheet]. Port of Spain Hindu Mandir, St. James, July 1973. Mimeo.

[Song Sheet]. Tenth Anniversary of the Sunday Morning Class, Port of Spain Hindu Mandir, St. James, n.d. Mimeo.

Songs of Worship: Sung by William Marrion Branham. Jeffersonville, Ind.: Spoken Word Publications, n.d.

Spencer, Peter. *World Beat: A Listener's Guide to Contemporary World Music on CD.* Pennington, N.J.: A Capella Books, 1992.

Spottswood, Richard. "Discography of West Indian Recordings," comp. Donald Hill. "Calypsonians Speak for the Record." University of the West Indies Library, St. Augustine, Trinidad, 1985. Manuscript.

Spradley, James P., ed. *Culture and Cognition: Rules, Maps, and Plans.* San Francisco: Chandler Publishing Co., 1972.

Srī Rāmcharitmānas (Manasa Lake Brimming over with the Exploits of Srī Rama). Hindi Text with English Translation. 3d ed. Gorakhpur, India: Gita Press, 1976.

Steward, John Othneil. "Coolie and Creole: Differential Adaptation in a Neo-Plantation Village—Trinidad West Indies." Ph.D. diss., University of California at Los Angeles, 1973.

Steward, Julian. *Theory of Culture Change: The Methodology of Multilinear Evolution.* Urbana: University of Illinois Press, 1956.

Stuempfle, S. "The Steelband Movement in Trinidad and Tobago: Music, Politics and National Identity in a New World Society." Ph.D. diss., University of Pennsylvania, 1990.

Swinton, Captain E., and Mrs. *Journal of a Voyage with Coolie Emigrants from Calcutta to Trinidad. By Captain and Mrs. Swinton, Late of the Ship "Salsette,"* ed. James Carlile. London: Alfred W. Bennett, 1859.

Tagore, Rabindranath. *The Gardener.* London: Macmillan, 1922.

———. *Gītānjalī (Song Offerings).* London: Macmillan, 1913.

Taylor, Patrick. "Ethnicity and Social Change in Trinidadian Literature." Pp. 254–74 in *Trinidad Ethnicity*, ed. Kevin A. Yelvington. Knoxville: University of Tennessee Press, 1993.

Tewari, Laxmi Ganesh. "Folk Music of India: Uttar Pradesh." Ph.D. diss., Wesleyan University, Middletown, Conn., 1974.

Thapar, Romila. "The Ramayan Syndrome." *Seminar*, no. 353 (January 1989): 74.

Tikasingh, G. I. M. "The Establishment of the Indians in Trinidad, 1870–1900." Ph.D. diss., University of the West Indies, 1973.

Tinker, Hugh. *The Banyan Tree: Overseas Emigrants from India, Pakistan, and Bangladesh.* Oxford: Oxford University Press, 1977.

———. "British Policy towards a Separate Identity in the Caribbean, 1920–1950." Pp. 33–47 in *East Indians in the Caribbean*, ed. Bridget Brereton and Winston Dookeran. London: Kraus, 1982.

———. "Indians Abroad: Emigration, Restriction, and Rejection." Pp. 15–29 in *Expulsion of a Minority,* ed. Michael Twaddle. London: Athlone, 1975.

———. *A New System of Slavery: The Export of Indian Labour Overseas, 1830–1920.* London: Oxford University Press, 1974. 2d ed. 1993.

———. *Separate and Unequal: India and the Indians in the British Commonwealth, 1920–1950.* London: C. Hurst and Co., 1976.

Tiwari, Udai Narain. *Bhāsāsāstra ki ruparĕkhā.* Allahabad: Bharti Bhandar Lidar Press, 1963.

———. "Bhojpuri Verb Roots." *Indian Linguistics* 14 (1954): 529–39.

———. "Intrusive Vowels in Bhojpuri." *Indian Linguistics, Turner Jubilee Volume,* 1 (1958): 49–51.

———. *The Origin and Development of Bhojpuri.* Calcutta: The Asiatic Society, 1960.

Trinidad Calypso 1977. Topic Publications, [Port of Spain, 1977].

Trinidad Carnival. Republication of "Trinidad Carnival Issue," *Caribbean Quarterly* 4, nos. 3–4 (1956). Port of Spain: Paria Publishing Co., 1988.

Trinidad and Tobago. Immigration Department. *The Protector's Report on Emigrant Ships and Immigrants Arrived During the Season of 1898.* Port of Spain: Government Printing Office, 1899.

———. *Trinidad and Tobago August 1962.* Port of Spain: Trinidad and Tobago Government, 1962.

Trollope, Anthony. *The West Indies and the Spanish Main.* London: Chapman and Hall, 1859.

Trotman, D. V. "The Image of Indians in Calypso: Trinidad 1946–1986." Pp. 385–98 in *Social and Occupational Stratification in Contemporary Trinidad and Tobago,* ed. Selwyn Ryan. St. Augustine: University of the West Indies, Institute of Social and Economic Research, 1991.

Tyson, John D. *Report on the Condition of Indians in Jamaica, British Guiana and Trinidad . . .* 1938–39. Simla: Government of India Press, 1939.

University of Sussex, School of African and Asian Studies. *Postgraduate Course: Social Anthropology Handbook, Fieldwork in Social Anthropology.* Mimeo.

Upadhyaya, Hari Shankar. *Bhojpuri Folksongs from Ballia.* Atlanta: Indian Enterprises, 1988.

———. "The Joint Family Structure and Familial Relationship Patterns in the Bhojpurī Folksongs." Ph.D. diss., Indiana University, 1967.

Upadhyaya, Krishna Deva. *Bhojpurī Lok-gīt (Bhag 1).* Allahabad: Hindi Sahitya Sammelan, 1954.

———. *Bhojpurī Lok Sāhita kā Adhyayan* ["A Critical Study, in Hindi, of Bhojpurī Folklore and Folk Literature"]. Banaras: Vishwavidyalaya Prakashan, 1960.

———. *Bhojpurī Lok-gīt (Bhag 2).* Allahabad: Hindi Sahitya Sammelan, 1966.

———. "An Introduction to Bhojpurī Folksongs and Ballads." *Midwest Folklore* 7 (1957): 85–94.

Upadhyaya, Ravi Shankar. *A Cultural Study of Bhojpuri Folksongs.* Varanasi: Lok Sankriti Shodha Sansthan, 1985.

Vatuk, Ved Prakash. "Craving for a Child in the Folksongs of East Indians in British Guiana." Bloomington, Ind., *Journal of the Folklore Institute* 2, no. 1 (1965): 55–77.

———. "Protest Songs of East Indians in British Guiana." *Journal of American Folklore* 77 (1964): 220–35.

———. *Thieves in My House: Four Studies in Indian Folklore of Protest and Change.* Banaras, 1969.

Vedalankar, Pandit Nardev, and Manohar Somera. *Arya Samaj and Indians Abroad.* Arya Samaj Centenary Publication. New Delhi: Sarvadeshik Arya Pratinidhi Sabha, Dayanand Bhavan, Ramlila Ground, 1975.

Vedananda, Swami. *The Prophet of the Age: A Short Life Sketch of Acharya Swami Pranavanandaji Founder of Bharat Sevashram Sangha.* Calcutta: Swami Nirmalananda, Bharat Sevashram Sangha, n.d.

de Verteuil, Anthony. *Eight East Indian Immigrants.* Port of Spain: Paria Publishing Co., 1989.

de Verteuil, Louis Antoine Aimé Gaston. *Trinidad, Its Geography, Natural Resources, Administration, Present Condition, and Prospects.* London: Cassell, 1884.

Vertovec, Steven. "Hinduism and Social Change in Village Trinidad." Ph.D. diss., Oxford University, 1987.

———. "Hinduism in Diaspora: The Transformation of Tradition in Trinidad." Pp. 157–86 in *Hinduism Reconsidered,* ed. Gunther-Dietz Sontheimer and H. Kulke. New Delhi: Manohar, 1989.

———. *Hindu Trinidad: Religion, Ethnicity, and Socio-Economic Change.* London: Macmillan; Warwick University Press, 1992.

Vidyarthi, D. N., ed. *Filmindia: The Fabulous Star Magazine* (Port of Spain).

Wachsmann, Klaus. "Criteria for Acculturation." International Musicological Society, 139–49. *Report of the 8th Congress,* New York, 1961.

Wade, Bonnie C. "By Invitation Only: Field Work in Village India," *Asian Music* 3, no. 2 (1972): 3–7.

———. "Songs of Traditional Wedding Ceremonies in North India." *Yearbook of the International Folk Music Council* 4 (1972): 57–65.

Wagley, Charles. "Plantation America: A Cultural Sphere." Pp. 3–13 in *Caribbean Studies: A Symposium,* ed. Vera Rubin. Seattle: University of Washington Press, 1960.

Wagley, Charles, and Marvin Harris. *Minorities in the New World: Six Case Studies.* New York: Columbia University Press, 1964.

Wallace, Anthony. "Revitalization Movements." *American Anthropologist* 58 (1956): 264–81.

Warner, Keith Q. "Ethnicity and the Contemporary Calypso." Pp. 275–91 in *Trinidad Ethnicity,* ed. Kevin A. Yelvington. Knoxville: University of Tennessee Press, 1993.

———. *Kaiso! The Trinidad Calypso: A Study of the Calypso as Oral Literature.* Washington, D.C.: Three Continents Press, 1958.

———. *The Trinidad Calypso: A Study of the Calypso as Oral Literature.* Port of Spain: Heinemann, 1982.

Waterman, Richard Alan. "African Patterns in Trinidad Negro Music." Ph.D. diss., Northwestern University, Evanston, Ill., 1943.

Weatherly, U. G. "The West Indies as a Sociological Laboratory." *The American Journal of Sociology* 29, no. 3 (November 1923): 290–304.

Weller, Judith Ann. *The East Indian Indenture in Trinidad.* Caribbean Monograph series, no. 4. University of Puerto Rico, Institute of Caribbean Studies, 1968.

———. "A Study of the Regulation of the East Indian Indenture System in Trinidad, 1845–1917." Ph.D. diss., Columbia University, New York, 1965.

White, Charles, S.J. "The Sai Baba Movement: Approaches to the Study of Indian Saints." *Journal of Asian Studies* 31, no. 4 (1972): 863–78.

Williams, Eric. *Capitalism and Slavery.* Chapel Hill: University of North Carolina Press, 1944; 2d rev. ed., London: André Deutsch, 1964.

———. *From Columbus to Castro: The History of the Caribbean 1492–1969.* London: André Deutsch, 1970.

———. *History of the People of Trinidad and Tobago.* New York: Praeger, 1962.

———. *Inward Hunger: The Education of a Prime Minister.* London: André Deutsch, 1969.

———. "Massa Day Done." Pp. 3–29 in *The Aftermath of Sovereignty: West Indian Perspectives,* ed. David Lowenthal and Lambros Comitas. Garden City, N.Y.: Anchor Books, 1973.

———. "Race Relations in Caribbean Society." Pp. 54–60 in *Caribbean Studies: A Symposium,* ed. Vera Rubin. Seattle: University of Washington Press, 1960.

Yelvington, Kevin A., ed. *Trinidad Ethnicity.* Knoxville: University of Tennessee Press, 1993.

Discography

Arawak Indian. *Bow & Arrow.* Tabla and ḍholak by Sham. Music arranged by Courtney. Lyrics by Arawak Indian. Recorded at Kingston Studio. Compact Cassette, stereo, 1990s. Produced by Ashley Enterprises, New York. AE005.

Arti Sangrah [*Ārtī* Collection]. Pandit Bishwanath, music direction. 12 in., LP, 2 sides, stereo, 1970s. The Indian Record Manufacturing Co., Ltd. (Calcutta), 3412-5015.

Babla and Kanchan. "*Laila.*" Prod. Mohan Jaikaran. Manufactured and distributed by Infinity Industries, Ltd., Point Lisas, Trinidad. Compact Cassette, stereo, 1990s.

Bejulah (Side A); Benny Sewnath (Side B). *Jazal Ghazal* (A); *Bhajan* (B). Accompanied by the Jit Seeshai's East Indian Orchestra. 10 in., STD, mono, 1940s. Recorded in Trinidad. Decca (U.S.A.), 166507A/16507B.

[*Bhajan Mala*] *Best in Bhajans.* 12 in., 2 sides, stereo, 1970s. Gramophone Company of India Ltd. (Dum Dum), ECLP 2885.

Bharatiya Vidya Sansthhaan of Trinidad and Tobago. *Melodies of Adesh. Sanskrita Shivir.* 7 in., 45 R.P.M., 2 sides, stereo, 1970s. Bhavisthhaan Records (Trinidad), A001.

———. *Reflections of Balandra (Melodies of Adesh): Dhun Jhanda Hamara (Inst.)* (Side A); *Dhun Shiver Geet (Inst.)* (Side B). 7 in., 45 R.P.M., stereo, 1970s. Bhavisthhaan Records (Trinidad), A003.

———. *Tamaso Ma Jyotirgamaga ("Lead Us from Darkness to Light"): Diwaalee Songs and Prayers. Melodies of Adesh.* 12 in., LP, 2 sides, stereo, 1970s. Bhavisthhaan Records (Trinidad), LP ALP 002.

Bharatiya Vidya Sansthhaan of Trinidad and Tobago and H. S. Adesh. *Echoes of Kashmir on Santoor by Adesh. Melodies of Adesh.* 12 in., LP, 2 sides, stereo, 1970s. Bhavisthhaan Records (Trinidad), ALP3, 111979.

Bharatiya Vidya Sansthhaan of Trinidad and Tobago with Sangeet Saarika Uma [Budram]. *Indian Music Across Seven Seas: Classical and Devotional Songs by Sangeet Saarika Uma. Melodies of Adesh.* 12 in., LP, 2 sides, stereo, 1970s. Bhavisthhaan Records (Trinidad), LP BVS 001.

Bodas, Kashinath Shanker, Purnima Thakur, Chatur Sai, Dhira Ghosh. *Aarti.* 12 in., LP, 2 sides, stereo, 1970s. Gramophone Company of India Ltd. (Calcutta), ECSD 3057.

Darshan Do Ghanshyam: Bhajans from Films. 12 in., LP, 2 sides, stereo, 1980s. Gramophone Company of India Ltd. (Dum Dum), ECLP 5818.

Dindial, Henry Tooloom, and Ramchaitar. *Memories of Masters.* Prod. Moean Mohammed. 12 in., LP, 2 sides, mono (labeled stereo), 1970s. Windsor Records (Port of Spain, Trinidad), LP/W012.

Doobe, Shrimati Ghisai. *Shrimati Ghisai Doobe Ki Sangheet* ["The Songs of Miss Ghisai Doobe"]. 12 in., LP, 2 sides, stereo, 1970s. Gayatri Records (Surinam), SG 001 Asss-SP:419.

Dropati. *Let's Sing and Dance with Dropati.* Prod. Moean Mohammed. 12 in., LP, 2 sides, mono, 1970s. Windsor Records (Port of Spain, Trinidad), LP/W006.

Drupatee. *Drupatee's Down in Sando.* Prod. S. E. D. Persad and Trevor Walker. Compact Cassette, stereo, 1990s. Disributed in the Caribbean by Kisskidee Records, Port of Spain. Spice Island Records, S.I. 0023.

Edwards, Sally. *Dil Diwana* ["Crazy Heart"]. Compact Cassette, stereo, 1990s. Distributed by Jamaican Me Crazy, Jamaica, N.Y.

Guyana Zindabad ["Long Live Guyana"](Side A); *Dudu Gal* (Side B). Prakash Orchestra. 7 in., 45 R.P.M., mono, 1970s. Jazam Records (Guyana), J-001 (223).

Har Har Mahadev. 12 in., LP, 2 sides, stereo, 1980s. West Indies Records (Barbados) Ltd., under license from the Gramophone Company of India Ltd., EMI / W-127.

Henry, Edward. *Chant the Names of God: Village Music of the Bhojpuri-Speaking Area of India.* 12 in., LP, 2 sides, mono, 1981. Rounder Records (Sommerville, Mass.), 5008. Pamphlet insert.

Hernandez, Liz. *Sugarcane.* Arr. Carlos Belfon; written by Johnny Jai; guitar Ronnie Kallicharan. 1990s. Recorded at Tracks (Rec.) Studio, Arima, Trinidad. JMC 1093.

Hosein, Jameer, Imim R. Ali et al. *Muslim Inspiration.* Harry Mahabir and the B.W.I.A. National Indian Orchestra; prod. Moean Mohammed. 12 in., LP, 2 sides, mono, 1970s. Windsor Records (Port of Spain, Trinidad), LP/W005.

Jaikaran, Basdeo, and the Saraswatie Cultural Group. *Satya Bhajans.* 12 in., LP, 2 sides, stereo, 1980s. Jaikaran Records (Trinidad), BJL 002.

Jai Shiv Shankar. 12 in., LP, 2 sides, stereo, 1980s. West Indies Records (Barbados) Ltd., under license from the Gramophone Company of India Ltd., EMI / W-125.

Jinkoe, Bahauw, and the Nowlakhaharr Sangeet Samar (Surinam). *Rahesmandal.* 12 in., LP, 2 sides, stereo, 1970s. K.D.R. Records (Port of Spain, Trinidad), 017-LP.

Kanchan. *Give Me Paisa!* Arr. Babla and Ed Watson; prod. Mohan Jaikaran. 12 in., LP, 2 sides, stereo, 1980s. Recorded at Platinum Factory (Fulton Street, Brooklyn, N.Y.), MO 6000.

———. *International Fame in Holland 1982. Kayse Banie.* Music by Babla. 12 in., LP, 2 sides, stereo, 1982. Distributed by Paloeloe Record Centre, The Hague, Holland, and West Indies Records (Barbados) Ltd.

———. *Kuchh Gadbad Hai* ["Something is Wrong"]. Sung by Kanchan. Music by Babla and his Orchestra. Prod. Rohit Hagessar and David Raffe. Recorded at Weston Outdoor, Bombay. 12 in., LP, 2 sides, stereo, 1984. A Rohit International Release, 021. Distributed by Rohit (Jamaica, N.Y.).

———. *Kuchh Kuchh Baby* ["Some Some Baby"]. (Rock. .It, D. Williams). Sung by Kanchan. Music by Babla. 12 in., LP, 2 sides, stereo, 1985. Rohit International Recording Organization. 12-100.

Kashiprasad Mishra, Pandit. *Ramayan.* Music by Navv Bharat Sangeet Orchestra. 12 in., LP, 2 sides, stereo, 1970s. Balroop (Tacarigua, Trinidad), B-0001.

[Kawalsingh], Geeta. *Chutney Lambada.* Music Director, Harry Mahabir. Recorded at Diron Studios. Music B.W.I.A.'s Indian Orchestra. 12 in., LP, 2 sides, stereo; Compact Cassette, stereo, 1990s. MO Records (Jamaica, N.Y.), MOG 007.

Keshavadesh, Sant Sri Bhadragiri. *Chants and Bhajans* (Side A); *Sri Ramacharitmanas of Sant Tulsidas* (Side B). 12 in., LP, stereo, 1970. D.S.C.T. (Toronto, Canada), SMT-70-3.

Khan, Yusuff. *Haunting Melodies of Yusuff Khan.* Moean Mohammed, prod. 12 in., LP, 2 sides, mono, 1970s. Windsor Records (Port of Spain, Trinidad), W/007.

———. *Tent Singing by Yusuff Khan.* Prod. Moean Mohammed. 12 in., LP, 2 sides, stereo, 1970s. Windsor Records (Port of Spain, Trinidad), LP/WO31.

Mahabir, Harry. *Modern Music of India.* B.W.I.A. National Indian Orchestra of Trinidad and Tobago. 12 in., LP, 2 sides, stereo, 1970s. Tropico (Port of Spain, Trinidad), TSI 2040.

———. *Music Loved by All.* B.W.I.A. National Indian Orchestra of Trinidad and Tobago. 12 in., LP, 2 sides, stereo, 1970s. Windsor Records (Port of Spain, Trinidad), LP/WOO2.

———. *Our Talent—Our Land.* B.W.I.A. National Indian Orchestra of Trinidad and Tobago. 12 in., 2 sides, LP, stereo, 1970s. Windsor Records (Port of Spain, Trinidad), LP/WOO2.

Maharajh, Nirmal, and the Maha Sabha Ramayan Group. *Excerpts from the Holy Ramayan.* 2 discs (4 sides), 12 in., LP, stereo, 1970s. Tropico (Port of Spain, Trinidad), TSI 2056.

Mangeshkar, Lata. *Ram Ratan Dhan Payo* ["The Prosperity of Rām Found"]. 12 in., LP, 2 sides, stereo, 1980s. Music India, BLP 2393 890.

Merchant [Denis Williams]. *Rock. . It.* Prod. Mackie Nelson. Recorded at KH Studio, Sea Lots, Port of Spain, Trinidad. 12 in., LP, 2 sides, stereo, 1980s. Benmac Records (Port of Spain), Benmac 0051.

Mohammed, Imtaz. *Local Amitabh in Soca Style.* Music by Ed Watson; ḍholak by Rager Sook Raj; guitar by Simeon Ramesar; Chorus, Shiela Basdeo. Recorded at Fuzz Studio. Compact Cassette, stereo, 1990s. A&A Productions, AA 12-10.

Mohammed, Sayyeed (Side A); Rambarose Pancham (Side B). *Nabi Ji Arp Ka. Goonaganay Walay* (A); *Kawalie* (B). Accompanied by Nazir Mohammed's Orchestra. Recorded in Trinidad. 10 in., STD, mono, 1940s. Decca (U.S.A.), 16508A/16508B.

Pancham, Rambarose (Side A); Jugrue Quawal (Side B). *Hindou Song: Telana Nath* (A); *Quawali Song: Sab Nabio Me Vo Allah* ["Allah is the Greatest of All the Prophets"] (B). Accompanied by the Jit Seeshai's East Indian Orchestra. Recorded in Trinidad. 10 in., STD, mono, 1940s. Decca (U.S.A.), 16500A/16500B.

Parsad, Pandit Kasi. *Parsuram Acamaan.* Accompanied by R. S. Narayansingh's Orchestra. Recorded in Trinidad. 10 in, STD, 2 sides, mono, 1940s. Decca (U.S.A.), 16513A/16513B.

Persad, Tarran (Side A); Ramdhani Shyama (Side B). *Apnay Gully Bolewanah* ["Call Me in Your Lane"]*: Hindu Bhajan* (A); *Marnay Ki Manjtay Hai Dowah: Urdu Ghazal* (B). Arr. Amrai Khan. Recorded in Trinidad. 10 in., STD, mono, 1940s. Bluebird (U.S.A.), B-29005-A/B.

———. *Tarran Persad Sings Movie Hits and Other Favourites.* Naya Zamana Indian Orchestra. 12 in., LP, 2 sides, stereo. Tropico (Port of Spain, Trinidad), TSI-2038.

Popo, Sundar. *Anup Jalota Presents Trinidad's Sundar Popo "Hot and Spicy" (Chutneys).* Prod. Moean Mohammed; music by Anup Jalota. 12 in., LP, 2 sides, stereo, 1980s. Windsor Records (Port of Spain, Trinidad), LP/W065.

———. *Come Dance with the Champ.* Prod. Moean Mohammed. 12 in., LP, 2 sides, stereo, 1970s. Windsor Records (Port of Spain, Trinidad), LP/W057.

———. *Screwdriver.* Music by Ed Watson; prod. Mohan Jaikaran. Recorded at York Studio. 12 in., LP, 2 sides, stereo, 1990s. Distributed in New York by Mohan Jaikaran, M.J. 5001.

Quaval, Jugrue (Side A); Master Rameswak (Side B). *Huckanee. Narw Bhawurr May* ["Boat in Whirlpool"] (A); *Dadra* (B). Accompanied by the Jit Seeshai's East Indian Orchestra (A); Gopi's East Indian Orchestra (B). Recorded in Trinidad. 10 in., STD, mono, 1940s. Decca (U.S.A.), 16503A/16503B.

Quaval, Jugrue (Side A); Master Rameswak (Side B). *Mara Nabee Mohammad Pyara* ["My Love Prophet Mohammed"] (A); *Hindi Kawali* (B). Accompanied by the Jit Seeshai's East Indian Orchestra (A); Gopi's East Indian Orchestra (B). Recorded in Trinidad. 10 in., STD, mono, 1940s. Decca (U.S.A.), 16505A/16505B.

Ramasar, Kissoon. *An Album of Devotional Songs.* 12 in., LP 2 sides, mono, 1970s. K.D.R. Records (Port of Spain, Trinidad), KDR-004.

———. *Amar Katha, Hanuman Chalesa and Beebha Geet* ["Immortal Story," "Hanuman Forty," and "Wedding Song"]. 12 in., LP, 2 sides, stereo, 1970s. K.D.R. Records (Port of Spain, Trinidad), 018-LP.

———. *Central Tempo* (Side A); *Mano Mano* ["Accept It"] (Side B). Trinidad Philharmonic Orchestra. 7 in, 45 R.P.M., mono. K.D.R. Records (Port of Spain, Trinidad), KDR-005.

———. *Dhanuk Yag ("Holi")* (Side A); *Sita-Bee-Bha* ["Sita's Wedding"] (Side B). 7 in., 45 R.P.M., mono, 1970s. K.D.R. Records (Port of Spain, Trinidad), KDR-002.

———. *Excerpts from the Holy Ramayan.* 3 vols. 12 in., LP, 6 sides, mono, 1970s. K.D.R. Records (Port of Spain, Trinidad), KDR-003-LP.

———. *Hanuman Chalesa* ["Hanuman Forty"]. Accompanied by the Trinidad Philharmonic Orchestra. 7 in., 45 R.P.M., 2 sides, stereo, 1970s. K.D.R. Records (Port of Spain, Trinidad), KDR-006.

———. *Hits of Kissoon Ramasar.* 12 in., LP, 2 sides, stereo, 1970s. K.D.R. Records (Port of Spain, Trinidad), KDR-020-LP.

———. *A Live Recording at Cami Hall New York, September 1975, with Favourites of Kissoon Ramasar.* 12 in., LP, 2 sides, stereo, 1975. K.D.R. Records (Port of Spain, Trinidad), KDR-015-LP.

———. *Prixie 62. Nacho Ji Nacho* ["Dance, Yes Dance"] (Side A); *Harmonica Tempo. Indian Twist Time* (Side B). Accompanied by the Trinidad Philharmonic Orchestra. 7 in., 45 R.P.M., mono, 1970s. K.D.R. Records (Port of Spain, Trinidad), KDR-001.

———. *Soono Bhabhana* (Side A); *Maai Mohay Largay* (Side B). Accompanied by the Trinidad Philharmonic Orchestra. 7 in., 45 R.P.M., mono, 1970s. K.D.R. Records (Port of Spain, Trinidad), KDR-011.

———. *Today is My Birthday* (Side A); *Mikey Cipiani* (Side B). Accompanied by the Trinidad Philharmonic Orchestra. 7 in., 45 R.P.M., mono, 1970s. K.D.R. Records (Port of Spain, Trinidad), KDR-011.

Ramasar, Kissoon, and Phoolbassia Ragoobir. *Bhajans and Folk Songs.* Accompanied by the Trinidad Indian Philharmonic Orchestra. 12 in., LP, 2 sides, stereo, 1970s. K.D.R. Records (Port of Spain, Trinidad), KDR-013-LP.

———. *Tribute to Mastana Bahaar* (Side A); *Chitawaniya May Naina* (Side B). 7 in., 45 R.P.M., mono, 1970s. K.D.R. Records (Port of Spain, Trinidad), KDR-010.

Ramasar, Kissoon, and Shantimala. *Nirgoon Bhajans.* Accompanied by the Trinidad Philharmonic Orchestra. 12 in., LP, 2 sides, stereo, 1970s.

Ramasar, Kissoon, and the St. James Ramayan Goal. *Excerpts from the Holy Ramayan.* 2 vols. Eric Michaud, eng. 12 in., LP, 2 sides, stereo, 1970s.

Ramaya, Narsaloo. *Cherished Melodies: Narsaloo Ramaya on the Violin.* Prod. Moean Mohammed. 12 in., LP, 2 sides, stereo, 1970s. Windsor Records (Port of Spain, Trinidad), LP/W013.

Rambachan, Surujrattan, and the Saraswati Kirtan Mandali. *Bhajans and Chants.* 12 in., LP, 2 sides, stereo, 1970s. Balroop (Tacarigua, Trinidad), B-4.

———. *Come Let Us Chant: Bhajans and Kirtan.* Prod. Surujrattan Rambachan. 12 in., LP, 2 sides, stereo, 1970s. Temple Records (Trinidad), SR-001.

Rambahal, Moon, and the Paradise Bell Tassa Group. *East Indian Traditional Drums.* Prod. Moean Mohammed. 12 in., LP, 2 sides, stereo, 1970s. Windsor Records (Port of Spain, Trinidad), SP/W009.

Ramballie, Pearl. *Bhajans in Living Stereo.* Lakhan Teemal, eng. 12 in., LP, 2 sides, stereo, 1970s. Balroop (Tacarigua, Trinidad), B-5.

Ramkissoon, Dev Bansraj. *Bhajans.* Prod. Moean Mohammed. 12 in., LP, 2 sides, stereo, 1970s. Windsor Records (Port of Spain, Trinidad), LP/W008.

———. *Tent Singing by Dev Bansraj Ramkissoon.* Wayne Jameson, eng.; prod. Moean Mohammed. 12 in., LP, 2 sides, stereo, 1970s. Windsor Records (Port of Spain, Trinidad), LP/W027.

Ramsaran, Amina. *Bina Bolai* ["Bina Speaks"]. Compact Cassette, stereo, 1990s. Produced and marketed by Prainsingh (Jamaica, N.Y.), JMC-069.

Raymond Family. *Oriental Music Songs.* 12 in., LP, 2 sides, stereo, 1970s. Raymond Records (Port of Spain, Trinidad), LP/W008.

Razack, Abdool "Kush." *Tent Singing by Abdool "Kush" Razack.* Wayne Jameson, eng; prod. Moean Mohammed. 12 in., LP, 2 sides, stereo, 1970s. Windsor Records (Port of Spain, Trinidad), LP/W026.

Razack, Abdool "Kush," and Roy Cooper. *Indian Classical Songs.* Prod. Moean Mohammed. 12 in., LP, 2 sides, stereo, 1970s. Windsor Records (Port of Spain, Trinidad), LP/W021.

Sai Bhajan: Om Sai Baba's Selected Bhajan Songs. 12 in., LP, 2 sides, mono, 1980s. Hindusthan Record (Calcutta, India), 1412-0001.

Salima. *Dhama Da Ma Dam.* Music by Ramdeo Seelochan's Gemini; prod. Michael, Steve, Raymond, and Ramdeo Seelochan. Compact Cassette, stereo, 1990s. Marketed and Distributed by Soca Records, Inc. (Queens, N.Y.).

Sansar Sangeet: Abum of Bhakti Bhajans. Helbert Clarke, eng.; prod. Pandit Reepu Daman Persaud. 12 in., 2 sides, mono, 1970s. Radio Demarara Studio (Guyana).

Sewnath, Benny (Side A); Sayyeed Mohammed (Side B). *Hindou Song: Kamach Bintee,* accompanied by the Jit Seeshai's East Indian Orchestra (A); *Quawal Song: Mora Ji Ghabarana,* Nazir Mohammed's Orchestra (B). Recorded in Trinidad. 10 in., STD, mono, 1940s. Decca (U.S.A.), 16501A/16501B.

Shankar, Ravi. *Meera.* 12 in., LP, 2 sides, stereo, 1970s. Philips/Polydor of India Ltd. (Bombay), 6405 636.

Sharan, Hari Om. *Souvenir of the West Indies: Devotionals.* 12 in., LP, 2 sides, stereo, 1970s. Sharan Records (Port of Spain, Trinidad), S-1.

———. *Souvenir of the West Indies: Excerpts from the Tulsidas Ramayan.* 12 in., LP, 2 sides, stereo, 1970s. Sharan Records (Port of Spain, Trinidad), S-2.

Shyma, Ramdhani (Side A); Tulsi Dass (Side B). *Hindi Ghazal* (A); *Urdu Ghazal* (B). Accompanied by Gopi's East Indian Orchestra. Recorded in Trinidad. 10 in., STD, mono, 1940s. Decca (U.S.A.), 16502A/16502B.

Singh, Charanjit. *Live in Europe: The Charanjit Singh . . . One Man Show.* Prod. Prakash Dalloesingh. Recording arrangements by Radio Studio Roshnie, Amsterdam. 12 in., LP, 2 sides, stereo, 1990s. Prakash Records, PDR 12 82.

Singh, Kung Beharry. *Tent Singing by Kung Beharry Singh.* Prod. Moean Mohammed. 12 in., LP, 2 sides, mono, 1970s. Windsor Records (Port of Spain, Trinidad), LP/W003.

Sookhraj, Sookdeo. *Hanuman Chalisa, Shawan Kumar-Katha and Bhajans.* ["Hanuman Forty, The Story of Shawan Kumar (*Ramayan*), and Bhajans"] 12 in., LP, 2 sides, mono, 1970s. Windsor Records (Port of Spain, Trinidad).

———. *Tent Singing by Sookraj.* David Beresford, eng.; prod. Moean Mohammed. 12 in., LP, 2 sides, stereo, 1970s. Windsor Records (Port of Spain, Trinidad), LP/W025.

Souvenir 1977: Mastana Bahaar Cultural Pageant. Prod. Moean Mohammed. 12 in., LP, 2 sides, stereo, 1977. Windsor Records (Port of Spain, Trinidad), LP/W035.

Tewari, Laxmi. *Folk Music of India (Uttar Pradesh).* 12 in., LP, 2 sides, stereo, 1970s. Lyrichord Records (New York), LLST 7271.

Tulsi Das. 12 in., LP, 2 sides, stereo, 1970s. West Indies Records Ltd. (Barbados), under licence from EMI India Ltd., EMI W-124.

Universal Mother Laxmi. 12 in., LP, 2 sides, stereo, 1970s. West Indian Records (Barbados) Ltd., under licence from the Gramophone Company of India Ltd., EMI/W-129.

Vastindian: Sma Antillerna [West Indies: Lesser Antilles]. 2 discs. Krister Malm, prod. 12 in., LP, stereo. With notes by Krister Malm. Caprice (Sweden), CAP 2004: 1-2.

Yankarran, Anand. *King of Kings.* Music by Anand Yankarran and Sadro; ḍholak by Aaron Jeewansingh and Sunil Ramsoon; ḍhantāl by Sunil Ramsoon; rhythm by Sadro. Prod. Anand Yankarran and Sadro. 12 in., LP, 2 sides, stereo; Compact Cassette, stereo, 1992. MO Records, Inc.

———. *Zindabad Trinbago* ["Long Live Trinbago"]. Music by Jerry George and Sunil Pitchan. Produced by Anand Yankarran. Recorded at Sarana Studios. Compact Cassette, stereo, 1980s. West Indian Records (Barbados, Ltd.), DY1.

Yankarran, Isaac. *Gems of Yankarran: A Tribute to the Late Isaac Yankarran.* Accompanied by the Beena Sangeet Orchestra of Tunapuna. 12 in., LP, 2 sides, mono, 1970s. Windsor Records (Port of Spain, Trinidad), LP/W003.

———. *Songs to Remember by the Late "Yankarran."* Accompanied by the Naya Zamana Orchestra. 12 in., LP, 2 sides, mono, 1970s. Balroop (Tacarigua, Trinidad), B-3.

Yankarran, Sharm. *Tent Singing by Sharm Yankarran.* Prod. Moean Mohammed. 12 in., LP, 2 sides, stereo, 1970s. Windsor Records (Port of Spain, Trinidad), LP/W032.

List of Songs

First lines of song texts are given in numerical order.

1. One day the swan will fly off the pond, 5
2. Seat yourself, my brother, on a sandal stool (Grierson 1886), 21–22
3. Be it wealth, or be it power, 65–66
4. A full moon has risen over us, 66
5. Sītā Rāma name day and night speak keep loving, 77–78
6. God of God ours false world is, 78
7. Fall in love no one happiness gains, 79
8. This is an epithet of Prayag, salvation giving happiness, 79–80
9. God already has written it down about Sītā and Rāwaṇ, 80–81
10. Phāgun has come and it is Holī, 81
11. The season of blooming of the marigold is come, 81–82
12. Beloved, do not go abroad; the spring season has come close (Arya 1968), 82–83
13. Oh, came Sāwan most charming, 84–85
14. My husband and king wetting the other side in the drops of the Sāwan rain, 85–86
15. Our lanes in come on lovers, 86
16. I am fair beautiful, you black cloud, 86
17. Blow eastern breeze, pain comes up, 86–87
18. Dr. William[s] well proud and glad, 97
19. Let us foreign land go now love, 130
20. Among all prophets is the great [Mīrābāī], 130
21. Will find Shyām own inside, 131
22. Hey Brindāban of living one, 132
23. Oh, Prophet, you who sing about *Haj* is, 132–133
24. Beloved, see my lord, 133–34
25. That life more beloved country to made into graveyard, 134–35
26. Boat whirlpool in has stuck, Lord [help to] cross, 135
27. Early in the morning separate will love, 136
28. Lord, how the elephant trouble from got released, 137
29. Do not know love keep doing, 137–38
30. Oh, Mother Saraswatī, grant me a boon of a new awakening, 142
31. May this country of Carnival be always green and prosperous, 142
32. The charming island of Trinidad is beautifully situated in the yard of the ocean, 143
33. Where of *haldī,* 154
34. Father, what bridegroom kept searching (1), 154–55
35. Night husband not arrived. Who bewitch, 164–65
36. On the bank of the river there is a bungalow, 169–70
37. On the paved road there is a bungalow, 170
38. Oh, bridegroom, if you wish to have a wife, 170–71
39. Sweep the way, Pandit Rāma, 176
40. Oh, elephant invite to sit, 176–77
41. "A long and noisy wedding party arrives at your gate, O father" (H. S. Upadhyaya 1967), 177
42. Father, what bridegroom kept searching (2), 177–78
43. Pandit Rāma, take a jug of water in your hand, 180
44. Ten female friends are in front, 185
45. Ten female friends walk ahead, ten female friends behind her, 186
46. Five matrons arranged the lamp with four wicks (Grierson 1883), 186–87
47. In the evening six stars come out, 189–91
48. Friend, come and see (Archer 1985), 191
49. Oh, oh, brother who plays the musical instruments, 193
50. Whose tent is pitched and whose tent is thatched, 193
51. Beat the drum, beat the drum (Barua 1963), 194
52. Brother seated on the cot, 194
53. Get the dung of a beautiful cow, 196–97
54. Crowd of the groomsmen, 197
55. Auspicious time, the day, the hour; auspicious is the lot of the lady Sītā (Grierson 1883), 198
56. Courtyard praises King Janaka of, 198–99

57. The wedding party has come, 200
58. Everyone comes, 200
59. The basket of ornaments came, oh father, basket came, 200–201
60. My father has cut green bamboo, 203
61. Mother kept this daughter as a ghee pitcher, 204
62. The *lotā* is trembling, the *ḍhotiā* is trembling, 204–5
63. Oh, oh, brother Rām, 205
64. O brother, pour the water (Archer 1985), 205
65. As the eclipse influenced moon at, 206
66. On the thatching grass the father sits (Archer 1985), 206
67. Brother, welcome the popped rice, 208
68. Mix the parched paddy [rice], O brother (Archer 1985), 208
69. She is calling, "father, father," but the father does not speak, 209–10
70. Daughter thy father calling, father does not speak, 210
71. "O father, the month of Chaiet ends and Baesakh begins" H. S. Upadhyaya 1967), 210
72. In the evening the clouds come in the sky, 211
73. *Samadhī*, my daughter is an innocent, 216
74. You go son, *gaurī* marry, *gaurī* marry, 217
75. King Janak a garden plant, 238–41
76. The male swan is feeding in half of the pond, the female swan is feeding in half of the pond, 244–45
77. The male cobra is moving in half of the pond, the female cobra is moving in half of the pond, 248–49
78. In half the pond male swans are pecking, in half female swans are pecking, 251
79. In half the pond the male swan Tch!, 251–52
80. In half the pond male cobras are pecking, in half female cobras are pecking, 252
81. In half the pond the female swan is pecking, in half the pond the male swan is pecking, 253
82. In half the pond the female swan is pecking, in half the male swan is pecking, 253–54
83. In half the pond the male swan is pecking, in half the female swan is pecking, 254–55
84. In half the pond the male swan is pecking, in half the female swan is pecking, 255–56
85. In all his escort (Archer 1985), 259–60
86. Oh, mother, she weak tear flowing, 261
87. Oh, eyes flooded tears, 262
88. Came Sāwan most charming, 264
89. Oh dear friend, my husband has gone abroad and I am lying alone in the month of Sāvana (Tewari 1974), 264
90. The raindrops are beginning to fall (Sahai-Achuthan 1987), 264
91. Sāwan and the eager river leaps (Archer 1985), 265
92. Beloved, do not go abroad; the soring (season) has come close (Arya 1968), 265
93. Gladly would I rub sandal paste upon my body and weave a garland of flowers (Grierson 1883), 266
94. In Chait, the Ṭesū tree flowers in the forest, and the fair one is sending a message to her beloved (Grierson 1884), 266
95. Often the peacock cries (Archer 1985), 267
96. My teenage is lap full, 268
97. "I served the meal on a golden plate" (H. S. Upadhyaya 1967), 268–69
98. Oh, *nanad*, if I knew your brother will go foreign (K. D. Upadhyaya 1966), 269
99. When I start planting the *mehadi* tree (H. S. Upadhyaya 1967), 269–70
100. My husband is in a distant land (H. S. Upadhyaya 1967), 270
101. O Mother-in-law, where should I sleep (Lewis 1958), 270
102. Both brothers, Rama and Lakshmana (Tewari 1974), 270–71
103. Wherever the sun rises, 271
104. The east wind blows, and yawning has come upon me (Grierson 1886), 272
105. Mahādeb has gone to the East to trade, 272
106. The easterly wind is blowing (H. S. Upadhyaya 1967), 272–73
107. In the deep shadows of the rainy July, with secret steps, thou walkest (Tagore 1913), 273
108. Rām is born in Chait in Ajodhyā, 275–76
109. Now call the midwife, go send for her (Rao 1991), 276
110. Oh, Shiva Shankar, where was the birth place of Rām, 277
111. Oh, Rām lifted up Shiva's bow, 277–78
112. Rām saw the assembled people and saw Jānakī [Sītā], 278–79
113. Where from Bipra arrive, 281
114. Turmeric who king letter write post, 282–83
115. Father, getting late to go to Janakpur, 283–84
116. Skinny Rām, skinny waist, 284

117. After dressing up the bridegroom stands, 284–86
118. Who rides an elephant (H. S. Upadhyaya 1967), 286
119. Soft bamboo cuts King Dasarath, 286–87
120. King Dasarath was cutting the green bamboo (Hertig-Skalická), 287–88
121. King Dassarth goes to cut bamboo in Mathur battlefield (H. S. Upadhyaya 1967), 288
122. My son, Sīṭā's food is sweet, 289
123. Rāmā! Without Sīṭā the world is lonely, 289–90
124. Sītā's eyes are big, and her hair is long (H. S. Upadhyaya 1967), 290
125. O Rama, the husband goes to a distant land (H. S. Upadhyaya 1967), 290
126. Heart Rām *charan* [feet] in came, 290–91
127. Rām of grandeur saints world in great is, 291–92
128. My Lord, come! Worship Govinda [Krishna], 302
129. Salutation to Shiva, 302
130. In my heart has settled Rām, Lord of the Raghus, 306
131. Oh, father of the world, beloved Lord, give us knowledge, 307–9
132. Salutations to Shiva as Shambū, 311–15
133. Rām, Rām, worship Rām, 326–27
134. Sing in praise the name of Niranjana [God free of illusion], 332
135. May the supreme being, lord of the world, be ever victorious, 334–35
136. Surrender to Lord Ganesh, 344
137. Oh Lord, grant me a vision of you, 344–45
138. One day this world will be left behind, 365
139. Oh, my Lord, do this for me, 365–66
140. I drinking to die, so I drinking to die, 368—69
141. You buy me the wedding ring, 369–71
142. My heart linked to you, 371–72
143. What does crow take from others, 372
144. O Cuckoo, where is the jungle (Archer 1985), 373
145. She was the prettiest thing I'd ever met (Rohlehr 1990), 373
146. An Indian man was holding a piece of wire (Rohlehr 1990), 373–74
147. Me work for me money, me go back to me country (Rohlehr 1990), 374
148. This is really true (Rohlehr 1990), 374–75
149. This song you hear, 376
150. They give me blows, 376
151. Oh sweetheart, oh sweetheart, oh sweetheart, oh sweetheart, 379–80
152. Would you like to rock it with me baby, 381–83
153. A party in girl came, 384–85
154. Nand Bābāji of son, 386–87
155. You, you, you, 389–91
156. One, two, one, two, three, four, 391–93
157. Mother-in-law is to me careless, very careless, 393–94
158. Quick not kill love, my darling, 394–96
159. My husband, on the day when my daughter was born I became sad (Grierson 1883), 407
160. A beautiful girl stepped near the canopy (Hertig-Skalická 1974), 408
161. O daughter-in-law, the pitcher symbolizes your married life and the mangoes symbolize children (H. S. Upadhyaya 1967), 410
162. Rama says, "I am like a lotus flower" (H. S. Upadhyaya 1967), 410
163. Who will tattoo the *kalsa?* (Barua 1963), 411
164. Under half the wedding tent jewels are inlaid, 411–13
165. Wedding tent full all people and all female relatives, 415
166. Pond full all male cobra and female cobra all, 417
167. In [my] father's pond behind [my] house (Hertig-Skalická 1974), 417–18
168. Male swan female swan both of them pond at trouble in, 418

Index

The page numbers for song themes and for terms from songs texts are given in italic type.

"Abide with me," 388. *See also* hymns
abīr, 72, 74, *276*
aboriginal populations, xvii–xviii, 23
absent husband, *164–65, 265–70, 272*
accelerando, 74–75, 344, 461n.15
accompaniment, 91, 98, 168. *See also names of instruments*
accordion, 173, 394–96
acculturation, xvii, xx, 32–33, 149–50, 258, 360, 377, 401–3; Hinduism and Christianity, 259, 301; in Hindu wedding, 152–53, 259; in music, 400–401; in Shango, 33–35
ãchalwā (ãchal, ãcharwā), 151–52, *193,* 217–18. See also *oḍhanī*
across seven seas, 6–7
Adesh, Guru H. S., 43, 59, 112, 138–46, *292,* 401; album in local record collection, 109; on melody, 256–57; and north Indian classical music, xxi; Rām *bhajan,* 291–92; reintroduced classical instruments, 120; teaching in Trinidad, 138–46, 148, 150
Adhikari, Pundit, 148
adjoupas, 45
Advaitananda, Swami, 295
aesthetics, xx, 109–10
Africa, 27, 30, 31, 35, 376; Afro-Bahian cult groups, xvii; Afro-Indian ethnicity, 37; to Caribbean, xviii; hourglass drums, 94–95; retentions in Shango, 34
Āghor Panthī, 295
Agni, *81;* in *havan,* 296, 300
agriculture, 61–88, 400
Ahīr, 107, 119, *277*
ahīrwā songs, 107
Ajodhya, 274, *275, 287*
alankār, 388
Alladin, M. P., 112
Allah, *65–66*
Alok, 310
amrit, 340–45
Anandnagar, xix, 221, 227–29, 231, 409
Andhra, 276
animal sacrifice, 33–34, 35
annual cycle, 61–88
antarā: in *dhun,* 107; Number One Song, Dube, 417; in wedding songs, 219; examples, 192, 195, 199, 202, 211, 248
anthropology, xvii, 32, 50; consensualism, 37–40; much researched communities, xviii; pluralism, 37–40; reinterpretation, xvii, 35; research in Trinidad, 31–42; theories, xx, 32–33, 37; social constructionist, 38; syncretism, xvii, 35–36
apartheid, 30
Arapesh, xviii
Arawaks, xviii, 23, 27
Archer, William: *bārāt* song, 176; Bhojpurī language, 214; Bhojpurī song studies, 263; bridegroom song, 191; *ḍhariā* song, 205; *kanyādān* song, 206; Sāwan song, 265; song of rainy season, 267; wedding gifts, 200; wedding song, 373
Archives and Research Center for Ethnomusicology, New Delhi, xxv
arectoe, xviii
arieto, xviii
arkatiā, 16–19, 29–30
arranged marriages, 263, 407–8; of Permanand sisters, 173
ārtī: bhajan, 309, 333; at funeral, 365; to greet groom, *178,* 183, 184; and Sai Baba, 345, 354; during *sanḍhyā,* 300; to Saraswatī, *142;* Sītā's mother to Rām, 281; at the wedding, *155,* 155–56, *185, 186*
Arya Samaj, 296, 333, 360, 400
Arya, Usharbudh, 74, 82–83, 265, 411, 413
Ascension, 8
Assam, 340
assawari, 147
astrology and wedding dates, 151–53
ātmān, 341
Attila the Hun, 373
Aum Hindutvam, 302
aunt, *186, 289*
Aurobindo, 297
"authenticity" of folk music, 402

avatars: Parsurām, 280; Sai Baba, 341–43; of Vishnu, 274
Awadhī: *chautāl,* 75; *Rāmcharitmānas,* 274; Tulsī Dās, 280
Ayodhya, *239, 270,* 274, *288, 306*
Azamgarh, U.P., 409, 418

Babla, 128, 378
Badian, 94
Bahadoor, Jang, 125
bahnoī, at wedding, 181
bahū, 407
Bala Joban, 123, 400
Bālakāṇḍa, 211–12, 280
Ballia, U.P., xxiv, 177, 210, 409, 418; lotus song (Hertig-Skalická), 417–18; mother's song, 407–8; song of Dasarath's boons, 287–88
balls swinging, 164, *170*
bamboo, 5, 68, 153, *177, 203, 210, 244, 253, 266*
bamboo splinter, song of Dasarath's boons, *286–87, 288*
bananas, *81–82,* 300
Banaras, 20, 21, 155, *201,* 227, 405; recruitment center, 16; *sohar* with swans, 418
band, 95, 127–28: Carnival, 71; *chautāl,* 74. *See also* brass band; steel band
bangles, 229, *384, 390*
Banpurwā, U.P., 405–6, 409, 410; Holī songs, 80–82, 267
bānsurī, 127
banyan tree, *79*
barahī, xxiii, 378; *kajarī* sung, 85
bārah māsas, 61, 274–76
bārāt, 153, 156, 162, 171, 178; "army of groomsmen," *197;* arrival, 197; *bāriātiyā, bariāta, 240–41, 283;* bridegroom's army, *284–86;* drums, 191; of Rām, 283–84; wedding songs, 174–76
barber, *286, 288;* in Number One Song, *249, 281, 282*
Barua: drum song, 193; *kalsa* song, 411
bass (drum), 158, 159, 161 ex. See also *tāssā*
bass (range), Sundar Popo, "Scorpion Gyul," 394–96
bata, 34
bationiers, 94
battlefield, *130, 288*
beat: fast, slow, 109–10; Indian, 100
Beatles, in local record collection, 109
bee, 263; in Holī songs, 78–79, *79, 80, 82*
Beethoven, 100
Begai, Bel, 147
beggars, on Shivrātrī, 72
Bejulah, 136–37
bele, 35
bell, *77,* 300, *366*
beloved, *82–83, 133, 134, 264, 265, 266*
bemba, 34
Bengal Awakening, 296
Bengali, 30, 399
Besant, Annie, 296
betel, *164, 177, 180,* 187, *191, 198, 203, 238, 269, 284, 287, 418*
betī, 407
Bhāgawad Gītā, 75, *132, 291,* 342
Bhāgawata Purāṇa, 301
bhāgwat (service), 43
bhāgwat song, 109
bhairav, 148
bhairavī, 100, 120, 148
bhajan, 52–54, 58, 105–7, 301–39, 399; accompanying instruments, 310; by Adesh, 142–44, 146; by Ameer Shah and Tarran Persad, 131–32; *ārtī,* 309, 333; by Benny Sewnath, 131; and *bhaktī,* 301; booklets, 60, 302–3; for Diwālī, 62, 63; fast or slow, 355–59; Felicity repertory, xxi; form, 303–39; at funeral, 365–66; *gamak,* 335; from Indian films, 124, 306, 309, 335; and *kīrtan,* 106–7; for Krishna, 87, 302; local classical music, 124; metric complexity, 332–33; *nām kīrtan,* 302; performing style, 332–33; *purvī,* 270–71; for Rām, 276, 290–92; Rāmlīlā, 88; response forms, 303, 306; rhythm, 310, 333; romanized texts, xxix; at Sai Baba *satsangh,* 345; and Sai Baba songs, 354–59; during *sanḍhyā,* 300; scores, xxviii; for Shiva, 302; for Shivrātrī, 72; social role, 401; strophic, 301, 400; sung by Adesh students, 146; translations, xxviii–xxix; Trinidad *chutney,* 368–97; verse and refrain, 399; at wake, 362
Bhajans and Chants of Satya Sai Baba, 60, 343, 354
bhaktī, 301, 342; and spice, 397; yoga, 343
bhandara feast, 363
bhāng, 75
Bharat (Rām's brother): song of Dasrath's boons, *287–88;* and wedding songs, 187
bhāratī, 160
Bharatiya Vidya Sansthhaan, 112, 138
Bharat Sevashram Sangha, 298, 401
Bhatkhande, Pandit V. N., 141, 145

bhatwān ki rāt, 153, 154, 156
bhaujī, in Number One Song, *242–62,* 419
Bhojpurī, xvii, 399; in British colonies, 30; demise, 373–76; grammar of songs, 215–16; lingua franca, 214; portrait of village women, 410; region, 21; romanization, xxix; villages, 405; wedding, 153
Bhojpurī songs: dramatic structure, 242; fundamental theme, 263; grammar, 215–16; at Holī, 74–83; *jhūmar,* 74, 107, 147, 155, 399; *kajarī,* xx, 83–87, *84,* 107, 147; kinship terms, 400; *lachārī,* xxi, 27, 108, 155, 162–72, 177, 303, 371–72, 398; language, 21, 214–15; love songs, 263–73; Phāguā, 74–83; poetry, xxviii, 214–18; repertory, 6, 90, 107–9, 404; *sohar,* 27, 36, 107, 147, 276–77, 359, *418;* transcription, xxvii–xxviii; from Uttar Pradesh, 27; wedding songs, 173–220, 242–62, 421–22
bihāg, 100, 147, 148
Bihar, 16, 20; Archer song, 191; *bārāt* song collected by Archer, 176; Barua *kalsa* song, 411; population explosion, 30; western, 409
Bipra, *281*
birahā, 21, 119, 147, 413
birds, 13, 22, 35, 51, *82, 142, 261, 265,* 282–84. *See also* crow; humming bird; swan(s); vulture
Bissoondialsingh, Usha, 108, 112, 138–40, 146–50
black cloud, *86, 264*
black magic, 35, 356
black water, 6
Blavatsky, Madam, 296
blink, *86,* 162, *169*
boat, *135, 269, 291, 415;* of life, *365*
Bombay, 20, 104, 258, 296, 378, 413, 424
Bombollywood, 124
bongos, 35, 70, 127
Boodram, Sharleen, 391–93, 400
bow, *21, 191, 278–79, 326*
Boxing Day, 68
Brahma, *283,* 299
brahman(s), 20, 31, 36, 63, *197, 275,* 341, 359, 408, 425; children in Rāmlīlā, 274; Dube family, 14, 221, 227
Brahmchārī, blessing *jhanḍī,* 60
Brahmo Samaj, 296
Braithwaite, Lloyd, 38
brass band, 153; brass in "Scorpion Gyul," 394–96
breast(s), *169,* 218, *265, 269,* 393
breeze, *84, 85–87,* 88
bride, *154,* 157, *196, 197,* 198–200, *208, 209,* 210, 216–17, *260, 407, 417–18. See also* Hindu weddings
bridegroom, *154, 154–55, 170–71,* 174, *177, 185–87,* 188, *190,* 194, *200, 205, 208, 209–10,* 216–17, *239–40, 259–60, 417–18;* "army," *284–86;* "broken," *415;* dressing bridegroom, 181; greeting bridegroom, 180–89. *See also* Hindu weddings
Bridglal, Basraj, 298
Brindāban (Brindābana), *61, 132, 365*
British Empire, 27, 29, 50
British Guiana, 295
brother, *21, 78, 176, 187, 190–91, 193, 194, 197, 204, 205, 208, 209, 244, 252, 253, 255, 261, 271, 284, 413, 418*
brother-in-law, *171, 245, 249, 251, 252, 254, 255, 415, 417, 418*
buffalo, *217*
bull, *315*
bumblebee, *265*
bumiputra, 30
bungalow, *86, 169, 170, 266*
Burma, 27–29
byāh ke gīt, 27, 108, 165, 168, 173–220, 218–19, 400; arrival of bridegroom, 187–91; *ārtī,* 155–56, 183–87; attitudes toward, 219–20; *bārāt,* 174–78, 194–97; compared with *lachārī,* 155; *ḍāl (ḍāla),* 199–201; *ḍharia,* 204–5; drum song, 191–94; greeting bridegroom, 180–82; *imili chumawan,* 194; for the *kalasā,* 242–62; *kanyādān,* 201–6; *kohabar,* 210–11; *lāwā,* 206–8; leader-chorus form, 256–57 (*see also* leader-chorus); melodic motifs, 219; musical style, 218–19; Number One Song, 242–62; omitted in recent years, 173; popular tune, 256; *sindūr,* 208–10; singers, 174. *See also* wedding song

Cacandee Settlement, 45–47
cadence. See *tāl*
cahakā, 74
Caird, Thomas, 19
calabash rattle. *See* shak shak
Calcutta, 7, 19, 20, 21
calendar, Hindu lunar, 461n.11
call-and-response, 284–86, 399; response form, 327; in *sanḍhya,* 298–300. *See also* leader-chorus

calypso, 39, 56–58, 69, 71, 94–98, *382,* 401; competitions, 401; about East Indians, 373–76; in Felicity, 401; Hindi, 401; in Indian songs, *143,* 150; influence on Indian music, 126; roots in *carieto,* xviii; soca, 380–83; social function, 95; west African traits, 95
calypso-steel band (*tāssā* hand), 160
camphor, *185,* 296, 297
Canadian Mission Schools, 52–54, 117–18
canboulay, 94
cannabis, 75
Cannes Brûlées Riots, 95
Capildeo, Pandit. *See* Kapil Dev
card games, 362–63
Caribbean culture, xvii–xviii
Caribbean Islands, *143*
Caribs, xviii, 23, 27
carieto, xviii
Carnival, 69–71, 94–95, 375, 381
carnival arts, xvii
Caroni, xviii, 22–23, 36, *376;* early Indian settlement, 14–15; savannah described by Morton, 48–49
Caroni, Ltd., 48
carpenter, *193*
Casacu, 45
Casals, Pablo, 71
cassettes, local classical, 50, 56–58, 100
caste, 31, 32, 35–37, 425; antibrahmanical ideals, 358–59; breakdown of system, 297; and Hinduism, 295–98; of indentured Coolies, 19–20; and mantras, 62–63; in marriage, 407–8; Rāmlīlā, 87. *See also* Ahīr; brahman; Chāmar; *other groups*
Ceylon, 27, 29
chachar tāl: in *byāh ke gīt,* 257; in Uttar Pradesh, 413
Chaguanas, 35, 45, 59, 71; described by Morton, 48–49, 460n.7; Sai Baba *satsangh,* 345
chaitī, 107
Chāmar, 20, 35, 36
change: Caribbean East and West Indians, xviii; in Hinduism, 301; in Indian music, 126, 400–403; in temple music, 359–60; in wedding songs, Tewari, 218
chant, 102; in *kīrtan,* 106; Sai Baba, 343, 345, 357; Vedic chants, 295–96, 300, 461n.11
chanting, 101–3
chantuelles, 94
Chapra, Bihar, 409
chatī, xxiii, 378; *kajarī* sung, 85
chatpatī, 396
chaturang, 148
chaupāī, 57–58; *Rāmāyaṇ, 278–79,* 280
chautāl, xx, 74–83, 107, 147, 303; competitions, 401; ecstasy, 75; leader-chorus, 399; by men, 399; *tāssā* hand, 159
childbirth celebrations, xxiii. See also *sohar; barahī*
children on shipboard, 9–12
children's songs, 52–54, 56, 57 ex., *274,* 354–55, 359; *kaseeda,* 65–66; wedding songs, Felicity school girls, 421–22
Chīnī, Chīnītāt, 6, 22, 138
Chota Nagpur, 20
Christian(s): attitude toward calypso, 95; Felicity churches, 59; Hindustani hymns, 112, 115–18; holidays, 66–69, 83, 424; proselytization, 39; school songs, 52–53; and Shango, 33–34; songs, 104–5
Christmas, 66–69, 424
chumawan, 187, 194
chupes, 156
Church of the Nazarene, 59
chutney, xxi, 108, 368–97, *391–92,* 402, 422–24; and alcohol, 371; in Brooklyn, 381, 388–89; clubs, 400; commercialism, 369–71; concept of spice, 396–97; hot songs, 56; as Indian music, 399; *jhūmar,* 389; knowledge of Hindi, 400; and *lachārī,* 170; *lambada,* 389; "'94 Summer Chutney Time," 391–93; 1980s and '90s, 376–96; 1994 season, 423; rap, 389; soca, 389; and tent singing, 401
cinema. *See* film
clappers, 344. See also *kartāl*
clarinet, 310, 312–15 ex.
Clarke, Colin, 38
classical music, 98, 100; described by Ramaya, 120–29; north Indian, xxi; revival, 401–2; Western, and steel band, 71. *See also* local classical
cloud(s), *61, 66,* 86, *143, 211,* 263, *264, 266, 267, 271, 418*
clubs, *chutney,* 377, 400
cobra: in Number One Song, Dube, 415–17, *415, 417;* in Number One Song, Surinam, *411;* in Number One Song, Trinidad, 242–62, *249, 252*
color-class hierarchy, 37–40
colors: for funeral, 362–64; for the wedding, 259–60. *See also* red

Columbus, Christopher, 22
competition, xviii, 127–28; *chautāl,* 74; *chautāl* and calypso, 401; *jawābī kīrtan,* 388; in local classical music, 122–23; *parang,* 67; steel band, 70–71; village folk song, 422
composed songs, 97–99, 402
concerts, 380
conch shells, 94
conch-shell trumpet, 300
congas, 70
congo drums, 34, 127
Conrad, Joseph, 26
consensualism, xx, 37–40, 44
contests, 122
contract labor systems, 27, 29. *See also* indentureship
Coolie(s), 14, 24, 459n.4
"copies," *bhajan,* 106
costumes: Carnival, 71, 95; of Rām, 181, 188; Hosay, 65; for Rāmlīlā, 87–88; for wedding, 151, 259
counting rhyme, 56, 57 ex.
cow, *196–97, 217, 277*
cowbells, 70
crapaud, 51; as example of marginal survival, 460n.8
cremation, xxi, 46, 48, 361–67
Creole, 35; attitudes toward East Indians, 36, 40; Carnival, 69–71; color-class hierarchy, 37–40; music, xx; pan (steel band), 58, 69, 375, *376;* population of Caribbean, xviii; song, calypso, 94–98
crescendo, 74–75, 344, 461n.15
crocodile, *133, 306. See also* elephant, and crocodile
crop time, 24, 61
crow, 372; foreshadows Rām's exile, *240, 282, 283–84;* and Rām's wedding, 282–84
Crowley, Daniel, 35, 41
crown *(māur),* 151, *185,* 188, *190, 191, 287, 306, 326, 365;* in Number One Song, *252*
crying (cried), 261, 364; in Number One Song, *245, 254, 255, 261*
cuatro, 67
cuckoo, *61, 267;* in Archer wedding song, 373; in *chutney, 371,* 372, *373*
cults, 33–36, 401
cultural persistence, 32, 33
culture change, xvii, 258, 360
Cunupia River, 45, 48, 363
"cut," *tāssā* style, 160
cutie-pie, *384–85*
cymbals, 344. See also *jhāl; manjīrā*

Dadra, 135–36
dādrā tāl: in *dhun,* 107; during the indentureship, 120; in *kīrtan,* 106; local classical, 100
ḍāl (ḍāla), 199–200
damarū, 302, 315
dance, 32, 33, 401, 420; Arawak, *arectoe,* xviii; in *chutney, 384–85,* 391–93; Coolies, on shipboard, 9; cuckoo, 373; at Holī, 72; at Hosay, 65; Indian classical, 165; jumping up, 94; Krishna, *365;* lewd, 355, 357, 371, 378; Lord of the, *315;* and *parang,* 67; described by Ramaya, 119, 123; part of *sangīt,* 90; Shango, 33; Shiva, 302; song, 396; war dances, 12, 32; at weddings, 123, 154, 155, 156, 162, 163
darshan, 134–35, *135,* 343
Dasarath (father of Rām), *238–41,* 276, *283, 286–88, 326*
das indriya, 363
daughter, *77, 154, 170, 176–77, 177, 180, 197, 198–99, 200, 201, 203, 204, 205, 208, 210, 216, 249, 255, 290, 407, 408*
daughter(s)-in-law, *177, 380, 410*
Dayananda, Swami, 296
Day, K. C., 125
death, 4–5, *135;* chant from *Rāmāyaṇ,* 276; East Indian customs, 361–67; Hindu concept of, 4–5; song, 366; spirit placated in Shango, 35
decorations: for *akhand Rāmāyaṇ,* 279; Christmas and New Year's Day, 69; Hosay, 64–65; Shivrātrī, 72
deep Hindi, 100, 103–4, 401. *See also* Sanskrit
dehatī gīt, 409
Delhi, *268*
desh, 147
Despres, Leo, 37
Devanagari script, 141–43
devī, daughters as, 407
Devi, Champa, 125
De Wolfe, Dr., 9
Dey, Manna, 128
dhamaar, 148
Dhangars, 20
ḍhantāl, 399, 166–67 ex., 350–51 ex.; Boodram "'94 Summer Chutney Time," 391–93; in calypso, *374; chutney,* 377; in local classical music, 120, 122; pictured, 321; Sai Baba, 345
ḍharia, in wedding, 203–6, *204, 205*
dharma, 326, 341, 425

Dhola, 119
ḍholak, xxiii, 27, 91, 147, 398, 399; to accompany *bhajan,* 106, 310; to accompany *lachārī,* 155, 398; Boodram "'94 Summer Chutney Time," 391–93; in *chautāl,* 74–75; *chutney,* 377; "Chutney Lambada," 389–91; in composed songs, 98; in examples, 166–67, 316, 319, 348, 350–51; exams by Adesh, 145; hands, 159–62; in Indian orchestras, 127; in local classical music, 120; Sai Baba songs, 344–45, 354; in Uttar Pradesh, 413
dhoti, 17–18, 42
Dhropatī, 75–77
dhrupad: during the indentureship, 120, 122; local classical, 100; in Trinidad, 146, 148–49
dhun, 107, 303; *Hare Rām,* 298; in Sai Baba 343, 356–57; in *sanḍhyā,* 298, 300
dhurpat. See *dhrupad*
diamond umbrella, *286*
dīpchandī tāl: in byāh ke gīt, 219, 257; in Uttar Pradesh, 413
disco, 381, 401; and calypso, 380
District Magistrate of Ghazipur, 17
Divine Life Bhajans, 60, 302, 359, 365
Divine Life Society, 54, 58–60, 298, 320; Ashram, 424; and Sai Baba, 343; Sai Baba songs, 354; weekly services, 59
Diwālī, 53, 62–64, 68, 298; lights from airplane, 405; in Naipaul, 37
diyā, 247; on Diwālī, 63; in *havan pūjā,* 297; in *Rāmāyaṇ* sessions, 279; in *sanḍhyā,* 300; at weddings, 153, 155
dogs, 13, 51, 294, 461n.10
dohā, 78; invocation to Saraswatī, 122; in *Rāmāyaṇ, 278–79*
donation, on Shivrātrī, 72. See also *kanyādān*
Doordarshan, *Rāmāyaṇ* series, 292–93
Dorman Nursery School, 53–54
doun doun, 94
"Dr. William," *97*
dowry, *282*
Dravidian languages, 30. *See also* Tamil; Telugu
dreams, *65, 273,* 345; Jesus and Sai Baba, 367; men in exile, 398; red sari, 366
drinking, 127, *137–38, 368–69,* 378; at Carnival, 71; *chutney, 368–69;* at Phāguā, 74; at weddings, 162
drone: harmonium, 332; Sai Baba songs, 358; in *sanḍhyā,* 298
drum(s): banned, 69, 95; box, 34; and *chutney,* 56; "coolie," *374;* and *kīrtan,* 106; in *lachārī,* 168; machine, 389–91; in Morton, 115–16; in Naipaul, 36; set, 173; at wedding, 153, 191, 197; in wedding songs, *193, 194, 197; tāssā,* 27. See also *damarū; ḍholak; nagārā;* steel band; *tāssā;*
drummers (drumming), 33–34, 74, 91, 109, 156, 399; Boodram "'94 Summer Chutney Time," 391–93; during the indentureship, 119–23; in local classical music, 123; in Morton, 118; Shango, 33–34; at wedding, 193
Drupatee, 376
dry season, 62, 88, *143*
Dube, xix; lineage, 221, 225, 230–36; Naipaul village, 178; Number One Song, 415–17; village of, 409. *See also* Mahadewā Dube
Duke of Normandy, 373
Durbin, Mridula Adenwala, 214
Durgā, 62, 223

earrings, *191,* 260, *306*
earth, 65, *291, 302*
Easter, 83
East Indians, 14–15; arrival in Trinidad, 20; attitudes toward Creoles, 36–40, 41; *chutney,* 377; and cultural change, 41–43; culture shock in India, 343; daily routine, 51–60; diet, 51–52; ethnic identity, 39–40, 41–42, 358–59; filmī culture influence, 41; forebears, 27; heritage, 40, 42; indentured laborers, 8; influx to Caribbean, xviii; isolation from India, effect on local singing, 124; language, 42; link with India, 149–50, 258; minority, 39–40; participation in Carnival, 69, 71; population growth, 15, 20; settlement, origins, early years, 14; taxonomy of music, 89–110, 92–93; term defined, 27; travel abroad, 49–50; world view, 50
eastern breeze, *86–87*
east wind, *135, 271, 272, 273;* love songs, 263, 270–73
eclipse, 205–6, *206*
electric instruments, xviii, 127, 173
elephant: and crocodile, 75, 76 ex., *77, 132,* 133–34, 136–37, *137;* in Hindu wedding, 174, *176, 197,* 211–12, *217;* Rām's *bārāt, 283, 286*
elephant pearls, *198, 275*
The Eleven Truths of Music, 420
Eliot, T. S., 3, 7, 12, 22, 25, 40, 424
embrace, *136*
engagement *(tilak),* 281
English, *134,* 399; "broken," 393; *chutney,* 368; classics, 100; in Felicity, 42–44; mixed with

Hindi, 374; and *Rāmāyaṇ*, 280; songs, 52–54, 91–94; song translations, 215
entertainment music, 401–2
epic, 274. See also *Rāmāyaṇ; Māhābharata; Rāmcharitmānas*
ethnographies, Felicity, 31
ethnomusicologist, xvii–xviii, 168, 402, 408, 413, 419
ethnomusicology, xx, 402–3, 459nn. 1, 3
extended family, 32

farmer, *249*
fast music, 110; characteristic of chant, 103; *chatpatī*, 396; *chautāl*, 74–75; *kīrtan* style, 106; Sai Baba songs, 110, 355, 357
Fatel Razack, 7, 20
father, *22, 154–55, 176, 177–78, 180, 187, 197, 200–201, 203, 204, 206, 209, 210, 244, 252, 253, 255, 261, 283, 285, 289, 290, 291, 335, 370, 413, 415, 417–18*
father-in-law, *84, 170, 244, 253, 277, 278, 379–80, 418*
Félicité estate, 21, 221, 360
Felicity, 3, 26, 45–50; abode of, 274; ancestral villages in India, xix; *Chautāl* Group, xxiii; Christians, 52–53; congregational worship, 38, 301; daily schedule, 51–60; death rites, 361–67; described by Morton, 48–49; districts, 45; ethnographic description, 45–50; founding of, 21, 45; Hindus, 52–53; Hindu School, 52–54, 63, 64, 354–55, 421; history of Hinduism, 295–99; Indian culture, 41; map, 46; Morton Klass's study, 32; musical history, 400–401; musical life, 398–403; primary schools, 48; research on, 31, 32, 50, 74, 343, 359–60; songs in India, 409–15; sounds and noise, 51–60; study of village, xviii–xx; taxonomy of music, 89–110, 92–93; temples, 38–39, 59, 72, 294–339, 355–60; visited by Morton, 460n.7; world view, 50
fertility, in Number One Song, 409, 410
festivals and fêtes. *See* Carnival; Holī; Hosay; Phāguā; *other celebrations*
fieldwork, 369; conditions, xvii; in India, 405; notes, xix, 58–60; techniques, xx
Fiji, 6, 27–31, 297
film *(filmī)*, Indian, xx; *Bala Joban*, 123; and *bhajan*, 107; learning tunes, 400; music, 126, 173; orchestration, 400; soca, 389; songs, 90, 123, 124, 125, 256–57, 399, 400, 409
finger cymbals. See *manjīrā*
Firamat, 147. *See also* Phiramat
firecrackers, 153
fire sacrifice. See *havan*
fish, *275, 418*
Five Rivers Islamia School, 65
flower(s), 81, *142, 238–39, 265, 266, 277;* in Mahadewā Dube song, *238–41;* sign of purity, 5, 82; in *sohar, 418*
flute, *86, 302,* 346–47 ex.; in film *bhajan,* 310; in Indian orchestra, 173; in Sai Baba songs, 344
folk songs, 53–54; *chutney,* 371, 377; defined, 419; in English, 91; indentureship period, 146–47, 400; as Indian music, 399; Rasiya and Dhola, 119; transcription and translation, xxviii
foreign, *130, 269*
forest, *61, 79, 132, 261, 264, 266, 270, 271, 275, 276, 287, 289, 326*
"Forged from the Love of Liberty," 94
French patois, in kalindas, 95
frog, *61, 84*
fulay, 160
full moon *kathā,* 59, 136
funk, 381
Furlonge Church, 59

gālī, 162, 177
gamak, 327–32, 335, 344
games, 12, 32, 61–62
Gandhi, Mahatma, 297
Ganesh, *78,* 340, *344,* 345
Gangeatic plain, 30
Ganges River (Ganga), 21, *22, 79, 197, 266, 268, 302, 311, 315, 363, 365*
Gangulee, Nagendranath, 18
garden, *82, 238–41, 418*
gardener, *81–82, 394*
garland, *131, 275, 315;* five colors, *190;* maker, *21;* snakes, *302;* skulls, *277–78*
gāyāk, 129
gāyan samay, 122, 123, 144
gazal, 120. See also *ghazal*
gharānā, 139
ghazal, 105, 401; described by Usha, 148–49; local classical, 100; by Ramdhani Shyma, 133–34; on records, 124; *tāssā* hand, 159; "Urdu Ghazal," *134–35*
Ghazipur, 17, 20, 409; *bārāt* song, 177; *kanyādān* song, 206
ghee, 60, *204, 277,* 296, 362, 366
gifts, *275;* as *neg,* 246; wedding, 154, 199–200, *282*

Gītā, 425
Gladstone Coolies, 27, 420
global communications, xviii
gobar (cow dung), *196, 277*
Gokhale, Veena, 413
Good Friday, 83
good song: hymns, 105; meaningful, 110
gold, golden, *66,* 199, *200, 203;* ball, bat, ring, *287;* bangle, *81, 255–56, 370, 390;* basket full, *282;* chain, in Number One Song, *254, 254–55, 255–56,* 256, 259; coin, in Number One Song, *249,* 256; dish, *239;* earring, *260;* gifts, *275; kalas, 275;* mantra, *376;* ornaments, *276;* pitcher, *196;* plate, *268;* ropes, *276;* and Sai Baba, 342; stool, *198;* threads, *275*
gopīs, 79, 165, 264–65, 301
Gopi's East Indian Orchestra; *Dadra,* 135–36; *Hindi Ghazal,* 133–34; Hindi Kawali, 137–38; on 78 R.P.M. records, 128; "Urdu Ghazal," 134–35
Gorakhpur, 7, 14, 20, 221, 226, 237, 409; Kapil Dev, 178; Number One Song, 415
gotra, 200
Govinda, *302, 365*
grandfather, *131*
graveyard, *134*
great tradition, little tradition, xxviii, 41
grey-out, cultural, 402–3
Grierson, Sir George Abraham, 19, 21; *bārah māsas,* 274–76; Bhojpurī language, 215; Bihārī song, 61; *birahā,* 21; crow, 283; love song, 266; *parichhan* song, 186; song of east wind, 272; song of the East, 272; song of mother's grief, 407; song of Sītā, 197–98; song of twelve months, 265–66; song studies, 263
gudanā, 36
guitar, 67, 127, *127,* 173
Gujarati, in India diaspora, 30, 31
Gulshan Bahar, 125
gunas, 363
gunshots at wedding, 53
Guru Pūrnimā, 145–46
Guyana, xvii, xviii, 37, 149, 258, 342

hair, Afro, 343
Haj, 132–33
Haley, Alex, 40–41
hand clapping: on the beat, 60; in examples, 319, 348; and fast singing, 357; in Felicity Hindu School, 354–55; and *karmas,* 357; Sai Baba songs, 344, 354–55, 357–58; in Shango, 34
hansā, 4, 5. *See also* swan(s)
hānsul in Number One Song, *251, 252*
Hanumān, 87, 224, *327,* 340, 345
Hardeo, 123
hardī (haldī): ceremony, lotus flowers, 414; *uthāway,* 153; at the wedding, 153–54, *154*
hardī song. *See* Number One Song
Hārichandra, *311*
Hari Rām, Brahmchārī. *See* Satchidananda, Swami
harmonium, 398; accompanying *bhajan,* xxviii, 310, 332; *chutney,* 377; drone in *sanḍhyā,* 298–99; equal-tempered pitch, 401; examples, 304, 319, 322–24, 336–39, 348–49, 350–51; heterophony, 333 ex. XXX; in local classical music, 120; in Naipaul, 36; and Sai Baba songs, 344–45
harmony, Western, 310
Harris, Marvin, 40
havan, xxiii, 299–301, *277;* booklets, 302–3; Divine Life Society, 354; mantras, 295; *pūjā,* 297; in *sohar,* 276–77; used in interview, 102
hawk cuckoo, *267*
heart, *22, 66, 78, 80, 82, 130, 135, 137, 142, 169, 177, 265, 266, 267, 289, 290–91, 307, 371–72, 379, 389–91, 395*
hermaphrodite singer, 418–19
Herskovits, Melville J., xvii, 35, 36; *Trinidad Village,* 33–34
Hertig-Skalická, Jitka, 263; Ballia mother's song, 407–8; lotus song, 417–18; song of boons, 287–88
Herzog, George, 250
hi-fi systems, 108–9
Hindi, 43–44, 53, 399; anti-Creole focus, 42; books and deep Hindi, 103–4; broken Hindi, 103–4; calypsos, xxi; compared with Bhojpurī, 215–16; decline in Trinidad, 149; dialects, 146; films brought to Trinidad, 123–24; hymns, described by Morton, 116–18; hymn book, 116–17; mixed with English, 374; pronunciation in song, 100; *Rāmāyaṇ,* 279; revival, 42; romanization, xxix; taught by Adesh, 138–39, 141, 144–46; taught by Morton, 117; school songs, 52–54
hindool, 100
Hinduism, 35, 58, 425; caste, 31; compared with Christianity, 38–39, 301, 363; congregational worship, 301; cremation, 48; darker side, 35; and death, 361–67; history in Felicity, 295–99; lunar calendar, 461n.11; mar-

riage, 31; missionaries, 295–96; musical practice, 299–339; purity and pollution, 31; renaissance, 296–301; songs, 105–7; worship, described by Morton, 115–16

Hindu(s): attitudes toward calypso, 95–96; in Felicity, 45, 48; holidays (*see* Diwālī; Holī; Rāmlīlā; Shivrātrī; *other holidays*); relations with Muslims, 128–29

Hindu weddings, 151–220, 242–62; auspicious date, 151–53; bride's vows taken by father, 213; calypso, 374–75; described by Morton, 116; described in song texts, 259–62; duties of brother, 259; groom's arrival, 174–78; local classical music, 123; Rām and Sītā, 280–86; recognized by British, 153; songs of Rām, 276; "under the bamboo," 153

Holas, Boodram, 377

Holī, 72–83, *81, 267,* 461n.15; *chutney,* 386–88. *See also* Phāguā

honey (endearment), *381–83*

honey (syrup), 340–45

hori, 120

horns, 94

horse: in Hindu wedding, 174, 176, *197,* 211–12; in Number One Song, 242–43, *244–56,* 259, *260, 413,* 414; racing, 68; Rām's *bārāt, 282, 283,* 286

Hosay (festival), 64–65

Hosay (*tāssā* hand), 160

hot music, 97

hot songs, 56; *lachārī,* 108

hourglass drum, *302*

humming bird, *143*

husband, *21, 85–86, 86–87, 164–65, 169–70, 170,* 218, *249, 261, 264, 265, 266, 268, 269–70, 278, 289, 290, 380, 394, 407, 408*

hymns, 105; analogous to *bhajan,* 401; Morton, Hindustani, 115–18; in the Presbyterian School, 52–53

Ian, 420–22, 421

idiophone, 168; Sai Baba songs, 344

Imami, 147; *sāraṇgī* player, 122

imiliā (imili), 176, 194

improvisation, 120, 327

indentureship, 7–25; abolished, 27; administration of system, 14, 19; *arkatiā,* 16–19, 29–30; caste of recruits, 19–20; Coolies' debts, 24; daily routine, 24; deception, 14, 16; factors for emigration, 29–30; fear of kidnapping, 17; history, 27, 30, 42–44; incentives, 16; Kingsley on, 24; laborers, xviii, 178, 420; mortality on estates, 24; music described by Ramaya, 119–23; music described by Usha, 146–49; pandits, 228; plantation life, 42–43; profile of population, 459n.5; recruitment, 7, 14, 16–20, 227–28; return passage, 14–15; role of famine, 29–30; stimulated by abolition, 23; teaching of songs, 178; work gangs, 24

Independence Day, 87

India, *77, 376,* 404–11; diaspora, 27–31, 460n.6; patriotic song, *134;* role of bride, *21–22*

Indian carnival, 72, 88. *See also* Phāguā

Indian classical music, 100; compared with Trinidad classical, 145, 146–50; Guru Adesh, 138–46, 401

Indian films: and *bhajan,* 301, 306, 309, 310, 335; "Chutney Lambada," 389–91; and culture change, 360; effect on Trinidad music, 126, 149–50; imported to Trinidad, 400; influence on local classical music, 149–50; about Rām, 274; religious, 62, 165; source of *bhajan,* 301; Sundar Popo, "Scorpion Gyul," 394–96; Trinidad orchestras, 173

Indian film songs, 88, 173, 401; acculturation, 91–94, 126, 128, 402; and *bārāt,* 171; playback singers, 309; studio techniques, 385–86. *See also* film, songs

Indian music, 56–58; defined, 399; and Indian languages, 399, 400; influence of Creole music, 118. *See also* Indian classical music

"Indian Music in Trinidad," 118–26

Indian orchestras, 39, 88, 125, 126–28, 377; and wedding songs, 173, 400

Indian records, 154, 400

Indian soca, 374, *376,* 377

Indian Talent on Parade, 125

Indic languages, translations, xxviii

Indo-African relations, 373–75

invocation, *sanḍhyā,* 298

Islam. *See* Hosay; *kaseeda;* Mohammed; Muslim

itinerant singers, 119–24

Jaan, Ali, 147

jahāj, 7

Jaiman, Pandit Mehta, 400

jajmānī, 31, 82

Jalota, Anup, 379, 380

jal tarang, 139

Jamaica, xvii, 27; song, 94

jamming, *381–82*

Jamuna River, 21, *79, 365, 387*

Janaka, *186, 198, 238–40,* 277, *281, 326*

Jānakī, *278*
Janakpur, *277, 281, 283–84*
Janamāshhtāmī, 87
janeū (janeua), 239, 281
Janglies, 20
Jangli Tola, 45–48
Janwasa, 123
jap, 101–2; *mālā,* 101–2, 131
jasmine, *22, 81–82, 266*
jawābī kīrtan, 388
jaykārā, 75, *77–78, 79, 279*
Jaywardena, Chandra, 41
Jesus Christ, 295, 342; Hindu attitudes toward, 104–5; in Vishram's dream, 367
Jhabwah, 123
jhāl, 74–75, 159, 160, 161 ex.
jhanḍi, 60
jhīl, 4
jhūmar (song) 74, 107, 147, 155, 399
jhūmar (*tāssā* hand), 159
jījā-sālī, 225
jingles, 348 ex.
Jit Seeshai's East Indian Orchestra; *Bhajan,* 131; "Hindou Song," 290–91; on 78 R.P.M. records, 128; *Jazal Ghazal,* 136–37; "Naarw Bhawurr May," 135; "Quawali Song," 130
jnana yoga, 301, 341–42
jogīrā, 74
John Morton of Trinidad, 112–18, 460n.7
jukeboxes, 48, 88, 401
jump up (jumping up) 58, 71, 94
jungle, *371,* 372, *373, 376*
Jyoti, 144

kabīr, 74, 159
Kabīr Das, 129, 148
kadam, 84, 176
kaffee, 148
kaharwā, 100
kaharwā tāl, 106–7, 257, 401
Kaikeyī (Kekaiya, Kekai), *200, 201, 286–88*
kajarī, xx, 83–87, *84,* 107, 147
Kakahieya, *186*
Kakandi, 21, 45, 48
Kakandi Settlement, 45, 460n.7
kālāpānī, 6
kalasā, 247; gold *(kalas), 275;* in *havan pūjā,* 297; at *mātīkonwā,* 153; in Number One Song, 242–62; tattoo, *411;* wedding pitcher, 410
Kālī, 277
kalindas, 94–95; *tāssā* hand, 160
kalingara (kalangara), 147
Kālī *pūjā,* 35, 107
Kalloo, 147
kāmdev, 5
Kamini, 42–44
Kanchan, 377, 378, 381, 402, 423, 424; authentic songs, 402; "Give Me *Paisā!*" 369–71; "Kuch Kuch Baby," 383–86; visit to Trinidad, 128
kangani, 29, 30
Kanhaiyā, *386–87*
kanyādān, 155, 201–6, 238
Kapil Dev, 14, 178, 221–23, 224, 227–28, 241
Karim, *292*
Karimganj (Karimpur), xviii, 4–5
karma, 78, 357, 425–26; yoga, 301, 341
kartāl, 155, 345, 399
Kārtik, 62–63, *266*
Kārtik Nahān, 63
kasakna, 272
kaseeda, 65–66
kathā, 59, 136
Kaushalyā (Kausilya), *200, 276, 288*
Kawal, Ustad Jhagroo. *See* Quaval, Jugrue
Kawali, 137–38
Kawalie, 132–33
Kekaī (Kekai), *275, 276, 287, 288*
kettledrums, 27, 212. See also *tāssā; nagārā*
key signatures, xxvii
khurma, 153
khyāl, 144, 148
kicharī, 155, 156
king, *85–86, 169, 170, 193, 208, 254, 255, 282, 284, 286–87, 288, 300, 306;* in Number One Song, *252*
Kingsley, Charles, 13, 14–15, 23–24, 33–34
kīrtan, 105–7, 109; leader-chorus, 399; on Shivrātrī, 72; style, in *dhun* and *bhajan,* 298, 300
kiss, *154, 395*
Klass, Morton, 31, 32, 50; Hinduism in Felicity, 359–60; Holī in 1958, 74; Sai Baba, 343, 359
kohabar, wedding song, 210, *211*
kohinur (*tāssā* hand) 160
Kōnsiliyā (Kōsilā), *186, 275*
Krishna, *79, 82–83, 131, 133,* 265, *292,* 342, *365–66, 387;* and Arjuna, 12, 342; *bhajan,* Janamāshhtāmī, 87; in *chautāl,* 74–79, 83; *chutney,* 386–87; elephant and crocodile, 131–34; in Felicity *bhajan,* 302; and flute, 356; as Gopala, 301; in Grierson song, 265–

66; and *lachārī,* 165; *nām kīrtan,* 302; in Phāguā song, 82–83; prayers at death, 363; in Rām *bhajan,* 291–92; *Shyāmla,* 86; in Surinam collection, 265; and *viraha,* 264
Kumar, Hemant, 128

lachārī, xxi, 27, 108, 162–72, 303, 398; and *byāh ke gīt,* 155; and *chutney,* 371–72, 380; and *gālī,* 177
Lachhiman, *289–90*
lachī, 155
La Guerre, John, 37
lahar pator skirts, 179, 414
laig (*tāssā* hand), 159
Lakhan, *238–41, 275, 279*
Lakshmaṇ; in *bhajan, 306;* in *Panchwatī,* 5–6, *270;* and Sītā, 280; social role, 216; song of boons, *287;* at wedding, 194; in wedding songs, 187, *196, 282, 283*
Lakshmī, 340, 355; Diwālī, 62–63, 64, 88
land grants, 14, 15
landowners, 30
Lankā, *133, 326;* Sītā's exile, 289–90
Latchuman, *284*
laughing, in Number One Song, *245*
lāwā: at *bhatwān ki rāt,* 154; ceremony, 206–8, *208; gālī,* 208
Laxuman, song of Dasarath's boons, *286–87*
leader-chorus, 254, *284–86;* in *bhajan,* 303, 310; in *chautāl,* 75; in the Divine Life Society, 60; examples, 76, 166–67, 304–35, 308–9, 312–15, 319, 322–25, 328–31, 346–47, 348–49, 350–54; in Felicity repertory, 399; in *lachārī,* 155; at large gatherings, 358; in Number One Song, 249–50; in *parang,* 67; Rām's *bārāt,* 284–86; response form, 327; in Sai Baba songs, 344; in Shango, 34; in syncretic forms, 35; in *tāssā* drumming, 160; in wedding songs, 218
learning: Indian classical music, 138–46; wedding songs, 178
leatherworker, *193*
Lewis, Oscar, 270
life cycle, songs, 400
light classical music, 124
lightning, *77, 264, 266, 267*
Lion House, 213, 223, 225, 226
līpā, 194
liquor, *137–38*
"local," 43, 401, 402
local classical, 99–100, 401; compared with Indian classical by Usha, 147–49; described by Ramaya, 120–29; development in, 124; modern change, 149–50; relationship to Indian classical music, 126
local composed, 98–99; *chutney,* 377
local music industry, 125
locket, in Number One Song, *245*
London, 69–70, *370*
Lord Executor, 373–74
Lord Kitchener, 39, 381
Lord Shorty, 56, 375, 381; Indian calypso example, 371
lorī, 107
lotus: and bee, *79;* in *birahā,* 21; flowers trembling, *417;* heart, *265;* metaphor, 419; in Naipaul, 36; in Number One Song, 242–62, *244–56,* 409, 415–17, *417;* pictured, 412, 414; Rām, *275, 410; samadhī, 216;* Tagore, 419; in Upadhyaya song, 410; in Uttar Pradesh ponds, 231, 413–14
love, *79, 80, 130, 133, 133–34, 136, 137–38, 142,* 164, *169–70,* 237, 241, *261,* 264, *266, 268,* 274, *368–69, 369–70,* 372, *390, 394–96, 407,* 420; and *bhaktī,* 301; in Hinduism, 223–26; sugar of, *411*
love marriages, 407; of Rām and Sītā, 238; and wedding dates, 152
lover, *86, 142–43, 267*
lovesickness, 273
love songs, 263–73, 371, 375; *kajarī,* 83–87
Lowenthal, David, 38, 39, 42, 44
lullabies, 27
lustful desire, *264*
Lutgendorf, Philip, 292

Madhuban (Madhuwan), *79, 289*
Madras, 19, 20, 258
Madrassee, 32
Madrassi dance, 119
Māhābhārata; chautāl texts, 74–79; in Indian films, 309; *jawābī kīrtan,* 388; *kathā,* 136–37; and *lachārī,* 165; Parsurām, 280
Mahādeva, *302*
Mahadewā Dube, 14, 221, 224, 227–29, 231, 241, 409
Māhākalī, *315*
Maharaj, Grace, 39
mahfil, local classical singing, 122
maistry, 29, 30
make-up (song), 402
Malaya (Malaysia), 27–30

mālī, 82
malkosh, 147
Malm, Krister, 33
mandolin, 67, 127, 145
Mangeshkar, Lata, 310
mango, *82, 84, 176, 265, 371,* 372, *410*
mangrove swamp, 13, 22, 23, 422
manjīrā (mangeera), xxix, 91, 319 ex., 346–47 ex., 350–51 ex.; in *bhajan,* 310; to accompany *lachārī,* 155; in local classical music, 120, 122, 147; Sai Baba, 345; self-accompaniment, 399
mantras, 100–103, *169,* 376; *aum namo,* 298; in *pūjā,* 62–63; in *sanḍhyā,* 299, 300; Vedic, 295
marawā, 153, 201, *239*
marfat, 120
marginal survival, xvii, xxi, 124, 419; bawling and ramage, 460nn. 8, 9; described by Naipaul, 36, 37; in the diaspora, 257–58; old English words, 51; Trinidad Bhojpurī, 214–15
Marīch, 3, 5
marigold, *81–82*
marriages: Hindu, described in song, *21–22* (*see also* Hindu weddings); India, 407–9; Trinidad, 31
mass media, xviii. *See also* radio; television
Mastana Bahaar, 39, 127, 401
Mathura, Pat, 125
mātīkonwā, 153
Mau, U.P., 409, 414
Mauritius, 3, 27, 30, 31, 246, 297
māyā, 341
Mecca, *66*
melody, *142, 374;* motif, example, 219 ex.; in Number One Song, 249–50, 257–59. *See also* tune
memorization, 218, 302–3
Merchant, 381, 385
meringue, 381
Merriam, Alan, xvii, xx, 34, 35, 359
midnight, *211*
midwife, *276*
The Mighty Killer, 374
Mighty Sparrow, 56, 375, 381
migration, Indian laborers, 27–31
mike, 154, 171; truck, 88, 361–62
milk, *82, 186, 187, 217*
milkmaids. See *gopīs*
mīnd, 327
Mīrābāī, 130, *130,* 148
miracles, and Sai Baba, 340–43, 356
Mirich Desh, 3
missionaries, Hindu, 295–99
modernization, xviii, 360. *See also* Westernization
mogalawa, 269
Mohammed, *66, 130*
Mohammedan, *133*
Mohammed brothers, 108, 125
Mohammed, Fakir, 147
Mohammed, Moean, 378
Mohammed, Sayyeed, 128–30
Mohan, Peggy, 214
moksha, 341, 397
money, *194, 200, 370–71, 374,* 377
monsoon season, xx; and love songs, 83–87, 264–65
moon, *66, 78, 190, 206, 266,* 299; moon-diadem, *302;* moonlight, *135;* moon-like face, *384*
Moon, 83–84, 97–98, 154, 177, 185, 193, 200, 203, 242–46, 251, 252, 256, 262, 281, 361, 409, 415, 426
Morisu, 3
Morton, John, 113; description of Caroni, 48–49; in Felicity, 460n.7; music, 112–18
Morton, Sarah, 112–18
mother, *22, 185, 186, 187, 193, 198, 204, 209, 217, 245, 261, 262, 276, 291, 335*
mother-in-law, *84, 169, 170, 270, 393–94*
Mouat, F. J., 9
mountain(s), *131, 142, 143, 177*
Mount Kailas, *277*
Mozart, 100, 397
mridang, 147
Mritungaya, Swami, 295
Mukesh, 58, 310
mūrtī, 300
music: change and, 149–50, 257–59, 359–60; competition, 38–40; defined, 89–90; Eleven Truths of, 420; ensembles (*see* Indian orchestras; steel band); feelings (*see* music, feelings); history, of Felicity, 400–401 (*see also* Ramaya, Narsaloo; Bissoondialsingh, Usha); industry, xxi, 99; as instrumental music, 90; instruments, xviii, *193, 194, 284;* musician, 194; notation, xxvii; patronage, 39; *sangīt,* 90; and Saraswatī, *142;* soca, *382;* social role, 401; soft style, 109; steeldrums, *376;* style, 218–19; teaching, 295; theory, 109–10; and welfare, 420
music, feelings, 357, 420, 426; ecstasy, 75; for Indian music, 58, 100; joy, 106; in local clas-

sical music, 120; spice, 397; for wedding songs, 185, 219–20
musicology, 398
Muslim(s): and Arabic language, 104; devotional songs, 65–66; in Felicity, 48; at Hosay, 64–65; indentured Coolies ("Mussulmans"), 20; in Rām *bhajan,* 291–92; relations with Hindus, 128–29; schools, 117; songs, 104, 129–30, 132–33
Mundas, 20
Myers, Helen, 413

nagārā, 399; accompany Ahīr dances, 119; hands, 159–62
naichal (*tāssā* hand), 159
naihar, 5, 408
Naipaul, V. S., xix, xxi; *An Area of Darkness,* 14, 36–37, 38, 227–28, 236–38, 241; aunts, 173 (*see also* Permanand sisters); on feelings of grandfather, 14; genealogy, 232–35; *havan,* 300; *A House for Mr. Biswas,* 223–26; *India: A Wounded Civilization,* 425; *The Middle Passage,* 226; trapdoors, 415; village attitudes toward, 50; *A Way in the World,* 300
nakaṭā, 155
nām kīrtan, 302
nanadī (nanad): in *lachārī,* 162, 166–67 ex., *168;* in Number One Song, *242–62, 269, 413,* 419
Nandalāla, *309*
naradī, Rāmāyaṇ singing style, 461n.15
national anthem, 36, 94
National Centre for the Performing Arts, 413
National Cultural Council, 118
nationalism, Indian, 297
Nau Jawan, 127
Navajī Haj, 133
Naya Zamana (orchestra), 118, 125, 127, 377
Naya Zamana (stage show), 125
Nazarene Church, 59
Nazir Mohammed's Orchestra: *Kawalie,* 132–33; "Quawal Song," 129–30; on 78 R.P.M. records, 128
Negro song, 98
Nepal, *284*
nephew, *244, 251, 252, 254, 255, 273*
neutral third, 256
Nevadomsky, Joseph, 31, 50
New World, 8
New Year's Day, 68–69
night blindness, *169–70, 170,* 218
Niranjana, *322*
Nolan Street, 48; temple, 294. *See also* Trinidad Sevashram Sangha
north Indian music: classical, xxi, 138–45, 461n.16; folk, 27, 119–23
Northern Hills, Trinidad, 13
North-Western Provinces, 16, 20. *See also* Uttar Pradesh
Number One Song, xxi, 3–4, 242–62, 402, 404, 422, 424, 425, 437–38, 440; imagery in Grierson, 21; in India, 419; in Mau, 414; mistakes, 253; poetic themes, 409–10; search, 413–15; Surinam version, 411–13; themes in *birahā,* 21; versions from India, 415–19
Nur-E-Islam Mosque, 65, *143*

obeah, 35
ocean, *131, 142;* of mercy, *335;* of trouble, *365*
oḍhanī: in *chutney, 391–92,* 400; at funeral, 362, 364; at *mātīkonwā,* 153; "orhnis," in Lowenthal, 42; at the wedding, 151, 191–93; worn by Coolie girls, 179; worn by Lord Shorty, 375. See also *āchalwā*
Old Year's Day, 68–69
olé (*tāssā* hand), 160
omen, *240, 281, 282, 283–84*
one-way drum (*tāssā* hand), 160
oral tradition, xxi, 419; in Bhojpurī folk songs, 27; described by Usha, 146–47; Sanskrit mantras, 62–63, 461n.12
orange tree, *290*
Oraons, 20
organ, 98; and *kīrtan,* 106. *See also* harmonium
Orinoco Delta, 13
Orissa, 16
ornaments (jewels, finery), 165; at the wedding, *187, 198,* 199, *200–201, 276, 282;* Rām, 282–83; wedding in *Rāmcharitmānas,* 212; women of Mau, 414
ornaments (musical), xxviii, 216, 327–32, 335, 344
Oropuche lagoon, 22
orthography, Trinidadian, xxix
Ostad, Ramcharan, 122
Oudh, 16, 20. *See also* Uttar Pradesh
Oudhī. *See* Awadhī
oumalay, 34
overseas populations, South Asian. *See* India, diaspora

pachrāt, 107
pāgal, 230, 236, 237, 241

palanquin, *249, 286, 417, 418*
pan (steel band), 58, 69, 375; yards, 401
panama hat, xxviii, *170*
Pancham, Rambarose, 128, 132–33, 268
panchāyat, 37
Panchwatī, 5, 289, *326*
Pandey, Umesh. *See* Umesh
Papiamento, xvii
parachhan (parichhagum, parichhan), 185, 186
parang, 67–68, 88, 461n.13; *jhūmar,* 389
Parmasad, K. V., 40–41
parrot, *84, 290*
Parsad, Pandit Kasi, 128, 278–79
Parsons, Talcott, 38
Parsurām, *278–79,* 280
pārv pūjā, 155
Patel people, 104
Patrā, 152–53
Peace Preservation Act (1884), 95
peacock, *84–85, 264, 267, 275;* in Archer wedding song, 373; in *chutney, 371–72*
pearl(s), *191, 196, 198–99, 206,* 293; to identify swan, 4; Number One Song, 413
pelu, 147
pentatonic, 344, 349
Permanand sisters, 173–76, 178–96, 199, 201–3, 206–14, 221–23, 226, 238, 409, 415, 426; genealogy, 232–35; portrait of Kalawatee, 222
Persad, Tarran, 124–25, 128; Hindu *bhajan,* 131–32
Peter's Field, 45, 48
petit carime, 61, 88
Phāguā, xx, 72–83, 107–8. *See also* Holī
Phāgun, *81, 266, 267, 276*
Pharenda, 236–37. *See also* Anandnagar
Phiramat (Firamat, Phiranta) 121, 122, 147
Piarco International Airport, 49
pitch, xxvii, 106, 109, 401
pitcher: of elephant pearls, *198;* wedding *(kalasā), 244–56, 410, 413*
Pitch Lake, 22
plantation Hindustani, 30
plantation system, 27
playback singer, 128, 309; Mukesh, 58
plowman, *208*
plural society, xx, 37–40; and Hinduism, 301
polyrhythm, 34
Poman, 123
pomegranate, *81*
pond, 5, 80; in Number One Song, *244–56, 415, 417, 418;* in *sohar, 418*
Pondicherry Mission, 297
poorvi (poorbi), 147
pop music, 97, 98, 108, 402
Popo, Sundar, 377, 402, 424; "Chaadar Bechawo Baalma," 379–80; Indian soca, 374; life story, 378; "Scorpion Gyul," 394–96; "Screwdriver," 393–94
pop tunes in Indian films, 126
Port of Spain, 13–14, 20, 94–95
post-crop time, 61
pot-hounds, 51. *See also* dogs
poverty in India, 165, 404, 423
pradhān, 405
Prākrit, 275
Prarthana Samaj, 296
prasād, 345
Prasad, Pandit Ayodhya, 400
prayers, 100–103; and music, 420; in *sanḍhyā,* 299, 300; in school, 52
Presbyterian School, 52–54
prophets, *130, 132–33*
Protector of Emigrants, annual reports, 19
pūjā: at Divine Life Society, 59–60; at Diwālī, 62–63, 64; Durgā, 59–60; *kanyādān,* 155; *mātīkonwā,* 153; described by Morton, 115–16; *sanḍhyā,* 298–301
punjabee chutney, 389
Punjabi, 30, 31, 41; songs, 119
purabiyas, 214
Purāṇas, 74, 79, *137, 291,* 296, 297, 309, *365*
Purnananda, Swami, 59, 294–99, 301, 302, 360, 401
purvī, 270–73
pushhpakvimān, 5
Puttaparthi, 341

qawwālī, 124
Quaval, Jugrue: in *Indian Talent on Parade,* 125; local classical music, 123, 147; in "Narw Bhawurr May," 135; "Quawali Song," 130; recording artist, 124–25; on 78 R.P.M. records, 128
Quaval, Pearu, 125
Quawal, 129–30
Quawali, 130
queen, 78, *132, 198, 244, 251, 252, 253, 288*

"race" calypsos, 375
Rada cult, 35
Rādha: in Grierson song, 265–66; and Krishna, 165, *387;* lament, *266; rāgamāla* miniature, 412
radio, *268–69;* calypso, 71; and *chutney,* 377;

learning tunes, 400; *parang,* 67–68; Radio Trinidad, 125; *Songs of India,* 125
Rafi, Mohammed, 128, 310
rāg: compositions by Adesh, 141, 143–44, 145; described by Ramaya, 120; *gamak,* 327; local classical, 100, 147–49
Raghunanandan, *277, 282*
Rahasmandal dance, 119
Rahim, *292*
rain, *85–86, 193, 211, 275, 418;* drops, *264, 275;* season, 83–87, *264, 271, 273*
Rajasthani songs, 119
rāju gun, 363
Rām (Rāmā, Rama), 5–6, 83, *131, 176,* 274–93, *284, 289, 290,* 342, *374, 386, 394; bārāt,* 283–86; *bhajan,* 303, *306, 326–27, 365;* birth, 276–77, *277;* and boatman, 280; breaks Shiva's bow, *278–79;* in *chautāl,* 74–81; defeat of Rāwaṇ, 274; exile, *270,* 274, 283–84, 286–88; feet, *275, 290–91;* glory, *291–92;* ideal bridegroom, 151; jealousy of stepmother Kaikeyī, 274; like lotus, *410;* loyalty of brothers, 274; in Mahadewā Dube song, 238–41; in Number One Song, Dube, *417; rām kevat sambād,* 280; Rāmlīlā, 87–88; Sai Baba, *345;* separation from Sītā, 290; *shyāmla,* 86; *sohar,* 276–77; superhuman strength, 274, *277–78;* Upadhyaya *bārāt* song, 286; wedding to Sītā, 274, 280–86; in wedding songs, 173, *180,* 183, *187, 190–91,* 194, *196–97, 198, 205, 208,* 210, *211,* 212, 216, 238–41
Rāmachandra, *77–78, 79, 289*
ramage, 51, 460n.9
Rāmakrishna, Brahmchārī, 295
Rāmakrishna Pramhansa, 297
Rāmanāndī Panthī, 295
Ramaya, Narsaloo, 108, 112, 118–26, 149–50
Rāmāyaṇ, 3–6, 36, 274–93; *akhand,* 279; and *byāh ke gīt,* 155, 165; Channu describes, 57–58; chanting at death, 401; *chautāl* texts, 74–79; *chutney,* Krishna, 388; Felicity tradition, xxi; in Indian films, 309; *jawābī kīrtan,* 388; leader-chorus, 399; in local record collection, 109; Mahadewā Dube song, 238; men's improvised songs, 413; *nāradi* style, 461n.15; nine-nights readings, 6; Parsurām, 280; on Shivrātrī, 72; and spice, 396; Trinidad Sevashram Sangha, 59; at wake, 362–63; and wedding, 183, 187; *yagya,* 276
Rambachan, Suruj, 280
Ramcharan, Ustad, 147
Rāmcharitmānas, 211–12, 274
Rameswak, Master, 135–38
Ramjattan, Loorkhoor, 123
Rāmlīlā, 6, 87–88, 274, 292, 298; *tāssā* hand, 160
Rām Naumi, 274
Ranade, Justice, 296
rap-style, 393
Rasdhari dance, 119
Rasiya, 119
Rasta, 94
rataunī, 162, *169*
rattles, 34, 94
Rāwaṇ (Rāwaṇa), 4, 5, *78, 80–81,* 87–88, *133,* 289–90, *326*
Raymond, Cyril, 126
records, xx; from India, 360; industry, 67, 125; learning tunes, 400; local classical, 100; local collection, 108–9; 78 R.P.M., xxi, 124, 128–38; Sundar Popo, 378
red: bangles, 229; in Hindu wedding, 171, 259–60; lips, *191;* on Phāguā, 72; sari, 155, 366; signifies death in dream, 366; water, *266*
reggae, 94, 391
reincarnation, 294–95
reinterpretation, xvii, 35
rejuvenation, 400–401
religion. *See* Hinduism; Muslim(s); Christian(s)
renaissance, Indian music in Trinidad, 146–49
research: in India, xix; social science, xvii (*see also* anthropology); West Indian music, xvii–xviii
response form, 60; *bhajan,* 318; calypso, 95; style (*see* leader-chorus)
reverb, 371, 386
revitalization, xviii, 41–42, 42–44, 400–401, 402, 403; in Felicity Hinduism, 301; from Indian sources, 401; inspired by India, 360; Sai Baba movement, 359
revival, 360, 400–401
rhythm, 102, *142, 376,* 377–78, 388, 401; of *bhajan,* 310, 332, 333; Sai Baba songs, 344; in soca, 381; and spice in *chutney,* 396–97; See also *tāl*
rice, 35, 54–55, 72, *142, 154, 187, 288;* cultivation, 22, 49, 61, 88; fields described by Morton, 48–49; puffed (see *lāwā*)
Richman, Paula, 292
river, *170–71, 265, 269,* 363. *See also* river bank
river bank, *130, 169, 269, 306, 372, 415*
Roberts, John Storm, 388
rocking, *382*
Rohlehr, Gordon, 373–75

romanization, xxix
ronā, 261
Roots, 40–41
rote, 54
Roy, Rām Mohun, 296
R. S. Narayansingh's Orchestra, 128, 278–79
ruby lamp, *198, 277*
rum, 35, 50, 51, *368–69, 373;* at Hosay, 65; at Phāguā, 75; at Shango, 35; shops, 48; at the wedding, 171. *See also* drinking
rūpak tāl, 141, 219
rupees, *203*
Russell, Lord John, 27

saarang, 147
Sacred Songs and Solos, 105
sacrifice, *135,* 300, *306.* See also *havan*
sādhanā, 341
Sahai-Achuthan, Nisha, 264
Sai Baba, 340–60, 423; ashram, 343; as avatar, 356; biography, 341–42; Felicity movement, xxiv; introduction to Trinidad, 342; in Rani's dream, 367; *satsangh,* 343, 345; *vibhūtī,* 342–43, 345; weekly group services, 59. *See also* Sai Baba, songs
Sai Baba, songs, 90, 343–55, 401; "Aum Bhagawān," 440; fast style, 110; fast or slow, 355–59; "Ganesh Sharanam," 440; introduction to Trinidad, xxi; in *kīrtan* style, 107; leader-chorus, 399; short Hindi texts, 400
Saigal, 125
sailor (Rām), *291*
St. Helena, 8, 11
salsa, 381
salvation, *79–80, 132, 291,* 302, *326,* 397
samadhī, 216
sanātan dharma, 165, 263
Sanatan Dharma Maha Sabha, 295, 298, 359
sandalwood, *275, 276;* door, *211*; heart, *416;* paste, *191, 266;* stool, *21–22, 155, 177, 253;* trunks, *198*
sanḍhyā, xxiii, 298, 299–301; booklets, 302–3; at change of light, 398; mantras, 295; and Sai Baba songs, 340, 345, 354
San Fernando Hosay Riots, 64
Sankey (hymnal), 105
Sanskrit, xxix, 62–63, 103, 274, 298, 300, 399; *bārah māsas,* 275; taught by Adesh, 138, 144; text of *sanḍhyā,* 299
Santals, 20
santūr, 139
Saptak, 140–44
sarang, 120
sāraṇgī; exams by Adesh, 145; Imami, 122; in local classical music, 120, 121; miniature, 147
Saraswatī (Saraswatee), 4, *77,* 122, *142,* 356
sargam, 141, 144; during the indentureship, 120; improvisation in, 122–23
sari, *77, 369, 384, 392;* in Number One Song, *245, 249,* 256
saṛū-bhāī, 225
sasurāl, 408–9; Naipaul, 223
Satchidananda, Swami, 298; *Divine Life Bhajans,* 60, 302, 359, 365; *Divine Life Sandhyaa Bandaanaa,* 299–300; and Sai Baba, 343
sāt samundar pār, 6–7
satsangh, Sai Baba, 343
satu gun, 363
satyāgraha, 297
savannah, 22, 45, 48
Sāwan *(Sāvana),* xx, 61, *84–85, 85–86, 264, 271, 275;* and love songs, 83–87, *264, 265, 266;* wedding in *Rāmcharitmānas,* 212
sax, 394–96
scale, xxvii
scarlet ibis, 22, 422
schools, 48, 52–54, 91. *See also* Felicity, Hindu School; Presbyterian School
scorpion, *395–96*
Scouting for Talent, 39
screw, 393, *394*
sea, *135, 142, 291, 361*
seasons, 61–88, *143, 193, 211, 264, 271, 273*
Seebalack, 123
Seetaa raama kaho, 52
Sewnath, Benny: *Bhajan,* 131; *Kamach Bintee,* 290–91; local classical music, 123; recording artist, 124–25; on 78 R.P.M. records, 128
sex (sexy), 162, 263–73, *373;* fire of, *81, 267; chutney,* 396
Shahabad, 186, 205, 265–66, 407
Shah, Ameer, 131–32
Shaivites, 30
Shakespeare, 4, 356, 413, 426
shak shak, 34, 67, 155, 166 ex.
Shāmala, *365*
Shambhu, *302, 311, 315*
Shango, 33–36
Shankar, Ravi, 100, 111
Shankara, *302, 315*
shankh, 300
Sharam, Hari Om, 138
Sharma, Ramdhani, 123–25
Shatrughn, 187

Shiva, 340, 345, *387;* avatar, Sai Baba, 340, 355; bow in *Rāmāyaṇ,* 274, *311;* in Felicity *bhajan,* 302; followers of, 30; Lord of the dance, *315;* mighty bow, *277, 278, 279;* Shankar, *277*

Shivrātrī, 72, 298, 301

Shouter Baptist, 35

shrimp fish, *418*

Shrī Shankar Mandir, 54–56, 59, 63, 295

Shyām, *78, 79, 131*

shyam-kalyan, 147

Shyma, Ramdhani, 133–34

Sikhs, 30

silver, *200, 203*

sindūr (sindurā), 284; at funeral, 366; Uttar Pradesh song, 409; at the wedding, 153, 162, 208–10

singing: class, 59; defined, 89–91; finger in ear, 119; and happiness, 426; at Holī, 72; to reach God, 397; in school, 52–54; on shipboard, 9; singers, itinerant, 119–20, 122; versus talking, 101–3; why, 426

sister(s), *22, 171, 194, 204, 205, 208, 244, 249, 253, 255, 417, 418*

sister(s)-in-law, *169, 170, 197,* 218, *418;* in Number One Song, 242–62, *244–56,* 419

Sītā, 5–6, *80–81,* 87, 274–93, *275, 278, 282–83, 284, 289, 290, 374;* in *bhajan, 306, 326;* duplicate Sītā, 280; exile in Lankā, 289–90; in Mahadewā Dube song, 238–41; "Sītā Rām" greeting, 55; wedding to Rām, 280–86; in wedding songs, 173, 183, *187,* 194, 197, *196–97, 198,* 210, 211, *211,* 212, *238–41, 410*

sitar, 312–15 ex., 346–47 ex.; by Adesh, 139, 145; in film *bhajan,* 310; in local classical music, 120, 147

Siūnārāynī Panthī, 295

Siwālā, 295, 298. *See also* Shrī Shankar Mandir

sixteen adornments (ornaments), *83, 201, 265, 282, 416*

ska, 381

sky, *211, 275, 277, 291, 302, 387*

slavery, 23; Middle Passage, 8

slow *bhajan,* 355, 357, 358

smallpox, 23

Smith, M. G., 37

Smith, R. T., 38

smrti, 296

snake, 275; garlands, *302;* in Number One Song, Dube, 415–17; in Number One Song, Trinidad, 242–62

sobbing, in Number One Song, *245, 252*

snow, *266*

soca, xxi, 371, 377, 380–83, 401; in Brooklyn, 388–89; Indian soca, 374, *376,* 377

social constructionist, xx, 38

social relationships: absent husband, *164–65, 265, 266,* 267–70, *267, 268–70, 272;* African-Indian, xxi; avoidance relationship, 225, 270; brother and sister, *21–22;* changed during Holī, 72; expressed in song, 215–16; Hindu family, 225; joking relationship, 225; male dominance, 225; in Number One Song, 259; in old classical song, 135–36; status in India diaspora, 31

social theories. *See* consensualism; social constructionist, *etc.*

society, plural, 301

sohar, 27, 36, 107, 147, 276–77, 359, *418;* for Rām, 276–77; from *Rāmāyaṇ,* 276; with swans, 418

Solo Sangeet Indian Orchestra, 39, 127

son, *22, 177, 216, 217, 380, 417, 418*

song(s): books, xix, 60; duels, 122; English, 53–54; songs, *407;* Spanish (see *parang*); variants, Number One Song, 242–62

songsters, 91, 119–29

soul, *5, 143, 266,* 367, *380,* 420

Southeast Asia, Indian population, 28

sparrow hawk, *81, 267, 275, 371–72*

spice, in Indian song, 396–97

spirit possession, 33–34

sponsorship, 39, 67

Srana, xvii

Sri Lanka, 3

sruti, 296

stage shows, 125

stamping tubes, 95

stars, *190, 217;* star-anklets, *302*

steel band (steeldrums), 69–71, 94, 126, *376,* 401

sthāyī, 107, 219; examples, 192, 195, 199, 202, 211, 248; *sthāyī-antarā* structure, Number One Song, 256–57

stick idiophone. See *ḍhantāl*

studio technology, 371, 380, 385–86, 389, 393, 394

sudarshan chakra, 133

sugar, 22; cane fields, 36; Caroni, Ltd., 48; at cremation, 362, 366; described by Morton, 48–49; eighteen-month cycle, 14; in the Empire, 27; estates, conditions, 20, 24–25; in Gorakhpur, 7; growing cycle, 61–88; and Indians, 36; labor conditions, 23–25; of love, *411;* slack season, 24, 61, 88

Sumitrā, *186, 200, 288*
sun, *66, 80, 133, 135, 196–97, 197, 206, 271, 282–83,* 299
Sunday Mid-Day, article on Helen, 413–14
Surinam, 37, 149, 258; love song, 265; Number One Song, 411–13; Phāguā, 74, 461n.15; Phāguā song, 82–83; Sai Baba, 342
swan(s), 4, 5, *5, 142,* 409, 415–18; in *birahā,* 21; as human soul, 4–5, 367; as judge of truth and justice, 4; metaphor, 419; in Number One Song, 242–62, *244, 251, 251–52, 253, 254, 255,* 413, *415;* in *sohar, 418;* spirit of prophecy, 294
sweep, *176*
sweet (sweeter), *384;* calypso, *382;* heart, *379–80;* Indian soca, 374; melody, *374;* memory, 26, 398–403; musical style, 56, 109; pan, 375; voice, 372
Swinton, Captain E., 9
Swinton, Jane, 11–12
syncopation, 333, 344
syncretism, xvii, xx, 33–36, 42, 301, 377
Syne, Bahadur, 147

tabla, 312–15 ex., 346–47 ex.; by Adesh, 139, 144–46; Amar playing, 140; in film *bhajan,* 310; in Indian orchestras, 127; in local classical music, 120, 121, 147, 148; Sai Baba songs, 344
Tagore, Rabindranath, *Gītānjalī,* 263, 266–67, 273, 419
take up (*tāssā* style), 160–61
Taki-Taki, xvii
tāl: in *byāh ke gīt,* 257; drum cadence, 162; during the indentureship, 120; local classical, 100, 126; notated in Devanagari script, 141; in *Saptak,* 144–45
talaiyā, 4
tālukdār, 30
tamarind, *176*
tamboo bamboo bands, 70, 95
tambourine, accompaniment, 348 ex.
tamburā (tanpura), 102, 144, 146, 147, 312 ex.
Tamil, in India diaspora, 30
tamo gun, 363
Tansen, 139
tape recording, xix, xxiv–xxv, 89–90, 110
tappa, 120, 148
tāpū, 3, 6
tarana, 148
tarz, 409; Number One Song, Dube, 415
tāssā, xxi, xxiii, 27, 116, 161 ex., 193, 391–93, 399, 400; hands, 159–62, 434; Hosay, 65; at the wedding, 153, 154, 155–62
tattoo, 36, *411*
taxonomy, folk, xx
taziya, 64–65
tears, 261, *261–62, 368, 408*
teenage, *268*
television, 39, 62, 87; Carnival, 71; and *chutney,* 377; Doordarshan *Rāmāyaṇ,* 292–93; *parang,* 67, 68; See also *Mastana Bahaar*
Telugu, in India diaspora, 30, 276
temple, *131;* of mind, *307;* repertory, 355–59; songs, 355–60, 401. *See also* Divine Life Society; Shrī Shankar Mandir; Trinidad Sevashram Sangha
tempo, 162, 355–60
tent singing, 100, 377, 401
tent, *85,* 153, 201, *239, 413, 415, 417*
Tepotzlán, xviii
tervī, 407
Tewari, Laxmi: *bārāt* song, 176; folk song, 250; *purvī bhajan,* 270–71; song loss, 218; song studies, 263; *viraha* song, 264
Thapur, Romil, 292
Theosophists, 296
ṭhumrī, 401; during the indentureship, 120, 122–23, 148–49; local classical, 100; *tāssā* hand, 159
thunder, *271, 275*
tikura: tāssā hand, 160; Rām and Sītā, 281
tilak, 281
tillānā: during the indentureship, 120, 122–23; *tāssā* hand, 159
timbre, 344
time signatures, xxvii
time theory of Indian music, 122, 123, 144
timing, in chant, 102
Tobago, *143*
Toco, 33–34
tom-toms, 115–16
tourist, *269*
translation, xxviii
transcription, xxvii–xxviii, 399
triangle, 70
tribal music, 20
Trinidad: aboriginal population, xvii–xviii, 23; in Adesh songs, *142–43;* African slavery, 23; agriculture, 23–24; anthropological research, 31–42; compared with Mauritius, Fiji, 31; cosmopolital society, 71; crops, 22; discovery of, 22; ethnic tension, 42; geography, 12, 22; Independence, 97; Indian music

history, xx; land grants, 14–15; musical competition, 38–40; race relations, 33–34, 36–40; seasons, 61–88; Spanish period, xvii, 22–23; West Indian setting, xvii
The Trinidad All Stars Percussion Orchestra, 69–70
Trinidad and Tobago, *97*
Trinidad Guardian, 118
Trinidad Sevashram Sangha, 59, 72, 296, 298–99, 401
Tripura, 193
trumpet, 127, 173
Tulsī Dās, Goswami, 129, 134, *137,* 148, 211–12, 274, *276,* 280, 291, 362, 396
tumhi ho maataa, 52
tune: of *byāh ke gīt,* 257–59; Felicity and India, 409, 419. *See also* melody
turban, *171, 177*
turmeric, 153, *239, 282*

ulārā, 74, 107, 147, 399; *tāssā* hand, 160
umbrella, diamond, *286*
Umesh: on absent husband, 267–68; Anup Jalota, 380; on *arkatiā,* 18–19; on Benny Sewnath, 290–91; Bhojpurī song texts, xxiv; on *chautāl,* 78–83; on *chutney* and *lachārī,* 372, 388; on *chutney* Holī song, 386–88; on Dasarath's song of boons, 286–88; on *dhotī-lotā,* 17–18; on the Doordarshan *Rāmāyaṇ,* 292–93; on the east wind, 271–72; The Eleven Truths of Music, 420; explains music from Felicity, 419–20; during fieldwork, 405, 406, 414; first plane ride, 405; his grandfather, 129, 138; on Krishna *chutney,* 387; language in Felicity, 419; in Mahadewā Dube, 226–41; on Mozart, 397; on Number One Song, 253; on old British silver ruppees, 18; portrait, 406 plate 46; on Rām, 282; on *Rāmāyaṇ,* 279; on *rām kevat sambād,* 280; searching for Number One Song, 413; on 78 R.P.M. records, 128–38; on Shiva and Kālī, 277; on social system, 267; on spice in Indian song, 396–97; on Sundar Popo, 380; on *tāpū* and *sāt samundar pār,* 3–7; transcription and translation, xxiv; on *viraha,* 264
uncle, *22, 178, 193, 197*
"under the bamboo," wedding, 153
Union Village, 45
University of the West Indies, 111–12
untouchability, 297
Upadhyaya, K. D., 263; song of absent husband, 269
Upadhyaya, Hari S., songs: absent husband, 268–70; *bārāt* song, 177; boons, 288; eastern wind, 272–73; *kalasā* song, 410; lotus song, 410; Rām's *bārāt,* 286; *sindūr* song, 210; Sītā, separation from Rām, 290; studies, 263
Upanishads, 79, 301, 341; *Chāndogya Upanishad,* lotus metaphor, 411
uṛan kharāmūn, 7
uṛan khatola, 6–7
urban genres, xviii
Urdu, 104, 123, 217; taught by Adesh, 138, 144; "Urdu Ghazal," 134–35
Usha. *See* Bissoondialsingh
Uttar Pradesh, eastern, 372, 405, 409; folk song tune, 409; harvest, 16; Holī songs, 74–75, 461n.15; love songs, 263; population explosion, 30; recruitment of Coolies in, 16; wedding song repertory, 258
Uttar Pradesh, western, 258; Holī, 461n.15

Vaishnavite, 30
Vālmikī, 274
vandanā, by Adesh, 141–42
variations, songs, 246
Vedas, 79, *80, 137, 198, 283, 291,* 297, 299, *307,* 341, *365; sanḍhyā* and *havan,* 295–96
veil, in Number One Song, *251, 252, 254–55, 256*
Venezuela, 67, 340–41
vermilion, *201, 209–10, 266, 284*
de Verteuil, Anthony, 221–22
vibhūtī, 342–43, 345
vibraphones, 70
vibration, 100, 341
vidā, 261
vimān, 5
vīṇā, 142, 356
violins, 67, 127, 145, 173, 310, 312–15 ex.
viraha, 264, 270
virgin, *176, 197, 203, 204, 206, 390, 394,* 409
Vishnu, 30, 62, *365;* in *Bhāgawata Purāṇa,* 301; Rām as avatar, 274; sixth incarnation, Parsurām, 278
vivāh (vivāha), 155, 238
Vivekananda, 297
vocal timbre, 164
voyage to Trinidad, 7–12; clothing, 19; courage of Coolies, 14; description by villagers, 9; hardship for women, 12; music and dance, 32; return passage, 14–15
vulture, *77, 80–81*

Wagley, Charles, 40
wail, 261, 364
wake (wakes, waking), 35, 67, 362–63, 401
Warner, Keith, 375–76
Waterman, Richard, xvii, 34, 35
wedding: Ahir dance, 119; arrange, *239–40;* basket, 199–201; *chutney,* 377; described by Morton, 116; grief, 185; honeymoon, *370;* local classical music, 123; outdoor music, 171; ring, *369, 395;* season, 88, 276; singers, 174; tent, *198, 244–56,* 419; white dress, Western, 171, 259. *See also* Hindu weddings
wedding songs, xxi, 107–8, 147, *198,* 151–220, 399; and broken Hindi, 103–4; Felicity school girls, 422; future prospects, 218; learning, 178; metaphors, 215–16; verse and refrain, 399. See also *byāh ke gīt; lachārī*
weeping, *22;* in Dasarath's song of boons, *287;* in Moon's song, *262;* in Number One Song, *252;* in Rajiah's song, *261*
west Africa: influence on calypso, 95; music, 35; in syncretized cults, 33–35. *See also* Africa
Westernization (Westernized), xviii, 36, 50, 126, 128, 401–3; impact on Caribbean, xviii; instruments, 173; Sai Baba movement, 359
West Indies, xvii–xviii; region defined, 27
whirlpool, *130, 135*
whistle, 51, 91
wife, *22, 170–71, 177, 208, 244–45, 249, 252, 253, 254, 255, 261, 268, 269, 290;* rival, *84*
Williams, Denis, 381, 385
wind, *266;* east, *271, 272, 273*
Windsor Records, 108, 377
women: and absent husband, *164–65,* 267–70; bride, in *sasurāl, 21–22,* 408–9; *chatī, barahī* for daughters, 85; daughters and wives, 407; daughters, role in village, 231; equality, 297; family reputation, 267; fear, 164; at funeral, 363, 367; grief of mother, 164, 185, 261–62; Indian versus Trinidadian, 261–62; laughter, 165; longing for a child, 272–73; love songs, 263–73; of Mau, 414; and quota system for indentureship, 19; Rādha as symbol, 165; rights of sister, 260–61; social importance in lineage, 231; songs of mother's grief, 407–8; suffering on voyage, 12; teen mothers, 267–68; *viraha,* 264; weeping, 261–62
World Parliament of Religions, 297
Wiley, Dr., 9

Yacoob, 123
Yama, 366
Yankarran, Anand, 377
Yankarran, Isaac, 125
yoga, and Sai Baba, 341–42. See also *karma; jnana; bhaktī*
Yoruba, 33–34; drums, 94
Yuman style, 250

zamidar, 30